LEGENDARY AND MYTHOLOGICAL ART

SPALATRO. BY WASHINGTON ALLSTON.

Drawn and Engraved by W. J. Linton.

LEGENDARY AND MYTHOLOGICAL ART

Clara Erskine Clement

Bracken Books
London

Legendary and Mythological Art

First published as *A Handbook of Legendary and Mythological Art* by Hurd and Houghton, New York, in 1876

This edition published in 1994 by Bracken Books, an imprint of Studio Editions Ltd, Princess House, 50 Eastcastle Street, London W1N 7AP, England

ISBN 1 85891 135 4

Printed and bound in Guernsey by The Guernsey Press Co. Ltd.

PREFACE.

This book, originating in my own experience of the want of some hand-book of reference, both in reading and in visiting art galleries when travelling, has been written with a threefold motive. I have endeavored to produce something that would interest and instruct my children, to whom this as well as all the labors of my life are dedicated; to acquire, for myself, a more exact knowledge of the subjects herein treated; and to make this effort to supply my own necessity the means of usefulness to others who feel the same need.

The study and research thus occasioned have accomplished the most selfish of my desires; if the others shall be realized, even imperfectly, my ambition will be satisfied.

Were I to make my acknowledgments to all the authorities which I have consulted, the book would be enlarged by some pages, but I would mention Alban Butler's "Lives of the Saints;" Didron's "Christian Iconography;" Mrs. Jameson's Works; "La Legende Dorée;" Perkins' "Tuscan and Italian Sculptors;" Miller's "Ancient Art and its Remains;" "Il Perfetto Legendario;" "History of Painting in Italy," by Crowe and Cavalcaselle; Winckelmann's "History of Ancient Art among the Greeks," and Westropp's "Handbook of Archæology, — Egyptian, Greek, Roman, and Etruscan," in connection with the first portion of the book.

The legends of place have been principally drawn from German literature. Most of the English translations of these legends that come within the reach of travellers, are the work of

Germans, and so imperfectly rendered, that a knowledge of their own language is almost necessary in order to comprehend their English.

The mythological portion embraces all subjects of that character which are illustrated in painting or sculpture in the galleries of Rome, Florence, the Louvre, Munich, Vienna, Dresden, and Berlin.

The illustrations are intended as a key or guide in the consideration of their subjects. I would call attention to the frontispiece as being the first example, so far as I am able to learn, of an American picture in any work connected with art.

The elegance of the book has been subordinated to the desire to make it compact and convenient as a hand-book in travelling; this being a purpose for which it was especially written.

C. E. C.

CLEMENT FARM, *August* 28, 1870.

TABLE OF CONTENTS.

LIST OF ILLUSTRATIONS.

SYMBOLISM IN ART.

St. Augustine calls the representations of art, "libri idiotarum" (the books of the simple), and there is no doubt that the first object of Christian art was to teach; and the aim of the artist was to render the truth he desired to present without regard to the beauty of the representation; he adhered to the actual, and gave no play to imagination or æsthetics. But later in its history, this art has been influenced by legends and doctrines in the choice of subjects, and these have been variously rendered, in accordance with the character, the æsthetic cultivation, and the refinement of the artist. But from its infancy to the present time, there have been certain characteristic figures, attributes or symbols, which have made a part of the language of what may be called Christian Art. These are meaningless, or worse, perhaps a deformity to the eye of one who understands them not; but they add much to the power of a representation, to the depth of sentiment and expression when rightly apprehended. These symbols are used in two ways: to express a general fact or sentiment, or as the especial attribute or characteristic of the person represented. My present limits allow but an imperfect and superficial consideration of this subject.

I. GENERAL SYMBOLS.

The Glory, Aureole, and Nimbus, all represent light or brightness, and are the symbols of sanctity. The nimbus surrounds the head; the aureole encircles the whole body, and the glory is the union of the nimbus and aureole. The nimbus belongs to all holy persons and saints as well as to the representations of divinity. The aureole, strictly speaking, belongs only to the persons of the Godhead, but the Virgin Mary is invested with it, — (1) when she holds the Saviour in her arms; (2) in pictures of the Assumption; (3) when she is represented as the intercessor for humanity at the last judgment; (4) when represented as the Woman of the Apocalypse. The aureole has also been used as a symbol of the apotheosis of holy persons; but this is a degeneration from its original design and the use assigned it in ancient traditions. The Glory also belongs especially to God and the Virgin. The oblong aureole is called in Latin, *vesica piscis;* in Italian, the *mandorla;* (almond). The cruciform or triangular nimbus, or the figure of a cross in the nimbus, belong properly to the persons of the Trinity; the nimbus of saints and lesser beings should be circular. A square nimbus is used for persons still living when the representation was made; the hexagonal nimbus for allegorical personages. These symbols did not appear in Christian art until the fifth century, and during the fifteenth and sixteenth centuries they disappeared. They are, however, employed in the present day, although not with the careful distinction in the employment of the various forms which characterized their earliest use. The color of these symbols in painting is golden, or that which represents light; in some instances, in miniatures, or on glass, they are of various colors. Didron believes these to be symbolical, but is not sure of the signification of the colors.

THE FISH. A fish, most frequently a dolphin, was the earliest and most universal of the Christian symbols. It has several significations. The Greek word for fish, ΙΧΘΥΣ, is composed of the initial letters of the Greek Ἰησοῦς Χριστός, Θεοῦ Υἱός, Σωτήρ, the Latin translation of which is, *Jesus Christus Dei filius Salvator* — thus forming the initial anagram of this title of Jesus; and these characters are found in many ancient inscriptions, and upon works of art. The fish is an emblem of water and the rite of baptism; of the vocation of the Christian apostle, or "fisher of men," especially in the hands of St. Peter and others who were eminently successful in making converts; it is emblematic of Christians generally, they being likened to fish in the call of the Apostles (Matt. iv. 19), and also typified by the miraculous draught of fishes (John xxi). But it is not true that the fish is always a Christian emblem; according to Didron it is never met as such in Greek art, and he believes that this emblem on the tombs in the catacombs at Rome, signified the occupation of the person buried in them.

THE CROSS has a deeper meaning than that of other symbols; it is in a certain sense not merely the instrument of the sufferings of Christ, but himself suffering — "*ubi crux est martyr ibi.*" In Christian iconography, the cross holds a most important place. According to the tradition or legend of the True Cross, it was coexistent with the world, and will appear at the last judgment. Chosroes believed that in possessing the cross of Christ he possessed the Saviour, and so it was enthroned at his right hand. Thus in early representations of the three persons of the godhead the cross without the figure was considered not only to recall Christ to the mind but actually to show him. There are four differently formed crosses: The Latin or Roman cross (1) is believed to be like that on which Christ suffered, and is the one placed in the hand of a saint. This cross is in the form of a man with the arms extended; the distance from the head to the shoulders being less than from the shoulders to the feet, and the length of the arms less than that of the whole figure. The Greek cross (2) has four equal branches. The cross of Saint Andrew (3) is a cross saltier or an X; and the Egyptian or "Tau" cross (4), has but three branches, like the letter T. This last is also called St. Anthony's Cross, because this saint is represented with a crutch in the shape of the "Tau," and it is embroidered on his vestments. It is also assigned as the cross of the Old Testament, and the brazen serpent is represented on a pole with this form. The Patriarchal Cross is of the same shape as the Latin Cross, but has two horizontal bars. There are numerous varieties of the Greek and Latin crosses, such as the Maltese Cross, the Cross of Dorat and various others which pertain in some cases to certain localities. The cross is often interlaced or combined with the first two letters of the name of Christ in Greek. This monogram itself is called the Labarum, or the Cross of Constantine, this being the form of the legendary cross which he saw in the sky, and which was inscribed, according to Eusebius, ΕΝ ΤΟΥΤΩ ΝΙΚΑ, "Conquer by this." Frequently when the cross was made of gold or silver, the five wounds of Christ were represented by inserting in it as many carbuncles or rubies, there being one in the centre and one at each extremity.

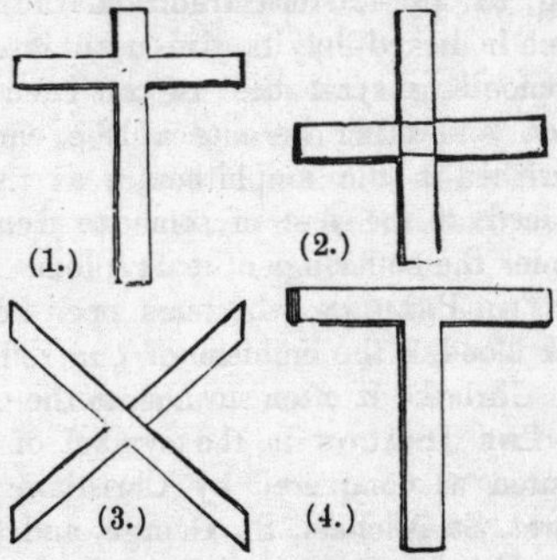

The Lamb has been an emblem of the Saviour from the earliest period of Christian art. It was the type of Him in the Old Testament and the name given Him by St. John the Baptist (John i. 28). When standing, bearing the cross or a banner, with a nimbus about the head, it is the Lamb of God, and is frequently inscribed, *Ecce Agnus Dei*. The Twelve Apostles are represented by as many lambs, while the thirteenth, the symbol of Christ, bears the cross or has a nimbus about the head, and is frequently larger than the others. The lamb, called the Apocalyptic Lamb, has seven horns and seven eyes (Rev. v. 6). The lamb is also a general symbol of modesty, purity, and innocence, as when made the attribute of St. Agnes.

THE LION is another symbol of Christ, the "Lion of Judah," and is sometimes represented with a cruciform nimbus. According to an Eastern tradition, the cub of the lion is born dead, and is licked by its sire until it comes to life on the third day. Hence it is symbolical of the resurrection. It is given to St. Jerome and other hermits as the emblem of solitude; to those who perished in the amphitheatre as the symbol of their death; and is placed at the feet of some to denote their courage and fortitude under the sufferings of martyrdom.

THE PELICAN, who tears open her breast to feed her young with her blood, is the emblem of our redemption, through the sufferings of Christ. It often surmounts the cross.

THE DRAGON is the symbol of sin and paganism. It is represented as conquered by Christianity, as in the legends of St. Margaret, St. Michael, St. George, and St. Sylvester. In the legend of St. Martha, it represents a flood and pestilence. The "jaws of hell" are represented by the open mouth of a dragon emitting flames.

THE SERPENT, another emblem of sin, is sometimes placed beneath the feet of the Virgin; sometimes twined around a globe, to indicate the power of sin over the entire world. In some symbolic pictures of the crucifixion the serpent lies dead at the foot of the cross, "or, if alive, looking impotently up at the second Adam upon the tree of our salvation, as before, according to art, he looked triumphantly down upon our first parents, from the tree of our fall."

THE HIND OR HART, is the especial attribute of St. Eustace, St. Procopius, St. Giles, and St. Hubert. It was made the symbol of religious aspiration by the "sweet singer of Israel' (Psalm 42), and is also an emblem of solitude and hermit life.

THE UNICORN. This fabulous creature was said to be able to evade all pursuers except a virgin of perfect purity in heart, mind, and life. It is only given as an attribute to the Virgin and St. Justina, and is the emblem of female chastity.

THE PEACOCK is seen on tombs, sarcophagi, and among funereal emblems. It symbolizes the change from life to immortality. It was borrowed from pagan art, where it represented the apotheosis of an empress. It was the bird of Juno, but was not the symbol of pride until modern times.

THE DOVE is the emblem of the soul when represented as issuing from the mouth of the dying; an emblem of purity, when given to the Virgin and certain female saints; also the symbol of the Holy Ghost and of spiritual inspiration. It symbolizes the divine spirit when it hovers over holy men, as the emblem of their heaven-sent inspiration; and is seen in pictures of the baptism of Christ, the Pentecost and the Annunciation.

THE OLIVE as the emblem of peace, is given to the Archangel Gabriel, and to some saints. It is seen upon the tombs of martyrs, and is sometimes borne by the angels who announce the nativity.

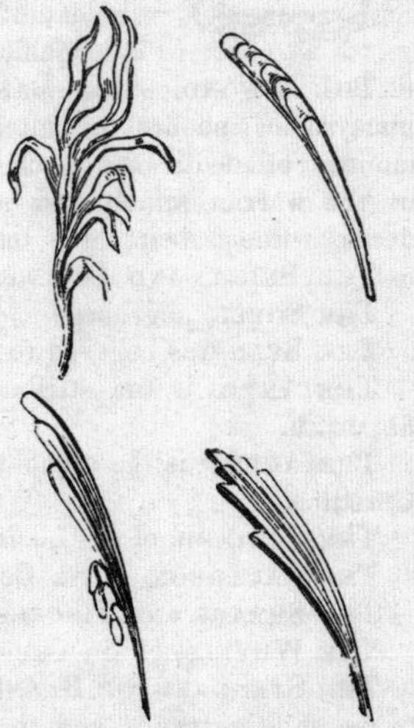

THE PALM. The use of the palm as the symbol of martyrdom is authorized by Scripture (Rev. vii. 9). It belongs to all the "noble army of martyrs." It is placed in their hands and carved on their tombs. It is sometimes brought to them by angels as if from heaven itself. It is very much varied in form and size.

THE LILY wherever seen, has but one signification, which is chastity and purity. It belongs especially to pictures of the Annunciation and to St. Joseph, whose rod was said to put forth lilies.

FRUIT OR FLOWERS, although frequently employed merely as ornaments, have under certain circumstances different significations. As the apple is an emblem of the fall in Paradise, in many pictures, so when presented to the infant Saviour, or in his hand, it signifies redemption. Roses are illustrative of the legends of St. Elizabeth of Hungary, St. Cecilia, and St. Dorothea, and a type of the Virgin as the "Rose of Sharon." A bursting pomegranate, is the symbol of a hopeful future. Any fruit in the hand of St. Catherine is a symbol of "the fruit of the spirit."

THE LAMP, LANTERN, OR TAPER is most frequently the symbol of piety. But the lamp as the attribute of St. Lucia, signifies heavenly wisdom, or spiritual light.

FIRE AND FLAMES are emblems of zeal and fervor of soul, or of the sufferings of martyrdom.

THE FLAMING HEART, is symbolical of fervent piety and spiritual love.

THE CROWN, when on the head of the Madonna, makes her the queen of Heaven and Regina Angelorum. When the attribute of a martyr, it signifies the victory over sin and death, or denotes that the saint was of royal blood; in the latter case it is usually placed at the feet.

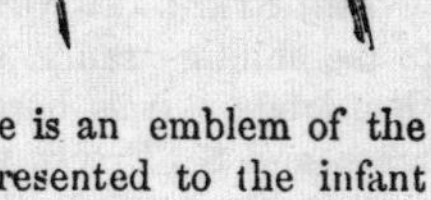

Among the Jews the crown was the ornament of a bride, and to the present time it is placed on the head of a nun when consecrated as the Bride of Christ. For this reason it is more frequently seen on the heads of female saints, while those of the other sex hold it in the hand. It is sometimes a mere circlet; often a chaplet of flowers, and again it is magnificent with gold and precious jewels.

THE SWORD, AXE, LANCE, AND CLUB are all symbols of martyrdom, and are the attributes of certain saints, and signify the manner of death they suffered. The sword is also an attribute of the warrior saints, and sometimes is an emblem of a violent death, without being the instrument employed.

THE SKULL AND SCOURGE symbolize penance.

THE SHELL, pilgrimage.

THE BELL was believed to exorcise evil spirits.

THE ANVIL is the attribute of St. Adrian, and is the symbol of his death.

THE ARROW is the attribute of St. Sebastian, St. Ursula, and St. Christina.

THE PONIARD, of St. Lucia.

THE CAULDRON, of St. Cecilia and St. John the Evangelist.

THE SHEARS AND PINCERS, of St. Agatha and St. Apollonia.

THE WHEELS, of St. Catherine.

THE STANDARD, OR BANNER, is the symbol of victory. It belongs to the military saints, and to those who carried the gospel to heathen lands. It is borne by Christ after the resurrection. St. Reparata and St. Ursula are the only female saints to whom it is given.

THE CHALICE is the emblem of faith and is an attribute of St. Barbara. With a serpent, it is that of St. John the Evangelist.

THE BOOK, in the hand of St. Stephen, is the Old Testament; in the hands of the evangelists it represents their own writings. In other cases it is the Scriptures, or the symbol of the learning and writings of the saint who bears it.

THE CHURCH, in the hand of St. Jerome, is the symbol of his love and care for the whole Christian Church. In other cases it is generally the model of some particular church, and the saint who bears it was its founder or first bishop.

THE SHIP. In early times the ark was the symbol of the Christian Church, but later any ship has had this significance. The boat of St. Peter, tempest-tossed and guided by Christ, is symbolical of his watchful care of his church.

THE ANCHOR is one of the earliest Christian symbols. It is seen in the catacombs and on very ancient gems. It is the emblem of immovable hope and untiring patience. It is an attribute of some saints in illustration of their legends, as in the case of St. Clement.

The Symbols of the Passion and Crucifixion are numerous, and although rarely seen in the catacombs and in early sculpture, they are constantly found in churches. They are, the two swords of the apostles, the ear of Malchus, St. Peter's sword, the pillar and cord, the scourge, the crown of thorns, the three dice, the spear, the sponge, the nails, the cross, the thirty pieces of silver, the hammer and pincers, the ladder, the lantern, the boxes of spice for embalming, the seamless garment, the purse and the cock: the five wounds are represented by the hands and feet with a heart in the centre, each pierced with one wound, or by a heart alone with five wounds.

Ears of Corn and Bunches of Grapes were symbols of the bread and wine of the Holy Eucharist; while the representations of the labors of the vintage were typical of those of Christians in the vineyard of the Lord; the vine and vine leaf was an emblem of the Saviour, the true vine.

The Candelabrum was an emblem of Christ and his Church, the light of the world. With seven branches it refers to the seven gifts of the Spirit, or to the seven churches (Rev. i. 20)

Little Naked Bodies are the symbols of the souls of men, and are seen in pictures of St. Michael when he is represented as the Lord of souls. They are also placed in the hand which symbolizes God the Father.

II. SYMBOLISM OF COLORS.

In ancient art each color had a mystic sense or symbolism, and its proper use was an important consideration, and carefully studied.

White is worn by the Saviour after his resurrection; by the Virgin in representations of the Assumption; by women as the emblem of chastity; by rich men to indicate humility, and by the judge as the symbol of integrity. It is represented sometimes by silver or the diamond, and its sentiment is purity, virginity, innocence, faith, joy, and light.

Red, the color of the ruby, speaks of royalty, fire, divine love, the holy spirit, creative power, and heat. In an opposite sense it symbolized blood, war, and hatred. Red and black combined were th. colors of Satan, purgatory, and evil spirits. Red and white roses are emblems of love and innocence, or love and wisdom, as in the garland of St. Cecilia.

Blue, that of the sapphire, signified heaven, heavenly love and truth, constancy and fidelity. Christ and the Virgin Mary wear the blue mantle, St. John a blue tunic.

Green, the emerald, the color of spring, expressed hope and victory.

Yellow or Gold was the emblem of the sun, the goodness of God, marriage and fruitfulness. St. Joseph and St. Peter wear yellow. Yellow has also a bad signification when it has a dirty, dingy hue, such as the usual dress of Judas, and then signifies jealousy, inconstancy, and deceit.

Violet or Amethyst signified passion and suffering, or love and truth. Penitents, as the Magdalene, wear it. The Madonna wears it after the crucifixion, and Christ after the resurrection.

Gray is the color of penance, mourning, humility, or accused innocence.

Black with white signified humility, mourning and purity of life. Alone, it spoke of darkness, wickedness, and death, and belonged to Satan. In pictures of the Temptation, Jesus sometimes wears black.

III. SYMBOLS OF GOD THE FATHER.

Before the twelfth century there were no portraits of God the Father, and the symbol used to indicate his presence was a hand issuing from the clouds. This hand when entirely open is in the act of bestowing and has rays from each finger. It was generally represented in the act of benediction, and the position showed whether it belonged to eastern or western, or to Greek or Latin art, for the benedictory gesture differs in the two churches. "In the Greek Church it is performed with the forefinger entirely open, the middle finger slightly bent, the thumb crossed upon the third finger, and the little finger bent. This movement and position of the five fingers, form more or less perfectly the monogram of the Son of God." The Latin benediction is given with the third and little fingers closed, the thumb and the other two fingers remaining open and straight. This is said to symbolize the three persons of the Trinity by the open fingers, and the two natures of Christ by the closed. The hand is frequently surrounded by the cruciform nimbus, which in the early centuries was given to God alone. The hand is most frequently seen in pictures of the Baptism of Christ; the Agony in the Garden; in the Crucifixion, where it is placed on the summit of the cross in the act of benediction; and when Jesus is represented as reascending to heaven after his death, bearing the cross in his hand, the right hand of the Father is extended to him as if "in a manner to assist him to rise." In another representation of the hand of God it is filled with little naked figures whose hands are joined as if in prayer. These are the souls of the righteous who have returned to God.

The next symbol of the Father was a face in the clouds, then a bust; and gradually by the end of the fourteenth century a figure and distinct characteristics represented the first person of the Godhead. In the beginning there was little or no distinction between the representations of the Father and Son; but gradually the Father was made older, while the place of honor, the royal crown on his head and the globe in his hand, indicated a superior dignity and consideration. From this time to that of the Renaissance, however, the representations of God were but little more than those of a pope or king; the triple tiara was indeed increased by the addition of two more crowns, and when in the garments of a king a nimbus encircled the crown. With the æsthetic genius and progress of the Renaissance, with Michael Angelo, Perugino, and Raphael, came representations of God that more satisfactorily embody that mental conception which can never be embodied, — the conception of God, of Jehovah, the Creator and Ancient of days. But at length it came to be remembered that no personal representation of the Father should ever be made. No man hath seen or can see Him; and Jesus being the Word, was the speech of God and was the fitting representation of the Father whenever he had spoken. Since the sixteenth century the Father has been symbolized by the triangle, which is his linear emblem, or some other geometrical figure inscribed with his name, and surrounded with rays of light. This radiating circle is itself an emblem of eternity. Sometimes a flood or blaze of light alone is the symbol of the "appearance of brightness" which the prophet describes (Ezek. viii. 2), but the triangle became extremely popular on account of the ideas or teaching which it embodied. Here the Father, represented by his name, in Hebrew, occupied the centre of the triangle which symbolized the Trinity, and all was contained in the circle of Eternity.

This abstruse symbol is often seen in the decorations of the churches of the present day and upon the vestments of bishops.

IV. SYMBOLS OF GOD THE SON.

The usual symbols of Christ have been mentioned under the head of general symbols, for they are capable of various significations and are employed as attributes of saints or to denote their characteristics. They are the glory, aureole, or nimbus, the fish, cross, lamb, and lion. The traditions of the earliest portraits of Christ will be found by referring to the legends of King Abgarus and St. Veronica. From the beginning of Christian art Christ has been represented by portraits rather than symbols, and in such a manner as to render them quite unmistakable. In the earliest representations of the crucifixion, it was surrounded with various symbols, and the aim of the artists who painted them was to portray the mysterious death which convulsed nature, raised the dead, and wrought mighty miracles, rather than the mere physical sufferings and human death which later art presents.

Among the symbols thus used were the sun and moon, represented by the classic figures of Sol and Luna, with the rays and crescent, or seated in their orbs surrounded with clouds, with their right hands raised to the cheek, an ancient sign of sorrow. Again, they bore torches reversed. Figures are seen rising from tombs and from the water, showing that the dead shall rise from sea and land. Earth and Ocean are also symbolized. In one ancient ivory, Earth is half nude and sits beside a tree; in one hand she holds a cornucopia, the symbol of abundance, while a serpent nurses at her breast, the emblem of life nourished by the earth. The ocean is as a river-god, riding on a dolphin, or holding a subverted urn, from which the water pours forth. The church and the synagogue are typified by females; the one on the right or place of honor, the church, holds a banner and gazes up at the Saviour, while on the left the synagogue turns her back as if rebellious. The Virgin and St. John are ever present at the crucifixion from earliest to latest time. Their hands are often raised to the cheek in token of affliction, and the disciple bears the Gospel in his hand. Angels sometimes hold a crown above the head of Christ, or hang from the cross in attitudes of anguish. The presence of the Father is shown by the hand before described, which holds the crown, or is in the act of blessing. Other symbols are the serpent twined about the foot of the cross; the pelican tearing her breast to feed her young, an emblem of redemption; a female figure crowned with towers supposed to represent Jerusalem; a skull symbolizes Adam; the sacrifice of a heifer typifies the Jewish rites; and sometimes the Evangelists are represented writing their Gospels while their winged symbols whisper in their ears. These are the most important accessories of the symbolical representations of the Crucifixion; the historical easily explain themselves. In many ancient crucifixions the figure of Christ is clothed in a robe. Some had a drapery from the hips to the knees. The draped figures are mostly if not all of Byzantine origin, and there is a legend which is given as a reason for this mode of representation: "A priest, who had exhibited to the people a figure of Christ only cinctured with a cloth, was visited by an apparition which said, 'All ye go covered with various raiment, and me ye show naked. Go forthwith and cover me with clothing.' The priest not understanding what was meant, took no notice, and on the third day the vision appeared again, and having scourged him severely with rods, said, 'Have I not told you to cover me with garments? Go now and cover with clothing the picture in which I appear crucified.'"

V. SYMBOLS OF THE HOLY GHOST.

From the sixth century to the present time, the dove has been the constant and universal symbol of the Holy Ghost. It appears in illustrations of the Scripture scenes, in which the Holy Spirit is mentioned from the "moving upon the face of the waters" to the Day of Pentecost. There are also many representations of his appearance in historical scenes, and in others which are partly or wholly legendary. The dove is often present at the Nativity and the Annunciation; it issues from the rod of Joseph, thus designating him to be the spouse of the Virgin; it hovers above the heads of holy men and saints, showing that their inspiration is heaven sent, — among which are David, St. John the Evangelist, St. Jerome. St. Theresa, and others. Another representation, intensely symbolical, is that of the Saviour surrounded by seven doves; they are of snowy whiteness, and have the cruciform nimbus; they are emblems of the seven gifts of the Spirit with which Christ was endowed: wisdom, understanding, counsel, strength, knowledge, piety, and fear (Isaiah xi.). These doves are frequently placed with three on each side and one at the top, thus forming a kind of aureole. It may not be out of place to observe that during the Middle Ages, seven was esteemed a sacred number. There were seven gifts of the Holy Ghost; seven sacraments; seven planets; seven days in the week; seven branches on the candlestick of Moses; seven liberal arts; seven churches of Asia; seven mysterious seals; seven stars and seven symbolic trumpets; seven heads of the Dragon; seven joys and seven sorrows of the Virgin; seven penitential psalms; seven deadly sins; seven canonical hours; and Mohammed says in the Koran, that "God visited the skies, and formed there seven heavens" (Koran ii. 27). Some cathedrals have seven chapels, as those at Rheims and Chartres. During the tenth century, the Holy Ghost was sometimes represented as a man; but this representation was never received with as much favor as the other. He was made of every age, from the earliest to the latest years of life. As a little child, he floated on the waters; as a young child he was in the arms of the Father; his age is according to the fancy of the artist, or the supposed requirements of the representation. Among the legendary pictures in which he was thus represented, is that of the reception of Christ in heaven, after his earthly mission was ended; the Holy Ghost is seated by the Father, and has a book, expressive of intelligence. He blesses Jesus, as does the Father; he also assists at the coronation of the Virgin. In some instances, the two representations of the Holy Ghost were combined, by the figure of a man with a dove on his head or hand. Still another symbol is that of a dove from which emanate rays of light, spreading out in every direction, forming a radiating aureole about it. The dove is also one of the general symbols of art, and as such is emblematical of purity and innocence, which signification was made most emphatic, by its use as the sacrifice for purification, under the Jewish law. As before mentioned, it is the attribute of certain female saints, denoting chastity and purity.

VI. SYMBOLS OF THE TRINITY.

Representations of the mystical Three in One were employed in art from its earliest ages. It was symbolized by the combination of three triangles, three circles, three fishes, and many other representations more obscure in their meanings. In later art, the three persons of the Trinity have been represented by three human figures, each with its special attribute, that of the Holy Ghost being the dove. Another mode represents the Father and Son with the dove between them; in the thirteenth and fourteenth centuries, the dove was often seen hovering between the first and second persons of the Trinity, with the tips of the wings touching the lips of each. This representation is called the double procession of the Spirit; illustrative of the sentence of the Nicene Creed, "proceeding from the Father and the Son." This representation belongs to the Latin Church. In these representations, when the locality is heaven, the figures are always seated. There is a device called the Italian Trinity, which was popular from the twelfth to the seventeenth century. In this the Father holds a crucifix by the ends of the transverse beam, the figure of Christ hanging between his knees; the dove proceeds downwards from the lips of the Father, and touches the head of the Son, or is merely sitting on the cross. Some attempts have been made to embody this mystery, by the representation of a body with three heads, or a head with three faces, but they are only frightful and monstrous.

VII. SYMBOLS OF ANGELS.

According to Dionysius, the Areopagite, there are three divisions of angels, and these each divided into three classes or choirs, making nine in all.

I. Councillors of God, consisting of—

1. The Seraphim, represented as covered with eyes.

2. The Cherubim, represented with six wings, and usually standing on wheels, according to the description of Ezekiel. Sometimes they have an open book. These two orders stand always before God, praising and adoring Him.

3. Thrones are represented carrying a throne or tower, and their duty is to support the throne of God.

II. Governors. — These rule the stars, and regulate the universe.

4. Dominations, represented with a sword, a triple crown and sceptre, or an orb and cross.

5. Virtues. — These carry a battle-axe and pennon or a crown and censer, and are in complete armor.

6. Powers. — These hold a baton, or are in the act of scourging or chaining evil spirits.

III MESSENGERS OF GOD.

7. PRINCEDOMS OR PRINCIPALITIES. — These are in armor, with pennons, or holding a lily.

8. ARCHANGELS. — These are seven in number, but the first three are those represented in art, and rarely the fourth. They are —

I MICHAEL (like unto God), captain-general of the host of Heaven, protector of the Hebrew nation, conqueror of the hosts of Hell; lord and guardian of souls, patron saint and prince of the Church Militant.

II. GABRIEL (God is my strength), guardian of the celestial treasury, the bearer of important messages, the angel of the annunciation, the preceptor of the patriarch Joseph.

III. RAPHAEL (the medicine of God), the chief of guardian angels, the conductor of the young Tobias.

IV. URIEL (the Light of God), the regent of the sun, the teacher of Esdras.

V. CHAMUEL (one who sees God) is believed by some to be the one who wrestled with Jacob, and appeared to Christ during his agony in the garden; but others believe that this was Gabriel.

VI. JOPHIEL (the beauty of God) the guardian of the tree of knowledge, and the one who drove Adam and Eve from the Garden of Eden, the protector of those who seek truth, the preceptor of the sons of Noah, the enemy of all who pursue vain knowledge.

VII. ZADKIEL (the righteousness of God), according to some authorities he stayed the hand of Abraham from sacrificing Isaac, but others believe that this was done by Michael.

The attributes of Michael are the sword and scales; of Gabriel, the lily; of Raphael, the staff and gourd of the pilgrim; of Uriel, a roll and book; of Chamuel, a cup and staff; of Jophiel, a flaming sword, and of Zadkiel, the sacrificial knife. When represented merely as archangels and not in their distinctive characters, they are in complete armor, holding their swords with points upwards, and sometimes with trumpets.

9. ANGELS. — Variously represented acccording to the purpose for which they are sent forth. The first great division of angels remain about the throne of God, and reflect the light and glory derived from Him upon the second division, who again reflect it upon the third division, who are the messengers of God and the guardians of mankind.

The Greek word for angel signifies literally "a bringer of tidings," therefore this term, though applied to all heavenly beings below the Godhead, belongs most properly to archangels and angels who are brought into communication with mankind. When Christ is represented with wings in Greek art, it is as "the great angel of the will of God." John the Baptist and the Evangelists, are angels, also, inasmuch as they were God's messengers, and they are sometimes represented with wings. A glory of angels is a representation in which the Trinity, Christ, or the Virgin, are surrounded by circles of angels, representing the different choirs. The interior circles, the Seraphim and Cherubim, are symbolized by heads with two, four, or six wings, and are usually of a bright red or blue color. Properly the Seraph, whose name signifies to love, should be red, and the Cherub, whose name signifies to know, should be blue. Angels should always be young, beautiful, perfect, but so represented as to seem immortal rather than eternal, since they are created beings. In early art, they were always draped, and although all colors are employed in the drapery, white should be the prevailing one. Wings are seldom wanting, and the representation of them as the attribute of celestial beings, did not originate in Christian art. This symbol of might, majesty, and divine beauty, is found in the remains of Egypt, Babylon, and Nineveh, as well as in Etruscan art.

VIII. SYMBOLS OF THE VIRGIN.

Among the symbols of the Blessed Virgin, the titles by which she is known, and from which certain pictures and effigies are named, are by no means the least interesting, showing as they do the estimation in which she is held, and the tenderness, as well as sacredness of the love she engenders in the hearts of her faithful worshippers. As the protector of the afflicted she is represented with her robe so spread out as to cover the votaries who pray for her gracious aid. In this character she has several titles, such as, —

Santa Maria di Misericordia, Our Lady of Mercy; and by this title, "Nuestra Señora de la Merced," she is known as the patroness of the Spanish Order of Mercy. When painted for their institutions, she frequently holds a badge of the Order on a tablet.

Santa Maria del buon Consilio, Our Lady of Good Counsel.

S. M. della Grazia, Our Lady of Grace.

S. M. Auxilium Afflictorum, Help of the Afflicted.

S. M. del Pianto, del Dolore, Our Lady of Lamentation or Sorrow.

S. M. del Soccorro, Our Lady of Succour, or of the Forsaken.

S. M. de buon Core, Our Lady of Good Heart.

S. M. Consolatrice, della Consolazione, or del Conforto, Our Lady of Consolation.

S. M. Refugium Peccatorum, Refuge of Sinners.

S. M. della Speranza, Our Lady of Hope.

She is invoked by women in travail as, —

S. M. del Parto, Our Lady of Good Delivery.

Again, by the people as, —

S. M. della Pace, Our Lady of Peace.

S. M. del Popolo, Our Lady of the People.

S. M. della Vittoria, Our Lady of Victory.

By students she is invoked as, —

S. M. della Sapienza, Our Lady of Wisdom.

S. M. della Perseveranza, Our Lady of Perseverance.

When painted for colleges and institutions of learning, she frequently holds a book.

By prisoners she is called, —

S. M. della Liberta, or Liberatrice, Our Lady of Liberty.

S. M. della Catena, Our Lady of Fetters.

There are also many titles derived from the circumstances of her life, or from certain accessories of the representation, as, —

S. M. della Cintola, Our Lady of the Girdle, when she gives her girdle to St. Thomas.

S. M. dell Libro, when she holds the book of Wisdom.

S. M. del Presepio, Our Lady of the Cradle, when in a Nativity.

S. M. della Lettera, the Madonna of the Letter, which illustrates the legend that she wrote a letter, A. D. 42, from Jerusalem to the people of Messina. This is her title as protectress of that city.

S. M. della Scodella, when with a cup she dips water from a fountain.

S. M. della Rosa, Our Lady of the Rose, when she holds a rose.

S. M. della Spina; this is her title as protectress of Pisa, when she holds the crown of thorns.

S. M. de Belem, Our Lady of Bethlehem. With this title she is the patroness of the Jeronymites.

S. M. di Loretto, Our Lady of Loretto. See legend of the Santa Casa.

S. M. del Pillar; this is her title as protectress of Saragossa. According to the tradition, she descended from heaven, standing on a marble pillar, and appeared to St. James when he was preaching in Spain. This legend is often seen in Spanish pictures, and the pillar is preserved in the cathedral of Saragossa.

S. M. del Carmine, Our Lady of Mount Carmel, under which title she is the protectress of the Carmelites.

S. M. della Neve, Our Lady of the Snow. See legend of Santa Maria Maggiore.

S. M. del Rosario, Our Lady of the Rosary. See the Rosary.

S. M. della Stella, Our Lady of the Star, when the star is embroidered on her mantle as an attribute.

S. M. del Fiore, Our Lady of the Flower. This is her title as protectress of Florence.

Certain prophets are sometimes represented as attending on Mary and the Infant Jesus. They are those who are supposed to have referred especially to the Incarnation. They are: —

Moses, because he beheld the burning bush.

Aaron, whose rod blossomed miraculously.

Gideon, whose fleece was wet with dew, when it was dry all around.

Daniel (Dan ii. 45).

David, both prophet and ancestor.

Isaiah, who prophesied that a virgin should conceive and bear a son.

Ezekiel (Ezek. xliv. 2). Frequently the figures of these prophets are omitted, and symbols of them introduced, as the burning bush for Moses; the dewy fleece for Gideon; the rod for Aaron, etc., etc.

Certain women, too, are regarded as types of Mary, and are often seated at her feet, or otherwise represented near her, as,—

Judith and Esther, who were emblems of the Virgin, in having brought deliverance to Israel.

Ruth, because she was the ancestress of David.

Bathsheba, because she sat on the right hand of her son.

Abishag, who was "the virgin who was brought to the king."

There are certain general symbols which are also given to Mary, with peculiar significations.

The Apple, when in the hand of the infant Saviour, signifies the sin of Paradise, which made his coming necessary; but in the hand of the Virgin, it designates her as the second Eve.

The Serpent, the general emblem of Satan and sin, has a peculiar meaning when placed beneath the feet of the Virgin, and is illustrative of the sentence, "Ipsa conteret caput tuum," "She shall bruise thy head."

The Globe, beneath the Virgin and intwined by a serpent, is the symbol of her triumph over a world fallen through sin.

The Pomegranate, the emblem of hope, is frequently given to the Virgin by the child Jesus.

Birds, in ancient pictures, figured the soul or the spiritual, as the opposite of the material. Thus the dove is the Holy Spirit hovering above her; while the seven doves, which typify the gifts of the Spirit, when surrounding the Virgin, make her the Mater Sapientiæ, or the Mother of Wisdom. When doves are near her while she reads or works, they express her gentleness and tenderness.

The Book, in the hand of Mary, if open, represents the book of Wisdom; if closed or sealed, it is a mystical symbol of the Virgin, which will be further explained.

Flowers were consecrated to the Virgin, and Fruits signify "the fruits of the Spirit,—joy, peace, and love."

Lastly, there are many symbols of the Virgin, derived from the Canticles and the Litanies of the Virgin, and which belong especially to her.

The Lily. (Cant. ii. 12.) "I am the rose of Sharon, and lily of the valleys."

The Rose is one emblem of love and beauty, and especially dedicated to Mary. A plantation or garden of roses is often represented.

The Enclosed Garden (Cant. iv. 12).

The Star is often embroidered on her veil or mantle. When she has a crown of twelve stars it is illustrative of the description in the Revelation. She is also called "Stella Maris," star of the sea; "Stella Jacobi," the star of Jacob; "Stella non Erratica," the fixed star; and "Stella Matutina," the morning star.

The Sun and Moon refer to her as the woman of the Apocalypse: "A woman clothed with the sun, having the moon under her feet, and on her head a crown of twelve stars."

The Stem of Jesse, is represented as a green branch twined with flowers (Isa. xi. 1).

The Porta Clausa, or closed gate (Ezek. xliv. 4).

The Well, Fountain, City of David, Temple of Solomon, and Tower of David, are all symbols borrowed from the Canticles.

The Olive, The Cypress, and Palm, are all emblems of the Virgin. The first signifies peace, hope, and abundance; the second points to heaven, and the third speaks of victory.

The Cedar of Lebanon, by its height, its perfume, its healing qualities, and its incorruptible substance, symbolizes the greatness, goodness and beauty of the Virgin.

The Sealed Book, in the hands of the Virgin, alludes to the text, "In that book were all my members written," and also to the sealed book described by Isaiah (xxix. 11, 12).

The Mirror is borrowed as an emblem from the book of Wisdom (vii. 25). "Specula sine maculâ."

The explanation of the seven joys and the seven sorrows of the Virgin, as well as that of the mysteries of the Rosary, will be found, by reference to them in their alphabetical order, in the next division of this book.

Tetramorph.

IX. SYMBOLS OF THE EVANGELISTS.

When the Evangelists are represented together, it is in their character of witnesses, upon whose testimony the whole truth of Christianity rests; when they are single they are usually presented as teachers or patrons. The earliest symbol of the Evangelists was a Greek cross, with a scroll or book in each angle, — emblems of the writers of the four Gospels. The second symbol was that of the four rivers, which rise in Paradise. Sometimes the Saviour with a lamb, or the symbolic Agnus Dei, was represented on an eminence, with the four streams, symbolizing the Evangelists, flowing from beneath him. Their next symbol was the four fiery creatures of Ezekiel's vision (Ezek. i. 5). These were interpreted by the Jews, as representing the archangels; also the prophets, Isaiah, Jeremiah, Ezekiel, and Daniel; but the early Christians explained them more satisfactorily to themselves, as emblems of the Evangelists.

The four "beasts" of the Apocalypse received the same explanation, and in the seventh century they had become the distinctive symbols of these inspired witnesses.

(Mosaic) St. Mark.

Jerome explains the individual application of these symbols thus:

1. The cherub, which most resembles a human being, was given to St. Matthew, because he speaks more of the human than of the divine nature of our Saviour.

St. Mark.

2. The Lion symbolizes St. Mark, for three reasons: —

(i.) He commences his epistle with the mission of St. John the Baptist, "The voice of one crying in the wilderness."

(ii.) The king of beasts is a type of the royal dignity of Christ, which St. Mark makes so apparent.

(iii.) According to an oriental tradition the young lions are born dead, and after three days are made alive, by the breath or the roar of the sire; thus they are an emblem of the Resurrection, of which St. Mark is called the historian.

(Mosaic, 5th Century.) St. Luke.

3. The Ox was given St. Luke because he especially sets forth the Priesthood of Christ, and the ox is symbolical of sacrifice.

4. The Eagle was given to St.

John as an emblem of the lofty flights of his inspiration.

(Mosaic, 11th Century.) St. John.

Others regarded these "Beasts" as shadowing forth the Incarnation, Passion, Resurrection, and Ascension of Jesus; and they are also believed to represent the fourfold character of Christ as man, king, high-priest, and God.

These symbolic creatures were always represented as winged. The union of all four "Beasts," forms that mysterious emblem called the Tetramorph. In another symbol a woman represents the new Law, or the Church. She is crowned and seated on a creature who has the four heads of these symbolic beasts, the body of a horse, and four feet, embracing one of each of the four creatures. Again, the Church is in a triumphal chariot, driven by a cherub or angel, and drawn by the lion, ox, and eagle. The next advance was the combination of the human form with the heads of these mystic beasts. Figures formed in this way were sometimes represented alternately, with the figures of the prophets, all forming a circle. These ideas seem to have been borrowed from the winged bulls, with human heads, found at Nineveh.

(Mosaic, A. D. 750.) St. Luke.

At length the only symbol retained in the representations of the Evangelists was the wings. These were attached to the human form; they bear their books, and the symbolic creatures were represented near them or at their feet.

The Evangelists were often represented together, with four prophets, thus symbolizing the old and new

(Fra Angelico.)

(Fra Angelico.)

law; or with four doctors of the Church, as witnesses to, and interpreters of the truth.

In later art the Evangelists appear without emblems or attributes; sometimes with their names inscribed above or beneath their representations. In speaking of the different stages of this symbolism, Mrs. Jameson says: "It will be interesting to pause for a moment and take a rapid, retrospective view of the progress, from first to last, in the expression of an idea through form. First, we have the mere fact; the four scrolls, or the four books. Next, the idea; the four rivers of salvation, flowing from on high, to fertilize the whole earth. Thirdly, the prophetic symbol; the winged cherub of fourfold aspect.

St. John.

(Hans Beham.)

"Next, the Christian symbol; the four beasts in the Apocalypse, with or without the angel-wings. Then the combination of the emblematical animal with the human form. Then the human personages, each of venerable, or inspired aspect, as becomes the teacher and witness; and each attended by the Scriptural emblem — no longer an emblem but an attribute marking his individual vocation and character.

"And, lastly, the emblem and attribute both discarded, we have the human being only, holding his gospel, *i. e.* his version of the doctrine of Christ." [1]

(Fra Angelico.)

X. SYMBOLS OF THE APOSTLES.

The earliest purely symbolic representation of the Twelve Apostles was that of twelve sheep surrounding Christ, the good Shepherd, while He

[1] Sacred and Legendary Art.

bore a lamb in his arms; or again, Jesus as the Lamb of God, is on an eminence, from which flow the four rivers of Paradise, while on one side six sheep leave Jerusalem, and on the other side the same number leave Bethlehem. They were very rarely represented by doves. The next advance was to represent them as men, and all bearing sheep; or in place of sheep, scrolls, and distinguished from each other by the inscription of their names above them.

According to tradition, the Apostles, before separating, composed the Apostles' Creed, of which each one furnished a sentence, or proposition. These are inscribed on their scrolls as follows: St. Peter, — Credo in Deum Patrem omnipotentem, creatorem cœli et terræ; St. Andrew, — Et in Jesum Christum Filium ejus unicum, Dominum nostrum; St. James Major, — Qui conceptus est de Spiritu Sancto, natus ex Maria Virgine; St. John, — Passus sub Pontio Pilato, crucifixus, mortuus et sepultus; St. Philip, — Descendit ad inferos, tertia die resurrexit a mortuis; St. James Minor, — Ascendit ad cœlos, sedet ad dexteram Dei Patris omnipotentis; St. Thomas, — Inde venturus est judicare vivos et mortuos; St. Bartholomew, — Credo in Spiritum Sanctum; St. Matthew, — Sanctam Ecclesiam Catholicam, sanctorum communionum; St. Simon, — Remissionem peccatorum; St. Matthias, — Carnis resurrectionem; St. Thaddeus, — Et vitam æternam. From the sixth century, each one of the Apostles had his especial attribute, which was taken from some circumstance of his life or death, and which will be found in the legends of each. These attributes are as follows: —

St. Peter, the keys or a fish.

St. Andrew, the transverse cross which bears his name.

St. James Major, the pilgrim's staff.

St. John, the chalice with the serpent is the proper attribute of the Apostle; but the eagle, which is his attribute as an Evangelist, is sometimes seen when he is with the Apostles.

St. Thomas, generally, a builder's rule; rarely, a spear.

St. James Minor, a club.

St. Philip, a small cross on a staff or crosier, surmounted by a cross.

St. Bartholomew, a knife.

St. Matthew, a purse.

St. Simon, a saw.

St. Thaddeus, a halberd or lance.

St. Matthias, a lance.

Sometimes St. Paul, St. Mark, and St. Luke are represented with the Apostles, and some others are left out, as the number is always twelve. In such cases, St. Paul bears either one or two swords.

The Apostles have also been represented seated on clouds, surrounding the Saviour, as they are supposed to be in heaven. Later art has not only distinguished each of the Apostles by his own attribute, it has also attempted to represent the character of each in the face and bearing; and the illustration of the legends which develop the characteristics drawn from the Scripture history, enables the artist to accomplish this object, sometimes with wonderful effect.

XI. SYMBOLS OF THE MONASTIC ORDERS.

To a student or lover of art, there is a world of interest connected with the monastic orders, with their founders, their artists, their pictures. While they instituted schools, built cathedrals, and founded hospitals, they were the most munificent patrons of art the world has ever seen. To them we are indebted for many of the rarest gems of painting. Intended for the seclusion of church and cloister, *they now belong to all the world;* for who that has gazed on the Madonna di San Sisto; on the spirit-moving pictures of Angelico the Blessed, and many, many others, does not feel that he has a possession in them; that they have imparted something to him that was *his;* something intended for him, and held in trust until he came to claim his own? There are certain peculiarities in what may be called monastic pictures, which were most fitting when in their proper places, but which seem incongruous when in the galleries of art, or on the walls of palaces. I refer especially to the representation of the personages, and the peculiar habits and symbols of the different Orders for which the pictures were painted. For instance, in pictures of the Annunciation, and other scenes from the life of the Virgin, or the Saviour, we see the founders of Orders and Institutions in their distinctive dress; and until we consider that they were painted for these Orders, and in honor of these very founders and saints, we wonder at and are disturbed by the seeming inappropriateness of the representations.

That these things are so, make it a necessity that some attention should be given to these symbols and habits. A knowledge of them enables one to decide for what Order a picture was intended, and explains much of its import and purpose.

There are certain general symbols which have a peculiar significance in monastic pictures: —

The Nimbus is given only to a canonized saint, never to a beato sometimes the picture is painted before canonization, and the nimbus added afterwards.

The Infant Christ is often placed in the arms of a saint, or, in some pictures of the Virgin, she bends down and places the child in the arms of holy men and women. These are generally representations of visions which these saints have had, or have arisen from legends like that of St. Anthony of Padua, which relates that the Saviour came in this form, and stood on his book while he preached the Gospel.

The Standard, surmounted by the cross, belongs especially to such as were missionaries and Apostles, and carried the Gospel to heathen nations. It is also an attribute of the warrior saints connected with the monastic orders.

The Crown at the feet of saints, indicates that they were of royal birth, or resigned their kingdoms for the monastery. If they retained their rank until death, they wear the crown; and female saints of royal blood frequently wear the diadem outside the veil.

A Seraph distinguishes the saints of the Seraphic Order.

The Stigmata, or wounds of Christ, belong properly to St. Catherine of Siena and St. Francis alone, but are sometimes given to St. Maria Maddalena de' Pazzi.

The Book in the hand has the general signification of the Gospel, but accompanied by the pen or ink-horn it indicates that the saint was an author, and the book is sometimes lettered with the proper titles of his works. The open book in the hand of a founder, is the symbol of the Rule of his Order, and is often inscribed with the first sentence of the rule.

The Crucifix in the hand, signifies a preacher; it is also an emblem of penance and faith.

The Flaming Heart is an emblem of divine love. The heart crowned with thorns belongs to St. Francis de Sales. The heart inscribed with I. H. S., is given to Jesuit saints, to St. Theresa, St. Bridget of Sweden, and St. Maria Maddalena de' Pazzi.

The Crown of Thorns on the head, or in the hands, is the symbol of suffering for Christ's sake.

The Palm is not a general symbol for the monastic saints, but is given to St. Placidus, St. Boniface, and St. Thomas à Becket, of the Benedictines; to St. Angelus and St. Albert, of the Carmelites, and to St. Peter Martyr, of the Dominicans, and but few others.

The Scourge is the symbol of self-inflicted penance.

Walking on the Sea represents a miracle attributed to the saint who is so painted.

The Cardinal's Hat is proper to St. Bonaventura. He is distinguished from St. Jerome by the Franciscan girdle.

The Mitre and Pastoral Staff belong to abbots and bishops. The staff without the mitre is proper only to abbesses.

Slaves with Broken Chains, as well as beggars, children, and lepers at the feet of a saint, signify beneficence.

Roses are significant of the name of the saint, or are connected with some circumstance in their lives, as with St. Elizabeth of Hungary, and St. Dorothea.

The Lily is an emblem of purity and chastity, and of very general use, but it belongs especially to St. Clara, St. Anthony of Padua, St. Catherine of Siena, as well as to those who made vows of celibacy, like St. Casimir and others. The crucifix twined with lilies belongs to St. Nicholas of Tolentino. The lily also belongs to such as devoted themselves especially to the Virgin.

THE STAR over the head or breast expresses the divine attestation to the sanctity of the saint.

THE SUN on the breast is the symbol of the light of wisdom.

THE DOVE is the emblem of the direct inspiration of the Holy Ghost.

THE FISH, as the emblem of baptism, belongs to some early missionaries and such as converted the heathen.

THE LAMB is proper to St. Francis as the symbol of meekness.

WILD BEASTS at the feet of a saint, signify that he cleared a wilderness or founded a convent in a solitude.

THE HIND OR STAG is the emblem of solitude.

THE DRAGON at the feet is sin conquered, but chained to a rock or led by a chain it is heresy vanquished.

The habits and special symbols of different orders are important. First, the *Benedictines* with St. Benedict as their general patriarch, embrace —

THE CAMALDOLESI, founded by St. Romualdo;

THE VALLOMBROSIANS, founded by St. John Gualberto;

THE CARTHUSIANS, founded by St. Bruno;

THE CISTERCIANS, founded by St. Bernard of Clairvaux;

THE OLIVETANI, founded by St. Bernardo Ptolomei;

THE ORATORIANS, founded by St. Philip Neri;

THE CLUNIACS, founded by St. Peter of Clugny;

And some other less important branches which are governed by the rule of St. Benedict.

The color of the habit is not especially determined in the Benedictine rule. In the early pictures of St. Benedict he wears black, but in some pictures painted for the reformed Benedictines, he is in a white habit. The black habit is given to St. Scholastica and the pupils of St. Benedict, St. Maurus, and St. Placidus, and to St. Flavia; also to St. Boniface, the Apostle of Germany; St. Bennett, Bishop of Durham; St. Benedict of Anian; St. Dunstan of Canterbury; St. Walpurgis of Eichstadt; St. Giles of Languedoc, St. Ildefonso of Toledo; St. Bavon of Ghent; and to nearly all Benedictines who lived before the year 1020.

THE CAMALDOLESI and their founder wear white.

THE VALLOMBROSIANS, gray or ash color.

THE CLUNIACS, black.

THE CISTERCIANS, white. Their habit is long and loose, with very wide sleeves.

THE CARTHUSIANS, white.

THE OLIVETANI, white.

These orders furnished the earliest artists and architects of Europe. The monastery of Monte Cassino was founded by St. Benedict. Its church and cloisters contain many works of art, and among them the statues in marble of the most noted members and benefactors of the community. The cave at Subiaco, the Sacro Speco, is of great interest, and painted with very ancient frescoes. They were done in 1219, and are important in the history of art. Among the finest edifices of the Benedictines may be mentioned the Basilica of San Paolo fuor-le-mure at Rome, San Severino at Naples, San Giustina at Padua, the monastery of Bamberg in Germany, St. Maur, Marmoutier, and Fontevrauld in France. For their convent at Piacenza, the Madonna di San Sisto was painted; for that at Grotta Ferrata, the life of St. Nilus by Domenichino; at San Severino, the life of St. Benedict by Antonio lo Zingaro. For the Vallombrosians, Perugino painted the Assumption. Taddeo Gaddi painted many pictures for the Camaldolesi; and for different Benedictine Orders, Ghirlandajo and Andrea del Sarto painted some of their finest pictures. The Certosa di Pavia is unequaled in many points, and has works of Luini, Borgognone, and many other famous masters. This is a Carthusian monastery, as is also the Certosa at Rome, built by Michael Angelo. Zurbaran and Carducho painted for the Spanish Carthusians, and Le Sueur the life of St. Bruno for those at Paris.

The Cistercians have many pictures of the Virgin, as they especially worship her and dedicate their churches in her name.

The beautiful church of San Lorenzo in Cremona, and that of Santa Maria in Organo at Verona, belong to the Olivetani, whose artists excelled in Tarsia or Intarsiatura, a beautiful style of inlaid work. In England many of the finest cathedrals were Benedictine foundations, and the word Abbey belonged especially to this order.

The Augustines.

These orders reverence St. Augustine of Hippo as their general patriarch and founder. They embrace —

The Servi, founded by St. Philip Benozzi;
The Order of Mercy, founded by St. Peter Nolasco;
The Brigittines, founded by St. Bridget of Sweden.

The Augustines reverence St. Joseph, the husband of the Virgin Mary, as their patriarch and patron saint. The habit of the Augustines is black. St. Augustine and his mother, St. Monica, are the principal personages in the pictures of the Order. St. Joseph and all the events of his life are also favorite subjects, and the earliest martyrs and bishops, though common to all orders, are especially honored by the Augustines. Their primitive hermits, St. Anthony and St. Paul, also receive much veneration; but their chief saint is Nicholas of Tolentino. The most important churches of the Agostini in Italy are the Sant' Agostino at Pavia, which contains the magnificent shrine of their founder, which has in all two hundred and ninety figures worked in marble. The principal events of the life of St. Augustine are represented, and there are also statues of the Evangelists, Apostles, and many saints. The Sant' Agostino at Rome is the church for which the Isaiah of Raphael was painted. The Eremitani at Padua and the San Lorenzo of Florence, are rich in works of art. The cathedrals at Cologne, Strasbourg, and Mayence belong to the Augustines, and churches everywhere which are dedicated to St. Laurence, St. Sebastian, St. Mary Magdalene, and St. Antonio Abbate usually are of this Order.

The Franciscans.

With St. Francis at their head, this order embraces the —

Capuchins;
Observants;
Conventuals, and
Minimes.

These monks, as well as the Dominicans, are called frati, or brothers, instead of padri, or fathers, and the humility of St. Francis caused him to add the word minori, or lesser, to his community. The habit of the Franciscans was first gray, and remained so for two centuries, when it was changed to dark brown. It is a plain tunic with long full sleeves, but not as ample as those of the Benedictines. This tunic is bound about the waist with a knotted cord, which is the emblem of a beast subdued; and this was the light in which St. Francis considered the body when subjected to the spirit. A scanty cape hangs about the shoulders, to which is attached a hood to be drawn over the head in cold weather. The nuns wear the same dress, with a veil in place of the hood. The third order of St. Francis are distinguished by the cord worn as a girdle. The Franciscans are barefooted or with a sandal known in Italy as the zoccolo, hence the name Zoccolanti by which these friars are sometimes called. The *Minimes* are distinguished by a scapulary which hangs a little below the girdle in front and is rounded at the ends; to this is attached a small round hood, while that of the Capuchins is pointed. The Franciscans aspired to extreme sanctity, and were greatly beloved by the people. They have several royal saints, but first are their eight principal saints, called, "I Cardini dell Ordine Serafico," — the chiefs of the Seraphic Order.

1. St. Francis, Padre Serafico, patriarch and founder.

2. St. Clara, Madre Serafica, first Franciscan nun and foundress of the Povere Donne or Poor Clares.

3. St. Bonaventura, il Dottore Serafico, the great prelate of the Order.

4. St. Antony of Padua, who is, next to St. Francis, the miracle-worker of the order.

5. St. Bernardino of Siena, their great preacher and reformer.
6. St. Louis, King of France.
7. St. Louis, Bishop of Toulouse.
8. St. Elizabeth of Hungary.

Then follow St. Margaret of Cortona, St Rosa di Viterbo, St. Felix de Cantalicio, and a host of others.

The churches of the Franciscans have been magnificently adorned. The parent convent and church at Assisi was three hundred years in the hands of the greatest artists of Italy. Raphael, Pinturicchio, Giotto, Taddeo and Angelo Gaddi, Giottino, Luca della Robbia, and Benedetto da Maiano, all contributed to the decoration of Franciscan edifices. The St. Antonio-di-Padova is filled with art treasures. It has bronzes of Donatello and Andrea Riccio; pictures by many of the great painters of Upper Italy, and marbles of Lombardi, Sansovino, and Sammichele. Murillo painted many of his wonderful pictures for this Order in Spain.

The Dominicans.

These are called the Preaching Friars, and have St. Dominick at their head. They wear a white woolen gown, fastened with a white girdle; over this a white scapular, which hangs to the feet from the neck, both before and behind, like a long apron; over all a black cloak with a hood. The scapular of the lay brothers is black. The Dominicans always wear shoes. Their traditions teach that this habit was adopted in accordance with the directions of the Blessed Virgin. The white symbolizes purity; the black, mortification and penance. Their four principal saints are St. Dominick, St. Peter Martyr; St. Thomas Aquinas, the Angelic Doctor; and St. Catherine of Siena. The Dominicans have embraced some of the most splendid artists and patrons of art. The shrine of St. Dominick is in the church of his Order at Bologna. It is called, in Italy, the "Arca di San Domenico." Niccolo Pisano built the church and executed the shrine, but the church has been rebuilt in modern style. At Rome, the Santa Maria-Sopra-Minerva is their most important church; and here sleeps Angelico da Fiesole, "Il Beato," and Leo X., with Cardinal Howard, Cardinal Bembo, and Durandus. This church is filled with beautiful pictures, and here is Michael Angelo's statue of Christ. At Florence, the Dominicans have the Santa Maria Novella. In this church is the Chapel Dei Spagnuoli, painted by Taddeo Gaddi and Simone Memmi. The Strozzi Chapel, by Andrea Orcagna; and here is the Madonna and Child, by Cimabue.

In Florence is the convent of St. Mark, where lived and painted Fra Angelico, and Fra Bartolomeo. The first of these entered this convent when twenty years old, and passed the remainder of his long life in painting the spiritual conceptions of his devout and gentle mind. He believed that God granted him his benediction on his labors, and so impressed was he with the religious importance of them, that he is said to have painted much upon his bended knees, as if performing an act of devotion. His principal works are in his own convent, in the Church of Santa Maria Novella, and in the Chapel of Nicholas V., in the Vatican. Fra Bartolomeo is also called Baccio della Porta and Il Frate.

At Siena the Dominicans have the Madonna by Guido da Siena, and the frescoes of Razzi. For this Order, Leonardo da Vinci painted his Last Supper, and Titian his San Pietro Martire.

Their churches were built without aisles, having a nave only, in order that the preaching, which was their especial duty, might be heard in every part; this form of edifice was very advantageous also for showing off their pictures.

The Carmelites.

This Order claim the prophet Elijah as their founder, and also that Mt. Carmel has been inhabited by a direct succession of hermits ever since the time of that prophet. They wear a brown tunic with a white mantle, and are also called White Friars. Their most interesting church is the Carmini at Florence, in which is the Brancacci Chapel, which was painted by Masaccio, Filippino Lippi, and Masolino. The Carmelites are not important as an Order in art.

The Jeronymites.

These monks claim St. Jerome as their founder, and adorn their edifices largely with pictures of that saint, and scenes from his life. The Escurial and the monastery of St. Just, in Spain; the Monastery of Belem in Portugal; and that of St. Sigismond near Cremona, in Italy, all belong to this Order, which is remarkable for the magnificence of its edifices.

The Jesuits.

The members of this Order are not easily distinguished in art. They wear the black frock buttoned to the chin, which is so unfavorable for a picture, that they are often represented in the dress of a priest. If the head is covered, it is by a square black cap. The Jesuits did not appear to value art as highly as many of the other monastic orders. They lavished large sums of money on their churches; but it was spent in brilliant decorations of gold and silver, rare marbles, and even jewels, rather than in pictures and statues; and yet they were (after some royal personages) the chief patrons of Rubens and Van Dyck, who decorated the splendid church of their Order at Antwerp.

XII. VOTIVE PICTURES, ANACHRONISMS, ETC.

There are large numbers of what are known as votive pictures, which are painted in fulfillment of a vow, in gratitude for some signal blessing, or to avert some anticipated danger. Many commemorate a recovery, or escape from sickness or accident. The donor, and sometimes his entire family, are seen in the picture, and are frequently represented as grouped about the Madonna and Child. In early art, the donor or votary was represented as very diminutive, to express humility, but in later times they appear a natural size. The figure of a bishop kneeling, while all others stand, signifies that he is the person who presents the picture; when he stands it is difficult to determine who he may be; for there are hundreds of bishop-martyrs and patrons, who are thus represented.

In many works of art, there is an apparent anachronism in the choice of the persons represented; as, for instance, when the Virgin is surrounded by those who lived either centuries before or after herself. It must be borne in mind that such pictures were not intended to represent physical facts, but are devotional in their character and meaning. And if the persons represented are not living, they know no more of time; for them it no longer exists, and that which, at a careless glance, appears to be the result of ignorance or bad taste, is in fact a spiritual conception of the "communion of saints," who belong no more to earth. When thus considered, there appears no incongruity in these representations, of which the Correggio at Parma is a good illustration. In it, St. Jerome presents his translation of the Scriptures to the infant Christ, while an angel turns the leaves, and Mary Magdalene kisses the feet of Jesus. Neither is the grouping in many pictures strictly in accordance with what might be termed propriety. The Sibyls dancing around the cradle of Jesus, and the representations of Greek poets and philosophers in ecclesiastical art, is explained by the fact that everything was regarded in but a single aspect, — that is, in its relation to Christ and his religion. And all those who had preceded Him were believed to have foreshadowed Him, and prophesied of his coming; in fact, these Greeks sometimes bear scrolls inscribed with sentences from their writings, which are interpreted as relating to the Saviour. In the examination of large numbers of religious pictures, chronology should be entirely forgotten, for time was not thought of in their arrangement, and many other considerations determined the artist in his association of persons. Certain saints are brought together, because they are joint patrons of the place for which they were painted, as in the Venetian pictures of St. Mark, St. George, and St. Catherine. Again, they are connected by the same attributes, or similar events, in their lives, as is the case with St. Roch and St. Sebastian, — the first having tended the sick who suffered from the plague, and the last being a patron against it. Or they were friends on earth, as St. Cyprian and St. Cornelius; or they rest together in death, as St. Stephen and St. Laurence. Some of these, or other like reasons, which were good and sufficient to the minds of artists and their patrons, always explained the apparent inconsistencies of these pictures, and were perfectly understood in the age to which they belonged. Again, some saints are so much more frequently represented than others, as to occasion surprise and remark. This may be explained in part, by the fact that some saints were universal patrons, worshipped everywhere, and belonged to Christendom, while the veneration for others was confined to localities or Orders. St. George, St. Sebastian, St. Christopher, St. Cosmo, St. Damian, St. Roch, St. Nicholas, St. Catherine, St. Barbara, St. Margaret, and St. Ursula, are all thus considered.

In particular schools of art this frequent representation of certain personages is governed by the locality in which they were painted, or that for which they were intended. Florentine artists would introduce St. Donato and St. Romulo; a Neapolitan, St. Januarius; a Frenchman, St. Denis, etc., etc., or as in an existing picture, St. Peter, St. Leonard, St. Martha, and St. Mary Magdalene, are united to indicate that the society for which it was painted, redeemed prisoners, ransomed slaves, labored for the poor, and converted the fallen and sinful.

Thus, it is apparent that it is for the advantage of the careful observer to consider, that however bizarre a picture may appear, there is some reason for its arrangement, which if understood and appeciated, adds meaning to it; helps to discern its intention and sentiment, and shows that what seems at first to be the result of chance, or an ignorance of the fitness of things, is in truth that of deep and earnest thought, of delicate and poetic conceptions, and a lofty desire to teach grand and holy truths, as well as to give pleasure and delight the eye.

Badge of the Order of Mercy

LEGENDS AND STORIES

WHICH HAVE BEEN ILLUSTRATED IN ART.

St. Abbondio was born at Thessalonica. He was the fourth Bishop of Como, in the time of Leo I. He is represented in the Cathedral of Como, and is the apostle and patron saint of that portion of Italy.

Abgarus, King. The apocryphal gospel spoken of by Eusebius, and called "Christ and Abgarus," commences with "A Copy of a Letter written by King Abgarus to Jesus, and sent to Him by Ananias, his Footman, to Jerusalem, inviting Him to Edessa." This letter commences with greetings to the Saviour, and goes on to urge Him to go to Edessa, to cure the king of a serious disease. It adds, "My city is indeed small, but neat, and large enough for us both." Jesus returned an answer, that He could not go, as He must fulfill his mission at Jerusalem, but promised that after his ascension He would send a disciple, who would cure the king and give life to him and to all who were with him. This account ends here; but up to the tenth century, there were a variety of additions made to it, until then it had assumed the following form: "Abgarus, King of Edessa, suffering from the twofold infliction of gout and leprosy, withdrew from the sight of men. Ananias, one of his servants, returning from a journey to Egypt, tells him of the wonderful cures by Christ, of which he has heard in Palestine. In the hope of obtaining relief, Abgarus writes to Christ, and charges Ananias, who was not only a good traveller but a skillful painter, that if Christ should not be able to come, he should at all events send him his portrait. Ananias finds Christ as He is in the act of performing miracles, and teaching the multitude in the open air. As he is not able to approach Him for the crowd, he mounts a rock not far off. Thence he fixes his eyes upon Christ, and begins to take his likeness. Jesus, who sees him, and also knows in spirit the contents of the letter, sends Thomas to bring him to Him, writes his answer to Abgarus, and gives it to him. But seeing that Ananias still lingers, Jesus calls for water, and having washed his face, He wipes it on a cloth, on which, by his divine power, there remains a perfect portrait of his features;

this He gives to Ananias, charging him to take it to Abgarus, so that his longing may be satisfied, and his disease cured On the way Ananias passes by the city of Hierapolis, but remains outside the gates, and hides the holy cloth in a heap of freshly made bricks. At midnight the inhabitants of Hierapolis perceive that this heap of bricks is surrounded with fire. They discover Ananias, and he owns the supernatural character of the object hidden among the bricks. They find, not only the miraculous cloth, but more still; for, by a mysterious virtue, a brick that lay near the cloth has received a second impress of the Divine image. And, as no fire was discoverable, except the light that proceeded from the picture, the inhabitants kept the brick as a sacred treasure, and let Ananias go on his way. He gives King Abgarus the letter and the cloth, who is immediately healed." This last legend was edited by the Emperor Constantine Porphyrogenitus, and in his time the original napkin was at Constantinople; two others at Rome and Genoa, while a false copy had been sent to the King of Persia. The brick, too, had remained in its first city, but had furnished images to other cities. In fact, the Roman one still exists in the Church of San Silvestro. But Constantine has given a third version, which is that Christ, on the way to Calvary, wiped his face on a piece of linen on which his impress was left, and gave it to Thomas, commanding that after his ascension Thaddeus should take it to Abgarus in order to fulfill the promise which Jesus had made. This was done, but Thaddeus first goes to the house of a Jew in Edessa, determined to do some miracles which shall attract the attention of the king. And he heals the sick, until Abgarus hears of him and sends for him, hoping that he is the disciple whom Christ had promised him should come. As Thaddeus enters the room, he lifts up the picture, and so great a light proceeds from it, that Abgarus springs from his bed, forgetting all his lameness, and goes to receive the picture. He touches it to his head and limbs, and receives strength. The leprosy disappears except from his forehead. He is converted, and when he is baptized, even the last marks of the leprosy disappear. This legend has been often represented in painting.

St. Achilleus and St. Nereus. These are Roman saints, and the church dedicated to them is near the Baths of Caracalla. They were chamberlains of Flavia Domitilla. They persuaded her not to marry Aurelian, the son of the consul, to whom she was betrothed, because he was an idolator. For this they were beheaded. Flavia Domitilla was the grand-niece of the Emperor Domitian. Her parents had been martyred because they were Christians. She also suffered death for the same cause, at Terracina. Nereus and Achilleus are represented in secular habits, standing on each side of Domitilla. She is dressed as a princess. They all bear palms. May 12.

St. Adelaide or **Alice of Germany** was the daughter of Ralph II. of Burgundy. Her father died when she was six years old, and at sixteen she married Lothaire, King of Italy. Her husband did not live long, and after his death Adelaide was imprisoned at Pavia, by Berengarius III. She at length escaped, and fled towards Germany. She was met by the Emperor Otho I., who was marching with his army to release her. Otho made a treaty with Berengarius, and married Alice. But the treaty was soon broken, when Otho sent Berengarius a prisoner to Germany, and he himself was crowned emperor at Rome. Adelaide made use of her rank and power to do good, and educated her son Otho II. with carefulness. The emperor died after a reign of thirty-six years; and his son suffered himself to be influenced by evil advisers, and especially by his second wife, Theophania, so that he banished his good mother from the court. But being overtaken by misfortune, he recalled her and attempted to atone for his wicked cruelty. He died after a reign of nine years, and his wife, so long as she lived, insulted St. Adelaide by the most disrespectful treatment; but she, too, soon died, and Adelaide became regent. From this time she devoted herself to good works, and built many religious edifices. The people, who loved her, were guided by her into virtue and piety. She died at Salcis, when on a journey. A part of her relics are preserved in a shrine in Hanover. December 16, A. D. 999.

St. Adelaide was the wife of St. Lupo, and the mother of St. Grata, who together with St. Alexander, the martyr, are saints belonging especially to Bergamo, the last two being the patron saints of that city. St. Grata, after the death of her husband, became a Christian, and converted her father, who was Duke of Bergamo, and her mother, St. Adelaide, to the same faith. Through the influence of St. Grata, St. Lupo founded the Cathedral at Bergamo. After the death of her parents, Grata governed Bergamo, and founded three churches and a hospital, where she herself ministered to the sick. St. Alexander was a soldier of the Theban Legion, and was beheaded outside Bergamo. Grata wrapped the head in a napkin, and gave honorable burial to the remains. St. Adelaide is represented with a crown and a long veil, St. Lupo with a royal crown, St. Alexander as a Roman warrior with a palm, and St. Grata as carrying the head of Alexander.

St. Adrian (*Gr.* Ἅγ. Ἀδριανός; *Lat.* Sanctus Adrianus; *Fr.* St. Adrien; *Ital.* Sant' Adriano) was a military saint, and for ages was considered next to St. George in Northern Europe. In the North of France, Flanders, and Germany, he was the patron saint of soldiers, and protector against the plague. He is also the patron of Flemish brewers. He was a noble Roman, son of Probus. At the time of the tenth persecution of the Christians at Nicomedia, a city of Bithynia (A. D. 290), he served in the guards of the Emperor Galerius Maximian. He was less than thirty years old, and was married to Natalia, who was a Christian secretly. She was exceedingly virtuous and beautiful. The imperial edict was torn down by St. George, which so infuriated the emperor that thirty-four Christians were sentenced to the torture at one time. It fell by lot to Adrian to superintend the execution of the sentence. When he saw the manner in which the Christians suffered for their faith, he was suddenly converted, and seating himself in their midst, exclaimed, "Consider me also as one of ye, for I, too, will be a Christian." He was immediately imprisoned. Natalia, hearing this, was full of joy, and, going to him, encouraged him to suffer for Christ. Adrian was soon condemned to die, and the night before his execution, he bribed his jailor to permit him to visit Natalia. She, hearing that her husband had left his prison, was in great sorrow, and tearing her garments, threw herself down, saying, "Alas! miserable that I am! I have not deserved to be the wife of a martyr! Now will men point at me and say, Behold the wife of the coward and apostate, who, for fear of death, hath denied his God.' But Adrian, who had now come, hearing these words, said, "O thou noble and strong hearted woman! O, bless God that I am not unworthy of thee! Open the door that I may bid thee farewell before I die." Joyfully she opened the door and embraced him, and returned to prison with him. The next day Adrian was scourged and tortured, and sent back to prison. The tyrants, hearing of the devotion of Natalia, ordered that no woman should be admitted to the prison. She then cut off her beautiful hair, and dressed as a man, and so gained admission to Adrian. She found him torn and bleeding. She took him in her arms, and said, "O light of mine eyes and husband of mine heart! Blessed art thou, who art called to suffer for Christ's sake!" Thus she so strengthened his heart that he was able to endure to the end. The next day his limbs were struck off on an anvil, and he was beheaded. Natalia supported him in his sufferings, and he expired in her arms before the last blow. Kissing him, she took one of his hands, which she wrapped in linen with spices and perfumes, and placed it at the head of her bed. His body was taken by Christians to Byzantium, since Constantinople. There is a tradition that in the ninth century it was removed to the convent which bears his name, at Grammont, in Flanders. After this the emperor threatened to marry Natalia to a tribune of the army. She fled to Argyropolis, near Byzantium, and passed her life near the tomb of Adrian. He often appeared to her in visions, and asked her to follow him, which she soon did; and when she died, Adrian with rejoicing angels met her, and together they entered the presence of God. An anvil is the attribute of Adrian, and is represented at his feet, or in his hand.

His sword was long kept as a relic, at Walbeck, in Saxony, but the Emperor Henry II. (St. Henry) girded it on himself, when preparing to go against the Turks and Hungarians. A. D. 290.

St. Afra was the daughter of St. Hilaria, and is the patroness of Augsburg. She was for a long time a courtesan in that city, and had three maidens as dissolute as herself, — Digna, Eunomia, and Eutropia. At length Narcissus, a holy man fleeing from persecution, came to her house, not knowing her character. When she found he was a priest, she was overcome with fear, and for the first time was ashamed of her life of sin. He told her of Christ, and at length she besought him to allow her to be baptized. He, knowing that Christ did not reject even the greatest sinners, baptized her and assured her of forgiveness. By her aid Narcissus escaped to his native Spain. Through her influence, her mother and the three maidens were also converted. Afra was seized, and accused of having assisted Narcissus to escape, and of being herself a Christian. The judge, Gaius, who had known of her former life, was amazed at her modesty, and the firmness with which she acknowledged her new faith, and asked her how one so vile could expect to be received by Jesus. To which she replied, "It is true I am unworthy to bear the name of Christian: nevertheless, He who did not reject Mary Magdalene, when she washed his feet with her tears, will not reject me." She was burned alive, and as she prayed in the midst of the fire, angels bore her spirit to heaven. Shortly after, her mother and the three maidens were executed for their faith, and suffered with constancy. August 5, A. D. 304.

St. Afra, Patroness of Brescia, is supposed to have been of noble family. She was converted by the works of San Faustino and San Giovita (Faustinus and Jovita), and suffered martyrdom with Calocerus. The church dedicated to her is one of the finest ornaments of Brescia.

St. Agatha. (*Lat.* Sancta Agatha; *Fr.* Sainte Agathe; *Ital.* Santa Agata; *Ger.* Die Heilige Agatha.) Virgin and martyr; patroness of Malta and Catamia, also patroness against fire and all diseases of the breast. The Emperor Decius strangled his predecessor, Philip, and desiring to make it appear that he did this because Philip was a Christian, and not for his own advancement, he instituted great persecutions of the Christians throughout his empire. He made Quintianus king of Sicily. Here, at Catania, dwelt Agatha, a maiden of great beauty, whom Quintianus tempted with presents, flattery, and promises, without success. He then gave her to Frondisia, who was a courtesan with nine daughters, all as wicked as possible, and promised her great riches if she would subdue Agatha to his wishes. Frondisia attempted to influence Agatha by every means in her power, for thirty-three days; but she remained fixed in her purity, and her faith in Jesus. At the end of that time

Frondisia said to Quintianus, "Sooner shall that sword at thy side become like liquid lead, and the rocks dissolve and flow like water, than the heart of this damsel be subdued to thy will." Then Quintianus in fury commanded her to be brought, and attempted to move her by threats; but she said: "If thou shouldst throw me to the wild beasts, the power of Christ would render them weak as lambs; if thou shouldst kindle a fire to consume me, the angels would quench it with their dews from heaven; if thou shouldst tear me with scourges, the Holy Spirit within me would render thy tortures harmless." Then the tyrant ordered her to be beaten, and her bosom to be torn with shears. After that she was thrown into a dark dungeon. At midnight there came an aged man bearing a vase of ointment, and a youth with a torch. It was St. Peter and an angel, but Agatha did not know them: and the light, which filled the dungeon, so frightened the guards that they fled, leaving the door open. Then one said to the maiden, "Arise and fly." But she replied: "God forbid that I should fly from my crown of martyrdom, and be the occasion that my keepers should suffer, for my flight, tortures and death; I will not fly." Then St. Peter healed all her wounds with celestial ointment, and vanished from her sight. The rage of Quintianus not being satisfied, he sent for her again, and was astonished at the wonderful cure of her wounds. "Who hath healed thee?" asked he; she replied, "He, whom I confess and adore with my heart and with my lips, hath sent his apostle and healed me, and delivered me." Then Quintianus ordered her to be burned; and as she was thrown in the fire, a great earthquake shook the city, and the people ran to the palace, crying, "This has fallen upon us because of the sufferings of this Christian damsel;" and they threatened to burn Quintianus, if he did not desist. So he ordered her to be taken from the flames, and she was borne again to prison, scorched, and in great agony. Here she entreated God to release her, and take her to heaven, which prayer was heard, for immediately she died. The Christians embalmed her body, and placed it in a tomb of porphyry. Near to Catania is a volcano which the people call Mongibello (Mt. Ætna), and about a year after the death of Agatha this mountain opened and sent forth streams of fire. When the fire had almost reached the city, the people took the veil of Agatha from her tomb, and, placing it on a lance, bore it in procession towards the fire, and when they came to it the fire was stayed and the city saved. When the heathen saw this miracle, they were all converted and baptized. There is in Malta a subterranean chapel dedicated to St. Agatha. It is cut out of the rock, and the walls are frescoed. Tradition teaches that the ground once belonged to the family of the saint. St. Agatha is usually represented with a palm in one hand and a salver in the other, on which is the female breast. Sometimes the shears are beside her. She wears a long veil. February 5, A. D 251.

St. Aglaë (*Gr.* Ἄγ. Ἀγλαις) was a Greek by birth, and lived with her lover, Boniface, in sin and luxury for many years. In the time of the last persecution of the Christians, they were both convicted of their sins, and became followers of Christ. Aglaë sent Boniface with great treasures, to assist the martyrs and to bury their remains. In his zeal, he exposed himself and suffered martyrdom. His body was brought to Aglaë. She built on the western side of the Aventine an oratory, where she placed the remains of Boniface, and she spent the remainder of her life in prayers and penitence. May 14, Boniface died, about 307; Aglaë, fifteen years later.

St. Agnes. (*Lat.* Sancta Agnus. *Ital.* Sant' Agnese, *Sp.* Santa Inez; *Fr.* Ste. Agnés.) St. Agnes was a Roman maiden of great beauty, and a Christian from her infancy. She was not more than thirteen years old, when the son of the prefect Sempronius saw her, and so loved her that he sought her for his wife. But she refused his request, saying that she was already affianced to a husband whom she loved, meaning Jesus. The young man knew not to whom she referred, and his jealousy and disappointed love made him sick, almost unto death.

(M. Schoen.) St. Agnes.

Then the physicians said, "This youth is sick of unrequited love, and our art can avail nothing." When the prefect questioned his son, he told his father of his love for Agnes, and that, unless she would be his wife, he must die. Then Sempronius begged of Agnes and her parents that she should marry his son; but she replied, as before, that she preferred her betrothed to the son of the prefect. When he had inquired her meaning, and found that she was a Christian. he was glad, for there was an edict against them, and he felt she was in his power. He then told her that since she would have no earthly husband, she must become a Vestal Virgin. But she refused with scorn the worship of vain images, and declared that she would serve none but Jesus. Sempronius then threatened her with the most horrid death, and put her in chains, and dragged her to the altars of the gods. But she remained firm. Then he ordered her to be taken to a house of infamy, to suffer the most fearful outrages. The soldiers stripped off her garments; but when she prayed, her hair was lengthened till it was as a cloak about her, covering her whole person, and those who saw her were seized with fear. So they shut her in a room, and when she prayed to Christ that she might not be dishonored, she saw before her a shining white garment, which she put on with joy and the room was filled with great light. The son of the prefect, thinking she must be subdued, now came to her. But he was struck blind, and fell in convulsions. Agnes, moved by his sufferings and the tears of his friends, prayed for his recovery, and he was healed. When Sempronius saw this, he wished to save her; but the people said, "She is a sorceress: let her die." So she was condemned to be burned, but the flames harmed her not, while her executioners were consumed by them. Then they cried out the more, "She is a sorceress: she must die." Then an executioner was commanded to ascend the pile, and kill her with the sword. This he did, and gazing steadfastly towards heaven, she fell dead upon the pile. She was buried on the Via Nomentana, and the Christians were accustomed to visit her tomb to weep. But she appeared to them, and forbade that they should sorrow for one, who was happy in heaven. St. Agnes is a favorite saint with Roman women. There is one church dedicated to her, on the Piazza Navona, on the spot where stood the house of infamy to which she was carried; and another of great interest beyond the Porta Pia, said to have been built by Constantine, at the request of his daughter, Constantina, to commemorate the burial place of St. Agnes. Next to the Evangelists and Apostles, there is no saint whose images are older than those of St. Agnes. She is most frequently represented with a lamb. January 21, A. D. 304. She was one of the four great virgin martyrs of the Latin Church.

St. Agnes of Monte Pulciano. This saint was remarkable for her piety from her very infancy. At nine years of age she was placed in a nunnery, and at fifteen was made abbess of a new convent at Procino, of the Dominican Order. She slept on the ground with a stone pillow, and lived on bread and water for fifteen years, until she was obliged to diminish her austerities on account of her health. At length the people of Monte Pulciano, being desirous that she should return to her native town, built a convent on a spot where they had destroyed a lewd house, of which St. Agnes became the superior. She had the gifts of miracles and prophecy, and was greatly beloved. St. Catherine of Siena made a pilgrimage to the tomb of St. Agnes with two of her nieces, who took the veil on that occasion. She is greatly venerated in Tuscany. April 20, A. D. 1317.

St. Alban was the first saint and martyr in England, on which account the Abbot of St. Alban's had precedence over all others. This saint was a native of Verulam. He lived in the time of Aurelian, and went to Rome. While an idolater he was noted for his hospitality, charity, and many virtues, as well as great learning. When the persecution of Diocletian invaded Britain, a priest found shelter with St. Alban, who was the means of his conversion, and baptized him. When the priest was pursued to his house, St. Alban put on his long robe and gave himself to the soldiers to save his guest. He was condemned to death, as he would not worship idols nor surrender the priest. He was first tortured, and then led out for execution. It was necessary to cross the river Coln to reach the place where he was to suffer. The crowd was large, and the bridge so narrow that they could not pass; but when the saint said a short prayer, the waters were divided, and all went over dry-shod. When on the hill of execution, he prayed for water to quench his thirst and a spring gushed out at his feet. He was beheaded. His burial place was forgotten, and disclosed in 793 by a miracle. An angel commanded King Offa in a vision that he should find the remains of this saint, and secure to them the veneration of the people. He found them at Verulam, and built a church for them, near which arose a great Benedictine monastery and the town of St. Alban's in Hertfordshire. His attributes are the sword and a fountain springing at his feet. June 22, A. D. 305.

St. Albert (*Lat.* Sanctus Albertus; *Ital.* Sant' Alberto) was Bishop of Vercelli and Patriarch of Jerusalem. He is reverenced as the founder of the Order of the Carmelites. He was murdered at Acre, when embarking to attend a council at Rome. On the cathedral at Cremona, is a vessel in which, tradition says, St. Albert kneaded bread for the poor. He is represented in his episcopal robes, and carries the palm.

Albertus Magnus, sometimes called Sant' Alberto Magno, was a teacher of St. Thomas Aquinas, and is represented in art in company with that saint.

St. Alexander (*Ital.* Sant' Alessandro; *Fr.* St. Alexandre). See St. Adelaide. March 18, A. D. 251.

St. Alexis (*Lat.* S. Aletius; *Ital.* Sant' Alessio; *Fr.* St. Alexis; *Ger.* Der Heilige Alexius). In the time of Pope Innocent I. and the Emperor Honorius, there lived on the Cœlian Hill a man of great rank and wealth named Euphemian. His wife was called Aglæ. For many years they had no child, and on this account prayed earnestly to God, until at length they had a son, whom they called Alexis. From his childhood he devoted himself to the service of God, and wore beneath his rich clothing a shirt of hair, and when in his own chamber bewailed his sins, and those of the whole world, and made a vow to serve God alone. At length Euphemian selected a beautiful maiden of noble rank to be the wife of Alexis. When he saw the loveliness of his bride and remembered his vow, he trembled. He did not dare to disobey his father, and the wedding was celebrated with great pomp. Then Alexis went to the chamber of his bride, and gave her a gold ring, a girdle of precious stones, and a purple veil, and bade her farewell, and was seen no more. His mother and his wife passed their time in the deepest grief, while his father sent through all the world to find him. Alexis, disguised as a pilgrim, reached the mouth of the Tiber in a small boat, and sailed from Ostia for Laodicea. From there he went to Edessa in Mesopotamia, where he dwelt, ministering to the poor and sick, until the people called him a saint. Fearing this flattery, he sailed for Tarsus to pay his devotions to St. Paul. But the vessel in a storm was driven to Ostia. So then Alexis went to his father's house, and begged that he might live upon his charity. Euphemian, not recognizing him, thought upon his son, that he too might be poor and in need, and gave orders that he should be provided for. But the servants ill-treated him, and gave him no lodging but a hole under the marble steps of the house. But the hardest thing he had to endure was to hear his wife and mother constantly lamenting for him and upbraiding his absence. By this was he sorely tempted, but he yielded not. Thus passed many years, till at length he knew that he must die. Then he asked for pen and ink, and wrote an account of all his life, and put it in his bosom. Now on a feast day, as Innocent was reading high mass before Honorius, and Euphemian was standing by the emperor, a voice cried out, "Seek the servant of God, who is about to depart from this life, and who shall pray for Rome," And the people fell on their faces, and another voice said, "Where shall we seek him?" And the answer was, "In the house of Euphemian the patrician." So they all went instantly, and Euphemian led the way; and as he came near home, they told him that the beggar had died, and they had laid him on the steps before the door. When he uncovered the face, it was as the face of an angel, and a great glory of light shone from it. Then he said, "This is the servant of God, of whom the voice spoke just now." And the pope took the letter from the dead hand of Alexis, and read it aloud. The father was overwhelmed with grief. The wife and mother rushed out and threw themselves on the dead body. Seven days they watched beside it, and many sick and infirm were healed by touching the sacred remains of Alexis. He is the patron of pilgrims and beggars, and on the spot where stood his father's house is now the Church of St. Alexis. The marble steps beneath which he lived and died, are preserved in the church; and a statue of the saint, in the dress of a pilgrim with a staff beside him, and a letter in his hand, is extended beneath them. July 17, A. D. 400.

St. Alphege was an English nobleman. He was a most holy man, and was made Archbishop of Canterbury in 1006. Six years later the Danes took the city and Cathedral of Canterbury. They put the people to death and burned the city. St. Alphege was kept seven months in prison, and then stoned to death because he refused to pay a large ransom for his life. The place where he met his death was at Greenwich, and the same as that on which the parish church now stands. It is said that ten years after death his body was found entire and incorrupt. It was removed from St. Paul's to the Canterbury Cathedral and enshrined near the high altar. He is represented with his chasuble full of stones. April 19, A. D. 1012.

St. Ambrose (*Lat.* S. Ambrosius; *Ital.* Sant' Ambrogio; *Fr.* St. Ambrose; *Ger.* Der Heilige Ambrosius). St. Ambrose was one of the Latin fathers of the church. He was born at Treves, A. D. 340, and was a son of a prefect of Gaul of the same name. He studied at Rome, and being at length appointed prefect of Æmilia and Liguria (Piedmont and Genoa), he resided at Milan. He was very eloquent, and the same story that is told of Plato and Archilochus is told of him, namely, that when an infant in his cradle a swarm of bees alighted on his mouth without injuring him. This was thought to indicate his future eloquence. Shortly after his going to Milan, the bishop died, and a great dispute arose between the Catholics and Arians concerning the succession, when Ambrose by his eloquence quieted them. In the midst of it a voice like that of a child cried out, "Ambrose shall be bishop." To this he greatly objected, especially as he had never been baptized. But the people would not listen to this refusal, and being baptized, in eight days he was consecrated Bishop of Milan. He first gave all his property to the poor, and then devoted himself to such studies as would fit him for his office. The two favorite doctrines of St. Ambrose were celibacy for both sexes, and the supremacy of the church above all other powers. He had no fear of man, forbidding even the Emperor Theodosius to enter the church until he had atoned for his sins by public penance. He founded the Basilica of Sant' Ambrogio Maggiore at Milan in 387, and dedicated it to all the saints. He is the patron saint of Milan. There are many wonderful and miraculous circumstances related in his life, and at his death it was said that Christ visited him, and that he ascended to heaven in the arms of angels. He is represented as a mitred bishop with the crosier; sometimes a beehive at his feet; but his usual attribute is a knotted scourge with three thongs. April 4, A. D. 397.

St. Anastasia (*Fr.* Ste. Anastasie; *Gr.* Ἅγ. Ἀναστασίη). Just under the Palatine Hill is the church dedicated to this saint, who, while she has great fame in the Greek Church, was a Roman lady. She was condemned to the flames in the persecution of Diocletian. She suffered greatly at the hands of her husband and family because she openly professed Christianity. St. Chrysogonus (Grisogono) is chiefly celebrated for his influence over Anastasia and the courage with which he inspired her. He was slain by the sword and thrown into the sea. They are said to have suffered at Illyria, but Anastasia was buried by Apollina, in her garden, near the Circus Maximus, where her church now stands. It is said that St. Jerome once celebrated mass in this church. There is also a beautiful church at Verona dedicated to St. Anastasia. The Church of Chrysogonus in the Trastevere, built in 599, was rebuilt in 1623 by Scipio Borghese, Cardinal of San Grisogono. December 25, A. D. 304.

St. Andrea of Corsini was born in 1302. He was of the Corsini family of Florence. He was extremely wild until he was sixteen years old, when his mother, in despair, told him of a dream which she had before his birth, in which she dreamed of giving birth to a wolf; but this wolf on entering a church was changed to a lamb. This greatly affected Andrea, and he went to a Carmelite church to pray, where such a change was begun in him, that at seventeen he became a friar. He was Bishop of Fiesole. The Florentines attributed to the protection of this saint their victory of the battle of Anghiari. February 4, A. D. 1373.

(Peter Vischer.)
St. Andrew.

St. Andrew (*Lat.* S. Andreas; *Ital.* Sant. Andrea; *Fr.* St. André; *Gr.* Ἅγ. Ἀνδρέας). St. Andrew was the first to be called to be an apostle. He was the brother of Simon Peter. Very little is said of him in Scripture. The legends teach that he travelled into Scythia, Cappadocia, and Bithynia, and converted multitudes by his preaching. The Russians believe that he preached to the Muscovites in Sarmatia. He returned to Jerusalem, and after visiting Greece came to Patras, a city of Achaia. Here, among many others he converted Maximilla, wife of Ægeus, the proconsul. He also persuaded her to make a public confession, which so enraged her husband, that he condemned St. Andrew to be scourged and crucified. There is a variety of opinions as to the form of the cross on which he suffered, but the one called by his name is generally believed to be like that on which he died. It is said that he was fastened with cords rather than nails. When he approached his cross, he adored it as having been sanctified by Jesus. He was gloriously triumphant in his death. In the fourth century, a part of the relics of St. Andrew were taken to Scotland, since when he has been the patron saint of that country and of its first order of knighthood. He is the patron of the Order of the Golden Fleece of Burgundy, as well as of Russia, and its great order of the Cross of St. Andrew. He is represented leaning on his cross, the Gospel in his hand; his hair and beard are silvery white and his beard divided. November 30, A. D. 70.

St. Angelus, the Carmelite, came from the East, and preached in Palermo and Messina. There was a certain Count Berenger who led an openly shameful life with his own sister. Being rebuked by Angelo, he commanded him to be hung upon a tree and shot with arrows. The legend, and in fact the very existence of this saint, has been disputed, but pictures said to represent him are seen at Bologna. May 5, A. D. 1225.

St. Anianus, or Annianus. In the Acts of St. Mark we are told that this saint was a shoemaker whom St. Mark healed when he first entered the city of Alexandria. He became so zealous a convert, and learned so rapidly that St. Mark made him bishop during his absence. He governed the church at Alexandria four years with St. Mark, and eighteen years after his death. There was a church in that city dedicated to him. April 25, A. D. 86.

St. Anna seated with the Virgin and Child.

St. Anna, the mother of the Blessed Virgin, whose name signifies gracious, is much honored in the Church, and numerous miracles have been attributed to her. About 550, Justinian I. built a church at Constantinople, and dedicated it to St. Anna. Her body was removed from Palestine to Constantinople in 710. July 26. See St. Joachim.

St. Ansano of Siena. This saint was a Roman, Ansanus Tranquillinus. His nurse, a Christian woman, named Maxima, had him secretly baptized. His faith was not disclosed until he was nineteen years old, when he began to preach with great success. He suffered much during the persecution of Diocletian, and was at last beheaded on the banks of the river Arbia. St. Ansano was, until the end of the thirteenth century, the great patron of Siena, and there is in the Duomo of that city a fine statue representing him as baptizing the Sienese converts.

St. Anthony (*Ital.* Sant' Antonio Abbate, or l'Eremita; *Fr.* St. Antoine l'Abbé; *Ger.* Der Heilige Anton or Antonius). St. Anthony, an Egyptian, was born at Alexandria. At eighteen years of age he was left an orphan, with one sister. He had great rank and wealth. Thoughtful from childhood, he feared the temptations of the world. Entering a church one day, he heard these words: "Every one that hath forsaken houses, or brethren, or sisters, or father, or mother, or wife, or children, or lands, for my name's sake, shall receive a hundred-fold, and shall inherit everlasting life;" and at another time, "If thou wilt be perfect, go and sell all thou hast, and give to the poor, and thou shalt have treasure in heaven." He was so impressed by these things that he took them as a warning from God. He divided his wealth with his sister, and gave all his share to the poor, and joined a company of hermits in the desert. Here he lived so pure a life as to arouse the hatred of Satan, who sent demons to tempt and torment him. They whispered to him of all he had left behind, and pictured before his mind the attractions of the world. But he prayed until great drops stood on his brow, and the demons despaired. They then placed delicious food before him, and, assuming the forms of lovely women, tempted him to sin. Again he resisted all their arts with prayer; but he suffered so much that he determined to go yet farther into the desert, and he found a cave where he thought Satan could not discover him. But here the demons came and tortured him with all kinds of horrible pains, and tore him with their claws, till a hermit who carried him food, found him lying as if dead. He bore him to his cell, but as soon as Anthony revived, he insisted upon returning to his cave, and when there, he cried out, "Ha! thou arch tempter! didst thou think I had fled? Lo, here I am again; I, Anthony! I have strength to combat still!" Then was Satan furious, and he set his demons to try all their powers to overcome him. They surrounded him with lions, tigers, serpents, scorpions, and all the horrible shapes they could conceive, and they were roaring and hissing all around him. But in the midst of all this came a great light from heaven, and the beasts vanished; while Anthony, looking up, cried out, "O Lord Jesus Christ! where wert Thou in those moments of anguish?" And Christ said gently, "Anthony, I was here beside thee, and rejoiced to see thee contend and overcome. Be of good heart; for

I will make thy name famous through all the world." Then he resolved to go even farther into the desert. As he travelled he saw heaps of gold and silver, but he knew they were the temptations of Satan; and when he looked away, they disappeared in the air. He was now thirty-five years old, when he shut himself in a cavern for twenty years, and saw no one, neither was he seen of any; but when he came forth, all could see that he had been miraculously sustained, for he was not wasted or changed, except that his hair was white and his beard long. And now he preached the love of God to all men; comforted the sick and afflicted, and expelled demons, over whom he had gained great power. Multitudes were converted and came to the desert, until there were five thousand hermits in the caves and ancient tombs, and St. Anthony did many miracles. At length, when he had lived in the desert seventy-five years, he began to be proud of his life of self-denial, and a voice said to him in a vision, "There is one holier than thou art, for Paul the hermit has served God in solitude and penance for ninety years." So he resolved to seek Paul; and as he journeyed he met a centaur, who pointed the way to him; and again a satyr, who besought him to pray for him and his people. The third day he came to the cave of Paul. At first Paul would not receive him, but at length, moved by his prayers and tears, he admitted him. Then they held communion together; and as they sat, a raven brought them a loaf of bread, when Paul blessed God and said, "For sixty years, every day, hath this raven brought me half a loaf; but because thou art come, my brother, lo! the portion is doubled, and we are fed as Elijah was fed in the wilderness." And they ate and returned thanks. Then Paul said, "My brother! God hath sent thee here that thou mightest receive my last breath, and bury me. Go, return to thy dwelling; bring here the cloak which was given to thee by that holy Bishop Athanasius, wrap me in it, and lay me in the earth." Then Anthony wondered, for the gift of the cloak was unknown to all. But he kissed Paul, and hastened to bring the cloak, for he feared he should not reach him again before his death. Returning, when he was about three hours from his cave, he heard heavenly music, and, looking up, saw the spirit of Paul, as a star, borne by prophets, apostles, and angels, to heaven. Then Anthony lamented, and went with haste to the cave where Paul was dead, in the attitude of prayer. Then he wept over him and recited the offices for the dead, and he thought how he could bury him, for he had not strength to dig a grave. Then came two lions across the desert, roaring, as if in sympathy, and with their paws they dug a grave, in which Anthony laid Paul, wrapped in the cloak of Athanasius. When he had returned to the convent, he told all these things, which were believed by the whole church, and Paul was made a saint. Fourteen years after, Anthony, being one hundred and four years old, felt that he must soon die; and after going to a lonely place with a few brethren, he charged them that they should keep secret the place of his burial. Gently his spirit passed away, and angels conveyed it to heaven. St. Anthony is represented with various attributes. He wears a monk's habit, as the founder of Monachism. In Greek pictures the letter Th. is on the cope on the left shoulder, and always in blue. It is the first letter of Theos, God. The crutch is a symbol of his age and feebleness. The bell signifies his power to exorcise evil spirits, as the sound of a bell is believed to overcome demons. The asperges, or rod for sprinkling holy water, is a symbol of the same idea. The hog represents the sensuality and appetites which he conquered. Flames of fire under his feet, or a city or house burning, signify that he is a patron against fire, in this world and the next also. Paul is represented as old, meagre, half clothed in palm-leaves, his hair long and white, seated on a rock in meditation, and a palm-tree near him. St. Anthony, January 17, A. D. 357.

(Pesillino.) Florence Academy.

St. Antony of Padua (*Lat.* Sanctus Antonius Thaumaturgus; *Ital.* Sant' Antonio di Padova, Il Santo; *Sp.* San Antonio de Padua, Sol brillante de la Iglesia, Gloria de Portugal, etc., etc.). This saint was a Portuguese by birth. He became a Franciscan, and stands in that Order next to its founder. After the martyrdom of the first missionaries in Morocco, Antony determined to be himself a missionary and martyr, and went to convert the Moors. But he was seized with an illness that compelled him to return to Europe. He was driven by the winds to Italy, and came to Assisi, where St. Francis was holding the first chapter of his Order. St. Francis found him a valuable assistant, and he preached at the universities of Padua, Bologna, Paris, and Toulouse, but at length he preached to the people. He did much good in Italy as a preacher. His imagination was vivid and his language effective. His similes were very beautiful. He died at thirty-six, after a ministry of ten years. Great honors have been paid his memory, and the Church of Sant' Antonio at Padua is wonderfully rich in adornments of both ancient and modern art. He performed many miracles, which are represented in pictures in various churches and convents, especially in Italy and Spain. One of these, which is represented in the accompanying picture, is thus related. When preaching the funeral sermon of a very rich man, he denounced his love of money and exclaimed, "His heart is buried in his treasure-chest; go seek it there, and you will find it." The friends of the man broke open the chest, and to their surprise found the heart; they then examined his body and found that his heart was indeed wanting. His attributes are the lily and crucifix. He is young, and wears the habit and cord of St. Francis. June 13, A. D. 1231.

St. Antonio, Archbishop of Florence, was a native of Florence. He was born about 1384. His thoughtfulness and studiousness caused his friends to regard him as fitted for a religious life. He went to Fiesole and asked admission to the Dominican Convent at fifteen. The prior, after talking with him, told him that when he had learned perfectly the Book of Decrees, he would receive him. This he did in one year, and then was sent to Cortona to pass his novitiate in study. He took his vows at Fiesole, and there formed a tender attachment to the wonderful painter-monk, Fra Giovanni, called Il Beato and Angelico. It is believed that the great learning of Antonio was of advantage to the heavenly mind of Angelico, and that their communion was not without its effects upon his pictures. The Archbishop of Florence dying, the pope wished to give the office to Angelico; but he begged that Antonio should have it instead, which the pope granted. This greatly pleased the Florentines, as he was not only much beloved, but a native of their city. He died at the age of seventy, thirteen years after he was made archbishop, during which time he was distinguished for his wisdom and holiness. He is always represented as an archbishop, and wears the pallium over the habit of the Dominicans. May 10, A. D. 1461.

St. Apollinaris of Ravenna (*Ital.* Sant' Apollinare; *Fr.* Saint Apollinaire). This saint came with the Apostle Peter from Antioch to Rome, and Peter, having laid hands on him, sent him to preach in the east of Italy. He became the first Bishop of Ravenna, and performed such miracles, and so preached, as to convert multitudes. At length he was seized and imprisoned. His jailer allowed him to escape, but his enemies pursued him, beat him, and wounded him so that he died. The Basilica of Apollinaris-in-Classe, is on the spot where he was martyred. July 23, A. D. 79.

St. Apollonia of Alexandria (*Fr.* Sainte Apolline). The parents of Apollonia were heathens, and had no children, though they constantly prayed the gods to grant them a child. Her father was a magistrate. At length there came three pilgrims to Alexandria, begging in the name of Jesus and the Blessed Virgin. The wife of the magistrate, hearing them, asked if the Virgin could grant her prayer for a child? Being told of her great power, she gave the pilgrims food and money, and full of faith, prayed to Mary, who answered the prayer by the birth of Apollonia. She was very beautiful; and as her mother constantly told her the story of her birth, she grew up a Christian, and sought St. Leontine that he might baptize her. As soon as he did so, an angel appeared with a garment dazzlingly white, which he threw over her, saying, "This is Apollonia, the servant of God! Go now to Alexandria and preach the faith of Christ." She obeyed and converted many, but others accused her to her father, who gave her to the heathen governor. He commanded her to worship the idol of the city. But she made the sign of the cross before the idol, and commanded its demon to depart. The demon broke the statue and fled, crying, "The holy virgin Apollonia drives me forth." Then they bound her to a column, and drew her teeth out one by one with pincers, and then, kindling a fire, they burned her. She is the patroness against toothache and all diseases of the teeth. Her attributes are a pair of pincers with a tooth, and the palm; sometimes a golden tooth suspended on her neck chain. February. 9, A. D. 250.

St. Athanasius (*Gr.* Ἅγ. Ἀθανασίος; *Lat.* St. Athanasius, Pater Orthodoxiæ; *Ital.* Sant' Atanasio; *Fr.* St. Athanase). This saint, the founder of the creed which bears his name, was an Alexandrian, and a pupil of St. Anthony. He first studied science and literature, but being converted, he was ordained deacon. His opposition to Arius at the Council of Nice gained for him the title of the "Father of Orthodoxy." He became Bishop of Alexandria, and during the great schism of his age, gained by his perseverance the victory of the Catholic Church. He was bishop forty-six years, but he was in exile during twenty years of that time. May 2, A. D. 373.

St. Augustine, or **St. Austin** (*Lat.* Sanctus Augustinus; *Ital.* Sant' Agostino; *Fr.* St. Augustin). The father of St. Augustine was a heathen; his mother Monica, was a Christian. He was born in Tagaste, Numidia. In his youth, he was so devoted to pleasure, that his mother feared the destruction of his character, and in her sorrow, sought advice of the Bishop of Carthage. He comforted her with the assurance that her prayers would be answered at last. At length Augustine went to Rome, and was famous as a lawyer. But he was restless and unhappy. He went to Milan, and was

(Murillo)

there converted by the preaching of St. Ambrose, who baptized him in the presence of his mother. The "Te Deum" which is now used was composed for this occasion. St. Augustine and St. Ambrose recited it as they approached the altar. He was Bishop of Hippo, and after thirty-five years Hippo was besieged by the Vandals, and St. Augustine perished at the age of seventy-five. It is said that his remains were removed to Pavia. He was the third doctor of the church, and his writings are celebrated. One of the scenes in his life most frequently illustrated in art, is that of a vision related by himself, and which he saw while writing his Discourse on the Trinity. He walked on the sea-shore, lost in meditation upon the great theme of his writing, when he saw a little child bringing water and endeavoring to fill a hole which he had dug in the sand. Augustine asked him the motive of his labors. The child said he intended to empty all the water of the sea into this cavity. "Impossible," exclaimed St. Augustine. "Not more impossible," answered the child, "than for thee, O Augustine, to explain the mystery on which thou art now meditating." He is the patron of theologians and learned men. August 28, A. D. 430.

St. Augustine of Canterbury is believed to have introduced the Benedictine Order into England. He was sent from Rome as missionary to Britain, by St. Gregory. Fearing the dangers thought to exist in England at that time, he and his companions were seized with dread, and Augustine went to beg the pope to recall his command. This Gregory refused to do. He made Augustine bishop over those who should be converted. They landed in Kent, where there was great hatred of Christianity, but Queen Bertha was a Christian, and for her sake King Ethelbert permitted them to enter Canterbury, which they did, singing praises, and carrying the image of Christ. Ethelbert and his people became Christians, and were baptized in a little chapel which Bertha had built near Canterbury, and, being a French princess, had dedicated to Martin of Tours. Augustine desired the conversion of the Britons as well as the Saxons, and this gave rise to great controversy. He deprived the bishops of their sees, and resorted to severe measures, being in fact accused of having excited King Ethelfred to destroy the monastery and the twelve hundred monks of Bangor. He should be represented in the Benedictine habit, with the staff and the Gospel, or as bishop, with pallium, cope, and mitre. A. D. 604.

St. Balbina was the daughter of the prefect Quirinus, and discovered the lost chains of St. Peter. The church dedicated to her at Rome is very ancient. She is represented veiled, with chains in her hand or near her.

St. Barbara (*Ital.* Santa Barbara; *Fr.* Sainte Barbe). This saint was of the East, and daughter of Dioscorus, who dwelt in Heliopolis. He was rich and noble, and loved his only daughter so fondly that he shut her up in a high tower lest she should attract suitors by her beauty. Here she passed her time in study, and while watching the wonders and beauties of the heavens, felt that the idols could not be gods, or the creators of the world. But she had heard of no other God. At length the fame of Origen reached her from Alexandria, and she sent him a letter by a trusty servant, asking that he should teach her. He sent a disciple disguised as a physician, who instructed her, and, after her conversion, baptized her. Her father had set workmen to make a bath-room in her tower; and when they had made two windows, she desired them to add another. They were afraid to do this, but she insisted, and when her father asked the cause, she said, "Know, my father, that through three windows doth the soul receive light — the Father, the Son, and the Holy Ghost; and the three are one." Then her father would have killed her with his sword, but she fled to the top of the tower, and angels concealed her and bore her away to a place of safety. A shepherd betrayed where she was hidden, and her father dragged her by the hair and put her in a dungeon. He then delivered her to the proconsul Marcian, who scourged and tortured her, but she did not yield; and at last her father carried her to a mountain near the city, and himself beheaded her. Immediately a great tempest arose, and the lightning entirely consumed the father. St. Barbara is the patroness of Ferrara, Mantua, and Guastala; also of fortifications and fire-arms, as well as of armorers and gunsmiths. She is also invoked as a protector against lightning and the explosions of gunpowder. A tower with three windows is her peculiar attribute. She also has the book, palm, and sword. December 4, A. D. 303.

St. Barnabas (*Ital.* San Barnabà; *Fr.* Saint Barnabé). The name of apostle is also given this saint; and if not fully entitled to it, he is at least next in holiness to the apostles with whom he labored. He was a native of Cyprus — a Levite and a cousin of St. Mark. He labored with Paul at Antioch and Lystra, and the legends teach that he was of so noble a presence that he was called Jupiter, while Paul was styled Mercurius. At length, on account of a difference concerning Mark, they separated, and Barnabas preached in Italy as well as in Asia Minor and Greece, and it is said he was the first Bishop of Milan. Tradition says he preached from the Gospel of St. Matthew, written by the evangelist himself, which he carried always with him, and that it had power to heal the sick, when laid upon their bosoms. He was at last seized by the Jews and cruelly martyred while preaching in Judæa. Mark and other Christians buried him, and in the time of the Emperor Zeno his resting-place was revealed in a vision to Antemius. He was found with the Gospel in his bosom. This was taken to Constantinople, and a church was built for the saint. June 11.

St. Bartholomew (*Lat.* S. Bartholomeus; *Ital.* San Bartolomeo; *Fr.* St. Barthélemi). The origin of this saint is doubtful, it being disputed whether he were the son of a prince, Ptolomeus, or of a husbandman. After the ascension of our Lord, he wandered through India, carrying the Gospel of St. Matthew. He preached in Armenia and Cilicia. He suffered a horrible death at Albanopolis, being first flayed, and then crucified. His attribute is a large knife. Sometimes he has his own skin hanging over his arm. August 24.

St. Basil the Great (*Gr.* Ἅγ. βασίλειος; *Lat.* S. Basilius Magnus; *Ital.* San Basilio Magno; *Fr.* St. Basile). This saint is the second in rank in the Greek Church, as well as the founder of the Basilicans, the only monastic order known in that church. He was born at Cæsarea, in Cappadocia, in 328, and was of a family of great sanctity — his grandmother, father, mother, two brothers, and a sister all being saints. He wrote many theological works. He attributes his early education to his grandmother, St. Macrina. He studied at Constantinople and at Athens, where he was associated with both St. Gregory of Nazianzen and with Julian, afterwards the Apostate. His great talents at one time so aroused his pride, that but for the influence of St. Macrina, his sister, he would have periled his salvation. He was then about twenty-eight, and after this gave himself entirely to the Christian service — passing some years in the desert, as a hermit, where he lost his health, from the austerity of his living. He was made a priest in 362, and eight years after Bishop of Cæsarea. The fourteenth of June, the day of his ordination, is a great feast in the Greek Church. He lived with the same abstinence on the throne as in the desert. He contended with the Arians for the doctrine of the Trinity; and when the Emperor Valens required him to use the rites of the Arians, he refused. The Emperor threatened him, even with death, without effect. At length he thought to awe Basil by coming to church in great state, with all his court and soldiers. It was on the day of the Epiphany. But Basil did not notice him, even when he advanced to the altar with his oblation. Valens swooned and fell into the arms of an attendant. The Emperor afterwards conferred with Basil, and, though he remained unconverted, he made some concessions to the Catholics. It is related of him, as of two other saints, that while he preached, the Holy Ghost, in the form of a white dove, rested on his shoulder, to inspire his words. June 14, A. D. 380.

St. Bavon (*Flem.* St. Bavo or St. Baf; *Ital.* San Bavone). He was born a nobleman; some authorities claim, Duke of Brabant. He was converted from idolatry by St. Amand of Belgium, first Bishop of Maestricht. Bavon was nearly fifty years old, a widower, and had led a dissipated life. He gave all his riches in charity, and was placed by St. Amand in a monastery in Ghent; but he left that, and lived a hermit in the forest of Malmedun. His shelter was a hollow tree, and he subsisted on herbs. It is related of him, that after becoming a Christian, he met one who had been his slave, and cruelly treated. Bavon besought him to bind and beat him, and cast him in prison, as he had formerly done to him. This was of course refused; but the saint so insisted, that finally it was done, and while in prison, he passed his time in penitence for his former sins. He is the patron of Ghent and Haerlem. His attribute is a falcon; he is sometimes represented as a hermit, and sometimes in his ducal robes. October 1, A. D. 657.

St. Bede, the Venerable, was born at Jarrow, in Northumberland, in 673. He was eminent for his learning and piety, and some even thought him superior in eloquence to St. Gregory. He died dictating the last words of a translation of the Gospel of St. John. He was called the "Venerable," and was known by this name at a Council at Aix-la-Chapelle. There is a legendary account of the way in which he received this title. It says that his scholars wishing to put an inscription on his tombstone, one of them wrote: —

"Hac sunt in fossa
Bedæ ossa,"

leaving the blank as above, because no suitable word occurred to him. He fell asleep thinking of it; and when he awoke, "venerabilis" had been inserted by an angelic writer. Other accounts of it are given, but this is the favorite one. His works are extant, and his "Ecclesiastical History" is the only authentic record we have of the early English Church. May 27, A. D. 735.

Bel and the Dragon. When Cyrus was King of Babylon, and Daniel was his friend, and greatly honored by him, the Babylonians had an idol called Bel, to whom was given every day "twelve great measures of fine flour, and forty sheep, and six vessels of wine." And the number of the priests who attended him were three score and ten, and they had wives and children. Now Cyrus worshipped Bel, but Daniel worshipped his own God; and when Cyrus demanded the reason of this, Daniel replied that he could not "worship idols made with hands, but the living God," who had created all men and the world in which they lived. Then Cyrus asked Daniel if Bel were not living, and reminded him of how much he ate and drank each day. Then said Daniel, "O king, be not deceived; for this is but clay within and brass without, and did never eat or drink anything." So the king was wroth, and said to the priests, "If ye tell me not who this is that devoureth these expenses, ye shall die. But if ye can certify me that Bel devoureth them, then Daniel shall die: for he hath spoken blasphemy against Bel." And Daniel replied, "Let it be according to thy word." Then the priests said to the king, "Lo we go out, but thou, O king, set on the meat, and make ready the wine, and shut the door fast, and seal it with thine own signet; and to-morrow when thou comest in, if thou findest not that Bel hath eaten up all, we will suffer death; or else Daniel, that speaketh falsely against us." Now they did this because they had an entrance which was hidden under the table, and by that they could go out and in as they liked. Then the king set the food before Bel, as the priests had said; and Daniel commanded the servants to bring ashes, and he strewed them upon the floor; and when all was ready they closed the temple, and the king sealed it with his own seal. Then in the night, the priests came with their wives and children, as they were accustomed to do, and consumed all that had been provided. Now in the morning the king came with Daniel, and they found the seals whole, and they broke them and went in. And when the king saw that the food was gone, he cried out, "Great art thou, O Bel, and with thee is no deceit at all!" Then Daniel laughed, and said to the king, "Behold now the pavement, and mark well whose footsteps are these." So when the king saw the footsteps of men, women, and children, he was angry, and took the priests with their wives and children, and these showed him the door where they had gone in and out. Then the king slew them, and gave the idol Bel to Daniel, and he destroyed both the god and his temple. Now in the same place was a great dragon, which was also worshipped by the Babylonians; and the king said to Daniel, "Wilt thou also say that this is of brass? Lo, he liveth, he eateth and drinketh; thou canst not say that he is no living God, therefore worship him." But Daniel declared that he would not worship him, and that he could slay him without sword or stave. And the king gave him leave. Then Daniel took pitch and fat and hair, and made lumps of it, and put them in the Dragon's mouth, until he burst in sunder. Then the people were filled with indignation, and they came to the king, and demanded that he should deliver Daniel to them, or they would destroy him and his house. Then the king, being sore pressed, gave up Daniel, and they threw him into the lions' den, where he remained six days. Now there were seven lions in the den, and each day they had given them two carcasses and two sheep, but now they gave them nothing, so that they might devour Daniel. There was in Jewry a prophet whose name was Habakkuk; and he had made him a mess of pottage, and had put bread in a bowl, and was about to give it to the reapers in the field; but the angel of the Lord came to him, and commanded that he should carry it to Babylon, and give it to Daniel, who was in the lions' den. Then Habakkuk said, "Lord, I never saw Babylon; neither do I know where the den is." Then the angel of the Lord took Habakkuk by the hair of his head, and set him in Babylon over the lions' den; and Habakkuk cried, saying, "O Daniel, Daniel, take the dinner which God hath sent thee." Then Daniel thanked God that he had not left him to perish, and arose, and ate the food which the prophet had brought, and the angel set Habakkuk again in his own place. Now, upon the seventh day, the king came to the den, to bewail Daniel, and he found him alive. Then cried the king, "Great art thou, O Lord God of Daniel, and there is none other beside thee." Then he took Daniel out of the den, and cast in those who had accused him, and they were devoured in a moment, before his face.

St. Benedict (*Ital.* San Benedetto; *Fr.* Saint Benoît; *Sp.* San Benito). This saint was the founder, the patriarch and the first abbot of the great Order of the Benedictines. He was of noble birth, and a native of Norcia, in the duchy of Spoleto. He studied at Rome, but soon wearied of the profligacy of those about him; and imbibing the ideas of St. Jerome and St. Augustine in favor of solitude, at fifteen he became a hermit. His nurse, who loved him extremely, followed him in his retirement, and ministered as much as possible to his comfort. But he, regarding this as a drawback to perfect holiness, fled from her to Subiaco, a wilderness, forty miles from Rome. Here he lived for three years, entirely unknown, except to Romano, another hermit, who shared with him his bread and water. Here he was greatly tempted by the recollections of the world he had left, and especially at one time, by the remembrance of a beautiful woman he had seen at Rome, when, to overcome his great desire to return to her, he flung himself into a thicket of briers and thorns, and rolled himself until he was torn and bleeding. At the monastery of Subiaco they show roses, said to have been propagated from these briers. The fame of his sanctity at last brought great crowds to him, who begged his prayers, and that he would heal their diseases, and a company of hermits near by requested that he would be their head. But when they saw the severity of his life, they attempted to poison him. When he made the sign of the cross before the poisoned cup, it fell to the ground in fragments. He then returned to his cave and again dwelt alone. But so many hermits came to Subiaco and lived in huts and caves, that at length, for the sake of order, Benedict commanded them to build twelve monasteries, and he placed twelve monks in each. Two senators of Rome brought to him their sons, Maurus and Placidus, to be educated as Christians. They were but twelve and five years of age, and they became the special charge of Benedict. But Satan, much troubled at all this, put it into the heart of a priest, Florentius, to traduce the character of St. Benedict, and to poison him with a loaf of bread. These plans failing, he at last brought seven young women into one of the monasteries to try the chastity of the monks. Then Benedict left Subiaco, and immediately Florentius was crushed to death beneath a falling gallery in his own house. Benedict even wept for his fate, and imposed a penance on Maurus when he rejoiced at it. There still remained at this time, on Monte Cassino, a temple of Apollo. Here Benedict went, and by his miracles and preaching converted the idolaters, so that they broke the statue and altar, and burnt the grove. Here he built up two chapels, and dedicated them to St. John the Baptist and St. Martin of Tours On the summit of this mountain he founded the monastery which has always been regarded as the parent of all others of the Benedictine Order. From here he promulgated the rules of his Order. His sister Scholastica followed him to Monte Cassino, and he visited her once a year during the last years of his life. In 540 Totila, King of the Goths, visited Benedict, and entreated his blessing. The saint reproved him for his past life, and it was thought that after this the Goth was less ferocious. Before his death monasteries of his order were instituted in all parts of Europe. He was at last seized with fever, and on the sixth day he ordered his grave to be dug, and after standing upon the edge of it, supported by his disciples, and in silent contemplation, he was borne to the altar of the church, and receiving the last sacrament there died. March 21, A. D. 543.

St. Benedict of Anian (*Fr.* Saint Benoît d' Aniane). This saint was page and cup-bearer at the court of Pepin-le-Bref, and a distinguished commander in the army of Charlemagne. He was born at Maguelonne, in Languedoc, and his original name is unknown. He had an extremely narrow escape from drowning, after which he commenced a religious life. He went first to the Abbey of St. Seine; but disapproving of the habits of the monks, he dwelt a hermit on the banks of the Anian. At length, a number of hermits having joined him, he founded a Benedictine monastery, with great severity of rule. He was called to Aix-la-Chapelle by Louis-le-Debonnaire. Here he founded another monastery. He presided at a council for the reformation of the monastic orders. William, Duke of Aquitaine, was a great warrior, and had vanquished the Saracens in the south of France. He was converted by St. Benedict, and built a monastery in which he lived and died, a monk. St. Benedict conferred upon him the monk's habit. February 12, A. D. 821.

Benedict, Bennet Biscop, or **St. Bennet of Wearmouth,** did much for art as well as piety in England. He was of a noble Northumbrian family. He founded the monasteries of St. Peter's at Wearmouth and St. Paul's at Jarrow. He had a cultivated taste, and went five times to France and Italy. He brought to England stone-workers and glaziers to introduce a new style of building. He brought, too, many books and pictures, and also a certain John, Abbot of San Martino, who was a teacher of music, and who introduced chanting into English cathedrals. St. Bennet wrote many books of instruction for monks, and died at an advanced age, celebrated for piety and munificence. January 12, A. D. 703.

St. Benno is noted especially for his connection with the Emperor Henry IV. He was a German Benedictine, and Bishop of Meissen; and when Henry, after being excommunicated, attempted to enter the cathedral, Benno locked the doors and threw the key in the river Elbe. He then went to Rome. On his return to Meissen, he ordered a fishermen to cast his net into the river, and a fish was taken, in which was found the key. His proper attribute is a fish with a key in its mouth.

St Bernard of Clairvaux (*Lat.* Sanctus Bernardus, Doctor mellifluus; *Ital.* San Bernardo di Chiaravalle, Abbate; *Ger.* Der Heilige Bernhard; *Fr.* Saint Bernard) was a man of great power and importance. He was born in 1190 at Fontaine near Dijon. He was the son of a noble, and his mother, Alice, was a remarkable woman. She had a large number of children, all of whom she nursed at her own breast, as she believed that infants imbibe with the milk the temperament of the nurse. According to all authorities she gave her son his early education. From the age of fifteen he practiced great self-denial, and from it his health suffered. He had great personal beauty. After studying at the University of Paris, he entered at twenty the Benedictine Monastery of Citeaux. He resisted all temptations, and it is related of him, that finding himself gazing on a beautiful woman with a feeling of pleasure, he rushed into a half-frozen pool and remained there until nearly frozen himself. The Abbey of Citeaux became so crowded, that Bernard was sent at twenty-five to found another monastery. He went with twelve companions to what was then called the "Valley of Wormwood," and there founded the Abbey of Clairvaux. In a few years Bernard became famous, and his abbey very much crowded. He was considered authority in matters of law as well as religion. He wrote the laws of the Templars. He was judge between Anacletus and Innocent II., and the whole church was satisfied with his decision. He also reconciled the disputes between the clergy of Milan and Rome. He preached a second Crusade, and succeeded in rousing the people to great enthusiasm, and was invited to assume the command. He was also the adversary of Abelard and Arnold de Brescia. St. Bernard is one of the Fathers of the Church. In his writings he sets forth with great power the perfections of the Blessed Virgin, especially in the "Missus Est," and

(Fra Angelico.)
St. Bernard of Clairvaux.

it was believed that she appeared to him twice: once, when ill and unable to write, she restored him by her presence; and again she moistened his lips with the milk of her bosom, so that his eloquence was irresistible. His health suffered greatly from his labors and fasts, and he died at sixty-three. His attributes are the demon fettered behind him; three mitres on his book or at his feet, emblems of three bishoprics which he refused; the bee hive, a symbol of eloquence. The mitre and crosier as Abbot of Clairvaux are given him but rarely. Aug. 20, A. D. 1153.

St Bernard writing the "Missus Est."

St. Bernard Ptolomei (*Ital.* San Bernardo dei Tolomei). He was of an illustrious family of Siena; born in 1272. He distinguished himself as a lawyer, but at length, seized with the religious passion of the age, he went into a mountain, called the Mount of Olives, about ten miles from Siena. Here he formed the order called "Olivetani." They were Benedictines in rule, and wore a white habit. August 21, A. D. 1348.

St. Bernard of Menthon was by birth a noble Savoyard. In his youth he was serious and studious, showing such traits of character as fitted him for a religious life. His father wished him to marry; but he preferred to study, and put himself under the teaching of Peter, Archdeacon of Aoust. In 966 Bernard was made archdeacon, which was at that time a responsible and laborious office, as its duties comprised the whole government of the diocese. By great devotion and constant preaching for forty-two years, he did much good in the dioceses of Aoust, Sion, Geneva, Tarantaise, Milan, and Novara. He destroyed an idol on a mountain in the Walais, and exposed the deception of the heathen priests. He founded two roads and two monastic hospitals, the Great and Little St. Bernard, the former of which was near the site of the heathen idol before spoken of. At these hospitals the monks, assisted by their dogs, search out and care for travellers who are lost in the passes of the mountains, where the storms are severe and the cold intense. St. Bernard died at Novara, at eighty-five years of age. His body is in the monastery at Novara, and his head is shown in a rich case at the monastery of Monte-Joye, in the diocese of Aoust. May 28, A. D. 1008.

St. Bernardino of Siena. This saint was of the family of Albizeschi. He was born at Massa, a Sienese town, in 1380. His mother dying, he was educated by an aunt, whose influence developed not only his talents, but great purity of character also. At seventeen he joined a brotherhood whose members were devoted to the service of the hospitals. A pestilence soon broke out, which destroyed great numbers, and among them physicians and priests. For four months, Bernardino with twelve others cared for the inmates of the plague hospital. His health suffered greatly from his labor. He became a Franciscan at twenty-three. He was a celebrated preacher, and went all over Italy. He endeavored to reconcile the Guelphs and Ghibellines. He was offered three bishoprics, which he refused. The duke of Milan, offended at his preaching, threatened him in vain; he then sent him money, with which he went to the prisons and liberated poor debtors. He founded the order called in Italy "Osservanti," and in France "Frères de l'Observance," because they observe strictly the rule of St. Francis, going barefoot and keeping absolute the vow of poverty. When preaching, he held in his hand a tablet on which was the name of Jesus in a circle of golden rays. A man who had lived by making cards and dice complained to the saint that on account of the reforms in religion, his occupation was gone. Bernardino advised him to carve tablets like his, to sell to the people. He did so; and a peculiar sanctity being attached to them, he sold large numbers, and

St. Bernardino of Siena.

made a fortune in this way. St. Bernardino is said to have founded those institutions called still in France "Monts-de-Piété," where money is loaned on pledges. In the commencement they were entirely charitable and for the benefit of the poor. He died at Aquila, in the Abruzzi, where his remains are preserved in a silver shrine in the church of San Francisco. May 20, A. D. 1444.

St. Bernardino da Feltri shares the honor of having founded the "Monts-de-Piété. He was a celebrated preacher, and preached at the Church of Santa Croce in Florence, against Jews and usurers, and the necessity that the poor should be protected from them. It is certain that the two Bernardinos labored in this matter, but not easy to decide to which belongs the greatest honor.

St. Bibiana was a Roman lady,. who, together with her father, mother, and sister, suffered martyrdom in the reign of Julian the Apostate. She was scourged, and then pierced with a dagger. The church dedicated to her is between the Santa Croce and the Porte Maggiore. The column to which she was bound, is shown within the church. December 2, A. D. 362.

St. Blaise of Sebaste (*Gr.* Ἁγ. Βλαισός; *Ital.* San Biagio; *Fr.* Saint Blaise; *Ger.* Der Heilige Blasius; signification, crooked.) This holy man was bishop over the Christians at Sebaste in Cappadocia, and, in the time when Agricolaus was governor, was obliged to flee to the mountains to escape persecution. There were great numbers of wild beasts there, but instead of harming the saint, they came to him in numbers each morning to receive his blessing; and when Agricolaus sent to obtain beasts for the amphitheatres, the hunters found St. Blaise surrounded with them. He nursed the sick ones, reproved the ferocious, and gave his benediction to all. The hunters, amazed at this, seized him and took him to the governor. As they went they met a woman, whose child was choking from a bone stuck in its throat. The mother cried out, "O servant of Christ, have mercy on me." He laid his hand on the throat of the child and prayed, and it was healed. Again, they met a woman whose pig had been carried off by a wolf, and as it was all she had of worldly goods, she was in much distress. St. Blaise commanded the wolf to bring back the pig unharmed; which was done. The governor sentenced him to be scourged and imprisoned without food; but the poor woman had killed her pig, and brought a part, with bread and fruit, to the holy man. A second time the governor tortured him by tearing his flesh with iron combs, such as are used to card wool; when, as he still remained firm in his faith, he was beheaded. He is the patron of Ragusa, also the patron of wool combers, of those who suffer from throat diseases, and of wild animals. He is a popular saint in France and England, and especially in Yorkshire, where once in seven years a festival is held in his honor. The iron wool comb is his proper attribute. February 3, A. D. 316.

St. Bonaventura was the great prelate of the Seraphic Order, and was styled "il Dottore Serafico." His fame is not confined to his Order, as he is considered one of the brightest lights of the whole Roman Catholic Church. His name was Giovanni Fidanga, and he was born at Bagnarea in Tuscany, in 1221. In his infancy he was so ill that his life was despaired of, and his mother took him to St. Francis to be healed. When the saint saw him, he exclaimed, "O, buona ventura," whereupon his mother dedicated him to God by the name of Bonaventura. His progress in study was amazing, and at twenty-two he became a Franciscan, and went to Paris to study theology. He soon became celebrated, but his humility was so great that he felt unworthy to receive the sacrament, and it is taught in the legends that the Host was presented to him by angels. Louis IX. (St. Louis) greatly honored him while at Paris, and he was chosen General of his Order at thirty-five. He was appointed Archbishop of York, but declined the honor. At length he was made Cardinal and Bishop of Albano When the pope's nuncios carried him the cardinal's hat, they found him in the garden of a convent, near Florence, washing the plate from which he had just eaten, and he requested them to hang the hat on a tree until he could take it. In 1274, when a council was held at Lyons to reconcile the Greek and Latin churches, he, being one of the most distinguished of preachers, first addressed the assembly. The fatigues of his labors here brought on a fever, of which he died, being fifty-three years old. He was buried in the church of the Franciscans at Lyons, but the Huguenots broke open his shrine and threw his ashes into the Saone. July 14, A. D. 1274.

(Raphael.) St. Bonaventura.

St. Boniface, martyr (*Lat.* and *Ger.* Sanctus Bonifacius; *Ital.* San Bonifaccio). The history of St. Boniface is one of the most authentic, as well as beautiful, of the legends of his age. Justice can by no means be done to his character in the space allotted him here. His name was Winfred, and he was born of a noble family at Crediton, in Devonshire. He taught literature and the Holy Scriptures at the Benedictine abbey of Nutsall, or Nuscella, near Winchester, until he was thirty-six years old. For some years he had not been happy in his quiet vocation, but was constantly haunted by a desire to preach the Gospel in Germany. He went first to Friesland, but it was in the days of Charles Martel, and a time when he could hope for no results from his labors; so he returned to Nutsall, but soon left England for the last time, and went to Rome to entreat the aid of the pope in his German labors. It is said to have been at this time that he changed his name. Receiving a commission from the pope, he now travelled through Bavaria, Thuringia, Saxony, and Friesland, preaching with great success. In 732, he was made Archbishop and Primate of all Germany, and soon after, King Pepin-le-Bref, whom Boniface had consecrated, made him the first Bishop of Mayence. But when seventy-four years old, he gave up all his honors, and girding on the plain habit of a Benedictine monk, devoted himself again to missionary labors. At length, while in his tent, on the banks of a small river in Friesland, where he awaited a company of proselytes, to whom he was about to administer the rite of confirmation, he was attacked by a band of pagans who had sworn to murder him. He always carried in his bosom a copy of the "De Bono Mortis" of St. Ambrose. This was stained with his blood, and was preserved as a sacred relic at Fulda. In 1835 King Louis of Bavaria, in honor of the twenty-fifth anniversary of his marriage, founded a magnificent basilica, and consecrated it to St. Boniface, in which are fine frescoes, representing the various scenes in the life of this wonderful man. June 5, A. D. 755.

St. Boniface. See St. Aglæ.

St. Brice (*Lat.* Sanctus Britius) was Bishop of Tours and successor to St. Martin. He is represented with coals in his hands, which he carries unhurt, to prove himself innocent of false accusations made against him; and again he carries a child in his arms. November 13, A. D. 444.

St. Bridget of Ireland. Although nearly every vestige of this saint is gone, she still lives as their patroness in the hearts of the Irish people. Her mother was very lovely, and the captive, taken in war, of a powerful chieftain. His wife, being jealous of her, turned her away before the birth of Bridget. But two disciples of St. Patrick took pity on them, and baptized the mother and child. Bridget grew up with such beauty of mind and person, that she became famous, and her father desired to have her, and to marry her to a chief. But Bridget devoted herself to God's service, especially to the instruction of women. She went to Kildare, "the cell or place of the oak," and not only taught and preached, but performed miracles. Her fame drew about her many women who lived in huts, and from this arose the first religious community of women in Ireland. The convent and city of Kildare, were afterwards both flourishing and famous. Here was preserved unextinguished, for many centuries, the sacred lamp which burned before her altar.

> " The bright lamp that shone in Kildare's holy fane,
> And burned through long ages of darkness and storm."

February 1.

St. Bridget of Sweden was the founder of the Order of the Brigittines, or Birgitta, and is one of the patron saints of Sweden. She was of royal blood, and married to the Prince of Norica, named Ulpho. She was very devout, and influenced her husband and their eight children to live religiously. After the death of Ulpho, she built the Monastery of Wastein and endowed it largely. Here she placed both nuns and brothers. Their rule was principally that of St. Augustine, though modified by directions Bridget received in visions, of which she had many. Her order was approved by the pope, under the title of the " Rule of the Order of our Saviour." She made many pilgrimages to Rome and Compostella.

St. Bruno was the founder and first abbot of the Carthusian Order. He was of a noble family of Cologne, and on account of his great talents was sent to Paris to study theology under Raymond. He afterwards taught in the school at Rheims; but, after long reflection, determined on a monastic life. With six companions, he went to Grenoble, when Hugo, the bishop, having been warned in a dream of their coming, gave them some barren land at Chartreux. Here Bruno founded his first monastery, and his order was confirmed by the pope. The robes and hoods of the Carthusians are white, and their whole heads shaven. Urban II. had been a pupil of Bruno at Rheims, and when he became pope, sent for him to aid him in his great cares, and desired to make him Archbishop of Reggio. But this Bruno refused, and not liking the life at court, retired to Calabria, where he founded another monastery. He died in 1200. The order which he established is of great interest. It is the most severe in its rule of all the monastic orders, and adds almost perpetual silence to the usual vows. Only once a week can these monks talk together. They never taste flesh, and make but one meal a day, of pulse, bread, and water, and this is eaten separately. They labor, too, with great diligence, and their

(Le Sueur.) Louvre. St. Bruno reading the Pope's Letter.

discipline has been described as most fearful in its severity. In spite of all this, they have an extreme love of the beautiful, and have done much for art. Their churches and gardens were wondrous in their perfection, and their pictures at La Grande Chartreuse (now in the Louvre); in the Chartreuse of Santa Maria de las Cuevas, near Seville; at Paular, and other places, possess a world of interest. July 18.

Cædmon the Poet lived in the monastery of the Abbess Hilda, as a servant, until past middle life. He knew nothing of literature or poetry; and when it came his turn to sing at table, he went away. Once as he did this, and went to the stable to care for the horses, he fell asleep, and an angel came in a dream and told him to sing. He answered that he could not sing, and for that reason had left the table. But the angel said, "You shall sing, notwithstanding;" and when he asked what he should sing, the reply was, "Sing the beginning of created beings." Then Cædmon began to sing praises to God; and when he awoke he remembered all he had sung, and was able to add more also. When he told this to Hilda, she believed him to be inspired, and received him into her community. He was instructed in Scripture; and as he read, he converted it into verse. His paraphrase of Scripture is still preserved in the Bodleian Library, at Oxford. He died peacefully, while making the sign of the cross.

St. Casimir, patron saint of Poland, was the son of Casimir IV. of Poland and Elizabeth of Austria. From his childhood he participated in none of the pursuits of his father's court; and as he grew up, he composed many religious hymns. He refused the crown of Hungary, and lived more and more secluded, devoting himself to religious pursuits, until his death in 1483. March 4.

St. Cassian (*Ital.* San Casciano) was a school-master of Imola, and being denounced as a Christian, the judge who condemned him to death allowed his scholars to be his executioners. They hated him on account of his severe discipline, and they tortured him most cruelly, by piercing him with the iron styles used in writing. He is the patron saint of Imola. August 13.

St. Catherine of Alexandria, virgin and martyr (*Lat.* Sancta Catharina; *Ital.* Santa Catarina dei Studienti, or Santa Catarina delle Ruote; *Fr.* Madame Saincte Catherine; *Sp.* Santa Catalina; *Ger.* Die Heilige Katharina von Alexandrien). This saint was the daughter of Costis (half brother to Constantine the Great) and Sabinella, Queen of Egypt. Before the birth of Catherine, her mother was prepared by a dream to find her a remarkable child; and at the moment of her birth, a halo of light played about her head. Her acquirements and her wisdom were most wonderful, and the philosophy of Plato was her favorite study while a child. She had seven learned masters, and chambers fitted with everything to aid her in her studies. Her father died when she was fourteen, leaving her heiress to the kingdom. She gave herself up to study and retirement, which displeased her subjects, and they begged her to marry. They said she was possessed of four notable gifts. That she was of the most noble blood in the world; that she surpassed all others in wealth, knowledge, and beauty; and they desired that she should give them an heir. She replied that as she had four gifts, so he whom she would marry, must likewise be of such noble blood that all would worship him; and so great as not to be indebted to her for being made a king, richer than any other; so

(Mücke.) St. Catherine borne to Mt. Sinai.

beautiful that angels should desire to see him; and so benign as to forgive all offenses. Such a one only could she marry. Then Sabinella and the people were sorrowful, for they knew of no such man. But Catherine would marry no other. Now a hermit who dwelt in a desert not far from Alexandria, was sent by the Virgin Mary, who appeared to him, to tell Catherine that her Son was the husband she desired to have, for he possesed all the requirements, and more. And the hermit gave Catherine a picture of Mary and Jesus. When she gazed on his face, she loved Him, and could think of nothing else, and her studies became dull to her. That night she had a dream, in which she went with the old hermit to a sanctuary on a high mountain; and when she approached it, angels came to meet her, and she fell on her face. But an angel said, "Stand up, our dear sister Catherine, for thee hath the King of glory delighted to honor." Then she stood up and followed them, and they led her to a chamber, where the queen was, surrounded by angels, saints, and martyrs, and her beauty none could describe. The angels presented Catherine to her, and besought her to receive her as her daughter. The queen bade her welcome, and led her to our Lord. But the Lord turned away, saying, "She is not fair and beautiful enough for me." At these words Catherine awoke, and wept till morning. She called the hermit and demanded what would make her worthy of her celestial Bridegroom. He,

(Titian.) Marriage of St. Catherine.

perceiving the darkness of her mind, instructed her in the true faith, and she, and also Sabinella, were baptized. That night, as Catherine slept, the Virgin and her Son, attended by many angels, appeared to her, and Mary again presented her to Jesus, saying, "Lo, she hath been baptized, and I myself have been her godmother." Then Christ smiled on her, and plighted his troth to her, and put a ring on her finger. And when she awoke, the ring was still there; and from that time she despised all earthly things, and thought only of the time when she should go to her heavenly Bridegroom. At length the good Sabinella died. At this time Maximin came to Alexandria and declared a great persecution against those who did not worship idols. Then Catherine came forth to the temple and held an argument with the tyrant and confounded him. He then ordered fifty learned men to come from all parts of the empire to dispute with her; but she, praying to God, overcame them all, so that they, too, declared themselves Christians. Then Maximin, enraged, commanded them to be burned; and Catherine comforted them when they could not be baptized, saying that their blood should be their baptism, and the flames glorious crowns for them. Then the emperor, admiring her beauty, tried to overcome her virtue; and when he could not do this, and was about to go to war, he commanded Porphyry, his servant, to cast her in a dungeon and starve her. But angels came to feed her; and when, after twelve days, they opened the dungeon, a bright light and a fragrance filled all the place. Then the empress and Porphyry, with two hundred others, fell at the feet of Catherine, and declared themselves Christians. When Maximin returned, he put the empress and all to death, and, admiring Catherine's beauty still more than at first, offered her to be mistress of the world if she would listen to him. When she still rejected his offers, he ordered the most dreadful tortures for her — wheels revolving in different directions, that should tear her in many pieces. When they had bound her to these, an angel came and consumed the wheels in fire, and the fragments flew around, and killed the executioners and three thousand people. But again Maximin ordered her to be scourged and beheaded. Then angels came and bore her body to the top of Mount Sinai, and there it rested in a marble sarcophagus. In the eighth century a monastery was built over her burial-place, and her remains are still greatly venerated. It is said by some that Maximin was consumed by an inward fire; by others, that wild beasts devoured him. Catherine is patroness of education, science, and philosophy, of all students and of colleges. As patroness of eloquence, she was invoked for all diseases of the tongue. She is also patroness of Venice, and a favorite saint of ladies of royal birth. She is represented as richly dressed, and her peculiar attribute is the wheel, either whole or broken. She has also the martyr's palm, the crown of royalty, the book which expresses her learning, and frequently tramples on the head of Maximin, which is a symbol of the triumph of her Christian faith over paganism and cruelty. The marriage of St. Catherine to the Saviour is a favorite and extremely beautiful subject of art. November 25, A. D. 307.

St. Catherine of Bologna, or Santa Caterina de' Vigri, has been greatly venerated in her own city for about two centuries. She was of noble family, and for a time a maid of honor at the court of Ferrara. She entered a convent of Poor Clares, and became distinguished as a painter. There are said to be several pictures of hers in Bologna. Her remains, dressed in brocade and jewels, are to be seen in her convent at Bologna. March 9, A. D. 1463.

St. Catherine of Siena (*Lat.* Sancta Catharina Senese, Virgo admirabilis, et gloriosa Sponsa Christi; *Ital.* Santa Caterina di Siena, la Santissima Vergine). She was the daughter of a dyer who dwelt near the Fonte-Branda, at Siena; his dwelling is now the Oratory of St. Catherine. She dedicated herself to a religious life as early as in her eighth year, and prayed Christ to be her Bridegroom, as He was that of Catherine of Alexandria. Her father and mother

(Razzi.) San Domenico, Siena. St. Catherine of Siena receiving the Stigmata.

were angry at her refusal to marry, and greatly persecuted her, putting the most menial labors upon her, and treating her with great harshness. But at length, her father saw her at prayer with a white dove resting upon her head, of whose presence she seemed unconscious. From this time, she was allowed to choose her own course in life. She never entered a convent as a professed nun, but she made a vow of silence for three years, and led a life of the greatest self-denial. She went each day to the Convent of St. Dominick to pray, and there she had many wonderful visions. She was greatly tempted of Satan —

she inflicted upon herself the most severe penances, and Christ came to her in visible presence to console her. She nursed the sick, even those who had the most loathsome diseases. Her fame spread through all Tuscany and to Milan and Naples. At length the Florentines, having rebelled against the Holy See, were excommunicated by the pope, and they sent Catherine to him as their mediator. The pope, then at Avignon, was so much pleased with Catherine that he left her to decide the terms of peace between himself and the Florentines Catherine felt it to be a great cause of misrule in the church, that the popes were absent from Rome, and she used all her powers to persuade Gregory XI. to return to the Lateran, which he did, Catherine accompanying him. In the great schism which followed the death of Gregory, Catherine took the part of Urban VI., who appointed her ambassadress to the court of Joanna II. of Naples. But the danger of the journey prevented her from fulfilling the mission. Catherine died at thirty-three, after great physical suffering — still full of zeal and faith. She was one of the most noted of female saints, and is known at Siena as La Santa. The facts of her history render her life interesting in many ways. She is represented in pictures in the habit of the Dominican Order, with the stigmata, which she is said to have received. April 30, A. D. 1380.

St. Cecilia (*Fr.* Saint Cécile). She is supposed to have lived in the third century, and the honor paid to her can be traced to that time. She was the daughter of a noble Roman, who, with his wife, had secretly become Christians. Cecilia was in childhood remarkably serious and pious. She early made a vow of chastity, and devoted herself to a religious life. She always carried a copy of the Gospels in her robe. She especially excelled in music, and composed and sung hymns so

(Raphael.) St. Cecilia

sweet that angels came to listen to her. But the instruments employed in secular music were insufficient to express the music of her soul, and she invented the organ, and consecrated it to God's service. Her parents desired her, when sixteen years old, to marry Valerian, a rich young noble. She did so, but beneath her bridal robes she wore a garment of penance, and, remembering her vow, prayed God to help her to preserve her chastity. He so answered her prayer, that when she told Valerian of her faith, he became converted, and was baptized, and respected her vow. Cecilia had told Valerian that she had a guardian angel, and when he returned from his baptism, he heard sweet music, and saw the angel standing near her with two crowns, made of the immortal roses which bloom in Paradise. Cecilia and Valerian knelt, and the angel crowned them with the flowers, and told Valerian, that because he had listened to Cecilia, and respected her vow, whatever he most desired should be granted him. Then Valerian said, " I have a brother, named Tiburtius, whom I love as my own soul; grant that his eyes also may be opened to the truth." This request was pleasing to God, and when Tiburtius entered soon after and perceived the fragance of the roses, he was surprised, for it was not the time of flowers. Then Cecilia told him of their faith, and he too was converted and baptized. They then gave themselves up to a religious life, and did much good to the poor and persecuted Christians. But the prefect, Almachius, commanded them to worship Jupiter, and when they would not, he cast the brothers into prison, and gave them a keeper, called Maximus, and he also became a Christian. This so enraged the prefect, that he commanded the three to be beheaded. Cecilia cared for, and buried their remains in the cemetery of Calixtus. Desiring to have her great wealth, the prefect then commanded Cecilia to worship Jupiter, and threatened her with fearful tortures. She only smiled her scorn. He then commanded her to be thrown into her bath, filled with boiling water. This did not hurt her at all; so he then sent an executioner to slay her with the sword. His hand trembled, so that he inflicted three wounds on her neck and breast, and yet did not kill her. She lingered three days. She gave her money to the poor, and desired that her house should be made a church. She died sweetly singing, and was buried beside her husband. In the ninth century, when Paschal repaired her church, he had a vision of St. Cecilia, in which she told him her burial place. Her body was found, and also those of Valerian, Tiburtius, and Maximus. They were placed in her church, now called St. Cecilia-in-Trastevere. Her bath-room is a chapel, and the stones and pipes for heating the bath still remain. In the sixteenth century the church was again repaired, and her coffin opened, when the celebrated statue of " St. Cecilia lying dead," was made, and represents her as she appeared in the coffin. She is the patroness of music and musicians. Her proper attribute is the organ and a roll of music. She also has the crown of roses and an attendant angel. She is richly dressed, and often has jewels. November 22, A. D. 280.

St. Celsus (*Ital.* San Celso). This was a young disciple of St. Nazarius, who was a converted Jew. Together they travelled through Gaul as missionary preachers. At Genoa the people threw them into the sea, but they were miraculously saved, and came at last to Milan, where Protasius and Gervasius had become Christians, whom they strengthened. Both Celsus and Nazarius were beheaded at Milan, where there is a beautiful church, San Nazaro Maggiore. There is also at Ravenna the remarkable Byzantine church of SS. Nazaro-e-Celso. They are always represented together, and bear the swords and palms of martyrs. Nazarius is old and Celsus quite young. July 28.

St. Cesareo, or Cæsarius. The veneration of this saint seems to be confined to Rome. He perished at Terracina because he opposed the worship of Apollo. He was famous both in the East and West in the sixth century. The Church of San Cesareo in Rome is also called "in Palatio," from its situation near the ancient palace and baths of Caracalla on the Via Appia, not far from the Porta St. Sebastiano. He was put into a sack, and cast into the sea, together with a priest named Lucian. November 1, A. D. 300.

St. Chad of Lichfield became, in 659, abbot of the Priory of Lastingham, which had been founded by his eldest brother, Cedd. He was famous for his religious life, and being made bishop of the Mercians and Northumbrians, he preached as a missionary through all the country. He had his episcopal see in Lichfield, "the field of the dead," and there he built a habitation where he lived with a few brethren, and a church where he baptized his converts. After living in this way more than two years, he had a vision in which he was warned of his death. He saw his brother with a troop of angels. They sang and called him to follow them to God, and still sweetly singing ascended to heaven. He advised the brethren how they should live, and soon died. His church may be considered the origin of the Cathedral of Lichfield, where the shrine of St. Chad was deposited in 1148, and is greatly venerated. March 2, A. D. 673.

Chantal, la Mère. Ste. Jeanne-Françoise de Chantal was the grandmother of Madame de Sevigné. She was a religious enthusiast even in childhood, and would not receive a gift from a Calvinist. In obedience to her parents, she married Baron Chantal, but made a vow to dedicate herself to a religious life, if she should ever be a widow. Her husband died when she was twenty-nine, and for ten years she devoted herself to her children and to the preparation for the fulfillment of her vow. She assisted St. Francis de Sales to establish the Order of the Visitation, and assumed the direction of it, as la Mère Chantal. Her children loved her passionately, and sought to keep her with them, but she remained firm in her determination. At the time of her death in 1641, there were seventy-five houses of her Order in France and Savoy. She was canonized in 1769. August 21, A. D. 1641.

St. Charles Borromeo (*Ital.* San Carlo). This saint was of one of the noblest families of Lombardy. Being the second son he was early dedicated to the Church. At twelve years of age he received the revenues of a rich Benedictine monastery, but would only reserve a mere pittance for himself, devoting the remainder to charity. At twenty-three he was made cardinal and Archbishop of Milan, by his uncle Pius IV. His elder brother died when Charles was twenty-six. He went at once to take possession of his diocese and estate. His incomes he dedicated to public uses, only spending for himself enough to buy his bread and water, and straw on which to sleep. He sent missionaries to preach in every part of his diocese, and went also himself to see that his people were cared for. In public he lived as became his rank, and gave feasts of which he never partook. His charities were most munificent. At the time of the plague at Milan, he went into the city, when all others fled, and tended the sick and performed all the duties pertaining to his office. His example inspired twenty-eight priests to join him, all of whom with St. Charles escaped unhurt. He lived in a time when the Church had fallen into great laxity of discipline, and he may be regarded as a powerful instrument in rescuing it from destruction. He was hated by the priests who had been in the habit of using the revenues of the Church for their own indulgence, and one, Fra Farina, attempted to kill him by firing upon him, while he was celebrating the evening service. He finished the prayer, although he believed himself mortally wounded, and the people considered him to be miraculously healed. He died November 4, 1584, and with his last breath exclaimed, "Ecce venio." His remains repose in a rich shrine at Milan. He is represented in cardinal's robes and barefooted, a rope about his neck and one hand raised in benediction, with a book in the other. November 4, A. D. 1584.

St. Charlemagne, whose history as Charlemagne the Great, Emperor of France, Italy, and Germany, is so familiar to all, stands at the head of royal saints in the countries over which he ruled, although if a strict chronology were observed, St. Clotilda and St. Sigismond would precede him. He is frequently represented with a book, in remembrance of his having caused the Scriptures to be correctly translated and widely promulgated. January 28, A. D. 814.

St. Cheron was a disciple of St. Denis, and was Bishop of Chartres. He was attacked by robbers and his head struck off, when on his way from Chartres to Paris to visit St. Denis. Taking his head in his hand he continued his journey. One of the windows in the Cathedral of Chartres represents the history of St. Cheron.

St. Christina (*Ital.* Santa Cristina; *Fr.* Ste. Christine). She is supposed to have been born at Tiro, a town on the borders of Lake Bolsena which has since been swallowed up in the lake. The legend of this saint has been rejected by the Church, but she is celebrated in Central and Northern Italy. She was the child of a

(Johan Schoreel. Munich Gal.) St. Christina.

Roman patrician who governed the city. She called herself Christina because she had been converted to the doctrines of Christ. As she stood, one day, watching those who begged alms, and had nothing to give, she thought of the golden idols of her father, and she broke them in pieces and gave them to the poor. Her father was furious, and ordered his servants to beat her and throw her in a dungeon. Here angels came and healed her wounds. Her father then commanded her to be thrown into the lake with a mill-stone tied to her neck. But angels bore her up, and God clothed her with a white robe, and led her safely to land. She was then thrown into a fiery furnace, where she remained unharmed five days and sung God's praises. Her father then ordered her head to be shaved, and that she should then be taken to the temple of Apollo to sacrifice, but when she came there the idol fell down before her, which so frightened her father that he died. But Julian, hearing that she sung in her prison, sent orders that her tongue should be cut out, when she still continued to sing, to the amazement of all. She was next shut up with poisonous reptiles, but she was not harmed. At last, in despair, he commanded her to be bound to a post and shot with arrows till she died. Thus was she martyred, and angels bore her soul to heaven. On an island in the lake of Bolsena, which few travellers visit, is a church dedicated to St. Christine, said to have been painted by the Caracci. The Cathedral of Bolsena is consecrated to her — Patroness of Bolsena and the Venetian States. Her proper attribute is the mill-stone, but she sometimes has arrows alone, when she might be mistaken for St. Ursula. She has also the martyr's palm and crown. July 24, A. D. 295.

St. Christopher (*Lat.* St. Christophorus; *Ital.* San Cristofero, or Cristofano; *Fr* St. Christophe, or Cristofle; *Ger.* Der Heilige Christoph). St. Christopher might well be called the giant saint. He was of the land of Canaan, and before performing the deeds which entitled him to his saintship was called Offero, which signifies the bearer. He was proud of his vast size and strength, but in spite of this, his poverty compelled him to become a servant. So he resolved that the most powerful monarch of the earth alone should be his master, and he went to seek him. At length after many days of wandering, he came to the court of a king said to excel all others in power and wealth, and to him he offered his services. The king accepted him gladly, for no other monarch of all the earth could boast of such a servant. Now Offero knew nothing of the power of Christ or Satan, and supposed his master to be afraid of no one, since he was the greatest monarch of the earth; but one day as he stood beside him, a minstrel who was singing, mentioned frequently the name of Satan, and each time he did so the king trembled and crossed himself. Offero asked the meaning of this, and when the king did not answer, he said, "If thou dost not answer me this, I leave thee." Then the king said, "I make this sign that Satan may have no power over me; for he is very mighty, and as wicked as strong, and I fear lest he shall overcome me." Then Offero felt himself deceived, and said, "Since there is one whom thou fearest, him will I seek and serve, for my master must fear no one." So he wandered again, seeking Satan; and crossing a great desert, he saw a terrible being with the appearance of great power, marching at the head of an armed legion. He did not seem to notice the great size of Offero, and with an air of authority said, "Whither goest thou, and for what dost thou seek?" Then said Offero, "I wish to find Satan, for I have heard he is the most powerful of all the earth, and I would have him for my master." Satan, well pleased, replied, "I am he, and your service shall be an easy and pleasant one." Offero then bowed before him, and joined his followers. After a time as they journeyed on, they came to a cross, erected by the wayside, where four roads met. When the Devil saw this he turned with great haste and fear, and went a long distance out of his way to avoid the cross. Then said Offero, "Why is this? What is this cross, and wherefore dost thou avoid it?" But Satan spoke not. Then said Offero, "Except thou tellest me I must leave thee." Being compelled, the wicked one replied, "I fear the cross, because upon it Jesus died, and when I behold it, I fly, lest he should overcome me." Then said Offero, "Tell me, who is this Jesus, for since thou fearest him, he is more powerful than thou, and him will I seek and serve." So he left Satan, and wandered many days in search of Christ. At length he came to a hermit, whom he entreated to tell him where Christ could be found. Then the hermit, seeing that he knew nothing of Jesus, began to teach him, and said, "Thou art right in believing that Christ is the greatest king, for his power extends over both heaven and earth, and will endure throughout eternity. But thou canst not serve him lightly, and if he accepts thee, he will impose great duties upon thee, and will require that thou fast often." Then said Offero, "I will not fast, for it is my strength that makes me a good servant: why should I waste it by fasting?" "And besides, thou must pray," said the hermit. "I know not how to pray, neither will I learn. Such a service is for weak ones, but not for me," said the proud giant. Then said the hermit, "If thou wilt use thy strength, knowest thou a deep, wide river, that is often swollen with rains, and sweeps away in its swift current many of those who would cross it?" Offero said, "I know such a stream." "Then go there," said the hermit, "and aid those who struggle with its waves; and the weak and the little ones, bear thou from shore to shore, on thy broad shoulders. This is a good work, and if Christ will have thee for this service, he will assure thee of his acceptance." Then was Offero glad, for this was a task which suited him well. So he went to the river and built upon its bank a hut of the boughs of trees. And he aided all who came, and many he bore upon his shoulders, and was never weary by day or night in assisting those who crossed the river. And after he began his work, not one perished, where before so many had been swept away. For a staff he used a palm-tree which he pulled up in the forest, and it was not too large for his great height and strength. As Jesus beheld this he was well pleased with Offero and his labor, for though he would neither fast nor pray, yet had he found a way to serve him. At length, after Offero had spent a long time, and did not weary of his toil, as he rested one night in his hut, he heard a voice like that of a weak child, and it said, " Offero, wilt thou carry me over ? " And he went out quickly, but he could find no one. But when he had again laid down, the same voice called as before, and at the third call he arose and sought with a lantern. At last he found a little child who besought him, " Offero, Offero, carry me over to-night." He lifted him up, and carrying his staff, began to cross the stream. Immediately the winds blew, the waves were tossed, and the roar of the waters was as many thunders, and the little child grew heavy and more heavy, until Offero feared he should himself sink, and both be lost. But with the aid of his palm staff, at length he crossed and put his burden safely down upon the other side. Then he cried out, " Whom have I borne ! Had it been the whole world, it could not have been more heavy ! " Then the child replied, " Me, thou hast desired to serve, and I have accepted thee. Thou hast borne not only the whole world, but he who made it, on thy shoulders. As a sign of my power and of my approbation of thee, fix thou thy staff in the earth, and it shall grow and bear fruit." Offero did so, and the staff was soon covered with leaves, and the dates hung in huge clusters upon it. But the wonderful child was gone. Then Offero knew that it was Christ whom he had borne, and he fell down and worshipped Him. After that, Offero went to Samos, where there was a great persecution of Christians, and in spite of his great strength a heathen struck him, when he said, " Were I not a Christian, I would take vengeance on thee." He permitted himself to be bound and taken to Dagnus, the King

(Albert Durer, 1521.) St. Christopher.

of Lycia, in which country was Samos. At the sight of the giant the king fainted. When he was himself again he said, "Who art thou?" and the giant answered, "My first name was Offero, the Bearer, but now I serve Christ, and have borne him on my shoulders; for this I am now called Christ Offero, the bearer of Christ." Dagnus sent him to prison, and tried to seduce him to idolatry by sending beautiful women to him, who urged him to sin. But Christopher was faithful, and by his influence the women became Christians, and suffered death because they too, worshipped Jesus. Then Dagnus tortured him greatly, and commanded him to be beheaded. When they led him to execution, he kneeled down and prayed, that all who beheld him and believed in Christ should be delivered from earthquake, fire, and tempest. It was believed that his prayer was effectual, and that all who look upon the figure of St. Christopher are safe for that day from all dangers of earthquake, flood, or fire. The sight of him is believed also to impart strength to the weak and weary, which idea is expressed in many inscriptions more or less similar to the following one, which accompany his pictures:—

> "Christophori Sancti speciem quicumque tuetur,
> Illo namque die nullo languore tenetur."

"Whoever shall behold the image of St. Christopher shall not faint or fail on that day." July 25 A. D. 364.

St. Chrysanthus (*Ital.* San Grisante). This saint came to Rome from Alexandria, and St. Daria came from Athens. They were betrothed, but Chrysanthus persuaded Daria that a state of virginity was more favorable to a religious life than that of marriage. They were remarkable for their devotion to their faith. They were at length accused and martyred, in the reign of Numerian, according to some, but Baillet believes in the persecution of Valerian. It is said that soon after their burial a large number of Christians who were praying at their tomb were walled up in the cave and thus buried alive. The part of the catacombs where they were interred was long called the cemetery of SS. Chrysanthus and Daria. The Greek Church honor them on March 19 and October 17. The Latins October 25. A. D. 237.

St. Chrysogonus. (*Ital.* San Grisogono.) See St. Anastasia.

St. Clair (*Lat.* S. Clarus) is one of the headless saints. He was an Englishman of noble extraction, and lived and labored in the county of Vexin in France. He preached with great faithfulness, and was murdered at a village which bears his name by ruffians hired by a lewd woman who could not overcome his chastity. This village is between Rouen and Pontoise. His shrine is greatly venerated and visited by pilgrims. He is represented on a window at St. Maclou in Rouen. November 4.

St. Clara (*Lat.* Sancta Clara; *Ital.* Santa Chiara; *Fr.* Sainte Claire). Clara d' Assisi was the daughter of a nobleman, Favorino Sciffo; her mother was named Ortolana. Her beauty and the great wealth of her family caused her to receive many offers of marriage. She had early dedicated herself to a religious life, and went to St. Francis to ask his advice. He encouraged her to renounce the world, and appointed Palm Sunday as the day for her to make her profession. She went to church with all her family richly attired, as was the custom on that day. When the others approached the altar she remained afar off, and St. Francis, admiring her humility, came down from the altar to give her the palm-branch. At evening she concealed herself in a veil, and escaped to the Porzioncula where St. Francis dwelt. She was conducted to the altar, where St. Francis cut off her hair with his own hands, and she, putting off her rich garments, was covered with the personal penitential robes of Francis, which he threw over her. Thus she became his disciple, and the "Madre Serafica," or the foundress of the Order of Franciscan nuns, or, as they are better known, the "Poor Clares." The rules of her order were severe in the extreme. Clara went, by the wish of St. Francis, to the Convent of St. Paolo. Her family and friends tried every means to induce her to return to them without effect, and in a short time she was followed by her sister Agnes, only fourteen years old, by many ladies of rank, among whom were three of the house of Ubaldini, and at length by her mother. Clara so strictly adhered to the rules of her order as to injure her health, and for a long time she was bedridden. On one occasion, when the Saracens, to whom Frederick had given the fortress of Nocera, came to ravage her convent of San Damiano, she arose from her bed where she had so long been confined, and placing the Pyx which contained the Host upon the threshold she kneeled down and began to sing, when the infidels threw down their arms and fled. Innocent IV. visited her and confirmed her Order; and before her death it had spread throughout Christendom and embraced many noble ladies. She died at sixty in a rapturous

(Portrait at Assisi). St. Clara.

trance, believing herself called to heaven by angelic voices. Her sister Agnes succeeded her as abbess. When the nuns removed from San Damiano to San Giorgio they bore her remains with them. This is now the Church of Santa Chiara d' Assisi, and is the most famous one of her order. St. Clara is a favorite saint all over Europe, but especially so in Spain. Her proper attribute is the Pyx containing the Host. She wears a gray tunic, and the cord of St. Francis with a black veil. She also bears the lily, the cross, and the palm. August 12, A. D. 1253.

St. Clara of Monte-Falco. This saint was of the Augustine order. In her own country she is called Saint Clara, but she was never canonized. She is properly the "Beata Clara della Cruce di Monte-Falco." Her birth took place in 1268, and she lived quietly in her own city, which from its height overlooks the Umbrian valleys. The fame of her miracles and the sweetness of her life was well known through all the country.

St. Clement (*Ital.* San Clemente) is supposed to be spoken of by the Apostle Paul (Philippians iv. 3). He was the third bishop of Rome. During the many years of his bishopric he made large numbers of converts, among whom was Domitilla, the niece of the Emperor Domitian, and by her influence he was protected during the reign of her uncle. In the persecution under Trajan, the prefect who governed Rome in the absence of the emperor, commanded Clement to worship the idols, and when he would not, he banished him to an island where there were large stone quarries worked by convicts. Many Christians had been sent there before him, and others went with him to share his exile. Clement found those on the island suffering for want of water; he knelt and prayed, and looking up saw a lamb on the summit of a hill, which was invisible to all others. He knew it to be the lamb of God. He went to the spot where he had seen it, and upon digging found a large, clear spring of water. After this miracle he was condemned to be cast into the sea bound to an anchor. But when the Christians prayed, the waters were driven back for three miles, and they saw a ruined temple which the sea had covered, and in it was found the body of the saint with the anchor round his neck. For many years, at the anniversary of his death, the sea retreated for seven days, and pilgrimages were made to this submarine tomb. At one time a woman was praying there, and her child had fallen asleep, when the waters arose, and she fled, forgetting the child in her fear. The next year the boy was found quietly sleeping as she had left him. The church of San Clemente in Rome is of remarkable interest, and the scenes of his life are represented in paintings of the twelfth century. According to tradition, the relics of the saint are now here, and also those of St. Ignatius of Antioch. His proper attribute is the anchor. November 23, A. D. 100. (See page 498.)

St. Clotilda (*Fr.* Sainte Clotilde). St. Clotilda was a Burgundian princess, and the wife of Clovis. She is famed as having Christianized France. Her husband, after long resisting her attempts for his conversion, called upon the God of Clotilda in the midst of an unfortunate battle. Immediately the fortunes of his arms were changed, and by this he was converted, and was baptized by St. Remi. At his baptism it is said that the oil was brought by a dove, or the Holy Ghost, and tradition says that an angel descended from heaven, bearing three lilies, which he gave to St. Remi, and he in turn gave them to Clotilda, and at this time the arms of France were changed from the three toads (crapauds) of earlier days, to the fleurs-de-lys, the emblems of purity and regeneration. June 3, A. D. 545.

St. Cloud, was a grandson of St. Clotilda, who, when his brothers were murdered, escaped to a convent, and became a monk of the Benedictine order. September 7, A. D. 560.

Constantine, Emperor. Constantine, while still an idolater and a persecutor of the Christians, was afflicted with a leprosy. The priests of the idols prescribed that he should bathe in children's blood. Three thousand children were collected to be slain, but as the emperor rode to the place where they were, the mothers of the children so entreated him, that he stopped his chariot and said, "Far better is it that I should die, than cause the death of these innocents." He then commanded the children to be restored to the mothers, and gave them large gifts to compensate for their sufferings. That night in his sleep, St. Peter and St. Paul appeared to him, and told him that because he had spared the innocents, Christ had sent them to him. They told him to send for Sylvester, who would show him a pool in which he could wash and be clean, and that from that time, he should cease to persecute the Christians, and himself worship their God. Now Sylvester was the bishop of Rome, who had hid away from the cruelties of Constantine and was in a cave near Monte Calvo. The emperor sent for him, and when the soldiers found him and led him away, he thought it was to his execution. They took him to the emperor, who asked him who the two gods were who had appeared to him the previous night. Sylvester replied, that they were not gods, but the apostles of Jesus. Constantine then desired to see the effigies of these apostles. Sylvester showed him some pictures of Peter and Paul, and Constantine saw that they were like those whom he had seen in the vision. Sylvester then baptized him, and he came out from his baptism cured of his disease. The next day Constantine commanded that Christ should be worshipped in all Rome as the only God; the next day, that those who blasphemed against him should lose their lives; the third day, that any one who insulted a Christian should forfeit half his goods; the fourth day, that the Bishop of Rome should be the first bishop of the world; the next day, he gave the privilege of sanctuary to the Christian churches; the sixth he ordered that no churches should be built without the consent of the bishop; the seventh, that the tithes of the domains of Rome should belong to the church; and the eighth day, he founded the Lateran, by digging himself, and carrying on his shoulders twelve hodfuls of earth, and laying the first stone. Another account of the manner of his conversion to Christianity, and one frequently illustrated in art, is, that during the campaign of 312, while on his march to Rome, he saw a luminous cross in the sky, with the inscription, "By this Conquer," and that on the night before his last battle with Maxentius, he was commanded in a vision to inscribe the sacred monogram of the name of Christ upon the shields of his soldiers. Three different localities claim the honor of having been the place where Constantine beheld the cross; these are, Autun, Andernach, and Verona. But to these miraculous directions and the success which followed his obedience to them, is attributed his belief in Christianity. The Empress Helena told him, that it would have been better to become a Jew than a Christian. So he wrote her to bring to dispute with Sylvester the most learned of the Jews. She came to Rome with one hundred and forty doctors of the law. A day was appointed for the discussion, and Zeno and Crato, Greek philosophers, were appointed arbitrators. Then Sylvester, praying for wisdom, utterly defeated these learned Rabbis. Then one of them, Zambri, who was a magician, desired that a fierce bull should be brought, and said that when he should speak in his ear the name of his God, he should fall dead. The bull was brought, and as the magician had said, he fell dead at his feet as soon as he had whispered to him. Then Sylvester was attacked with fury; the arbitrators were as tonished, and Constantine was shaken in his faith, but Sylvester said that the name he had spoken was that of Satan, for Christ did not destroy but gave life. He desired that Zambri should restore the bull to life. This he could not do, but Sylvester made the sign of the cross, and commanded him to rise, when the bull obeyed and rose up as gentle as he had been fierce. Then all who saw this believed and were baptized. A while after this it was told the emperor, that the dragon which dwelt in the moat had since his conversion killed three hundred persons each day by his poisonous breath. Then Sylvester went down to the dragon and exorcised him in the name of Christ, and bound up his mouth with a thread and sealed it with the sign of the cross. Sylvester also gave aid in his house to a Christian, who was afterward slain for his faith. The governor believed that Sylvester had riches which belonged to the martyr, and threatened him with tortures if he did not give them up. Sylvester told him that his soul should be in torments that night, and as he ate his dinner he was choked to death. There is no need to remind one that history and the legends greatly differ regarding Constantine. As for Sylvester, he was at the great Nicene Council, and after governing the Church for nearly twenty-four years, he died and was buried in the cemetery of Priscilla at Rome. The proper attribute of St. Sylvester is the bull. Sometimes the portraits of St. Peter and St. Paul. His festival is December 31, and he died in 335.

St. Cosmo and **St. Damian** (*Latin* SS. Cosmus et Damianus; *Ital.* SS. Cosimo e Damiano gli santi medici Arabi; *Fr.* SS. Côme et Damien). These brother saints are seldom separated in thought or representation. They were Arabians, but dwelt at Ægæ, in Cilicia. Their father died early, and their mother, Theodora, trained them in Christian virtue. Their charities were extensive, and they studied medicine for the purpose of relieving suffering, and refused all compensation for their labors. They did not refuse to relieve even animals, when in their power. They became most skillful physicians. In the time of Diocletian they were seized by the proconsul Lycias, and thrown into the sea, but were saved by an angel. They were also put in the fire, which would not burn them, and bound to crosses and stoned, but none of the stones reached them, so that at last they were beheaded. They were patrons of medicine, and succeeded to the honors of Æsculapius among the Greeks. They have also the title of Anargyres (without fees). They were patrons of the Medici family, as is seen on the coins of Florence. September 27, A. D. 301.

St. Costanzo Bishop of Perugia. Nothing is known of this saint but that he suffered martyrdom in the reign of Marcus Aurelius. The country between Perugia and Foligno is called the "Strada di Costanza," and he is much venerated in that portion of Italy.

St. Crispin and **St. Crispianus** (*Ital.* San Crispino e San Crispiano; *Fr.* SS. Crespin et Crespinian). These saints were brothers, who went with St. Denis from Rome to preach in France. They supported themselves by making shoes, and were supplied with leather by angels to make shoes for the poor. Being denounced as Christians, they were cruelly tortured, and then beheaded at Soissons. The Roman tradition fixes their death in A. D. 300, but other authorities give the date thirteen years earlier. Their proper attributes are the awl and shoemaker's knife. October 25.

St. Cunegunda. March 3, A. D. 1040. See St. Henry of Bavaria.

St. Cunibert, to whom one of the most ancient churches of Cologne is dedicated, was bishop of that city. He was the adviser of King Dagobert and some of his successors, and an intimate friend of Pepin d'Heristal. He held his diocese thirty-seven years. According to the legend, St. Cunibert was directed by a dove to the spot where St. Ursula and her companions were buried. He is represented in the episcopal dress, holding in his hand the model of a church. The dove is his attribute. November 12, A. D. 660.

St. Cuthbert of Durham, was a shepherd in his youth, in the valley of the Tweed. In his childhood an angel appeared to him and urged him to a pious life. He was instructed at a monastery near his home, where St. Aidan was the prior. One night as Cuthbert tended his flocks, he saw a dazzling light, and looking up beheld angels bearing St. Aidan to heaven. He then entered the monastery and soon became a noted preacher. He not only made converts, but he preached much to such Christians as lived unworthy lives. It was said that when he appealed to them an angelic brightness shone in his face, and none could deceive him or conceal the sin of their hearts. He wandered among the mountainous regions, and preached in villages considered almost inaccessible. He dwelt on an island on the coast of Northumberland, called afterwards Holy Island, in memory of his sanctity. Here he supported himself upon what he raised by his own labor, and it is said that angels brought him bread from Paradise. He was afterwards Bishop of Landisfarne. Miraculous things are told of him during his life, and of his relics after his death. His shrine became a place of pilgrimage. His relics are now in the Cathedral of Durham. His attribute is the head of St. Oswald which was buried in the tomb of St. Cuthbert, when he was slain in battle. He also has the otter, which was said to have licked him into life when almost perished from cold and exposure. March 20, A. D. 687.

St. Cyprian, and **St. Justina of Antioch** (*Ital.* San Cipriano il Mago e Santa Giustina; *Fr.* St. Cyprien le Magicien et Sainte Justine.) The histories of these saints cannot be separated. Saint

Justina was an exceedingly lovely and virtuous Christian maiden of Antioch. Her father was a priest of the idols, but she converted both him and her mother to her own faith. A nobleman, named Aglaides, sought her love in vain, and at length he applied to the fa-

(Belvedere, Vienna.) St. Justina and Alphonso I. of Ferrara. (Il. Moretto.)

mous magician, Cyprian, for his aid in winning her heart. Now Cyprian was very learned in astrology and necromancy, and doubted not his power to overcome all obstacles. But when he saw Justina, he also loved her and determined to win her for himself. He sent demons to her to fill her mind with unchaste and voluptuous images, but she remained unaffected. At length he sent the prince of evil spirits to tempt her, but all without success. Then Cyprian was so astonished at the power of her virtue, that he resolved to serve the God of this pure maiden. So he went to her filled with repentance, and confessed himself a Christian. Justina, in her joy at so great a victory for Christ, cut off her beautiful hair, and made of it an offering to the Virgin. Cyprian was soon baptized, and became as famous for his piety as he had before been for his wickedness. When the last persecution of the Christians broke out, the governor of Antioch commanded these saints to be thrown into boiling pitch, which, by a miracle, had no power to harm them. He then sent them to Diocletian at Nicomedia, who ordered them to be instantly beheaded. September 26, A. D. 304.

St. Cyprian of Carthage, and archbishop of that place, perished in the persecution of Valerian. His martyrdom is one of the most authentic in history. He is very rarely represented in works of art, and perhaps the picture by Paul Veronese, in the Brera at Milan, is the only one likely to come within the observation of the traveller. September 16, A. D. 258.

St. Cyril (*Lat.* S. Cyrillus; *Ital.* San Cirillo; *Fr.* S. Cyrille). This saint was patriarch of Alexandria from the year 412 to 444. He wrote much upon theology, and was earnestly engaged in the contests of the early Church. His fame as patriarch is sullied by the terribly cruel murder of Hypatia, the female mathematician and philosopher. She was put to death in his church by his followers, and many believed it to have been done with his connivance. He is more highly venerated in the Greek than in the Latin Church, and is the only bishop whom they represent with his head covered. January 28, A. D. 444.

St. Cyril and **St. Methodius.** St. Cyril was a philosopher, and Methodius an artist. They were of the Order of St. Basil, and were sent by the Patriarch of Constantinople as missionaries to the people who lived on the borders of the Danube. Bogaris, the king of Bulgaria, desired Methodius to paint a picture in the hall of his palace that should impress his subjects with awe. Methodius painted the "Last Judgment," with Christ enthroned and surrounded with angels; also the happiness of the blessed and the miseries of the lost. When finished, the king desired an explanation of this terrible picture, and Cyril gave it with such power that the monarch, and all who listened, were converted. So they labored among the neighboring nations with success. Methodius painted, and Cyril so explained his pictures as to convince large numbers of the truth of the Christian faith. St. Cyril also learned their languages, made an alphabet for them, and translated a part of the gospels. He obtained, too, the privilege of celebrating the mass in the Sclavonic tongue. They are generally represented together; St. Cyril with a book and St. Methodius with a tablet on which is a picture. The Greeks honor St. Cyril March 9, and St. Methodius May 11. The Latins both March 9.

Dale Abbey, Legend of. This legend is represented in five pictures. In the first, the abbot shoots the deer with a cross-bow, because it had eaten his wheat. In the second, the foresters complain of him, and the king commands him to be brought before him. In the third and fourth, he is in the presence of the king, who grants him as much land as he can encircle by a furrow from sun to sun; the plough to be drawn by two wild stags from the forest. In the fifth he ploughs with the stags.

St. Damian. See St. Cosmo.

St. Daria. See St. Chrysanthus.

Dead Nuns, the legend of. There were two noble ladies who joined the sisterhood of St. Scholastica who were fond of scandal and vain talk. St. Benedict hearing of this, reproved them, and sent them word that unless they reformed he would excommunicate them. For a while they remembered it, but fell again into the habit, and so died. They were buried in the church near the altar. One day as Benedict celebrated mass, when the deacon said, "Let those who are excommunicated, and forbidden to partake, depart and leave us," these nuns arose from their graves, and with sad appearance left the church. This occurred each time the mass was celebrated there, until St. Benedict, pitying them, absolved them from their sins and they rested peacefully.

St. Delphine. See St. Eleazar de Sabran.

St. Denis of France (*Lat.* Sanctus Dionysius; *Ital.* San Dionisio or Dionigi; *Fr.* Saint Denis). The truth of the legend which makes St. Denis the same with Dionysius the Areopagite, will not be confirmed upon a critical examination of facts, but as they are thus represented in works of art, it is necessary to be given in order to understand the representations of them. Dionysius was an Athenian philosopher. He was a judge of the Areopagus, and for his wisdom in heavenly things was called Θεόσοφος, Theosophus. He went to Egypt to study astrology, and was at Heliopolis at the time of the crucifixion of Our Lord. He was greatly troubled at the darkness which endured for three hours, because he could not understand it. He was converted at Athens by Paul, and became first bishop of that city. In his letters he tells of going to Jerusalem to visit the Virgin; of his astonishment at the dazzling light which surrounded her, and of being present at her death and burial. He went to Rome and attended Paul at his martyrdom. He was then sent by Pope Clement to preach in France with two deacons,

Rusticus and Eleutherius. After his arrival in France he was called Denis. He found Paris a beautiful city, seeming to him like another Athens. He dwelt here, and by his preaching converted many. He sent missionaries to all parts of France and to Germany. At length he was accused of his faith to the Roman Emperor, who sent Fescennius to Paris to seize him, with his companions. They were condemned to death. At the place of execution St. Denis knelt down and prayed, and the deacons responded in a loud Amen. Their bodies were left as usual, to be devoured by wild beasts. But St. Denis arose, and taking his head in his hands, walked two miles, to the place now called Mont Martre, the angels singing as he went. This miracle converted many, and among them Lactia, wife of Lubrius, who was afterwards beheaded also. The bodies of St. Denis and his deacons were buried, and a church erected over them by St. Geneviève, but in the reign of Dagobert they were removed to the Abbey of St. Denis. He is the patron saint of France, and his name the war-cry of its armies. The oriflamme, the standard of France, was consecrated on his tomb. When Stephen II. became pope, the name of this saint began to be venerated in all Europe. Stephen had been educated at the monastery of St. Denis. There is a beautiful life of the saint in the royal library of Paris, with a large number of exquisite miniatures. His attribute is the severed head. October 9.

St. Digna. See St. Afra of Augsburg, whose handmaiden she was.

St. Diego d'Alcala was an humble Capuchin brother in a convent of Alcalà, who never dreamed of being a saint. It was said that the infant Don Carlos was healed through his intercession, when severely wounded. Philip II. obtained his canonization on this account. About 1600, a wealthy Spaniard residing at Rome dedicated a chapel to this saint in the Church of San Giacomo degli Spagnuoli, which was painted by Annibal Caracci, and Albano who was then his pupil. These frescoes were transferred to canvas. There are also pictures of him by Murillo.

St. Dominick (*Lat.* Sanctus Dominicus, Pater Ordinis Prædicatorum; *Ital.* San Domenico, San Domenico Calaroga; *Fr.* Saint Dominique, Fondateur des Frêres Prêcheurs; *Sp.* San Domingo). This saint was a Castilian of noble descent. His mother dreamed before his birth, that she had brought forth a dog with a torch in his mouth. At his baptism a star descended from heaven to crown his brow. He studied at Valencia, and joined the Order of St. Augustine at an early age; indeed, he performed penance from the age of six years. When thirty years old he went to France, and being shocked at the heresies of the Albigenses, he preached with such effect as to convert many. He went the second time to France with his bishop to conduct to Castile the young princess who was to espouse Prince Ferdinand. Her death, just as he arrived, was a great shock to him, and from that time his zeal and religious devotion were very great. He obtained permission of the Pope in 1207 to preach to the Albigenses in the Vaudois. He wrote out articles of faith, and it is said, that when this book was thrown in the fire it would not remain, but leaped out, uninjured. As the heretical books were burned, this miracle had the effect to convince and convert many. It cannot be known what part he took in the persecution of the Albigenses, but it is certain that he was extremely earnest in his prayers and endeavors to secure the triumph of the Church. He united with several priests, who went about to preach barefooted. From this arose his Order, which was confirmed in 1216. St. Dominick, though not the inventor of the Rosary, instituted its use, made an arrangement of the chaplet, and dedicated it to the Virgin. A rosary should have fifteen large, and one hundred and fifty small beads. The large represent the Paternosters, and the small the Ave-Marias. This use of the rosary was a great assistance to St. Dominick in his labors. In 1218 St. Dominick was commissioned by the Pope to reform the nunneries at Rome. From this originated the Order of the Dominican Nuns, for he made a new Rule which they adopted. He founded many convents in the principal cities of Europe, none of which are more famous than the splendid one of his Order in the Rue St. Jacques at Paris. It is from the situation of this convent that the Dominicans were called Jacobins in France. At length he returned to his convent at Bologna, where he died of a fever, brought on by his arduous labors. Two years after his death he was canonized, and his remains placed in the magnificent "Arca di San Domenico" at Bologna. It is said his true portrait was brought from heaven by St. Catherine and Mary Magdalen to a convent of Dominican nuns. His attributes are, the dog by his side; the star, on or above his head; a lily in one hand and a book in the other. There are many interesting legends of his wonderful

St. Dominick.

miracles. At one time, it is said, he restored to life the young Lord Napoleon, nephew of Cardinal Stephano di Fossa-Nova, when he had been killed by a fall from his horse. When, at the convent of St. Sabina, they had not sufficient food, St. Dominick pronounced the blessing upon the little they had, and immediately two angels appeared with bread and wine which was celestial food, and sweeter than any of earth. St. Dominick had a vision, in which he saw the Saviour with the arrows of divine wrath in his hand. The Virgin asked him what he would do, and when he replied that he would destroy the earth on account of its wickedness, she besought him to wait, and presented to him St. Francis and St. Dominick, saying, that they would traverse the whole earth and subdue it to Christ. August 4, A. D. 1221.

St. Donato of Arezzo (*Lat.* St. Donatus; *Fr.* Saint Donat). This saint was of noble birth, and in childhood a companion of the Emperor Julian. After the apostasy of Julian, he put many Christians to death, and among them the father of Donatus. Donatus then fled from Rome to Arezzo, and had for his companion the holy monk, Hilarion. They preached, and performed many miracles. At one time a tax-gatherer of the province went on a journey and left the money which he had with his wife Euphrosina. She died suddenly and told no one where she had hidden the treasure. When her husband returned he was in great distress, and fearing to be punished as a defaulter, he appealed to Donatus, who went to the tomb and called upon Euphrosina to tell him where the money was. She answered him, and this was heard by many. He was made bishop of Arezzo, and as he celebrated the Holy Mass, the cup which held the wine, and was of glass, was broken by some idolaters. When Donatus prayed, it was made whole, and not a drop of wine spilled. This miracle was the cause of the conversion of so many, that the pagans, in their rage, tortured and beheaded him. Hilarion was scourged to death, and both are interred beneath the high altar of the Cathedral of Arezzo. August 7.

St. Dorothea of Cappadocia, Virgin and Martyr (*Ital.* Santa Dorotea; *Fr.* Sainte Dorothée). She was a noble virgin, and the most beautiful of the city of Cæsarea. She was a Christian, and devoted to prayer, fasting, and almsgiving. Sapritius or Fabricius, the governor, hearing of her beauty, sent for her, and threatened her with death if she would not worship the idols. She depicted to him the joys of heaven, and declared that she preferred the death which would give her these to a life of idolatry. She was taken to prison, and two sisters, Calista and Christeta, who had renounced Christianity through fear of torture, were sent to induce Dorothea to follow their example. But she so influenced them that they left her, declaring themselves again Christians. Then Fabricius commanded the sisters to be burned, and Dorothea to witness their sufferings. She encouraged them through all, and was then condemned to be tortured and beheaded. She endured the tortures with great bravery. As she was led to execution, a young lawyer, called Theophilus, jeered her and asked her to send him fruits from the gardens to which she was going. She told him that his request should be granted. When at the place of execution, she knelt and prayed, and suddenly there was beside her a beautiful angel with a basket, in which were three roses and three apples. She commanded him to take them to Theophilus and tell him she had sent them, and should await him in the gardens from which they came. Then she was beheaded. When Theophilus received the fruit and tasted of it, he too became a Christian, and at last suffered martyrdom. Her attributes are roses in the hand or on the head, or a basket with three apples and three roses held by an attendant angel. February 6, A. D. 303.

(German.) St. Dorothea.

St. Dunstan was born in 925. He became a monk at Glastonbury. He was a fine scholar, a remarkable musician, a painter, and a worker of metals. He went to court when quite young, and was a great favorite of King Edmund, who admired his musical talents. He had such an influence over the king that he was accused of sorcery and driven from the court. One day as the king was hunting the stag, his dogs leaped down a fearful precipice. The king feared that he could not rein his horse and must follow to death. He prayed, and thought of his cruelty to Dunstan. The horse stopped on the bank. The king soon sent for Dunstan to return to him. It is related that as he labored one night at his forge, the Devil came to tempt him in the form of a beautiful woman. Dunstan seized the Devil by the nose with his red-hot tongs. One day his harp hanging on the wall played to him the hymn, "Gaudete animi." Dunstan was made the king's treasurer and Abbot of Glastonbury, but when Edwin came to the throne and lived a shameless life with Elgiva, he drove Dunstan again from court. When Edgar was king, he was again honored. He was made Bishop of Worcester, and then Archbishop of Canterbury. In 960 he went to Rome, and received great honors as Primate of the Anglo-Saxon nation.

(Bod. Lib. Oxford.) A pen-drawing of St. Dunstan at the feet of Christ. Drawn by himself.

On his return he founded numerous schools and monasteries. He relates in his writings a vision, in which he beheld his mother espoused to Christ while angels sung around them. One of the angels asked Dunstan why he did not sing, and when he replied that he was ignorant and could not sing, the angel taught him the hymn, and the next day he could sing the same to his monks. May 19, A. D. 988.

Duns Scotus was a Franciscan, and a rival in theological controversy of St. Thomas Aquinas. Their opinions gave rise to the parties called Thomists and Scotists. He was one of the most stubborn defenders of the doctrine of the Immaculate Conception. He was an Englishman, and went to Paris about 1304, where he wrote his commentaries. He was sent to Cologne in 1308, where he was received with great honor; and there he died in the same year. There was a fable of his having been buried alive, which is disputed by good authorities.

St. Ebba of Coldingham. This saint was abbess of the largest monastery which existed in her time, and had monks as well as nuns under her rule. About the year 870, there was an incursion of Danish pirates, and St. Ebba was alarmed for her chastity and that of her nuns; she assembled them in the chapter-house and made an appeal to them; she then took a razor and cut off her nose and upper lip. Her example was followed by the whole community, and when the pirates came, the frightful spectacle they presented protected their virginity. The pirates in their disappointment set fire to the monastery and the nuns perished in the flames. April 2.

St. Edith of Wilton, daughter of King Edgar. Her mother was a beautiful nun, Wilfrida, whom the king took from her convent by force. As soon as she could escape from him she returned, and Edith was born in the nunnery. She refused to go to court, and was celebrated for her sanctity, learning, and beauty. She spent the fortune her father gave her in founding a nunnery at Wilton, which has since been the seat of the earls of Pembroke. Edith was remarkable for the costliness and elegance of her attire, and when she was rebuked for it by St. Ethelwold she insisted that this was of no importance, for God regarded the heart alone, and that He could read beneath any garment. "For," answered she, "pride may exist under the garb of wretchedness; and a mind may be as pure under these vestments, as under your tattered furs." She died at the age of twenty-three. She lived to see the consecration of the church she had built in honor of St. Denis, but died forty-three days after. St. Dunstan was warned of her approaching end, while celebrating mass on the occasion of the consecration. September 16, A. D. 984.

Edith of Polesworth. See St. Modwena.

St. Edmund. King and Martyr. The ecclesiastical legend of King Edmund is this: Ragnar Lodbrog was a Dane of royal blood. He went out fowling in a small skiff, and a storm coming on he was driven upon the English coast in Norfolk. He was taken to King Edmund, who much admired the strength of the Dane, and his skill as a huntsman, while Lodbrog was dazzled by the accomplishments of the young king, and the splendor of his court. The huntsman of Edmund became jealous of the Dane, and killed him. A dog which

Lodbrog had reared watched over his body until it was discovered The huntsman confessed his crime, and as a punishment was put adrift in the same boat which had brought Lodbrog to England. He was carried to the home of the Dane, where his two sons, seeing the boat of their father, and supposing him to be murdered, were about to kill the huntsman. But he told them that Edmund had done the deed. Then they swore vengeance, and collecting a great fleet, went to invade England. They landed in Northumbria, and destroyed everything within their reach as they advanced to the territory of Edmund. They demanded of him one half his kingdom. He took counsel with Bishop Humbert and determined never to submit to a heathen power. He then prepared for battle and met the Danes near Thetford, where they fought. King Edmund was surrounded by his enemies, and with Humbert, took refuge in the church. They were dragged out, and the king was bound to a tree and scourged; his body was then filled with arrows from the Danish bows, and finally he was beheaded. Humbert also was martyred. At length when the Christians who had hidden came forth, they found a large, gray wolf watching the head of the king. This they buried in a spot where was afterwards built a church and monastery, and then a town, which was called in memory of the king, Bury St. Edmunds, which name it still retains. November 20, A. D. 870.

St. Edward the Martyr was the son of King Edgar. One day when he was hunting he went to Corfe Castle, where his stepmother, Elfrida, was living with his brother Ethelred. His mother received him kindly, but commanded one of the servants to stab him in the back as he was drinking. He, finding himself wounded, rode away, and died in the forest. Elfrida and her son gave him a shameful burial, and instituted rejoicings at his death. But God shed a celestial light on his grave, and those who came to it were healed of all infirmities. Multitudes made pilgrimages to his grave, and when St. Dunstan reproved Elfrida as a murderess, she was struck with remorse, and desired herself to go there. But when she mounted her horse for the journey, he would not move, and no power could make him, so Elfrida, perceiving the will of God in this, walked barefooted to the place. His remains were removed, with great honors, to the nunnery at Shaftesbury, which Alfred the Great had endowed. March 18, A. D. 978.

St. Edward, King and Confessor. This saint was son of King Ethelred, who had before his birth two other sons. But when it was near the time for this third one to be born, Ethelred called upon his council to decide who should succeed to the throne. St. Dunstan was present, and he prophesied the early death of those already born, so the council decided in favor of the expected prince, who was afterwards the saint of whom we speak. All the nobles took the oath of fealty to him, dans le sein de sa mère. The coronation of Edward was on Easter day, 1043. He freed his subjects from the tax called Danegelt, because when a large sum of this tribute was brought to the palace, and the king was called to look at it, he beheld a rejoicing demon dancing upon the money. This saint had many visions during his life, and also possessed miraculous powers of healing. His history is told in bas-reliefs in his chapel in Westminster Abbey. January 5, A. D. 1066.

St. Eleazar de Sabran was a Franciscan. His mother was a woman of remarkable character and great piety. He was early married to Delphine, heiress of Glendènes. She was as pious as her husband, and they were both enrolled in the Third Order of St. Francis. As Count of Sabran, he administered his affairs with great ability and justice. He died at twenty-eight. St. Delphine then resided for some time with Sancha, queen of Naples, but at last withdrew to perfect seclusion. St. Eleazar is represented in art holding a package of papers to commemorate a noble act of his life. After the death of his father, he found papers which had been written to induce his father to disinherit him, and which attributed to him all manner of evil. Instead of taking revenge on the writer of these calumnies, he sent for him, and burned the letters in his presence. He thus converted his bitter enemy to a devoted friend.

St. Elisabeth, mother of John the Baptist. (*Lat.* Sancta Elisabetha; *Ital.* Santa Elisabeta; *Sp.* Santa Isabel; *Ger.* Die Heilige Elizabeth.) The Hebrew signification of this name is Worshipper of God, or Consecrated to God. The Gospel describes Elisabeth as walking in all the commandments of the Lord blameless. A woman "well stricken in years," when she was "exalted to a miraculous motherhood," and chosen for high honors by God. She should not, however, be represented as decrepit and wrinkled, but as elderly, dignified, and gracious. She appears as an important personage in art, and yet in most cases as the accompaniment to those of still greater importance. She is first seen in pictures of the Visitation or Salutation, when with prophetic utterance she exclaims, "Whence is this to me, that the mother of my Lord should come to me?" Then the representations of the birth of John the Baptist, and in various scenes from his life; one of which illustrates the legend that as Elisabeth fled from the massacre at Bethlehem, a huge rock opened, and received her and St. John, whom she bore in her arms, into its bosom, where they were concealed until the danger was past. Again, St. John is taking leave of his parents to go away to his wilderness life. But the Holy Families in which St. Elisabeth appears are far more numerous than any other representations of her. And none could be more pleasing than these. Elisabeth is frequently presenting her child to the Saviour, and teaching him to kneel and fold his hands as if in worship. The matronly age, the dark complexion, and coifed head of Elisabeth are in beautiful contrast with the virgin bloom, the abundant hair, and youthful grace of the Madonna.

St. Elizabeth of Hungary (*Lat.* Sancta Elizabetha, Mater Pauperum; *Ital.* Santa Elisabeta di Ungheria; *Fr.* Madame Saincte Elisabeth; *Sp.* Santa Isabel; *Ger.* Die Heilige Elizabeth von Ungarn, or, von Hessen; Die liebe Frau Elizabeth). This legend is almost entirely historical, with just enough of the marvelous to entitle it to a place in "legendary lore." She was the daughter of the King of Hungary, and was born in 1207. The year of her birth was full of blessings to her country, and from her earliest days she was regarded as an especial favorite of God and one who should bring good to her people. The first words she uttered were those of prayer, and at three years old she showed her charity by giving her toys and garments to those less fortunate than herself. When Herman of Thuringia heard of these things he desired this princess as a wife for his son, Prince Louis, and sent an embassy to solicit her of her father. His ambassadors were of great rank, and with them went the noble Bertha of Beindeleben, with a train of knights and ladies, and many rich presents. Their request was granted, and the little Elizabeth, only four years old, was given to them. Her father gave her a silver cradle and bath; a rich wardrobe and a train of twelve maidens. He also sent to Herman, and his wife Sophia, many splendid and precious things which he had obtained from Constantinople. The princess was received at the Castle of Wartburg, at Eisenach, with great and imposing ceremony. The next day she was betrothed to Louis, and being laid in the same cradle, they smiled and played in such a manner, as that it was considered an omen of a happy marriage. From this time they were never separated, and grew together in perfect love. Elizabeth was soon seen to be very different from all other children; her mind was devoted to heavenly things, and charity was her chief characteristic. As long as Herman lived, Elizabeth was happy, and he was her true friend and father; but after his death, which happened when she was nine years old, the mother and sister of Prince Louis did all they could to prevent the marriage, because they did not like her devotion and piety. But although she suffered many insults, she never resented them, and Louis remained true to her in spite of all. Sometimes he feared she was too pure and holy to be any other than the bride of Heaven, but at length when he was twenty the marriage took place. They lived a life of most perfect love. but she continued all her religious penances. Louis sometimes remonstrated, but he secretly felt that he and his people should receive, in some way, great blessings from the sanctity of his wife. Her confessor had told her that the imposts for the support of the royal table were unjust, and from that time, while others feasted she ate bread and drank only water; but one day Louis took the cup from her hand and tasted, and he thought he drank wine more delicious than he had ever had before. He questioned the cup-bearer, who declared he had given Elizabeth only water. Louis said nothing, for he believed that angels attended her. At another time when Louis entertained a company of princes, he desired Elizabeth to dress magnificently. When she was attired and about to enter the apartment of Louis, a wretched beggar sought her charity. She told him she could not attend to him then, but he entreated her in the name of John the Baptist. Now this was her patron saint, and she could not refuse what was asked in his name, so she tore off her costly mantle and gave the beggar, and sought her chamber fearing what her husband might say. Just then Louis came to seek her, and as he hesitated whether to blame or praise her, a servant brought the mantle, saying she had found it hanging in its place. Then Louis led her forth to his guests with his heart full of love and wonder. And a bright light was about her and the jewels on her mantle glowed with celestial brilliancy. Tradition teaches that the beggar was none other than our blessed Lord. Another time when visiting the poor of Eisenach, she found a leprous child whom none would care for. She carried him in her arms and laid him in her own bed. This enraged the mother of Louis, and when he returned she told him what sort of person was in his bed in his absence. Almost out of patience, he went to see, and behold! when he looked he found a sweet infant, and as they gazed it vanished away from their sight. This too, was believed to have been Jesus. When Louis was absent she spent all her time in visiting the poor, and as she one day descended to Eisenach carrying food in her robe, she met her husband. The path was icy, and she bent with the weight of her burden. When Louis demanded what she did, she did not like to show him, and pressed her robe more firmly together. He insisted and opened her mantle, when he saw only red and white roses, more lovely than the earthly roses of summer; and this was in winter. Then he was about to embrace her, but such a glory seemed to surround her, that he dared not touch her, but put one of the roses in his bosom and went on, thinking of all these wonders. In 1226, Louis went to Italy with the Emperor Frederick II. A great famine afflicted all Germany, but especially Thuringia. Elizabeth was untiring in her charities and labors. The famine was followed as usual by a plague, and again she labored, with her own hands tending the sick. She founded several hospitals, and went constantly from one to the other. She exhausted the public treasury, and gave away her own robes and jewels. When Louis returned, his counselors made great complaints of Elizabeth, but he, only thankful that she was still spared to him, said, "Let her do as she will." But she kissing him many times, said, "See! I have given to the Lord what is his, and he has preserved to us what is thine and mine!" The next year Louis went to the Crusades. The grief of the hearts of this husband and wife at parting was such that Elizabeth was carried home more dead than alive, for she had gone two days on his journey with him, before she could find strength to leave him. It was their final parting, for Louis died in Calabria in the arms of the Patriarch of Jerusalem. He commanded his retainers to carry his body to his wife, and to defend her and his children, even with their lives, from all wrong. Her grief was so great that God alone could sustain her by miraculous comfort. The brother of Louis, Henry, now drove her forth with her children, and took possession of the Wartburg. It was winter time; she carried her newly born baby in her arms, and was followed by her three other children and her women. It is said that she fell, and that one whom she had cared for in the hospital mocked at her. She found a shelter for her children, and supported herself by spinning wool. But when the knights returned with the body of Louis, they obliged Henry to accept the office of regent until her son, Herman, could reign; and Elizabeth received as her dower the city of Marbourg. And now she gave herself up to the direction of her rigid and bigoted confessor, Conrad. She lived a life of penitential humiliation, and even separated herself from her children lest she should love them too well. She drank the very dregs of the cup of penance, and clothed in rags and mocked by the children in the streets as a mad woman, she spun wool until she had no strength remaining. It is said that she was comforted by celestial beings, and that even the Blessed Virgin talked with her. When dying she sang sweet hymns, and at last she said, "Silence," and died. Tradition says that angels bore her spirit to heaven, and as they ascended were heard to chant, "Regnum mundi contempsi." She was twenty-four years old, and Louis had been dead three years and a half. She was canonized four years after her death. Her shrine in the church at Marbourg, which bears her name, was visited by pilgrims, and its stone steps worn away by their knees. In the Reformation this shrine was desecrated, and her remains scattered, no one knows where. The shrine is still preserved as a curiosity in the sacristy of the church. The castle of Wartburg is in ruins. But here since the days of Elizabeth, Luther found a refuge, and labored on his translation of the Bible, and he himself relates that here he contended bodily with demons, and the stain is shown on the wall which was made by his inkstand when he threw it at the head of Satan. There are many pictures of this lovely saint, but the most celebrated was painted by Murillo for the church of the Caritad, at Seville. November 19, A. D. 1231.

St. Elizabeth of Portugal (*Sp.* Sant' Isabel de Paz). This Elizabeth was the daughter of the King of Aragon, and grand-niece of Elizabeth of Hungary. She was married to Dionysius, King of Portugal. He was most faithless and cruel as a husband, but a good king to his subjects. After forty years of great domestic trials she was left a widow. She died at sixty-five, and can be distinguished from the other Saint Elizabeth, of whom we have spoken, by her age, as the former is always represented as young, while this one is old and venerable. She was so patient, and so often reconciled the troubles of her family, as to acquire in Spain the title Sant' Isabel de Paz. She is the heroine of Schiller's "Fridolin," though the scene is in Germany, and her name "Die Gräfin von Savern." July 8, A. D. 1336.

St. Eloy of Noyon (*Lat.* Sanctus Eligius; *Eng.* St. Loo; *Ital.* Sant' Alò or Lò; Sant' Eligio). This saint was born at the village of Chatelas. He was of humble origin. He was at school at Limoges, and there learned the trade of a goldsmith, in which he so excelled, that when he went to Paris he attracted the attention of the treasurer of the king, Clotaire II. The king desired to have a throne of gold set with jewels, and it was important to find a skillful and an honest man. Eloy was selected, and of the material furnished him for one throne he made two. The king was so pleased with the beauty of the work, and the probity of the workman, that he from that time employed him in state affairs. His successor, Dagobert, made Eloy Master of the Mint. He cut the dies for the money, and there are known to be thirteen pieces bearing his name. He was at length, after the death of Dagobert, made Bishop of Noyon. He was remarkable for his eloquence, and was sent to preach in Belgium, and by some he is believed to have been the first to carry the Gospel to Sweden and Denmark. In spite of all the duties of his high position, he still labored as a goldsmith, and made many beautiful shrines for saints, and holy vessels for churches. The Devil tempted St.

(Or-San-Michele.)
Florence. Statue. St. Eloy.

Eloy, as he did so many of the saints, and it is said of him as of St. Dunstan, that he seized the Devil's nose with his hot tongs. One of the miracles attributed to this saint, and represented on the exterior of Or-San-Michele at Florence, is that a horse being brought to him to be shod, which was possessed by the devil, he cut off the leg and quietly put on the shoe; this being done, he made the sign of the cross, and replaced the leg, to the great astonishment of all. He is patron of Bologna and Noyon, of goldsmiths and all other metal workers, and of farriers and horses. December 1, A. D. 659.

St. Elphege. See St. Alphege.

St. Enurchus, or Evurtius, was sent into France by the Church at Rome, to attend to the redeeming of captives. The people were electing a Bishop of Orleans. A dove alighted twice upon the head of Enurchus, and this was considered as showing such a remarkable sanctity in him that he was made bishop, which office he held more than twenty years. One of the miracles which he did, was this: when laying the foundations of his Church of the Holy Cross, he directed the men to dig in a certain place, and they there found a pot of gold which was enough to pay for the church. September 7, A. D. 340, or about that time.

St. Ephesus and **St. Potitus** are represented on the walls of the Campo Santo at Pisa, and seem to belong especially to that city. St. Ephesus was an officer under Diocletian, and was sent to destroy all the Christians in Sardinia. But he was so warned by a dream that he became himself a Christian, and turned his arms against the Pagans. He suffered martyrdom with his friend Potitus.

St. Ephrem of Edessa, who on account of his writings is one of the Fathers of the Greek Church, was a hermit of Syria. He is represented in a very curious Greek picture, called the "Obsequies of St. Ephrem," which is one of the best representations of hermit life. Greek festival, January 28; Latin, February 1, about 378.

St. Erasmus of Formia (*Ital.* Sant' Elmo or Erasmo; *Sp.* St. Ermo or Eramo; *Fr.* St. Elme). This saint suffered a most horrible martyrdom under Diocletian at Formia, now Mola di Gaeta. He so withstood all common tortures that he was cut open and his entrails wound off like a skein of silk on wheels. He was a bishop, and is represented as such with the implement of his torture in his hand. There is an altar dedicated to him in St. Peter's, over which a mosaic represents his death. It is a copy of a picture by Poussin. St. Erasmus is invoked under the name of Elmo by the mariners on the shores of the Mediterranean, in Spain, Sicily, and Calabria, and is believed to have power over the tempests. At Naples a monastery and fortress bear his name. June 3, A. D. 296.

St. Ercolano (Herculanus) was Bishop of Perugia, at the time of the invasion of the Goths under Totila. He labored hard and encouraged the people through the siege of Perugia, and when the city was taken, by order of Totila, he was beheaded on the ramparts. He was thrown into the ditch, and was found lying beside a dead child who was buried in the same grave with the saint.

St. Ethelberga. Of this saint there is little known but the one fact that she was the abbess of the first Benedictine nunnery in England, which was at Barking in Essex. October 11.

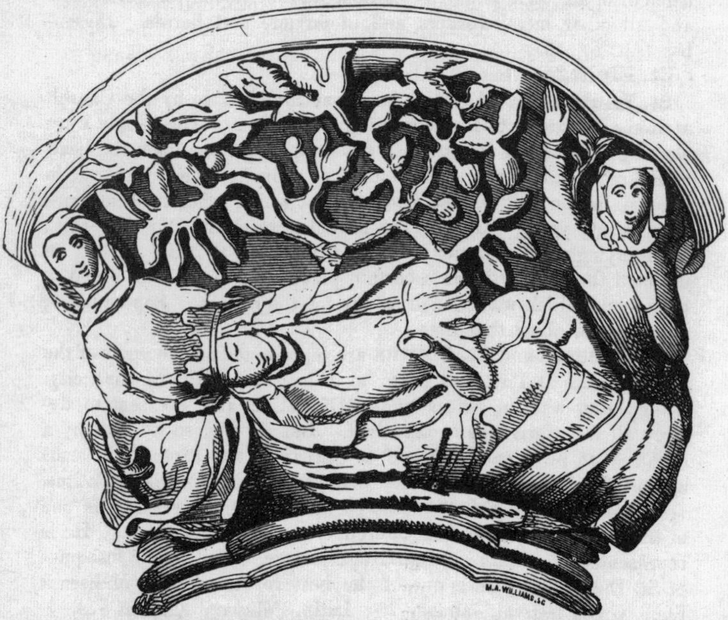

(Ancient Sculpture, Ely Cathedral.) St. Ethelreda's Dream.

St. Ethelreda. This saint is also called St. Audrey. She was the foundress of the magnificent Cathedral of Ely. Her father was Ina, king of the East Angles, and when she married Toubert, or Touberch, prince of the Gervii, the isle of Ely was her dowry. She had a second husband, Egfrid, king of Northumbria, but after living with him in a state of continency for twelve years, she took the veil at Coldingham, with his consent. King Egfrid then repented, and attempted to drag her from the convent. She fled to a rocky point called St. Ebb's Head. Egfrid pursued her, but the tide suddenly rose, and made the rock inaccessible. He married another wife. She crossed the Humber with two virgins, who watched beside her while she slept, and had a miraculous dream, in which she thought that her staff, being stuck in the ground, had put forth branches and leaves, and become a large tree. She is related to have performed a miracle about four hundred years after her death. A wicked man Britstan, being very sick, repented, and desired to dedicate himself to God in the monastery at Ely; but on his way there he was arrested and imprisoned. He implored the aid of St. Ethelreda, and at night she, with St. Benedict, came to him, and when she touched his fetters they fell from his feet. After being buried sixteen years in the common cemetery, she was placed in a beautiful sarcophagus of marble, which was probably a relic of the Romans, but the people believed it to have been wrought for the saint by angels. June 23, A. D. 679.

St. Eugenia was the daughter of Philip, proconsul of Egypt in the reign of Commodus. She was very learned. She was converted to Christianity, and put on the attire of a man and became the monk Eugenius. She went to Rome, and was put to death in the time of the Emperor Severus. December 25.

St. Eulalia, of Merida. The story of this saint is told by Prudentius. Eulalia was but twelve years old, at the time of the publication of the edict of Diocletian. She went to the prefect who judged the Christians, and reproached him for his cruelty and impiety. The governor immediately seized her, and placed on one side of her the instruments of torture, and on the other the offerings for the idol. She trampled the offerings under her feet, threw down the idol, and spat at the judge. She was then tortured to death, and as she died, a white dove issued from her mouth and flew to heaven. She is much venerated in Spain, and is buried at Merida. Another St. Eulalia is buried at Barcelona. December 10.

(Andrea Mantegna.) St. Euphemia.

St. Eunomia. See St. Afra, of Augsburg.

St. Euphemia, of Chalcedonia (*Gr.* Ἁγ. Εὐφημία; signification, praise; *Ital.* Sant' Eufemia; *Fr.* Sainte Euphémie). She was a Greek saint, and in the Eastern Church is styled Great, for such was the fame of her beauty and her courageous endurance. There is a homily upon St. Euphemia among the writings of Asterius, whc wrote about A. D. 400. She suffered death not far from Byzantium, about 307. She was very beautiful in person. After suffering many tortures she was thrown to the lions, who licked her feet, and refused to do violence to her. Priscus, her judge, was so enraged at this, that one of the soldiers, who desired to please him, killed the maiden with his sword. Within a century from the time of her death there were many churches dedicated to her, both East and West. In Constantinople alone, there were four. Leo, the Iconoclast, ordered her relics to be cast into the sea, but they appeared again in the Island of Lemnos. From here different portions of her remains were carried to many places. September 16, A. D. 307.

(Domenichino.) St. Eustace.

St. Eustace (*Lat.* Sanctus Eustatius; *Ital.* Sant' Eustachio; *Fr.* Saint Eustache). Before his conversion this saint was called Placidus. He was captain of the guards of the Emperor Trajan. He was a lover of hunting, and one day when in the forest, he pursued a white stag, which fled and ascended a high rock. As he looked, he saw between the horns of the stag a radiant cross, and on it an image of Jesus. He fell on his knees, and a voice seemed to come from the figure on the cross, announcing itself as the Redeemer, and demanding of Placidus that he should believe. He answered, "Lord, I believe." He was then told that he should suffer much for Christ, but he declared himself ready to do so. He returned to his home, and was baptized, together with his wife and two sons, and was called Eustace. Misfortune soon came. His property was taken by robbers, and his wife carried away by pirates, and he wandered in poverty with his sons. One day he wished to cross a stream, and swam over with one child, whom he left on the bank, while he returned for the other. But when he was in the midst of the river, there came on one side a lion, and on the other a wolf, and carried off the two boys. He went to a village where he labored for his support for fifteen years. At that time the Emperor Adrian required the services of Placidus, and searched for and found him. He was put again at the head of his troops, and his honors restored to him with new power and riches. But his heart was lonely, and he mourned for his wife and sons. Now they had been rescued from their dangers, and at last they were all again united. Then Eustace believed that his troubles were ended; but soon Adrian ordered a great sacrifice to the gods, and when Eustace refused to join in it with his household, they were shut up in a brazen bull, and a fire was kindled beneath it. September 20, A. D. 118.

St. Eutropia. See St. Afra, of Augsburg.

St. Ewald the Black and **St. Ewald the Fair.** These saints were twins, and Saxons. They left England in the days of St. Boniface, and went to Ireland to study. They then went through Friesland to Westphalia, where they were to preach. Here they sought out the prince of the country. and asked permission to preach, but they were murdered by the barbarians and their bodies thrown into the river. A light was seen above the spot where they were, and their remains were recovered and carried to Cologne, and buried in the church of St. Cuthbert. They are patron saints of Westphalia. October 3, A. D. 695 or 700.

St. Fabian was made Bishop of Rome in A. D. 236. Eusebius says he was chosen because a dove alighted on him while the people and clergy were choosing a Pope. At the time, he was a stranger to all present. He died a martyr in the persecution of Decius. January 20, A. D. 250.

St. Faith (*Lat.* Sancta Fides) was born at Agen in Aquitaine. She had great beauty, but from her youth was insensible to the pleasures of the world. Because she refused to sacrifice to Diana, while still very young, Dacian, the Prefect of the Guards, subjected her to the most fearful tortures. She was beaten with rods, then half roasted on a brazen bed, and at length beheaded. The crypt of old St. Paul's in London was dedicated in the name of this saint. October 8, A. D. 290.

St. Faustinus and **St. Jovita** (*Ital.* San Faustino and San Giovita). These were brothers who were converted by the preaching of St. Apollonius, at Brescia. They preached, ministered to the poor, and zealously devoted themselves to a Christian life. By the command of Adrian they were seized and thrown into the amphitheatre. The beasts did not attack them, and they were afterwards beheaded outside the walls of Brescia, of which city they are the patron saints. February 15, A. D. 121.

St. Felicitas and her seven sons (*Ital.* Santa Felicità, *Fr.* Sainte Félicité.) This saint was of an illustrious Roman family. A widow, she devoted herself to the care of her children, and to pious works of charity. She had great riches, which made her enemies anxious to accuse her as a Christian, so that they might share the spoils; and her influence having converted many to her religion, gave them a powerful plea against her. It was in the time of the great persecution of the Emperor Marcus Aurelius Antonius. She was called before Publius, a prefect of Rome, who commanded her to sacrifice to the gods she had rejected. This she refused, and when reminded of the dangers which threatened her children no less than herself, she replied, that they knew how to choose everlasting life in preference to eternal death. She witnessed the tortures and death of her sons, never ceasing to exhort them to remain true to their faith. Januarius, the eldest, was scourged with thongs loaded with lead. Felix and Philip were beaten with clubs. Sylvanus was thrown from a rock. Alexander, Vitalis, and Martial were beheaded. After they had all thus suffered martyrdom, Felicitas praised God that she had been the mother of seven sons whom He had deemed worthy of being saints in Paradise. Her only desire was that she might quickly follow them. But she was kept four months in prison, with the hope that this prolonged agony would destroy her faith and strength. But at length she was tortured and killed. Some say she was beheaded, and others that she was thrown into a cauldron of boiling oil. In art she is represented as hooded or veiled like a widow, with the martyr's palm, and surrounded by her sons. The representations of this Roman family are sometimes confounded with those of the Seven Maccabees and their heroic mother. The only guide by which to distinguish them is, that St. Felicitas was not recognized in the East. In Byzantine art, seven young martyrs with their mother probably represent the Jewish rather than the Roman saints. St. Felicitas is the patroness of male heirs. November 23, A. D. 173. Festival of the sons, July 10.

St. Felix de Valois. November 20, A. D. 1212. See St. John de Matha.

St. Felix de Cantalicio. This saint was a native of Citta Ducale in Umbria. He was born in 1513. His parents were very poor. He entered a Capuchin monastery as a lay brother, but afterwards took the habit, and was sent to the Capuccini at Rome. Here, for forty-five years he daily begged the bread and wine for his convent, and such an abundance of these articles was never known there, as during his time. On this account he is represented in the habit of his order, with a beggar's wallet, which has two ends like a purse thrown over his shoulder, to contain the alms begged for his convent. The extreme devotion of his life won the admiration not only of the brotherhood to which he belonged, but of all who saw him. It is told of him, that as he went out on a stormy night to beg, he met an angelic child, who gave him a loaf of bread and a benediction, and then vanished from his sight. He was the first saint of the Order of the Capuchins. May 21, A. D. 1587.

St. Felix de Cantalicio.

St. Felix or **Felice**. July 12. See St. Nabor.

St. Ferdinand of Castile (*Sp.* El Santo Rey, Don Fernando, III). This great king, warrior and saint, was the eldest son of Alphonso, king of Leon, and Berengaria of Castile. His parents were separated by the Pope, because being within the prohibited degrees of consanguinity they had married without a dispensation. Their children were, however, declared legitimate. Berengaria returned to her father's court and lived in retirement. The influence she had over Ferdinand was extraordinary, and endured throughout his life. Berengaria, when she came into possession of Castile, gave up her rights to her son, and when at his father's death he succeeded to the throne of Leon, the two kingdoms were united. Ferdinand was married to Joan, countess of Ponthieu, who was as obedient and loving to Berengaria as was her husband. Ferdinand fought bravely against the Moors, and expelled them from Toledo, Cordova, and Seville. It is related that at the battle of Xeres, St. Iago appeared at the head of the troops, conducting the fight.

St. Ferdinand. (Murillo.)

Thousands of Moors were slain, but there was only a single Christian killed, and he was one who had gone into battle refusing to forgive an injury. At the time of his death, Ferdinand was planning an expedition to Africa. In the "Annals of the Artists of Spain," we are told that he founded the Cathedral of Burgos, "which points to heaven with spires more rich and delicate than any that crown the cities of the Imperial Rhine. He also began to rebuild the Cathedral of Toledo, where during four hundred years artists swarmed and labored like bees, and splendid prelates lavished their princely revenues to make fair and glorious the temple of God intrusted to their care." When urged to tax his people, in order to recruit his army and fill his empty coffers, he made a reply which reflects more glory upon his character than his victories or his cathedral foundations can give. "God," he replied, "in whose cause I fight, will supply my need. I fear more the curse of one poor old woman, than a whole army of Moors!" He died as a penitent, with a cord about his neck and a crucifix in his hand. His daughter, Elenora, was married to Edward I. of England. She possessed the piety and courage of her father. It was she who sucked the poison from her husband's wound. When the bull which canonized Ferdinand reached Seville, the greatest religious festival ever held there took place. He was buried in the Cathedral of Seville. There is a portrait of St. Ferdinand, thought to be authentic, in the convent of San Clemente at Seville. May 30, A. D. 1152.

St. Filomena (*Lat.* Sancta Philumena; *Fr.* Sainte Philomène). Recently, within a quarter of a century, this saint has come to be very popular. Her story is vague and fanciful in the extreme. In the beginning of the present century a sepulchre was discovered in the Catacomb of Priscilla at Rome, in which was the skeleton of a young girl. It was adorned with various rudely painted symbols, and a portion of an inscription, the beginning and end of which were gone. It was,

—lumena pax te cum fi—

These remains, supposed to be those of a martyr, were placed in the treasury of relics in the Lateran. When Pius VII. returned from France, a Neapolitan prelate was sent to congratulate him. One of the priests in his train begged for some relics, and the remains described above were given him. The inscription was translated, "Saint Philomena, rest in peace. Amen." Another priest had a vision, in which St. Filomena appeared, with great glory, and revealed that she had suffered death for preferring the Christian faith and her vows of chastity to marriage with the emperor, who wished to make her his wife. Afterwards a young artist was told in a vision that this emperor was Diocletian, but it is also thought to have been Maximian. These two visions so established the claims of the saint, that the priest, Francesco da Lucia, carried the relics to Naples. They were inclosed in a case made in the form of a human body. It was dressed in a crimson tunic and a white satin petticoat. The face was painted, a garland of flowers put upon the head, and a lily and a javelin, with its point reversed, emblematic of her purity and her martyrdom, were put in her hand. She was placed, half sitting, in a sarcophagus with glass sides. After lying in state in the church of Sant' Angiolo, she was carried in procession to Mugnano, amid the acclamations of the people, performing miracles on the way. Jewels of great value now decorate her shrine. Her image is found in Venetian churches, in Bologna and Lombardy. At Pisa, in the church of San Francisco, and at Paris in the churches of St. Gervais and St. Merry, there are chapels dedicated to St. Filomena. The Jesuits are said to receive this saint. August 10, A. D. 303.

St. Fina of Gemignano. This saint was not a martyr, but received the honor of canonization on account of her patience and cheerfulness during long and fearful sufferings from disease. She labored as long as was possible for the relief of all the poor and wretched within her reach. She is scarcely known outside of the little town where she dwelt, but there her name is typical of patience, fortitude, and charity. She was warned of her death by a vision of St. Gregory, whom she especially honored, and at the moment of her decease all the bells in San Gemignano were miraculously tolled. As her body was borne to the grave, she raised her hand as if to bless her aged nurse, who from that time was healed of a troublesome disease. The life of this saint is beautifully painted on the chapel dedicated to her in the Cathedral of San Gemignano. March 12, A. D. 1253.

St. Flavia was the daughter of a Roman Senator, and sister of St. Placidus, who was taken by his father at the age of five years to Subiaco to be educated by St. Benedict. Flavia followed her brother to Sicily, where he was sent by his superior, and she, with Placidus and thirty of their companions, was slain by the barbarians outside of their convent near Messina. This legend is not considered as canonical by later Benedictine writers. October 5, A. D. 540.

St. Florian is one of the guardian saints of Austria. He was a Roman soldier, who, on account of his Christian faith, was put to death in the reign of Galerius. A millstone was tied round his neck, and he was thrown into the river Enns. Many miracles were attributed to him, one of which was, that with a single pitcher of water he extinguished a large conflagration. Representations of this saint are frequent in Austria and Bohemia, and often adorn pumps and fountains. A magnificent monastery bearing his name commemorates his life, and its painful end. A picture of St. Florian, by Murillo, is in St. Petersburg. May 4.

St. Francesca Romana. The church dedicated to this saint in Rome was the scene of her fasts and vigils, and is now called by her name rather than that of S. Maria Nuova, which it formerly bore. In the Torre de' Spechi is her convent, which has been the best school in all Rome for the girls of the higher classes. Her father was Paolo di Bassi. She was born in 1384. She was extremely pious from her childhood, and would have preferred the veil of the nun to that of a bride; but her father married her to Lorenzo Ponziano, a rich nobleman. She shunned the society and pleasures belonging to her station, and devoted herself as far as possible to a religious life. Every day she recited the entire Office of the Virgin, and went in disguise to her vineyard beyond the gate of San Paolo to gather fagots, which she brought on her head into the city, and distributed to the poor. During the lifetime of her husband she collected the company of women, whose superior she became after his death. Their principal labor was teaching the young, and their vows were not irrevocable. She spent so much time in prayer that she was frequently interrupted by the demands of her family. Once it happened that while reciting the Office of Our Lady she was called away four times at the same verse; when she returned the fifth time she found this verse written on the page in golden light. This was done by a guardian angel who attended her always, and was visible only to herself. Many wonderful works are attributed to her: the raising a dead child to life, the staying of an epidemic by her prayers, and the increasing of bread by prayer, when there was not enough for the inmates of her convent, are some of the most important results of her power to work miracles. She died of a fever at the house of her son, whom she had gone to comfort on the occasion of some affliction. Her fame was not by any means confined to Rome, but was great in all Italy. March 9, A. D. 1440.

(Domenichino — fresco at Grotta Ferrata.)
St. Francesca Romana.

St. Francis of Assisi (*Lat.* Sanctus Franciscus, Pater Seraphicus; *Ital.* San Francisco di Assisi; *Fr.* Saint François d'Assise). St. Francis, called the Seraphic, from the peculiar favor in which he was held by Heaven, was the founder of the Franciscans, one of the three Mendicant Orders of Friars. His father, Pietro Bernardone, was a rich merchant. His baptismal name was Giovanni, but he acquired the title of Francisco (the Frenchman), from the fact that his father had him early instructed in French as a preparation for business. In his early years Francis was beloved for his generous and compassionate heart, and remarkable for his prodigality and love of gay pleasures. In a quarrel between the inhabitants of Assisi and those of Perugia, Francis was taken a prisoner, and held for a year in the fortress of Perugia. On reaching home he was very ill for months, and it was during this sickness that his thoughts were turned to the consideration of the wicked uselessness of the life he had lived. Soon after his recovery he met a beggar, in whom he recognized one who had formerly been known to him as rich and noble. Francis exchanged garments with him, putting on the tattered cloak of the mendicant, and giving him the rich clothes in which he was dressed. That same night, in a vision, he thought himself in a splendid apartment, filled with all kinds of arms and many rich jewels and beautiful garments, and all were marked with the sign of the cross. In the midst of them stood Christ, and he said, "These are the riches reserved for my servants, and the weapons wherewith I arm those who fight in my cause." From this, Francis thought that he was to be a great soldier, for he knew not as yet of the spiritual weapons Christ gives his disciples. Afterwards, when he went to pray in the half ruined church of San Damiano, as he knelt he heard a voice say, "Francis, repair my Church which falleth to ruin." Taking this in its most literal sense he sold some merchandise, and took the money to the priests of San Damiano for the repairing of their church. His father was so angry at this that Francis hid himself many days in a cave in order to escape from his wrath. When he returned to the city he was so changed, so haggard, and so ragged, that he was not recognized, and the boys hooted him in the streets. His father believed him insane and confined him, but his mother set him at liberty, begging him at the same time to return to his former mode of life, and not to provoke his father and disgrace them all by his strange conduct. At length his father took him to the bishop, to be advised by him. When Francis saw the holy man, he threw himself at his feet; he abjured his former life, and throwing his garments to his father, said, "Henceforth I recognize no father but Him who is in Heaven." The bishop wept with joy and admiration, and taking from a beggar who stood by a coarse cloak, he gave it to Francis, who gladly received it as the first fruits of the poverty on which he was resolved. He was now twenty-five years old. The first labor he performed was that of caring for the lepers in a hospital, and this was considered the more meritorious from the fact that before this he could not look on a leper without fainting. The next years of his life were passed in prayer and penitence. He wandered among his native mountains, begging alms, every penny of which that could be spared, after supplying the imperative wants of nature, was given for the reparation of churches. He dwelt in a cell near the chapel of S. Maria degli Angeli; and several disciples, attracted by the fame of his piety, joined him here. Poor as he was, his attention was attracted to the text, "Take nothing for your journey, neither staves, nor scrip, nor bread, nor money, nor two coats," and he cast

(School of Giotto.)
St. Francis espouses Poverty, Chastity, and Obedience.

about him to see if he had any superfluous comfort. He could find nothing that he could spare, save his leather girdle; and casting that away, he used instead a rope of hemp. This has also been adopted by his followers, from which peculiarity they are called Cordeliers. He preached with marvelous effect, and soon had many followers. Among his female converts none are of greater note than the first, Clara d'Assisi, the beautiful "Gray Sister," the foundress of the Order of the "Poor Clares." The vow of poverty, the most complete and absolute, was insisted upon by St. Francis in his Order. One of the Franciscan legends is, that as he journeyed to Siena, "St. Francis was encountered by three maidens, in poor raiment, and exactly resembling each other in age and appearance, who saluted him with the words, 'Welcome, Lady Poverty!' and suddenly disappeared. The brethren not irrationally concluded that this apparition imported some mystery pertaining to St. Francis, and that by the three poor maidens were signified Chastity, Obedience, and Poverty, the beauty and sum of evangelical perfection — all of which shone with equal and consummate lustre in the man of God, though he made his chief glory the privilege of Poverty." This legend has been illustrated by various pictures, and Giotto made Poverty the bride of him, who did indeed woo the sufferings which she brought, with a more devoted ardor than that with which most lovers seek the sweet and sometimes *glittering* rewards of more attractive mistresses. At length Francis went to Rome to obtain the confirmation of his Order. At first the pope, Innocent III., considering him as an enthusiast, repulsed his suit. That night in a vision the pope saw the walls of the Lateran tottering, and only kept from falling by the support of the very man to whom he had refused his aid. He immediately sent for Francis, and granted him the privileges he desired for his Order, and full dispensation to preach. He then built cells for his disciples, near his own, and gave his brotherhood the name of "Frati Minori," to signify that humility should be their chief attribute, and that each should strive for the lowest, rather than the highest place — while in his own eyes he was himself the basest of men, and he desired to be thus considered by all. His fear that his disciples should seek any other than the deepest poverty led him to forbid the building of any convent, and he commanded that the churches built for them should be the plainest and most inexpensive. Another marked peculiarity of this holy man was what is termed the "gift of tears." He wept and prayed continually, on account of his own sins and those of the whole world; and he resolved to go to preach to the heathen, and indulged the hope that God would grant him the great glory of martyrdom. He attempted at different times to go to Syria and Morocco; but he was driven back by a storm the first time, and the second was arrested by sickness. But he did many miracles, and founded convents in Spain. Ten years after the establishment of his Order he held the first general chapter, at which there assembled five thousand friars. They seemed to be thoroughly inspired with the spirit of their leader, and even he found it necessary to caution them against an excess of austerities and penances. From this assembly he sent forth missionaries to other countries, and again started himself to preach in Egypt and Syria. He only succeeded in reaching Damietta, where he was taken before the sultan, who would neither allow him to preach nor to suffer martyrdom in his territory, but sent him back to Italy, looking upon him with oriental regard and kindness, as one insane or wanting in mental capacity. A few years later, having obtained from Pope Honorius the confirmation of his Order, he resigned his office as its head, and retired to a cave on Mount Alverna. Here he had many trances and visions of our Saviour and his blessed mother, and it is said that the saint was sometimes raised into the air in ecstatic raptures of devotion. Here it was that he had the wonderful vision, and received the especial marks of the favor of God, which obtained for him the title of The Seraphic. "After having fasted for fifty days in his solitary cell on Mount Alverna, and passed the time in all the fervor of prayer and ecstatic contemplation, transported almost to heaven by the ardor of his desires, — then he beheld, as it were, a seraph, with six shining wings, bearing down upon him from above, and between his wings was the form of a man crucified. By this he understood to be figured a heavenly and immortal intelligence, subject to death and humiliation. And it was manifested to him that he was to be transformed into a resemblance to Christ, not by the martyrdom of the flesh, but by the might and fire of Divine love. When the vision had disappeared, and he had recovered a little from its effect, it was seen that in his hands, his feet, and side he carried the wounds of our Saviour." It has remained an article of belief that these wounds were really impressed by a supernatural power. Francis in his humility desired to conceal the great favor and honor he had received, but, notwithstanding his endeavors, they were seen by many. His last days were full of suffering. As death approached, he commanded those about him to place him on the earth. He attempted to repeat the 141st Psalm, and at the last verse, "Bring my soul out of prison," he breathed his last. He had requested that his body should be buried with those of the malefactors, at a place called the Colle d'Inferno, outside the walls of his native city. This request was fulfilled, and as his body was borne past the Church of San Damiano, Clara and her nuns came out to take a farewell of all that remained of him who had shown her the true religion. Only two years passed before his canonization, and the commencement of the church which covers his remains. These are still entire and unviolated in their tomb, which is in a hollow rock. There are numberless legends connected with St. Francis, a vast number of which are written in picture history. Many of them are illustrative of his love for all lower animals and even insects; for he felt that love of Christ in our hearts should fill us with sympathy for everything that can suffer pain, or be benefited by kindness. When in Rome, he had always with him a pet lamb. One instance of his tenderness is thus given: "One day he met, in his road, a young man on his way to Siena to sell some doves, which he had caught in a snare; and Francis said to him, 'O good young man! these are the birds to whom the Scripture compares those who are pure and faithful before God: do not kill them, I beseech thee, but give them rather to me;' and when they were given to him, he put them in his bosom and carried them to his convent at Ravacciano, where he made for them nests, and fed them every day, until they became so tame as to eat from his hand. And the young man had also his recompense; for he became a friar and lived a holy life from that day forth." There is in the church at Assisi a picture of St. Francis, painted soon after his death, under the oversight of those who had known him well. It has almost the value of a portrait. October 4, A. D. 1226.

St. Francis de Paula. This saint, though a native of Paola, a small city of Calabria, is more important in France, and in connection with French history, than in his own country. It was for this saint that Charles VIII. founded the Church of the Trinità-di-Monti at Rome. At the age of fifteen he went with his parents to the shrine of St. Francis at Assisi. On his return he became a hermit and lived in a cave near Reggio. His fame drew disciples about him, for whom the people built cells and a little chapel. He called his little band Minimes, or the Hermits of St. Francis, for they followed the Franciscan rule, adding to it even greater austerities than it already prescribed. They kept Lent all the year, and they called themselves, as their title indicated, the least of all the disciples of the Church. King Louis XI. of France had heard of

St. Francis de Paula.

the many wonderful cures performed for the sick by St. Francis de Paula, and sent for him to come to him at Plessis-le-Tours, where he was dying. The saint felt that he had not been summoned in the right spirit, and refused to go, when Louis applied to Sixtus IV. for aid in the matter. At the command of the pope, Francis went, and he was received at Amboise, by the dauphin and court, with all the honors possible. When he arrived at the castle, the king knelt to him, and prayed him to obtain from God the return of health and a longer life. Francis rebuked him, and reminding him that God alone could give life or death, and that submission to his will was man's first duty, he performed for him the last offices of religion. Francis was kept in France by Charles VIII. and Louis XII., and his influence was very great. The courtiers gave him the title of "Le Bonhomme," in derision of his mode of life, but this became the title of his Order in France, where his disciples became very popular, and were to the people "Les Bons-hommes" in every good sense of the term. Francis was godfather to Francis I., and they are frequently represented together in pictures. Before the Revolution the effigies of Francis de Paula were very common in France. His tomb was broken open by the Huguenots in 1562 and his remains burnt. He died at Plessis, and Louise d'Angoulême prepared his winding-sheet with her own hands. April 2, A. D. 1507.

St. Francis de Sales. This saint is famous for his religious and devotional writings, which are held in great esteem by Protestants as well as by those of his own church. He was also known as very charitable, tolerant, and gentle towards those who disagreed with him, as well as those who lived lives of wickedness. When others remonstrated against his charitable tenderness, he would reply, "Had Saul been rejected, should we have had St. Paul?" He was made Bishop of Geneva in 1602. He was very remarkable for his personal beauty and the almost angelic expression of his face. January 29, A. D. 1622.

St. Francis Xavier was a Jesuit, the friend and disciple of Ignatius Loyola, and was sent by him as the leader of a band of missionaries to the Indies. He was of an illustrious family, and was born at a castle in the Pyrenees. He studied at Paris. When young he was gay and enthusiastic in his temperament, and it was not until after many struggles that he was able to take the vow of obedience; but having once done so, he was more ardent in the pursuit of his duties than he had ever been in seeking the accomplishment of his own desires and ends. He was thirty-five years old when he went to the East, and most of the remainder of his life was spent in Japan. His self-denial and sufferings were very great, and yet he always wrote of happiness, and died believing that he had done great good. He conferred the rite of baptism upon an almost innumerable host. He appointed other teachers over their churches, and saw the crucifix erected in many homes, as a token of the results of his labors, and of the conversion of the heathen to the religion of Christ. He would have hailed the martyr's death with joy, but his end, though a painful one, was not brought about by the violence of his enemies. He attempted to go to China. He had succeeded in reaching the island of Sancian, where he was seized with fever and died. He suffered very greatly for want of shelter and care. He regretted that he must die a natural death, but at length experienced a willingness to depart in God's way, and felt that his desire for martyrdom was sinful, since it was not according to the Divine will. His body was interred near the shore, where there is still a cross to mark the spot; but his remains were carried to Malacca and finally to Goa, where a magnificent church has been built to the honor of this great missionary saint. December 3, A. D. 1550.

St. Francis Borgia stands as the third among the saints in the Jesuit Order. He belonged to a family most illustrious in rank, and equally as infamous in their lives. In youth he was surrounded with all that would seem to make life desirable and happy, — wealth, station, and power, — while he was fondly in love with his beautiful wife, and had a large family of promising children. But he was thoughtful and melancholy, and cherished in his heart deep religious feeling. Circumstances combined to strengthen these emotions. His friend, Garcilasso de la Vega, the poet, died; he was himself more than once brought near to death by severe sicknesses. At length, when the Empress Isabella died, it was his duty to raise the winding-sheet from her face at the moment the body was to be buried, and to swear to the identity of the remains. He did so, and took the oath, and at the same moment made another vow to forsake the service of the kings of earth, and from that hour to serve only the King of Heaven. But this he could not fulfill literally at once. He was Governor of Catalonia, and administered the affairs of the province with great care and faithfulness; but through the acquaintance of a Jesuit named Aroas, he became a disciple of Loyola, and corresponded with him. His wife died, and he then resolved that after providing for his children in the best manner, he would renounce the world and every human affection. For six years he devoted himself to settling his affairs, and then went to Rome, and became an humble Jesuit. He gave all his life and energy to perfecting the system of education of his Order, and never granted his approbation to the Inquisition. For seven years he was general of his society, being the third who had held that high position. He died at Rome, and was buried in the Gesu, near Loyola; but his grandson, the Cardinal Duke of Lerma, removed his remains to Madrid. October 10, A. D. 1572.

St. Frediano of Lucca (*Lat.* Sanctus Frigdianus). This

saint was a native of Ireland. He was made Bishop of Lucca, to which place he had gone, in 560. The principal occurrence in his life which is represented in art, is his turning the course of the river Serchio, when it threatened to deluge Lucca. This he did by drawing a harrow along the ground, and the river followed the course he thus marked out. His whole history is painted in a church at Lucca called by his name.

St. Gabriel (*Gr.* Ἅγ. Γαβριήλ; *Lat.* Sanctus Gabriel; *Ital.* San Gabriello, San Gabriele, L'Angelo Annunziatore; *Fr.* St. Gabriel). This saint, whose name signifies "God is my strength," is the second in rank among the archangels, or the seven who stand before God. (Rev. viii. 2.) His name is mentioned four times in the Bible (twice in Daniel, viii. 16 and ix. 21; twice in Luke, i. 19, 26), and always as a messenger, bearing important tidings. First he announces to Daniel the return of the Jews from their captivity, and then makes him understand the vision which shows forth the future of the nations. Next he tells Zacharias of the child that should be born to his old age, and lastly he comes to tell the mother of our Lord that she is *the one* highly favored and blessed among women. These four authenticated acts make him of such importance as to command our deepest interest in all relating to him; and in addition to these he is believed to have foretold the birth of Samson, and that of the Virgin Mary. He is venerated as the angel who especially watches over childbirth. The Jews believe him to be the "chief of the angelic guards," and the keeper of the celestial treasury. The Mohammedans regard him as their patron saint, as their prophet believed him to be his inspiring and instructing angel. Thus is he high in the regard of Jews, Christians, and the followers of Islam. It is as the angel of the Annunciation that he is most frequently and beautifully represented. The spirit in which these pictures are painted has changed with the belief of the Romish Church.

Archangel Gabriel.

In the earlier ones both the Angel and the Virgin are standing, and the manner of the Virgin is expressive of humility and of reverence for a superior being. She has been painted as kneeling. But after the thirteenth century, *she* becomes the one to be exalted. She is from this time the *Regina angelorum;* and as his queen, Gabriel often kneels before her. His attributes are, — the lily; a scroll inscribed "Ave Maria, Gratia Plena;" a sceptre and sometimes an olive branch, typical of the "peace on earth" that he announced. March 18.

St. Gaudenzio (*Lat.* Sanctus Gaudentius) was one of the early bishops of Rimini. His effigy is found on its coins. He was scourged and then stoned to death by the Arians. He is patron saint of Rimini. October 14, A. D. 359.

St. Gaudentius of Novara was the bishop, and is now patron saint of that city.

St. Geminianus (*Ital.* San Geminiano). This saint was Bishop of Modena in the middle of the fifth century. So great was the fame of his miracles that he was sent for to go to Constantinople to heal the daughter of the emperor, who was possessed of an evil spirit. It is supposed to have been the Princess Honoria. (See Gibbon, 35th chapter.) When Modena was threatened with destruction by Attila, King of the Huns, it was spared on account of the intercession of Geminianus; and after his death he preserved the Cathedral from destruction by a flood. He is represented on the coins of Modena, and worshipped as the patron saint and especial protector of that city.

St. Geneviève of Paris (*Eng.*; *Ger.*; *Ital.* Saint Genoveva). This saint is essentially French, and one of very great importance and interest among those of *le moyen âge*. The village of Nanterre was her birthplace, and during her childhood she tended a flock of sheep. When she was about seven years old, St. Germain spent a night at Nanterre. The inhabitants flocked to receive his benediction. When his eyes rested on the little Geneviève, he was made aware by inspiration of the sanctity of her character, and the glory for which God had chosen her. He talked with her; and with a manner which at her age showed her to be the especial child of God, she declared her wish to be the bride of Christ. The bishop hung round her neck a coin marked with the cross, and blessed her as one consecrated to God's service. From this time she believed herself to be separated from all worldly, and devoted to all heavenly interests. There are many wonderful stories told of her childhood. On one occasion, her mother struck her in a fit of anger. She was struck blind, and remained so for twenty-one months, when Geneviève made the sign of the cross above the water with which she bathed her mother's eyes, and her sight was restored. Geneviève remained with her parents during their lives, and then went to a relative in Paris. Although she did not enter a convent, she vowed perpetual chastity at fifteen years of age. It was many years before God gave any public and unmistakable proof of his approbation of Geneviève. During this time, while some venerated her for the holiness of her life, others regarded her as a pretender and hypocrite. She was tormented too, by demons, who, among other things, constantly blew out the tapers she had lighted for her nightly vigils. But she was able to relight them by faith and prayer.

(Guérin.) St. Geneviève of Paris.

At length Attila threatened the destruction of Paris, and the people in their alarm would have fled from the city; but Geneviève addressed them, begged them to remain, and assured them that God would not allow this pagan to overcome his followers. Immediately the news was brought that Attila had marched away. And again wher Childeric took possession of Paris, and the people suffered from want of food, Geneviève took command of the boats which went to Troyes for aid, — a tempest arose, which was calmed by her prayers, and the provisions they had received brought safely to the sufferers. Childeric respected the saint, and Clovis, even before he thought of being a Christian, venerated Geneviève, and granted any requests she made of him. She influenced his own mind and that of his queen, Clotilde, so that the first Christian church was erected, and the pagan worship forbidden in the city of Paris. It was that which is now known by her name. Ever after the miraculous manifestation of her power in the deliverance of Paris from Attila, her prayers were sought by all the people, whenever they were afflicted, and the miracles attributed to her are both wonderful and numerous. One of these was the staying of a plague, called the *mal ardent.* Until 1747, there was a little church called Ste. Geneviève des Ardents, which was on the site formerly occupied by the house of the saint. She was eighty-nine at the time of her death. She was buried beside King Clovis and his wife. St. Eloy made a magnificent shrine for the remains of the saint, but in the Revolution it was destroyed, and the relics burned in the Place de Grève. January 3, A. D. 509.

St. Geneviève of Brabant. The story of this saint has furnished the subject for poems, plays, and pictures which are anything but religious in their character. But there are many representations in art of her romantic life and sufferings. She was the wife of Count Siegfried, who was led by his steward to believe her to be wanting in fidelity to himself and her marriage vows. He ordered her to be executed, but those charged with the task of putting her to death, left her alone in the forest. She gave birth to a child, which was nursed by a white doe. A number of years having passed, her husband, while hunting, came to her abode. Explanations made plain her innocence. The steward was really put to death, while the wife was restored to her home and happiness. There is a picture by Albert Durer, which is sometimes called by the name of Geneviève of Brabant, but it is in truth the "Penance of St. John Chrysostom."

St. George of Cappadocia (*Lat.* Sanctus Georgius; *Ital.* San Giorgio; *Fr.* Saint Georges, le très-loyal Chevalier de la Chrétienneté; *Ger.* Der Heilige Jorg, Georg, or Georgius). The legend of this saint, as most generally represented in art, makes him a native of Cappadocia. His parents were of the nobility, and Christians. He was a tribune in the army, and lived in the time of Diocletian. There is a disagreement as to the scene of his most wonderful conquest of the dragon. By some it is believed to have been Selene in Libya; by others, Berytus or the modern Beyrout of Syria; but the story is ever the same. Being on his way to join his legion, he came to a city whose inhabitants were in great terror on account of a terrible dragon who lived in a marsh near the walls. This fearful monster had devoured all the flocks and herds, and the people, having retired into the city, gave him daily two sheep until all they had were gone. Then, in order to prevent his approaching the city, they commenced to send out daily two children to be devoured by this insatiable monster. Terrible as this was, it was better than that he should come near them, for his breath poisoned the air for a great distance about him, and all who breathed it, perished from its pestilential effects. The children were chosen by lot, and were less than fifteen years old. Now the king had a daughter, named Cleodolinda, whom he loved exceedingly. At length the lot fell to her. The king offered all he possessed, even to the half of

(Raphael—Louvre.) St. George of Cappadocia.

the kingdom, that she might be spared; but the people said that as it was by his own edict that their children had been sacrificed, there was no reason for allowing him to withhold his own, and they threatened to take the princess by force, if she was not delivered to them. Then the king asked that she might be spared to him eight days longer. This was granted, and at the end of that time Cleodolinda went forth to the sacrifice, clothed in her royal robes, and declaring herself ready and willing to die for her people. She moved slowly towards the place where the dragon came daily for his victims, and the way was strewed with the bones of those who had already perished. Just then St. George came to the place; and seeing her tears, he stopped to learn the cause of her sorrow. When she had told him, he said, "Fear not, for I will deliver you!" but she replied, "O noble youth! tarry not here, lest thou perish with me! but fly, I beseech thee!" Then St. George answered, "God forbid that I should fly! I will lift my hand against this loathly thing, and will deliver thee through the power of Jesus Christ!" Even as he spoke, the dragon approached them. Then the princess again entreated him, "Fly, I beseech thee, brave knight, and leave me here to die!" But St. George, making the sign of the cross, rushed to combat with the monster. The struggle was terrible, but at length the dragon was pinned to the earth by the lance of the brave knight. He then bound the dragon with the girdle of the princess; and giving it to her, she was able to lead the conquered beast like a dog. In this manner they approached the city. The people were filled with fear; but St. George cried out, "Fear nothing; only believe in the God through whose might I have conquered this adversary, and be baptized, and I will destroy him before your eyes." And in that day were twenty thousand people baptized. After this St. George slew the dragon and cut off his head. Then the king gave him great treasures, but he gave all to the poor, keeping absolutely nothing for himself; and he went on his way towards Palestine. This was the time of the publication of the edict of Diocletian, which declared the persecution against the Christians. All who read it were filled with terror, but St. George tore it down and trod it into the dust. For this he was carried before the proconsul Dacian, and condemned to eight days' torture. He was first bound to a cross, and his body torn with sharp nails; next he was burned with torches, and then salt rubbed into his wounds. Seeing that all these horrible and devilish cruelties had no power to vanquish the spirit of the saint, Dacian sent for an enchanter, who invoked the aid of Satan, and then poisoned a cup of wine which St. George drank. Before doing so, however, he made the sign of the cross, and the poison had no effect on him. The magician was converted to Christianity by this miracle, and, upon his declaring the fact, was immediately beheaded. St. George was next bound upon a wheel filled with sharp knives, but two angels descended from heaven and broke it in pieces. They then put him in boiling oil. Believing that he must be now subdued, he was taken by the judges to assist at the sacrifices in the heathen temple. Crowds came to witness his humiliation. But the saint knelt down and prayed, and instantly there came thunder and lightnings from heaven.

The temple was destroyed; the idols were crushed; while the priests and many of the people perished. Now at last Dacian commanded him to be beheaded. He met death with joy and courage. The story of St. George bears great resemblance to those of Apollo, Bellerophon, and Perseus, while the destruction of the temple and his persecutors is very like that of the Philistines when they called Samson out of his prison-house to make sport for them. The Greeks give St. George the title of the GREAT MARTYR, and his worship is very ancient in the East. In Europe little was thought of him until the Crusades, when the aid he gave to Godfrey of Boulogne established his fame as a military saint. When Richard I. made holy war, he placed his army under the protection of St. George, and from this time he has been patron saint of England. His feast was ordered to be kept through all England in 1222, and the Order of the Garter was instituted in 1330. April 23, A. D. 303.

St. Gereon, one of the commanders of the Theban legion. When St. Maurice and the greater part of the legion were at Aganum (now St. Maurice), Gereon with his command reached Cologne. Verus, the prefect, by order of the Emperor Maximin commanded them to renounce Christianity. Upon their refusal, Gereon and many of his soldiers were put to death and thrown into a pit. The veneration of this saint extends back to the fourth century, but he is little heard of outside the part of Germany which was the scene of his sufferings. Many of the representations of St. Gereon are in sculpture, and upon the stained glass in the oldest of the German churches.

St. Gervasius and **St. Protasius** (*Ital.* Gervasio e Protasio; *Fr.* St. Gervais et St. Protais). These were twin brothers who suffered martyrdom in the time of Nero. They were sent bound to Milan, together with Nazarus and Celsus. They were brought to Count Artesius, who bade them sacrifice to the idols. They refused, and Gervasius was condemned to be beaten to death with scourges loaded with lead, and Protasius to be beheaded. A man named Philip obtained their bodies and buried them in his garden, where they remained until the place of their burial was revealed in a vision to St. Ambrose. It happened after this wise. When Ambrose founded the church at Milan (A. D. 387), the people were anxious that it should be consecrated by holy relics. While Ambrose was much engaged in thought of this, and very anxious to please his people, he went to the Church of St. Nabor and Felix to pray; while there a trance came over him, and in it he beheld St. Paul and St. Peter, and with them were two young men clothed in white, and of wonderful beauty. It was revealed to Ambrose that these were two martyrs who had been buried near the spot where he was. Assembling his clergy, he made search, when the two bodies were found. They were gigantic in size. The heads were separate from the bodies, and in the tomb was a writing which told their story. These sacred relics were carried in procession to the basilica, and those sick ones who could touch them as they passed along the street, were instantly healed. Among these was a man named Severus, who had been many years blind. As he touched these bones his sight was restored. This miracle was seen by so many of the people, that it established beyond a question the great efficacy of these relics. St. Ambrose, as he laid them beneath the altar, blessed God and cried out, "Let the victims be borne in triumph to the place where Christ is the Sacrifice: He upon the altar, who suffered for all; they beneath the altar who were redeemed by his suffering." The enemies of Ambrose accused him of duplicity in this matter, and even said that Severus was bribed to play a part, but the authority of the father was sufficient to inspire confidence in spite of all, and the church was dedicated to SS. Gervasius and Protasius. Since the death of St. Ambrose, this church, which is one of the most wonderful and famous in the world, is called "Sant' Ambrogio Maggiore." The veneration of these saints was introduced into France, where they became very popular, by St. Germain in 560. He carried some part of the relics to Paris. Many cathedrals and parish churches have been dedicated to them. It would be natural to expect their pictures to represent their vast size, but this is not the case. There are few Italian and many French paintings of them. June 19, A. D. 69.

(Lucas V. Leyden.) St. Giles

St. Giles (*Gr.* Ἅγ. Γίλλος — ; *Lat.* Sanctus Ægidius; *Ital.* Sant' Egidio; *Fr.* Saint Gilles; *Sp.* San Gil) was an Athenian of royal blood. Some miracles which he performed, one of which was throwing his mantle over a sick man and thus healing him, had gained for him the veneration of the people. St. Giles left his country and became a hermit. After long wanderings, he came to a cave in a forest near the mouth of the Rhone, about twelve miles south of Nismes. Here he subsisted upon herbs and wild fruits, and the milk of a hind. This gave rise to his attribute of a wounded hind, for it came to pass, that as a party, said by some to be that of the King of France, and by others the King of the Goths, were hunting, this hind was pursued by the dogs. It led to the cave and nestled in the arms of the saint. A hunter sent an arrow after it, and when they came to look in the cave, they found the holy man wounded by the arrow. Their sorrow was great, and they entreated his forgiveness, even on their knees. He resisted all their endeavors to draw him out of the cave, and there he soon died. Above this cave was built a magnificent monastery. A city sprung up about it bearing the name of the saint, and the counts of that district were called Comtes de Saint-Gilles. The church which still remains upon the spot is an extraordinary remnant of the Middle Ages. It is covered with bas-reliefs on the outside, and has a remarkable staircase in the interior. Queen Matilda dedicated a hospital, which she founded outside of London, to St. Giles. This was in 1117, and the name now belongs to an extensive parish. In Edinburgh, too, the parish church bore his name in 1359. He is patron saint of Edinburgh, of Juliers in Flanders, and of the woodland everywhere. September 1, A. D. 725.

Glastonbury, Abbey of. The origin of this famous abbey is lost in antiquity, but the legend connects it with the introduction of Christianity into England. The wondrous story tells that when Philip, who was one of the twelve Apostles, came to France, he sent Joseph of Arimathea with his son and eleven other disciples to Britain. King Arviragus so admired the beauty of their lives, and so appreciated the dangers which they had overcome in their long journey from Palestine, that he gave them an island called Avalon. Here they built a church by twining wands, and consecrated a place of burial. They limited their number to twelve, and lived in imitation of the Master and his disciples. By their preaching many Britons were converted. It is a wonderful old place. It is here King Alfred found a refuge from his Danish foes. Here King Arthur was buried, and here ever bloomed the "mystic thorn" at the feast of the Nativity. It is upon the strength of this legend that the kings of England have claimed precedence of the kings of France in the religious councils of Pisa, Constance, Siena, and Basle. They declared that Joseph of Arimathea came to England in the fifteenth year after the assumption of the Virgin Mary, and that France received not the religion of Christ until the time of St. Denis, and that for this reason they did "far transcend all other kings in worth and honor, so much as Christians were more excellent than Pagans."

Godiva, the Countess, was the wife of Leofric, Earl of Murcia. Godiva had a great affection for Coventry, and often entreated her husband, that for the love of God and the Blessed Virgin he would free that place from the servitude to which it was subject. Leofric was not willing to grant a request which so ill agreed with his profit, and forbade her speaking again of the subject. But she again made her appeal, when he said, that if she would ride on horseback, naked, from one end of the town to the other, in sight of all the people, her wish should be fulfilled. And she replied, "But will you give me leave so to do?" Then when he answered, "Yes," she appointed a certain day, and rode naked through the town with her hair loose about her which concealed all her body save her legs. And she returned with joy to her husband, who gave the inhabitants a charter of freedom on account of this deed of Lady Godiva. It is said that the countess had commanded that on that day and hour every citizen should keep within his house, and away from the window on pain of death. But one person could not control his curiosity, and it cost him his life. From this circumstance arose the term of "Peeping Tom of Coventry," and an image of him was long preserved there. The representations of Lady Godiva are quite unmistakable.

St. Grata. See St. Adelaide.

St. Gregory, or **Gregory The Great** (*Lat.* Sanctus Gregorius Magnus; *Ital.* San Gregorio Magno or Papa; *Fr.* St. Grégoire; *Ger.* Der Heilige Gregor; signification, watchman), was born at Rome in 540. His father, Gordian, was a senator. His mother, Sylvia, was a woman of remarkable character, and like many of the mothers of that time, who bore sons destined to act a great part in the world, she had a vision while he was but a baby in her arms, in which St. Antony revealed to her that this son should be the head of the earthly Church. When grown he studied and practiced law, and was prætor of Rome for twelve years. His character was, however, always deeply religious, and the piety of his mother seemed to have descended to, and been intensified in the son. On the death of his father he devoted his wealth to religion and charity. He made his home on the Celian Hill a hospital and monastery, and dedicated it to St. Andrew. He then took a cell within it, and taking the habit of a Benedictine, devoted himself to studies which fitted him for his duties in later life. This monastery is now the Church of San Gregorio. When a fearful plague broke out in Rome, Gregory devoted himself to the nursing of the sick. One of the victims of the pestilence was Pope Pelagius. The people desired to have Gregory as his successor, but he shrank from the office, and even entreated the Emperor not to assent to the wishes of the people. When finally his election was confirmed, he hid himself in a cave away from Rome. Those who sought for him were led by a celestial light about the place where he was hidden, and he was brought again to Rome. He soon proved that the choice of the people had been a wise one. He was the most humble of men, and was the first to call himself, "Servant of the servants of God." He introduced many reforms into the Church, and showed a spirit of toleration and charity far in advance of his time. He disapproved all persecution; he restored the synagogues of Sardinia to the Jews, from whom they had been taken; he abolished slavery, and was so moved at the sight of some wretched British captives who were to be sold in Rome, that he sent missionaries to England. It is not certain that the belief in purgatory originated with Gregory, but he first preached it. He also instituted the celibacy of the clergy. He reformed the services of the Church, arranged the garments of the priests, and the Roman liturgy has ever remained as he modeled it. The chants which he arranged are used in all churches, and have ever borne his name. He even trained the choristers. He felt the responsibilities of his office so much as to consider himself literally the father of each individual of the Church, and on one occasion, he fasted and interdicted himself from any sacerdotal function for several days, because a beggar had died in the streets of Rome. His charities were boundless. When a monk, a beggar asked alms at the monastery, and receiving something came again and again until Gregory had nothing to give him but a silver porringer, which Sylvia had sent to her son, and this he did not withhold. When pope he had twelve poor men to sup with him each evening. One night he saw thirteen at his table, and calling his steward, he demanded the reason of this. The steward replied, after counting, "Holy Father, there are surely twelve only!" Gregory said no more, but at the end of the meal, he asked the uninvited one, "Who art thou?" and he said, "I am the poor man whom thou didst formerly relieve; but my name is the Wonderful, and through me thou shalt obtain whatever thou shalt ask of God." Then Gregory believed him to be an angel, and some say, Christ himself. The painting of this legend is called the "Supper of St. Gregory." John the deacon, who was his secretary, has left an account in which he declares that he has seen the Holy Spirit seated on his shoulder in the shape of a dove, while he wrote. This explains why the dove is so frequently one of his attributes. "The Mass of St. Gregory," so often painted, is founded upon a legend, that as the saint was officiating some one doubted the real presence in the elements. The saint prayed, and instantly a vision was revealed of the crucified Saviour, surrounded with all the instruments of his passion, upon the altar.

Another painting represents the miracle of the Brandeum. The Empress Constantia sent to Gregory, desiring a portion of the relics of SS. Peter and Paul. Gregory replied that he dared not disturb the sacred remains, and sent her the Brandeum, or a part of a consecrated cloth which had enfolded the remains of St. John the Evangelist. The empress disappointed, rejected this gift with scorn. Then Gregory, wishing to show that it was not so much the relics themselves, as the faith of the believer which worked the miracles, placed the cloth upon the altar, and after praying, pierced it with a knife, and blood flowed from it as from a living body. St. Gregory's doctrine of purgatory is illustrated in the legend which recounts the manner in which the saint released Trajan from torment. It is said that on one occasion, when that emperor was leading his soldiers to battle, he was stopped by a poor widow who threw herself before his horse, and demanded vengeance for the death of her son, who had been killed by the son of Trajan. The emperor promised that on his return he would attend to her request, "But Sire," replied the widow, "should you be killed in battle, who then will do me justice?"—"My successor," said Trajan. Then she replied, "What will it signify to you, great emperor, that any other than yourself should do me justice? Is it not better that you should do this good action yourself than leave another to do it?" Then the emperor alighted, and listened to her story, and finally gave his own son to her, and bestowed upon her a large dowry. Now, as Gregory was one day thinking of this story he became greatly troubled at the thought that so just a man as this should be condemned as a heathen to eternal torments, and he entered a church and prayed most earnestly, that the soul of the emperor might be released from suffering. While still at prayer he heard a voice, saying, "I have granted thy prayer, and I have spared the soul of Trajan for thy sake; but because thou hast supplicated for one whom the justice of God had already condemned, thou shalt choose one of two things: either thou shalt endure for two days the fires of purgatory, or thou shalt be sick and infirm for the rest of thy life." This is given as the explanation of the great weakness, and the many infirmities suffered by Gregory, for he chose the sickness in preference to the two days of purgatory. The last two years he lived he was not able to leave his couch. His bed, and a scourge with which he kept his choristers in order, are still preserved in the Church of the Lateran. Gregory the Great was the last pope who has been canonized. March 12, A. D. 604.

St. Gregory Nazianzen (*Gr.* Ἀγ. Γρηγορέω Θεολόγος; *Lat.* Sanctus Gregorius Nazianzenus; *Ital.* San Gregorio Nazianzeno; *Fr.* S. Grégoire de Naziance; *Ger.* S. Gregor von Nazianz), was born about 328. His father, St. Gregory, was Bishop of Nazianus. St. Nonna was his mother, and St. Gorgonia and St. Cesarea his sisters. While a boy he had a dream, which in a great measure influenced all his course in life. He thought there came to him two celestial virgins of dazzling beauty. They took him in their arms, and kissed him. He asked who they were, and from whence they came? and one said, "I am called Chastity, and my sister here is Temperance; we come to thee from Paradise, where we stand continually before the throne of Christ, and taste ineffable delights: come to us, my son, and dwell with us forever." When this was said they flew into heaven. He stretched out his arms to them, and awoke. This dream was to him like a direct command from God, and he took vows of perpetual continence and temperance. He studied in Athens, where St. Basil and Julian, who though a Cæsar, is only known as the Apostate, were his fellow-students. He was not baptized until almost thirty years old. He devoted himself to religious studies, and to austerities which he declared were ever most repugnant to him. But if they have any virtue it must have been increased by this fact. He was ordained the coadjutor of his father, and succeeded to his bishopric in 362. He was invited to preach against the Arians at Constantinople. The disputes ran very high, and were carried on by all classes, and even by the women, who argued in public as well as at home. Gregory was small in stature, and every way insignificant in his appearance. At first he was stoned when he attempted to speak, but his earnest eloquence overcame all obstacles, and though he at length gave up the bishopric of Constantinople, to which Theodosius had appointed him, because he could not endure the contests in the church, yet he had gained the respect of enemies and the confidence of friends. Leaving Constantinople, he lived on a small estate of his father's in great strictness and self-denial. St. Gregory Nazianzen is the earliest Christian poet of whom we have any knowledge. In his retirement he wrote hymns and lyrics which express all the struggles and aspirations of his naturally intense and imaginative nature. May 9, A. D. 390.

St. Gudula, called in Flemish Sinte-R-Goelen, and in Brabant St. Goule or Ergoule. The patroness of the city of Brussels. She was daughter of Count Wittiger. Her mother was St. Amalaberga, and St. Gertrude of Nivelle, her godmother. She was educated by the latter. There are many miracles told of her, but that of her lantern is the one best known and oftenest painted. It was her custom to go to the church of Morselle in the night, to pray. It was a long distance, and she carried a lantern. Satan was very envious of the influence she gained by her piety, and frequently put out her light, hoping that she might be misled. Whenever this was done, Gudula immediately relighted it by her prayers. January 8; about A. D. 712.

St. Guthlac of Croyland. The legend relates, that "at the time of his birth a hand of ruddy splendor was seen extended from Heaven to a cross which stood at his mother's door." Although this was thought to indicate future sanctity in the child, he grew up wild and reckless, and at the age of sixteen organized a band of robbers, and was their leader; but "such was his innate goodness that he always gave back a third part of the spoil to those whom he robbed." He lived thus eight years, when he saw the sinfulness of his life, and the remainder of it was devoted to penance and repentance. At the monastery of Repton he studied the lives of the hermits, and learned to read. He went at length to a wilderness, where he encountered evil spirits as numberless as those which tormented St. Anthony. St. Bartholomew was the chosen saint of Guthlac, and he often came to his rescue and drove the demons into the sea. The place of his retreat was a marsh. At first a little oratory was built, and at length a splendid monastery was raised on piles, and dedicated to St. Bartholomew. The marshes were drained, and labor and cultivation changed the appearance of the place, and put to flight the demoniac inhabitants of the former solitude. The ruins of Croyland Abbey cover twenty acres. The country is again neglected, and an unhealthy marsh. The remains of a beautiful statue, said to be St. Guthlac, may still be seen. St. Pega, the sister of St. Guthlac, gave to the monastery the whip of St. Bartholomew. April 11, A. D. 714.

(Boisserée Gallery.)
St. Helena.

St. Helena. It is admitted by all authorities, that St. Helena was born in England, but the exact location of her birth is a matter of dispute and doubt. She married Constantius Chlorus, ("the Pale"), and was the mother of Constantine the Great. When her son embraced Christianity she was much distressed, and declared that it would have been better to be a Jew than a Christian. When she at length became a convert, her wonderful zeal, and the great influence she had over the mind of her son, conduced to the rapid growth and the strength of the Church. In 326 she made a journey to

Palestine, and when she arrived at Jerusalem, she was inspired with a strong desire to discover the cross upon which Christ had suffered. The temple of Venus stood upon the spot supposed to be the place of the crucifixion. She ordered this to be taken down, and after digging very deep, three crosses were found. There are two accounts given of the manner in which the true cross was selected. Some say they were all applied to a sick person. The first two without effect, while the third caused an instantaneous cure. Others say, that they were carried to a dead person, and that at the application of the third, life was restored. Constantine erected a basilica upon the spot where the crosses were found, and it was consecrated September 13, A. D. 335. The following day was Sunday, and the Holy Cross was elevated on high for the veneration of the people. It is with the "Invention of the True Cross," as it is called, that St. Helena is most frequently considered; but she did many other things which either in themselves or their effects still speak of her active zeal for the Church. The Church of the Nativity at Bethlehem was erected by her in 327, and is the oldest church edifice in the world. August 18, A. D. 327.

Heliodorus. This apocryphal legend is found in the third chapter of the second book of Maccabees. It is frequently illustrated in art, and is as follows. When Onias was high-priest at Jerusalem and all was prosperous there, a certain Simon, governor of the temple, became disaffected toward Onias on account of some trouble in the city. So he went to Apollonius, the governor of Cœle-Syria, and told him "that the treasury in Jerusalem was full of infinite sums of money, so that the multitude of their riches, which did not pertain to the account of the sacrifices, was innumerable, and that it was possible to bring all into the king's hand." When Apollonius told this to the king he sent his treasurer Heliodorus, with commands to bring to him this money. When Heliodorus came to Jerusalem, he was courteously received by Onias; and when he told him what they had heard, and demanded if it was true that so much money was there, the high-priest told him that much money was indeed there, but that it was laid up for the relief of widows and orphans. Some of it belonged to Hircanus the son of Tobias, and it did not in truth belong to the treasury as the wicked Simon had said. Onias said that the sum was four hundred talents of silver and about two hundred talents of gold, and "that it was altogether impossible that such wrong should be done unto them that had committed it to the holiness of the place, and to the majesty and inviolable sanctity of the temple, honored all over the world." But Heliodorus said that the king had given him commands, that in any wise it should be brought into the treasury. So a day was set when he should receive the treasure. Now the whole city was in agony, and the priests prostrated themselves before the altars and entreated God that this should not be allowed, and called unto Him that the law which he had made should be kept, and the money preserved for those who had committed it to their care. "Then whoso had looked the high-priest in the face, it would have wounded his heart; for his countenance and the changing of his color declared the inward agony of his mind. For the man was so compassed with fear and horror of the body, that it was manifest to them that looked upon him what sorrow he had now in his heart. Others ran flocking out of their houses to the general supplication, because the place was like to come into contempt. And the women girt with sackcloth under their breasts, abounded in the streets, and the virgins that were kept in, ran, some to the gates, and some to the walls, and others looked out of the windows. And all holding their hands toward heaven made supplication. Then it would have pitied a man to see the falling down of the multitude of all sorts, and the fear of the high-priest being in such an agony. But in spite of all, Heliodorus went to the temple to execute his intentions. Now as he was there present himself with his guards about the treasury, the Lord of spirits, and the Prince of all power caused a great apparition, so that all that presumed to come in with him were astonished at the power of God, and fainted and were sore afraid. For there appeared unto them an horse with a terrible rider upon him, and adorned with a very fair covering, and he ran fiercely, and smote at Heliodorus with his fore feet, and it seemed that he that sat upon the horse had complete harness of gold. Moreover, two other young men appeared before him, notable in strength, excellent in beauty, and comely in apparel, who stood by him on either side, and scourged him continually, and gave him many sore stripes. And Heliodorus fell suddenly unto the ground, and was compassed with great darkness: but they that were with him took him up, and put him into a litter. Thus him, that lately came with a great train and with all his guard into the said treasury, they carried out, being unable to help himself with his weapons: and manifestly they acknowledged the power of God. For he by the hand of God was cast down and lay speechless without all hope of life. But they praised the Lord that had miraculously honored his own place; for the temple which a little afore was full of fear and trouble, when the almighty Lord appeared, was filled with joy and gladness. Then straightways certain of Heliodorus' friends prayed Onias, that he would call upon the Most High to grant him his life, who lay ready to give up the ghost. So the high-priest, suspecting lest the king should misconceive that some treachery had been done to Heliodorus by the Jews, offered a sacrifice for the health of the man. Now as the high-priest was making an atonement, the same young men in the same clothing, appeared and stood beside Heliodorus, saying, 'Give Onias, the high-priest, great thanks, insomuch that for his sake the Lord hath granted thee life. And seeing that thou hast been scourged from heaven, declare unto all men the mighty power of God.' And when they had spoken these words, they appeared no more. So Heliodorus, after he had offered sacrifice unto the Lord, and made great vows unto him that had saved his life, and saluted Onias, returned with his host to the king. Then testified he to all men the works of the great God, which he had seen with his eyes. And when the king asked Heliodorus who might be a fit man to be sent yet once again to Jerusalem, he said, 'If thou hast any enemy or traitor, send him thither, and thou shalt receive him well scourged, if he escape with his life; for in that place, no doubt there is an especial power of God. For He that dwelleth in heaven hath his eye on that place and defendeth it, and he beateth and destroyeth them that come to hurt it.' And the things concerning Heliodorus, and the keeping of the treasury fell out on this sort."

St. Henry of Bavaria was born in 972. He married Cunegunda, daughter of Siegfried, Count of Luxembourg. Both are saints, and both obtained that glory by their perfect and entire devotion to the Church. This was so marked a feature of Henry's character and reign that it caused a revolt among the princes of his empire, as they thought he had no right to lavish so much treasure for the purposes of the Church. Henry was no less a soldier than a devotee, and after defeating the seditious nobles, he restored to them their possessions and treated them as if nothing had occurred. When he went to war to subject and convert Poland and Sclavonia, he put himself and his army under the protection of SS. Laurence, George, and Adrian. He girded on the sword of the latter, which had long been preserved in Walbeck Church. The legend teaches that the

(I. v Melem.)
St. Henry

three saints were visible, fighting by the side of Henry, and that through their aid he conquered. The Church of Merseberg was built to commemorate this victory. He also fought in Italy and drove the Saracens from Apulia. Henry had an especial veneration for the Virgin, and when on his expeditions, upon entering a place, always repaired first to some church or shrine dedicated to

St. Cunegunda tested by the Ordeal.

her. On one occasion at Verdun, he was seized with such a disgust and weariness of his imperial life and duties that he desired to become a monk. The prior told him his first duty would be that of obedience, and when Henry declared himself ready to obey, he made it his command that the emperor should retain his office and discharge his duties. Henry and Cunegunda together founded and richly endowed the cathedral and convent of Bamberg in Franconia, as well as many other religious edifices in Germany, and also in Italy. After they had been united several years, during which time, by mutual consent, they lived in the strictest continence, Cunegunda was suspected of unfaithfulness to her husband. Henry believed in the purity of his wife, and she would have looked upon these reports as trials sent from Heaven to test her patience, but she felt that her position demanded her justification, and she asked to be allowed the trial by ordeal. She walked over burning ploughshares uninjured. Henry tried to make amends to her by showing her the greatest respect and tenderness, but she preferred to retire to the cloister; to which he consented. Henry died in 1024, and was buried in the Cathedral of Bamberg. His wife then took the Benedictine habit, and led a life of incessant prayer and labor, working with her hands for the poor and sick. She died in 1040, and was interred by the side of Henry. Festival of Henry, July 14. Cunegunda, March 3. For St. Henry, see also St. Laurence.

St. Herman-Joseph was a native of Cologne. His mother was very poor, but brought up her son piously. It was his custom each day, when on his way to school, to go to the Church of St. Mary, and repeat his prayers before the image of Our Lady. One day when an apple was all he had for his dinner he offered it humbly to the Virgin, and the legend says that this so pleased "Our Blessed Lady, that she put forth her hand and took the apple and gave it to our Lord Jesus, who sat upon her knee: and both smiled upon Herman." When still young, Herman took the habit of the Premonstratensians. He had many beautiful visions, in one of which the Virgin descended from heaven, and putting a ring on his finger, called him her espoused. From this vision he acquired the additional name of Joseph. April 7, A. D. 1236.

St. Hermengildus was the son of King Leovigild, and during the contest between the Catholics and Arians, he was put to death by his father for relinquishing the Arian faith. He is one of the most famous Spanish martyrs. The chef-d'œuvre of Herrera is the apotheosis of this saint. He is carried into glory, while St. Isidore and St. Leander stand on each side, and the young son of Hermengildus gazes upwards as his father is borne to heaven. The saint holds a cross, and wears a cuirass of blue steel and a scarlet mantle. April 13, A. D. 586.

St. Hilarion. See St. Donato of Arezzo.

St. Hilary (*Ital.* Sant' Ilario; *Fr.* Saint Hilaire), was Bishop of Poitiers. Although French, he is greatly reverenced in Italy, and is one of the patrons of Parma, where it is said a part of his relics repose. January 14, A. D. 363.

St. Hilda, of Whitby, was the great grand-daughter of King Edwin. She was abbess of Whitby, and celebrated for her piety and learning and the excellent training which she gave all under her charge. Six bishops were elected out of her convent. She presided at a council held at her monastery. She was bitterly opposed to the observance of Easter according to the ritual of the Romish church, to the tonsure of priests, and to the extension of the papal jurisdiction to England. These questions were discussed at the said council and decided against her, to which decision she yielded. Her wisdom was so great that kings and princes sought her guidance. She was adored by the people, and many wonderful miracles are attributed to her. Fossils having the shape of coiled serpents have been found which were believed to have been venomous reptiles changed by the prayers of St. Hilda. Bede thus tells of her death, "And in the year of the incarnation of Our Lord, 680, on the 17th of November, the abbess Hilda, having suffered under an infirmity for seven years, and performed many heavenly works on earth, died, and was carried into Paradise by the angels, as was beheld in a vision by one of her own nuns, then at a distance, on the same night: the name of this nun was then Bega; but she afterwards became famous under the name of St. Bees." November 18, A. D. 680.

St. Hippolytus (*Ital.* Sant' Ippolito; *Fr.* Saint Hyppolyte; *Gr.* Ἅγ. Ἱππόλυτος: signification, "one who is destroyed by horses," of which animal this saint is the patron). There is great obscurity in the legends of Hippolytus. He was a Roman soldier and was appointed a guard over St. Laurence. He became a Christian from the influence of his prisoner, and his entire family were also converted. After the fearful martyrdom of St. Laurence, Hippolytus took the body and buried it. On account of this he was accused of being a Christian, which he denied not, but declared himself ready to meet any death, rather than deny his Saviour. He saw nineteen of his family suffer death, among whom was his aged nurse, Concordia, who was so bold in declaring her faith that she was scourged to death, while the others were beheaded. Hippolytus was tied to the tails of wild horses, and thus torn to pieces. The Brescians claim that his relics repose in the convent of Santa Giulia. The legends also say that in the eighth century his remains were carried from Rome to the Church of St. Denis, and on this account he is a popular saint in France. August 13, A. D. 258.

Holofernes. See Judith.

St. Hubert of Liége was a very gay nobleman. He was of Aquitaine, and lived at the court of Pepin d'Heristal. He participated in all the pleasures of the court, but was especially fond of the chase, and even hunted on the days appointed by the Church for fasting and prayer. As he hunted in the forest of Ardennes one day in Holy Week, there came to him a milk-white stag, with a crucifix between his horns. Hubert was overcome with awe and surprise. He became sensible of the wickedness of his life, and lived a hermit in the very forest where he had so often sought his amusement. There were bands of robbers, and large numbers of idolaters in and around the forest of Ardennes, and to them St. Hubert preached Christianity, and also introduced social reforms and civilization among them. At length he studied with St. Lambert, and became a priest. He was afterwards bishop of Liége. He requested that he might be buried in the Church of St. Peter at Liége. Thirteen years after his death his remains were found to be perfect, and his robes unstained. The Benedictines of Ardennes desired to have his body, and it was removed to their Abbey church about a century after his death. St. Hubert is patron of the chase and of dogs, and chapels are erected to him in the forests where the devout huntsman may pray. Bread consecrated at his shrine is believed to cure hydrophobia. November 3, A. D. 727.

(Wilhelm von Köln, 1380.) St. Hubert.

St. Hugh of Grenoble. This saint was Bishop of Grenoble at the time when St. Bruno founded the first Chartreuse. Hugh often retired to the monastery, and devoted himself to the life of the most humble and penitent brother. One of the miracles related as being performed by him is the changing of fowls into tortoises, when his Carthusian brethren could eat no flesh and could obtain no fish. It is said that Satan tempted Hugh forty years, by whispering continually in his ear doubts of God's Providence, on account of his permitting sin in the world. The saint fasted and did penance continually on account of this temptation, and it never obtained dominion over him sufficiently to weaken his faith in God. April 1, A. D. 1132.

St. Hugh, Bishop of Lincoln, was also a Carthusian. He was sent to England in 1126, and made Bishop of Lincoln. The cathedral, which had been destroyed by an earthquake, was rebuilt by St.

Hugh. It is a fine specimen of the best Gothic architecture. Of all the munificent gifts of its founder, the only one remaining is the glass in one window, which is painted with scenes from his life. His proper attribute is a swan, typical of solitude, which was his delight. November 17, A. D. 1189.

(Boisserée Gallery.)
St. Hugh presenting a votary.

St. Hugh, Martyr. The legend connected with this martyr is one of the latest of the monkish fables, and relates that this child, who is represented as about three years old, was stolen by the Jews and crucified by them in ridicule of the Saviour of the Christians, and in revenge for the cruelties which the Jews suffered in Christian countries. There are three other saints who have been canonized on account of having suffered the same martyrdom: St. William of Norwich, A. D. 1137; St. Richard of Pontoise, A. D. 1182; and St. Simon of Trent, A. D. 1472. The date of St. Hugh's death is in 1255, August 27.

St. Hyacinth belonged to the family of the Aldrovanski, one of the most noble in Silesia. He was educated in Bologna, and was distinguished not only for his intellectual superiority, but for his piety, and his prudence and judgment in everything he attempted to do. Soon after the completion of his studies, with his cousin Ceslas, he accompanied his uncle Ivo, who was Bishop of Cracow, to Rome. There they listened to the preaching of St. Dominick, which so moved the heart of Ivo that he besought the saint to send one of his Order on a mission to his far-off and half heathen coun try. But Dominick had no disciple to send, as all were engaged elsewhere. Then the young Hyacinth declared his intention to become a monk, and to preach to his ignorant and barbaric countrymen. Ceslas joined him, and they took the vows and the habit of the Dominicans in the Church of St. Sabina at Rome. For forty years Hyacinth travelled and preached in all the northern countries. It is said that his wanderings extended from Scotland to the Chinese boundaries. He founded various monasteries, and it is related of him that his convent in Kiov in Russia, being sacked, he escaped bearing the Pyx and the image of the Virgin, which he had taken from the altar. He reached the banks of the Dniester, pursued by the Tartars. The river was much swollen, but being determined to preserve the precious objects from desecration by the pagans, he prayed to Heaven, and plunged into the river. The waters sustained him, and he walked over as on dry land. He died at his monastery in Cracow, to which he returned worn out by his labors and exposures. Anne of Austria, after her marriage, requested the King of Poland to send her some relics of St. Hyacinth. This he did, and they were placed in the Dominican Convent at Paris. From this time the saint became an object of veneration in France, where many pictures of him are seen. September 11, A. D. 1257.

St. Ignatius of Antioch (*Lat.* Sanctus Ignatius; *Ital.* Sant' Ignazio; *Fr.* Saint Ignace: *Ger.* Der Heilige Ignaz. His Greek title is *θεόφορος* (inspired)). Tradition teaches that Ignatius is the same, whom Jesus presented, when a child, to his disciples, with the words, "Whosoever shall receive one of such children in my name, receiveth me." He was a disciple of St. John the Evangelist, and the dear friend of Polycarp. It is also said that on account of his perfect purity of thought and life, he was permitted to hear the music of the angels, and that from the angelic choirs he learned the singing of God's praises in responses, which he introduced into his church after he was Bishop of Antioch. The Emperor Trajan, after one of his victories, commanded sacrifices to the gods in every province of his empire. The Christians refused to obey. Trajan came to Antioch, and sending for Ignatius charged him with the perversion of the hearts of his people, and promised him great favors if he would sacrifice in a pagan temple. But Ignatius scornfully refused, and said he would worship only the true and living God. Then Trajan asked how he could call Him living who had died upon a cross. But Ignatius spurned the idea of any God but the Lord, and Trajan commanded him to be imprisoned, and reserved for the amphitheatre at Rome. Ignatius rejoiced in his sentence, and set out on his journey with great courage. At Smyrna he saw Polycarp and other Christians, whom he encouraged to labor for the church, and if need be to die for it. Arrived at Rome, on a feast day he was set in the midst of the amphitheatre. He addressed the people thus, "Men and Romans, know ye that it is not for any crime that

I am placed here, but for the glory of that God whom I worship. I am as the wheat of his field, and must be ground by the teeth of the lions, that I may become bread worthy of being served up to Him." According to one tradition he fell dead before the lions reached him, and his body was not touched by them. Another says that they tore him and devoured him, leaving only a few bones.

(From Greek MS. 9th century.) Martyrdom of St. Ignatius.

Whatever remained of him was carried by his friends to Antioch, and it is said his relics were brought again to Rome, and placed in the Church of St. Clement in 540, or near that time. February 1, A. D. 107.

St. Ignatius Loyola, who was the founder of the Order of the Jesuits, was in his youth a page in the court of Ferdinand the

Catholic, and then a brave and gay soldier. His family was one of the most noble, and Ignatius was filled with pride of race, and was vain of his handsome person. At Pampeluna, when thirty years old, he was wounded in both legs, and although he endured the most torturing operations to prevent lameness, they were in vain. While confined by these sufferings, he read the Life of Christ and other

(Rubens.) St. Ignatius Loyola.

books, which resulted in his resolving to devote himself to the service of the Blessed Mother of God, and that of her Son, whose soldier he would be. As soon as possible he laid his sword and lance upon the altar of Our Lady of Montserrat, and went to Manresa. Here he was subject to great temptations, and Satan so tormented him with doubts as to make him almost a maniac; but at length by visions he was assured of his salvation as well as instructed in the faith. He then attempted to go to Jerusalem, but was prevented, and obliged to remain in Spain. Not being allowed to teach on account of his ignorance of theology, he submitted to a tedious course of study. After a time he went to Paris, where he made the acquaintance of five men who sympathized with his views, and who with a few others, formed themselves into a community under his direction. In addition to the usual monastic vows of poverty, chastity, and obedience, they promised unreserved obedience to the pope, and to go to any part of the globe where he should send them. There were three especial duties belonging to this Order, which was called the "Company of Jesus": first, preaching; second, the guidance of souls in confession; and third, the teaching of the young. It was three years before Ignatius obtained the confirmation of the Order of which he was the first General The usual number of miracles, visions, penances, and temptations are attributed to him. On his way to Rome, it is said the Saviour appeared to him, bearing his cross, and saying, "Ego vobis Romæ propitius ero," and again an angel held before him a tablet thus inscribed, "In hoc vocabitur tibi nomen." July 31, A. D. 1556.

St. Ildefonso or **Alphonso** (*Ger.* Der Heilige Ildephons). This saint was one of the first Benedictines in Spain. He devoted himself to the service of the Virgin Mary, and wrote a book to prove her perpetual virginity. He had two remarkable visions. In one St. Leocadia, to whom he had vowed particular devotion, rose out of her tomb to assure him of the favor of the Virgin, and of the approval of his treatise in her praise. The saint wore a Spanish mantilla, and Ildefonso cut off a corner of it, which was preserved in her chapel at Toledo. Again, as he entered his church at midnight, at the head of a procession, he saw a great light about the high altar. All were alarmed save himself. Approaching, he beheld the Virgin seated on his ivory throne, surrounded by angels, and chanting a service. He bowed before her, and she said, "Come hither, most faithful servant of God, and receive this robe, which I have brought thee from the treasury of my Son." Then she threw over him, as he knelt, a cassock of heavenly substance, and the angels adjusted it. From that time he never occupied the throne or wore the garment. Archbishop Sisiberto died on account of his presumption in endeavoring to wear the robe, and sit on the throne. He was archbishop and patron saint of Toledo. January 23, A. D. 667.

Innocents, The Massacre of (*Ital.* Gli Innocenti Fanciulli Martiri, I Santi Bambini Martiri; *Fr.* Les Innocents; *Ger.* Die Unschuldigen Kindlein). These murdered infants are regarded with especial homage by the Church, as being the first Christian martyrs, and in a sense they are so. While we connect willingness to suffer for Christ with martyrdom, still it is true that unconsciously these children suffered for him, since it was on account of his birth that they were destroyed. They are represented with martyrs' palms. Sometimes they sustain the cross and the instruments of torture, again they surround the Madonna and Child, or are received into heaven by the Infant Saviour.

St. Isabella of France, who founded the convent at Longchamps, was sister to the saintly King Louis. She was educated with her brother by their mother, Blanche of Castile. She dedicated her convent to the "Humility of the Blessed Virgin," and gave to it all her dowry. As long as the convent existed, the festival of this saint was celebrated with great splendor. February 22, A. D. 1270.

St. Isidore the Ploughman (*Ital.* Sant' Isidoro Agricola; *Sp.* San Isidro el Labrador). The Spanish legend teaches that this saint could not read or write. His father was a poor laborer, and he himself was the servant of a farmer, named Juan de Vargas. Isidore spent much time in prayer, and his master went one day to the field determined to forbid what he considered a waste of time. As he came near he saw two angels guiding the plough, while the saint knelt at his devotions near by. One day when his master thirsted, Isidore struck a rock with his goad, and pure water flowed out. He restored a child to life by his prayers, and performed various other miracles. May 10, A. D. 1170.

St. Isidore, Bishop of Seville, is styled the "Egregius Doctor Hispaniæ." His brother Leander, who preceded him in his bishopric, is called the "Apostle of the Goths," and they are both distinguished for their opposition to the Arian doctrines. In Spanish pictures they are represented with Ferdinand of Castile and St. Hermengildus. In the Church of St. Isidore, at Seville, is a magnificent picture (el Transito de San Isidoro), which represents him dying on the steps of the altar, having given all his property to the poor. Both these brothers are patron saints of Seville. April 4, A. D. 606.

St. Ives of Bretagne (*Ital.* Sant' Ivo; on account of his profession, he is styled "Saint Yves-Helori, Avocat des Pauvres"). He belonged to a noble family, and from his mother, Aza du Plessis, who conducted his early education, he derived his remarkable piety. As a boy he had an ambition to be a saint. He was but fourteen when he went to Paris, and here and afterwards at Orleans he devoted himself to legal studies. It has been said that lawyers have chosen him as their patron rather than pattern, as he was distinguished for his love of justice and its vindication under all circumstances. All through his years of study he gave many hours to religious duties, and especially to the labors of charity. He also at this time made a vow of celibacy. After returning home he studied theology. At the age of thirty he was made judge advocate. He always attempted to reconcile contending parties without resorting to law, and was always ready to plead for the poor without recompense. At length he entered the ministry. Before assuming his priestly garments he gave those he had worn to the poor, and went out from the hospital where he had distributed them with bare head and feet. When a priest, he continued to be l'Avocat des Pauvres, and his double duties wore on his health. He died at the age of fifty. He is the patron of lawyers in all Europe. May 19, A. D. 1303.

St. James the Great (*Lat.* Sanctus Jacobus Major; *Ital.* San Giacomo, or Jacopo, Maggiore; *Fr.* St. Jacques Majeur; *Sp.* San Jago or Santiago, El Tutelar). St. James, called the Major, the Great or the Elder, is presented to us in two very different charac-

(Carreño de Miranda.) Santiago

ters, each being important and full of interest. First, in the Gospels as the brother of the Evangelist, and a near kinsman and favorite disciple of our Lord. He was much with Jesus, and present at many of the most important events in his life, such as his transfiguration and the agony of the Garden. Still, after the Saviour's ascension nothing is told of him, save that he was slain by Herod. But in his second character, as patron saint of Spain, we can make no complaint of the meagreness of the writings concerning him. The legends of him and his works would fill a volume; and he is said to have appeared after death at the head of the Spanish armies on thirty-eight different occasions. The Spanish legend, while it makes Santiago the son of Zebedee and a native of Galilee, does not represent him as a poor fisherman, who followed that vocation for a livelihood, but as a nobleman's son, who accompanied his father and brother in a boat, attended by servants, merely for pastime and sport. But so heavenly minded was this young nobleman, that he was greatly attracted to Jesus, and chose to follow him in all his labors, witnessing his wonderful miracles, and imbibing his spirit and teaching. After the ascension of Christ, James preached first in Judæa, and then travelling as a missionary, to bear the news of the Gospel to all the earth, came at last to Spain. Here he made few converts, on account of the dreadful ignorance and idolatry of the people. At length as he was standing one day on the banks of the Ebro, the Virgin appeared to him, and commanded him to build there a church for her worship, assuring him that in the future this pagan land should devoutly worship her divine Son and herself. He obeyed, and having established the faith in Spain, he returned to Judæa, where he preached until his death, many years after. The Jews were very bitter in their persecutions of James, and one Hermogenes, a sorcerer, especially opposed him. He sent one of his pupils, Philetus, to oppose him in argument. James signally defeated the Jew, and moreover converted him to his own doctrines. This greatly enraged Hermogenes, who in revenge bound Philetus by his spells, and then told him to let his new teacher deliver him. Philetus sent his servant to James, who, when he heard his story, sent his cloak to his new disciple, and as soon as Philetus touched it he freed himself and went to James with haste. Hermogenes then sent a band of demons with orders to bind both James and Philetus and bring them to him, but on the way they met a company of angels, who punished them severely. St. James then ordered the demons to bring Hermogenes bound to him. They obeyed, and besought him as they laid the sorcerer at his feet, that he would be revenged for them and himself on a common enemy. But James assured them that his Master had taught him to do good for evil, and so released the prisoner. Hermogenes cast all his books into the sea, and entreated James to protect him from the demons who had been his slaves. The apostle gave him his own staff, and from that time the persecutor became the earnest and faithful disciple, and preached his doctrines with effect. At length the Jews were determined to destroy him, and sent to drag him before Herod Agrippa. His gentleness, and the miracles which he did on the way, so touched the soul of one of his tormentors that he begged to die with him. James gave him a kiss, saying "Pax vobis," and from this arose the "kiss of peace," which has been used as a benediction in the Church from that time.

The saint and his last convert were then beheaded. The legend of the dead body of James is far more wonderful than any of his life. His disciples took his body, but not daring to bury it, put it on a ship at Joppa. Many accounts are given of this miraculous vessel. Some say it was of marble, but all agree that angels conducted it to Spain. In seven days they sailed through the Pillars of Hercules and landed at Iria Flavia, or Padron. They bore the body on shore and laid it on a large stone, which became like wax and received the body into itself. This was a sign that the saint desired to remain there. But the country was ruled by a very wicked queen, who commanded that they should place the stone on a car and attach wild bulls to it, thinking that they would dash it in pieces. But the bulls gently drew the car into the court of Lupa's palace. Then she was converted, and built a magnificent church to receive the body of James. Afterwards the knowledge of his burial-place was lost until the year 800, when it was revealed to a priest. The remains were removed to Compostella, which became one of the most famous of shrines, on account of the miracles done there. The Order of St. Jago was instituted by Don Alphonso, for its protection, and was one of the most honorable and wealthy in all Spain. The fame of the shrine of Compostella spread over Europe, and in some years it was visited by a hundred thousand pilgrims. One of the most curious of the legends of this saint, and one frequently treated in art, is connected with three of these pious pilgrims. A German with his wife and son made a pilgrimage to the shrine of St. James, and lodged at Torlosa on the way. The son was a handsome youth, and the daughter of the Torlosa innkeeper conceived a wicked passion for him. He being a virtuous young man, and moreover on a pious pilgrimage, repulsed her advances. She determined to revenge this slight to her charms, and hid her father's silver drinking-cup in his wallet. As soon as it was missed, she directed suspicion to the young pilgrim. He was followed, and the cup found in his sack. He was then taken to the judge, who sentenced him to be hung, and all that the family had was confiscated. The afflicted parents continued on their pilgrimage, and sought consolation at the altar of Santiago. On their return, they stopped at the gibbet where their son had hung for thirty-six days. And the son spoke to them and said, "O my mother! O my father! do not lament for me; I have never been in better cheer. The blessed apostle James is at my side, sustaining me, and filling me with celestial comfort and joy." The parents being amazed, hastened to the judge. He was seated at the table. The mother rushed in, and exclaimed, "Our son lives!" The judge mocked them, and said, "What sayest thou, good woman? thou art beside thyself! If thy son lives, so do those fowls in my dish." He had hardly spoken, when the two fowls, which were a cock and a hen, rose up feathered in the dish, and the cock began to crow. The judge called the priests and lawyers, and they went to the place of execution, and delivered the young man to his parents. The miraculous cock and hen were placed under the protection of the Church, and their posterity religiously preserved for a long time. The most notable occasion upon which St. James appeared to lead the soldiers of Spain, was in the year 939, when King Ramirez determined not to submit longer to the tribute of one hundred virgins, which was annually paid to the Moors. He defied Abdelraman to a battle which took place on the plain of Alveida, or Clavijo. After a furious contest, the Christians were driven back. That night St. James appeared to Ramirez and promised to be with him the following day, and give him the victory. The king related this to his officers, and also to his soldiers when they were ready for the field. He recommended them to trust to the heavenly aid which had been promised. The whole army caught the spirit of their king, and rushed to battle. Immediately St. James appeared at their head on a milk-white charger, waving a white standard. He led them to victory, and sixty thousand Moors were left dead on the field. From that day "Santiago!" has been the Spanish war-cry. In early works of art St. James is usually, if not always, represented with the other disciples, and may be known by his place, which is the fourth. But later he has been portrayed in all the different scenes of his life, and very frequently as a pilgrim of Compostella. In this character he bears the pilgrim's staff and wallet, the cloak and shell, while his hat is often on his shoulder. The most effective representation of this that I have seen is the statue by Thorwaldsen in the Church of Our Lady at Copenhagen. July 25, A. D. 44.

St. James Minor (*Fr.* S. Jaques Mineur; *Ital.* San Jacopo or Giacomo Minore; *Lat.* S. Jacobus Frater Domini; *Gr.* Ἀδελφόθεος, brother of God). This saint has another most honorable title of "The Just." He was the son of Cleophas and Mary, the sister of the Virgin Mary; in reality cousin-german to the Saviour, but often styled "the Lord's brother." The epistle which he wrote beautifully speaks the piety and love for which he was venerated. He is distinguished as the first Christian Bishop of Jerusalem. The Jews threw him down from one of the terraces of the Temple, and as he fell his brains were beaten out with a fuller's club, which instrument of his death is his proper attribute in works of art. When the disciples are all represented, St. James the Less is the ninth in order. The legends teach that James bore a striking resemblance to Jesus, so much so that they were at times mistaken for each other, and that it was this circumstance which made necessary the kiss of Judas. James made a vow that he would not eat bread from the time that he partook of the Last Supper until he should see Jesus raised from the dead. Soon after his resurrection, the Saviour went to show himself to James, and asked for a table and bread. He blessed the bread, and gave it to James, saying, "My brother, eat thy bread; for the Son of man is risen from among them that sleep." May 1.

St. Januarius (*Ital.* San Gennaro; *Fr.* Saint Janvier). This saint, who was Bishop of Benevento, came in the tenth persecution to Naples with six of his disciples, to comfort and cheer the Christians. They were seized and thrown to the beasts of the amphitheatre, but they would not harm them. Januarius was then thrown into a fiery furnace, which hurt him not; and at last he was beheaded. He is represented as a bishop with the palm, and usually with Mt. Vesuvius in the distance; for he is the patron saint of Naples, and its protector from the fearful eruptions of the volcano. The miracle of the blood of Januarius is too well known to need description here. September 19, A. D. 305.

(Titian.) Penance of St. Jerome.

St. Jerome (*Lat.* Sanctus Hieronymus; *Ital.* San Geronimo or Girolamo; *Fr.* Saint Jérome, Hiérome, or Géroisme; *Ger.* Der Heilige Hieronimus). St. Jerome has universal importance and consideration on account of "The Vulgate," or his translation of the New Testament into Latin, and also that which his wonderful piety and learning must inevitably command; but in the Romish Church he is additionally venerated as the father of Monachism in the West.

He was the son of Eusebius, a rich Dalmatian of Stridonium, and was born about A. D. 342. Being a scholar of more than usual promise, he was sent to Rome to complete his studies. There for a time he led a life of pleasure, but at length he became distinguished as a lawyer, and especially so on account of his eloquence in pleading his cause. At about thirty years of age he was baptized, and at the same time took a vow of celibacy. After having journeyed into Gaul, he went in 373 to the East, to gratify an insatiable desire to live among the scenes where Christ had dwelt. He became so enamored of the hermit life, which was then so common in the Orient, that he retired to a desert in Chalcis, where he passed four years in study and seclusion. But this time was not without its recollections of another life, and longings for both the sins and pleasures of the past. He says: "O, how often in the desert, in that vast solitude which, parched by the sultry sun, affords a dwelling to the monks, did I fancy myself in the midst of the luxuries of Rome! I sat alone, for I was full of bitterness." But one thing which caused him severe trials was his love of learning and his appreciation of all that was elegant and beautiful in the ancient classics. This gave him a disgust for the crudeness of the Christian writers, and it was a fearful struggle for him to master the Hebrew. All this appeared to him as dreadful sin. He says that he fasted before he read Cicero, and he describes a vision which these mental struggles undoubtedly caused. He thought he heard the last trumpet sounded, and that he was commanded to appear before God for judgment. "Who art thou?" was the first question. Jerome replied, "A Christian." Then came a fearful reply: "'Tis false! thou art no Christian; thou art a Ciceronian. Where the treasure is, there will the heart be also." After ten years of wearisome temptation and struggle, of weary controversy and labors, he returned to Rome. Here he preached with all the enthusiastic eloquence he could command, against the luxury of the Roman clergy and laity, and maintained the doctrines of extreme self-denial and abstinence. He especially influenced the Roman women, some of the most distinguished becoming converts to his doctrine, and being ready to follow him in any self-sacrifice. Paula, a descendant of the Scipios and Gracchi, whose cell is shown in the monastery at Bethlehem, was perhaps the most celebrated of these converts, but Marcella is another name handed down to us with his. She is by some held to be the first who founded a religious community for women, while others give this high dignity to St. Martha. Jerome remained but three years in Rome, when he returned to his monastery at Bethlehem. Here he died; and when he knew that death was approaching, he desired to be borne into the chapel, where he received the sacrament, expiring soon after. He left many epistles and controversial writings, and the cell in which he wrote at Bethlehem is regarded with great veneration. The Jeronymites were distinguished for the magnificence of some of their churches and convents. The Escurial was theirs, as well as the Monastery of Belem, in Portugal, and that of St. Just, to which Charles V. retired when he gave up his throne. The proper attributes of St. Jerome are books, illustrative of his writings, and the lion, which is emblematic of the boldness and watchfulness of the saint; but there is also a legend which accounts for the association of the lion with the holy man. One evening he was sitting at the gate of his monastery when a lion entered, limping, as if wounded. The monks were all terrified, and fled, except Jerome, who went to meet him. The lion lifted his paw, and in it Jerome found a thorn which he extracted, and then tended the wound till it was well. The lion remained with the saint, and he made it the duty of the beast to guard an ass which brought wood from the forest. One day, while the lion slept, a caravan of merchants passed, and they stole the ass and drove it away. The lion returned to the convent with an air of shame. Jerome believed that he had eaten the ass, and condemned him to do the work of the ass, to which the lion quietly submitted, until the ass was again discovered by himself in the following manner: One day after his task was ended, he saw a caravan approaching, the camels of which (as is the custom of the Arabs) were led by an ass. The lion immediately saw that it was his stolen charge, and he drove the camels into the convent, whither the ass gladly led them. The merchants acknowledged the theft, and St. Jerome pardoned them for it. Hence the lion is so often associated with the saint; but its appropriateness as a type of his wilderness life, and his zealous and vehement nature, is a more satisfactory thought than the fanciful wildness of this legend can give. The introduction of the cardinal's hat into the pictures of this saint is a glaring anachronism, as there were no cardinals until three centuries later than that in which he lived. St. Jerome, as a penitent, is the subject of numberless pictures, and his last communion by Domenichino (Vatican) is one of the most celebrated of all pictures. St. Jerome is the special patron of students in theology. September 30, A. D. 420.

Jew, The Wandering. See Wandering Jew.

St. Joachim (*Ital.* San Gioacchino; *Fr.* St. Joakim) was the husband of Anna, and the father of the Virgin Mary. He was of Nazareth, and his wife of Bethlehem, and both of the royal race of David. Joachim was rich, and an extremely devout man. He was childless, and it happened that on a certain feast day when he brought his offering to the Temple it was refused by Issachar, the high-priest, who said, "It is not lawful for thee to bring thine offering, seeing that thou hast not begot issue in Israel." Joachim went away sorrowful, and he searched the registers of Israel, and he found that he alone of all the righteous men had been childless. And he went away and would be seen by no one, and built a hut, and fasted forty days and nights, saying, "Until the Lord look upon me mercifully, prayer shall be my meat and my drink." And Anna mourned grievously, for her barrenness, and for the absence of her husband. At length her handmaid, Judith, wished to cheer her, and tried to persuade her to array herself, and attend the feast. But Anna repulsed her in such a way as that Judith was angry, and told her mistress that she could wish her nothing worse than that which God had sent her, since he had closed her womb, that she could not be a mother. Then Anna arose and put on her bridal attire, and went forth to her garden, and prayed earnestly. And she sat beneath a laurel-tree, where a sparrow had a nest, and Anna said, "Alas! and woe is me! Who hath begotten me? Who hath brought me forth? That I should be accursed in the sight of Israel, and scorned and shamed before my people, and cast out of the temple of the Lord! Woe is me! to what shall I be likened? I cannot be likened to the fowls of heaven; for the fowls of heaven are fruitful in thy sight, O Lord! Woe is me! to what shall I be likened? Not to the unreasoning beasts of the earth, for they are fruitful in thy sight, O Lord! Woe is me! to what shall I be likened? Not to these waters, for they are fruitful in thy sight, O Lord! Woe is me! to what shall I be likened? Not unto the earth, for the earth bringeth forth her fruit in due season, and praiseth thee, O Lord!" And immediately she beheld an angel standing near her. And he said, "Anna, thy prayer is heard, thou shalt bring forth, and thy child shall be blessed throughout the whole world." And Anna replied, "As the Lord liveth, whatever I shall bring forth, be it a man child or maid, I will present it an offering to the Lord." And another angel came to tell her that Joachim was approaching. For an angel had also spoken to him, and he was comforted. Then Anna went to meet her husband, who came from the pasture with his flocks. And they met

(A. Durer.) Joachim meeting Anna

by the Golden Gate, and Anna embraced him, and hung on his neck, saying, "Now know I that the Lord hath blessed me. I who was a widow, am no longer a widow. I who was barren, shall become a joyful mother." Then they returned home together. And when her time was come, Anna brought forth a daughter, and she called her Mary, which in Hebrew is Miriam. The Franciscans in their devotion to the Virgin have endeavored to teach that her birth was not only immaculate, but altogether miraculous, and that the joyful kiss with which Joachim met Anna, was the source of her being. This the Church did not receive, but it would seem that the sentiment of the idea had influenced some artists in the representations of this meeting. March 20.

St. John the Baptist (*Ital.* S. Giovanni Battista; *Fr.* St. Jean Baptiste; *Ger.* Johann der Taüfer). In Scripture this saint, the herald of Christ, is presented in three characters; as Preacher, Prophet, and Baptist. Parts of his story are given by all the Evangelists, from the miraculous circumstances attending his birth to the awfully sinful horrors of his death. To these tradition has added his miraculous deliverance from the assassins of Herod, by being inclosed with his mother in a rock, when she fled from the massacre with him in her arms. Art has represented him as leaving his home, while yet a child, to begin his desert life. Legends tell that the scene of his death was the royal fortified palace of Macheronta, near the Dead Sea, on the river Jordan, that he was buried at Sebaster, and that his head was brought to Europe in 453. He is venerated almost universally, and is the connecting link between the Old and New Dispensations, being the last prophet of the former and the first saint of the latter. The most ancient pictures represent him as meagre and wasted, with unshorn beard and hair. This would seem the true way; but often in later times he is made beautiful, and even dressed in rich mantles which cover the garment of camel's hair. When painted as the Messenger, he wears the hairy garment, and bears a cup, a reed cross, and a scroll with the inscription, "Vox clamantis in deserto," or "Ecce Agnus Dei!" The Greek signification of Messenger is Angel, and this is rendered in Byzantine art by painting him with wings. As a witness to the divinity of Christ, he is represented at various ages. He is introduced into Holy Families in this character in many different positions, all expressive of worship to the Holy Child. He is patron of all who are baptized, and also patron saint of Florence. In baptisteries he is very frequently represented in sculpture. In the historical pictures of this saint, which easily explain themselves, there is but one peculiarity to be noticed. That to which I refer is the representation of the legend that Mary prolonged her visit to Elizabeth until the birth of the child. In these pictures Mary usually receives or holds the babe, and is known by the glory about her head. The Greek legends teach that his death took place two years before that of Christ, and that he descended to Hades to remain until the Saviour's death should give him deliverance. He bore to the departed spirits the tidings of the approaching redemption, at which they all rejoiced, while the devils were filled with fearful rage. Nativity of St. John the Baptist, June 24.

St. John the Evangelist (Greek title, θεολόγος (Word cf God); *Lat.* Sanctus Johannes; *Ital.* San Giovanni Evangelista; *Fr.* Saint Jean, Messire Saint Jehan; *Ger.* Der Heilige Johan). More is known of this "disciple whom Jesus loved" than of the other Evangelists. He was son of Zebedee, and brother of James the Great. His life seems to have been almost inseparable from that of the Master, ever after his call to follow Him. He saw the Transfiguration. He leaned on the bosom of Our Lord at the Last Supper. He stood by the cross, and received the charge of Jesus concerning the Virgin Mary, and he laid the body of the Saviour in the tomb. He went with Peter through Judæa, to preach the Gospel, after the death of Mary. He then went to Asia Minor, living chiefly at Ephesus, and founding the seven churches. During the persecution of Domitian he was taken, bound, to Rome, and the Romish traditions tell that he was thrown into a cauldron of boiling oil without injury. The scene of this miracle was outside the Latin Gate, and the Chapel of San Giovanni in Olio commemorates the event. Being afterwards accused of magic, he was exiled to Patmos, where he is believed to have written his Revelation. Upon the death of Domitian, he was allowed to return to his church at Ephesus. Here, when ninety years old, he is said to have written his Gospel. He died at Ephesus, at the age of a century, or very little less. One of the Church legends teaches that he never died, and is founded upon the words which Jesus spoke to Peter (John xii. 21, 22); but it is not generally taught or believed. This idea is represented in art by his descending into an open grave, and lying down in sleep, rather than death. The Greek tradition is that he died without pain, and immediately arose again without change, and ascended to heaven to rejoin Jesus and Mary. The legends of the life and miracles of this saint are extremely interest

(Raphael.) St. John.

ing. St. Isidore relates that at Rome an attempt was made against the life of John, by poisoning the sacramental cup. When he took the cup, the poison came forth in the form of a serpent, and he drank the wine unhurt, while the poisoner fell dead at his feet. It is said to have been done by order of Domitian. Another account says that he was challenged to drink of a poisoned cup, in proof of the authority of his mission, by Aristodemus, the high-priest of Diana at Ephesus, and that while John was unhurt, the priest fell dead. Clement of Alexandria relates that when John was first at Ephesus, he took under his care a young man of great promise. When he was taken away to Rome he left this youth to the care of a bishop. But the young man became dissipated in his life, and at length was the leader of a band of robbers. When John returned, he asked of the bishop an account of his charge, and when he knew the truth, he blamed the unfaithful guardian, and suffered great grief on account of the young man. He then went in search of him, and when he came where he was, the captain of the robbers tried to avoid his old friend. But John prevailed on him to listen to his words. As John talked to him, he tried to conceal his hand, which had committed many crimes. But John seized it, and kissing it, bathed it with his tears. He succeeded in reconverting the robber, and reconciled him to God and to himself. At another time two rich young men sold their possessions to follow the Apostle. Afterwards they repented, seeing which John sent them to gather stones and fagots, and changed these to gold, saying: "Take back your riches, and enjoy them on earth, as you regret having exchanged them for heaven." When John returned to Ephesus from Patmos, he met a funeral procession as he approached the city. When he asked whom they bore, and heard that it was Drusiana, he was sad, for she had been one rich in good works, and John had dwelt in her house. He ordered them to put down the bier, and he prayed earnestly to God, who restored the woman to life; and she arose and John returned with her, and dwelt again in her house. Two wonderful miracles are related of John, as being performed after his death. King Edward the Confessor reverenced John next to the Saviour and the Virgin Mother. One day he attended a mass in honor of St. John, and as he returned he met a beggar, who asked him an alms in the name of God and St. John. The king drew from his finger a ring, and gave it to the man, unknown to any one beside. When Edward had reigned twenty-four years, two Englishmen, who had been as pilgrims to the Holy Land, met on their return a man, also in the garb of a pilgrim. He asked them of their country, and said, "When ye shall have arrived in your own country, go to King Edward, and salute him in my name. Say to him that I thank him for the alms which he bestowed on me in a certain street in Westminster; for there, on a certain day, as I begged of him an alms, he bestowed on me this ring, which till now

I have preserved, and ye shall carry it back to him, saying, that in six months from this time he shall quit the world, and come and remain with me forever." Then the pilgrims said, "Who art thou, and where is thy dwelling-place?" And he replied, "I am John the Evangelist. Edward, your king, is my friend, and for the sanctity of his life I hold him dear. Go now, therefore, deliver to him this message, and this ring, and I will pray to God that ye may arrive safely in your own country." Having said this, St. John gave them the ring, and vanished out of their sight. Then thanking God for this glorious vision, the pilgrims kept on their way, and went to King Edward, and delivered the ring and the message. He received them gladly, and entertained them as royal guests. He also made preparations for death, and gave the ring to the Abbot of Westminster, to be forever preserved as a holy relic. This legend is represented in sculpture in the Chapel of Edward the Confessor. Again, in A. D. 425, when the Empress Galla Placidia returned to Ravenna from the East, she encountered a fearful storm. She vowed to St. John, and being safely landed, she built in his honor a splendid church. After it was done she was greatly desirous of having some relics of the saint to consecrate the sanctuary. One night as she prayed earnestly, the saint appeared to her, and when she threw herself down to kiss his feet, he vanished and left his sandal in her hand, which was a long time preserved. The Church of Galla Placidia at Ravenna, though greatly changed, yet remains, and on it may be traced in sculpture, both the storm and the Empress taking her vow, and the miracle of the slipper. St. John is represented in art as an evangelist, an apostle, and a prophet. The Greeks represented him, whether apostle or evangelist, as an old, gray-bearded man; but in Western art he is never beyond middle age, and often young. As a prophet, and the author of the Revelation, he is an aged man, with flowing beard. The scene, a desert with the sea, to represent Patmos, while the eagle is beside him. His proper colors are a blue or green tunic, with red drapery; and his attributes, beside the eagle are the pen and book, and the cup either with the serpent or the consecrated wafer, which last typifies the institution of the Eucharist. Sometimes the eagle has a nimbus or glory. This figures the Holy Ghost, as the Jews made the eagle a symbol of the spirit. When the Baptist and Evangelist are introduced in the same picture, as frequently occurs, the latter may be known from his more youthful look, as well as by the above attributes. When associated with the other apostles he is distinguished by his youth and flowing hair, or by his nearness to the Saviour, and frequently by some token of peculiar love in the position or aspect of the Master. On great occasions, at the Church of the S. Croce, at Rome, a cup is exhibited as that from which John, by command of Domitian, drank poison without injury. December 27, A. D. 99.

St. John Capistrano was a Franciscan friar, who after the capture of Constantinople by the Turks, was sent out to preach a crusade for the defense of Christendom. At the siege of Belgrade, in 1456, when Mohammed was repulsed by the Hungarians, this saint was seen, with his crucifix in hand, in the midst of the battle encouraging and leading on the soldiers. He died the same year, and in 1690 he was canonized in commemoration of the deliverance of Vienna from the infidels, which took place in 1683. His attribute is the crucifix or the standard with the cross. A colossal statue of him is on the exterior of the Cathedral at Vienna. He is trampling a Turk under his feet, while he has in one hand a standard, and a cross in the other. October 23, A. D. 1456.

St. John Chrysostom (*Lat.* Sanctus Johannes Chrysostom; *Ital.* San Giovanni Crisostomo, San Giovanni Bocca d' Oro; *Fr.* St. Jean Chrysostome). This saint is always called by his Greek appellative, which signifies, " Of the golden mouth." He was born at Antioch in 344. He was of an illustrious family. His father died while he was still young, and his mother, Arthusia, remained a widow that she might devote herself entirely to her son. At twenty he had won renown by the eloquence of his pleas, for he was an advocate, but he greatly desired to retire from the world as a hermit. The entreaties of his mother prevented this until he was about twenty-eight, when in spite of all he fled to the wilderness near and led a life of such rigor as to destroy his health and oblige him to return to Antioch. Soon after this, Flavian ordained him a priest, and tradition teaches that at the moment of his consecration a white dove descended on his head. This signified his peculiar inspiration of the Spirit, and truly from this time, he seems, as a Christian orator, to have been assisted of God. Only Paul is ranked beyond him. He saved the people of his native city by his eloquence, when they had so offended the Emperor Theodosius that he had threatened them with dreadful punishment. So much was he beloved at Antioch, that when chosen Patriarch of Constantinople he had to go away secretly before the people could interfere to retain him. At Constantinople he lived a life of humble self-denial, but entertained the stranger and the poor with kind hospitality. His eloquent enthusiasm, his poetic imagination, and elegant scholarship, added to his great earnestness caused him to speak as one inspired of God, and he preached so fearlessly against the irregularities of the Empress Eudoxia, the monks, and all the customs of the court, that he was banished from the city. The people obliged the emperor to recall him, but again he was inexorable in his denunciations, and again was sent into exile. His guards treated him so cruelly that he perished from exposure and fatigue. He was sixty-three years old and had been bishop ten years. It was thirty years after his death when his remains were removed to Constantinople, and the Emperor Theodosius advancing as far as Chalcedon to meet them, fell prostrate on the coffin and implored the forgiveness of the saint in the names of Arcadius and Eudoxia, his guilty parents. The most peculiar of the representations of this saint is that called "The Penitence of St. John Chrysostom." The legend upon which it is founded is given in Italian, French, and German, and differs a little in each, but the principal points and the sentiment are the same. I give the German version. When John Chrysostom was baptized, the pope (signifying simply a priest) stood godfather. At seven years old he went to school and was so dull that he became the butt of his schoolmates. Greatly troubled at their ridicule he went into a church to pray to the Virgin, and a voice said, "Kiss me on the mouth, and thou shalt be endowed with all learning." This he did, and when he returned to school his companions were amazed at the manner in which he surpassed them all. When they looked they saw a golden circle about his mouth, and when he told them of how it came there they were filled with wonder. His godfather loved him very much and ordained him a priest when still young. The first time he offered the sacrifice of the mass he was so overcome with a sense of his unworthiness that he threw off his priestly robes and fled to a rocky cave, where he dwelt a long time in prayer and meditation. Not far from his retreat was the capital of a powerful king. One day as the princess was walking with her maidens she was lifted by the wind, and carried far into the forest. She came to the cave of Chrysostom and asked for admission, but he, thinking it a messenger of the Devil, refused to let her in. She assured him that she was no demon, but a Christian woman, and that if left there the beasts would devour her. So he admitted her. Then he drew a line in the middle of his cell and said, "This is your part, this is mine, and neither shall pass this line." But all was in vain. Passion and temptation overcame his resolution; he passed the line and sinned. Both bitterly repented, and Chrysostom fearing further sin took the maiden to a precipice and threw her down. Then he was seized with remorse, and went to the pope at Rome and confessed all, begging absolution. But the pope did not know him, and being filled with horror drove him out, refusing him pardon. Then the unhappy one made a vow never to rise from the earth, nor look upward, but to crawl on his hands and knees until his crime should be expiated and he should be absolved by Heaven. After fifteen years, the queen gave birth to a son, and when the pope went to baptize it, the child cried out, "I will not be baptized by thee, but by John." This was repeated three times, and although none could understand the meaning of this, the pope was afraid to baptize the child. Now it happened that the huntsmen had gone to the forest for game for the christening feast, and as they rode they saw an unknown animal creeping on the ground, and they threw a mantle over it, and chained it, and brought it to the palace. Many came to look at this beast, and among them the nurse with the infant in her arms, and immediately the child cried out, "John, come thou and baptize me." He answered, "If it be God's will, speak again." And the child a second and third time repeated the words. Then John arose and the

(A. Durer.) Penance of St. John Chrysostom.

moss and hair fell from him, and they brought him garments, and he baptized the child with great devotion. Then he confessed to the king, who thought, "Perhaps this was my daughter, who was lost and never found." And he sent to seek her remains, that they might be properly buried. When the messengers came to the foot of the precipice they found a beautiful, naked woman, seated with a child in her arms. And John said, "Why sittest thou here alone in the wilderness?" And she answered, "Dost thou not know me? I am the woman who came to thy cave by night, and whom thou didst hurl down this rock." Then they brought her home to her parents with great joy. The principal interest in this extravagant legend is that it shows the feeling which existed towards Chrysostom before he incurred the displeasure of the monks by his plain preaching. The pictures illustrative of it are quite incomprehensible until it is understood. Some of them are valuable works of art. They usually represent a woman and child in the foreground, while "the savage man" is seen crawling in the distance. St. John Chrysostom died September 14, A. D. 407. The Greeks keep his festival November 13th, and the Latin Church the 27th of January.

St. John Gualberto (*Ital.* San Giovanni Gualberto; *Fr.* S. Jean Gualbert or Calbert) was born at Florence. His family was rich and noble, and he received an education befitting his rank. He had but one brother, Hugo, whom he passionately loved. While John was still young, Hugo was slain by a gentleman with whom he had a quarrel. John, with the consent and encouragement of his parents, determined to pursue the murderer to the death. It happened that on Good Friday, at evening, as John left Florence for his father's country-house, he took the road which leads to the Church of San-Miniato-del-Monte. In ascending the hill he met his brother's assassin, and drew his sword to kill him, feeling that a just God had thus delivered him into his hand. The wretched man fell on his knees, imploring mercy. He extended his hand in the form of a cross, and reminded John that Jesus had died on that praying for pardon to his murderers. John felt himself moved by a great struggle, and the conflict between his desire for revenge and his wish to act as a Christian was so great that he trembled from head to foot. But at length, praying to God for strength, he lifted his enemy, and embracing him, they parted. John, overpowered with emotion, had scarcely strength to enter the church, where he knelt before the crucifix at the altar. Here he wept bitterly, and all the horror of the crime he had been about to

(F. Angelico.) St John Gualberto.

commit was vividly impressed on his mind. He supplicated for pardon, and as he raised his eyes to the face of Jesus, he believed that the holy head was bowed in token of his forgiveness. This miracle completed the great change already begun in him, and he determined to leave the world. He took the Benedictine habit, and entered the monastery of San Miniato. When the abbot died, John was elected to succeed him, but he would not accept the office, and, leaving the convent, retired to the Vallombrosa, in the Apennines, about twenty miles from San Miniato. At first he had but two companions in his retreat, but the fame of his sanctity attracted numbers to him, and thus originated the Order of Vallombrosa, of which this saint was the founder. They adopted the rule of St. Benedict, but revived some of the severities which had fallen into disuse, and instituted others, especially that of silence. The pope confirmed this new Order, and before the death of the saint twelve houses were filled with his followers, in different places. The Church of the Trinità at Florence belonged to them, and in it is preserved the miraculous crucifix before which John knelt on that memorable Good Friday night. The ruins of the monastery of Salvi, near Florence, which was of the Vallombrosa, show by their extent what its importance must have been. John was most strict in his humility and simplicity, and was so shocked at the way in which his disciples at Moscetta embellished their convent, that he prophesied some fearful punishment for them. Shortly after an inundation destroyed a large part of their buildings. He is also distinguished for his determined opposition to the practice of simony, which disgraced the Church in his time. Pietro di Pavia had purchased the archbishopric of Florence. He was a man of notoriously bad character. John denounced him publicly. Pietro sent soldiers to burn and pillage San Salvi, and several monks were murdered. Still Gualberto would not be silent, and it is probable that his order would have been destroyed by the powerful wickedness of Pietro, had not one of the monks, called Peter Igneus, demanded the ordeal by fire. He stood the test triumphantly, and the archbishop was deposed. Several miracles, like that of multiplying the food when they were in want, are attributed to this saint. The Vallombrosans had fine libraries and many works of art, before they were despoiled. These pictures are now scattered in galleries. Cimabue painted his famous Madonna for them, and Andrea del Sarto his Cenacolo. Gualberto meeting the murderer is represented in a little tabernacle which has been erected on the spot where the encounter took place. July 12, A. D. 1073.

St. John de Matha (*Sp.* San Juan de Mata) was a native of Faucon in Provence. He was born in 1154, and his parents were of noble family. Like so many saints, he was consecrated to God by his mother, whose name was Martha. He was a student in the

University at Paris, and after becoming famous for his piety was ordained a priest. The first time he celebrated the mass he had a vision of an angel, whose hands crossed over each other rested on the heads of two slaves who knelt on each side of him. On the breast of the white robe which the angel wore, was a cross of red and blue. Felix de Valois, another holy man, was a friend of the saint, and when John had told him the vision, and that he regarded it as an intimation from heaven that he was to labor for the relief of prisoners and captives, the two determined to found a new Order, having this labor for its object. It was called "The Order of the Holy Trinity for the Redemption of Captives." John and Felix went to Rome for their confirmation, and were most kindly received, for the pope had also had a vision of an angel with two captives chained, one of which was a Moor, while the other was a Christian, which taught that all races and religions were to be benefited by this new brotherhood. The parent institution of the Order was that of Cerfroy, but they were called Mathurins, and had a monastery in Paris near the street still called by their name. At Rome they were given the church and convent on Monte Celio, so beautifully situated, and from the ancient bark in front of it called, S. Maria della Navicella. Having obtained followers and money, John sent his disciples, and went himself to various places in Africa and Spain, and exchanged and ransomed prisoners and brought them home. This was a most noble work, for no class of Christians so needed assistance as those who had been made prisoners and then slaves during the fierce wars of those times. He had delivered hundreds, when, being about to sail with one hundred and twenty slaves, the infidels became furious and tore up his sails and broke his rudder. But he used his mantle and those of his disciples as sails, and praying God to be his pilot, the ship was quietly wafted to Ostia. But the health of the saint was so feeble that he was not able to go even to Paris, and after two years of suffering he died at Rome. February 8, A. D. 1213.

St. John Nepomuck (*Ital.* San Giovanni Nepomuceno; *Ger.* Heil. Johannes von Nepomuk; *Sp.* San Juan Nepomuceno). This saint was the confessor of the beautiful and good Princess, Joan of Bavaria, who was unfortunately married to the cruel Wenceslaus IV. of Germany. John knew there was no earthly recompense for such woes as his empress endured, and he earnestly endeavored to so lead her religiously, that she might suffer with patience the hardness of her life. At length Wenceslaus commanded him to reveal the confession of the empress. This he refused to do, and was imprisoned and tortured without effect on his silence. At length the empress by prayers and tears obtained his release. She dressed his wounds and nursed him with her own hands. Then he returned to court and preached as usual, but knowing the uncertainty of his life he first chose the text "Yet a little while and ye shall not see me." He endeavored to prepare himself and all who heard for death. Not long after, as he approached the palace, the emperor saw him from the window, and being seized with one of his tempers, he ordered him brought before him. Again he demanded the confession of the empress. The saint felt his end near, and kept perfect silence. Then the emperor commanded the guards to throw him over the parapet of the bridge into the Moldau. The legend relates that as he sank five stars hovered over the spot; which, when the emperor saw them, so distracted him that he fled and hid for some time in the fortress of Carlstein. The empress greatly mourned, and the people carried his body in procession to the Church of the Holy Cross. When Prague was besieged in 1620, it is believed that St. John Nepomuck fought with his people. The empress did not long survive her faithful friend and confessor. He was canon regular of St. Augustine. He is patron saint of bridges and running water in Austria and Bohemia. His statue stands on the bridge at Prague on the very spot where he was thrown down. Five stars are his proper attribute. Sometimes he has his finger on his mouth; sometimes a padlock on his mouth or in his hand in token of silence. He is patron of discretion and silence and against slander. May 16, A. D. 1383.

St. John and St. Paul were brothers and Roman officers in the service of Constantia. They were put to death by Julian the Apostate. Their church on the brow of the Cœlian Hill is on the spot where their house stood, which is one of the most lovely in ancient Rome. It has existed since 499. The church at Venice which bears their name was built by emigrants from the convent of St. John and St. Paul at Rome. It is filled with most interesting monuments, but none exist in honor of these saints. In art they are always represented together, and their attributes are the military dress with the sword. June 26, about 362.

St. Joseph (*Lat.* Sanctus Josephus; *Ital.* San Giuseppe; *Fr.* St. Joseph; *Ger.* Der Heilige Josef). Joseph was not made a saint in his own right until the sixteenth century, and all his glory seems to be a reflected one, coming from the more sacred characters with whom he was so intimately associated. The great honor which God conferred upon him in selecting him to be the guardian of the Virgin and her Divine Son is sufficient proof that he was a holy man. The Scripture account leads us to conclude that he was gentle and tender as well as just. He was of the lineage of David and tribe of Judah — a carpenter, and dwelt in Nazareth. This is the sum of the positive knowledge we have of him. Legends are the source of all other opinions concerning him. In these there is great difference regarding his age. All agree that he was a widower when he espoused Mary. In early art he is made very old, and some monks taught that he was more than fourscore at the time of his second marriage. In later years he has been represented of mature middle-age, strong and able to fulfill the duty of providing for his charge. One attribute of age has however been handed down from the earliest time, the crutch or cane, and is seldom omitted. The legend of the marriage of Mary and Joseph is given in the Protevangelion and History of Joseph, in these words: "When Mary was fourteen years old, the priest Zacharias (or Abiathar, as he is elsewhere called) inquired of the Lord concerning her, what was right to be done; and an angel came to him and said, 'Go forth and call together all the widowers among the people, and let each bring his rod (or wand) in his hand, and he to whom the Lord shall show a sign, let him be the husband of Mary.' And Zacharias did as the angel commanded, and made proclamation accordingly. And Joseph the carpenter, a righteous man, throwing down his axe, and taking his staff in his hand, ran out with the rest. When he appeared before the priest, and presented his rod, lo! a dove issued out of it, a dove dazzling white as snow, and after settling on his head, flew toward heaven. Then the high-priest said to him, 'Thou art the person chosen to take the Virgin of the Lord, and to keep her for Him.' And Joseph was at first afraid, and drew back, but afterward he took her home to his house, and said to her, 'Behold, I have taken thee from the Temple of the Lord, and now I will leave thee in my house, for I must go and follow my trade of building. I will return to thee, and meanwhile the Lord be with thee and watch over thee.' So Joseph left her, and Mary remained in her house." Jerome makes a difference which artists have followed. He relates that among the suitors for Mary was the son of the high-priest, and that they all deposited their wands in the Temple over night. Next morning Joseph's rod had blossomed. The others in their disappointment broke their wands and trampled on them, while one, Agabus, who was of noble race, fled to Mt. Carmel and became an anchorite. In many pictures the espousals take place in the open air, and various places outside the Temple, having no appearance of the sacrament of marriage. This is explained by the truth that among the Jews marriage was a civil contract rather than a religious ceremony. Many believe that Joseph was in reality only the guardian of Mary. His next appearance, in the legends, is on the journey to Bethlehem. The way, so long and weary to the suffering Virgin, is described, and the Protevangelion tells that "when Joseph looked back, he saw the face of Mary, that it was sorrowful, as of one in pain; but when he looked back again she smiled. And when they were come to Bethlehem there was no room for them in the inn, because of the great concourse of people. And Mary said to Joseph, 'Take me down, for I suffer.'" Another legend relates that Joseph sought a midwife, but when he returned with her to the stable Mary was sitting with her

Infant on her knees, and the place was filled with a light far brighter than that of noonday. And the Hebrew woman in amazement said, "Can this be true?" And Mary replied, "It is true: as there is no child like unto my son, so there is no woman like unto his mother." Four times God sent angelic messengers to guide Joseph in the execution of his important mission. First, he assured him of the purity of Mary, and that he need fear nothing in taking her to wife. The legends say that after waking from this vision, he "entreated forgiveness of Mary for having wronged her even in thought." The second dream commanded him to flee into Egypt. The pictures of the Flight, and of the Repose, which is an incident of the flight, represent the watchful care of Joseph. The duration of the sojourn in Egypt is differently given, and ranges from two to seven years. The third vision told Joseph to return to Judæa, and a fourth guided him on the journey. After the return to Nazareth, Joseph is only associated with a quiet, industrious life, and the training of his foster-son to the trade of a carpenter. The time of Joseph's death is also a disputed point. Some assert that it occurred when Jesus was eighteen years old, while some make it nine years later. One of the most interesting accounts of this event is found in an Arabian history of Joseph the Carpenter. Jesus is supposed to relate it to his disciples. He tells that Joseph acknowledged him as the "Redeemer and Messiah," and speaks thus of Mary: "And my mother, the Virgin, arose, and she came nigh to me and said, 'O my beloved Son, now must the good old man die!' And I answered, and said unto her, 'O my most dear mother, needs must all created beings die; and Death will have his rights, even over thee, beloved mother, but death to him and to thee is no death, only the passage to eternal life; and this body I have derived from thee shall also undergo death.'" Then after giving an account of the death scene, he says, "I and my mother Mary, we wept with them," alluding to the sons and daughters of Joseph who were about him weeping. Then follows an account of a struggle between good and bad spirits for the soul of Joseph, but at last Gabriel comes to clothe it with a robe of brightness and bear it to heaven. On account of this triumphant end, Joseph came to be invoked as the patron of death-beds. His death is often represented in family chapels which are consecrated to the dead. The twentieth of July had been observed in the East with great solemnity as the anniversary of Joseph's death for many years before he was popular in the West. It was the custom to read publicly homilies upon his life and death, and many of them are very curious and ancient, dating from the fourth century in some cases. There is great significance in the different modes of representing this saint, and in the attributes given him. He regards Mary with veneration mingled with tender care and thoughtfulness. In the pictures of the Nativity, the Adoration of the Magi, and in many

Holy Families, he is in an attitude of quiet and contemplative admiration; and while treated with dignity is never made an important point in the picture. In the flight and repose in Egypt he is the caretaker and guide, and the importance of his trust is made apparent. He sometimes holds the Infant or bears him in his arms, in token of his high office of providing for him, and at the same time carries a lily, the emblem of chastity, or his budded rod, in token of the purity of the relation between himself and Mary. Sometimes he gathers dates, leads the ass which bears the Virgin and Child, and carries the wallet and staff of the pilgrim. When he kneels before the Infant and presents a flower, it is an act of homage on the part of the saint. His dress should be a gray tunic and saffron-colored mantle. March 19.

St. Jovita or Giovita. See St. Faustinus.

St. Juan de Dios was the founder of the Order of the Hospitallers or Brothers of Charity; in fact he may be said to be that of the same class of institutions in all countries. Our own hospitals and asylums for the poor, the "Maisons de Charité" of France, the "Barmherzigen Brüder" of Germany, the "Misericordia" of Italy, and the "Caritad" of Spain. He was the son of poverty, born in Monte-Mayor, Portugal, in 1495. He had no education, but was piously reared by his mother. When Juan was but nine years old he was so charmed by the stories of a priest who was entertained by his parents, and who had travelled far and wide, that he went away with him without the knowledge of his family. The priest for some reason abandoned him, and he was left utterly alone in Oropesa, a village of Castile. He entered the service of a shepherd, where he remained until he entered the army. He was reckless and dissipated as a soldier, and yet at times was greatly moved by recollections of the piety of his mother and the lessons of his childhood. He met with many adventures, and narrowly escaped death from wounds and accidents. Being set to guard some booty taken from the enemy, he fell asleep, and the prize was carried off. His commanding officer ordered him hanged on the spot, but after the rope was around his neck, a superior officer who chanced to pass released him on the condition that he should leave the camp. He returned to his old occupation in Oropesa, but his restless mind gave him no peace, and in 1532 he joined the troops raised for the Hungarian war. At the end of the strife he returned to his native place, making a pilgrimage to Compostella on his way. Here he was so seized with remorse, when he learned that his parents had died of grief for his desertion of them, that his reason was impaired. Having no money he became the shepherd of a rich lady near Seville. Here he gave much time to meditation and prayer, and determined to do some good in order to atone as much as possible for his past sins. He remembered the sad and wretched condition of the poor, and of captives and prisoners, of whom he had seen many during his wanderings. At length he determined to devote himself to their relief, and even, if possible, to be a martyr. He went to Gibraltar, and there saw a Portuguese noble, who, with his family were exiled to Ceuta in Africa. He entered the service of these distressed people. They suffered much from sickness and poverty, and Juan became their only support. He hired himself as a laborer and toiled for them until they received aid elsewhere. Then returning to Spain he travelled about, selling religious books and pictures, and doing all in his power for the poor until he was told in a vision, "Go, thou shalt bear the cross in Granada." The miraculous bearer of this message was a radiant child who held a pomo-de-Granada (pomegranate) in his hand. Juan came into Granada at the time of the celebration of Saint Sebastian's festival. He was already much excited in mind, and the additional effect of the enthusiasm of a famous preacher who was there drove him to frenzy. He was taken to a mad-house, and, as the custom was, scourged each day until the blood flowed freely from his wounds. The same preacher referred to was filled with pity for him, and by patient attendance restored him to reason and liberty. He obtained a little shed for his home, and here founded the first Hospital for Charity, for he commenced the practice of bringing here the most wretched ones he could find, and of begging for their support. At first he could provide for but two or three, but would himself lay outside on the ground for the sake of caring for an additional one. Soon he succeeded in obtaining a large circular building, in the centre of which was kept a great fire, and here he often gathered two hundred homeless wretches. He gave up the idea of martyrdom, and devoted himself with wonderful zeal to the relief of the misery about him. He made no rules for any Order, and does not appear to have contemplated the establishment of one, and yet he "bequeathed to Christendom one of the noblest of all its religious institutions. In France he has the title of "le bienheureux Jean de Dieu, Père des Pauvres." His proper attributes are the pomegranate and cross. Often he is painted with a beggar kneeling before him. "The Charity of San Juan de Dios," painted by Murillo for the Church of the "Caritad" at Seville, represents him staggering beneath the burden of a dying beggar, whom he is bearing through a storm to his hospital. It is said that few behold this picture without tears. March 8, A. D. 1550.

St. Juan de la Cruz. He is mentioned by Mr. Stirling as "A holy man who was frequently favored with interviews with our Saviour, and who, on one of these occasions, made an uncouth sketch of the Divine apparition, which was long preserved as a relic in the convent of the Incarnation at Avila." He was the first barefooted Carmelite, and is famous for his terrible austerities and penances. He was the ally of St. Theresa in all her reforms, and is frequently represented with her. Books with the titles of his writings are often introduced into his pictures. November 24, A. D. 1591.

Judas Iscariot (*Ital.* Giuda Scariota; *Fr.* Judas Iscariote). The silence of the Gospel concerning the life of Judas before he became a disciple is more than filled by the legends of the Middle Ages. They relate that he was of the tribe of Reuben, and that his mother dreamed before his birth that he would murder his father, commit incest with his mother, and betray his God for money. Horrified at this prospect, his parents determined that he should not live to fulfill such prophecies, so they put him in a chest and threw it in the sea, but the chest was washed on shore and the child taken by a certain king and reared as his son. This king had a son whom Judas hated from the natural ugliness of his disposition. At length he killed him in a quarrel and fled to Judæa and was employed as a page by Pontius Pilate, who was attracted by the comeliness of his person. In course of time he fulfills the dreadful prophecies regarding his parents, and at length learns from his mother the secret of his birth. He is filled with horror of himself, and having heard of the power of Christ to forgive sins, he seeks to become his follower. Jesus received him, knowing all, in order that the destined betrayal should take place. He now adds avarice to his other vices, and becomes so completely corrupt as to fit him for the end. The bribery, betrayal, repentance, and death follow according to the Scripture account. His repentance is in some cases most vividly portrayed. Remorse is made a real person who seizes and torments him until he invokes Despair, who brings to him all kinds of implements of death and bids him choose from them. He is represented, too, with an imp upon his shoulder, figuring the Satan that entered into him. The Mohammedans believe that Christ ascended alive into heaven, and that Judas was crucified in his likeness. But his death has been variously represented in art. Those who have painted him as hanging with his bowels gushing out have seemingly made a mistake. The more reasonable version is, that having hanged himself he fell, and from the fall he "burst asunder." One tradition is that he was found hanging and thrown over the parapet of the Temple and dashed in pieces. Expression has been given to the wildest imaginations concerning him. An old miniature makes demons toss his soul from hand to hand like a ball. The horror of this restlessness is a fearful thought. The "bursting asunder" was considered a special judgment, in order that his soul should escape from his bowels, and not be breathed out through the lips that had betrayed Christ. The idea is represented by a demon taking the soul, in the usual form of a little child, from the bowels. The ugliness of person and expression given to Judas in pictures appeals to our feeling, although not in harmony with the legend. And it does not seem that such a man would have been allowed in the company of the twelve. The proper color for him is a dirty yellow. At Venice the Jews were formerly compelled to wear hats of this Judas color, while in Spain and Italy malefactors and galley slaves are clothed in it.

St. Jude. See St. Simon.

Judith and Holofernes. In the seventeenth year of the reign of Nabuchodonosor, king of Nineveh, he went out to battle with King Arphaxad of Ecbatane; and he sent to all the people round that they should join his army and help him to conquer the Medes. But the people scorned the commands of Nabuchodonosor, and did not join his army. Then was he wroth, and he swore to destroy those nations which would not acknowledge him for the king of the whole earth. So he sent Holofernes, who was the chief captain of the army of the Assyrians, and gave him commands to go forth and destroy the cities and exterminate the people who had scorned his authority. Holofernes did so; and when he came to the city of Bethulia he sat down before it to besiege it. And he was advised not to attack the city, which was so high up in the mountains as to be almost impregnable, but to seize the fountain outside the city and thus cut off their water, so that the people of Bethulia would fall dead in their own streets from thirst. Holofernes received this advice, and seized the fountain. Now when all the water in the city was gone, the women and children began to drop with faintness, and the men were ready to perish; then came they to Ozias, the chief of the city, and they said it is better that we deliver us up to the Assyrians than that we die thus; and Ozias reasoned with them that God would deliver them, but they would not hearken. Then Ozias said, "Let us wait five days, and if God does not send rain to fill our cisterns, neither deliver us in any other way, then we will deliver us up to the enemy." Now there was in Bethulia a widow, Judith, and she was exceeding beautiful and very pious. She had been a widow three years and four months, and she had "fasted all the days of her widowhood, save the eves of the Sabbaths and the eves of the new moons, and the feasts and the solemn days of the house of Israel." She was moreover very rich in lands and servants, cattle and money, and beautiful apparel and jewels. Now she was thought very wise, and her opinion greatly esteemed. She did not approve of the decision of the people, and told Ozias and the other chief men that they had done wrong; that God was not a man that his counsels should be limited or a time set for him to deliver them; and she said she would go forth out of the city with her waiting woman, and that before the time they had promised to deliver up the city should come, God would give their enemies into her hand. So she went and prayed God to be with her; to allow her to sway the heart of Holofernes by the pleasant words she would speak, and by the sight of her beauty. Then she put off her widow's garments, and she dressed herself in the apparel which she wore in the days of Manasses her husband; she plaited her hair, and put a tire upon it, "and she ook sandals upon her feet, and put about her her bracelets, and her chains, and her rings, and all her ornaments, and decked herself bravely, to allure the eyes of all men that should see her." And when she had taken wine and figs and bread and parched corn, she put them in a bag and gave to her waiting woman, and they proceeded to the gate of the city; and Ozias and all who saw her wondered at her great and dazzling beauty. So went she forth; and when she was come to the camp of Holofernes, those who saw her admired her greatly, and they took her to their captain with great honor. Now when Holofernes saw her, from that moment he desired to have her; but he questioned her of herself, and why she had thus come. Then she told him that her people were wicked, in that they did not submit to his command, and that to this sin they were about to add that of drinking the wine which had been kept for the use of the Temple, and that she, foreseeing the destruction which must come for all this sin, had sought his presence; she added that she would remain with him, going out each night into the valley to pray, and that when the wicked designs of her people were accomplished, she would tell him, and then he could go forth with his army and con quer them without difficulty. So she remained, and Holofernes offered her food; but she said, "I will not eat thereof, lest there be an offense; but provision shall be made for me of the things that I have brought." And when he said "If thy provision should fail?" she answered, "As thy soul liveth, my lord, thine handmaid shall not spend those things that I have, before the Lord work by mine hand the things that he hath determined." So he gave her a tent, and she and her waiting woman dwelt there, going out each night into the valley. Now on the fourth day Holofernes made a feast for his own servants, and called none of his officers to it. And he sent Bagoas, the eunuch who had charge of all that he had, to invite Judith to this feast; and she arose and decked herself and went. "Now when Judith came in and sat down, Holofernes his heart was ravished with her, and his mind was moved, and he desired greatly her company; for he waited a time to deceive her, from the day that he had seen her." Then Holofernes urged her to eat and drink, which she did, such things as her maid prepared for her; and she said, "I will drink now, my lord, because my life is magnified in me this day, more than all the days since I was born." "Holofernes took great delight in her, and drank much more wine than he had drank at any time in one day since he was born." At last when evening was come the servants retired, and Bagoas shut the tent, and Judith was alone with Holofernes, and he was drunk with the wine. Then Judith, praying to God to assist her, took down his fauchion which was at his head, and she took hold of the hair of his head and said, "Strengthen me, O Lord God of Israel, this day." And she smote him twice upon his neck, and took away his head. Then she pulled down the canopy, and went forth and gave the head to her maid, and she put it in her meat bag, and they went forth into the valley as was their custom. But now they kept on till they came to Bethulia; and Judith called to the watchman when they were still afar off. And when her voice was heard, all the city hastened to hear what news she might bring. And she commanded them to praise God, and showed them the head of Holofernes, and the silken canopy. Then Judith gave an order that they should hang the head on the highest part of the wall, and when the morning should come every man should take his weapon and go forth as if to battle; then the Assyrians would go to the tent of Holofernes, and fear should fall upon them, and they would flee before the men of Bethulia. And it was all as she said. Now when Bagoas knocked at the door of the tent, he had no answer — he went not in, for he thought that Holofernes had slept with Judith — but when he could hear no one he entered and found the body from which the head had been cut away. Then was the Assyrian camp filled with dismay, and they "fled into every way of the plain and of the hill country." And the children of Israel fell upon them and smote them and chased them beyond Damascus. And the tent of Holofernes with all its rich appointments they gave to Judith; and the men of Bethulia spoiled the camp of the Assyrians. Then Judith sang a song of triumph; and she went to Jerusalem and gave the tent and all its belongings to the sanctuary, and they feasted there for three months. And Judith lived to be one hundred and five years old; but she would not marry, though many desired her. And the people of Israel esteemed her according to her worth, and when she died they of Bethulia mourned her seven days, and buried her by the side of her husband, Manasses.

St. Julia (*Fr.* Sainte Julie; *Ital.* Santa Giulia) was a noble virgin, who is often represented with the Brescian saints. She was martyred at Corsica, and her relics carried to Brescia, where a church and convent were dedicated to her. She is painted young, lovely, and richly attired. She died in the fifth century. May 22.

Julian the Apostate. Julian, Flavius Claudius, Emperor of Rome, nephew of Constantine the Great. Famous for his attempt to reëstablish Paganism. Born at Constantinople in 331, died of a wound received in battle near Ctesiphon, when fighting against Sapor, king of Persia, being thirty-two years old. When young he was kept in obscurity by his cousin Constantius, from jealousy. He was first taught by Christian bishops, and was then a pupil of the school at Athens, and intimately associated with men distinguished for wonderful piety and learning. It is said that he revolted from the Church on account of its intolerance of philosophy. But if he hated intolerance, how must he have hated himself! for he persecuted those he called persecutors, and became a fanatic in his opposition to religion. For the legend of his death, see St. Mercurius.

St. Julian Hospitator (*Ital.* San Giuliano Ospitale; *Fr.* St. Julien l'Hospitalier) was a count and lived in great state. He hunted and feasted continually. One day as he pursued a deer it turned on him and said, "Thou who pursuest me to the death, shalt cause the death of thy father and thy mother!" He stopped affrighted, and resolved to flee from his parents in order not to fulfill the prophecy. So he went into a far country. The king of this country received him kindly and gave him a rich and lovely widow for his wife, with whom he lived so happily as to forget his home and the prophecy. But his father and mother had put on the attire of pilgrims and set out to find their son. Now while Julian was absent at court, they arrived at his house, and Basilissa, his wife, showed them every kindness, and put them in her own bed to sleep. The next morning while she was gone to church to thank God for having brought them to her, Julian returned. He entered his chamber, and in the dim light saw two people in bed, and one of them a bearded man. Seized with furious jealousy he drew his sword and slew them both. Rushing out he met his wife. Astonished, he asked who was in his bed, and hearing the truth was as one dead. He then wept bitterly, and exclaimed, "Alas! by what evil fortune is this, that what I sought to avoid has come to pass? Farewell, my sweet sister! I can never again lie by thy side, until I have been pardoned by Christ Jesus for this great sin!" But she replied, "Nay, my brother, can I allow thee to depart, and without me? Thy grief is my grief, and whither thou goest I will go." So they travelled till they came to a stream swollen by mountain torrents in which many who tried to cross were drowned. Here Julian built a cell for himself and a hospital for the poor. And he constantly ferried the travellers over the river without reward. At length one stormy night in winter, when it seemed that no boat could cross the stream, he heard a sad cry from the opposite bank. He went over and found a youth who was a leper dying from cold and weariness. In spite of his disease he carried him over and bore him in his arms to his own bed, and he and Basilissa tended him till morning, when the leper rose up and his face was transformed into that of an angel, and he said, "Julian, the Lord hath sent me to thee, for thy penitence is accepted, and thy rest is near at hand." And he vanished from sight. Then Julian and his wife fell down and praised God for his mercies, and soon they died, for they were old, and full of good works. He is patron saint of ferrymen and boatmen, of travellers and of wandering minstrels. His dress should be that of a hermit; his attribute a stag, which may be distinguished from that of St. Hubert by the absence of the crucifix between the horns. January 9, A. D. 313.

St. Julian of Rimini was of Cilicia, and but little is known of him beyond the fact that he endured a prolonged martyrdom with unfailing courage. Of this St. Chrysostom writes. He is represented as young and graceful — melancholy. He is richly dressed, and carries the palm, the standard of victory, and the sword. March 16.

Julian. There are twelve saints of this name, but the two given above are the most important, and most frequently represented in art.

(Murillo.) St. Justa and St. Rufina.

St. Justa or **Justina** and **St. Rufina,** patronesses of Seville. These were the daughters of a potter of Seville. They sold earthenware, and gave away all they made after supplying their bare necessities. Some women went to buy of them some vessels to be used in the worship of Venus. They answered that they would not sell them for that purpose, when the women broke all their ware, and the populace seized them and bore them to the prefect, but not until they had destroyed the image of Venus. They were condemned to the torture. Justa died on the rack, and Rufina was strangled. The Giralda is their especial care, and it was believed that this beautiful tower was preserved by them in the terrible thunder-storm of 1504. They are sometimes painted as *muchachas* (or of the lower class), and sometimes beautifully attired. They always bear palms and *alcarrazas*, or earthen pots. July 19, A. D. 304.

St. Justina of Antioch. See St. Cyprian. September 26. A. D. 304.

St. Justina of Padua (*Lat.* Sancta Justina Patavina Urbis Protectrix; *Ital.* Santa Giustina di Padova; *Fr.* Sainte Justine de Padoue) was a daughter of King Vitalicino, who was a Christian, and brought up his child in the same faith. After the death of her father she was accused before the Emperor Maximian, who ordered her death by the sword. She opened her arms, was pierced through the bosom, and died. She is patroness of Padua and Venice, and in the former city there is a sumptuous church in her honor, which was founded in 453, and rebuilt in the sixteenth century. Her proper attribute is the sword transfixing her bosom. Sometimes the unicorn, which belongs to Justina of Antioch, is also given to this saint, which causes confusion between the two. The unicorn attending a female is also the emblem of chastity; when it accompanies Justina of Padua, the Venetian costume, or Venice itself, or else St. Mark in the distance, will usually decide, but when the female is alone or with a company of martyrs and the unicorn, it is Justina of Antioch. October 7, A. D. 303.

St. Lambert of Maestricht (*Ital.* San Lamberto; *Fr.* and *Ger.* Lambert, Lanbert, or Landbert). This name signifies, illustrious with landed possessions. He was Bishop of Maestricht, but was exiled and recalled in 677. It is said that when an acolyte he carried burning coals in the folds of his surplice to kindle the incense; this typifies his fervor. The cause of his death is given in two ways. One account is that two brothers who had robbed the Church of Maestricht, were slain without the knowledge of the bishop, and their kinsmen in revenge entered the house of Lambert, and murdered all within. He was killed with a dart or javelin. The other story is, that having boldly reproved Pepin d'Heristal for his love of his mistress, the beautiful Alpaïde, the grandmother of Charlemagne. one of her relatives entered his dwelling and slew him. His attributes are the palm and javelin. September 17, A. D. 709.

Lamech. There is a Jewish tradition that after Lamech became blind, he was hunting in a forest where Cain had concealed himself, and mistaking the vagabond for a wild beast, he slew him with an arrow, and afterwards killed his son, Tubal-Cain, who had pointed out to him the thicket in which Cain had been. This is said to explain Genesis iv. 23, "For I have slain a man to my wounding, and a young man to my hurt." This legend has been illustrated in an engraving by Lucas von Leyden, and in sculpture in the cathedrals at Amiens and Modena, as well as in the Campo Santo at Pisa.

Last Supper (*Ital.* Il Cenacolo, Le Cena; *Fr.* La Cène; *Ger.* Das Abendmal Christi). This subject occupies a most important place in art when illustrating the history of Christ, as the Redeemer. It has been treated in two distinct modes. First, as a mystery, and "the spiritual origin of the Eucharist," and again as illustrative of the detection and exposure of Judas. Keeping this distinction in mind will help to explain the differences in treatment of the various artists, and influence the judgment in deciding points connected with them; as what seems irreverent, and out of place in a religious and devotional picture, is quite admissible in one that is barely historical.

(Pinturicchio.) St. Laurence.

St. Laurence (*Lat.* S. Laurentius; *Fr.* St. Laurent; *Ital.* and *Sp.* San Lorenzo; *Ger.* Der Heilige Laurentius, or Lorenz). Historically, but little is known of this saint. Even the time and place of his birth are matters of doubt, but that he existed, and was martyred according to the general belief, is undoubtedly true. His legend relates, that he was a Spaniard, and a native of Osca, or Huesca in Aragon, where his parents are honored as SS. Orientius and Patienza. He went to Rome when quite young, and by his exemplary life so pleased Sixtus II., then Bishop of Rome, that he made him his archdeacon, and gave the treasures of the Church into his care. When Sixtus was condemned to death as a Christian, St. Laurence clung to him, and desired to accompany him, saying, among other things, "St. Peter suffered Stephen, his deacon, to die before him; wilt thou not also suffer me to prepare thy way?" Sixtus assured him that in three days he would follow him, and that his sufferings would be far the greatest, because being younger and stronger he could longer endure. He also commanded Laurence to distribute the property of the Church to the poor, so that the tyrant should never possess it. So Laurence took the treasures and sought through all Rome for the poor, and he came at night to the Cœlian

Hill, where dwelt Cyriaca, who was a devout widow, who often concealed the persecuted Christians, and cared for them. She was sick, and St. Laurence healed her by laying his hands on her, and also washed the feet of the Christians in the house, and gave them alms. Thus from house to house he dispensed his charities, and prepared for his hastening martyrdom. The tyrant, learning that the treasures were in his hands, ordered him to be brought to the tribunal. He was required to tell where the treasures were, to which he would not reply, and was put into a dungeon under the care of Hippolytus, whom he converted to Christianity with his whole family, so that they were baptized. Being questioned again by the prefect concerning the treasures, he promised that in three days he would show them. The time arriving, he gathered the poor ones to whom he had given aid together, and showed them to the tyrant, saying, "Behold, here are the treasures of Christ's Church!" The prefect then ordered him to be tortured until he should tell what he wished to know. But no horrors could subdue the saint, and the prefect ordered him to be carried by night to the baths of Olympias, which were near the villa of Sallust, and a new torment inflicted on him, which was, that he should be stretched on an iron bed, made of bars like a gridiron, and roasted over a fire kindled beneath. This was done, and all who saw were filled with horror of the tyrant who could conceive such cruelty, and condemn so gentle and comely a youth to such suffering. But Laurence was not now subdued, and cried out, "Assatus est: jam versa et manduca" (I am done or roasted, — now turn me and eat me). And all were confounded by his endurance. Then he looked to heaven, and said, "I thank thee, O my God and Saviour, that I have been found worthy to enter into thy beatitude!" and so he died. The prefect and executioners went away, and Hippolytus took the body and buried it in the Via Tiburtina. For this the tyrant commanded him to be tied to the tail of a wild horse, and so he was martyred. Soon after this prefect, as he sat in the amphitheatre, was seized with pangs of death, and cried out to St. Laurence and Hippolytus, as he gave up the ghost. In Rome six churches have been dedicated to him; in Spain the Escurial; in Genoa a cathedral; and in England about two hundred and fifty churches, besides many others in all Christendom. St. Laurence is connected with the death of the Emperor Henry II., by the following legend. One night as a hermit sat in his hut he heard a sound as of a host rushing past. He opened his window, and called out to know who they could be. The answer came, "We are demons. Henry the Emperor is about to die at this moment, and we go to seize his soul." The hermit then begged that on their return they should tell him the result of their errand. This they promised, and after a time that same night they came again, and knocked at the window. When the hermit questioned of their success, the fiend swore that all had gone ill, for they arrived just as the emperor expired, and were about to seize his soul when his good angel came to save him. After a long dispute the Angel of Judgment (St. Michael) laid his good and evil deeds in the scale, and the latter descended and touched the earth, and the victory was to the demons, when lo! the roasted fellow (for so he wickedly called the saint) appeared, and threw into the other scale the holy cup, which changed the balance, and defeated the fiends. But the demon had avenged himself by breaking the handle off the cup, and this he gave the hermit. In the morning the hermit hasted to the city and found Henry dead, and one handle gone from the cup he had given the Church, and this had disappeared in the night. St. Laurence is usually painted in the rich dress of an archdeacon bearing the palm, and *la graticola* or gridiron. But sometimes he carries a dish full of money, and the cross to signify his office of treasurer to the Church, and also of deacon, for they bore the cross in processions. The gridiron varies in form and size. Sometimes it is embroidered on his robe, suspended round his neck, or borne in the hand; and again he puts his foot on it in triumph. Patron of Nuremberg, the Escurial, and Genoa. August 10, A. D. 258.

St. Lazarus (*Lat.* and *Ger.* same as *Eng.; Fr.* St. Lazare; *Ital.* San Lazarro; *Sp.* San Lazaro, Lazarillo. Signification: God will help). This saint is venerated as the first Bishop of Marseilles. When seen in any pictures other than those of his resurrection, he wears in common with many other saints the bishop's dress, but as he is most frequently associated with Mary and Martha, he is not easily mistaken. In rare instances a bier is seen in the background. September 2.

St. Leander. February 27, A. D. 596. See St. Isidore.

St. Leocadia was a native of Toledo. She was thrown into prison during the persecution of Diocletian. While there she was told of the death of St. Eulalia, who was her friend, and she earnestly prayed that death might reunite them. Her prayer was soon answered, and she died in prison. Another legend relates that she was thrown down from a height of rocks, and a chapel was built on the spot where she fell, and in it she was buried. When St. Ildefonso had written his treatise defending the doctrine of the perpetual virginity of the Virgin Mary, angels rolled the stone from the tomb of St. Leocadia, and she went to St. Ildefonso to tell him of the approbation of his work in heaven. Before she could disappear he cut a piece from the mantilla which she wore, and this relic was preserved as one of the church treasures. She is patroness of Toledo, and her statue surmounts the gate (Puerta del Cambron). She is only seen in Spanish pictures. December 9, A. D. 304.

St. Leonard (*Lat.* Sanctus Leonardus; *Ital.* San Leonardo; *Fr.* Saint Léonard or Lionart. Signification: Brave as a Lion) was a courtier of the court of King Theodobert, and was much beloved by the king for his cheerfulness and amiability. He was a Christian, and especially delighted in visiting and relieving prisoners and captives, and oftentimes the king pardoned those for whom he pleaded. At length, being weary of court, he retired to a desert near Limoges, and became a hermit. One day as the king and queen, with all the court, rode to the chase, the queen was seized with the pains of child-bearing, and seemed likely to die. The spot where they were was near the house of Leonard, and he, hearing, of this distress, came and prayed for the queen, and she was soon safely delivered. Then the king gave St. Leonard a portion of the forest, and he founded a religious community, but he would never accept any office above that of deacon. His dress is that of a Benedictine or of a deacon, and his attribute a chain. Sometimes he bears a crosier as founder of a community, and often slaves or captives are near him. November 6, A. D. 559.

(Old fresco.) St. Leonard.

St. Leopold of Austria (*Ger.* Der Heilige Leopold, Luitpold, or Leupold. Signification: Bold for the People). Leopold, Margrave of Austria, was born in 1080. At twenty-six he married Agnes, widow of Frederic, Duke of Suabia. She bore him eighteen children, and eleven of them were living at his death. He was canonized on account of his having founded the splendid monastery of Kloster-Neuberg, on the Danube. The legend relates that soon after his marriage, he stood with Agnes on the balcony of his palace of Leopoldsberg. They regarded the extensive view before them, with Vienna near by, and hand in hand, they vowed to build and endow an edifice for the service of God in gratitude to Him who had blest their love. Just at that moment the wind lifted, and bore away the bridal veil of Agnes. Eight years from this time, when hunting in a forest near by, Leopold found this veil on a tree. He remembered his vow, ordered the forest cleared, and built the monastery of Kloster-Neuberg. A flourishing town was built around it, and some of the finest vineyards in Austria were here. The whole life of Leopold was that of a virtuous and just man. He is one of the patron saints of Austria, and is represented in armor. Sometimes he has a rosary in his hand. November 15, A. D. 1136.

St. Lieven, or **Livin,** was a poet, and a Benedictine missionary. He was born in Ireland, and educated in the schools of that country, famous in those days for their superiority. While pursuing his labors near Ghent, he was cruelly martyred. His tongue was pulled out and then his head cut off. The mother of St. Brice had been his hostess, and both she and her son were killed with St. Lieven. He had written a hymn in honor of St. Bavon, within whose church at Ghent he was buried, and there his relics still repose. He is sometimes painted holding his tongue with tongs. Rubens painted this martyrdom with terrible truthfulness. November 12, A. D. 656.

St. Lioba. This saint was the most distinguished companion of St. Walburga. She was a poetess, and very learned for the time in which she lived. Charlemagne, and his Empress Hildegarde, were very fond of Lioba, and would gladly have kept her with them as a companion and counselor, but she preferred her convent life. She was buried at Fulda by the side of St. Boniface. September 28, A. D. 779.

St. Longinus (*Ital.* San Longino; *Fr.* Saint Longin, Sainct Longis). This saint is known as being the "first fruits of the Gentiles." He is said to be the centurion who pierced the Saviour's side. The legend relates, that soon after this act he touched his eyes with his blood-stained hands and instantly the weakness of sight or blindness from which he had long suffered was cured. He then sought the Apostles and was baptized. After this he preached in Cæsarea and converted numbers, but being commanded to sacrifice to the pagan deities he refused. He was desirous of the martyr's crown, and assured the governor, who was blind, that after his own death his sight should be restored. Upon this he was beheaded, and immediately the governor was healed, and became a Christian from the time of this miracle. This legend is repudiated by the Church, but the knowledge of it explains the importance given to the centurion in many works of art. His dress is that of a Roman soldier, and his attribute a spear or lance. He has been patron saint of Mantua since the eleventh century, when his relics were said to have been brought to that city. His statue is under the dome of St. Peter's in Rome, because tradition says that his lance or spear is still among the treasures of the Church. March 15, A. D. 45.

St. Lorenzo Giustiniani was a Venetian of noble family. He was born in 1380, and from his youth was enthusiastic in his piety. Quirina, his mother, though young and beautiful, remained a widow that she might devote herself to her son. At nineteen he believed that he was called to a religious life by a miraculous vision. His family desired him to marry, but he retired to the cloister of San-Giorgio-in-Alga. He came to his mother's palace to beg, "per i poveri di Dio." She filled his wallet, and hid herself in her chamber. He became so distinguished for his piety that he was made Bishop of Castello. When the patriarchate of Grado was removed to Venice, Lorenzo was the first to fill the office. The people so revered him that they believed that his prayers had saved them from war, famine, and plague, and they exalted him as a saint without canonization, and built churches and altars to him two centuries before he was made a saint, by Alexander VIII. September 5, A. D. 1455.

(Venice. S. Maria dell Orta. Gentil Bellini.)
St. Lorenzo Giustiniani.

St. Louis Beltran, or Bertrand (*Ital.* San Ludovico Bertrando), was born at Valencia. He became a celebrated Dominican, and was a missionary. He lived in the sixteenth century. He was a friend of St. Theresa. Feeling called to preach to the heathen he went to Peru, but he declared that he encountered greater trials from the wickedness of the Christians than from the ignorance of the heathen. He has no especial attribute, but Peruvians or Peruvian scenery often determine his personality. Espinosa placed himself and his family under the care of this saint during the plague in Valencia in 1647, and in consideration of their protection from harm he painted a series of pictures, and placed them in the chapel of the saint in the convent of San Domingo at Valencia. October 9, A. D. 1581.

St. Louis Gonzaga, or **St. Aloysius,** was born in 1568. He was the oldest son of the Marchese di Castiglione. He entered the Society of Jesus when not yet eighteen years old. He became eminently distinguished for his learning, piety, and good works, and died of fever at Rome in 1591, which was contracted while nursing the sick. He has no particular attribute, but his youth distinguishes him from most saints of his order. A. D. 1591.

St. Louis, King of France (*Lat.* Sanctus Ludovicus Rex; *Ital.* San Luigi, Rei di Francia). Son of Louis VIII. and Blanche of Castile. Born in 1215 at Poissy. The holiness of Louis, his talents and virtues, combined to make him respected and beloved by all, and even Voltaire said of him: "Il n'est guère donné à l'homme de pousser la vertu plus loin!" The Franciscans claim that he put on their habit before embarking on his first crusade, and that in it he died. He was a great collector of relics, for which he had an extreme veneration. Baldwin II. secured his aid by surrendering to him the crown of thorns, and when it was brought from Constantinople Louis carried it from Sens to Paris, bareheaded and barefooted. Having also a piece of the "True Cross," he built the beautiful chapel, La Sainte Chapelle, in honor of these precious relics. In 1247, being very sick, he laid in a trance for hours. When he awoke he exclaimed, "La Lumière de l'Orient s'est répandue du haut du ciel sur moi par la grâce du Seigneur, et m'a rappelé d'entre les morts!" He then called the Archbishop of Paris, and in spite of all remonstrance from his priests and friends he commanded the cross of the crusade to be affixed to his dress. The archbishop obeyed with tears and sobs. As soon as his health allowed, he sailed for Egypt. His wife and brothers went also; and his army of fifty thousand men embraced the flower of the French nobility. After many disasters Louis was made prisoner. But his zeal never cooled, and he regarded all his soldiers who perished as martyrs of a noble type. When ransomed he spent three years in Palestine and returned to France, where he remained sixteen years. He was a wise ruler, and repaired his losses and enlarged his kingdom. At the end of this time he set out on a second crusade. Those whom he left as children when he went at first now made his army. After more trials by disease and suffering he died in his tent, lying upon ashes, and wearing the dress of a penitent. A portion of his relics were taken to Palermo and placed in the Church of Monreale. The remainder were laid in St. Denis, but did not escape the destroyers of the first revolution. His proper attributes are the crown of thorns, his kingly crown and sword. August 25, A. D. 1270.

(Ancient French stained glass.)
St. Louis.

St. Louis of Toulouse (*Ital.* San Ludovico Vescovo) was the nephew of the last-named saint, son of the King of Naples and Sicily. Like his kingly uncle-saint, he was piously reared by his mother. When he was but fourteen his father, being made prisoner by the King of Aragon, gave Louis and his brothers as hostages. He became wearied of everything but religion, and in 1294, when he was made free, he gave all his royal rights to his brother Robert, and became a monk of the Order of St. Francis. He was then twenty-two years old. Soon he was made Bishop of Toulouse, and he went barefooted and clothed as a friar to take his new office. He went into Provence on a charitable mission, and died at the Castle of Brignolles, where he was born. He was first buried at Marseilles and removed to Valencia, where he was enshrined. His pictures represent him as young, beardless, and of gentle face. He has the fleur-de-lys embroidered on his cope or some part of his dress. The crown which he gave away lies at his feet, while he bears the mitre of a bishop. August 19, A. D. 1297.

Sœur Louise de la Miséricorde, who was first the lovely Louise de la Vallière, was never canonized as a saint, except in the hearts of those to whom her sorrow and suffering, her repentance and charities, have made her martyr and saint. She became a Carmelite nun at thirty years of age, in 1674. She commanded Le Brun to paint "Mary Magdalene renouncing the World," as an altarpiece for her convent. It has been thought a portrait of her, but many believe that another Magdalene by the same artist, which is in Munich, is probably the best likeness of La Vallière.

St. Lucia (*Eng.* St. Lucy or Luce; *Fr.* St. Luce or Lucie). When Diocletian was emperor and Pascasius was governor of Sicily, this saint dwelt in Syracuse. She was a noble and virtuous maiden. Her mother was named Eutychia. Lucia, without the knowledge of her mother, had made the vow of chastity, but her friends had her betrothed to a rich young man who was not a Christian. Eutychia being ill, her daughter persuaded her to visit Catania to pay her devotions at the shrine of St. Agatha. While Lucia knelt beside the tomb she had a vision of the saint, who addressed her thus, "O, my sister handmaid of Christ," — and assured her that her mother was healed, and that as Catania had been blessed by her, so Lucia should obtain the favor of Heaven for Syracuse. Now when her mother was healed, Lucia persuaded her to allow that she should remain single, and wished her dowry to give to the poor. Her mother feared lest she should be a beggar before she died, and hoped to die soon if Lucia thus distributed her wealth. But the daughter so entreated and argued that at length Eutychia consented willingly. Then Lucia gave to the poor all she had. This so enraged the young Pagan to whom she was betrothed that he accused her to Pascasius as a Christian. She was taken to this cruel governor, who ordered her to sacrifice to the gods, and when she would not, he condemned her to be taken to a vile place and treated with indignity. She assured him that he could not make her sin, although he could control her body, for that was not sin to which the mind did not consent. Then the tyrant in fury commanded her to be taken away, but when they tried they could not move her. Then they fastened ropes to her, and pulled her, but still she remained fixed. All the magicians and sorcerers were brought, but their spells had no power on her. Then they kindled a great fire about her, but she prayed that these heathen might be confounded, and the fire did not harm her. At this Pascasius was so enraged that a servant, in order to please him, murdered her by piercing her throat with a poniard.

(Crivelli.) St. Lucia.

Her body was buried by the Christians on the very spot where she died, and not long after a church was erected there and dedicated in her name. This legend, which is one of the most ancient, does not speak of the loss of her eyes, but more modern ones relate the following additional story. There dwelt in Syracuse a youth, who having seen her but once was so enamored of her that he took every means to woo her, and constantly protested that it was her wonderfully beautiful eyes which so haunted him, and possessed his soul that he could not rest. Whereupon Lucia, considering the Scripture saying, "If thine eye offend thee, pluck it out," took out her eyes and sent them to the young man on a dish, with this message, "Here hast thou what thou hast so much desired; and for the rest, I beseech thee, leave me now in peace." The young man was so affected by this that he became a convert to Christianity and an example of virtue and chastity. But Lucia did not remain blind, for as she was one day praying, her eyes were restored and were more beautiful than at first! The legend advises those who doubt this to consult the writings of various learned men, where they will find these facts related. There is another legend which makes the loss of her eyes a part of her martyrdom, but there is little authority for this. Her attributes are a light, which is the signification of her name, her eyes on a dish, with or without an awl by which they were bored out, and a poniard as the instrument of her death. Sometimes light proceeds from wounds in her neck, and again she is being pulled by men and oxen, with no effect. In her apotheosis an angel carries her eyes to heaven while others bear the saint. Patroness of Syracuse; protectress against all diseases of the eye; and of the laboring poor. December 13, A. D. 303.

St. Ludmilla was the grandmother of St. Wenceslaus or Wenzel, who is venerated in the north of Germany. Ludmilla was converted by the preaching of St. Adelbert, and she educated her grandson in the Christian faith. His brother Boleslaus was a pagan and instructed by his mother, Drahomira. Bohemia at length became divided between Christians and Pagans, and Boleslaus and his mother determined to kill Ludmilla, who protected the Christians. They hired assassins who strangled her with her veil when she was praying in her oratory. Wenceslaus was then persuaded to visit his mother, and was slain by his brother when he too was in the act of paying his devotions at the altar. Ludmilla was the first martyr saint of Bohemia. September 16, A. D. 927.

St. Luke (*Lat.* Sanctus Luca; *Ital.* San Luca; *Fr.* St. Luc). We are told but little of St. Luke in the Gospel. It would seem that he was not converted until after the Ascension of our Lord. He was a disciple of Paul, and was with him until his death. Some say he was crucified at Patras, and others that he died a peaceful death. That he was a physician may be inferred from the fact that Paul speaks of him as "Luke, the beloved physician;" but the general belief that he was an artist rests on Greek traditions, and can only be traced to the tenth century. A picture of the Virgin found in the Catacombs with an inscription, to the import that it is "one of seven painted by Luca," is regarded as a confirmation of this belief concerning the Evangelist Luke.

Tradition teaches that he carried always with him two portraits, one being that of the Saviour and the other of Mary. These he had painted, and he made many converts by displaying these faces, which inspired those who saw them with devotion, and besides he worked miracles with them. In the Church of Santa Maria, in Via Latâ at Rome, a small chapel is shown as that where Luke wrote his Gospel and multiplied images of the Virgin, which it was his delight to do. From these legends he has been chosen the patron saint of artists and academies of art. He is often represented as painting the Virgin. His attributes are the ox, given him because he wrote especially of the priesthood of the Saviour, and the ox is the emblem of sacrifice; the book, signifying his writings, and a portrait of the Virgin placed in his hand. Sometimes the ox has wings; and again the head of an ox is placed on the figure of a man as a symbol of this Evangelist. In the Church of San Domenico and San Sisto at Rome, there is a tablet which is inscribed thus: "Here at the high altar is preserved that image of the most blessed Mary, which, being delineated by St. Luke the Evangelist, received its colors and form divinely. This is that image with which St. Gregory the Great (according to St. Antonine), as a suppliant, purified Rome; and the pestilence being dispelled, the angel messenger of peace, from the summit of the Castle of Adrian, commanding the Queen of Heaven to rejoice, restored health to the city." Another picture in the Ara Cœli claims to be the one which was thus honored. Both of them are dark and far from beautiful, and if they are the work of St. Luke, I would much prefer the *word-picture* of Mary which he gives in his Gospel, to those of his brush. October 18.

St. Lupo. See St. Adelaide.

St. Macarius (of Alexandria) was one of the most famous hermit saints of Egypt. He is represented in the great fresco by Pietro Laurati in the Campo Santo at Pisa. He is in the centre looking down at a skull which he touches with his staff. This is explained by the following legend: As Macarius was wandering among the Egyptian tombs he saw a skull of a mummy. He turned it over and asked to whom it belonged. It answered, "To a pagan." He then said, "Where is thy soul?" And the skull replied, "In hell." Macarius then said, "How deep?" "The depth is greater than the distance from heaven to earth," answered the skull. Then Macarius asked, "Are there any deeper than thou art?" and the skull replied, "Yes, the Jews are deeper still." And again the hermit said, "Are there any deeper than the Jews?" "Yes, in sooth!" replied the skull, "for the Christians whom Jesus Christ hath redeemed, and who show in their actions that they despise his doctrine, are deeper still!" January 2, A. D. 394.

Madonna, La, or **Our Lady** (*Fr.* Notre Dame; *Ger.* Unser liebe Frau; *Eng.* The Virgin Mary; *Lat.* Virgo Gloriosa, Virgo

Sponsa Dei, Virgo Potens, Virgo Veneranda, Virgo Prædicanda, Virgo Clemens, Virgo Sapientissima, Sancta Virgo Virginum; *Ital.* La Vergine Gloriosa, La Gran Vergine delle Vergini; *Fr.* La Grande Vierge; *Greek*, Θεοτόκη).

(Early Florentine Sculpture.) Head of the Virgin.

Taking the legends connected with the life of Mary in order, the first is the legend of *Joachim and Anna* (*Ital.* La Leggenda di Sant' Anna Madre della Gloriosa Vergine Maria, e di San Gioacchino). See St. Joachim.

The next historical picture is *The Nativity of the Blessed Virgin.* (*Fr.* La Naissance de la S. Vierge; *Ital.* La Nascità della B. Vergine *Ger.* Die Geburt Maria.) As tradition teaches that Joachim and Anna were "exceedingly rich," the room in which the birth is represented is usually rich in furniture and decorations. A glory sometimes surrounds the head of the child. Most artists have also painted attendants, and a number of friends and neighbors who have come to rejoice with St. Anna that her prayers are answered and a child born to her, while she herself reclines on her bed and receives the attentions of the handmaidens and the congratulations of her friends. September 8.

The Presentation of the Virgin (*Ital.* La Presentazione. ove nostra Signora piccioletta Sale i gradi del Tempio; *Ger.* Die Vorstellung der Jungfrau im Tempel, Joachim und Anna weihen ihre Tochter Maria im Tempel). The legend says, "And when the child was three years old, Joachim said, 'Let us invite the daughters of Israel, and they shall take each a taper or a lamp, and attend on her, that the child may not turn back from the temple of the Lord.' And being come to the temple, they placed her on the first step, and she ascended alone all the steps to the altar: and the high-priest received her there, kissed her, and blessed her, saying, 'Mary, the Lord hath magnified thy name to all generations, and in thee shall be made known the redemption of the children of Israel.' And being placed before the altar, she danced with her feet, so that all the house of Israel rejoiced with her, and loved her. Then her parents returned home, blessing God because the maiden had not turned back from the temple." There are various pictures of the life of Mary in the Temple. She is represented as instructing her companions, as spinning and embroidering tapestry. She is sometimes attended by angels, and tradition teaches that her food was supplied by them, and that Mary had the privilege, which none other of her sex ever had, of going into the Holy of Holies to pray before the ark of the covenant. Presentation of B. V. November 21.

The Marriage of the Virgin (*Ital.* Il Sposalizio; *Fr.* Le Mariage de la Vierge; *Ger.* Die Trauung Mariä). When fourteen years old Mary was told by the high-priest that it was proper for her to be married. But she replied that her parents had dedicated her to the service of the Lord. Then the high-priest told her of a vision he had had concerning her, and she submitted herself to the Lord's appointment with sweet humility. The manner in which her husband was selected is told in the legend of St. Joseph. In the representations the Virgin is attended by a train of maidens, and the disappointed suitors are often seen. The priest joins her hand to that of Joseph, or Joseph is placing the ring on her finger. Joseph frequently carries his blossomed wand, while the other suitors break or trample on theirs. The Cathedral of Perugia is said to contain among its relics the nuptial ring of the Virgin Mary. The return of Joseph and Mary to their house is also a subject of art, and Luini represents them as walking hand in hand, Joseph regarding her with veneration, and she looking down, modestly serene. January 23.

The Annunciation (*Fr.* La Salutation Angélique, L'Annonciation; *Ger.* Die Verkündigung, Der englische Gruss; *Ital.* L'Annunciazione, La B. Vergine Annunziata). In addition to the Gospel account of this event, artists have been influenced by legends. One relates that as Mary went forth at evening to draw water, she heard a voice which said, "Hail, thou that art full of grace!" but could see no one. Being troubled, she returned to her house and her work, which is said to have been purple and fine linen. St. Bernard relates the event in this wise: Mary was studying the

(J. Van Eyck.) Annunciation.

book of Isaiah, and as she read the verse, "Behold, a Virgin shall conceive and bear a son," she thought within herself, "How blessed the woman of whom these words are written! Would I might be but her handmaid to serve her, and allowed to kiss her feet!" And instantly the angel appeared to her, and in her the prophecy was fulfilled. The time is sometimes just at evening, in reference to which belief that hour has been consecrated as the "Ave Maria." But others believe it to have been midnight, and that Christ was born at the same hour the following December. The place is usually within the house and rarely by a fountain as the legend presents it. Sometimes Gabriel flies in from above, or is borne by a cloud. Sometimes he walks, but is always young, beautiful, and yet thoughtful in look. He has wings, and in the early pictures full drapery. He either bears the lily (Fleur de Marie), or it is in some other part of the picture. Sometimes he has the olive, typical of peace, or a sceptre with a scroll inscribed, "Ave Maria, gratia plena!" Very rarely he has the palm. The Holy Spirit, as a dove, is sometimes poised over the head of Mary, sometimes hovers toward her bosom, or enters the room through the window. A less agreeable introduction is that of the Eternal Father, above the sky, surrounded by a glory and sending forth celestial light. The spirit or sentiment of the picture depends in a great measure upon the age in which it was painted. Before the fourteenth century Mary is usually represented as humble and submissive, as if listening to the mandate of God, and that from the lips of a superior being. But after that time the increased veneration paid by the Church to the Virgin, makes *her* the superior being, and her manner is that befitting the "Regina angelorum." The work-basket, typical of the industry of Mary, is seldom omitted, and to express her temperance a dish of fruit and pitcher of water are frequently introduced. There are certain mystical or allegorical representations of the Annunciation difficult to be understood. One represents a unicorn taking refuge in the bosom of the Virgin, an angel near by winds a hunting-horn, while four dogs crouch near him. Its signification is given thus in an ancient French work: The fabulous unicorn, who, with his single horn, was said to wound only to free the part wounded from all disease, is an emblem of Jesus, the great physician of souls. The four dogs represent Mercy, Truth, Justice, and Peace, as the four considerations which influenced the Saviour to undertake the salvation of men. The remainder of the explanation is so peculiar that no translation can give the exact idea. It is thus: "Mais comme c'étoit par la Vierge Marie qu'il avoit voulu descendre parmi les hommes et se mettre en leur puissance, on croyoit ne pouvoir mieux faire que de choisir dans la fable, le fait d'une pucelle pouvant seule servir de piége à la licorne, en l'attirant par le charme et le parfum de son sein virginal qu'elle lui présentoit — enfin l'ange Gabriel concourant au mystère étoit bien reconnoissable sous les traits du veneur ailé lançant les lévriers et embouchant la trompette." Another mode of representation is that of Mary, standing with her hands folded over her breast and her head bowed. She is beneath a splendid portico. Gabriel kneels outside and extends the lily. Above the Padre Eterno appears and sends forth the Saviour, who is in the form of the Infant Christ bearing his cross, who floats downward toward the earth, preceded by the Holy Spirit in the form of the Dove. These ideal pictures usually, if not always, date earlier than the seventeenth century. March 25.

The Visitation (*Fr.* La Visitation de la Vierge; *Ital.* La Visitazione di Maria; *Ger.* Die Heimsuchung Mariä). This scene, which represents the meeting of Mary and Elizabeth, is also called "The Salutation of Elizabeth." This picture is not easily mistaken however painted: sometimes the scene is in the garden of Zacharias, where the legend relates that Mary often retired to meditate upon the great honor God had bestowed upon her. It is told that one day while in this garden the Virgin touched a flower which before then had no perfume, but since that time its odor is delicious. Again the two favored women meet at the entrance of the dwelling of Elizabeth. She is of course much older than Mary, but should not be feeble and wrinkled. Her manner fitting one who recognizes the Mother of her Lord, with glad humility, but showing also a certain dignity, being herself appointed by God to an exalted motherhood. Zacharias and Joseph as well as servants are frequently introduced, and sometimes the ass on which Mary has ridden. Zacharias is robed as a priest and Joseph as a traveller. Sometimes Elizabeth kneels, as if to make more impressive her words, "And whence is this to me, that the mother of my Lord should come to me?" July 2.

The Nativity (*Fr.* La Nativité; *Ital.* Il Presepio, Il Nascimento del Nostro Signore; *Ger.* Die Geburt Christi). An ancient legend relates that about the same time that Cæsar Augustus decreed "that all the world should be taxed," he was warned by a sibyl of the birth of Jesus. The pictures and sculptures representing this legend are not improperly considered in connection with those of the nativity to which they so distinctly point. The legend relates that the emperor consulted the sibyl Tiburtina, to know if it were right that he should accept the divine honors which the Senate had decreed to him The sibyl, after meditating some days, took the emperor alone, and showed him an altar.

Nativity.

Above this altar the heavens opened, and he saw a beautiful virgin bearing an infant in her arms, and he heard a voice saying, "This is the altar of the Son of the living God." Then Cæsar

Augustus erected on the Capitoline Hill an altar, and inscribed it, " Ara primogeniti Dei." The Church called the Ara-Cœli stands on the same spot as that on which the altar was built, and in it is a bas-relief representing this legend, to which an incredible antiquity is attached by the Church. There are other paintings of the same subject. The Nativity, when treated as an historical event, is represented in a stable, at midnight, and in winter. The earlier pictures give Mary an appearance of suffering, but from the fourteenth century it is not so. Sometimes she kneels by the child, or points to the manger in which he lays, or bending over him is bright with the light which comes from the child, and, according to the legend, illuminated the place with supernatural light. Joseph is sitting, or leaning on his staff, and frequently holds a taper or other light to show that it is night. The angels who sang the " Gloria in excelsis," were at first represented as three, but in later pictures their number is larger, as of a chorus. The ox and ass are invariably seen. The old monks had various ideas associated with these animals. They regarded them as the fulfillment of prophecy (Habakkuk iii. 4), and as typical of the Jews and Gentiles, — the ox representing the former and the ass the latter. And one old writer relates that they warmed the heavenly babe with their breath. Sometimes the ass is with open mouth, as if proclaiming in his way the light that had come to lighten the Gentiles. The shepherds are frequently in the background. When treated as a mystery, the virgin adores the child who is her son and God. It is sometimes difficult to distinguish between this and a " Madre Pia," but usually something is introduced to denote the Nativity. The babe lies in the centre with his finger on his lip, as if to say, " Verbum sum," and looks upward to the angels, who in the heavens sing his glory. His hand rests sometimes on a wheat-sheaf, emblem of the bread of life. Mary kneels on one side, and Joseph, if present, also kneels; and often angels adore and sustain the child. When other figures are introduced they are saints or votaries for whom the picture was painted. December 25.

The Adoration of the Shepherds (*Fr.* L'Adoration des Bergers; *Ger.* Die Anbetung der Hirten; *Ital.* L'Adorazione dei Pastori). The shepherds present their offerings of fruits, lambs, or doves, and with uncovered heads show their devotion with rude simplicity. Women, dogs, and sheep sometimes accompany them, and there is a legend that the apostles Simeon and Jude were of their number. Sometimes the child sleeps, and the Virgin or Joseph raise the covering to show him to the shepherds. When angels scatter flowers, they are those gathered in heaven.

The Adoration of the Magi (*Ger.* Die heilige drei Königen; Die Anbetung der Weisen aus dem Morgenland; *Ital.* L'Adorazione de' Magia; L'Epifania; *Fr.* L'Adoration des Rois Mages). This picture, while it makes one of the historical series in the life of the Virgin, has another deep interest in the consideration that it is the expression of the Epiphany; of the manifestation to Jews and Gentiles of God in man. The legend follows the Scripture account, and the reasonable inferences to be deduced from it, more closely than many others. It is, that these Magi were not men who knew the arts of magic, but wise princes of some eastern country. The prophecy of Balaam had been held in remembrance by their people, "I shall see him, but not now; I shall behold him, but not nigh: there shall come a Star out of Jacob, and a sceptre shall rise out of Israel;" and when they saw a star differing from those which as learned astronomers they had studied, they recognized it as the star of the prophecy,

(Taddeo Gaddi) Adoration of the Magi.

and at once followed where it led. It has been said that the star when first seen had the form of a child bearing a sceptre or cross. The wise men said farewell to their homes and friends, and took numerous attendants for their long journey. After many perils, the climbing of mountains, the crossing of deep streams, and many difficulties, they came to Jerusalem. On inquiry for the King they sought, they were directed to Bethlehem, and asked by Herod to bring him news on their return of where the child could be found, that he too might worship him. At length the star stood still over the lowly place where Jesus was. No matter how different may have been their previous imaginations from the reality they found, their faith was equal to the demand upon it, and they bowed down, thus giving themselves first, and then presented the gold, which signified that Jesus was king; the frankincense, that he was God; and the myrrh, that he was suffering man, and must yield to death. In return for their gifts Christ gave them charity and spiritual riches in place of gold; perfect faith for their incense; and for myrrh truth and meekness of spirit. The Virgin gave them as a precious memorial, one of the linen bands in which she had wrapped the divine child. Being warned in a dream they returned not to Herod, but went another way. There is a legend that their homeward journey was made in ships; and in a commentary on the psalms of the fifth century it is said that when Herod found that they had escaped from him "in ships of Tarsus," he burned all the vessels in the port. But however they returned, the legend relates that the star guided them to the East as it had led them from it, and they reached their homes in safety. They never again assumed their former state, but in imitation of their new sovereign they gave their wealth to the poor, and went about to preach the new gospel of peace. There is a tradition that after forty years, when St. Thomas went to the Indies, he met there these wise men and baptized them; and afterwards as they continued to preach they went among barbarians and were put to death. Long after their remains were found, and the Empress Helena had them removed to Constantinople. During the first Crusade they were carried to Milan, and lastly the Emperor Barbarossa placed them in the cathedral at Cologne, where they remain in a costly shrine, and have performed many wonderful miracles. The names of these three "Kings of Cologne," as they are often called, are Jasper or Caspar, Melchior, and Balthasar. In the pictures they are of three ages: the first, Jasper, very old with gray beard; Melchior of middle age; and Balthasar always young, and sometimes a Moor or black man, to signify that he was of Ethiopia, and that Christ came to all races of men. Sometimes this idea is manifested by making his servant black. Their costumes, attendants, and various appointments vary with the time in which the pictures were painted and the nationality of the artist. Now they have all the usual paraphernalia of royalty as it was seen in the continental capitals; again the knowledge acquired in the Crusades was employed, and all about them is oriental in style; and elephants, leopards, and even monkeys are introduced into the scene. The holy child is sometimes held by his mother, and sometimes sits alone, but usually raises his hand as if in blessing. In early days Joseph was seldom present, but as more veneration was accorded him by the Church he was more frequently made an actor in this scene; he sometimes only looks on quietly, again he receives the treasure, and in some instances the Magi seem to congratulate him. The various modes of representing this inexhaustible subject would fill a volume if described. January 6.

The Purification of the Virgin; The Presentation of Christ in the Temple (*Ital.* La Purificazione della B. Vergine; *Ger.* Die Darbringung im Tempel). The Virgin, after the birth of her son, complied with all the requirements of the law, and the scene in the Temple is sometimes called the Purification, but more frequently it is regarded as referring especially to the Saviour; and many representations present the prophecy of Simeon as the important event in the scene. It is also considered as the first of the seven sorrows of the Virgin, and the words, "Yea, a sword shall pierce through thy own soul also," may well have saddened the heart of Mary, and given her a warning of all the *glorious sorrows* which were before her. The legend of Simeon is so closely connected with this scene as to be better given here than elsewhere. Two hundred and sixty years B. C., Ptolemy Philadelphus requested the high-priest of the Jews to send him scribes and interpreters to translate for him the Hebrew Scriptures, so that he might place them in his library. Six learned Rabbis from each tribe were sent, seventy-two in all, and among them Simeon, who was full of learning. His portion was the book of Isaiah, and when he came to the sentence, "Behold a Virgin shall conceive," he feared the translation might offend the Greeks, and after much consideration he rendered it a *young woman*, but when it was written, an angel effaced it, and wrote the word Virgin, as it should be. Then Simeon wrote it again and again, and each time it was changed. When this was done three times he was confounded, and as he meditated on this it was revealed to him that the prophecy should not only be fulfilled, but that he "should not see death till he had seen the Lord's Christ." So he lived until these things were come to pass, and then he was led to the temple on the very day when this Virgin Mother came to present there her god-son. And there it was that he exclaimed, when his prophecy was ended, "Lord, now lettest thou thy servant depart in peace, according to thy word." Anna the prophetess acts her part in this picture. She prophesied of him who should bring redemption to Israel, but she did not take the child; from this she has been regarded as an image of the synagogue, which had prohpesied much of the Messiah but failed to embrace him when he came. This picture is frequently called the *Nunc Dimittis*, which is its title in Greek art. February 2.

The Flight into Egypt (*Ital.* La Fuga in Egitto; *Fr.* La Fuite de la Sainte Famille en Egypte; *Ger.* Die Flucht nach Ægypten). There are various legends connected with this journey of the Holy Family which have been illustrated by artists. One is, that when escaping, and fearing lest they should be overtaken by the officers of Herod, they came to a place where a man was sowing wheat. Mary said to him, "If any shall ask you whether we have passed this way, ye shall answer, 'Such persons passed this way when I was sowing this corn.'" And then, by a miracle of the infant Jesus, the corn grew in one night, so as to be fit for the harvest. Next day the officers did indeed come, and the man who was cutting his wheat in great wonder and thankfulness answered as he had been instructed, and the pursuers turned back. Another legend relates that the Holy Family encountered a band of robbers, of which there were large numbers in that country in those days. One of the robbers was about to attack them, when another said, "Suffer them, I beseech thee, to go in peace, and I will give thee forty groats, and likewise my girdle." This offer the first robber accepted. The second then took the travellers to a safe place, where they passed the night. The Virgin said to him, "The Lord God will receive thee to his right hand and grant thee pardon of thy sins!" And this was done, for (according to the legend) these were the two thieves who were crucified with Jesus, and the merciful one was the same who went with Christ to Paradise. Another popular incident of this journey in legendary writings is that the palm-tree bent its branches at the command of the child, to shade the Blessed Virgin. It is also related that a tree which grew at the gate of Heliopolis and was venerated as the home of a god, bowed itself at the approach of the Saviour, and that all along their route wherever there were idols, they fell on their faces and were broken in fragments. And this is assented to by religious authorities as well as writers of legends. There are many ways of representing the three travellers on this remarkable journey, but all easily recognized. There are a few in which they are either embarking, or are in a boat crossing one of the streams or lakes which intercepted the course of their journey. Sometimes an angel assists the Virgin to enter and sometimes steers the boat. See, also, St. Joseph.

(Zuccaro.) The Robber.

The Repose of the Holy Family (*Ital.* Il Riposo; *Ger.* Die Ruhe in Ægypten; *Fr.* Le Repos de la Sainte Famille). The subject of this picture is really an incident of the Flight, but it is not found in very early art, rarely, if at all, before the sixteenth century. When other figures than those of the Virgin and child with Joseph are introduced it is not a *Riposo*, but a *Holy Family.* The legend teaches that the Holy Family reposed beneath a sycamore grove near the village of Matarea, and that near the same village a fountain sprang forth miraculously for their refreshment. This gave a religious interest to the sycamore, and the Crusaders brought it to Europe, and this same "Fountain of Mary" was shown me by the Arab

(N. Poussin.) Flight into Egypt.

guides, a few miles from Cairo. Mary is sometimes painted dipping water, and again washing linen in this fountain, which the legend also teaches that she did. In pictures of the Repose, angels often minister to the comfort of the travellers, in various ways and with beautiful propriety. There is a wild ballad legend, which probably originated in the East, which gives an account of the meeting of Mary and a Zingara or gypsy. The gypsy crosses the palm of the child and tells his future, according to their customs. Her prophecy of all his sufferings quite overcomes the Virgin, but the Zingara consoles her with the assurance of the redemption of mankind through all these sorrows, and ends by asking forgiveness of her sins, instead of the usual gold or silver piece, the gypsies love so well. This affords a fine subject for art, and has been painted. When the Holy Family are seen as on a journey, and the Saviour represented as walking, it is the return from Egypt that is intended.

The Holy Family (*Fr.* La Sainte Famille; *Ital.* La Sacra Famiglia, La Sacra Conversazione). From the return to Nazareth until Jesus is twelve years old, the Gospels record no events of the life of the Virgin or her Son. Under the title of Holy Family, there are hundreds of pictures representing the imaginary life of these exalted ones, whose every act was full of interest to all the world. The simplest form is that of two figures, the Virgin and Child, and frequently she is nursing the babe, sometimes kisses him, or amuses him with playthings, and again watches him asleep, and ponders in her heart upon her wonderful child; which last are called "Il Silenzio," or "Le Sommeil de Jésus." Where there are three figures it is generally St. John who is added, but sometimes St. Joseph makes the third. Four figures include either St. John and Elizabeth, or more rarely St. Joseph and St. John. Five figures include all who have been named, and Zacharias sometimes makes the sixth. More than these are unusual, although there are pictures in which large numbers surround the Holy Family proper, and are supposed to represent the relatives of the Saviour, especially those who were afterwards to be his disciples and followers. But any description of these pictures would fill volumes. Many of them are designated by some prominent peculiarity, and bear such names as "La Vierge aux Cerises," "Vierge à la Diadème," "La Vierge à l'Oreiller Verd," "La Madonna del Bacino," "Le Ménage du Menuisier," "Le Raboteur," etc., etc.

The Dispute in the Temple (*Ital.* La Disputa nel Tempio; *Fr.* Jésus au milieu des Docteurs). While this is the representation of a very important act in the life of Jesus, it is quite as frequently made one of the series from the life of the Virgin, and "is one of the sorrowful mysteries of the Rosary." And in regarding these pictures it will aid one to consider whether it is the wonderful knowledge of Jesus or the grief of Mary which is most forcibly portrayed.

The Death of Joseph (*Ital.* La Morte di San Guiseppe; *Fr.* La Mort de St. Joseph; *Ger.* Josef's Tod). See St. Joseph.

The Marriage at Cana in Galilee (*Ital.* Le Nozze di Cana; *Fr.* Les Noces de Cana; *Ger.* Die Hochzeit zu Cana). Although Jesus performed his first miracle at this marriage feast, it was not a favorite subject in early art on account of the low estimation of marriage among the monks and early writers of the Church. But those who would exalt the Virgin regard it as greatly to her honor that this miracle was done at her request. His answer, that his hour had not yet come, and his performing the miracle immediately after, is construed to mean, that although the period had not fully arrived for the use of his power, still out of regard to his mother and her wishes, the power was put forth. In some pictures the bride is dressed as a nun about to make her professional vows, and an ancient legend taught that this was the marriage of St. John the Evangelist with Mary Magdalene, and that immediately they separated, and led chaste and austere lives, devoting themselves to Christ's service. After this marriage the Virgin is not mentioned in the Gospels until the time of the Crucifixion.

In the Rosary two scenes from the Passion of Our Lord make two of the mystical sorrows: the *Procession to Calvary*, or "Il Portamento della Croce," and the *Crucifixion*. It was in the Via Dolorosa, through which Christ bore his cross, that Mary is said to have fainted at the sight of his sufferings, and this incident is frequently a subject of painting. The celebrated "Lo Spasimo di Sicilia" of Raphael, represents Mary as "Notre Dame du Spasme," or "du Pâmoison," as the French call the mournful festival which they keep in Passion Week to commemorate this event. The Italians call these representations "Il Pianto di Maria," or "La Madonna dello Spasimo." But in all these pictures, and those of the Crucifixion, Mary is a prominent figure. There has been much said and written upon the impropriety of representing the Virgin as too much overcome with her grief, as it is thought to detract from the grandeur of her character; and it would seem, that although the time had come when Simeon's prophecy was fulfilled, yet her heaven-given patience and hope should have sustained her, and she should have endured where any other mother might have fainted. The legend relates, that in *The Descent from the Cross*, when Joseph of Arimathea and Nicodemus removed the nails from the hands of the Saviour, St. John took them away secretly, that Mary might not see them, and while Nicodemus drew forth those which held the feet, Joseph so sustained the body that the head and arms of Jesus hung over his shoulder. Then Mary arose, and kissed the bleeding hands of her beloved Son, and clasping them tenderly sank to the earth in anguish; and this action is usually represented in pictures of the Descent from the Cross. In the *Deposition*, or the act of laying down the body of Christ, the Virgin supports her son, or bends tenderly over him. In older pictures she is fainting here, which does not meet with the same censure from critics in this case, as in the Procession to Calvary. The Virgin is also seen in the representations of the *Entombment*, although this is not painted in the series of the Life of the Virgin; and in this as in the others her sorrow is often expressed by fainting. The next subject in course is, "*John conducting the Virgin to his Home*," which, beautiful as it is, did not appear in works of art until the seventeenth century, so that it is not frequently seen. Although not recorded in Scripture, the traditions teach that Jesus appeared first of all to his mother, and the story is thus told: After all was finished Mary retired to her chamber, and waited for the fulfillment of the promise of Christ's resurrection. And she prayed earnestly, "Thou didst promise, O my most dear son, that thou wouldst rise again on the third day. Before yesterday was the day of darkness and bitterness; and, behold, this is the third day. Return then to me, thy mother. O my son, tarry not, but come!" And while she prayed, a company of angels surrounded her, and they waved palms, and joyously sang the Easter hymn, "Regina Cœli lætare, Alleluia!" Then Christ entered, bearing the standard of the cross, and followed by the patriarchs and prophets whom He had released from Hades. All knelt before Mary, and thanked her, because their deliverance had come through her. But she greatly desired to hear the voice of Jesus, and He raised his hand in benediction, saying, "I salute thee, O my mother!" And she fell on his neck, exclaiming, "Is it thou indeed, my most dear son?" Then He showed her his wounds, and bade her be comforted since He had triumphed over death and hell. Then Mary on her knees thanked Him that she had been his mother, and they talked together until He left her to show himself next to Mary Magdalene. The representations of the Apparition of Christ to the Virgin, are in the most matter-of-fact style, and poorly portray the spirit of this beautiful legend. *The Ascension of Christ* is the seventh of the mystical sorrows of the Virgin, for by it she was left alone. The legends teach that she was present, and gazing at the departing Saviour prayed, "My Son, remember me when thou comest to thy kingdom. Leave me not long after thee, my Son!" Mary, when represented in the pictures of the *Descent of the Holy Ghost*, is placed in the centre or in front, as Regina et Mater Apostolorum. It has been objected that as Mary was Wisdom, or the Mother of Wisdom, she needed no accession of understanding. But if the testimony of Scripture is taken, it would seem proper that she should be represented here (Acts i. 14, and ii. 1). There is no authoritative record of the life of Mary after the ascension of Jesus, but there are many legends which speak of circumstances of her life, and a very curious one of her death and assumption. One which has been the subject of pictures is the Communion of Mary, in which she receives the sacrament from the hand of St. John. The traditions relate that when the persecution began at Jerusalem, the Virgin went with St. John to Ephesus, accompanied by Mary Magdalene; also, that she dwelt on Mount Carmel in an oratory which the prophet Elijah had built, and from this she became the patroness of the Carmelites, and the sixteenth day of July is set apart by the Church as that of the Blessed Virgin Mary of Mount Carmel.

The Death and Assumption of the Virgin (*Lat.* Dormitio, Pausatio, Transitus, Assumptio, B. Virginis; *Ital.* Il Transito di Maria, Il Sonno della Beata Vergine, L'Assunzione; *Fr.* La Mort de la Vierge, L'Assomption; *Ger.* Das Absterben der Maria, Mariä Himmelfahrt). Sometimes these two events are represented together, the death making the lower, and the apotheosis the upper portion of the picture. But so many circumstances of the legend are portrayed in these pictures that they cannot be well understood without a knowledge of it. It is thus given by Mrs. Jameson in the "Legends of the Madonna": "Mary dwelt in the house of John upon Mount Sion, looking for the fulfillment of the promise of deliverance; and she spent her days in visiting those places which had been hallowed by the baptism, the sufferings, the burial and resurrection of her divine Son, but more particularly the tomb wherein he was laid. And she did not this as seeking the living among the dead, but for consolation and for remembrance. And on a certain day, the heart of the Virgin being filled with an inexpressible longing to behold her Son, melted away within her, and she wept abundantly. And, lo! an angel appeared before her clothed in light, as with a garment. And he saluted her, and said, 'Hail, O Mary! blessed by Him who hath given salvation to Israel! I bring thee here a branch of palm gathered in Paradise; command that it be carried before thy bier in the day of thy death; for in three days thy soul shall leave thy body, and thou shalt enter into Paradise, where thy Son awaits thy coming.' Mary answering, said: 'If I have found grace in thy eyes, tell me first what is thy name; and grant that the apostles, my brethren, may be reunited to me before I die, that in their presence I may give up my soul to God. Also, I pray thee, that my soul, when delivered from my body, may not be affrighted by any spirit of darkness, nor any evil angel be allowed to have any power over me.' And the angel said, 'Why dost thou ask my name? My name is the Great and the Wonderful. And now doubt not that all the apostles shall be reunited to thee this day; for He who in former times transported the prophet Habakkuk from Judæa to Jerusalem by the hair of his head, can as easily bring hither the apostles. And fear thou not the evil spirit, for hast thou not bruised his head, and destroyed his kingdom?' And having said these words, the angel departed into heaven; and the palm branch which he had left behind him shed light from every leaf, and sparkled as the stars of the morning. Then Mary lighted the lamps and prepared her bed, and waited until the hour was come. And in the same instant John, who was preaching at Ephesus, and Peter, who was preaching at Antioch, and all the other apostles who were dispersed in different parts of the world, were suddenly caught up as by a miraculous power, and found themselves before the door of the habitation of Mary. When Mary saw them all assembled round her, she blessed and thanked the

Lord, and she placed in the hands of St. John the shining palm, and desired that he should bear it before her at the time of her burial. Then Mary, kneeling down, made her prayer to the Lord, her Son, and the others prayed with her; then she laid herself down in her bed, and composed herself for death. And John wept bitterly. And about the third hour of the night, as Peter stood at the head of the bed, and John at the foot, and the other apostles around, a mighty sound filled the house, and a delicious perfume filled the chamber. And Jesus himself appeared accompanied by an innumerable company of angels, patriarchs, and prophets; all these surrounded the bed of the Virgin, singing hymns of joy. And Jesus said to his mother, 'Arise, my beloved, mine elect! come with me from Lebanon, my espoused! receive the crown that is destined for thee!' And Mary, answering, said, 'My heart is ready; for it was written of me that I should do thy will!' Then all the angels and blessed spirits who accompanied Jesus began to sing and rejoice. And the soul of Mary left her body, and was received into the arms of her Son; and together they ascended into heaven. And the apostles looked up, saying, 'O most prudent Virgin, remember us when thou comest to glory!' and the angels who received her into heaven, sung these words, 'Who is this that cometh up from the wilderness leaning upon her Beloved, she is fairer than all the daughters of Jerusalem.' But the body of Mary remained upon the earth; and three among the virgins prepared to wash and clothe it in a shroud; but such a glory of light surrounded her form, that though they touched it they could not see it, and no human eye beheld those chaste and sacred limbs unclothed. Then the apostles took her up reverently, and placed her upon a bier, and John, carrying the celestial palm, went before. Peter sung the 114th Psalm, 'In exitu Israel de Egypto, domus Jacob de populo barbaro,' and the angels followed after, also singing. The wicked Jews, hearing these melodious voices, ran together; and the high-priest, being seized with fury, laid his hands upon the bier, intending to overturn it on the earth; but both his arms were suddenly dried up, so that he could not move them, and he was overcome with fear; and he prayed to St. Peter for help, and Peter said, 'Have faith in Jesus Christ, and his Mother, and thou shalt be healed;' and it was so. Then they went on, and laid the Virgin in a tomb in the Valley of Jehoshaphat. And on the third day, Jesus said to the angels, 'What honor shall I confer on her who was my mother on earth, and brought me forth?' And they answered, 'Lord, suffer not that body which was thy temple and thy dwelling to see corruption; but place her beside thee on thy throne in heaven.' And Jesus consented; and the Archangel Michael brought unto the Lord the glorious soul of our Lady. And the Lord said, 'Rise up, my dove, my undefiled, for thou shalt not remain in the darkness of the grave, nor shalt thou see corruption;' and immediately the soul of Mary rejoined her body, and she arose up glorious from the tomb and ascended into heaven, surrounded and welcomed by troops of angels, blowing their silver trumpets, touching their golden lutes, singing and rejoicing as they sung, 'Who is she that riseth as the morning, fair as the moon, clear as the sun, and terrible as an army with banners?' (Cant. vi. 10.) But one among the apostles was absent; and when he arrived soon after, he would not believe in the resurrection of the Virgin; and this apostle was the same Thomas, who had formerly been slow to believe in the resurrection of the Lord; and he desired that the tomb should be opened before him; and when it was opened it was found to be full of lilies and roses. Then Thomas, looking up to heaven, beheld the Virgin bodily, in a glory of light, slowly mounting towards the heaven; and she, for the assurance of his faith, flung down to him her girdle, the same which is to this day preserved in the cathedral of Prato. And there were present at the death of the Virgin Mary, besides the twelve apostles, Dionysius the Areopagite, Timotheus, and Hierotheus; and of the women, Mary Salome, Mary Cleophas, and a faithful handmaid, whose name was Savia." The French legend gives Mary Magdalene and Martha among those who witnessed the Virgin's death. The full illustration of this legend requires seven different scenes, namely, 1. The Angel announces her death, and presents the palm. 2. She takes leave of the Apostles. 3. Her Death. 4. The bearing to the Sepulchre. 5. The Entombment. 6. The Assumption. 7. The Coronation in Heaven. Frequently two or three of these scenes are represented together, as, the Death below, and the Assumption above, and sometimes the Coronation above all. The angel who announces the death frequently presents a taper to the Virgin. It was customary to place a taper in the hand of one dying. The death of the Virgin is sometimes called the Sleep (Il Sonno della Madonna), as it was in early times a belief that she only slept before her assumption. This doctrine has since been declared a heresy. There are two modes of treating the Assumption: one represents the assumption of the soul, and in these, Christ receives the Spirit, standing near the death-bed of the Virgin. The other portrays the union of the soul to the body, when it rises from the tomb, and leaving earth and all earthly things, the Mother soars to meet the Son, and to share his glory and his throne for evermore. She is represented in a mandorla, or aureole, crowned or veiled (sometimes both), her dress spangled with stars, and surrounded by adoring angels. These are the more ideal or devotional pictures. The strictly historical ones, have the wondering apostles, the doubting Thomas, and the blossoming tomb below; while Mary, "quasi aurora consurgens" is borne toward heaven. *The Legend of the Holy Girdle* belongs properly to the consideration of the pictures of the Assumption of the Virgin. It is of Greek origin, and relates that St. Thomas, when about to go to the far East, gave the girdle to one of his disciples for safe keeping. The girdle remained for a thousand years guarded from profane eyes, and was in the possession of a Greek priest, to whom it had descended from a remote ancestry. He had one daughter, dearly beloved, to whom he gave the care of the sacred girdle. It happened that Michael of Prato, who had gone on the Crusade of 1096, had remained in Jerusalem after the war was ended, and lodged in the house of this priest. He too loved the daughter, and wished to marry her, but the father would not consent. Then the mother assisted the lovers to be married, and gave them the precious girdle as a dowry. They fled, and embarked for Tuscany. They landed at Pisa, and sought the home of Michael at Prato, bearing always with them the casket which held the sacred relic. Michael so venerated his treasure, and so feared lest he should be robbed of it, that he lighted each night a lamp in honor of it, and besides placed it beneath his bed for safety. Now although he did this without knowing that it was wanting in respect to so holy a relic, it displeased his guardian angels, and they each night lifted him out of his bed, and laid him on the bare earth. At length Michael fell sick, and knowing that he was near death he delivered the girdle to Bishop Uberto, commanding him, that the girdle should be preserved in the Cathedral of Prato, and from time to time shown to the people. This injunction Uberto obeyed, and carried it in a solemn procession to the church. There it remained until 1312, when an attempt was made to carry it away, and sell it to Florence. This attempt was discovered, and Musciatino, the would-be thief, was put to death. Then the people of Prato resolved to erect a shrine for the safe keeping of the girdle, which they did, and the chapel containing it is painted to represent all the circumstances of this legend.

(Cimabue. S. Maria. Novella. Florence.)

The Coronation of the Virgin is not always easily distinguished from the allegorical picture called the "Incoronata." When the historical scene is intended, the last of the life of Mary, the death-bed, the tomb, the apostles, and weeping friends are seen on the earth, while above the Saviour crowns his Mother, or she is seated beside him on his throne.

Regina Virginum.

Having thus briefly considered the historical pictures of Our Lady, the mystical, allegorical, or strictly devotional ones remain. These are: —

The Virgin Alone (*Lat.* Virgo Gloriosa; *Ital.* La Vergine Gloriosa; *Fr.* La Grande Vierge). Pictures representing the Virgin Mary alone, and placing her before us as an object of religious veneration, are painted in a variety of ways, and to illustrate the different attributes which are accorded to her by the Church. When she stands alone, with saints or apostles apparently subordinate to her, she is THE WOMAN; THE MOTHER OF HUMANITY, a second Eve; and the VIRGIN OF VIRGINS. When she has a book she is the representation of HEAVENLY WISDOM, — Virgo Sapientissima. When she has a sceptre, or wears a crown over her veil, or is enthroned alone, she is the QUEEN OF HEAVEN, — Regina Cœli. When represented as above and surrounded by worshipping angels, she is QUEEN OF ANGELS, — Regina Angelorum. When veiled, with folded hands, and face full of purity, sweetness, and all imaginable beauty, she is The Madonna, The Blessed Virgin, — Santa Maria Vergine.

Virgo Sapientissima. (Van Eyck.)

L'Incoronata; The Coronation of the Virgin (*Lat.* Coronatio Beatæ Mariæ Virginis; *Ital.* Maria Coronata dal divin suo Figlio; *Fr.* Le Couronnement de la Sainte Vierge; *Ger.* Die Krönung Mariä). This picture is entirely different in its spirit and object from the historical coronation of the Virgin before described. That picture makes the closing scene in the life of Mary, and as before remarked, has the apostles, the tomb of flowers, and the death-bed to distinguish it. But the intent of the devotional coronation is to represent the Virgin as the type or emblem of the Spiritual Church. She is received into glory and exalted above all created beings, angels and men, as the Espoused, the Bride of Christ, — THE CHURCH. Frequently the Saviour has an open book with the inscription, "Veni, Electa mea, et ponam te in thronum meum," etc., "Come, my Chosen One, and I will place thee upon my throne." Many chapels are dedicated to the Virgin in this character. "Capella dell' Incoronata." The dress of the Virgin is most beautiful, and frequently embroidered with suns, moons, and golden rays, recalling the "woman clothed with the sun,' which John describes (Rev. xii. 1). When Mary holds the child and is crowned, it is not a coronation, but an adoration of her as the Mother of God.

(Guido.) Immaculate Conception.

Our Lady of the Immaculate Conception (*Lat.* Regina sine labe originali concepta; *Fr.* La Conception de la Vierge Marie; *Ital.* La Madonna Purissima; *Sp.* Nuestra Señora sin peccado concepida, La Concepcion; *Ger.* Das Geheimniss der unbefleckten Empfängniss Mariä). This picture is unknown in the early days of art, but has been almost miraculously multiplied since the beginning of the seventeenth century, when Paul V. instituted the office for the commemoration of the Immaculate Conception of the Virgin, and forbade teaching or preaching the opposite doctrine. The question had been in agitation a decade of centuries, and in the fifteenth century the Sorbonne had declared in its favor; but the opposition of a large portion of the Church prevented its actual promulgation as a doctrine necessary to be believed, and even that did not satisfy the opposers of the dogma, as a much later controversy proves. The last papal ordinance concerning it was promulgated in 1849 by Pius IX. The model for the Virgin in this representation is the woman of the Apocalypse. She is young, about twelve or fourteen, her robe of white with blue mantle, her hands folded as if in prayer. Her beauty, " all that painting can express." The sun, a vivid light about her, the moon beneath her, and a starry crown above her head. Sometimes the same idea of the Madonna Purissima is represented by the head alone. It is painted very young, with white vesture and flowing hair. Before the authorization of the doctrine of the Immaculate Conception, there was another mystical representation of Mary, which might be confounded with those of the Madonna Purissima. It is the embodiment of the idea that the redemption of the human race existed in the mind of the Creator before the beginning of the world. And this is expressed by the Virgin surrounded by the same attributes as in the Conception, and sometimes setting her foot on the serpent. Mary, made thus a second Eve, is sometimes painted as an accompaniment to the picture of Eve holding the apple. The date of the picture will decide the question between these subjects. December 8.

(Miniature. 16th cent.) Predestination.

The Mater Dolorosa (*Ital.* La Madre di Dolore, L'Addolorata; *Fr.* Nôtre Dame de Pitié, La Vierge de Douleur; *Sp.* Nuestra Señora de Dolores; *Ger.* Die Schmerzhafte Mutter). There are three distinct modes of representing the "Mourning Mother," to whom the afflicted of the Roman Catholic world address their prayers, feeling that she has felt the deepest pangs of earthly sorrow. As the *Mater Dolorosa,* she is alone, seated or standing, and frequently only a head or half figure; of middle age, with bowed head, clasped hands, sorrowful face, and streaming eyes. Often the bosom is pierced with one, and sometimes with seven swords. As the *Stabat Mater,* she stands on the right of the crucifix while St. John is on the left. The whole figure expresses intense sorrow. She is usually wrapped in a dark violet or blue mantle. *La Pietà,* the third Sorrowing Mother, when strictly rendered, consists only of the

Virgin and the dead Christ. Occasionally lamenting angels are introduced. This representation has been varied in every possible way which could express sorrow, resignation, tenderness, love, and dignity. But usually the son is in the arms, on the lap, or lying at the feet of the Mother.

(Greek Mosaic. A. D. 642. Lateran.)
Virgin of San Venanzio.

The Virgin of Mercy. Our Lady of Succor (*Ital.* La Madonna di Misericordia; *Fr.* Nôtre Dame de Miséricorde; *Sp.* Nuestra Señora de Gracia; *Ger.* Maria Mutter des Erbarmens). This picture represents the Virgin as the Merciful Mother of Humanity. In it she sometimes stands with outstretched arms, crowned or veiled; her ample robe extended by angels, over kneeling votaries and worshippers. Sometimes these embrace all ranks and ages, and again those of some particular Order who seek her aid. But these instances are rare, as she usually bears the child in her arms, signifying that from her maternity itself a large portion of her sympathy is derived. In pictures of the Day of Judgment, the Virgin is also represented as Our Lady of Mercy. She is on the right hand of the Saviour, while John the Baptist kneels on the left. Mary is usually a little lower than the Saviour, but has been represented in ancient pictures seated by his side. She appears as a mediator and intercessor for mercy, whatever her position. In one instance this inscription is painted beneath her: "Maria Filio suo pro Ecclesia supplicat."

The Virgin and Child Enthroned (*Lat.* Sancta Dei Genitrix, Virgo Deipara; *Ital.* La Santissima Vergine, Madre di Dio; *Fr.* La Sainte Vierge, Mère de Dieu; *Ger.* Die Heilige Mutter Gottes). The very title of these pictures, which are numberless, explains their signification. They are devotional, and represent the mother and child in

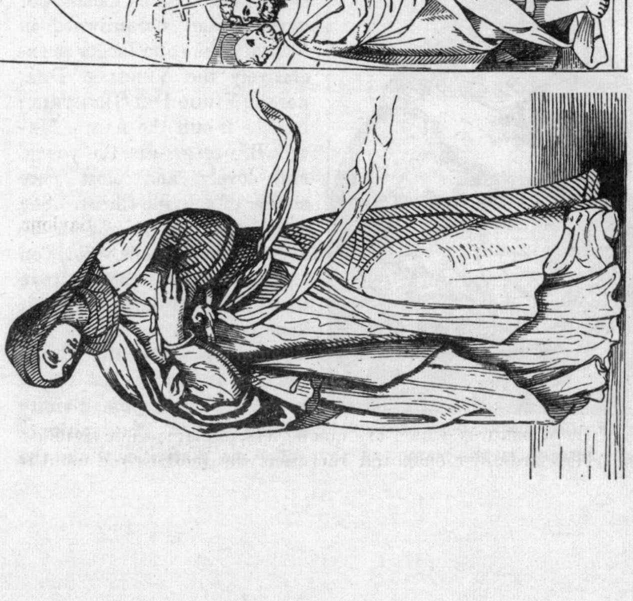

(Moretto of Brescia.) The Blessed Virgin

(Garofalo.) Enthroned Madonna.

(Martin Schoen.) Virgin and Child.

various positions, and with such differences of expression and sentiment as must inevitably result from the vast number of artists who have treated this subject. Its beauties are as inexhaustible as they are indescribable, and there are few hearts that have not been filled with emotion and admiration by some of these representations of what is purest and holiest in woman.

In addition to the Madonnas already mentioned, there are numerous votive Madonnas both public and private. Their titles usually indicate the objects for which they were painted, as those painted for the Carmelites, which are called "La Madonna del Carmine." Others denote especial acts, as "La Madonna della Vittoria," or deliverance from dangers, such as pestilence, floods, fire, and tempests, as the "Madonna di San Sebastiano," which was an offering of the city of Modena against the plague. Family votive Madonnas usually bear the name of those who offer them, as the "Madonna di Foligno," which was consecrated by Sigismund Conti of Foligni, in fulfillment of a vow made when in danger from a severe storm. There is scarcely a church or religious institution of the Romish Church that does not possess at least one votive Madonna.

The Mater Amabilis (*Ital.* La Madonna col Bambino; *Fr.* La Vierge et l'enfant Jésus; *Ger.* Maria mit dem Kind). This is the representation of the Virgin as THE MOTHER alone, and its exquisite beauty and feeling, when painted as it should and may be, is only to be *felt*, it cannot be *told*. Here "she is brought nearer to our sympathies. She is not seated in a chair of state with the accompaniments of earthly power; she is not enthroned on clouds, nor glorified and star-crowned in heaven; she is no longer so exclusively the VERGINE DEA, nor the VIRGO DEI GENETRIX; but she is still the ALMA MATER REDEMPTORIS, the young, and lovely, and most pure mother of a divine Christ. She is not sustained in mid-air by angels; she dwells lowly on earth; but the angels leave their celestial home to wait upon her." A version of this Madonna is styled the Madre Pia, and represents the Virgin as acknowledging the divinity of her Son. The spirit of these pictures is the same as that of some Nativities where the

(Fra Bartolomeo.) Mater Amabalis.

Virgin worships the babe, but the accessories determine the difference between them. And lastly there are the Pastoral Madonnas, in which numerous persons, such as the relatives of the Virgin or St. Joseph, the saints and holy personages, are introduced as participating with the Virgin in the adoration of the child.

(Francesco Francia.) The Madonna, St. Dominick, and St. Barbara.

La Madonna della Sedia. The pretty and poetical legend of this famous picture relates that centuries ago there dwelt among the Italian hills a venerable hermit, whom the people called Father Bernardo. He was renowned for wisdom and holiness, and many visited him for advice and consolation. He often remarked that though his solitude was deep, yet he was not entirely alone, for he had two daughters, one that spoke to him, and one that was dumb. Now the first was the daughter of a vine-dresser, named Mary, who dearly loved the old man, and often brought him little presents of such things as would add to his comfort, and cheered him with loving words and caresses. But his dumb daughter was a "brave old oak," that grew near his hut and sheltered it with its branches. This tree old Bernardo greatly loved, and in the heat of summer he brought water to its thirsty roots, and tended and talked to it as if it could hear and feel. At morning and evening he fed the birds which lived in its branches, and in return was cheered by their songs. Many times some woodman had desired to cut down this oak, but the prayers of the old man deterred him from the deed. There came at last a terrible winter when the mountains were laden with heavy snow, and then the sun shone warm, and fearful freshets came down like torrents, and swept away flocks and trees and even hamlets in their course. After the worst had subsided, Mary and her father went to see how it had fared with the good hermit, fearing that he had perished. But his dumb daughter had saved his life; for when the thaw came on he had sought the roof of his hut, but he was soon convinced that there was no safety for him there, and as he lifted his eyes in prayer it seemed that the limbs of the oak beckoned him to come to them. Then he climbed with confidence among its branches, and there he stayed three days. While below him his hut and everything else was swept away, still his daughter stood firm. But he only had a few dry crusts to eat, and when Mary arrived he was fainting and ready to die from cold and exposure. Then this talking daughter comforted him, and took him to her home until his hut could be rebuilt. And now with great fervor Bernardo thanked God for his preservation, and called down blessings upon his two children who had both been instruments in his deliverance; and he prayed Heaven to distinguish them in some way from the other works of his hand. Years passed on and the hermit was laid to rest; his hut was in ruins forever, and the oak was converted into wine-casks for Mary's father. One day one of these casks was in an arbor where Mary, now a wife and mother, sat with her two boys. As she pressed her baby to her breast and watched the elder one at play, she thought of the old hermit and wondered if his blessing would ever be fulfilled in her or these children; just then the older child ran towards her with a stick to which he had fastened a cross; and at the same time a young man approached, whose large dreamy eyes were such as feast on beauty, but his air was that of one restless and weary. And he was so; for he had long been seeking a model which could be used to assist him in painting a picture of the Blessed Virgin and her son which floated before his vision; just real enough to haunt his thoughts continually, and just unreal enough to refuse to be rendered by his brush. This was Raphael Sanzio d'Urbino. Now at last as he gazed on Mary the wish of his heart was realized. But he had only a pencil! On what could he draw? Just then the smooth cover of the huge wine-cask presented itself to him, and eagerly he drew upon it the outlines of Mary and her babe. This he took away with him, and rested not till with his very soul he had painted his wondrous "Madonna della Sedia." Thus was the blessing and desire of the old monk realized, and together his two daughters were distinguished for all time.

St. Marcella is represented with Lazarus and his sisters. All that is known of her is that she accompanied these saints from the East, wrote the life of Martha, and preached the gospel in Sclavonia.

St. Marcellinus. See St. Peter Exorcista.

St. Margaret (*Ital.* Santa Margarita ; *Fr.* Sainte Marguerite ; *Ger.* Die Heilige Margaretha ; Greek Ἁγ. Μαργαρίτης. Signification : A pearl.) This saint was the daughter of a priest of Antioch. She was a delicate child, and was therefore sent to a nurse in the country. This woman was a Christian, and brought Margaret up in her own faith. She was seen one day by Olybrius, who was governor of Antioch, and her beauty so impressed him that he commanded that she should be brought to his palace, and he determined to marry her if he should find that she was free born. But Margaret declared herself a Christian, to the great horror of the governor and her relatives. The latter deserted her, and Olybrius attempted to subdue her by torments of so fearful a nature, that he could not endure the sight of her agony. Still she yielded not. She was then imprisoned, and in her dungeon Satan appeared to her in the shape of a hideous dragon, and endeavored to confound her with fear. But Margaret held up a cross and he fled from her—or (as another legend teaches) he swallowed her, and instantly burst asunder, and she remained unhurt. He then came in the form of a man, to tempt her still further, but she overcame him, and placed her foot upon his head, and compelled him to confess his vile purpose and to answer her questions. Again she was taken before the governor and tortured, but her firmness was so great that she not only remained true to Christ herself, but she converted many who witnessed her devotion, so that in one day five thousand converts were baptized. Then it was determined

(Lucas v. Leyden.) St. Margaret.

that she should be beheaded, and as they led her away to death she prayed that in memory of her deliverance from the womb of the dragon, all who called on her in childbirth should be safely delivered. And a heavenly voice assured her that her prayer should be granted.

The attributes of Margaret are the palm and the dragon. She is young and girlish, and thus easily distinguished from St. Martha, who also has the dragon. Sometimes she has pearls around her head, and rarely the daisy, or marguerite, which is so named in memory of her. She is especially the type of maiden innocence and humility.

(Henry VII's Chapel.) St. Margaret.

"Si douce est la Marguerite."

In the picture by Lucas v. Leyden, she is rising from the back of the dragon, while a piece of her robe remaining in his mouth indicates that he had swallowed her. She is the patroness of women in childbirth, and patroness of Cremona. July 20. A. D. 306.

St. Margaret of Cortona, whose church is on the highest part of the hill upon which that city is built, was the Magdalene of that locality. She was born in Alviano in Tuscany. Her mother died when she was still in infancy, and the cruelty of a step-mother and the unkindness of her father drove her to desperation, and she led an evil life for several years. One of her lovers was assassinated when returning from a visit to her. A little dog which was with him returned to Margaret and attempted to lead her to the body of his master, by pulling at her robe and piteously whining. Wondering at length that her lover returned not, she went with the dog, and was horrified to find the murdered body of him she sought. She was overcome with terror and repentance, and went to her father's house. But the step-mother persuaded her father to refuse to admit her. She then retired to a vineyard near by, and here in her lonely wretchedness she was tempted to return to her sinful life. But she prayed God to be to her more than all earthly friends could be, and while so praying she had a revelation that her prayer was answered, and she was directed to go to the Franciscan convent at Cortona. This she did, and entering barefooted and with a cord about her neck, she threw herself before the altar and begged to be admitted to the Order as an humble penitent. She was refused this privilege until she should prove her penitence by a more worthy life. But at length she took the habit of St. Francis in 1272. Tradition relates that as she knelt one day before the crucifix, Christ bowed his head in answer to her prayers, and from that time she was held in great reverence by the people of Cortona. She is painted young and beautiful, her dress not always that of the nun, but usually with the cord for a girdle, which indicates the Third Order of St. Francis. Her attribute is a dog, which is seldom omitted. February 22, A. D. 1297.

St. Marina. The sad story of this saint presents a touching illustration of self-sacrifice and unbounded humility, for which she was greatly reverenced. Her father was an eastern hermit, and when he first went to the desert he so longed for this daughter whom he had left that he dressed her in male attire, and charged her that she should never reveal her sex. He then took her with him to his retreat, and there she grew up as Brother Marinus. She was frequently sent to the shores of the Red Sea with a wagon and oxen to get supplies for the monks. The man to whom she went had a daughter who was found to be with child, and she wickedly accused Marinus of being her seducer. Marina did not deny the charge, and the abbot ordered her to be scourged and driven out of the walls of the monastery, and the wicked woman came with her child, and putting it in the arms of Marina said, "There, as you are its father take care of it." Then Marina cared for the child. She remained outside the gate of the convent and begged a support, which was given her with many insults, as to a vile sinner. But when she died and the truth was discovered, there was great mourning on account of all she had endured, and she was reverenced for her humility. She is represented with the dress of a monk and the face of a beautiful woman with a child in her arms. June 18. Eighth century.

Santa Maria Maddalena de' Pazzi was of the noble Florentine family whose name she bears. No events of her life are related, but she was a Carmelite nun, and of extreme sanctity and humility, for which she was canonized. May 27, A. D. 1607.

Maria Maggiore, Santa. This splendid church at Rome is said to owe its origin to a vision related in a legend, called that "of the Snow!" in Italian, "della Neve." Giovanni Patricio, a Roman who was rich and childless, prayed the Virgin to direct him how he should dispose of his wealth. On the fifth of August, A. D. 352, Mary came to him in a dream, and commanded him to build a church in her name on the spot where he should find snow the next morning. His wife and the Pope Liberius each had the same vision; and early next day they all went to the Esquiline, where they found miraculous snow, in spite of the heat of the season. Liberius traced upon it, with his crosier, the plan of the church, and here the church was built. Murillo painted two beautiful pictures of this legend, called in Spanish S. Maria la Blanca.

St. Mark (*Lat.* S. Marcus; *Ital.* San Marco Evangelista; *Fr.* St. Marc; *Ger.* Der Heilige Marcus). This Evangelist was not an apostle, but a convert and beloved disciple of St. Peter, according to the tradition of the Roman Church. He journeyed with Peter even to Rome, where he wrote his Gospel, and many believe it to have been dictated by St. Peter. He went afterwards to preach in Egypt, and after spending twelve years in Libya and the Thebais, he founded his church at Alexandria. On account of his miracles the heathen accused him of being a magician, and at length when celebrating the feast of their god Serapis, they seized St. Mark and dragged him through the streets with cords until he died. Then immediately there fell a storm of hail, and a tempest of lightning came with it which destroyed his murderers. The Christians buried his remains, and his tomb was greatly venerated. But in A. D. 815, some Venetian merchants despoiled the tomb of its sacred relics and took them to Venice, where the splendid Cathedral of San Marco was erected over them. There are many legends of this saint which have afforded subjects for representations in art. One day as he walked in Alexandria, it is said that he saw a poor cobbler who had wounded his hand so severely with an awl, that he could no longer support himself. St. Mark healed the wound, and the man, who was called Anianus, was converted and afterwards became Bishop of Alexandria. The famous legend of the preservation of Venice is thus related: It was on the twenty-fifth of February in 1340. The waters had been rising for three days, and on this night there was a fearful storm, and the height of the water was three cubits more than ever before. An old fisherman, with difficulty, reached the Riva di San Marco with his little boat, and determined to wait there for the ceasing of the tempest. But there came to him a man who entreated him to row over to San Giorgio Maggiore. After great persuasion, the fisherman, believing it to be the will of God, consented. Having arrived at San Giorgio, the stranger landed and commanded the fisherman to await his return. He came bringing with him a young man, and they told him to row again to San Niccolo di Lido. The poor man doubted his ability to do this, but they assured him he might row boldly and strength would be given him. Then they came at last to San Niccolo di Lido, where the two men landed. When they returned to the shore there was a third one also. Then they ordered the fisherman to row beyond the two castles. When they came to the sea, they saw a bark filled with frightful demons rapidly approaching. They were coming to overwhelm the city with water. Then the three men in the boat made the sign of the cross and bade the demons depart, and instantly the bark vanished, the sea became calm, and the waters began to subside. Then the men commanded the boatman to land them at the places from which they had come. He did so, but in spite of the great wonder he had seen he demanded of the third that he should pay him. Then the man replied, "Thou art right; go now to the Doge and to the Procuratori of St. Mark; tell them what thou hast seen, for Venice would have been overwhelmed had it not been for us three. I am St. Mark the Evangelist, the protector of this city; the other is the brave knight St. George; and he whom thou didst take up at the Lido is the holy bishop St. Nicholas. Say to the Doge and to the Procuratori that they are to pay you; and tell them likewise that this tempest arose because of a certain schoolmaster dwelling at San Felice, who did sell his soul to the Devil and afterwards hanged himself." The fisherman answered that his story would not be believed. Then St. Mark took from his finger a ring, and gave it to the man and said, "Show them this, and tell them when they look in the sanctuary they will not find it." And he then disappeared. The next morning the fisherman did as he had been commanded, and it proved as he had been told, and the ring was not found. Then the man was paid, a procession was ordained with great solemnity, and they gave thanks to God and the three saints for their miraculous deliverance. The fisherman received a pension, and the ring was given to the Procuratori, who replaced it in the sanctuary. Another legend relates that a certain slave, whose master resided in Provence, persisted in going to the shrine of St. Mark to pray, for which he was condemned to be tortured. As the sentence was about to be executed, St. Mark descended to save his votary. The executioners were confounded, and the instruments of torture broken and made unfit for use. The tradition which makes St. Mark the amanuensis of St. Peter is frequently illustrated in paintings. The attribute of St. Mark is the lion either with or without the wings, but generally with them. This enables one to distinguish him from St. Jerome, who has the lion unwinged. He often wears the robes of a bishop. April 25, A. D. 68.

St. Martha (*Ital.* Santa Marta, Vergine, Albergatrice di Christo; *Fr.* Sainte Marthe, la Travailleuse). St. Martha is highly venerated on account of having persuaded her sister Mary to listen to the words of Jesus, thus becoming the instrument of her conversion. The old story in "Il Perfetto Legendario" goes on to say of this, "Which thing should not be accounted as the least of her merits, seeing that Martha was a chaste and prudent virgin, and the other publicly contemned for her evil life; notwithstanding which, Martha did not despise her, nor reject her as a sister, but wept for her shame, and admonished her gently and with persuasive words, and reminded her of her noble birth, to which she was a disgrace, and that Lazarus, their brother, being a soldier, would certainly get into trouble on her account. So she prevailed and conducted her sister to the presence of Christ, and afterwards, as it is well known, she lodged and entertained the Saviour in her own house." The Provençal legends relate that Martha was the first who founded a convent for her own sex, and the first one after the Blessed Virgin who consecrated her virginity to God. While Mary Magdalene made converts in Marseilles, Martha preached at Aix. In those days there was a fearful dragon who inhabited the river Rhone, and ravaged the country by night. He was called the Tarasque, and on the scene of his life the city of Tarascon now stands. Now Martha sprinkled this monster with holy water and bound him with her girdle, and then he was speedily killed by the people. When after many years of labor, death approached, she desired to be borne to some spot where she could see the sun in the heavens. She wished the story of the Passion of Our Lord to be read to her, and as she died she said, "Father, into thy hands I commend my spirit." Her attribute is a dragon, and she may be known from St. Margaret by the pot of holy water, while the latter has the cross. St. Martha also bears sometimes, a cooking utensil. Patroness of cooks and housewives. June 29, A. D. 84.

St. Martial was Bishop of Limoges. St. Valérie or Valère was a beautiful virgin who was converted by his teaching. She refused to listen to the addresses of the Duke de Guyenne. This so enraged the duke that he "luy fit trancher la teste, couronnant sa virginité d'un martyre bien signalé, car à la venuë d'un chacun elle prit sa teste, et la porta jusques au pied de l'Autel ou S. Marcial disect la messe; le bourreau, la suivant pas-à-pas, mourut dans l'Eglise, après avoir clairement protesté qu'il voyoit les anges à l'entour de son corps." This legend is illustrated in the Cathedral of Limoges. She is represented with a streak around the neck. Her festival is December 10.

St. Martin of Tours (*Lat.* Sanctus Martinus; *Ital.* San Martino) was one of the most popular saints of the Middle Ages. He was born at Saberia in Pannonia in the time of Constantine the Great; and tradition relates that on one occasion the Empress Helena, who was the daughter of a wealthy lord of Caernarvonshire, prepared for him a supper with her own hands, and waited on him while he ate it, in the same manner as that of the humblest servant; and at the end gathered up the crumbs, estimating them as more precious than any meal she could eat at the emperor's board. From a child St. Martin was of a religious disposition, but became a soldier before he was baptized. In the army he won the love and respect of his comrades, by the great excellences of his character and the purity of his life. He was especially noted for his benevolence and charities to the poor. The winter of 332 was so severely cold that large numbers perished in the streets of Amiens where the regiment of St. Martin was quartered. One day he met at the gate a naked man, and taking pity on him he divided his cloak (for it was all he had), and gave half to the beggar. That night in a

(Martin Schoen.) St. Martin.

dream Jesus stood before him, and on his shoulders he wore the half of the cloak that Martin had given the beggar. And he said to the angels who attended him, "Know ye who hath thus arrayed me? My servant Martin, though yet unbaptized, hath done this." Then Martin was immediately baptized; and he was at the time twenty-three years old. At forty years of age, he desired to leave the army that he might devote all his time to God's service. Then the legend tells, that Julian the Apostate being now emperor, accused him of cowardice, saying that he wished to be dismissed to avoid a coming battle. But Martin replied, he would be set naked in the front of the fight, armed only with the cross, and not fear to meet the enemy

Then the Emperor commanded men to guard him and see that this was done; but before the time of battle peace was made, and it was not attempted. After leading a religious life for years he was made Bishop of Tours in 371. He did many miracles, healing the sick, and even restoring to life the son of a poor widow. One day as he celebrated mass in his cathedral he asked his deacon to clothe a naked beggar before him. The deacon did not comply readily, and St. Martin took off his priestly robe and gave it to the wretched man; and while he officiated at the altar a globe of fire was seen above his head, and as he elevated the Host, his arms (being exposed on account of the absence of the garment) were covered by a miracle, with chains of gold and silver, which angels fastened upon them. His evenness of temper was an especial virtue, and he was never angry, neither spoke he ever unkindly. In spite of all he was greatly tempted, and Satan one day ridiculed him, because he so soon received the sinful who repented. St. Martin replied, "O, most miserable that thou art! if thou also couldst cease to persecute and seduce wretched men, if thou also couldst repent, thou also shouldst find mercy and forgiveness through Jesus Christ!" It is due to the wonderful energy of St. Martin that paganism was rooted out of that portion of Gaul where he ruled the Church. He destroyed temples, demolished the images of the gods, and was impervious to all threats and dangers which he incurred by so doing. The demons whom he thus disenthroned often appeared to him, sometimes in hideous forms, and again with all the beauty of Venus; but he overcame all fear and all temptation, and steadfastly served God. At length he wearied of the numbers who pressed about him, and he built himself a cell away from Tours, between the rocks and the Loire. From this the monastery of Marmoutier arose. St. Martin not only opposed heathenism, he battled against blind superstition as well. There was near Tours a chapel where the people worshipped a martyr, as they believed. But Martin thought them mistaken. He went and stood on the sepulchre and prayed that it might be revealed to him, if any martyr rested there. Soon a dark form appeared and told St. Martin that he was a robber whose soul was in hell, and whose body rested beneath him, where he stood. Then the saint destroyed the chapel and altar as he did those of the pagans. He was once invited to sup with the emperor. The cup was passed to Martin before his majesty drank, with the expectation that he would touch it to his lips, as was the custom. But a poor priest stood behind Martin, and to the surprise and admiration of all, the saint presented the full goblet to him, thus signifying that a servant of God deserved more honor, however humble his station, than any merely earthly rank. From this legend he has been chosen the patron of drinking and all joyous meetings. It is said that on an occasion when St. Martin sought an interview with the Emperor Valentinian, his majesty did not rise from his chair as the saint approached, whereupon the chair took fire beneath him, and necessity compelled him to do what reverence had no power to effect. This unique legend has been represented in art. St. Martin died after being bishop more than thirty years, and many heard the songs of the angels who bore him to Paradise. From the time of his death he has been an object of extreme veneration. In art he is usually represented with a naked beggar at his feet. A goose when introduced alludes to the season of his feast, which occurs at the time when geese are eaten, and is called in England, Martinmas-tide. In France this festival was kept like the last day of the Carnival, — a time of feasting and excess. November 11, A. D. 397.

St. Martina was a Roman virgin. A church dedicated to her stands at the foot of the Capitoline Hill. It is on the left as we descend to the Forum from the Ara Cœli. Here from very ancient times there was a chapel where the people venerated this saint, who was martyred in the time of Alexander Severus. In 1634, when repairing this chapel, a sarcophagus was discovered built into the foundations, which contained the body of a young woman, while the head was in a separate casket. This being regarded as the body of the saint, called the attention of all Rome to the place, and even the Pope was filled with enthusiasm at the discovery. Cardinal Francesco Barberini undertook to rebuild the church, and Pietro da Cortona very solemnly dedicated his talents to the work of adorning the same. The church was given to the academy of painters and consecrated to St. Luke, their patron. It now bears the name of " San Luca e Santa Martina." Pietro da Cortona left all his fortune to the chapel of St. Martina, which he had himself painted. She is represented as young and beautiful, with different instruments of torture, signifying the manner of her death. January 30.

St. Mary of Egypt (*Ital.* Santa Maria Egiziaca Penitente; *Fr.* Sainte Marie l'Egyptienne, La Gipesienne, La Jussienne). The legend of this Mary Egyptiaca is much older than that of Mary Magdalene. It was in a written form, and fully believed in the sixth century, for a very ancient tradition taught that a female hermit had dwelt for years in Palestine, and there died. The legend as now given is rested on the authority of St. Jerome, and relates that a woman named Mary, whose wickedness far excelled that of the Magdalene, dwelt in Alexandria, and after seventeen years of abandonment to sin, in the year 365, as she walked one day near the sea, she saw a vessel about to depart well filled with pilgrims. On inquiry she found that they were going to Jerusalem to keep the feast of the true cross. She was seized with anxiety to go also, but had no money to pay her passage. Then she sold herself to the sailors and pilgrims and so accomplished the journey. Arriving at Jerusalem she thought to enter the church with the others, but when she reached the entrance some invisible power held her so that she could not go in, and as often as she tried to cross the threshold, so often was she driven back. Then a sense of all her sins came over her and she was overcome with sorrow, and prayed to God for grace and pardon. Then the restraining power was taken away, and she entered the church on her knees. She then bought three loaves of bread and went into the desert, even beyond Jordan. Here she remained in deepest penitence. She drank only water, and subsisted

(Pietro da Cortona.) Death of St. Mary of Egypt.

on roots and fruits, and her three loaves, which were constantly renewed by a miracle. Her clothing wore out and dropped from her; then she prayed God to clothe her and her prayer was answered, for her hair became a cloak about her, or as others say, a heavenly robe was brought her by an angel. She had lived thus forty-seven years when she was found by Zosimus, a priest. She begged him to keep silence concerning her, and to return at the end of a year and bring with him the holy wafer that she might confess her sins and receive the communion before her death. Zosimus complied with her desires and returned to her in a year. He was not able to cross the Jordan, and Mary was miraculously assisted to cross to him. After receiving the sacrament she requested him to leave her again to her solitary life, and to return at the end of another year. When the year was passed and he went again to meet her, he found her lying dead, with her hands folded as in prayer. And upon the sands these words were written: "O, Father Zosimus, bury the body of the poor sinner, Mary of Egypt! Give earth to earth, and dust to dust, for Christ's sake!" When he endeavored to do this he found he had not sufficient strength, for he was an old man. Then a lion came and assisted him, digging with his paws; and when the body of Mary was in the grave the lion went quietly away and Zosimus returned home, praising God for the mercy He had shown to the penitent woman. She is represented in art as old, worn, and wasted, with long hair, and three loaves of bread in her hand. When united with Mary Magdalene the contrast of age, appearance, and dress is very striking. The pictures of her penance are sometimes mistaken for the Magdalene, but if the vase, skull, and crucifix are wanting it is the Mary of Egypt. A chapel in the Church of St. Merry in Paris is painted with scenes from her life. April 2, A. D. 433.

(Statue, Donatello, Florence.) St. Mary Magdalene.

St. Mary Magdalene (Lat. Sancta Maria Magdalena; *Fr.* La Madeleine; La Sainte Demoiselle pécheresse; *Ital.* Santa Maria Maddalena; *Sp.* Santa Maria Magdalena). The writings which would fill volumes, the numberless sermons which have exhausted the talents of the preachers and the patience of the hearers, the learned arguments of tongue and pen, and the wild, imaginative legends which have each and all essayed to give and establish the truth about this saint, have left her, in the *heart of the world*, what the gospel alone and unaided makes her, — the *first* sinning and repenting woman forgiven through the love of Jesus, a glorious beacon of hope, shining down through all ages, *silently saying* to every other magdalene, "go and sin no more." It has never been decided whether she was differently spoken of as "Mary of Bethany," the "woman who was a sinner," and she "out of whom Jesus cast seven devils," or whether she was but one of these; but the legend as it is generally represented in western art is as follows: Mary Magdalene was the daughter of noble, if not royal parents, and the sister of Martha and Lazarus. Syrus, their father, had vast riches, and at his death they were divided equally between the three. The castle of Mary, called Magdalon, was in the district of Magdala on the shore of the sea of Tiberias. Lazarus was by profession a soldier. Martha was virtuous and discreet, but Mary, giving herself up to luxury and idleness, became at length so wicked as to be called "THE SINNER." Martha, loving her sister, and filled with sorrow by her sinful life, continually rebuked her and finally persuaded her to listen to the teachings of Jesus. The seven evil spirits which Jesus cast out were the seven deadly sins, to which she had been subject before her conversion. The entertainment of the Saviour at the house of Martha, the supper at the house of Simon the Pharisee, the devotion of Mary to Jesus, and the scenes connected with his death and resurrection, are given in the legend as in the Gospels. It then adds, that after the ascension of Christ, Lazarus and his sisters with their handmaid Marcella, Maximin who had baptized them, and the blind man to whom Jesus had given sight, called Cedon, were placed in a boat with no rudder to steer and no oars or sails to speed them, and set adrift. This was done by the heathen. They were carried by winds and waves to a harbor which proved to be that of Marseilles. The people of that place were also heathen, and they refused to give the castaways food or shelter. Then they found a resting-place in the porch of a temple, and Mary began to preach of Christ, and to urge the people to forsake their idols. And both the sisters did such miracles that many were converted and baptized. When Maximin was dead, Lazarus was made first bishop of Marseilles. But Mary desired to live in solitude, and retired to a frightful wilderness, where she lived thirty years a life of penitence and sorrow for the sins she never ceased to regret and bewail. It was supposed she was dead, but at length a hermit whose cell was in the same desert as her own saw a miraculous sight which disclosed the truth that she still lived. It appears that often in her hunger and exhaustion angels had ministered to her, and during the last years of her life they bore her, each day, up into regions where she could hear celestial harmonies, and see the glory prepared for those who repent and believe in God. It was this daily ascension that the hermit saw, and he hastened to the city to relate the wonderful vision. Legends disagree concerning the place and manner of her death. Some relate that it occurred in the desert, where angels watched over her and cared for her, while others say she died in a church, after receiving the last sacrament from St. Maximin. The scene of her solitary penance is said to be the site of the monastery of La Sainte Beaume, or the Holy Cave, between Marseilles and Toulon. In the thirteenth century some remains, believed to be those of St. Lazarus and Mary Magdalene, were found about twenty miles north of Toulon, at a place called St. Maximin. Here a church was built in 1279 by Charles count of Provence, brother of St. Louis king of France. A few years later Charles was made prisoner by the king of Aragon, and he ascribed the praise of his liberation to Mary Magdalene, who was his chosen protectress. She performed many miracles, one of which has been frequently represented in pictures. A certain prince of Provence came to Marseilles with his wife to sacrifice to the pagan gods. They listened to the preaching of Mary, and were persuaded to leave the service of the idols. One day the husband told Mary of his strong desire to have a son. And Mary asked him if he would believe if his prayer were heard. And he promised that he would believe. Not long after this prince decided to go to Jerusalem to see St. Peter, and to ascertain if the doctrines of the Magdalene were the same as those of that saint. The wife determined to go also, but he said, "How shall that be possible, seeing that thou art with child, and the dangers of the sea are very great?" But she so entreated him that he granted her request, and they departed. After a day and night had passed a terrible storm arose. The pains of childbirth came upon the woman, and in the midst of the tempest the babe was born and the mother died. The sailors wished to throw the body into the sea, believing that the storm would not cease while it remained in the ship; but the prince persuaded them with entreaties and money to retain it awhile. Soon they arrived at an island, where he laid his wife on the shore, and placing the babe on her breast he covered them with his cloak and wept bitterly, and said, "O, Mary Magdalene! to my grief and sorrow didst thou come to Marseilles! Why didst thou ask thy God to give me a son only that I might lose both son and wife together? O, Mary Magdalene! have pity on my grief, and if thy prayers may avail, save at least the life of my child!" Then he proceeded to Jerusalem and remained there two years. And he was instructed by St. Peter and saw the places which had been hallowed by the life and death of the Saviour. Now on his return he landed at the island where he had left the body of his wife, that he might weep at her last resting-place. Who can tell his surprise when he saw his child running about on the shore? And when the infant saw the strange man, he was afraid and hid beneath the cloak that covered his dead mother. Then when the father approached, the mother also opened her eyes and smiled, and put out her arms to embrace her husband. Then did the prince greatly rejoice, and they all returned to Marseilles and threw themselves at the feet of the Magdalene and were baptized. There are legends (though never accepted by the Church) which relate that an attachment existed between St. John the Evangelist and Mary Magdalene; and even that the feast which Jesus attended at Cana of Galilee was on the occasion of the marriage of these two saints. Donatello's famous statue, carved in wood, stands above her altar in the baptistery in Florence. It represents her as the wasted, sorrowing penitent, and is strangely in contrast with the loveliness of many representations of her. Her proper attribute is the jar of ointment. This signifies either the ointment which she brake upon the feet of the Saviour, or that which she prepared for the anointing of his crucified body. It varies in size and form; is usually either in her hand or standing near her, though sometimes borne by an attending angel. The colors of the dress of the Magdalene are red, expressing love; violet, penitence and mourning; and blue, constancy. Sometimes she wears a violet tunic and red mantle. Some Spanish pictures represent her with dark hair; but it should be luxuriant, fair, and golden. Patroness of frail and penitent women; — of Provence and Marseilles. July 22, A. D. 68.

St. Mary the Penitent (*Ital.* Santa Maria Penitente; *Fr.* Sainte Marie, la Penitente). This Mary was the niece of the hermit Abraham, and her life was mostly spent in the deserts of Syria. She too was a sinner and became a penitent, to whose prayers God granted miraculous answers. Her father had large riches and lived in splendor. When he died the daughter was carried to her hermit uncle to be religiously instructed. She was seven years old when taken to the desert. Abraham built a cell close to his own and opening into it by a window, and there placed the child. Here he taught her to pray, to sing praises, to recite psalms, and to despise the pleasures of the world. Thus Mary lived until she was twenty years old. At this time there came a young hermit to the cell of Abraham to receive his instructions. The beauty of the face which he beheld by chance through the window, and the music of the voice which chanted holy praises so near him, inflamed his heart with love for the maiden, and he tempted her to sin, forgetting his vows. When she at length reflected on what she had done, she so feared her uncle that she fled from his sight and went to a remote place where for two years she lived a shameless life of sin. Now on the very night that she fled, Abraham dreamed that a hideous dragon came to his cell and found there a white dove and took it away with him. When he awoke the dream troubled him. Again when he slept he saw the same dragon, and he crushed his head with his foot, and took the dove from its maw and put it in his bosom. Then the dove came to life, and spreading its wings, flew to heaven. Then the hermit knew that this dream referred to his beloved Mary. He took his staff and went forth seeking her through all the land.

After a long time he found her, and when she was overcome with shame and sorrow he encouraged her, and promised himself to do penance for her. Then she cried out, "O, my father! if thou thinkest there is hope for me, I will follow thee whithersoever thou goest, and kiss thy footsteps which lead me out of this gulf of sin and death!" Then he comforted her, and leaving behind all her jewels and gay attire she returned with him to the cell in the desert. Here she ministered to her aged uncle and lived a life of contrition and penance. And for many years after his death she still continued the same life, and so great was the virtue of her prayers that the sick who were brought to her were cured when she prayed. When she died she was borne by angels to Paradise. Conversion of Mary the Penitent, October 29.

St. Matthias (*Ital.* San Mattia; *Fr.* St. Mathias; *Lat.* Sanctus Matthæus) was the last apostle, chosen to take the place made vacant by the treachery of Judas. St. Denis relates that he was selected by the Apostles on account of a beam of divine splendor which pointed to him. This has been represented in art. He preached in Judæa and was martyred by the Jews. His attribute is a lance or an axe. February 24.

St. Matthew (*Lat.* S. Mattheus; *Ger.* Der Heilige Matthäus; *Fr.* St. Matthieu; *Ital.* San Matteo). Among the Evangelists St. Matthew holds the first place on account of having written his Gospel first. In representations of the disciples he is the seventh or eighth. He has not been a popular subject of art. The Scripture account only tells that his name was Levi, and his office that of tax-gatherer. A Hebrew by birth. When Christ called him, he immediately left all else to obey; and he also made a great feast in his house, at which Jesus with his disciples sat with publicans and sinners to the horror of the Jews. After the separation of the Apostles, Matthew preached twenty-three years in Egypt and Ethiopia. At the capital of Ethiopia, he was honorably entertained by that eunuch whom Philip had baptized. He raised the son of the King of Egypt from the dead, and cured his daughter, called Iphigenia, of leprosy, and placed her at the head of a society of young maidens, dedicated to the service of God. A heathen king determined to take her away from this community, on

St. Matthew.

account of which his palace was burned, and he became a leper. When this saint was in Ethiopia a terrible fear was over the people, on account of two skillful magicians who put many under their spells, and afflicted them with dreadful diseases. St. Matthew overcame these sorcerers, and ended their power by baptizing the people. All this is related in the "Perfetto Legendario." The manner of his death is doubtful. The Greek legend says he died a peaceful death, but the western traditions teach that he suffered martyrdom in the time of Domitian. His proper attributes are the purse when represented as an apostle; the pen and book, with an attendant angel, when he is the Evangelist. The angel holds the inkhorn or the book; or points to heaven, or dictates. Greek pictures of his death show him dying peacefully, while an angel swings a censer; other representations give the martyrdom by the sword. September 21, A. D. 90.

(Hemshirk.) St. Maurice.

St. Maurelio or **Maurelius** was the first bishop, and is the patron saint of Ferrara and Imola. His image is on the coins of Ferrara. He was beheaded.

St. Maurice (*Lat.* Sanctus Mauritius; *Ital.* San Maurizio; *Ger.* Der Heilige Moritz; *Fr.* St. Maurice). The legend of St. Maurice and the Theban Legion is one of the most ancient of all legends, and has been so received as to have almost the same importance, as if it were a strictly historical fact. The Theban Legion was so called because levied in the Thebaïd. It was composed of 6,666 men, all of whom were Christians. It was commanded by Maurice, who was of illustrious descent. This legion was so characterized by valor, piety, and fidelity, that it had received the title of *Felix*. When Maximin was about to enter Gaul, he ordered this legion to accompany him thither. When they had passed the Alps the legion was divided: a part went to the Rhine, and the remainder halted on the banks of Lake Geneva. Here Maximin ordered a great sacrifice to the gods, with all the games and festivities which accompanied the pagan rites. There Maurice and his soldiers separated themselves from the army, and pitched their camp at a place now called Saint Maurice, but then Aganum. Maximin then made it known that the purpose of his expedition was the extermination of the Christians, and threatened the Theban Legion with his vengeance if they did not join in the sacrifices. They steadfastly refused to do so or to assist in the persecution of the Christians. Then Maximin commanded the men to be decimated. Those to whom the lot fell rejoiced in being thus chosen to testify to their faith, and those who were left were still so determined that they were decimated the second time. Even when the third summons came Maurice replied, "O Cæsar! we are thy soldiers, but we are also the soldiers of Jesus Christ. From thee we receive our pay, but from Him we have received eternal life. To thee we owe service, to him obedience. We are ready to follow thee against the Barbarians; but we are also ready to suffer death, rather than renounce our faith, or fight against our brethren." Then Maximin commanded that the rest of the army should surround these men, and murder every one with the sword. He was obeyed, — not one was left alive. But some were trampled to death, some hanged, and some shot with arrows. Maurice knelt down and was beheaded. At Cologne, and in other places, many more who belonged to the Theban Legion suffered martyrdom. Savoy, Piedmont, and parts of Germany abound in these soldier saints. The name of Maurice signifies "a Moor," and he is represented as one in some pictures. He is dressed in armor, and bears the standard and the palm. In Italian pictures he wears a red cross on his breast, which is the badge of the Sardinian Order of St. Maurice. September 22, A. D. 286.

St. Maurus was the son of a Roman senator, and was placed under the care of St. Benedict at Subiaco, when only twelve years old. He became one of the most famous disciples of his great Master. At one time Maurus expressed his satisfaction at the death of one Florentius, who had attempted to poison St. Benedict, and had committed many crimes which disgraced his office (for he was a priest); this expression so shocked his teacher that he commanded him to atone for his sin by a severe penance. After the death of Benedict, Maurus introduced the Benedictine Order into France, and founded the monastery of St. Maure-sur-Loire (then called Glanfeuil), where he died. His attribute is the book or censer. January 15, A. D. 584.

St. Mercuriale was the first Bishop of Forli in the second century. His attribute is a dragon, representing sin, which the saint had vanquished. He is patron saint of Forli.

St. Mercurius (*Gr.* Ἅγ. Ἑρμῆς. Signification: God's Messenger). The representations of this saint belong especially to Greek art. He was an officer whom Julian the Apostate put to death on account of his Christian faith. When Julian afterwards fought against the Persians, St. Basil had a vision in which he saw a woman seated on a throne, and surrounded by angels. To one of these she said, "Go forthwith, and awaken Mercurius, who sleepeth in the sepulchre, that he may slay Julian the Apostate, that proud blasphemer against me and against my Son!" As soon as the vision had passed Basil went to the tomb of Mercurius, but neither the body nor the armor which had been buried with him were in the tomb. But the next day the body of the saint and all the armor was as before, except that the lance was stained with blood. "For on the day of battle, when the wicked emperor was at the head of his army, an unknown warrior, bareheaded, and of a pale and ghastly countenance, was seen mounted on a white charger, which he spurred forward; and, brandishing his lance, he pierced Julian through the body, and then vanished as suddenly as he had appeared. And Julian being carried to his tent, he took a handful of the blood which flowed from his wound, and flung it into the air, exclaiming with his last breath, 'Thou hast conquered, Galilean! Thou hast conquered!' Then the demons received his parting spirit. But Mercurius, having performed the behest of the Blessed Virgin, re-entered his tomb, and laid himself down to sleep till the Day of Judgment."

St. Methodius. See St. Cyril.

(Cathedral of Cortona, about 7th century.) St. Michael.

St. Michael (*Lat.* Sanctus Michael Angelus; *Fr.* Monseigneur Saint Michel; *Ital.* San Michele, Sammichele; Ἅγ. Μιχαήλ). St. Michael, whose name signifies "like unto God," or Michael the Archangel, is regarded as the first and mightiest of all created spirits. He it was whom God commissioned to expel Satan and the rebellious angels from heaven. His office now is believed to be twofold, — including that of patron saint of the Church on earth, and Lord of the souls of the dead; deciding their merits, presenting the good to God, and sending the evil and wicked away to torment. It is believed to have been St. Michael who appeared to Hagar (Gen. xxi. 17), to Abraham to forbid the sacrifice of Isaac (Gen. xxii. 11); who brought the plagues on Egypt, led the

Israelites on their journey, contended with Satan for the body of Moses (Jude 5), put blessings instead of curses in Balaam's mouth (Num. xxii. 35), was with Joshua at Jericho (Josh. v. 13), appeared to Gideon (Judges vi. 11), brought the pestilence to Israel (2 Sam. xxiv. 16), destroyed the Assyrian army (2 Chron. xxxii. 21), delivered the three faithful Jews from the fiery furnace (Dan. iii. 25), and sent Habakkuk to feed Daniel in the lion's den (Bel and the Dragon, 32). The legends also relate that St. Michael appeared to the Virgin Mary to announce to her the time of her death, and that he received her soul and bore it to Jesus. And again, that during the sixth century, when a fearful pestilence was raging in Rome, St. Gregory advised that a procession should be made, which should pass through the streets singing the service which since then has been called the Great Litanies. This was done for three days, and on the last day, when they came opposite to the tomb of Hadrian, Gregory beheld the Archangel Michael hovering over the city; and he alighted on the top of the Mausoleum and sheathed his sword, which was dripping with blood. Then the plague was stayed, and the Tomb of Hadrian has been called the Castle of Sant' Angelo from that day, and a chapel was there consecrated, the name of which was Ecclesia Sancti Angeli usque ad Cœlos. St. Michael is also said to have appeared to command the building of two churches. The first was on the eastern coast of Italy, and was called the Church of Monte Galgano. The legend relates that in the fifth century there dwelt in Siponte a man named Galgano, who was very rich in herds which were pastured on the mountain. At one time a bull strayed away and Galgano took his servants and went to find him, and when he was seen he was on the very summit of the mountain, near the mouth of a cave. And Galgano was angry with the bull and ordered a servant to kill it; but the arrow came back to the bosom of him who sent it, and killed him instantly. Then Galgano being troubled, sent to the bishop to know what he should do. Then the bishop fasted and prayed for three days, at the end of which time, St. Michael appeared to him and told him that the spot where the bull had been was especially sacred to him, and he could not permit it to be violated by blood, and he commanded that a church should be built there and sanctified to his service. And when they entered the cave they found a stream of water running from the rock, which cured all manner of diseases; and three altars were already built there, and one was covered with a rich cloth embroidered in crimson and gold. So the fame of this vision spread through all Europe, and the church which was there built became a resort for numerous pilgrims. Again in the reign of Childebert II. St. Michael appeared to St. Aubert, Bishop of Avranches, and commanded that a church should be built on the summit of a rock in the Gulf of

Avranches, in Normandy. This rock is inaccessible at high water, and has been celebrated as an impregnable fortress. The bishop was also told that a bull would be found concealed there and a spring of pure water, and the church should be made to cover as much ground as the bull had trampled. St. Aubert considered this as but a dream, but it was repeated again and again, and the third time the Archangel pressed his thumb upon the head of the bishop

(Martin Schoen.) St. Michael.

and left there a mark which never disappeared. After this a small church was built which was afterwards replaced by a magnificent abbey, commenced by Richard, Duke of Normandy, and completed by William the Conqueror. Mont-Saint-Michel became one of the most celebrated places of pilgrimage, as it is one of the most picturesque in scenery, but the legend seems only a poor repetition of that of Monte Galgano. From this time St. Michael was greatly venerated in France. He was selected as patron saint of the country and of the Order which St. Louis instituted in his honor. An old French writer also makes him the angel of good counsel, and says, "Le vrai office de Monseigneur Saint Michel est de faire grandes revelations aux hommes en bas, en leur donnant moult saints conseils," and particularly "sur le bon nourissement que le père et la mère donnent à leurs enfans." St. Michael is always represented as young and beautiful. As patron of the Church Militant he is "the winged saint," with no attribute save the shield and lance. As conqueror of Satan, he stands in armor, with his foot upon the Evil One, who is half human or like a dragon in shape. The angel is about to chain him or to transfix him with the lance. But the treatment of this subject is varied in many ways, all however easily recognized. As lord of souls St. Michael is unarmed; he holds a balance, and in each scale a little naked figure representing the souls; the *beato* usually joins the hands as in thankfulness, while the rejected one expresses horror in look and attitude. Frequently a demon is seizing the falling scale with a Plutonic hook, or with his talons. In these pictures the saint is rarely without wings. When introduced in pictures of the Madonna and Child he presents the balance to Christ, who seems to welcome the happy soul. Whether with or without the balance, he is always the lord of souls in pictures of the death, assumption, or glorification of the Virgin Mary, for tradition teaches that he received her spirit and cared for it until it was reunited to her body and ascended to her Son. The old English coin called an angel was so named because it bore the image of this archangel. September 29. Apparition of St. Michael, May 8.

St. Miniato or **Minias.** The Florentine legend relates that this saint was an Armenian prince who belonged to the Roman army and served under Decius. When that emperor was encamped outside the city of Florence, Miniato was denounced as a Christian and condemned to be thrown to the beasts of the amphitheatre. A panther was first set upon him, but the saint was delivered from him in answer to his prayers. He was then hanged, put in boiling oil, and stoned without being destroyed, for an angel descended to comfort him, and clothed him in a garment of light. Finally he was beheaded. It is said that this occurred in 254. He is represented dressed as a prince with scarlet robe and a crown. His attributes are the palm, the lily, and javelins.

St. Modwena was an Irish virgin who had power to heal diseases. King Egbert had a son who was epileptic, and no physician of his court could heal him. Now the king hearing of the power of Modwena sent his son over seas to her with many and rich gifts. The virgin refused the presents but she healed the sick boy. Then the king sent for her to come to England. He was surprised at her learning and piety, and he built for her a convent at Polesworth, in Warwickshire, and gave his daughter Edith into her care. This Edith of Polesworth, as she is called, also became famous and was canonized. St. Modwena is represented in the black habit of a Benedictine nun with a white veil. In one hand a crosier, as first abbess of her monastery, and in the other a book. July 5, A. D. 1387.

St. Monica (*Fr.* Sainte Monique) was the mother of St. Augustine and a Christian, while his father was a heathen. Monica was sorely troubled at the dissipated life of her young son; she wept and prayed for him, and at last sought the advice and aid of the Bishop of Carthage. He dismissed her with these words: "Go in peace; the son of so many tears will not perish." At length she had the joy to behold the baptism of St. Augustine by the Bishop of Milan, in which city it took place. She is venerated as the first Augustine nun. She is represented in many of the pictures illustrative of the life of St. Augustine. Her dress is a black robe with veil or coif of white or gray. In one picture in Florence she is seated on a throne and attended by twelve nuns or saints. This represents her as the foundress of the Augustine Order of nuns. May 4, A. D. 387.

Moses, The Patriarch. There are some legends concerning Moses, so entirely outside all connection with the Scripture account of him that the pictures which are painted to represent them are quite incomprehensible without the traditions. According to these the daughter of Pharaoh Valid went to the Nile, in order to heal some disease from which she suffered, by the use of its waters. And when Thermutis (for so she was called) touched the babe she found she was immediately well. One legend relates that the king had seven daughters, and all of them lepers, and that all were made whole by the touch of the infant, and that therefore the king allowed them to rear the child in the palace. But art represents the first version, and the legend goes on to say that Thermutis having no children, grew so fond of the boy, that she desired that he should succeed to the throne of Egypt. Now when the child was three years old, she brought him to the king who caressed him, and sportively placed the crown on his head. Moses pulled it off and dashed it to the ground, it is said, because it was engraved with the figures of idols, which even then Moses abhorred; again, it is said that it was the covering of the king's beard that he pulled off and threw down. But be it as it may those who stood by looked upon it as a bad omen, and advised the king that he should be slain; but others said he was too young to know right from wrong; while others still thought there was something very uncommon in the babe. Then the third counselor said, let a ruby ring and a burning coal be set before him; if he should choose the ring it will show that he knows right from wrong and so let him be slain; but if he choose the coal it will show he is too young to distinguish the right, and so let him live. Then this was done, and the ring was the king's signet which was large and shining. Then at first the child reached out for the ring, but the angel Gabriel, who took the form of one of the attendants, turned his hand aside, so that he took the coal and put it into his mouth, and his tongue was so burned that he could never speak distinctly while he lived; but his life was spared. This appears in art from the fourteenth century.

St. Nabor and **St. Felix.** Little is known of these two saints beyond the fact that they were Christians, and were martyred on account of their faith in the reign of Diocletian. They suffered at Milan, and were buried by a Christian named Philip. A chapel was built over their remains, and it was in this church that St. Ambrose prayed when he had the vision which led to the discovery of the relics of SS. Gervasius and Protasius. They are represented in art both in armor and in secular costume. July 12.

St. Narcissus. See St. Afra of Augsburg.

St. Natalia. See St. Adrian.

St. Nazarius (*Ital.* San Nazaro). See St. Celsus.

St. Neot was the preceptor as well as kinsman of King Alfred. He was a very learned monk of Glastonbury. It is said that he journeyed to Rome seven times. He is described as "humble to all, affable in conversation, wise in transacting business, venerable in aspect, severe in countenance, moderate even in his walk, upright, calm, temperate, and charitable." He dwelt at one time in a wild solitude in Cornwall. He died in 878. Two towns in England bear his name. His attributes are the pilgrim's staff and wallet. October 28.

St. Nereus (*Ital.* San Nereo). See St. Achilleus.

St. Nicaise (*Lat.* Sanctus Nicasius) was Bishop of Rheims, and was famed for the success of his preaching. When Rheims was besieged in A. D. 400 by the Vandals, St. Nicaise went forth to meet them attended by his clergy, and singing hymns. A barbarian soldier struck off the upper part of his head; but still the saint marched on and continued to sing, until after a few steps he fell dead. He is represented in his bishop's robes, carrying a part of his head upon which is the mitre. December 14.

St Nicholas of Myra (*Lat.* Sanctus Nicholaus; *Ital.* San Niccolò or Nicola di Bari; *Ger.* Der Heilige Nicolaus or Niklas). Very little of historical fact is known of this saint. There was a bishop of this name, much venerated in the East as early as the sixth century; a church was dedicated to him in Constantinople about A. D. 560; in the Greek Church he ranks next to the great Fathers. He began to be reverenced in the West in the tenth century, and since the twelfth has been one of the most popular of all saints in Italy, Russia, and in fact all Catbolic Europe. But what history does not tell is more than supplied by tradition. The stories of St. Nicholas are numberless, and many of them have been treated in art. According to these legends Nicholas was born of illustrious Christian parents, when they had been many years married without having children, — and it was thought that this son was given by God as a reward for the alms which they had bestowed upon the Church and the poor, as well as for the prayers they had offered. Their home was in Panthera, a city of Lycia in Asia Minor. The very day of his birth this wonderful child arose in his bath, and joining his hands, praised God that he had brought him into the world. And from the same day he would only take the breast once on Wednesday and Friday; thus knowing how to fast from the time that he knew hunger. On account of his holy dispositions his parents early dedicated him to the service of the Church. While still young Nicholas lost both father and mother; and he regarded himself as but God's steward over the vast wealth of which he was possessed. A certain nobleman of Panthera who was very rich lost all his property, and became so destitute that he could not provide for his three daughters, and he feared that he should be driven to sacrifice their virtue for money to keep them from starvation. The daughters were filled with grief, and having no bread knew not where to look for aid. Now Nicholas heard of this and resolved to relieve them. So he took a good sum of gold and tied it in a handkerchief, and went to the house by night to try how he could give it to them and not be himself seen. As he lingered near the dwelling the moon shone out brightly and showed an open window. Then Nicholas threw the gold inside the house and hastened away. The money fell at the feet of the unhappy father, and with it he portioned his eldest daughter and she was married. Again Nicholas did the same, and the second daughter received this sum. But now the nobleman resolved to watch, in order to know who was thus kind to him; and when Nicholas went the third time he seized him by his robe, saying, "O Nicholas! Servant of God! why seek to hide thyself?" Then Nicholas made him promise that he would tell no man. And this was but one of the many charities which he did in Panthera. At length he determined to go to Palestine. On the voyage a sailor fell overboard and was drowned, but St. Nicholas restored his life; and when a storm arose, and they were about to perish, the sailors fell at his feet and implored him to save them; and when he prayed the storm ceased. After his return from Palestine Nicholas dwelt in the city of Myra, where he was unknown, and he lived in great humility. At length the Bishop of Myra died, and a revelation was made to the clergy to the effect that the first man who should come to the church the next morning was the man whom God had chosen for their bishop. So when Nicholas came early to the church to pray, as was his custom, the clergy led him into the church and consecrated him bishop. He showed himself well worthy of his new dignity in every way, but especially by his

(Angelico da Fiesole.) Charity of St. Nicholas of Myra.

charities, which were beyond account. At one time a dreadful famine prevailed in his diocese, and when he heard that ships were in the port of Myra laden with wheat, he requested the captains that they should give him a hundred hogsheads of wheat out of each vessel. But they dared not do this, for the grain was measured at Alexandria and would be again measured at Constantinople where they were to deliver it. Then Nicholas said that if they obeyed him it should happen by the grace of God that their cargoes should not be diminished. So they complied, and when they were arrived at the granary of the emperor they found as much wheat in their ships as when they left Alexandria. And moreover that which they gave St. Nicholas was miraculously increased; for he fed the people so that they had enough to eat, and still sufficient remained to sow their fields for the next year. During this time of hunger, as St. Nicholas was travelling through his diocese he did one of his greatest miracles. He slept in the house of a man who was a most loyal son of Satan, for in this time of want he was accustomed to steal children, to kill them and serve them up as meat to those who stopped at his inn. Now Nicholas no sooner had this abominable dish placed before him than he knew what it was and understood the horrible wickedness of the man. Then he accused the host, and went to the tub where the children were salted down and made the sign of the cross over it, when lo! three children rose up whole and well. All the people were struck dumb at this miracle, and the three children were restored to their mother, who was a widow. At one time Constantine sent certain tribunes to put down a rebellion in Phrygia. On their journey they stopped at Myra, and Nicholas invited them to his table; but as they were about to sit down he heard that the prefect of the city was preparing to execute three innocent men, and the people were greatly moved thereat. Then Nicholas hastened to the place of execution, followed by his guests. When they arrived the men were already kneeling with their eyes bound and the executioner was ready with his sword. St. Nicholas seized his sword and commanded the men to be released. The tribunes looked on in wonder, but no one dared to resist the good bishop. Even the prefect sought his pardon, which he granted after much hesitation. After this when the tribunes went on their way they did not forget St. Nicholas, for it happened that while they were absent in Phrygia their enemies poisoned the mind of Constantine against them, so that when they were returned to Constantinople he accused them of treason and threw them into prison, ordering their execution on the following day. Then these tribunes called upon St. Nicholas and prayed him to deliver them. That same night he appeared to Constantine in a dream and commanded him to release those whom he had imprisoned, and threatened him with God's wrath if he obeyed not. Constantine not only released them, but he sent them to Myra to thank St. Nicholas, and to present him with a copy of the Gospels which was written in letters of gold and bound in covers set with pearls and rare jewels. Also certain sailors who were in danger of shipwreck on the Ægean Sea, called upon Jesus to deliver them for the sake of St. Nicholas, and immediately the saint appeared to them saying, "Lo, here I am, my sons! put your trust in God whose servant I am, and ye shall be saved." And the sea was calm and he took them into a safe harbor. Now the fame of these miracles so went abroad through the world, that since that time those who are in peril invoke this saint, and find aid in him. And so his life was spent in doing all manner of good works, and when he died it was in great peace and joy; — and he was buried in a magnificent church in Myra. The miracles attributed to St. Nicholas after his death were quite as marvelous as those he did while yet alive. A man who greatly desired to have a son made a vow that if this wish could be realized the first time he took his child to church he would give a cup of gold to the altar of St. Nicholas. The son was granted, and the father ordered the cup to be made; but when it was finished it was so beautiful that he decided to retain it for his own use, and had another less valuable made for St. Nicholas. At length he went on the journey necessary to accomplish his vow, and while on the way he ordered the little child to bring him water in the cup which he had taken for himself. In obeying his father, the boy fell into the water and was drowned. Then the father repented sorely of his covetousness and repaired to the Church of St. Nicholas and offered the second cup; but when it was placed upon the altar it fell off and rolled on the ground, and this it did the second and third time; and while all looked on amazed, behold, the drowned child stood on the steps of the altar with the beautiful cup in his hand; and he told how St. Nicholas had rescued him from death and brought him there. Then the joyful father made an offering of both cups, and returned home full of gratitude to the good St. Nicholas. This story has often been told in prose and poetry as well as represented in art. Again, a Jew of Calabria, having heard of all the wonderful deeds of St. Nicholas, stole his image from the church and set it up in his house. Whenever he left his house he put the care of his goods in the hands of the saint, and threatened that if anything should befall them in his absence he would chastise the saint on his return. One day the robbers came and stole his treasures. Then the Jew beat the image and cut it also. That night St. Nicholas appeared to the robbers all wounded and bleeding, and commanded them to restore what they had stolen; and they being afraid at the vision did as he bade them. Then the Jew was converted by this miracle and was baptized. Another rich Christian merchant who dwelt in a pagan country had an only son who was made a captive, and was obliged to serve the king of the country as cupbearer. One day as he filled the king's cup he remembered that it was St. Nicholas' day, and he wept. Then the king demanded the cause of his grief, and when the young man told him he answered, "Great as is thy St. Nicholas he cannot save thee from my hand!" And instantly the palace was shaken by a whirlwind, and St. Nicholas appeared and caught the youth by the hair, and set him in the midst of his own family with the king's cup still in his hand. And it happened that the very moment when he came there was that in which his father was giving food to the poor and asking their prayers for his captive son. It is necessary to keep these traditions in mind when regarding the pictures of St. Nicholas, for in two different pictures there appears a boy with a cup, so that it is important to distinguish them by the accessories. Sometimes it is a daughter who is rescued from captivity. The tomb of St. Nicholas was a famous resort for pilgrims for centuries. In 807 the church was attacked by Achmet, commander of the fleet of Haroun Al Raschid. But the watchfulness of the monks prevented him from doing any harm, and putting to sea, he and his whole fleet were destroyed in punishment for their sacrilegious attempt. The remains of the saint rested in Myra until 1084, although several attempts were made by different cities and churches to possess themselves of these sacred relics. At length in the year mentioned some merchants of Bari who traded on the coast of Syria resolved to obtain these remains of which they had heard so great wonders. At this time Myra was desolated by the Saracens, and the ruined church was guarded by three monks. The remains were taken without difficulty and carried safely to Bari, where a splendid church was erected for their resting-place. The Venetians however claim that they have the true relics of St. Nicholas, brought home by Venetian merchants in 1100. But the claims of Bari are generally acknowledged, and the saint is best known as St. Nicholas of Bari. In Greek pictures he is dressed like a Greek bishop, with no mitre, the cross in place of the crosier, and the persons of the Trinity embroidered on his cope. In western art he has the bishop's dress, the mitre, the cope very much ornamented, the crosier, and jeweled gloves. His attributes are three balls, which are on the book, at his feet or in his lap. They are said to represent the three purses of gold which he threw into the window of the poor nobleman; or three loaves of bread, emblematic of his feeding the poor; or again, the persons of the Trinity. The first interpretation is the most general. He is chief patron of Russia. Patron of Bari, Venice, and Freiberg, as well as of many other towns and cities, numbers of them being sea-port places. He is protector against robbers and losses by violence. He is patron of children and school-boys in particular; of poor maidens, of sailors, travellers, and merchants. December 6, A. D. 326.

St. Nicholas of Tolentino, was born in the little town of St. Angelo, near Fermo, in 1239. His parents had prayed earnestly to St. Nicholas for a son, and as they believed that this son was given to them through the intercession of this saint, they named him Nicholas, and dedicated him to the service of the Church. At an early age he took the habit of an Augustine friar, and so great was the austerity of his life that it has been said, that "he did not live, but languished through life." He was successful as a preacher, and his miracles and visions are numberless. He never allowed himself to taste animal food, and when he was very weak he refused a dish of doves that his brethren brought him, and waved his hand above the dish, when the doves rose up and flew away. Tradition teaches that at the hour of his birth a brilliant star shot through the heavens from Sant' Angelo, where he was born, and rested over the city of Tolentino, where he afterwards lived. In the year 1602, a plague visited the city of Cordova, and according to the legend the governor caused the image of St. Nicholas of Tolentino to be carried through the city in solemn procession, on the day which was observed as the festival of that saint. Father G. de Uavas bearing a crucifix, met the procession, when the figure of Christ stooped from the cross, and embraced that of St. Nicholas, and immediately the plague was stayed. He is also represented in art as restoring a child to life, and doing many other miracles. He is painted in the black habit of his Order, with a star on his breast; he often bears a crucifix wreathed with lilies typical of the purity and austerity of his life. September 10, A. D. 1309.

St. Nicholas of Tolentino.

St. Nilus of Grotta Ferrata (*Ital.* San Nilo; *Fr.* Saint Nil le jeune). St. Nilus was connected with many interesting events in Roman history in life, and since his death is associated with art in an interesting manner. He was a Greek, born near Tarentum. It was not until after the loss of his wife, whom he loved devotedly, that he embraced a religious vocation. He took the habit of the Greek Order of St. Basil, and was soon made the superior of his community on account of his worth and learning. The chances of war drove him to the west of Italy, and he fled to the convent of Monte Cassino at Capua, which was of the Benedictine Order. He was received with great kindness, and a small convent assigned to him and his followers by the abbot. At this time Capua was governed

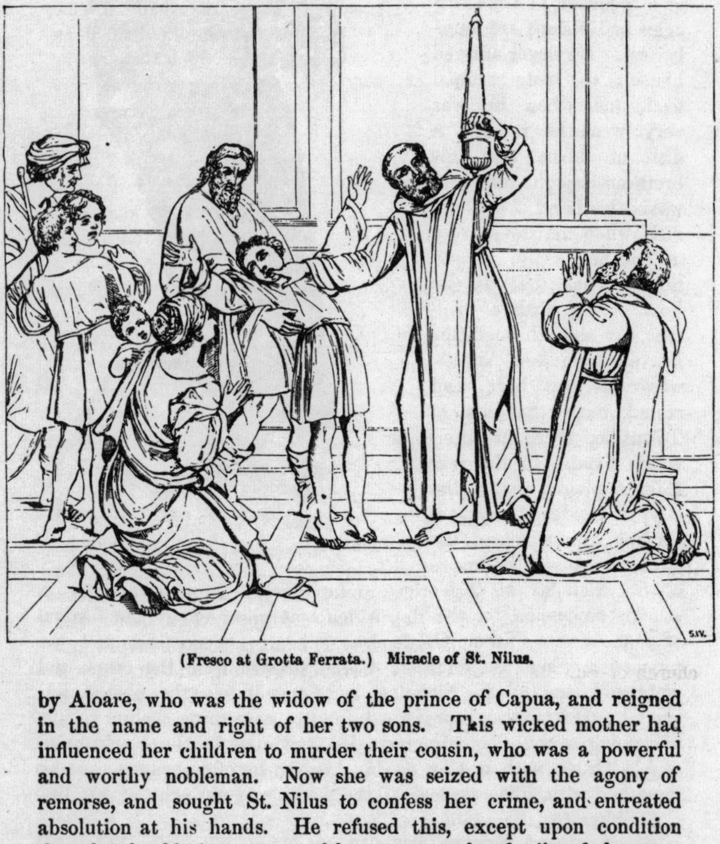

(Fresco at Grotta Ferrata.) Miracle of St. Nilus.

by Aloare, who was the widow of the prince of Capua, and reigned in the name and right of her two sons. This wicked mother had influenced her children to murder their cousin, who was a powerful and worthy nobleman. Now she was seized with the agony of remorse, and sought St. Nilus to confess her crime, and entreated absolution at his hands. He refused this, except upon condition that she should give up one of her sons to the family of the murdered man, to be dealt with as they saw fit. This she would not consent to do. Then St. Nilus denounced her unforgiven, and told her that what she would not give, Heaven would soon exact of her. She offered him large sums of money, and begged him to pray for her; but he threw down her money in scorn and left her. Not long after this the youngest son killed the elder in a church, and for this double crime of fratricide and sacrilege, he was put to death by command of Hugh Capet. Nilus afterwards went to Rome, and lived in a convent on the Aventine, where large numbers of sick people visited him, and he did many and great miracles. Among others, his cure of an epileptic boy forms a subject for art. Crescentius was consul at this time, and John XVI., who was a Greek like St. Nilus, was Pope. Then Otho III. came to Rome and made a new pope, with the title of Gregory V. He put out the eyes of Pope John, and laid siege to the Castle of St. Angelo to which Crescentius had retired. After a short siege the castle was given up on honorable terms; but not heeding these Otho ordered that Crescentius should be thrown headlong from the walls, and Stephanie, his wife, given up to the outrages of the soldiers. So great was the influence of Nilus in Rome at this time that the emperor and the new pope endeavored to conciliate him, but he fearlessly rebuked them, and declared that the time would soon come when they should both seek mercy without finding it. He then left Rome and went first to a cell near Gaeta, but soon after to a cave near Frascati, called the Crypta or Grotta Ferrata. Pope Gregory died a miserable death soon after. Otho went on a pilgrimage to Monte Galgano. When returning he visited Nilus, and on his knees besought his prayers. He offered to erect a convent and endow it with lands, but this Nilus refused, and when Otho demanded what boon he could grant him, the saint stretched out his hand, and replied, "I ask of thee but this: that thou wouldst make reparation of thy crimes before God, and save thine own soul!" Soon after Otho returned to Rome, he was obliged to fly from the fury of the people, and was poisoned by Stephanie, the widow of Crescentius. When St. Nilus died, he desired his brethren to bury him immediately, and to keep secret the place where they laid him. This they did; but his disciple, Bartolomeo, built the convent which Nilus had not wished to do, and received the gifts he had refused. The magnificent convent and church of San Basilio of Grotta Ferrata, was built, and St. Nilus is regarded as its founder. Their rule is that of St. Basil, and their mass is recited in Greek, but they wear the Benedictine habit as a dependency of Monte Cassino. The finest Greek library in all Italy was here, and is now in the Vatican, and Julius II. changed the convent to a fortress. In 1610, Domenichino was employed by Cardinal Odoardo Farnese, to decorate the chapel of St. Nilus, which he did with paintings from the life of the saint. September 26, A. D. 1002.

St. Norbert (*Ital.* San Norberto, Fondatore de' Premostratesi; *Ger.* Stifter der Prämonstratenser-Orden). This saint was a relative of Henry IV. He was born at Cologne, and early dedicated to the Church. But he led a dissolute life as a young man. At last, as he was one day riding, he was overtaken by a tempest, and a ball of fire fell from heaven and exploding at the feet of his horse, sank into the earth. He was terrified when he reflected upon what his state would have been had he been killed by it, and he resolved to lead a different life from that time. He bestowed his money on the poor, and determined to be a missionary. He only reserved a mule to carry the sacred utensils for the altar and the vestments, and ten marks of silver. He dressed himself in skins with a cord as a girdle, and thus he went forth to preach. After preaching for some years there were many who desired him to form a community, and lead them in a life of austerity and severe discipline. He prayed to the Blessed Virgin for direction, and she pointed out to him a spot called Pré-montré (Pratum Monstratum), in the valley of Coucy, where he should establish his monastery. The Virgin also directed what habit they should wear; that it should be a coarse black tunic, with a white woolen cloak, in imitation of angels who are clothed in white; and a four-cornered cap of white also, but in form like the beret of the Augustine canons. The rule was that of Augustine in extreme severity. St. Norbert was made Bishop of Magdeburg, and before his death his Order embraced twelve hundred souls. According to the legend, one day when he had consecrated the holy wine, and was about to drink it, he saw a large and poisonous spider in the cup. For a moment he hesitated; but he reflected that he could not spill the consecrated wine, — it would be sacrilege; so he drank it, and remained unharmed. This was considered as a miraculous recompense of his faith, and is often seen represented in art. When at Antwerp, there was one Tankelin who preached most heretical doctrines, saying, that the sacraments were unnecessary; the priesthood a cheat; and a community of wives as well as goods the true doctrine. St. Norbert confronted this heretic, opposed him, and triumphed over him with great effect. He wears in pictures the dress of an archbishop with mitre, crosier, and cope. Sometimes he bears the sacramental cup over which is a spider. He also has, in some instances, a demon at his feet, representing the sin and error which he had overcome. May 6, A. D. 1134.

St. Omobuono was a citizen saint of Cremona. He was a merchant, and married to a good and prudent wife, so though a saint he was not monk or priest. From his youth all his affairs prospered greatly, and his wealth was only equaled by his charity. He not only fed and clothed but he comforted the poor, and tried to encourage the erring ones to repent and lead virtuous lives. His wife often feared lest his generosity should make his children poor, but his money seemed to be miraculously increased, and it is related that being on a journey with his family he gave all the wine and bread he had provided for their use to some poor pilgrims whom he met; but when he took his wine-flasks to a spring and filled them with water, most excellent wine was poured from them, and his bags were filled with bread by angels. He died peacefully while kneeling before a crucifix in the Church of St. Egidio, just as the choir sang the "Gloria in Excelsis." He is represented clothed in a loose tunic and a cap, both of which are trimmed with fur. He usually distributes alms to the poor; wine-flasks stand near him.

St. Onuphrius (Onofrio, Honofrio, Onuphre) was a hermit. He went out from Thebes and passed sixty years in the desert, during which time he never uttered a word except in prayer, nor saw a human face. His clothing was of leaves and his hair and beard were uncut. He was thus seen by Paphnutius, who when he first saw him was filled with fear, believing him to be some strange wild beast; but when he saw that it was a man, he fell at his feet filled with reverence of his sanctity. Then Onuphrius recounted all he had endured in his solitude: how he had been tempted; had suffered from cold, heat, hunger, thirst, and sickness, and how God had sent angels to comfort, strengthen, and minister unto him. Then he begged Paphnutius to remain with him, as he was near to death. It was not long before he died, and Paphnutius covered his remains with one half of his cloak. Then he had a revelation that he should go into the world and make known the wonderful life and merits of him who had died. Many convents where silence and solitude are practiced, are placed under the protection of this saint. Tasso died and is buried in the convent of St. Onofrio in the Trastevere in Rome. He is represented as meagre and old; a stick in his hand and a branch with leaves twisted about him. In many old pictures he looks more the beast than the man. Sometimes money is lying at his feet to signify his scorn of it. June 12.

Ordeal. The trial by ordeal was used for the decision of cases where the oath of the accused person was not considered worthy of reliance. It was called the great purgation. The word Ordeal is from two Saxon words. *Or*, great, and *deal*, judgment. There were three tests used in these trials. 1. By red-hot iron. This the person held in the hand, or walked on barefooted. 2. By boiling water; the person dipped the hand to the wrist or the arm to the elbow and took out a stone. 3. By cold water or compelling persons to swim. This was chiefly used for detecting witches, and was also employed not only by judges, but at length by the people and especially by foresters to discover criminals.

St. Oswald. This king being moved with a desire to live a truly Christian life asked that a teacher might be sent to instruct him and his people. The first man who was sent was severe in disposition and had no success with the unlearned. Then Aidan came, and by means of his mildness and great discretion he had much influence with the king and his people. Aidan was afterwards prior of Melrose. According to the legends, it happened that as Oswald sat at dinner one Easter day with Aidan by his side, he was told that there were those at his door who begged for bread. Now there was before him a silver dish filled with delicate and savory meat. Oswald told the servant to give the beggars the meat, and then to break the dish and divide it among them. Then Aidan took his right hand saying, "May this hand never wither!" And his prayer was granted; for at his death his heathen enemies cut off his head and hands and set them on stakes; but his head was taken to the church of Landisfarne and buried in St. Cuthbert's tomb, between the arms of that saint: his right hand was carried to Bamborough Castle where it was a long time preserved, free from decay. At one time Oswald was driven from his throne by Cadwallader. At length he determined to regain his kingdom. He raised an army, and when in sight of his enemies he ordered his men to make a large wooden cross, and helped himself to place it in the ground. Then he cried out, "Let us all kneel down and beseech the living God to defend us from the haughty and fierce enemy, for He knows that we have undertaken a just war, for the safety of our nation." And when they fought Oswald was victorious. The greatest proof of his charity of heart is shown in the fact that as he died he prayed for those who killed him. "May God have mercy on their souls, as Oswald said when he fell," was a proverb for many years in England. And the legend tells that "in the place where he was killed by the pagans, fighting for his country, infirm men and cattle are healed to this day; nor is it to be wondered at, that the sick should be healed in the place where he died, for whilst he lived he never ceased to provide for the poor and infirm, and to bestow alms on them and assist them." His remains were carried to Bardney in Lincolnshire by Osthrida, and afterwards to St. Oswald's in Gloucestershire by Elfleda, the daughter of King Alfred. He is dressed as a king, in his pictures; wears a crown and carries a cross. August 5, A. D. 642.

St. Ottilia was the blind daughter of the Duke of Alsace. Her father, who was a pagan, commanded that on account of her infirmity she should be left out, and exposed to death. Her nurse then fled to a monastery with the child. Then Erhard, a bishop of Bavaria, was told in a vision that he should go to a certain monastery where he would find a little girl of noble birth who was blind. He was commanded to baptize her and call her name Ottilia, and promised that her sight should be given her. All this was done according to the vision. Her father repented of his wickedness before his death, and gave her all his wealth. Then Ottilia, knowing that for his cruelty her father was tormented in purgatory, determined to deliver him by prayers and penance. She built a convent at

Hohenburg, of which she was abbess, and there she gathered one hundred and thirty nuns. She is ranked as a martyr on account of her extreme austerities. She is represented in the black Benedictine habit. Her attributes are the palm or crosier, and a book upon which are two eyes. She is patron saint of Alsace, and especially of Strasbourg. She is also protector of all who suffer with diseases of the eye. December 13. A. D. 720.

(Old German Missal.) St. Ottilia.

St. Pancras (*Ital.* San Pancrazio ; *Fr.* St. Pancrace). This saint when only fourteen years old, offered himself as a martyr. He boldly defended the Christians and their faith before Diocletian, and was beheaded. His remains were buried by Christian women. His church at Rome, near the gate which bears his name, was built in the year 500. French kings formerly confirmed their treaties in his name, for he was regarded as the avenger of false swearing, and it was believed that all who swore falsely in his name were immediately and visibly punished. May 12, A. D. 304.

St. Pantaleon of Nicomedia (*Ital.* San Pantaleone ; *Gr.* Ἅγ. Παντaλέων) was born (according to tradition) at Nicomedia in Bithynia. He was remarkable for his personal beauty and elegant manners, on account of which, after completing the study of medicine, he became the favorite physician of the Emperor Galerius Maximian. The father of Pantaleon was a pagan and his mother a Christian ; but at the heathen court the son forgot all the instructions that his mother had carefully given him. At length he heard a priest, Hermolaus, preach, and was converted. When the persecution broke out he knew he could not conceal himself, and he prepared to suffer a cruel martyrdom. He went about to the sick and needy, and well earned the title of the "all merciful," which is the Greek signification of his name. When accused before the emperor he was condemned to be beheaded, together with the aged and venerable Hermolaus, who came forth from his retreat, desiring to suffer with Pantaleon. The latter was bound to an olive-tree, and as soon as his blood flowed to the roots of the tree it burst forth with leaves and fruit. He is especially venerated at Venice. There have been some who doubted his existence, and believed his name to have been derived from the war-cry of the Venetians, — Pianta Leone (Plant the Lion)! But Justinian erected a church in his honor in Constantinople, and he was celebrated in the Greek Church at that time, when Venice would have been more likely to introduce his worship from the East than to have originated it in any other way. Patron of physicians. He is represented as young, beardless, and handsome. As a martyr he is bound to an olive-tree with his hands nailed to it above his head, a sword at his feet. Without observation he might be mistaken for St. Sebastian. When he is painted as patron he wears the physician's robe and bears the olive or palm, or both. July 27. Fourth century.

St. Patrick (*Lat.* S. Patricius) was the son of Christian parents. He was carried a captive to Ireland when a boy, and tended the herds of his master. He was greatly moved at the ignorance and heathenism of the people about him, and when at last he made his escape and returned to his home he had visions in which it appeared, that the children of Ireland not yet born, stretched forth their hands to him and cried for salvation. Patrick resolved to become a missionary and prepared himself for his labor. He received his mission from Pope Celestine and returned to Ireland. He labored there forty years. He gained many disciples, and preached with the greatest success. He baptized the kings of Dublin and Munster, and the seven sons of the king of Connaught. Having found Ireland in a state of profound ignorance, he left it Christianized; with schools which became famous, and sent forth many learned scholars. The familiar story of the expulsion of the reptiles from Ireland, by this saint, has the signification of many other legends and allegories, and figures the triumph of good over evil. He died and was buried at Down in the province of Ulster. His resting-place is still venerated by the people, and his remains were preserved many years, but his church at Down was destroyed in the reign of Henry VIII. and such relics of him as remained were scattered either by the soldiers of Elizabeth or those under Cromwell. When represented as bishop, he wears the usual dress with the mitre, cope, and crosier, while a neophyte regards him with reverence. As the Apostle of Ireland he should wear a hooded gown and a leathern girdle. The staff, wallet, standard with the cross, and the Gospel, are all his proper attributes. A serpent should be placed beneath his feet. March 17, A. D. 464.

St. Paul (*Lat.* S. Paulus; *Ital.* and *Sp.* San Paolo; *Fr.* St. Paul; *Gr.* Ἁγ. Παυλος). St. Paul and St. Peter occupy the first place among the Apostles. St. Peter more especially represented the converted Jews and St. Paul the Gentiles; together they represent the Universal Church. There are few legends connected with St. Paul, but the scenes of his life as given in the Gospel have furnished inexhaustible subjects for the illustrations of art. St. Paul is so often represented with St. Peter that it is necessary to be able to distinguish the one from the other. Augustine and other early writers allude to portraits of St. Paul as existing in their time, and it is supposed that the traditionary picture of him which is so strictly followed, had its origin in those portraits. He is small of stature, with high forehead, sparkling eyes, and aquiline nose. His hair and beard are brown, and the latter long and flowing. Later artists have varied the head of St. Paul more than that of St. Peter, but the most ancient pictures are exact in these particulars. When the two apostles are together, their proper place is on each side of the Saviour, or of the Virgin enthroned. Their pictures should be placed on each side the altar, or of the arch over the choir. The dress is the same for both: a blue tunic and white mantle in Greek pictures, a blue or green tunic and yellow mantle in later works of art. Paul bears the sword in a double sense, signifying his spiritual warfare and the manner of his death. He also has a book or scroll and sometimes twelve rolls, representing his epistles. When he leans on his sword it is his death which is represented; when he holds it aloft, it signifies the "good fight" which he fought. If two swords are given him, both the manner of his death and that of his life are signified. The events in the life of this apostle are so well known to all, that they are easily recognized in art. The church called "San Paolo delle Tre Fontane" near Rome, is built over three fountains which are said to have sprung up at the three places where the head of St. Paul fell and bounded, after being cut off by the executioner. It is said that the fountains vary in the warmth of the water: the first, or the one where the head fell, being the hottest; the next, or that of the first bound, cooler; and the third still cooler; but probably time

(Greek, 11th century.) St. Paul.

has equalized the temperature, for I could not distinguish the difference. Formerly a magnificent monastery existed here, but three old churches and ruins, with a few sickly looking monks, are the only remains of its former splendor. The body of St. Paul was interred where the Church of "San Paolo-fuori-le-mura" stands, between the Ostian Gate and the Aqua Salvias; but traditions relate that they were removed with those of St. Peter to the Catacombs, and laid in the same tomb, during the reign of Heliogabalus. Two hundred years later the Oriental Christians endeavored to possess themselves of them, but the Roman Christians contended for them with success, and they removed them to the Church of the Vatican, and placed them together in a magnificent shrine. SS. Peter and Paul, June 29. Conversion of St. Paul, June 30. See also St. Peter.

St. Paul. Hermit. See St. Anthony.

Sts. Paul and John. See Sts. John and Paul, brothers.

St. Paula (*Gr.* Ἁγ. Παυλα) was a noble Roman matron, a pupil and disciple of St. Jerome. Though descended from the Scipios and the Gracchi, and accustomed to luxurious self-indulgence, she preferred to follow her saintly teacher to Bethlehem and devote herself to a religious life. The church dedicated to St. Jerome at Rome, is said to be upon the spot where the house of Paula stood, in which she entertained that holy man during his stay in Rome, A. D. 382. She studied Hebrew, in order to understand the Scriptures better. She built a monastery, hospital, and three nunneries at Bethlehem. Her daughter St. Eustochium was with her. The rule for these convents was very strict, and her own austerities so severe that she was reprimanded for them by St. Jerome. Her granddaughter Paula was sent to her at Bethlehem to be educated, and she succeeded her as superior of the monastery. She died making the sign of the cross on her lips, and was buried in the Church of the Holy Manger, where her empty tomb is now seen near that of St. Jerome. Her relics are said to be at Sens. January 26, A. D. 404.

St. Paulinus of York was sent from Rome to England in 601, to assist St. Augustine in his mission. He became the first Primate of York, where he founded the Cathedral. Wordsworth gives a word-picture of him thus: —

> ——— "of shoulders curved, and stature tall,
> Black hair and vivid eye, and meagre cheek,
> His prominent feature like an eagle's beak."

By the preaching of Paulinus, Coifi, the Druid and high-priest of Thor, was converted. King Edwin had renounced idolatry, and given Paulinus license to preach. When the king asked Coifi who would destroy the idols, the priest answered, "I! for who can more properly than myself destroy those things which I worshipped through ignorance!" It was not lawful for the high-priest to ride, except on a mare, or to bear arms, but now he asked Edwin to give him a horse and sword. This was done, and he rode to the temple and thrust his spear in, and commanded the temple and idols to be burned. Paulinus is often seen in pictures of St. Augustine. October 10, A. D. 644.

St. Perpetua was one of the martyrs who suffered at Carthage during the persecution of Severus. This saint manifested miraculous courage in devoting herself to her fate. She was tossed by a wild cow in the amphitheatre, but was not quite killed, and after great tortures was put to death in the spoliarium, or place where the wounded were dispatched by the gladiators. She had a vision of a narrow ladder which reached to heaven, beset with spikes, and a dragon lay at the bottom on whose head she must tread in order to mount the first step. One scene from her life represented in modern art, is her farewell to her infant child. There are many incidents in her story which would be most interesting subjects for the artist, that as yet remain without representation. In her pictures a cow stands by her side or near her. March 7, A. D. 203.

St. Peter (*Lat.* Sanctus Petrus; *Ital.* San Pietro or Piero; *Fr.* Saint Pierre; *Sp.* San Pedro. Signification: A rock). St. Peter

(Sarcophagus, 3d century.) Repentance of St. Peter.

and St. Paul are so associated in history that it is quite impossible to separate them in our minds, or entirely to do so in descriptions of them. And in works of art they are constantly associated. St. Peter is a strong man, old, with gray hair, and curling, silvery beard, a broad forehead, and an expression of courage and confidence. Sometimes he is bald; and there is a legend that the Gentiles shaved his head in mockery, and from this originated the tonsure of the priests. His dress is a blue tunic and white mantle in the oldest pictures and mosaics, but in later art it is a blue or green tunic with a yellow mantle. In the earliest pictures Peter only bears a scroll or book, and there is nothing to distinguish him from Paul except the difference in the head and features. The keys are not assigned as his attribute until the eighth century. He has usually two keys, one golden and one silver; they are interpreted as signifying his power to bind and to loose; or again, one as the key of heaven the other of hell, when the first is of gold and the second iron, and sometimes a third is added to express dominion over earth also. When the traditional differences in the two men are well represented, the contrast is marked and impressive. In some early representations, from the middle to the end of the fourth century, Peter bears a cross and stands on the left of Christ, with Paul on the right. This cross is said to be the emblem of the death he should die. When St. Peter and St. Paul occur together in strictly devotional pictures, they are represented as the founders of the Universal Church. Since the Protestant Church has separated from the Roman Church, a distinction is made between these saints. The Roman Church regards St. Peter as the saint of saints; of all most holy; while among Protestants St. Paul has come to be greatly venerated, and his clear, subtle, philosophical, reasoning religion can never be too much exalted by them. When St. Peter is represented in company with all the apostles he frequently has a fish, which is the symbol of his early vocation; but if the fish is given him when alone, it is symbolical of Christianity and the Rite of Baptism. When represented as the Head of the Roman Church he is seated on a throne; one hand raised in benediction, while in the other he holds keys, and often a book or scroll inscribed, "Thou art Peter, and on this rock have I built my Church." Sometimes he wears the papal tiara. When another apostle without attributes is seen with him it is Mark, who was his interpreter and amanuensis at Rome; and a tradition relates that St. Mark's Gospel was written after the dictation of Peter. The historical pictures, or those which represent scenes in the life of Peter, are of great interest and almost numberless, but all easily recognized. Of the legendary pictures those connected with Simon Magus are important. The story is, that Simon was a magician of great fame among the Jews. He did wonderful things at Jerusalem, and greatly astonished the people; but the miracles of Peter far excelled the inventions of the sorcerer. Then Simon endeavored to buy from the apostles the secret by which these miracles were done. These offers much enraged Peter, who rejected them with great indignation. Simon then threw away his wand, and casting his books into the Dead Sea he fled to Rome, where he became a favorite of Claudius, and again of Nero. Peter also came to Rome and afterwards Paul. Simon asserted that he was a god and could raise the dead. Peter and Paul challenged him to prove his skill before the emperor. His arts failed, and not only then, but many times he was vanquished by the apostles. At last Simon attempted to fly to heaven in the sight of the emperor and all Rome. He was crowned with laurel and supported by demons, and thus precipitated himself from a tower. He appeared to float in the air for a time, but Peter knelt and commanded the demons to let go their hold of him, when he fell to the earth and was dashed in pieces. This legend is not without some foundation in history, as there existed a Samaritan magician by that name who assumed to be God. Irenæus calls him, the father of all heretics. He carried about with him a beautiful woman called Helena, whom he said was the first conception of his divine mind. He presented her as being the resuscitation of Helen of Troy. In the Church of St. Francesca Romana at Rome, there are two stones let into the wall, bearing a double depression, made it is said by St. Peter's kneeling on them when Simon Magus was attempting his heavenly flight. Another legend relates that after the burning of Rome Nero accused the Christians of having fired the city. This was the origin of the first persecution. The Christians besought St. Peter to save himself by flight, which he at length consented to do. He departed by the Appian Way, and when about two miles from the city he met a vision of Our Saviour. Peter exclaimed, "Lord, whither goest thou?" Looking sadly upon him Christ replied, "I go to Rome to be crucified a second time." Peter understood this as a warning that he ought to return to Rome, which he did. This is called the "Domine, quo vadis?" when illustrated. In the little church erected on the spot sanctified by this miracle, a slab is shown containing footprints, said to be those made by the feet of Christ, as he talked with Peter. After Peter's return to Rome, he preached and labored as usual until he was seized with St. Paul and thrown into the Mamertine Prison. Here the centurions who guarded them, Processus and Martinian, and many prisoners, were converted. When St. Peter wished to baptize them and there was no water, he prayed to God and a fountain sprung up from the stone floor, which may still be seen. It was not long till the two apostles were martyrized. The traditions disagree in regard to the place where St. Peter suffered. According to one, he was crucified with his head downward in the court-yard of a military station on the summit of Mons Janicula, where the Church of San Pietro in Montorio now stands; but according to another, his crucifixion took place in the Circus of Caligula, at the foot of the Vatican. The legends make St. Peter the keeper of the entrance to Paradise and give him power to grant or refuse admission. The Church of San Pietro in Vincoli at Rome, was built by Eudoxia, wife of Valentinian III., to preserve the chains with which St. Peter was bound at Jerusalem. The chains are preserved in a bronze tabernacle in the sacristy, and are shown to the people on the festival of St. Peter in Vinculis on the 1st of August. Here is the picture of the deliverance of St. Peter by Domenichino. St. Peter and St. Paul, June 29.

St. Peter of Alcantara.

St. Peter of Alcantara was not canonized until 1669. According to the legend he walked on the sea by faith. In a picture in the Munich Gallery, he not only walks himself, but a lay brother goes with him, whom Peter seems to encourage by pointing to heaven. October 19, A. D. 1562.

St. Peter Exorcista and Marcellinus (*Ital.* SS. Pietro e Marcellino). These saints are always represented together. According to the legend they were imprisoned during the last persecution of Diocletian. Their jailer, Artemius, had a daughter, Paulina, who was sick. Peter promised to restore her to health if Artemius would believe in God. Then Artemius ridiculed him, saying, "If I put thee into the deepest dungeon, and load thee with heavier chains, will thy God then deliver thee?" Then Peter told him that it mattered little to God whether he believed or not, but that Christ might be glorified he desired that it should be done. And it was so; and in the night Peter and Marcellinus, dressed in shining white garments, came to Artemius in his own chamber. Then he believed, and was baptized with all his family and three hundred others. When they were to die it was ordered that the executioner should take them to a forest three miles from Rome, in order that the Christians should not know of their burial place. So when they were come to a solitary place and the executioner pointed it out as the spot where they were to die, they themselves cleared a space and dug their grave, and died encouraging each other. They are represented in priestly habits bearing palms. June 2. About 304.

St. Peter Martyr. St. Peter the Dominican (*Ital.* San Pietro (or Pier) Martire; *Fr.* St. Pierre le Dominicain, Martyr). This saint is esteemed next to St. Dominick by his Order. He was born at Verona about 1205. His parents were of the heretical sect called Cathari, but Peter went to a Catholic school. He was beaten at home for reciting the creed. St. Dominick found him a zealous disciple, when at Verona, and he persuaded him to unite with his Order at the early age of fifteen. He became a most intolerant man, and a successful preacher. He greatly delighted in the persecution of the Cathari. He was made Inquisitor General under Pope Honorius III. Two Venetian noblemen whom he had accused, and whose property was confiscated, resolved to be revenged on him. They hired assassins who watched that they might kill him in a forest where they knew he would pass un-

(Fra Bartolomeo.)
Jerome Savonarola as St. Peter Martyr.

accompanied, save by a single monk. When he appeared one of the murderers struck him down with an axe. They then pursued and killed his attendant. When they returned to St. Peter he was reciting the Apostles' Creed, or as others say, was writing it on the ground with his blood, when the assassins completed their cruel work. Fra Bartolomeo painted the head of his beloved Jerome Savonarola as St. Peter Martyr. He is represented in the habit of his Order, and bears the crucifix and palm. His more peculiar attribute is either the axe stuck in his head or a gash from which the blood trickles. April 28, A. D. 1252.

(Claude de Mellan.) St. Peter Nolasco.

St. Peter Nolasco (*Sp.* San Pedro Nolasco) was a convert of St. John de Matha. When young he enlisted in the crusade against the Albigenses. He was the son of a noble of Languedoc, and became the tutor of the young king James of Aragon, or Don Jayme el Conquistador. But being much moved at the consideration of the sufferings of captives he founded a new Order called, "The Order of Our Lady of Mercy" (Nuestra Señora de la Merced). At first the Order was military, consisting of knights and gentlemen, and the king placed himself at their head and gave them his arms as a device or badge. The Order was very popular, and soon extended itself on all sides. Peter Nolasco was the Superior, and spent his life in expeditions to the provinces under the Moors, from which he brought back hundreds of redeemed captives. In time the Order changed its character from that of a military to that of a religious institution. According to tradition, when Peter was old, he was taken from his cell by angels, and borne to and from the altar where he received the Holy Eucharist. He is represented as old; with a white habit and the shield of King James on his breast. January 13, A. D. 1258.

St. Peter Regalato. This saint appears in the later Italian and Spanish pictures of the Franciscans, to which Order he belonged. He was especially distinguished for his "sublime gift of prayer." March 30, A. D. 1456.

St. Petronilla (*Fr.* Sainte Pernelle) was the daughter of St. Peter. When at Rome with him, she was deprived of the use of her limbs by sickness. One day when some of his disciples sat at dinner with the Apostle, they asked why it was that when he healed others his own child remained helpless. Peter replied, that it was good for her to be ill, but that his power should be shown, he commanded her to rise and serve them. This she did, and when the dinner was over laid down helpless as before. Years after, when she had become perfected by suffering, she was made well in answer to her earnest prayers. Now Petronilla was very beautiful, and a young noble, Valerius Flaccus, desired to marry her. She was afraid to refuse him, and promised that if he returned in three days, he should then carry her home. She then earnestly prayed to be delivered from this marriage, and when the lover came with his friends to celebrate the marriage, he found her dead. Flaccus lamented sorely. The attendant nobles bore her to her grave, in which they placed her crowned with roses. May 31.

St. Petronius was Bishop of Bologna, and distinguished himself by banishing the Arians from that city. He was a Roman of an illustrious family. His pictures are confined to Bologna; and there is in that city a beautiful church dedicated in his name. He is represented in episcopal robes, with mitre and crosier. He has a thick black beard in an ancient representation, but generally is without it. His attribute is a model of Bologna, which he holds in his hand. October 4, A. D. 430.

St. Philip (*Ital.* San Filippo Apostolo; *Fr.* Saint Philippe). St

Philip was born at Bethsaida. Beyond the fact that he was the first called to follow the Saviour, little is told of him in the Gospel. After the ascension of Christ he preached in Scythia twenty years. Then going to Hieropolis in Phrygia, he found the people worshipping a huge serpent or dragon, whom they thought to be a personification of Mars. Then Philip took pity on their ignorance. He held up the cross and commanded the serpent to disappear. Immediately it glided from beneath the altar, and as it moved it sent forth so dreadful an odor that many died, and among them the son of the king; but Philip restored him to life. Then the priests of the serpent were so wroth with him that they crucified him, and when he was fastened to the cross they stoned him. The Scriptures state that Philip had four daughters who did prophesy (Acts xxi. 9). St. Mariamne, his sister, and his daughter St. Hermione, are martyrs in the Greek Calendar. St. Philip is represented as a man of middle age, scanty beard, and benevolent face. His attribute is a cross which varies in form, — sometimes a small cross in his hand; again, a high cross in the form of a T, or a staff with a small cross at the top. It has three significations: it may represent the power of the cross which he held before the dragon; or his martyrdom; or his mission as preacher of the cross of Christ. Patron of Brabant and Luxembourg. May 1.

St. Philip, Deacon (*Gr.* Ἅγ. Φίλιππος). It is necessary to distinguish him from the Apostle. It was Philip the deacon, who baptized the chamberlain of Queen Candace. This baptism has been beautifully illustrated in art. June 6.

St. Philip Benozzi (*Ital.* San Filippo Beniti, or Benizzi) stands at the head of the Order of the Servi or Serviti at Florence. He was not the founder of the Order, not having joined it until fifteen years after its establishment, but he is their principal saint. The history of the origin of this Order is full of interest, and an outline of it may be given in few words. It originated about the year 1232. Seven rich Florentine nobles, in the prime of life, were accustomed to meet every day in the Chapel of the Annunziata to sing the Ave, or evening service to the Blessed Virgin, whom they especially venerated. They became so well known for these pious acts that the women and children cried out as they passed, "Behold the servants of the Virgin!" ("Guardate i Servi di Maria!") At length they resolved to dispense their goods to the poor and forsake the world. They retired to Monte Senario, about six miles from Florence, where they built huts, and lived for the service of the Virgin. Their first habit was plain white in honor of the immaculate purity of Mary, but one of the number was warned in a vision that they should change it to black, in remembrance of her "maternal sorrow, and the death of her divine Son." These men, being allied to the proudest families of Florence, drew much attention to their Order, and the city became proud of them. St. Philip Benozzi had studied medicine at the Universities of Paris and Padua, and was a very learned man; but after receiving his degrees and commencing the practice of surgery in Florence, he became greatly wearied and oppressed with the sight and knowledge of human suffering. One day as he listened to the service in the Chapel of the Annunziata, he was impressed by the words, "Draw near, and join thyself to the chariot." He went home full of thought upon these words, and when he slept he had a vision of the Virgin seated in a chariot, and she told him to draw near and join her servants. Then he retired to Monte Senario, but such was his modesty that it was long before the brethren knew that he was so learned a man. He distinguished himself as a preacher, but far more as a peace-maker, for he did much to reconcile the then opposing factions of Tuscany. He obtained the confirmation of his Order, and preached with great success through Italy and France. He was General of his Order at the time of his death. The pictures of Andrea del Sarto in the cloisters of the Annunziata at Florence, have still further immortalized this saint. These were painted after his beatification by Leo X., A. D. 1516; but his canonization did not take place until 1671. August 23, A. D. 1285.

St. Philip Neri (*Ital.* San Filippo Neri), who was the founder of the Order of the Oratorians, was a Florentine, and born in 1515. His father was of one of the oldest Tuscan families, and a lawyer. When eighteen years old, Philip went to Rome, and became a tutor in a noble family. By his intellect, eloquence, and purity of character, he became very influential in the religious movements of his time. He was the intimate friend and almoner of St. Charles Borromeo, and in this capacity did much good. He was ever employed in works of charity, and gathered about him young men, members of the nobility and the learned professions, who went about reading and praying with the sick and needy, founding and visiting hospitals, and various charities. They were bound by no vows, and were not secluded from the world. They called themselves Oratorians, and from them arose the Pères de l'Oratoire of France. St. Philip Neri was the spiritual adviser of the Massimi family, and it is related that when the son and heir of Prince Fabrizio Massimi died of a fever, St. Philip came into the chamber where the family were lamenting over his dead body. Philip laid his hand on the head of the boy, and called his name; he opened his eyes and sat up. Philip then said, "Art thou unwilling to die?" "No," replied the boy. "Art thou resigned to yield thy soul to God?" "I am." "Then go," said Philip, and the boy sank back and expired with a sweet smile upon his face. On the 16th of March the Palazzo Massimi at Rome, is dressed for a festival in honor of this event, and services are held in the chapel at which the Pope sometimes officiates. A picture illustrative of this miracle is in the Church of S. Maria della Vallicella, which was given to the Oratorians when their Order was confirmed. In this church a chapel was dedicated to St. Philip Neri, and a mosaic copy of Guido's picture of this saint was placed there by Nero de' Neri of Florence. The bed, the crucifix, the books, and other relics of the saint are preserved in the oratory. May 26, A. D. 1595.

St. Phocas of Sinope (*Ital.* San Focà). This saint lived in the third century. He had a cottage and garden near the Gate of Sinope in Pontus. His cottage was open to all who needed shelter and lodging, and the produce of his garden was distributed to the poor after his own slight wants were supplied. As he sat at supper one night some strangers knocked at his door. He asked them to enter, gave them water to wash, and set food for them. Later in the evening they told him they had been sent to find Phocas, who had been accused as a Christian, and they had been commanded to kill him wherever he should be found. The saint betrayed no emotion, and gave them a chamber in which to sleep. When all was at rest, he went to his garden and made a grave among the flowers he loved. In the morning he announced that Phocas was found. The guests rejoiced, and said, "Where is he?" But when he answered, "I am he," they were unwilling to betray their host. Then he said, "Since it is the will of God, I am willing to die in his cause." Then they beheaded him on the border of the grave, and buried him. This saint is only represented in Byzantine Art. He is in the garb of a gardener, and has a spade as his attribute. Patron of gardens and gardeners. July 3, A. D. 303.

St. Placidus was the son of Tertullus, a Roman Senator, who placed this child under the care of St. Benedict at Subiaco, when only five years of age. Placidus was sent by his superior to preach in Sicily, when he was still quite young. According to tradition his sister Flavia and two young brothers joined him, and they dwelt in a convent near Messina. This was attacked by brigands, who massacred Placidus and Flavia, with thirty of their companions. The later Benedictine writers do not believe the account of this massacre. He is represented in the black habit of his Order, or with the rich dalmatica above a black tunic. The palm is his attribute. January 15, A. D. 584.

Plautilla, though not a saint, is seldom omitted in representations of the martyrdom of St. Paul. According to the legend, she was a Roman matron, and one of the converts of St. Peter and St. Paul. She placed herself on the way by which she knew that St. Paul would pass to his martyrdom in order to see him for the last time. When he came she besought him to bless her, and wept greatly. Then Paul seeing her faith asked her to give him her veil, that he might bind his eyes with it when he was beheaded, and promised that he would return it to her after his death. Then all who heard mocked at this promise, but Plautilla gave him the veil; and after his death St. Paul did indeed appear to her, and gave her again the veil which was stained with his blood.

St. Potitus of Pisa (*Ital.* San Potito). See St. Ephesus.

St. Praxedes and **St. Pudentiana** (*Ital.* Santa Prassede e Santa Pudenziana; *Fr.* Sainte Prassède et Sainte Potentienne). When St. Peter came to Rome he dwelt in the house of Pudens, who was a patrician of great wealth. Not long after the coming of the apostle, Pudens and Sabinella, his wife, with Novatus his son, and his two daughters, Praxedes and Pudentiana, were all converted and baptized. Soon after the parents and brother died, and the sisters, left alone, inherited all the riches of the family. They had houses and public baths at the foot of the Esquiline. Then began the first great persecution, in which St. Peter perished. Now the sisters determined to devote themselves to the relief and care of the suffering Christians, and to the burying of the bodies of such as were slain. They had the assistance of a holy man named Pastorus, who was devoted in their service. They shrank from nothing that came in the way of their self-imposed duties. They sought out and received into their houses such as were torn and mutilated by tortures. They visited and fed such as were in prison. They took up the bodies of the martyred ones which were cast out without burial, and carefully washing and shrouding them they laid them reverently in the caves beneath their houses. All the blood they collected with sponges, and deposited in a certain well. Thus boldly they showed forth the faith which was in them, and yet they escaped persecution and martyrdom, and died peacefully and were buried in the cemetery of Priscilla. Pastorus wrote a history of their deeds and virtues. Their house, which was made sacred not only by their lives but by the preaching of St. Peter, was consecrated as a place of Christian worship by Pope Pius I. Their churches are among the interesting remains of ancient Rome. In the nave of the Church of Santa Prassede is a well, in which she was said to have put the blood of those who suffered on the Esquiline, while the holy sponge is preserved in a silver shrine in the sacristy. In the Church of St. Pudentiana there is a well, said to contain the relics of three thousand martyrs. These sisters are richly draped in pictures, and the sponge and cup are their especial attributes. July 21, and May 19, A. D. 148.

St. Prisca. The church of this saint at Rome on the Aventine, is supposed to occupy the spot on which stood the house of Aquila and Priscilla, where St. Peter lodged; which site was thought to be also that of the Temple of Diana founded by Servius Tullius. And here is shown the font in which St. Peter baptized the earliest converts in Rome, and among others St. Prisca. According to the legend, she was a virgin of illustrious family, and was exposed to the beasts of the amphitheatre when but thirteen years of age. A fierce lion, who was let loose upon her, humbly licked her feet, to the joy of the Christians. She was then beheaded, and an eagle watched over her body until it was buried. She is represented bearing a palm with the lion beside her, and sometimes the eagle, thus being honored by the kings of both beasts and birds, as the legend remarks. The name of St. Prisca is retained in the calendar of the English Church. January 18, A. D. 275.

St. Procopius was King of Bohemia. He relinquished his crown and became a hermit. Many years passed without his being known, but at length as a certain Prince Ulrich was hunting, he pursued a hind which fled for safety to the arms of St. Procopius, and so he was discovered. On account of the similarity of the attribute, his pictures are sometimes mistaken for those of St. Giles. July 8, A. D. 303.

St. Proculus is the military patron of Bologna. In the time of the tenth persecution, a cruel man named Marinus was sent to Bologna to enforce the edict of the emperor. Proculus was so filled with indignation, which might almost be called holy, that he entered the house of Marinus and killed him with an axe, which axe is the attribute given him in art. He sometimes carries a head in his hands which may be either that of Marinus or his own.

St. Protasius of Milan. See St. Gervasius.

St. Pudentiana (*Ital.* Santa Pudenziana; *Fr.* Sainte Potentienne). See St. Praxedes.

Quattro Coronati, or the Four Crowned Brothers. According to tradition these were four Christian brothers, workers in wood and stone, who dwelt in Rome at the time of Diocletian. They refused to employ their art in fashioning gods or building temples for them, and for this suffered martyrdom. Some were scourged; some beheaded; and some put in iron cages and cast into the sea. The "Cinque Martiri" were also of the same trades and their fate the same. The names of the Coronati are given as SS. Carpophorus, Severus, Severianus, and Victorianus. The church dedicated to them is on the part of the Cœlian Hill which extends from the Lateran to the Coliseum. It is said that their remains were found here during the fourth century. Their title of Coronati alludes to the crown of martyrdom. The five martyrs (I Cinque Martiri) are honored at the same time and place with the Coronati, and they are represented in art with the implements of their profession: the mallet, chisel, square, and rule, bearing palms and wearing crowns. November 4, A. D. 400.

St. Quintin was the son of Zeno. He became converted, and gave up a high command which he held in the Roman army in order to preach. He labored especially in Belgium and at Amiens. He was accused before the prefect Rictius Varus, and suffered death by being impaled on an iron spit. This instrument of his torture is his attribute, which is not always represented. October 31, A. D. 287.

St. Quirinus was a soldier in the army of Aurelian. He became a Christian, and preached so openly as to especially exasperate his officers, who were pagans. His martyrdom was extreme in cruelty. His tongue was first taken out and thrown to a hawk. He was then dragged to death by horses. He is represented in armor with a horse, and a hawk, and a shield, with nine balls as well as the martyr's palm.

St. Quirinus, Bishop of Sissek in Croatia. He was martyred by being drowned with a millstone about his neck. One of the eight guardian saints of Austria. June 4, A. D. 309.

St. Radegunda was the daughter of the King of Thuringia, Berthaire, and the wife of Clothaire V. of France, who first carried her captive with all her family and afterwards married her. This queen was devoted to prayer and alms-giving, and often wore beneath her royal garments, one of penitential hair-cloth. One day as she walked in her garden she heard the prisoners, who were only separated from her by a wall, weeping and imploring pity. She thought of her own sorrows in the past, and she prayed earnestly for them, not knowing how else to aid them. And as she prayed their fetters burst in sunder and they were freed from captivity. Later in life Radegunda took the religious habit, and founded a monastery at Poitiers. She is represented with the royal crown, and beneath it a long veil. A captive kneels before her with his broken fetters in his hand. August 13, A. D. 587.

Ragnar Lodbrog. See St. Edmund.

St. Ranieri (*Ital.* San Ranieri; *Fr.* St. Regnier). The whole life of this saint was full of poetry and mystery. He was born in or about the year 1100. His family was that of the Scaccieri of Pisa. In his youth an eagle appeared to him bearing in his beak a blazing light, and said, "I come from Jerusalem to enlighten the nations." But Ranieri lived a life devoted to pleasure. At length as he one day played the lyre surrounded by beautiful damsels, a holy man passed by who turned and looked on Ranieri; and there was so much of sorrowful sadness in his gaze that the young man threw down his lyre and followed the man of God, bewailing and weeping on account of his sins and wasted life. Soon he embarked for Jerusalem, where he took off his own garments and wore the schiavina, or slave-shirt, and this he wore ever after in token of his humility. He lived the life of a hermit, in the deserts of Palestine, for twenty years. During this time he had numberless visions. On one occasion he felt his vows of abstinence to be almost more than he could keep. He then had a vision of a golden vase set with precious stones and full of oil, pitch, and sulphur. These were kindled to fire and none could quench the flames. Then there was put into his hands a small ewer of water, and when he turned on but a few drops the fire was extinguished. This vision he believed to signify the human passions, by the pitch and sulphur; but the water was the emblem of temperance. He then determined to live on bread and water alone. His reverence for water was very great, and most of his miracles were performed through the use of it, so that he was called San Ranieri dell' Acqua. But when he tarried with a host who cheated his guests by putting water in his wine, the saint did not hesitate to expose the fraud, for he revealed to all present the figure of Satan sitting on one of the wine-casks in the form of a huge cat with the wings of a bat. He did many miracles after his return to Pisa, and made converts by the sanctity of his life and example. When he died many miraculous manifestations bore witness to his eminent holiness. All the bells in Pisa were spontaneously tolled, and the Archbishop Villani, who had been sick in bed for two years, was cured to attend his funeral. At the moment in the funeral service when it was the custom to omit the "Gloria in Excelsis," it was sung by a choir of angels above the altar, while the organ accompanied them without being played by any perceptible hands. The harmony of this chant was so exquisite that those who heard it thought the very heavens were opened. He was buried in a tomb in the Duomo. After the plague in Pisa in 1356, the life of this saint was painted in the Campo Santo by Simone Memmi and Antonio Veneziano. These frescoes are most important in the history of art, and consist of eight scenes from the life of St. Ranieri. (1.) His conversion. (2.) He embarks for Palestine. (3.) He assumes the hermit's dress. (4.) He has many temptations and visions in the desert. (5.) He returns to Pisa. (6.) He exposes the fraud of the innkeeper. (7.) His death and funeral obsequies. (8.) His miracles after death. July 17, A. D. 1161.

St. Raphael, the Archangel (*Lat.* Sanctus Raphael; *Ital.* San Raffaello; *Fr.* St. Raphael; *Ger.* Der Heilige Rafael. Signification: The Medicine of God). Raphael is considered the guardian angel of humanity. He was sent to warn Adam of the danger of sin and its unhappy consequences.

"Be strong, live happy, and love! but first of all
Him whom to love is to obey, and keep
His great command; take heed lest passion sway
Thy judgment to do aught, which else free-will
Would not admit; thine, and of all thy sons
The weal or woe in thee is placed; beware!" — *Milton.*

He was the herald who bore to the shepherds the "good tidings of great joy which shall be for all people." He is especially the protector of the young, the pilgrim, and the traveller. In the apocryphal romance, his watchful care of the young Tobias during his eventful journey is typical of his benignity and loving condescension towards those whom he protects. His countenance is represented as full of benignity. Devotional pictures portray him dressed as a pilgrim, with sandals; his hair bound with a diadem or a fillet; the staff in his hand, and a wallet or *panetière* hung to his belt. As a guardian spirit he bears the sword and a small casket or vase, containing the "fishy charm" (Tobit vi. 6) against evil spirits. As guardian angel he usually leads Tobias. The picture of Murillo in the Leuchtenberg Gallery,

(Leuchtenberg Gallery, Murillo.) St. Raphael.

represents him as the guardian angel of a bishop who appears as a votary below. September 12.

St. Raymond (*Sp.* San Ramon). On account of the circumstances of his birth this saint is styled Nonnatus. He belonged to the Order of Mercy, and labored for the captives among the Moors. According to tradition his lips were bored through with a red-hot iron and fastened with a padlock. He was a cardinal, and the General of his Order. He presided at a chapter held at Barcelona. Pope Gregory IX. and King James of Aragon assisted at his funeral obsequies. August 31, A. D. 1240.

St. Raymond of Peñaforte was born at the castle belonging to his family at Peñaforte in Catalonia. He was allied to the royal house of Aragon, and his family were of Barcelona. He early entered upon a religious life, and became a model in his zealous devotion to the church and his charity to the poor. He assumed the habit of the Dominican Order, and was the third General of the Order. His zealous preaching against the Moors was thought to be the first cause of the final expulsion of the infidels from Spain. A miracle which he is said to have performed, and which is attested to in the bull of his canonization, is related thus: Raymond was the spiritual director of King James of Aragon (el Conquistador). This king was an accomplished gentleman, and did not incline to allow his confessor to interfere with his pleasures. Now he was greatly in love with a beautiful woman of his court from whom Raymond attempted to separate him in vain. The king summoned the priest to attend him to Majorca, but he refused to go unless the lady remained behind. James affected to comply, but the lady accompanied him in the dress of a page. Raymond soon discovered the deceit and remonstrated severely with the king, who was very angry. The priest threatened to return to Spain, but James forbade any vessel to leave the port, and passed sentence of death upon any who should aid Raymond to go away. St. Raymond then said, "An earthly king has deprived us of the means of escape, but a Heavenly King will supply them." Then walking up to a rock which projected into the sea, he spread his cloak on the waters, and, setting his staff upright and tying one corner to it for a sail, he made the sign of the cross, and boldly embarked in this new kind of vessel. He was wafted over the surface of the ocean with such rapidity that in six hours he reached Barcelona." This miracle was attested to by five hundred persons, who saw him land at Barcelona and take up his cloak perfectly dry from the water and wrap it round him, and then with an air of great humility retire to his cell. Don Jayme, overcome by this miracle, repented of his obstinacy and afterwards governed his kingdom and his life by the advice of St. Ramon. He is represented in the black habit of his Order, and kneels on his mantle while he is borne over the sea, or else the miracle is represented in the background. January 23, A. D. 1275.

St. Regulus was an African bishop. He fled from his diocese in the time of the contentions between the Arians and Catholics. He came to Tuscany and lived the life of an anchoret. In the invasion of Totila he was beheaded. According to tradition he took up his head and proceeded two stadia, when he sat down. Being found thus by two of his disciples he gave them his head, and they buried him there with great reverence and (what is not strange) *unspeakable awe.*

St. Reparata was a virgin of Cesarea in Cappadocia. In the persecution under Decius she was martyrized, though only twelve years old. As she died her spirit was seen to issue from her mouth in shape like a dove, and to fly to heaven. This saint was for six hundred years the chief patroness of Florence, and the Duomo was dedicated in her name; but it was re-dedicated to Santa Maria del-Fiore. She is represented in various colored robes, and bears the crown, palm, book, and a banner with a red cross on a white ground.

St. Roch (*Lat.* Sanctus Rochus; *Ital.* San Rocco; *Fr.* St. Roch or Roque) was the son of noble parents. Montpelier, in Languedoc, was his birthplace. When he was born, there was a small red cross on his breast. His mother interpreted this as a sign that he should be consécrated to God's service, and educated him with great care. The saint too was of the same mind; but he inclined to follow the example of Jesus,—to go about to do good in preference to that of many holy men, who flee from the world to serve God. His parents died when he was less than twenty years old, and left him vast estates. He sold all, and gave the money to hospitals and to the poor. He then went on foot to Rome in the garb of a pilgrim. When he arrived at Aquapendente a terrible plague was raging there. St. Roch offered to attend the sick in the hospitals. He was especially successful in his care of the plague-stricken, and it appeared that some peculiar blessing attended him; so prevalent was this idea that, considering his youth and gentleness, the people were ready to believe him an angel; and he himself was not without the thought that a special blessing was on his efforts. He then went to Cesena and Rimini, where he labored in the same manner, and then he arrived at Rome in the midst of a fearful pestilence, and for three years more devoted himself to the care of the most

(Carotto.) St. Roch.

hopeless cases He constantly prayed that God might find him worthy to die as a martyr to this care for others. Years passed thus, and he went from city to city, wherever he heard of any dreadful disease and suffering. At length at Piacenza he was himself struck down by an unknown epidemic then raging there. One night he sank down in the hospital weary with nursing, and fell asleep. When he awoke he found himself plague-stricken with a horrible ulcer on his thigh, the pain of which compelled him to shriek aloud. He feared lest he should disturb others, and crawled into the street; but he was not allowed to remain there. He then dragged himself to a wood outside the city, and lay down to die. But a little dog which had attended him in all his wanderings now cared for him, and brought him each day a loaf of bread. According to the legend an angel also dressed his wound and cared for him, but others doubting this, believe that it was a man named Gothard, who did this for him; but be this as it may, as soon as he was able he set out for his home. When he arrived at a little village near Montpelier, where the land belonged to his estates, and the people were the vassals of his family, no one knew him, and they regarded him so suspiciously that they took him before the judge as a spy. The judge was his uncle, but even he did not recognize him, and condemned him to be imprisoned. St. Roch regarded all this as the will of God, and said nothing, desiring that all should be as Providence should direct. So he was cast into a dungeon. There was no one to plead for him, and he adhered to his resolve of silence; thus he remained five years. One morning when the jailer went to his cell it was filled with a glory of light, and the prisoner lay dead with a paper beside him, which told his name, and these words also: "All those who are stricken by the plague, and who pray for aid through the merits and intercession of St. Roch, the servant of God, shall be healed." Then the judge, when he saw this paper, wept and was filled with remorse. He was honorably buried midst the prayers of the whole city. Nearly a century elasped before St. Roch was heard of outside his native city, where he was held in the greatest possible veneration. But at the time of the great church council at Constance, the plague broke out in that city, and the priests were about to fly from it in consternation when a German monk, who had been in France, advised that the power of St. Roch should be tested in this emergency. His counsel was followed, and the image of the saint borne through the city accompanied by a solemn procession, with prayers and litanies. Then the plague ceased, and to this the enlarged consideration of St. Roch may be traced. Towards the close of the fifteenth century the Venetians, who were especially exposed to the plague from their commercial intercourse with the East, resolved to possess, if possible, the relics of St. Roch. The men appointed to accomplish the purpose went to Montpelier as pilgrims. They succeeded in carrying away the sacred remains, and were received with joy by all Venice, from the Doge down to the poorest beggar. Then the splendid Church of San Rocco was built under the auspices of a society which already existed in Venice for the care of the sick, and which had been formed under his protection. In this society many of the nobility enrolled themselves. Many votive pictures are seen of this saint, in which he is represented as interceding for the sick person, who is introduced in the painting. In devotional pictures, St. Roch is represented as a man in middle age, of refined and delicate features, with an expression of benevolence and kindness. He is dressed as a pilgrim, with the cockle-shell on his hat, the staff in his hand, and the wallet at his side. With one hand he points to the plague spot on his side, or lifts his robe to show it. His dog also attends him. Patron of all who are in prison; of all sick persons in hospitals, but especially of those afflicted by the plague. August 16, A. D. 1327.

St. Romain, whose whole history is painted on the windows of the Cathedral of Rouen, was bishop of that city in the time of Clovis I. He is considered as the great Apostle of Normandy, for he preached there with remarkable zeal and overthrew paganism. The Seine at one time so overflowed its banks as to threaten the destruction of the city. St. Romain commanded the waters to retire, but of the slime and mud which remained a poisonous dragon was born, called by the French, la Gargouille; this monster spread consternation all along the shores of the river. Then the saint, by the aid of a wicked murderer, went forth and slew the beast. From this time it was the privilege of the chapter of Rouen to pardon a criminal condemned to death; and this was so until the time of the Revolution. February 28, A. D. 639.

St. Romualdo was born at Ravenna, of the noble family of the Onesti, about the year 956. He was trained like other young noblemen, and loved the chase, but often as he rode on the hunt in the forests of Ravenna, he was soothed and charmed by the beauty of the scenery, and would slacken his pace, and become absorbed in the thought of the quiet peace of those who dwelt alone with Nature. Then he would breathe a prayer, and return to his busy life of pleasure. But his father, Sergius, was a man of very different mettle. He was proud and self-willed, and could brook no opposition. Having disagreed with a relative concerning the succession of a certain pasture, he challenged him to combat and slew him. Romualdo was present at the time, and was so overpowered with horror that he believed it his duty to expiate his father's crime. He retired to a monastery near Ravenna, Sant' Apollinare in Classe, and assumed the habit of the Benedictines. But to his enthusiastic and sensitive temperament, the irregularities of the monks were unendurable; after seven years passed here he conceived the idea of establishing new monastical institutions, according to the pure spirit which he felt should control them, and of reforming the old ones and raising them to the same standard. Henceforth his life was a continuous battle. He was hated and reviled by monks everywhere, and even his life was in danger from the bitterness of their enmity to him. But he scorned all danger, and despised all persecution, and fought most bravely by prayer and labor for the cause he had undertaken to maintain. His first monastery was founded near Arezzo in the Apennines; in a glen called Campo-Maldoli, from the name of the family to whom it belonged. From this the new Order was called that of the Camaldoli. The members of this Order are consecrated to perpetual service to God; they strictly practice solitude, silence, and contemplation; they do not even eat together, but each lives in a separate hut with his own garden, in order to comply with the requirements for manual labor. The Camaldolesi are among the most severe of all monks, and are in fact hermits in societies. According to the legend the color of the habit of his Order was changed in this wise: Not long before his death the saint fell asleep beside a fountain not far from his cell, and he beheld a vision of a ladder reaching from earth to heaven, on which the brethren of his Order ascended by twos and threes, and all dressed in white. So he immediately changed the color, which had been black, and white has ever since been worn by the Camaldolesi. Thirty years after his secession from his first convent he had become famous throughout the north of Italy, and had communities of reformed monks numbering hundreds. He is represented with a loose white habit, and a full beard which falls to his girdle, and leans upon a crutch. February 7, A. D. 1027.

(National Gallery.) St. Romualdo.

St. Romulo (*Lat.* Sanctus Romulus) was a noble Roman, whom, according to the legend, St. Peter sent to preach to the people of Fiesole, which was then a most important Etruscan city. After thus being the apostle he became the first bishop of Fiesole. He was at length accused before the prætor, as a Christian, and was sentenced to suffer death. This was in the time of Nero. After suffering the most cruel tortures, he was slain with a dagger. The old cathedral of Fiesole is dedicated to St. Romulo. He is represented in the episcopal robes, and bears the palm. July 23.

Santa Rosa di Lima was born at Lima in Peru, and is the only canonized female saint of the New World. The principal thing by which she is distinguished is the extreme hatred she had of vanity, and consequently of beauty, which she regarded as the root of vanity. The severities of her life also, were very great. She was especially beautiful in her complexion, on account of which she was named. She rejected many suitors, and at last destroyed her great charm with a compound of pepper and quicklime. When her mother commanded her to wear a wreath of roses she so arranged it that it was in truth a crown of thorns. Her food was principally bitter herbs. She was a model of filial devotion, and maintained her parents by her labor after they had become poor, toiling all day in her garden, and all night with her needle. She took the habit of the Third Order of St. Dominick. The Peruvian legend relates, that when Pope Clement X. was asked to canonize her, he refused, exclaiming, "India y Santa! así como llueven rosas!" ("India and saint! as likely as that it should rain roses!") Instantly a shower of roses commenced in the Vatican, and did not cease till the Pope acknowledged his mistaken incredulity. Stirling's "Artists of Spain," thus speaks of Santa Rosa: "This flower of Sanctity, whose fragrance has filled the whole Christian world, is the patroness of America, the St. Theresa of Transatlantic Spain." In a picture by Murillo, she is represented with a thorny crown; holding in her hand the figure of the Infant Saviour, which rests on full-blown roses. August 30, A. D. 1617.

St. Rosa di Viterbo was a member of the Third Order of St. Francis. She lived in the thirteenth century, and was remarkable for the influence she exercised in Viterbo, as well as for her extensive charities and the eloquence of her speech. She lived a life of great austerity. She is now the patroness of that city, to which while living she was a benefactress. She is represented in a gray tunic, with knotted girdle, and a chaplet of roses. May 8, A. D. 1261.

St. Rosalia of Palermo, whose statue towers upon the summit of Monte Pellegrino, overlooking the Mediterranean, and cheering the mariners who consider her their protectress, was a Sicilian virgin of noble birth. When scarcely sixteen years old she withdrew from her home and friends secretly, and lived in a cave in

Monte Pellegrino, near the summit. She had rejected many suitors, and longed for the solitude where nothing could distract her mind from the service of God. She died without having been discovered, and twice after she had ascended to her heavenly bridegroom, she interceded for Palermo, and saved it from the ravages of the pestilence. At length her remains were discovered lying in her cave, and such was the purity of this unsullied virgin, that they remained uncorrupted, even in death! Her name was inscribed above her in the rock, and on her head was a crown made of the roses of Paradise, and placed there by angels. Her cave has become a chapel to which pilgrims resort. She is usually represented reclining in her cave, which is bright with celestial light; angels crown her with roses, and she holds a crucifix upon her breast. Again, standing and inscribing her name upon the rock. She wears a brown tunic, sometimes ragged, and her hair is loose about her. September 4, A. D. 1160.

Rosary, The. The beads used by Romanists and called by this name are so often represented in art, that an explanation of its use and signification will not be out of place. The use of beads to assist the memory in regard to the number of prayers recited, is of very ancient date and of eastern origin. They are used by the Mohammedans, and were employed by the Benedictines before their use became general in the Church. The rosary in its present accepted form was instituted by St. Dominick. He invented a new arrangement of the beads and dedicated it to the Blessed Virgin. The festival of the Rosary was instituted by Gregory XIII. after the battle of Lepanto, A. D. 1571, and from this time it became popular as a subject of art, and there are large numbers of pictures which relate to its institution. A complete rosary has one hundred and fifty small beads and fifteen larger ones. The latter represent the Pater-nosters and the former the Ave-Marias. The large beads divide the rosary into fifteen decades, each one consisting of ten Ave-Marias, preceded by a large bead, or Pater-noster, and all concluded with a Gloria Patri. Five decades make a chaplet, which is a third part of a rosary. To these beads a crucifix is added. The "Mysteries of the Rosary," consist in the assigning of a certain event in the life of the Virgin, or in the life of the Saviour to each decade. There are five joyful mysteries, which are, — the Annunciation, the Visitation, the Nativity, the Purification, and Christ found in the Temple. Five dolorous or sorrowful mysteries: Our Lord in the Garden of Gethsemane, the Flagellation, Christ Crowned with Thorns, the Procession to Calvary, and the Crucifixion. Five glorious mysteries: the Resurrection, the Ascension, the Descent of the Holy Ghost, the Assumption, and the Coronation. The rosary in the hand or about the person of a saint signifies that they obtained aid "per intercessione dell' Sacratissimo Rosario." When held before the Madonna it indicates that by the use of it she is to be propitiated; in short, the Rosary was intended to excite and assist devotion in various ways, and its representations illustrate the same idea. Festival of the Rosary, October 1.

St. Rufina. See St. Justina of Seville.

St. Sabina, to whom a church is dedicated at Rome, was a noble matron who suffered martyrdom during the reign of Hadrian. The church, which dates from the early part of the fifth century, is said to occupy the site of her house, and the altar-piece represents a soldier dragging the saint up the steps of a temple, with a sword in his hand. With her, Seraphia, a Greek slave, who had converted Sabina, was also executed. Her attribute is the palm. August 29. Second century.

Santa Casa. This is the title given to the house in which the Virgin Mary was born at Nazareth. According to the legend this house was threatened with profanation or destruction at the time of the invasion of the Saracens, when four angels took it and bore it over sea and land to the coast of Dalmatia; but there it was not safe, and the angels again removed it to a spot near Loretto; but here the brigands invaded it, and it was again removed to the spot where it now remains, — said to have been done in 1295. The Madonna di Loretto is represented as holding the Infant Saviour, and seated upon the roof of a house which is borne by four angels. Loretto became one of the most celebrated places of pilgrimage, and many chapels have been dedicated to Our Lady of Loretto.

St. Scholastica. Very little is known of this saint. She was the sister of St. Benedict, and followed him to Monte Cassino, and there gathered about her a small community of nuns. Benedict visited her but once each year. At one time when he arose to take leave of her, she begged him to remain longer, and when he refused she bent her head and prayed that God would interfere to detain her brother with her. Then immediately a furious storm arose and he was forced to remain for several hours. This was their last parting, for two days after St. Scholastica died, and Benedict saw her soul ascend to heaven in the form of a dove, while he was praying in his cell. She is represented in a black habit with a dove at her feet or pressed to her bosom, and a lily in her hand. February 10. About 543.

St. Sebald is one of the most distinguished among the early German saints, and is especially venerated in Nuremberg. The legends relate that he was the son of a Danish king, and left England with St. Boniface. His name in English is Seward, Siward, or Sigward. He travelled through the north of Germany, preaching as a missionary, and at last lived permanently in Nuremberg. While he dwelt in a cell not far from the city he went there almost daily to teach the poor. He was in the habit of stopping to rest in the hut of a cartwright. One day when it was very cold he found the family in the hut nearly frozen, and they had no fuel. Then Sebald commanded them to bring in the icicles which hung from the roof and use them to feed the fire. They obeyed and were thus miraculously warmed. Again the saint desired fish for a fast-day and sent the same cartwright to buy it. Now the lord of Nuremberg had commanded that no person should buy fish until the castle was supplied; so the poor man was punished by having his eyes put out. But St. Sebald restored his sight. His wonderful shrine in the Church at Nuremberg was made, according to its inscription, by Peter Vischer and his five sons. These sons with their families all dwelt with the father Peter, and shared alike his labors, his rewards, and his fame. It was commenced in 1508, finished in 1523, and remains undisturbed. He is represented in his statue by Peter Vischer as a pilgrim with shell in hat, rosary, staff, and wallet. He holds in his hand a model of his church. About A. D. 770.

(Nuremberg Statue. Peter Vischer).
St. Sebald.

St. Sebastian (*Lat.* Sanctus Sebastianus; *Ital.* San Sebastiano or Bastiano; *Fr.* St. Sébastien; *Sp.* and *Ger.* Sebastian). The legend of this saint, though very old, has the advantage of being better authenticated by history than many antique traditions. Sebastian was descended from a noble family which had been honored with high offices in the empire. He was born at Narbonne, and when still quite young was made commander of a company of the Prætorian Guards, and was thus always near the emperor, Diocletian, with whom he was an especial favorite. Now Sebastian was secretly a Christian, and while from this very fact he conscientiously fulfilled all his duties to the emperor, he also protected the Christians, and endeavored to make converts; and in this last he was very successful. Among those whom he had thus influenced were two young soldiers, of noble family, called Marcus and Marcellinus. They were accused as Christians and condemned to the torture; this they firmly endured and were led out for execution. Then their families, their wives and children, besought them to recant and live. That which the tortures could not effect, these prayers and tears were about to do, — they wavered; then Sebastian, regardless of himself, rushed forward and eloquently exhorted them, that they should not betray their Redeemer. So earnest was he, and so great was his power, that the two soldiers went boldly to their death, while their friends, many of the guards, and even the judge himself, were also converted and secretly baptized. Now Sebastian's time had come; but before his public accusation, the emperor so loved him, that he sent for him to see if privately he could not influence him to save his life And he said, "Have I not always honored thee above the rest of my officers? Why hast thou disobeyed my commands, and insulted my gods?" Then answered the young saint, with courage, but also with meekness, "O Cæsar, I have ever prayed, in the name of Jesus Christ, for thy prosperity, and have been true to thy service; but as for the gods whom thou wouldst have me worship, they are devils, or, at best, idols of wood and stone." After this, Diocletian ordered that Sebastian should be bound to a stake, and shot to death with arrows, but that it should be inscribed on the stake, that he had no fault but that of being a Christian. Then the archers did their duty, and he was left for dead, being pierced with many arrows. At night, Irene, the widow of one of his friends who had been martyred, came with her companions to take his body away to burial. And lo! it was found that he was still alive, for none of the arrows had entered a vital part. Then Irene took him home, and carefully tended him until he was well again. When his friends saw him they begged that he would fly from Rome and save his life; but Sebastian went to the palace and stood where he knew the emperor must surely see him, and he plead for certain condemned ones, and plainly told the emperor of his cruelty and wickedness. Then Diocletian, being amazed, exclaimed, "Art thou not Sebastian?" And he said, "I am Sebastian, whom God hath delivered from thy hand, that I might testify to the faith of Jesus Christ and plead for his servants." Then was Diocletian doubly infuriated; and he commanded that Sebastian should be taken to the circus and beaten to death with clubs, and his body thrown into the Cloaca Maxima, and thus hidden from his friends. But in spite of all this, a lady named Lucina, who was a Christian, found means to obtain his remains and they were laid with reverent care in the Catacombs at the feet of St. Peter and St. Paul. Apollo was the heathen god whom it was believed afflicted men by the plague; and he it was whom men invoked against it, and the arrow was the emblem of pestilence. It would seem that from the association of the arrow with St. Sebastian must have arisen the belief that he was especially powerful to grant aid against this curse; for there are, according to tradition, many cities which have been thus saved by his intercession. A century after the great plague in the time of Gregory the Great, another fearful pestilence ravaged Rome. In the Church of San Pietro-in-Vincoli is an ancient mosaic of St. Sebastian, and on a tablet the following inscription in Latin: "To St. Sebastian, Martyr, dispeller of the pestilence. In the year of salvation, 680, a pernicious and severe pestilence invaded the city of Rome. It was of three months' duration, July, August, and September. Such was the multitude of the dead, that, on the same bier, parents and children, husbands and wives, with brothers and sisters, were borne out to burial-places, which, everywhere filled with bodies, hardly sufficed. In addition to this, nocturnal miracles alarmed them; for two angels, one good and the other evil, went through the city; and this last, bearing a rod in his hand, as many times as he struck the doors so many mortals fell in those houses. The disease spread for a length of time, until it was announced to a holy man, that there would be an end of the calamity, if, in the Church of S. Peter ad Vincula, an altar should be consecrated to Sebastian the Martyr; which thing being done immediately, the pestilence, as if driven back by hand, was commanded to cease." From this time Sebastian became the universal patron against pestilence, which honor has been shared in later years by St. Roch. The pictures of St. Sebastian are innumerable and unmistakable. He is young, beautiful, without drapery, bound to a tree, and pierced by arrows. He looks to heaven, from whence descends an angel with palm and crown. He is the favorite saint of Roman women and indeed of women of all Italy. January 20, A. D. 288.

Notre Dame des Sept Douleurs.

St. Secundus, especially venerated at Asti, is one of the saints of the Theban legion. See St. Maurice.

Seven Joys, The, and The Seven Sorrows of the Blessed Virgin, are often represented in series of pictures. The subjects of the seven joys are,—(1.) The Annunciation. (2.) The Visitation. (3.) The Adoration of the Magi. (4.) The Presentation in the Temple. (5.) Christ found by Mary, disputing with the Doctors. (6.) The Assumption. (7.) The Coronation. The seven sorrows represent, (1.) The Prophecy of Simeon. (2.) The Flight into Egypt. (3.) Christ lost by his mother. (4.) The Betrayal of Christ. (5.) The Crucifixion, (St. John and the Virgin only present). (6.) The Deposition from the cross (7.) Ascension of Christ, leaving Mary on earth.

Seven Sleepers of Ephesus, The (*Ital.* I Sette Dormienti; *Fr.* Les Sept Dormants, Les Sept Enfants d'Ephèse; *Ger.* Die Sieben Schläfer). This tradition is of great antiquity. Gibbon says it can be traced to within fifty years of the time of the miracle it relates. There is scarcely a written tongue in which it is not found. Syriac, Latin, and Scandinavian relate it, and the writer of the Koran has given it a place. In the time of the persecution of Decius there dwelt in Ephesus seven young men who were Christians. Their names were Maximian, Malchus, Marcian, Dionysius, John, Serapion, and Constantine. Having refused to offer sacrifice to the gods they were accused before the tribunal. They fled to Mount Cœlian and hid in a cave. They were pursued and discovered. Then it was ordered that great stones should be rolled against the mouth of the cave, and they should thus be left to die of starvation. They resigned themselves to this dreadful fate, and embracing each other went to sleep. Time passed on until one hundred and ninety-six years had passed. Then, in the reign of Theodosius, a heresy arose denying the resurrection of the dead. The Emperor, greatly afflicted at this, retired to his palace and dressed himself in sackcloth and sprinkled ashes on his head. And God for his sake restored these seven sleepers. For a certain man of Ephesus went to Mount Cœlian to build him a stable, and he discovered this cavern and rolled the stones away. When the light entered there, the sleepers awoke, and thought they had slept but for a night. Then it was determined that Malchus should venture into Ephesus to obtain food. He went with fear and caution, and was surprised to find the gates of the city surmounted by crosses. Then when he entered within the walls he heard the name of Christ, which he had been accustomed to sigh forth only with his breath, boldly spoken everywhere. He believed himself in a dream. He entered a baker's shop, and in payment for his loaf he offered a coin of the time of Decius. He was regarded with great astonishment, and suspected of having robbed some hidden treasure. When accused he knew not what to say, and he was dragged to the bishop with contumely and reproaches. When the bishop had talked with him the truth was discovered. Then went out the emperor, the governor, the bishop, and hosts of the people, and the six other sleepers were found in the cave. Then when the emperor was come, one of them said, "Believe in us, O Emperor! for we have been raised before the Day of Judgment, in order that thou mightest trust in the resurrection of the dead!" Then they all bowed their heads and gave up the ghost. Representations of this legend are very common among works of art of the thirteenth and fourteenth century, in glass, miniatures, and sculpture. They are usually extended in their cave side by side. Their names are inscribed above their heads and they have the martyr's palm. June 27.

Sibyls, The were prophetesses, who foretold the coming of Christ to the Gentiles as the prophets did to the Jews. They are in the art of the Latin Church what the sages of antiquity were to the Greeks, and are in fact a kind of witnesses to the truth of Christianity. It may be shown that the Church accepted the witness of the sibyls by an extract from the hymn "Dies Iræ," said to have been written by Pope Innocent III. It is translated thus in the English version of the Missal:—

The dreadful day, the day of ire,
Shall kindle the avenging fire
Around the expiring world.
And Earth as Sibyl said of old,
And as the prophet king foretold,
Shall be in ruin hurled."

Their origin was obscure; they were regarded as holy virgins, who lived in caves and grottoes. They were believed to have the power to read the future, and were interrogated by their votaries upon important matters, and their answers were considered authoritative. Varro, who wrote about one hundred years B. C., gives their number as ten, and their names as taken from the localities of their habitations: The Sibylla Persica from Persia; the Sibylla Libyca from Libya; the Sibylla Delphica from Delphi; the Sibylla Erythræa from Erythræá; the Sibylla Cumana from Cumæ; the Sibylla Samia from Samos; the Sibylla Cimmeria from the Black Sea; the Sibylla Tiburtina from Tivoli; the Sibylla Hellespontina from the Hellespont; the Sibylla Phrygia from Phrygia. Two others called the Agrippa or the Hebraica, and the Europa were added in later times, as well as others seldom referred to. Sometimes the Queen of Sheba is represented as one of these wonderful beings. There have been serious disagreements in the opinions of the Church regarding the sibyls and the worth of their prophecies. Some of the early fathers considered them as agents of Beelzebub, while others, including St. Jerome and St. Augustine, believed them to be inspired of God. The two most interesting traditions of the sibyls in this connection are those of the Cumæan and Tiburtine Sibyls who appeared to King Tarquin and the Emperor Augustus. The first, the Cumæan, presented herself to Tarquin with nine books which she desired to sell him. They contained Sibylline Oracles. Tarquin refused her request. She went away and burned three of them and returned with six. Again he refused; again she burned three, and again returned with the three remaining. Then Tarquin sought the advice of the soothsayers, and they assured him that the destinies of the world depended upon the preservation of these oracles. So they were bought, and for centuries after were consulted on all great emergencies of the Roman nation. They were preserved in the Capitol under the care of priests, but during the wars of Marius and Sylla they perished. Then messengers were sent far and

(Baldassare Peruzzi.) Prophecy of the Sibyl.

wide all through the empire to collect the scattered Sibylline leaves, and as many as were found were again carefully preserved. The idea of the ancient Romans, as recorded by Tacitus and Suetonius, that those who should rule the world should come out from Judæa, is believed to have been derived from these Sibylline leaves. Again, when the Roman Senate decreed divine honors to Augustus, he consulted the Tiburtine Sibyl whether he ought to receive them. She replied that it was more becoming for him whose power was declining to go away from her silently, for a Hebrew child should be born who should reign over the gods themselves. Or, that a king should come from heaven whose kingdom should never end. Another version relates that the heavens were opened and a vision of the Virgin with the Infant Saviour in her arms, standing on an altar, was shown him, and a voice was heard saying, "Hæc ara filii Dei" (This is the altar of the Son of God). The emperor adored the vision and reported it to the Senate. And in remembrance of it he erected upon the Capitol an altar inscribed, "Ara primogeniti Dei." On this spot stands the Church of S. Maria in Capitolio, or the "Ara cæli." A passage of Virgil, who wrote forty years B. C., is also quoted as proving that the advent of Christ was foretold in Sibylline prophecy. It is thus translated: "The last age of the Cumæan song now approaches; the great series of ages begins again; now returns the Virgin (Astræa), now return the Saturnian kingdoms, now a new progeny is sent from high heaven. Be but propitious, chaste Lucina, to the boy at his birth, through whom the iron age will first cease, and the golden age dawn on the whole world." The Sibyls do not appear in the earliest art. They were not represented in the Catacombs. In the fourteenth century the vision of Augustus was employed as a symbol of the appearing of the star to the Magi, or the manifestation of Christ to the Gentiles. They were employed in the cyclical decorations of churches with the prophets. Often they were about the principal entrance, or if inside near the door; their position being typical of their having been "forerunners of the Lord." Their number varies. In the Eastern Church there is but one "*la sage Sibylle.*" They should be recognized by their scrolls, but the inscriptions have been so varied that they are not always guides. The sibyls of Michael Angelo on the ceiling of the Sistine Chapel are too well known to need any description, and it has been said that these representations are "the highest honor that art has rendered to the sibyls." Their various attributes, dress, and age, as nearly as it is possible to give them, are as follows: —

The Sibylla Persica was supposed to be a daughter-in-law of Moses. She predicted the coming of the Messiah. She is old, and her attributes are a serpent beneath her feet, and a lantern in her hand.

The Sibylla Libyca prophesied the manifestation of Christ to the Gentiles. She is twenty-four years old, and bears a lighted torch.

The Sibylla Erythræa is the prophetess of Divine vengence. She predicted the Trojan War; in this character she holds a naked sword. But it is also said that she foretold the Annunciation, and in this representation she has a white rose. She is old.

The Sibylla Delphica, her attributes are a horn or the crown of thorns.

The Sibylla Samia, attributes a reed or a cradle. She lived, it is supposed, in the time of Isaiah.

The Sibylla Cimmeria prophesied the Crucifixion. She is eighteen years old, and has a cross or crucifix.

The Sibylla Cumana is fifteen years old, and her attribute is a manger, having foreseen the Nativity in a stable.

The Sibylla Hellespontina prophesied the Incarnation, and also the Crucifixion. Her attributes are the crucifix and a budding rod.

The Sibylla Phrygia prophesied the Resurrection. Attributes, a banner and cross.

The Sibylla Tiburtina symbolizes the mocking and the flagellation of Christ. She is dressed in skins and bears a rod.

The Sibylla Agrippa. Attribute, a scourge; fifteen years old.

The Sibylla Europa prophesied the Massacre of the Innocents. Attribute a sword, fifteen years old. Sometimes all the Sibyls have books in which they read; or they bear torches or lanterns; and some have a sun on the head.

St. Sigismond.

St. Sigismond of Burgundy (*Ital.* San Gismondo) was the son of Gondubald and the cousin of St. Clotilda, wife of Clovis, King of France. Gondubald, was an Arian, and had murdered the parents of Clotilda. Sigismond was a Catholic, and though greatly distinguished for his piety, he put to death his eldest son on the accusation of his second wife, who hated and falsely accused the son of her predecessor. But Sigismond was seized with remorse, and sorely repented his crime. He prayed that his deserved punishment might be inflicted in this world rather than the next; and his prayer was granted, for the sons of Clotilda invaded his kingdom, took him prisoner, and finally, in revenge of the death of their grandparents, they murdered Sigismond. His body was thrown into a well, but was at length removed to the convent of St. Maurice. In a chapel dedicated to St. Sigismond in Cremona, Francesco Sforza was married to Bianca Visconti, and in witness of his love and gratitude he adorned this chapel with great beauty. St. Sigismond is represented in the splendid altar-piece, by Giulio Campi. He is patron saint of Cremona. May 1, A. D. 525.

Simeon, The Prophet. See the Madonna. The Presentation in the Temple.

St. Simon Zelotes, or the Zealot; **St. Jude,** Thaddeus or Lebbeus (*Ital.* San Simone, San Taddeo; *Fr.* St. Simon le Zelé, St. Thaddée; *Ger.* Judas, Thaddäus). The contradictions concerning these saints render it impossible to give any clear account of them. One tradition teaches that they were mentioned as brethren or kinsmen of Jesus by Matthew. Another that they were two brothers who were among the shepherds to whom the birth of Jesus was revealed. There is but one point of agreement concerning them. That is, that they preached the Gospel in Syria and Mesopotamia, and were martyred in Persia; but in what manner is not known, although it is believed that St. Simon was sawn asunder, and St. Jude killed with a halberd. They therefore bear the saw and halberd as their attributes. They are sometimes represented as young, and again as old, according to which tradition the artist follows. In Greek art, Jude and Thaddeus are different persons, Jude being young and Thaddeus old. They have rarely been represented as members of the Sacra Famiglia, and when so introduced have their names in the glories about their heads. May 1.

St. Siro, or **Syrus,** whose statue is in the Cathedral of Pavia, was first bishop of that city and governed the church fifty-six years. His effigy appears on the coins of Pavia.

The "Spalatro," or the Vision of the Bloody Hand, is a picture painted by Washington Allston, in illustration of a scene from "The Italian," by Mrs. Radcliffe; the story of which book is as follows: Vincentio di Vivaldi, the only son of the oldest and one of the most noble Neapolitan families, was determined upon marrying Ellena Rosalba, a lovely girl, and every way worthy of his admiration, but his inferior in rank. The Marchesa di Vivaldi, an ambitious and heartless woman, was resolved to prevent this union at all hazards. She had for her confessor a monk called Father Schedoni, whose early life had been so fearful in its wickedness as to render him a fitting instrument for any crime. He too, was ambitious, and in consideration of a church preferment which the Marchesa could obtain for him, he promised to render her son's marriage impossible by destroying Ellena. For this purpose he employed Spalatro, a man of many crimes who had before served Schedoni as an assassin. Ellena was seized and conveyed secretly to the house of Spalatro, in a lonely situation by the sea, and at night Schedoni and Spalatro proceeded towards her apartment to accomplish their dreadful designs. The beauty and innocence of Ellena had already softened the heart of the assassin, and as he contemplates this new crime, all those of his past life rise before him, and Macbeth-like he imagines that he sees a vision of a bloody hand beckoning him on to this new horror. He is seized with uncontrollable agony and fear. This is the moment represented by the artist, and this the word-picture of the scene: "At the foot of the staircase he again stopped to listen. 'Do you hear anything?' said he in a whisper. 'I hear only the sea,' replied the man. 'Hush! it is something more,' said Schedoni; 'that is the murmur of voices.' They were silent. After a pause of some length, 'It is, perhaps, the voice of the spectres I told you of, Signor,' said Spalatro, with a sneer. 'Give me the dagger,' said Schedoni. Spalatro instead of obeying now grasped the arms of the confessor, who looking at him for an explanation of this extraordinary action, was still more surprised to observe the paleness and horror of his countenance. His starting eyes seemed to follow some object along the passage, and Schedoni, who began to partake of his feelings, looked forward to discover what occasioned this dismay, but could not perceive anything that justified it. 'What is it you fear?' said he at length. Spalatro's eyes were still moving in horror. 'Do you see nothing?' said he pointing. Schedoni looked again, but did not distinguish any object in the remote gloom of the passage whither Spalatro's gaze was now fixed. 'Come, come,' said he, ashamed of his own weakness, 'this is not the moment for such fancies. Awake from this idle dream.' Spalatro withdrew his eyes, but they retained all their wildness. 'It was no dream,' said he, in the voice of a man who is exhausted by pain and begins to breathe somewhat more freely again. 'I saw it as plainly as I now see you.' 'Dotard! what did you see?' inquired the confessor. 'It came before my eyes in a moment, and showed itself distinctly and outspread.' 'What showed itself?' repeated Schedoni. 'And then it beckoned, yes, it beckoned me, with that blood-stained finger! and glided away down the passage, still beckoning, till it was lost in the darkness.' 'This is very frenzy!' said Schedoni, excessively agitated. 'Arouse yourself and be a man.' 'Frenzy! would it were, Signor, I saw that dreadful hand. I see it now; it is there again! there!' The representation of the lonely corridor, the horror and fright of the remorse-crazed villain, and the stern determination of the cold-hearted monk is most powerful and true to nature. The *chiaro-scúro* effect of light and shade and the whole coloring of the picture, is such as must command the admiration of the artist, and sensibly impress the less critical observer. [This picture is now the *possession* of Mr. John Taylor Johnston of New York, and makes one of the attractions of his rich and elegant art gallery. His generous kindness in allowing an engraving of it to be made, has enabled me to give my readers an idea of this gem of American art.]

St. Stanislas Kotzka, a young Polish nobleman, was among the earliest converts of the Jesuits. He was distinguished for his piety as a child. His mother educated him until he was fourteen, when he went to Vienna. He entered the Society of Jesus through the influence of Francis Borgia. He died at Rome when but seventeen. It is said that he fell sick at Vienna, and an angel brought to him the Eucharist on account of his being in the house of a Protestant. He is represented in art on a couch with an angel at his side. He is one of the patron saints of Poland, and as such his attribute is the lily. November 13, A. D. 1589.

St. Stephen, Proto-martyr (*Lat.* S. Stephanus; *Ital.* San Stefano; *Fr.* St. Etienne; *Ger.* Der Heilige Stefan). Little has been added to the Scripture account of this holy deacon by tradition or the fancy of his votaries. His name is significant of faith, devotion, zeal, and enduring love; it commands the veneration of the world, standing as it does at the *head* of the "noble army of martyrs." He was chosen deacon during the first ministry of Peter, and did great wonders and miracles. He was falsely accused of speaking blasphemously of the Temple and the Jewish law. For this he was condemned to death, and stoned by the people outside of the gate at Jerusalem, now called by his name. The legend concerning his relics relates, that it was not known for four hundred years what had become of his body. Then a certain priest of Carsagamala in Palestine, named Lucian, had a vision in which Gamaliel, the same who had instructed Paul in all the learning of the Jews, appeared to him, and revealed the burying-place of Stephen. Gamaliel himself had taken up the body and had placed it in his own sepulchre, where he also interred Nicodemus and other holy men and saints. This dream or vision was repeated a second and

(V. Carpaccio.) St. Stephen.

third time. Then Lucian, with the sanction of the bishop, dug in a garden that had been pointed out, and found the relics of St. Stephen, and their wonderful sanctity was proved by many miracles. They were first placed in the Church of Sion at Jerusalem; then carried by Theodosius to Constantinople; and lastly by Pope Pelagius to Rome, where they were deposited in the same tomb with St. Laurence. The legend adds that when the sarcophagus was opened to receive these sacred remains, St. Laurence moved to the left, thus giving the honorable right hand to St. Stephen. On this account St. Laurence is called by the populace of Rome, "Il cortese Spagnuolo," "The courteous Spaniard." St. Stephen is represented as young and beardless, in the dress of a deacon. The dalmatica is square and straight at the bottom, with large sleeves and heavy gold tassels hanging from the shoulders; it is crimson and richly embroidered. He has the palm almost always, and the stones are his special attribute, and when given to him it is impossible to mistake him; but when they are left out he is like St. Vincent. December 26.

St. Stephen of Hungary was the son of Duke Geysa. His father and mother were baptized late in life by St. Adelbert the Northumbrian missionary. They gave their son the name of the Protomartyr. Stephen was thus the first Christian king of Hungary. He found his country in ignorance and heathenism; he not only Christianized it, but he subdued other pagan nations about him and brought them also into the Church. He sent to Rome requesting the pope to grant him the title of king and to give him his benediction. The pope sent him a crown, and a cross to be borne before his army. Maria Theresa was crowned with this diadem, which was preserved at Presburg. St. Stephen married the sister of St. Henry, called Gisela. No child survived him, and his son St. Emeric is associated with him in the veneration of the Hungarians. He is represented in armor with his crown. As apostle of Hungary he bears the standard with the cross and the sword. September 2, A. D. 1038.

Sudarium. See St. Veronica.

St. Susanna was the daughter of Gabinius, brother of Pope Caius, and nearly related to the Emperor Diocletian. She was remarkable for her beauty, but more so for her learning. Diocletian desired her as a wife for his adopted son Maximus. She had made a vow of chastity, and refused even these tempting offers. Then Diocletian desired his empress, Serena, to try her influence with the maiden. But Serena was herself a Christian, and sympathized with Susanna in her determination. At length Diocletian became exasperated at her obstinate firmness, and sent an executioner who killed her in her own house. Her attributes are the sword and palm. August 11, A. D. 290.

Susanna. The illustrations of the apocryphal history of Susanna, are often seen among works of art; indeed, "Susanna at the Bath" is seen at least once in almost every picture gallery of any size. She was of Babylon, the daughter of Chelcias, and of exceeding beauty. She was married to Joacim, a very rich man, and greatly respected; and unto his house all the Jews resorted. There was a fair garden adjoining this house, and there Susanna was often seen walking with her maids. Now there were two judges, elders of the people, and both wicked men, who came each day to Joacim's house, and they both desired to possess Susanna, for her beauty had inflamed their hearts. So it happened that one day, when all the people departed at noon, they departed also, but they both returned and went into the garden to watch for Susanna; and when they met there, being surprised, they each questioned the other of what he sought. Then they acknowledged their wicked purposes, and agreed together that they would hide, and wait for the coming of the woman. Then came Susanna with two maids, and it was warm, and she thinking the garden empty save of herself, sent her maids to bring oil and washing balls, that she might bathe there. So they left her to bring these things, and they shut the door of the garden as she had also told them. Then the two judges laid hold of her, and they told her their wicked designs upon her, and they said, "If you consent not unto us we will accuse you, and say that we saw a young man with you here, and the doors were shut, and the maids sent away." Then Susanna sighed, and said, "I am straitened on every side: for if I do this thing, it is death unto me; and if I do it not, I cannot escape your hands. It is better for me to fall into your hands and not do it, than to sin in the sight of the Lord." Then she cried out, and the elders cried out against her, and they opened the door, and the servants of the house rushed in; then the elders declared against her, and all were sorrowful, "for there was never such a report made of Susanna." Now the next day when all the people were assembled, these elders came, and they called for Susanna, and Joacim was there, and his wife came with her children, and her parents and friends. Then the elders made accusation against her that they had seen her with the young man, and that he had escaped, but her they had retained. And they compelled her to raise her veil, and expose her beauty to the people. Now the assembly believed the accusation, and she was condemned to death, and all her friends were weeping and filled with grief; but she raised her eyes to heaven, and cried, "O everlasting God! that knowest the secrets, and knowest all things before they be; thou knowest that they have borne false witness against me, and behold, I must die, whereas I never did such things as these men have maliciously invented against me." Then the Lord heard her cry, and there arose a young man called Daniel, and cried out, "I am clear from the blood of this woman." Then the people asked the meaning of his words, and he declared that it was not just to condemn a daughter of Israel without examination, and he begged them to return again to the place of judgment. So they returned, and Daniel desired that the elders might be separated, that he might question first one, and then the other. And it was so, and taking them separately, Daniel asked them of the place where they had seen that of which they accused Susanna. And they contradicted each other; for one said it was beneath a mastic tree, and the other said the tree was an holm. Then Daniel said that having thus lied, they could not be trusted, and the whole accusation was false, and he desired that they might be punished for their false witness according to the law of Moses. So they were put to death, even as they had intended to kill Susanna. Then the family of the woman and Joacim, her husband, rejoiced greatly because there was no dishonesty found in her, and Daniel from that day forth had great reputation in the sight of the people.

St. Swidbert, who was a Benedictine monk, left England to lead the life of a missionary in Friesland, and the Duchy of Berg. He built a large monastery in Kaiserwerdt (about six miles below Dusseldorf), on the Rhine. He is represented as a bishop holding a star, which probably signifies the rising light of the Gospel which he preached to the pagans. March 1, A. D. 713.

St. Swithen was associated with St. Neot, in educating Alfred the Great. He was Bishop of Winchester. It is told of him, that when superintending the building of a bridge near Winchester, a poor woman complained to him that a workman had broken the eggs in her basket; whereupon St. Swithen made the eggs whole. He went to Rome with Alfred. He desired that his body should be buried with the poor people, outside the church, "under the feet of the passengers, and exposed to the droppings of the eaves from above." When the clergy attempted to remove his body to a more honorable tomb inside the church, there came on a storm of rain, which prevented their doing so; and this continued forty days until the project was abandoned. It would seem that there could have been no necessity of suffering from want of rain in Winchester, in those times. St. Swithen is represented as a bishop. July 2, A. D. 862.

St. Sylvester, Pope (*Ital.* San Silvestro; *Fr.* Saint Silvestre). He is represented in pontifical robes, with the plain mitre or the triple tiara, with the book and crosier as bishop. His proper attribute is the bull, which crouches at his feet; his dress distinguishes him from St. Luke, who has the ox. Sometimes he holds the portraits of St. Peter and St. Paul. December 31, A. D. 335.

For legends, see Constantine, Emperor.

St. Thecla (*Ital.* San Tecla; *Fr.* St. Thècle; *Ger.* Die Heilige Thekla). Although more especially a Greek saint, Thecla has been accepted and reverenced in the Latin Church. St. John pronounced the book called the "Acts of Paul and Thecla" to be spurious;

but in the earliest days of the Church it was thought the highest praise of any woman to compare her to St. Thecla. The legend relates that when St. Paul preached in the house of Onesiphorus at Iconium, Thecla could hear his sermons in her own house, by sitting at the window, and she became so entranced by what she heard that she would not turn her head or leave the window for any purpose. Now she was betrothed to Thamyris, who loved her with great devotion. Her mother, Theoclea, sent for the youth and told him how intent the maiden was upon the words of Paul; that she would neither eat nor drink; and seemed to care for nothing but what she heard from the Apostle. Then Thamyris also entreated her with words of love, but she would not heed him. Then he complained to the governor, and the governor imprisoned Paul, until he should have time to hear him in his own defense. But Thecla went to the prison and bribed the turnkey with her earrings, and the jailer with a silver looking-glass, and so gained admission to Paul. She sat at his feet and listened to his instructions, and kissed his chains in her delight. Then when the governor heard all this, he commanded that Paul should be scourged and driven out of the city, and that Thecla should be burned. So the young people of the city gathered wood for the burning of Thecla, and she was brought naked to the stake, where her beauty moved the hearts of all, and even the governor wept at the thought of the death she was to suffer. But when the fire was kindled, although it was very large, the flames did not touch her, and she remained in the midst of it uninjured. At length the fire was extinguished, and she made her escape.

(Lorenzo Costa.) St. Thecla.

Then Paul took her to Antioch, where she was again accused before the governor, who condemned her to be thrown to the beasts of the amphitheatre. When this sentence was known it created great indignation, and the people cried out, saying, "The judgments declared in this city are unjust." But Thecla submitted without reproaches, only asking of the governor that her chastity might be respected until the time of her martyrdom. Now when the time arrived the amphitheatre was crowded with spectators; Thecla was deprived of her garments and a girdle fastened about her waist, and the beasts were let in upon her. And murmurs of rage and disapprobation arose from the populace. The women cried out, "O unrighteous judgment! O cruel sight! The whole city ought to suffer for such crimes!" and a woman named Trissina wept aloud. But a fierce lioness bounded towards Thecla, and when she reached her laid down at her feet; all the bears and the he-lions also stretched themselves out as if asleep. Then the governor called Thecla and asked, "Who art thou, woman, that not one of the beasts will touch thee?" And Thecla replied, "I am a servant of the living God, and a believer in Jesus Christ his Son." And the governor ordered that her garments should be brought, and saying to her, "Put on your apparel," he released her. Then Trissina took Thecla to her own home. But Thecla desired much to see Paul, and determined to go in search of him. Trissina gave her much money and clothing for the poor, in order that Paul might be aided in his work. Thecla found him at Myra in Lycia, where he preached and labored for the conversion of the people. Thecla returned to Iconium, and after years spent in the service of Christ, she was led by the Spirit to retire to a mountain near Seleucia, where she lived in solitude, and was beset with great temptations. While she lived in this mountain she did many miraculous cures, and it was so that when the sick were brought to her cave they were healed, and the physicians of Seleucia were of no account. Then they consulted and said, "This woman must be a priestess of Diana. It is by her chastity she does these cures. If we could destroy that her power would be overthrown." So they sent evil men to do her violence. And Thecla ran from them praying for aid from Heaven, and lo! a great rock opened before her, leaving a space large enough for her to enter, and when she went in, it closed and she was seen no more, but her veil which one of the men had seized remained in his hand. The legend adds, "Thus suffered the blessed virgin and martyr Thecla, who came from Iconium at eighteen years of age, and afterwards partly in journeys and travels, and partly in a monastic life in the cave, lived seventy-two years, so that she was ninety years of age when the Lord translated her." Thecla is honored as the first female martyr in the Greek Church. St. Martin of Tours greatly venerated her, and assisted to make her popular in the Latin Church. She is represented in brown or gray drapery, and bears the palm. Wild beasts are about her. Patroness of Tarragona. September 23. First century.

St. Theodore (*Lat.* S. Theodorus; *Ital.* San Teodoro; *Ger.* Der Heilige Theodor). This is a warrior saint. He held a high rank in the army of Licinius. He was converted to Christianity and set on fire the temple of Cybele. He was burned alive or beheaded. He is represented in armor with a dragon beneath his feet. He was patron saint of Venice before St. Mark. There is another St. Theodore sometimes represented in Greek art, called St. Theodore of Heraclea. He is painted as an armed knight on horseback. The Venetian saint is represented in the more ancient pictures as young and beautiful, and often in company with St. George. January 11, A. D. 300.

St. Theonestus was one of the saints of the Theban Legion. See St. Maurice.

St. Theophilus (*Gr.* Ἅγ. Θεόφιλος; *Lat.* Sanctus Theophilus; *Ital.* and *Sp.* San Teofilo: *Ger.* Der Heilige Theophilus, Gottlieb; *Fr.* Saint Théophile). Signification; A lover of God. See St. Dorothea.

St. Theresa (*Ital.* Santa Teresa, Fondatrice dei Scalzi; *Fr.* Sainte Thérèse de Jésus des Carmes-Déchaussés; *Sp.* La Nuestra Serafica Madra Santa Teresa de Gesù). The father of this saint was Don Alphonso Sanchez de Cepeda, and her mother was named Beatrix. She herself is called Theresa d'Avila, on account of the place of her birth, which was Avila, in Castile. She was born March 28, 1515, and was one of twelve brothers and sisters. Her father was exceedingly pious, and her mother extremely romantic. Under these differing influences the character of the saint was formed. Among her brothers was one of ardent temperament, sympathetic with her own, whom she dearly loved. They especially delighted in reading

St. Theresa.

the lives of the saints and martyrs, and they conceived a passionate desire to obtain the crown of martyrdom themselves. When but eight or nine years of age they went into the country of the Moors begging, hoping to be taken and sacrificed by the infidels. They were disappointed in this, and then resolved to become hermits, but were prevented from thus pleasing themselves. But they bestowed all their pocket-money in alms, and whenever they played with other children always took the characters of monks and nuns; walked in processions and sang hymns. When Theresa was twelve years old her mother died. During her girlhood she seems to have forgotten her religious impressions, and to have given herself up to dress, and pleasure, pride of position, and self-love. She ardently longed to be loved and admired. Her father saw the dangers which surrounded her and placed her in a convent, commanding that she should be strictly secluded from the world. Again her religious nature was aroused, and she felt that a convent was the only haven of peace and safety for her A marriage which was disagreeable had been proposed to her. The conflict between her differing tastes and inclinations was so serious that she fell ill. Again upon recovering the struggle was renewed, and a second time she was prostrated by sickness. All this shows the extreme sensitiveness and ardor of her nature. At length the writings of St. Jerome decided her to lead a religious life. Her father consented, but again her mental sufferings on parting from her family nearly cost her her life. She entered the convent of Carmelites at Avila at twenty. Here her mind became more settled, although not at rest, and her health was for a long time enfeebled. She herself writes, that for twenty years she did not find the repose for which she had hoped. But she adds, "At length God took pity on me. I read the 'Confessions of St. Augustine.' I saw how he had been tempted, how he had been tried, and at length how he had conquered." From this time there was a change in her life and feeling. About the year 1561 Theresa set her mind upon reforming the Order of the Carmelites. From the people of Avila she obtained money, and there she founded her convent. She dedicated it to St. Joseph, whom she had chosen for her patron saint. When she entered her convent she had but eight nuns with her; before her death there were thirty convents established according to her rule. She met with great difficulties, but she overcame them; and during the later years of her life she travelled from convent to convent, promulgating the new regulations of her Order, and settling all points of difficulty. Her labors were not only for nunneries; she also effected changes in monasteries, and, indeed, founded fifteen convents for men. It was she who made the Carmelites barefooted or sandaled. From this arises the term "Barefooted Carmelites;" in Italy they are called Scalzi, the unshod, and also Padri Teresiani. St. Theresa wrote many essays and exhortations for her nuns; some mystical and poetical writings, and a history of her life written at the command of her spiritual directors. She never recovered the perfect use of her limbs after the repeated sicknesses of her youth, and with years her infirmities increased. She was attacked with her last illness at the palace of the Duchess of Alva. She desired to be removed to her own convent of San José. In her last moments she repeated the text from the Miserere, "A broken and a contrite heart, O Lord, thou wilt not despise." Her shrine at Avila in the church of her convent is a very holy place, and many pilgrims visit it. The nuns of the convent always sit on the steps and not on the seats of the choir, because they believe that the angels occupied these seats whenever St. Theresa attended mass. She is represented kneeling, and a flame tipped arrow pierces her breast, a symbol of the fervor of Divine love which possessed her soul. Sometimes she is gazing upwards towards the holy dove, a symbol of inspiration. This was never claimed by St. Theresa. Philip III. declared her to be the second patron saint of Spain, ranking next to Santiago. The Cortes confirmed this declaration. October 17, A. D. 1582.

St. Thomas.

St. Thomas (*Ital.* San Tommaso; *Sp.* San Tomé) was a Galilean fisherman; he is called Didymus, the twin, and is the seventh in the series of the Apostles. From the Scripture his character appears to be affectionate, and self-sacrificing: "Let us go also, that we may die with him." But so great was his incredulity that he has always been remembered for that, rather than for his other characteristics. According to tradition he travelled very far into the East; founded a church in India, and met the three Magi, whom he baptized. The legend, called that of "La Madonna della Cintola," relates, that when the Virgin ascended to heaven, Thomas was not present with the other Apostles. Three days later when he returned, he could not believe their account, and desired her tomb to be opened. It was empty; then the Virgin, that he might be satisfied, dropped her girdle to him from the heavens. (See also the Madonna; the Assumption.) According to another legend, when Thomas was at Cæsarea, he had a vision in which Christ appeared, and told him that Gondoforus, the king of the Indies, had sent his provost to find an architect to build him a palace more gorgeous than that of the Roman emperor. And Jesus desired St. Thomas to go to undertake this labor. Then

Thomas went, and Gondoforus gave him much treasure, and commanded the building of the magnificent palace, and went to a dis tant country and remained two years. Thomas built no palace, but gave all the riches with which he had been intrusted to the poor and sick. When the king returned he was very wroth, and ordered that St. Thomas should be cast into prison, and reserved for a terrible death. Now at this time the brother of the king died, and four days after his death he sat upright, and spoke to the king, saying, "The man whom thou wouldst torture is a servant of God: behold, I have been in Paradise, and the angels showed to me a wondrous palace of gold and silver, and precious stones; and they said, 'This is the palace that Thomas the architect hath built for thy brother, King Gondoforus.' Then the king ran to the prison to liberate Thomas. Then the Apostle said, "Knowest thou not that those who would possess heavenly things, have little care for the things of this earth? There are in heaven rich palaces without number, which were prepared from the beginning of the world for those who purchase the possession through faith and charity. Thy riches, O king, may prepare the way for thee to such a palace, but they cannot follow thee thither." According to tradition the Portuguese found at Meliapore an inscription, saying, that Thomas was pierced with a lance at the foot of a cross, which he had erected in that city, and that his body had been removed to Goa in 1523. When represented as an Apostle, his attribute is the builder's rule or square. As a martyr, he bears the lance. The two principal scenes in which he is represented, "The Incredulity of Thomas," and the "Madonna della Cintola," are easily recognized. Patron of Portugal and Parma. December 21.

St. Thomas à Becket. St. Thomas of Canterbury (*Lat.* Sanctus Thomas Episc. Cantuariensis et Martyr; *Ital.* San Tommaso Cantuariense; *Fr.* St. Thomas de Cantorbéri). Mrs. Jameson, in her "Legends of the Monastic Orders," gives a *resumé* of the principal events in the life of this saint, which is at once so concise and so comprehensive that I cannot do better than to quote it: "The whole of his varied life is rich in materials for the historical painter, offering all that could possibly be desired, in pomp, in circumstance, in scenery, in costume, and in character. What a series it would make of beautiful subjects, beginning with the legend of his mother, the daughter of the Emir of Palestine, who, when his father, Gilbert à Becket was taken prisoner in the Crusade, fell in love with him, delivered him from captivity, and afterwards followed him to England, knowing no words of any Western tongue, except 'Gilbert' and 'London,' with the aid of which she found him in Cheapside; then her baptism; her marriage; the birth of the future saint; his introduction to the king; his mission to Rome; his splendid embassy to Paris; his single-handed combat with Engleran de Trie, the French knight; the king of England and the king of France at his bedside, when he was sick at Rouen; his consecration as archbishop; his assumption of the Benedictine habit; his midnight penances, when he walked alone in the cloisters bewailing his past sins; his washing the feet of the pilgrims and beggars; his angry conference with the king; their reconciliation at Friatville; his progress through the city of London, when the grateful and enthusiastic people flung themselves in his path, and kissed the hem of his garment; his interview with the assassins; his murder on the steps of the altar; and, finally, the proud king kneeling at midnight on the same spot,

(After a print by Vostermann.) St. Thomas à Becket.

submitting to be scourged in penance for his crime." It was his martyrdom which made him a saint, and gave him a place in art. When he was made archbishop he ceased to be chancellor, and became a different man, and especially so to King Henry. He maintained his rank as spiritual father of the king and people with great determination. Henry was at last desperate at the continued opposition of the courageous priest, and in a moment of more than usual temper exclaimed, "Of the cowards that eat my bread, is there none that will rid me of this upstart priest?" This was enough; as powerful as a death warrant: and four Normans, attendant upon the king, bound themselves by oath to murder the archbishop. They went to Canterbury, and from the time of their appearance before him he divined their awful errand. At first they were not armed; he spoke to them with great spirit, and declared that he feared not their swords, and would die sooner than retract what he had said or done. This enraged them, and they rushed out to summon their followers. Then was heard the singing of the Vesper Hymn, and his friends urged Becket to go into the church as a place of safety. He ordered the cross of Canterbury to be borne before him, and passed through the cloister into the church. His friends barred the gates behind him, but he commanded them to be reopened, saying, that God's house should never be fortified as a place of defense. As he ascended the steps of the choir, the four knights with twelve attendants, all armed, burst into the church. "Where is the traitor?" demanded one of the number. All was silent. "Where is the archbishop?" asked Reginald Fitzurse. Then Becket replied, "Here I am; the archbishop, but no traitor! Reginald, I have granted thee many favors; what is thy object now? If you seek my life, let that suffice; and I command you in the name of God, not to touch one of my people." He was then told that he must absolve the Archbishop of York and the Bishop of Salisbury, whom he had excommunicated. "Till they make satisfaction, I will not absolve them," he firmly answered. "Then die!" said Tracy. The first blow aimed at his head was broken in its force by his cross-bearer, so that he was but slightly wounded. Feeling the blood on his face he bowed his head, and said, "In the name of Christ, and for the defense of his Church, I am ready to die." The assassins then wished to remove him from the church, in order to lessen the horrible sacrilege they were committing, but Becket declared that he would die there, and desired them to hasten their work. He said, "I humbly commend my spirit to God, who gave it," and instantly he was struck down, and soon dead; but so many blows were lavished on him that his brains strewed the pavement before the altar. His monks buried him in the crypt at Canterbury. According to tradition, as they bore him to the tomb, angels were heard singing the beginning of the Service of the Martyrs, "Lætabitur justus." The monks were for a moment amazed; they ceased their funeral hymn; then as if inspired they joined their voices with the angelic hymn, and bore him in triumph to his grave. The Church canonized him. His remains were inclosed in a splendid shrine, and his votaries from all parts of the world made pilgrimages to the scene of his martyrdom. But the power of the kings, the power he had despised, burned his relics, and threw the ashes into the Thames. He was fifty-two years old when he died. He is represented as a bishop, with the crosier and Gospels in his hand; as a martyr he is without the mitre, and a sword or axe is struck into his head; or the blood trickles from a wound over his face. December 29, A. D. 1170.

St. Thomas Aquinas (*Ital.* San Tommaso di Aquino, Dottore Angelico) was born at Belcastro in the year 1226. His father was Count of Aquino, Lord of Loretto and Belcastro. Thomas was grand nephew of Frederick I., and a kinsman of the emperors Henry VI. and Frederick II. The sweetness of temper, for which as a child he was remarkable, was preserved through life. When ten years old, the teachers at Monte Casino declared they could instruct him no farther, so great was his learning. His mother, the Countess Theodora, desired that he should have a private tutor, but his father placed him at the University of Naples. His own inclination and his mother's counsels kept him free from the temptations around him. At seventeen he assumed the Dominican habit at Naples. His mother hastened to persuade him not to take the final vows. He, fearing he could not resist her appeals, fled towards Paris, but his brothers, Landolfo and Rinaldo, seized him near Acquapendente; they tore off his monk's habit, and took him to his father's castle of Rocca-Secca. Then his mother came, and when her entreaties would not prevail, she had him guarded, and allowed no one to see him save his two sisters, who were instructed to persuade him to give up the idea of a religious life. The result was that Thomas so influenced his sisters that they sympathized with him, and aided him to escape. He was lowered from a window in a basket; some monks waited for him below, and not a long time elasped before he took his final vows. He was as eminent for his humility, and the quietness of his manner by which he concealed his acquirements, as for his learning. He was surnamed Bos, the Ox. On one occasion when it was his duty to read in the refectory, the superior corrected him, and told him to read a word with a false quantity. St. Thomas knew that he was right and the superior wrong, but he did as directed instantly. Being told that he should not have yielded, he replied, "The pronunciation of a word is of little importance, but humility and obedience are of the greatest." Pope Clement IV. desired to make him an archbishop, but he declined all preferments. He was the most learned man of his time in the Church. Being sent on a mission to Naples he was taken ill at Fossa-Nova, on his journey. He was carried to a Cistercian abbey, where he died. When extreme unction was administered to him, he requested to be laid on ashes on the floor. He is represented in the Dominican habit. His attributes are: a book or books; the pen or inkhorn; the sacramental cup, on account of his having composed the Office of the Sacrament; on his breast a sun, and sometimes an eye within it; frequently he looks up at a dove, or writes. March 7, A. D. 1274.

St. Thomas of Villanueva, surnamed the Almoner. He was born in 1488. His parents were of moderate fortune, but distinguished for their charities. They supplied seeds for the fields of the poor, and lent their money without interest. The son inherited this virtue to an intense degree. As a child he would take off his own clothes to give away to children in the street. He showed from his infancy a singular fitness for the ministry of the Church. He studied fourteen years at Alcala and Salamanca, and entered the Augustine Order at thirty. In his life it is related that he pronounced his vows in the self-same hour in which Luther publicly renounced his. He passed two years in penance and prayer, and then became an eloquent and distinguished preacher. Charles V. the Emperor of Spain, held St. Thomas in great veneration, and when he would not listen to the entreaties of friends or the requests of his son Don Philip, he yielded to St. Thomas, saying, that he considered his request as a divine command. In 1544 Charles made him Archbishop of Valencia. He was reluctant in accepting the office, and arrived in Valencia so poorly clad and provided for, that his canons sent him four thousand crowns to buy him an outfit; he thanked them and sent it to the hospital for the sick; and this, when the only hat he had, had been worn twenty-six years! His whole life was but a grand series of beneficent deeds. He divided the poor into six classes; 1. The bashful poor, who had been independent, and were ashamed to beg. 2. The poor girls, whose poverty exposed them to temptation to sin and shame. 3. The poor debtors. 4. Orphans and foundlings. 5. The lame, sick, and infirm. 6. Strangers and travellers who came to the city without the means to pay for food and lodging. For these he had a large kitchen always open where they could have food; rooms where they could sleep; and in addition a small sum of money when they went on their way. And in the care of all this he did not forget his duties as a spiritual teacher. When he died he had given away everything except the pallet on which he laid, and this was to be given to a jailer who assisted him in executing his benevolent designs. It was so surprising that in spite of all he had given away he still left no debts, that it was believed that his money had been miraculously increased according to his wants. Thousands of poor people followed him to his grave. When he was made a Beato it was also decreed that he should be represented with an open purse, in place of the crosier; but the latter is not always omitted. He is usually surrounded by poor people, who kneel. The finest pictures of this saint are Spanish. One of Murillo's of great beauty, represents him as a child dividing his clothing among four ragged little ones. The one called the "Charity of San Tomas de Villa Nueva," Murillo called "his own picture," and preferred it to all his other works. In this he stands at the door of his cathedral relieving a lame beggar kneeling before him. September 17, A. D. 1555.

St. Tibertius. April 14. See St. Cecilia.

Tobias, the son of Tobit. The pictures of the Archangel Raphael, are so often illustrative of his journey with the young Tobias, that the story of their companionship rightly belongs here. Now Tobit was a rich man and just; and he and his wife Sara were carried away into captivity by the Assyrians. He then gave alms to all his brethren that he could help and lived a just life, not eating the bread of the Gentiles. But in one way and another, his misfortunes were increased and he became blind, and nothing was left to him but his wife Sara and his son Tobias. And he was so afflicted that he prayed for death. At this same time there dwelt in the city of Ecbatane a man called Raguel, and he had an only daughter who had had seven husbands, and they were all killed by the evil spirit Asmodeus, as soon as they were married to her. And her maids reproached her and said she had strangled her husbands. And she was so wretched at this, that she too prayed for death that she might be at peace. So God sent his angel Raphael that he might take away the blindness of Tobit and the reproach of this unhappy woman. Then Tobit remembered that he had given to Gabael in Media, ten talents in trust, and he determined to send Tobias to ask for this money. So he called him and gave him directions concerning it. Then Tobias said, "But how can I receive the money, seeing I know him not?" Then Tobit gave him the handwriting and commanded him to seek for a guide who would show him the way. So Tobias sought a guide, and Raphael offered to go with him, and he was so that Tobias knew not that he was an angel. So he took him to his father, and they agreed upon the wages of the guide; and Tobit gave directions for their journey, and they departed. And Sara was much grieved to part from her son Tobias. At evening they came to the river Tigris and they lodged there, and when Tobias went to wash himself a fish leaped out at him. And the angel told him to take the fish, and take out the heart and the liver and the gall and preserve them carefully. This Tobias did, and they roasted the fish and ate it. Then Tobias asked the use of the parts they had kept, and the angel said, the heart and the liver were able to cure any one vexed with an evil spirit if a smoke was made of them before the person, and the gall would take away blindness from one who hath whiteness in the eyes. Now when they were come near to Rages the angel said, "Brother, to-day we shall lodge with Raguel who is thy cousin; he also hath one only daughter named Sara; I will speak for her that she may be given thee for a wife;" and he added, that according to the laws she belonged to Tobias, and as she was fair and wise, he could marry her on their return. Then Tobias said, he had "heard that she had been married to seven husbands who all died in the bridal chamber, and he feared that he too should die and thus bring his parents to their grave in sorrow, since he was their only son." But Raphael assured him that she was the wife intended for him by the Lord, and he should be preserved if when he came into the marriage chamber he should make a smoke with the heart and liver of the fish, for at the smell of it the devil would flee to come back no more. "Now when Tobias had heard these things he loved her, and his heart was effectually joined to her." So when they were come to Ecbatane they met Sara and she took them to the house of Raguel her father, and when they made themselves known unto him he rejoiced to see them and wept to hear of the blindness of his cousin Tobit, and Edna his wife and Sara wept also. And they killed a ram of the flock and prepared a supper; but Tobias said unto Raphael, "Speak of those things of which thou didst talk in the way, and let this business be dispatched." So they asked Raguel for Sara, that he should give her to Tobias as his wife. Then Raguel answered and told of the fate of the seven husbands she had had already; but he could not deny the request of Tobias, for by the law of Moses she belonged to him. And so it was settled before they did eat together, and Raguel joined their hands and blessed them. Then Edna prepared the marriage chamber and brought her daughter in thither, and Sara wept, but her mother comforted her and blessed her. Then when Tobias went in he took heed to make the smoke with the heart and liver of the fish as Raphael had said; and when the evil spirit perceived the odor thereof he fled away to return no more. Then Tobias and Sara knelt down, and Tobias prayed as Raphael had commanded him, and Sara said, Amen. And in the morning Raguel went out and dug a grave, for he counted Tobias as one dead, and he desired to bury him quietly that none should know what had taken place. And he sent a servant to see if he were dead; and the servant found them both quietly sleeping. Then did Raguel and Edna rejoice, and they prepared to keep the marriage feast of their daughter. And this feast kept fourteen days. Meanwhile the angel went to Gabael and received from him the money that Tobit had left with him. And when the feast was ended, Tobias with Sara and the angel departed to go to his father. And Raguel and Edna blessed them and gave them half of their goods, servants and cattle and money. Now as they approached to the city of Nineveh the angel said to Tobias, "Let us haste before thy wife and prepare the house; And take in thine hand the gall of the fish." So they went, and the little dog which they took away went with them. Now Anna was watching for them, and when she saw them she told Tobit that they were coming, and they were exceeding glad, for they had both been troubled at their long absence and feared lest some evil had overtaken them. Then said Raphael to Tobias, "I know that thy father will open his eyes; therefore anoint thou his eyes with the gall, and being pricked therewith, he shall rub and the whiteness shall fall away and he shall see thee." Then Tobias did so, and it was as the angel said, and the sight of Tobit was restored to him. Then they all rejoiced and blessed God, and Tobias recounted what had happened to him. And they went out to meet Sara and the servants and all that he had brought with him. And the people wondered when they saw Tobit and he was no more blind. And they brought in Sara and made a feast which they kept for seven days. Then Tobit said to his son, "See that the man have his wages that went forth with thee, and thou must give him more." And Tobias answered, "O father! it is no harm to me to give him half of those things which I have brought, for he hath brought me again to thee in safety, and made whole my wife and brought me the money, and likewise healed thee." And Tobit said, "It is due unto him." So they called Raphael and made known unto him their intentions. Then told he them to praise God, and glorify Him for all this good. And he told Tobit that all his acts and his goodness had been known in heaven, and his weariness of life and desire for death; and also that of Sara, who had so great troubles. Then he said, "And now God hath sent me to heal thee, and Sara thy daughter-in-law. I am Raphael, one of the seven holy angels, which present the prayers of the saints, and which go in and out before the glory of the Holy One." "Then were they both troubled and fell upon their faces; for they feared. But he said unto them, "Fear not, for it shall go well with you; praise God therefore." And after a few more words he vanished, and when they arose they could see no one. And from this time forth all did go well with Tobit and Sara his wife, with Raguel and Edna his wife, and with their children. And while they lived they never ceased to praise God for all the wonderful things He had showed them. And when Tobit and Sara were dead, Tobias took his wife and children and went to Ecbatane to Raguel his father-in-law. And when Raguel died he inherited his riches and lived with honor; and he lived to hear of the destruction of Nineveh, and died at Ecbatane, being an hundred and seven and twenty years old.

St. Torpè, or **Torpet,** is a Pisan saint. According to the legend he was a Roman, and served in the guards of Nero. He was converted by Paul. He was beheaded. When there was no water in the Arno and all were suffering for want of rain, the head of the saint was carried in procession, and so effectual was his intercession that the rain fell in floods and swept away a portion of the procession, and, mirabile dictu, the head of the saint also! The people knew not what to do, when two angels appeared, dived beneath the water, and brought again the head of the saint and gave it to the archbishop. Saint Torpè was the patron of Pisa before St. Ranieri. For a time he was eclipsed by the latter, but his fame again revived in the seventeenth century. He is represented as a Roman soldier, and bears a white banner with a red cross.

True Cross, The History of. A long time after Adam was driven out of Paradise, he grew so weary of his life of toil and hardship that he longed for death, and he sent his son Seth to the angel who guarded the Tree of Life to ask him to send him the oil of mercy which God had promised him when he was driven out of Paradise. And when his father had pointed out the way Seth went, and when he had asked the angel for the oil, he replied, "The oil of mercy which God promised to Adam can only be given after five thousand five hundred years shall have elapsed; but take these three seeds, they will bear fruit for the good of mankind." Then he gave him three seeds, believed to have been from the same tree of which Adam had eaten. And the angel told Seth that his father should die after three days, and commanded that after his death these seeds should be put under his tongue. Then Adam was joyous, for he much desired to die. And on the third day he died, and Seth buried him in the Valley of Hebron, and the three seeds were under his tongue. These seeds soon sprung up, and the three saplings thus formed united into one, thus becoming a symbol of the Trinity. It was with a part of this tree that Moses sweetened the waters of Marah; and with it also he struck the rock without calling on God; for which sin he was forbidden to enter the Promised Land. David also did miracles with this tree, and at last brought it to Jerusalem, and placed it in his garden, and built a wall about it. When Solomon was building the Temple, he saw that this tree was good and strong, and it was cut down for a beam; but the workmen could never make it fit in any place: sometimes it was too long, and again too short, so at last it was given up and thrown aside. After some years a woman, Sibylla, sat down upon it and immediately her clothes took fire; and she prophesied concerning it, that it would be for the destruction of the Jews. And some men who were near by cast it into a pond and it rose to the surface of the water, and formed a bridge upon which many passed. But when the Queen of Sheba came to visit Solomon, as she came to this bridge she had a vision of its future, and she would not step upon it, but knelt down and worshipped it; and she took off her sandals and walked through the stream, and she told Solomon that one should hang on that tree who should redeem the human race. Then Solomon took it and cased it in silver and gold and put it above the door of the Temple that all who came in might bless it. But when Abijah, the son of Rehoboam, reigned, he desired the gold and silver, and he took it away and buried the wood deep in the earth. Now after a time a well was dug over the spot where the Tree of Mercy was buried, and its waters were powerful to heal the sick, and it was called the Pool of Bethesda. As the time for the death of Jesus drew near, this beam was cast up to the surface of the waters, and the Jews took it and made from it *The Cross*; so was the tree which had grown from the seeds from Paradise, and which had been nourished by the decaying body of Adam, become at length the tree of the death of the second Adam. Another legend relates that the Jews believed that the body of Jesus would hang as long as the cross would last, and that it was made of four different kinds of wood, but the stem was of cypress wood, because this would not decay in earth or water. After the crucifixion the cross was buried deep in the earth and there remained for more than three centuries, until Constantine and his mother the Empress Helena were converted to Christianity; and she made a pilgrimage to Jerusalem, where she was seized with an uncontrollable desire to discover the Cross of Christ. So Helena commanded that all the wise men of the Jews should come to her palace. And they were alarmed, and questioned one with another why this should be. And there was one named Judas who said, "Know my brethren, that the empress hath come hither to discover the cross on which Jesus Christ suffered. But take heed that it be not revealed, for in the hour that the cross comes to light, our ancient law is no more, and the traditions of our people will be destroyed. My grandfather Zaccheus taught this to my father Simon, and my father Simon hath taught me. Moreover he told me that his brother Stephen had been stoned for believing in him who was crucified, and bid me beware of blaspheming Christ or any of his disciples." Then the Jews obeyed his injunction, and when the empress questioned them they all declared that they knew not where the cross was hid. So Helena commanded that they should all be buried alive. Then were they alarmed, and they said, "Here is a just man, and the son of a prophet, who knoweth all things pertaining to our law, and who will answer all questions." Then she released the others, but Judas she retained. And when she questioned him he exclaimed, "Alas! how should I know of these things which happened so long before I was born?" Then the empress was so filled with wrath that she declared he should be starved to death, and for that purpose he was cast into a dry well. Here he endured hunger and thirst for six days, but on the seventh day he yielded and led the empress to the Temple of Venus, which Hadrian had built above the place where the cross was buried. Then Helena commanded that the temple should be destroyed. And after that Judas began to dig, and when he had dug twenty feet he found three crosses; but they were all alike and no one knew which was that of Jesus. And as Helena and Macarius the bishop of Jerusalem were consulting as to what should now be done, behold, a dead man was carried past to his burial. And Macarius desired that he should be laid on the crosses, and it was done. Now when he was put upon the first and the second he stirred not, but when he was put upon the third he was restored to life, and the demons were heard to lament in the air above because Satan was overpowered and Christ reigned, while the man went on his way rejoicing. Then was Judas baptized, and his name was Syriacus or Quiriacus. But the nails of the cross were still wanting, and when Helena prayed for them they appeared on the surface of the earth shining like gold. Then Helena divided the cross, and left a part at Jerusalem, and a part she carried to Constantinople. Constantine kept a portion of it which was inserted into a statue of himself, and the rest was carried to Rome, where the Church of Santa Croce *in* Gerusalemme was built to receive and preserve it. One of the nails she had placed in the crown of Constantine, another she had made into a bit for his horse, and the third she threw into a whirlpool in the Adriatic, and immediately the sea was calm. In the year 615 Chosroes, King of Persia, came to Jerusalem and carried away the portion that had been left there. Then the Emperor Heraclius gathered his army together and defied Chosroes to battle. When they met the king and the emperor decided to settle their difficulties by single combat. Heraclius overcame Chosroes, and when he refused to be baptized he cut off his head. Then the emperor returned to Jerusalem in great triumph, and bearing the cross with him; but when he would, he could not enter, for the walls were all closed up by a miracle. He was astonished at this and an angel came to him and said, "When the King of Heaven and Earth entered through this gate to suffer for the sins of the world, he entered not with regal pomp, but barefooted and mounted on an ass." Then Heraclius wept that pride should have so led him to sin, and he descended to the earth, took off his crown, and also his shoes, and took the royal robes off even to his shirt. Then he put the cross on his shoulder, and the wall opened that he might pass in. Then was the cross exalted on an altar and displayed to the people. There is scarcely a point in this legend which has not been the subject of art. It is also related in the legends that *The Title* of accusation was found and sent to Rome by St. Helena; that it was placed on an arch in the Church of Santa Croce, and was there found in a lead box, in 1492. The inscriptions in the Hebrew, Greek, and Latin were in red letters, while the wood on which they were painted was white. Since then it has faded, and the words Jesus and Judæorum are eaten away. The board is now only nine inches long, but was originally about twelve. *The Sponge* which was used for the vinegar, to wash the wounds of Christ, as was the custom in crucifixions, is preserved with great veneration at the Church of St. John Lateran at Rome. *The Lance* which pierced his side is also at Rome, but the point is at Sainte Chapelle in Paris. According to various authorities it was buried with the cross. St. Gregory of Tours and Venerable Bede agree that in their day this lance was at Jerusalem. In order to guard it from the Saracens it was buried at Antioch, and there it was found in 1098, when it wrought many wonderful miracles. It was then carried to Jerusalem and from there to Constantinople. Baldwin II. sent the point of it to Venice in order to raise money for his necessities. St. Louis of France obtained it by paying the um Baldwin had received. The rest of the lance remained at Constantinople after it was taken by the Turks until 1492, when the Sultan Bajazet inclosed it in a beautiful case and sent an ambassador with it to Rome to present it to Pope Innocent VIII.

The Crown of Thorns was given to St. Louis by Baldwin, both on account of his kindness to him, and the friendly sentiments he entertained for him, and because Constantinople was no longer a safe place for it. St. Louis with his mother-in-law, his brother, and many priests and members of his court, met the ambassadors who carried it to him five leagues from Sens. St. Louis and his brother Robert of Artois were barefooted and in their shirts; thus they bore it to Sens and to the Cathedral of St. Stephen; there it was received with great ceremony. It was taken to Paris in the same manner, and Louis built for its reception the Sainte Chapelle, to which was attached a rich foundation for a chapter of canons. St. Louis also received the portion of the cross which was at Constantinople, and other relics which St. Helena had given her son. Some of the thorns from this crown have been given to other churches, and they have been imitated many times. They are very long.

The Nails of the cross have already been spoken of. These have been multiplied by imitation, and many made in this way and touched to the true nail were considered sacred.

The Pillar to which Christ was bound to be scourged, or a portion of it, is preserved at Jerusalem. The inscription above it says that it was placed there in 1223 by Cardinal Columna.

The Blood of Christ. Alban Butler says that this relic "which is kept in some places, of which the most famous is that of Mantua, seems to be what has sometimes issued from the miraculous bleeding of some crucifix, when pierced in derision by Jews or Pagans, instances of which are recorded in authentic histories. Representations of all these different relics, of circumstances connected with their discovery, of the ceremonies which have taken place on account of them and of the miracles they have performed, are very numerous in works of art.

St. Umilita, or **Humility,** was the wife of Ugolotto Caccianemici of Faenza. She was the foundress of the Vallombrosan nuns. She had desired to remain a virgin, but was compelled to marry on account of the avaricious interests of her family. Her husband was also virtuous and pious. Not long after their marriage, Rosane, for this was her name, thus addressed her husband, "Dost thou not feel that we can find no real permanent happiness here on earth, and should we not aspire to that peace and bliss which we can attain in heaven? Let us therefore, separate for a while, and in the silence of some cloister make a sacrifice of ourselves to God, for our country, our kindred, and for all those whom we love. Time fleets by with lightning speed, and we shall soon be reunited in the kingdom of heaven, where we shall enjoy all that felicity which has been denied us here below." Ugolotto consented, and they both lived strict lives according to the Vallombrosan rule. This legend has been illustrated in a series of eleven pictures by Bufalmacco. One of them represents Rosane persuading her husband to the separation. Her face is alight with the inspiration of the project of self-sacrifice she has conceived, while that of Ugolotto is sad at the thought of parting with her.

St. Ursula, and her Virgin Companions (*Lat.* id.; *Fr.* Sainte Ursule; *Ital.* Santa Irsola). This legend, which from its very improbability and surpassing strangeness is so fascinating, can be traced to the year six hundred. All the discussions as to its signification, have not (happily) changed the legend, and the Cologne version is the one followed by most painters who have attempted to depict its wonderful incidents. The manner in which this legend is told is so charming in its quaintness of thought and expression, that even when I consider the brevity that is here desirable, I cannot find it in my heart to do other than give it *verbatim et literatim.* "Once on a time there reigned in Brittany a certain king, whose name was Theonotus, and he was married to a Sicilian princess, whose name was Daria. Both were Christians, and they were blessed with one daughter, whom they called Ursula, and whom they educated with exceeding care. When Ursula was about fifteen, her mother, Queen Daria,

(Bruges. Hans Hemling.) St. Ursula.

died, leaving the king almost inconsolable; but Ursula, though so young, supplied the place of her mother in the court. She was not only wonderfully beautiful, and gifted with all the external graces of her sex, but accomplished in all the learning of the time. Her mind was a perfect storehouse of wisdom and knowledge: she had read about the stars, and the courses of the winds; all that had ever happened in the world from the days of Adam she had by heart; the poets and the philosophers were to her what childish recreations are to others; but, above all, she was profoundly versed in theology and school divinity, so that the doctors were astonished and confounded by her argumentative powers. To these accomplishments were added the more excellent gifts of humility, piety, and charity, so that she was esteemed the most accomplished princess of the time. Her father, who loved her as the light of his eyes, desired nothing better than to keep her always at his side. But the fame of her beauty, her virtue, and her wondrous learning, was spread through all the neighboring lands, so that many of the neighboring princes desired her in marriage; but Ursula refused every offer. Not far from Brittany, on the other side of the great ocean, was a country called England, vast and powerful, but the people were still in the darkness of paganism; and the king of this country had an only son, whose name was Conon, as celebrated for his beauty of person, his warlike prowess, and physical strength, as Ursula for her piety, her graces, and her learning. He was now old enough to seek a wife; and his father, King Agrippinus, hearing of the great beauty and virtue of Ursula, sent ambassadors to demand her in marriage for his son. When the ambassadors arrived at the palace of the King of Brittany, they were very courteously received, but the king was secretly much embarrassed, for he knew that his daughter had made a vow of perpetual chastity, having dedicated herself to Christ; at the same time he feared to offend the powerful monarch of England by refusing his request; therefore he delayed to give an answer, and, having commanded the ambassadors to be sumptuously lodged and entertained, he retired to his chamber, and, leaning his head on his hand, he meditated what was best to be done; but he could think of no help to deliver him from this strait. While thus he sat apart in doubt and sadness, the princess entered, and learning the cause of his melancholy, she said with a smile, 'Is this all? Be of good cheer, my king and father! for if it please you, I will myself answer these ambassadors.' And her father replied, 'As thou wilt, my daughter.' So the next day, when the ambassadors were again introduced, St. Ursula was seated on a throne by her father's side, and, having received and returned their salutations with unspeakable grace and dignity, she thus addressed them: 'I thank my lord the King of England, and Conon his princely son, and his noble barons, and you, sirs, his honorable ambassadors, for the honor ye have done me, so much greater than my deserving. I hold myself bound to your king as to a second father, and to the prince his son as to my brother and bridegroom, for to no other will I ever listen. But I have to ask three things. First, he shall give for me as my ladies and companions ten virgins of the noblest blood in his kingdom, and to each of these a thousand attendants, and to me also a thousand maidens to wait on me. Secondly, he shall permit me for the space of three years to honor my virginity, and, with my companions, to visit the holy shrines where repose the bodies of the saints. And my third demand is, that the prince and his court shall receive baptism; for other than a perfect Christian I cannot wed.' Now you shall understand that this wise princess, Ursula, made these conditions, thinking in her heart, 'either the King of England will refuse these demands, or, if he grant them, then eleven thousand virgins are redeemed and dedicated to the service of God.' The ambassadors, being dismissed with honor, returned to their own country, where they made such a report of the unequaled beauty and wisdom of the princess that the king thought no conditions too hard, and the prince his son was inflamed by desire to obtain her; so he commanded himself to be forthwith baptized; and the king wrote letters to all his vassals in his kingdom of France, in Scotland, and in the province of Cornwall, to all his princes, dukes, counts, barons, and noble knights, desiring that they would send him the required number of maidens, spotless and beautiful, and of noble birth, to wait on the princess Ursula, who was to wed his heir the Prince Conon; and from all parts these noble virgins came trooping, fair and accomplished in all female learning, and attired in rich garments, wearing jewels of gold and silver. Being assembled in Brittany, in the capital of King Theonotus, Ursula received them not only with great gladness and courtesy, but with a sisterly tenderness, and with thanksgiving, praising God that so many of her own sex had been redeemed from the world's vanities; and the fame of this noble assembly of virgins having gone forth to all the countries round about, the barons and knights were gathered together from east and west to view this spectacle, and you may think how much they were amazed and edified by the sight of so much beauty and so much devotion. Now when Ursula had collected all her virgins together, on a fresh and fair morning in the spring-time, she desired them to meet in a meadow near the city, which meadow was of freshest green, all over enameled with the brightest flowers; and she ascended a throne which was raised in the midst, and preached to all the assembled virgins of things concerning the glory of God, and of his Son, our Lord and Saviour, with wonderful eloquence; and of Christian charity, and of a pure and holy life dedicated to heaven. And all these virgins, being moved with a holy zeal, wept, and, lifting up their hands and their voices, promised to follow her whithersoever she should lead. And she blessed them and comforted them; and as there were many among them who had never received baptism, she ordered that they should be baptized in the clear stream which flowed through that flowery meadow. Then Ursula called for a pen, and wrote a letter to her bridegroom, the son of the King of England, saying, that as he had complied with all her wishes and fulfilled all her demands, he had good leave to wait upon her forthwith. So he, as became a true knight, came immediately; and she received him with great honor; and in presence of her father, she said to him, 'Sir, my gracious prince and consort, it has been revealed to me in a vision that I must depart hence on my pilgrimage to visit the shrines in the holy city of Rome, with these my companions; thou meanwhile shalt remain here to comfort my father and assist him in his government till my return; or, if God should dispose of me otherwise, this kingdom shall be yours by right.' Some say that the prince remained, but others relate that he accompanied her on her voyage; however this may be, the glorious virgin embarked with all her maidens on board a fleet of ships prepared for them, and many holy prelates accompanied them. There were no sailors on board, and it was a wonder to see with what skill these wise virgins steered the vessels and managed the sails, being miraculously taught; we must, therefore, suppose that it was by no mistake of theirs, but by the providence of God, that they sailed to the north instead of the south, and were driven by the winds into the mouth of the Rhine as far as the port of Cologne. Here they reposed for a brief time, during which it was revealed to St. Ursula, that on her return she and her companions should on that spot suffer martyrdom for the cause of God; all which she made known to her companions; and they all together lifted up their voices in hymns of thanksgiving that they should be found worthy so to die. So they proceeded on their voyage up the river till they came to the city of Basil; there they disembarked, and crossed over the high mountains into the plains of Liguria. Over the rocks and snows of the Alps they were miraculously conducted; for six angels went before them perpetually, clearing the road from all impediments, throwing bridges over the mountain torrents, and every night pitching tents for their shelter and refreshment. So they came at length to the river Tiber, and descending the river they reached Rome, that famous city, where is the holy shrine of St. Peter and St. Paul. In those days was Cyriacus Bishop of Rome; he was famous for his sanctity; and hearing of the arrival of St. Ursula and all her fair and glorious company of maidens, he was, as you may suppose, greatly amazed and troubled in mind, not knowing what it might portend. So he went out to meet them, with all his clergy in procession. When St. Ursula, kneeling down before him, explained to him the cause of her coming, and implored his blessing for herself and her companions, who can express his admiration and contentment! He not only gave them his blessing, but commanded that they should be honorably lodged and entertained; and, to preserve their maidenly honor and decorum, tents were pitched for them outside the walls of the city, on the plain towards Tivoli. Now it happened that the valiant son of king Agrippinus, who had been left in Brittany, became every day more and more impatient to learn some tidings of his princess-bride, and at length he resolved to set out in search of her, and, by a miracle, he had arrived in the city of Rome on the self-same day, but by a different route. Being happily reunited, he knelt with Ursula at the feet of Cyriacus, and received baptism at his hands, changing his name from Conon to that of Ethereus, to express the purity and regeneration of his soul. He no longer aspired to the possession of Ursula, but fixed his hope on sharing with her the crown of martyrdom on earth, looking to a perpetual reunion in heaven, where neither sorrow nor separation should touch them more. After this blessed company had duly performed their devotions at the shrine of St. Peter and St. Paul, the good Cyriacus would fain have detained them longer; but Ursula showed him that it was necessary they should depart, in order to receive the crown 'already laid up for them in heaven.' When the bishop heard this, he resolved to accompany her In vain his clergy represented that it did not become a pope of Rome and a man of venerable years to run after a company of maidens, however immaculate they might be. Cyriacus had been counseled by an angel of God, and he made ready to set forth and embark with them on the river Rhine. Now it happened that there were at Rome in those days two great Roman captains, cruel heathens, who commanded all the imperial troops in Germania. They, being astonished at the sight of this multitude of virgins, said one to the other, 'Shall we suffer this? If we allow these Christian maidens to return to Germania they will convert the whole nation; or if they marry husbands, then they will have so many children,— no doubt, all Christians,— that our empire will cease; therefore let us take counsel what is best to be done.' So these wicked pagans consulted together, and wrote letters to a certain barbarian king of the Huns, who was then besieging Cologne, and instructed him what he should do. Meantime St. Ursula and her virgins, with her husband and his faithful knights, prepared to embark; with them went Pope Cyriacus, and in his train Vincenzio and Giacomo, cardinals; and Solfino, Archbishop of Ravenna; and Folatino, Bishop of Lucca; and the Bishop of Faenza, and the patriarch of Grado, and many other prelates; and after a long and perilous journey they arrived in the port of Cologne. They found the city besieged by a great army of barbarians encamped on a plain outside the gates. These pagans, seeing a number of vessels filled, not with fierce warriors, but beautiful virgins, unarmed youths, and venerable bearded men, stood still at first, staring with amazement; but after a short pause, remembering their instructions, they rushed upon the unresisting victims. One of the first who perished was Prince Ethereus, who fell, pierced through by an arrow, at the feet of his beloved princess. Then Cyriacus, the cardinals, and several barons, sank to the earth or perished in the stream. When the men were dispatched, the fierce barbarians rushed upon the virgins just as a pack of gaunt hungry wolves might fall on a flock of milk-white lambs. Finding that the noble virgins resisted their brutality, their rage was excited, and they drew their swords and massacred them all. Then was it worthy of all admiration to behold these illustrious virgins, who had struggled to defend their virtue, now meekly resigned, and ready as sheep for the slaughter, embracing and encouraging each other! O, then! had you seen the glorious St. Ursula, worthy to be the captain and leader of this army of virgin martyrs, how she flew from one to the other, heartening them with brave words to die for their faith and honor! Inspired by her voice, her aspect, they did not quail, but offered themselves to death; and thus by hundreds and by thousands they perished, and the plain was strewed with their limbs and ran in rivers with their blood. But the barbarians awed by the majestic beauty of St. Ursula, had no power to strike her, but carried her before their prince, who, looking on her with admiration, said to her, 'Weep not, for though thou hast lost thy companions, I will be thy husband, and thou shalt be the greatest queen in all Germany.' To which St. Ursula, all glowing with indignation and a holy scorn, replied, 'O thou cruel man! blind and senseless as thou art cruel! thinkest thou I can weep? Or dost thou hold me so base, so cowardly, that I would consent to survive my dear companions and sisters? Thou art deceived, O son of Satan! for I defy thee, and him whom thou servest!' When the proud pagan heard these words, he was seized with fury, and bending his bow which he held in his hand, he with three arrows transfixed her pure breast, so that she fell dead, and her spirit ascended into heaven, with all the glorious sisterhood of martyrs whom she had led to death, and with her betrothed husband and his companions: and there, with palms in their hands and crowns upon their heads, they stand around the throne of Christ; and live in his light and in his approving smile, blessing Him and praising Him forever, Amen!" It has been very troublesome for the artists who have represented this legend to devise any means by which they could represent the idea of the eleven thousand virgins, and in spite of all their ingenuity, several thousands still remain to whom justice has never been done. The attributes of St. Ursula are the crown of the princess; the staff of the pilgrim; the arrow as a martyr; the white banner with the red cross as the victorious Christian; and the dove, because a dove disclosed her burial place to St. Cunibert. She is frequently represented as spreading out her broad mantle, underneath which many virgins cluster. There are many series of paintings giving the scenes of her life. Patroness of all young maidens; especially of school girls and of such women as instruct the young of their own sex. October 21.

St. Valerian. See St. Cecilia.

St. Valerie. See St. Martial.

Vera Icon, The. See St. Veronica.

St. Verdiana is seen in Florentine pictures. She is in the habit of a Vallombrosan nun, and bears a basket from which serpents feed. A. D. 1222.

St. Veronica (*Ital.* Santa Veronica; *Fr.* Sainte Véronique). There are two quite different legends concerning this saint. The most ancient relates that she was the woman who was healed by touching Christ's garment, and that she greatly desired a picture of his face. She first took a cloth to St. Luke and he painted a picture that both he and Veronica thought to be like Christ, but when next she saw him, she found his face quite different. Then the Saviour said to her, "Unless I come to your help, all Luke's art is in vain, for my face is known only to Him who sent me." Then he told her to go to her house and prepare him a meal, and before the day ended he would come to her. Veronica did this joyfully, and when Christ came he first desired water to wash. Veronica gave him this with a cloth whereon to wipe. He pressed the cloth to his face and his image remained on it. He then gave it to Veronica saying, "This is like me, and will do great things." About this time the Emperor of Rome was ill of a dreadful disease. Some say it was Vespasian, and others Tiberius; that he had worms in his head, or a wasp's nest in his nose. It was a fearful sight. Now the emperor hears that a great physician performs wonderful cures in Judæa. So he sends his messengers to Jerusalem and finds that Jesus, the physician, had been slain three years before. Then Pilate is filled with alarm and ac-

(Andrea Sacchi.) St. Veronica.

cuses the Jews of the deed, while they in turn, make him responsible for it. Then the messenger inquires for the followers of Jesus, and at last Veronica is brought to him. He then desires to see the portrait. At first she denies having it, but at length acknowledges that she treasures it with great care, and brings it to him. The messenger desires to take it to Rome, but she will not consent except she goes also. They therefore depart, and arrive after a very short and prosperous voyage. When all is explained to him of the death of Jesus, the miracle of the picture, and the powers it has, the emperor regards it believing, and is healed. Pilate, who has been brought to Rome, is then cast into prison; he kills himself and his body is thrown into the Tiber, where demons attack it. Then the emperor determines to avenge the death of Christ upon Jerusalem. He besieges the city, and so many Jews are slain, that they cannot be buried. Captives are crucified, the thieves who divided the garments of Jesus are cut in quarters, and many are sold for thirty pence each. Now this cloth, which is the subject of this legend, is the "Volto Santo," or "God's image," and these words were used as an imprecation in the Middle Ages. Vera Icon, another name for it, signifies, "The Sacred Picture," and is the same as the name of the saint, and in fact the picture is sometimes called "a Veronica." It is well to compare this legend with that of King Abgarus, as they probably came from the same source, and are very likely different versions of one legend. The later legend of St. Veronica does not make her the healed woman, but merely a woman of Jerusalem whose house Christ passed when bearing his cross. Seeing his sufferings she pitied him, and gave him her veil to wipe his brow. When he returned it to her it was impressed with the sacred image. This is recognized by the Roman Church. The house of St. Veronica is shown at Jerusalem on the Via Dolorosa. This last legend also takes Veronica to Rome, but the emperor has died before her arrival, and she remains with St. Peter and St. Paul, and at last suffers martyrdom under Nero. Still another version makes her go to Europe with Lazarus and his sisters, and suffer death in Provence or Aquitaine. The image is the Vera Icon, or the true image, and the cloth is the Sudarium. (*Ital.* Il Sudario; *Fr.* Le Saint Suaire.) A chapel in St. Peter's at Rome is dedicated to this saint, and there is kept an image painted on linen, and regarded by the people as the veritable Vera Icon. St. Veronica is unmistakable in art, as she is represented holding the napkin. The festival of St. Veronica (*Fr.* La Sainte Face de J. C.) is held on Shrove Tuesday.

St. Victor of Marseilles (*Ital.* San Vittore) was a soldier under Diocletian and suffered martyrdom in the tenth persecution. He endured terrible tortures with wonderful strength and devotion. In the midst of them a miniature altar was brought him on which to sacrifice to Jupiter and thus save himself, but he dashed down the image and destroyed it. He was then crushed with a millstone and afterwards beheaded. When he died angels were heard to sing, "Vicisti, Victor beate, vicisti!" He is represented as a Roman soldier with a millstone near him. July 21, A. D. 303.

St. Victor of Milan (*Ital.* San Vittore) was another Roman soldier who suffered also in the tenth persecution. He was a native of Mauritania but suffered at Milan, where there is a church dedicated to him. He is the favorite military saint of Northern Italy. It is said that he was thrown into a heated oven, and an oven with flames bursting out, is sometimes near him in pictures, but he is more frequently represented as the Victorious, sometimes on horseback, and always in the dress of a soldier. May 8, A. D. 303.

St. Vincent, Deacon and Martyr (*Lat.* S. Vincentius Levita; *Ital.* San Vincenzio Diacono, San Vincènzino; *Fr.* Saint Vincent). The principal facts concerning this saint are so established by good authorities that they cannot be denied, but imagination has had great license in the legend, as it is illustrated by those who paint; whether it be with brush or pen, artist or poet. It is as follows: — Vincent was born in Saragossa. At the time of the terrible persecution under Diocletian he was about twenty years old, and already a deacon. The proconsul Dacian caused all the Christians of Saragossa to be brought together, with a promise of immunity, and then ordered them all to be massacred. St. Vincent did all in his power to encourage and sustain the people of God, and at length was himself arrested, and brought before the tribunal. With him was his bishop, Valerius. When they were accused Valerius answered first; but he had an impediment in his speech, and was moreover old and feeble, so that his answers were almost unintelligible; then Vincent exclaimed, "How is this, my father? canst thou not speak aloud, and defy this pagan dog! Speak, that all the world may hear; or suffer me, who am only thy servant, to speak in thy stead!" When the bishop, therefore, gave him leave, he proclaimed his faith aloud, and defied all tortures and sufferings. Then was Dacian very wroth, and he commanded that the young man should be reserved to the tortures, but the old man be only sentenced to banishment from the city. The most fearful tortures were invented for Vincent, to which he submitted with miraculous strength. Prudentius says, in his celebrated hymn to St. Lawrence, "When his body was lacerated by iron forks, he only smiled on his tormentors; the pangs they inflicted were to him delights; thorns were his roses; the flames a refreshing bath; death itself was but the entrance to life." After his terrible sufferings they laid him on the floor of his dungeon strewed with potsherds; but angels came and ministered to him, and when his jailers looked in they beheld the place filled with celestial light, and a sweet perfume came out from it; they heard the songs of angels, in which Vincent joined with thanksgiving; and he called to the jailers to come in and partake of his bliss. And then they fell on their knees and were converted. After this, Dacian being convinced that tortures could not conquer his spirit, resolved to try the seductions of luxury. He had him placed on a bed strewn with roses; his friends were admitted to him, and everything was done to ease his pain. But no sooner was this done than he died, and angels bore his soul to glory. Then the furious Dacian ordered his body to be thrown to the wild beasts; but God sent a raven to guard them, and they remained untouched for many days. Then the Consul commanded that it should be sewed up in an ox hide, as was done to the bodies of parricides, and thrown into the sea. So it was thus prepared and carried out in a boat, and thrown over with a millstone attached to it; but lo, when the boatmen reached the shore it was returned before them, and lay upon the sands! Then they ran away terrified, and the waves hollowed out a grave and buried it. Here it remained for many years, until at last it was miraculously revealed to certain Christians of Valencia, where he was buried, and they removed him to their own city. When the Christians of Valencia fled from the Moors, they bore with them these sacred relics. The vessel in which they were was driven upon a promontory on the coast of Portugal, where they stopped, and interred the body, and that point has been called Cape St. Vincent from that day. Here too the ravens guarded the remains, and a portion of the cape is called in remembrance of them, "el Monte de las Cuervas." When in the year 1147, Alonzo I. removed the remains to Lisbon, two crows accompanied the vessel, one at the prow and one at the stern; these crows multiplied greatly in Lisbon, until rents were assigned to the chapter for their support. Vincent has been surnamed *the Invincible*, both on account of his character and the signification of his name. St. Vincent is represented as young and beautiful, in a deacon's dress, and his proper attribute is a crow or raven. Patron of Lisbon, Valencia, and Saragossa; of Milan; of Chalons, and many other places in France. January 22, A. D. 304.

St. Vincent Ferraris was born at Valencia in 1357. His parents denied themselves greatly in order to educate him and his brother Boniface. He was a Dominican, and took the habit when only eighteen. He became one of the most celebrated preachers and missionaries. He went all through Spain, Italy, and France, and by invitation of Henry IV. to England. He so moved the hearts of his hearers that he was often obliged to pause that the sobbing and weeping might subside. He did many miracles, and it is related that when he preached in Latin, he was understood by all who heard him, of whatever nation, learned or unlearned. He spent the last two years of his life in Brittany and Normandy, and died at Vannes. Jeanné de France, Duchess of Brittany, washed his body, and prepared it for the grave with her own hands. His proper attribute is the crucifix, which he holds aloft in reference to his labors as missionary. He sometimes has wings as symbols of his fervor, but with the Dominican habit they have a strange effect. April 5, A. D. 1419.

St. Vincent de Paule, who, as a saint, is so popular in Paris, should as a man be highly venerated everywhere. He was born in 1576, at Puy, in Gascony. His father was a farmer, and he tended the flocks. But his temper was so sweet, and his mind so active, that his father desired an education for him; so he was sent to a convent of Cordeliers, and assumed the habit of the Franciscans when twenty years old. He was sent to Marseilles, and when returning by sea, was seized by African pirates and carried into slavery. He remained thus two years, and had several masters. The wife of the last one pitied him, and when she spoke to him was charmed by his conversation. One day she asked him to sing, and he bursting into tears, sang, "By the waters of Babylon, we sat down and wept," and then the glorious "Salve Regina." This woman was converted, and in her turn preached to her husband, who also received the truth. Then they all escaped, and came to Aiguesmortes. Vincent placed his companions in a religious house, and went himself to Rome, from which place he was sent by the pope to Paris. This was in 1609. He had been greatly moved at the sight of the sufferings of the galley slaves. He had been in captivity. He was not able to do much for them, but he preached, and comforted them as much as possible. He then turned his attention to the Magdalenes of Paris, and founded the hospital of "La Madaleine." He also founded the Order of the Sisters of Charity, and established a foundling hospital. This is no place to speak of all the good he thus did, and indeed, who can tell it? He was a friend of Richelieu, until his death. He was called to the side of Louis XIII. in his last moments. During the wars of the Fronde, he ministered to the sufferers; and greatly desired to do something for the Catholics of Ireland, who were then suffering great oppression. In short he has been named by general consent, "L'Intendant de la Providence et Père des Pauvres." He died at St. Lazare. He is represented in the Franciscan habit, with a new-born infant in his arms, and a Sister of Charity kneeling before him. July 19, A. D. 1660.

St. Vitalis of Ravenna, was the father of SS. Gervasius and Protasius. He was condemned to be buried alive for having taken up and cared for the body of a Christian martyr. He was a soldier in the army of Nero, and had been converted by the preaching of St. Peter. His wife, Valeria, fled with her two sons to Milan. The church dedicated to him, and erected over the spot where he was buried, is a remarkable monument of Byzantine architecture. The fame of this saint extended all over Europe. He is represented as a soldier with the martyr's crown, and sometimes on a white charger, with the standard of victory. April 28; about 62.

St. Vitus (*Ital.* San Vito; *Fr.* St. Vite or St. Guy; *Ger.* Der Heilige Veit, Vit, or Vitus) was the son of a noble Sicilian, who was a pagan, but the nurse and foster-father of Vitus were secretly Christians, and they brought him up in the faith, and had him baptized. When only twelve years old, he declared himself a Christian, which so enraged his father and the governor, that they attempted to compel him to retract. They shut him in a dungeon after beating him; but when his father looked through the key-hole, he saw him dancing with seven beautiful angels, and so dazzling was the sight that the father was made blind, and only restored to sight at the intercession of his son. Again after this he persecuted Vitus, and he fled with his nurse and her husband in a boat which was steered by an angel to Italy. But here they were again accused as Christians, and were thrown into a cauldron of boiling oil. He is represented as a beautiful boy. He has many attributes: the palm; the cauldron of oil; a lion, because he was once exposed to them; a wolf, because his remains were guarded by one; and a cock, the reason of which is not known; but on account of which he is invoked against too much sleep. He is one of the fourteen Noth-helfers or patron saints of Germany. Patron saint of dancers and actors; and is invoked against the nervous disease, St. Vitus' dance. Patron of Saxony, Bohemia, and Sicily. June 15, A. D. 303.

St. Walburga, whose Anglo-Saxon name is the same as the Greek Eucharis, and signifies "gracious," is also called Walpurgis, Walbourg, Valpurge, Gualbourg, and Avangour. When her uncle, St. Boniface, and her brother, St. Willibald, determined to take a company of religious women from England to the continent, to assist in teaching the pagans, Walburga left the convent of Winburn, where she had lived twenty-seven years, and went with ten other nuns to Mayence. She was afterwards made first abbess of the convent of Heidenheim. After the death of Willibald, on account of her learning and talents she was called to Eichstadt, and governed the two communities there; the monks as well as the nuns. She wrote a history of her brother in Latin. She had studied medicine, and did some wonderful cures. After her death, she was entombed in a rock near Eichstadt, from which exuded a bituminous oil. For a long time the people about believed this oil to proceed from the remains of the saint, and it was called Walpurgis oil, and thought to effect wonderful cures. The cave became a place of pilgrimage, and a church was built on the spot. On the night of her festival, Walpurgis' night, the witches held their orgies at Blocksberg. Her chief festival is on the first of May. She is represented in the Benedictine habit with a crosier, and a flask; the latter a symbol of the Walpurgis oil. May 1; about 778.

Wandering Jew, The. This legend is given in several different ways. According to Matthew Paris, an Armenian archbishop came to England to visit its shrines, and was entertained at the monastery of St. Albans. He was questioned in regard to his own country and his travels, and was asked if he had ever known anything of a miraculous person who was present at the crucifixion of Christ, and who still lived. The archbishop testified that it was true that such a man lived, and that he knew him well. He said he had been the porter of Pontius Pilate, and was named Cartaphilus. When the Jews were dragging Jesus from the judgment hall, Cartaphilus struck him with his fist, saying, "Go faster, Jesus, go faster, why dost thou linger?" Then Jesus turned and said, "I indeed am going, but thou shalt tarry till I come." Afterwards he was converted, and baptized by the name of Joseph. At the end of every century he falls ill, and is incurable; at length he goes into a fit of ecstasy, and when he comes out of it he is the same age that he was when Christ died, which was about thirty. He is a grave and holy man. He remembers all the circumstances of the crucifixion, the resurrection, and ascension; of the composing of the Apostles' Creed, and their separation when they went forth to preach.

Another legend gives his name as Ahasuerus, and relates that as Jesus was bearing his cross he stopped before his door to rest, and Ahasuerus drove him away with curses. Then Jesus told him that he should wander until he came to judgment; and ever since he wanders, bowed down with grief and remorse, and unable to find a grave.

St. Wenceslaus of Bohemia. See St. Ludmilla.

St. Werburga figures among the early Benedictine saints in England. She was abbess of Repandum, and had jurisdiction over monks as well as nuns. She was the niece of St. Ethelreda, and was brought up with her at Ely. She founded several monasteries, and had the care of them besides that of Repton,— Weedon, Trentham, and Hanbury. The Cathedral of Chester was dedicated to her in 800, and a part of her shrine now supports a pew erected for the bishop of the diocese. About 708.

St. William of Aquitaine. See St. Benedict of Anian.

St. Zeno of Verona, was bishop of that city in the fourth century, and was remarkable for the wisdom with which he governed his diocese during those troublous times. He is represented in one picture holding a long fishing-rod, and the legend of Verona says, he was fond of fishing in the Adige; but it is quite probable that the fish which hangs from the line, is symbolical of baptism. It is doubtful whether he was martyred, although he is said to have been, by Julian the Apostate. It is related that King Pepin desired to be buried in the same grave with St. Zeno, so great was his esteem for him. April 12, A. D. 380.

St. Zenobio of Florence was the son of noble parents, Lucian and Sophia, but they were pagans. He was born in the last year of the reign of Constantine. He was converted while at school, and succeeded in converting his parents. He lived in Rome, and was a deacon, and the secretary of Pope Damasus I. He was sent to Florence in a time of great distraction, but both Catholics and Arians

(Masaccio.) St. Zenobio revives a dead child.

desired to have him for their bishop. He restored to life a man who had fallen down a mountain precipice, when on the way to bring some sacred relics to him, sent by St. Ambrose. A lady on her way to Rome stopped at Florence, to see this good man of whom she had heard much, and she left her son in his care until she should return. The day before her return the child died, but when she took it and laid it at the feet of St. Zenobio, he restored it to life. He led a most holy life, and died in the reign of Honorius. When he was being borne to his grave the people so pressed about his bier that in the Piazza del Duomo his body was thrown against the trunk of an elm that was withered. It immediately put forth buds and leaves. He is represented in his episcopal robes; his attribute is frequently a tree which is putting forth leaves. May 25, A. D. 417.

LEGENDS OF PLACE.

Adolphseck was the name of a castle at Eichthal near Schwalbach, built by Adolphus of Nassau. This legend is not entirely historical, but gives a good picture of the romance of love and the sorrows of war, mingled as they so frequently were during the adventurous Middle Ages. A war had broken out between France and Germany. The Bishop of Strasbourg made a traitorous league with the French king. He then challenged the Emperor of Germany. Adolphus of Nassau, who was a brave soldier and an excellent commander, entered Alsace to punish this treachery. His ardor carried him too far, as it had often done, and he so exposed himself to danger that he was borne wounded from the field, and taken to a convent. Here he was nursed by a novice, Imagina, whose lovely face and tender gentleness robbed the Duke of his heart while her devoted care restored him to health and strength. When she was near him his soul was soothed into an unutterable calm. At length he declared to her his love. Imagina made no answer, but withdrew from his sight, weeping. Then three days passed, and she returned not. When summoned to perform her accustomed duties she declared herself sick. Alas! how truly, for who are more sick than those whose hearts are tortured by the soul struggles between love and duty, even though the latter be, as in this case, imaginary? In these three days Adolphus heartily repented the rashness of his declaration, and could neither rest or sleep. At last, in the middle of the third night his door opened noiselessly and Imagina entered, disturbed with painful emotion, but far more lovely in her expressive grief than when calm and peaceful as she was wont to be. "Fly! I beseech you, my prince!" exclaimed she; "the Bishop of Strasbourg is at hand to make you his prisoner. You have not a moment to lose!" The emperor rose hastily and dispatched his servant to warn the commander of his troops. Then he proceeded with Imagina, through the deserted, echoing corridors of the convent, into the church and to a small door of which the maiden had obtained the key. "Heaven be praised, and the Blessed Virgin also, that she has heard my prayer, and you are saved!" murmured the maiden. "Farewell, most noble prince! God grant thee happiness! Do not forget Imagina," and she was about to leave him. But Adolphus detained her, and declaring that life without her was valueless, begged, even on his knees, that she would fly with him and be his bride rather than that of Heaven. She could not refuse, and wrapped in cloak and hood she followed her lover to the Rhine, which they were soon able to cross in safety. Adolphus shortly after concluded a peace with France, and built the Castle of Adolphseck in which to dwell with his faithful Imagina. Here they lived happily, but the unrestful spirit of the age soon made it necessary for the emperor to take the field again in order to retain his crown. Imagina followed her husband, and awaited him at the Convent of Rosenthal. The battle took place at Göllheim near Donnersberg. Adolphus was forgetful of all save the duty of a soldier, and rashly risked his life. He fell pierced with a lance. Thus Albert of Austria was made emperor. Imagina had listened with heavy heart to the resounding war-cries, and when at night her husband came not, she went to seek him. As she passed over the battle-field, its ghastly scenes, disclosed by the pale moon, filled her with fear and horror. At length the hound of Adolphus ran to her and led her to his master. He was carried to the Convent of Rosenthal and there interred, and in his grave, not only his dead body, but the living heart of Imagina was buried. She took the veil, and was not long separated from him she loved; for Death soon comes to the release of those whose hearts he has already broken. The Castle of Adolphseck was destroyed by the new emperor, and a cross erected by his command on the spot where Adolphus died.

Aix-la-Chapelle. "*The Foundation of the City.*" The Emperor Charlemagne governed an immense empire, and he moved about in it, living sometimes in one portion and again in another, in order that he might make himself acquainted with all his subjects and understand their hearts and their necessities; and to this end he was always accessible to all who desired to see him. At one time he held his court at Zurich, and had erected there a column upon which was fastened a small bell, and any who wished to see the emperor had but to ring it and he would himself appear. One day the bell was rung, but when Charlemagne came to the place there was no person in sight. Again on the following day the same thing occurred. Then the emperor set a servant to watch, where he could not be seen, and his surprise cannot be imagined when he saw an immense serpent issue from a cave near by and ring the bell. Charlemagne, who was dining, was told of this, and he immediately left the table to hasten to the spot, saying, "Be it animal or man I will have justice done to every one who demands it from me." Now when the serpent saw the emperor it bowed before him three times and went slowly to its cave. The emperor and his suite followed there also, and before the opening of the cave sat a monstrous toad that stopped the entrance of the serpent. It seemed that the serpent desired its removal; so Charlemagne ordered that it should be killed. A few days after as the emperor and his guests were about to sit down to dine, the same serpent came into the banqueting-hall and bowed to Charlemagne as before. It then crawled up to a drinking-cup and dropped therein a splendid jewel of wonderful size and beauty, and retired amidst universal surprise. The emperor gave this jewel to his wife, and she wore it as an ornament for her hair. It proved a magic stone, and to have the power of fixing the heart of the emperor upon whoever possessed it. Ever after the empress received it, Charlemagne could not endure to be absent from her, and his whole life and thought was devoted to her and her happiness. Now as the empress felt the approach of death she feared lest this treasure should fall into the hands of some one unworthy of the love of Charlemagne; so she hid it under her tongue, and there it remained. Then was the fondness of the emperor for the dead body of his wife as great as it had been for her when living; and he had it embalmed, and carried it with him wherever he went. At length this wonderful devotion excited a suspicion in the mind of Archbishop Turpinus that there must be something supernatural connected with it, and as he was the constant companion of Charlemagne, he took an opportunity to examine the dead body, and soon found the jewel. This he took and the love of the emperor was transferred to himself, and he would not be separated from him any more than formerly he would be from the empress. After a time this became very tiresome to Turpinus and in a fit of impatience he threw the jewel into some water they were passing in the western part of Germany. Then Charlemagne was fascinated with the country which contained his jewel; for nothing destroyed its magic art. So he built here the town of Aix-la-Chapelle, and the magnificent cathedral there still bears his name. Here he loved to stay, and he would sit for hours and days in happy, restful thought beside the quiet waters which held the miraculous gem, and it is believed that it is from the wonderful effects of this magic stone that the baths of Aix-la-Chapelle receive their healing properties and are so beneficial to those who use them.

The Cathedral. When the splendid Cathedral of Aix-la-Chapelle was not more than half finished, all the funds that could be raised for its building were exhausted, and those who had it in charge knew not how to obtain more money. One day as the Senate was considering this matter, and its members could not agree upon any course of action, there appeared to be great danger that the work would be abandoned. At this juncture of the affair a stranger was announced, who said he had an important proposal to make to the full Senate. His appearance was a singular combination of the repulsive and the agreeable. His costume was bizarre in the extreme, and there was an indescribable expression in his face of mingled calculation and mockery. But his address was faultless, and so courtly and pleasing was he in his speech that it was impossible to listen to him without a certain kind of pleasure. He told the Senate that he quite understood their difficulties; that he appreciated their sorrow at the prospect of being obliged to abandon the glorious work they had undertaken, and he also knew that as honest men they could not proceed without more money. Therefore he had come to offer them the full amount that they desired, and was ready at any time to give it to them in solid gold, if they could agree to his terms. The senators regarded him with astonishment, and wondered what could be the end of this strange affair. Did he know of what he spoke, and if so, who was he that spoke of millions as if they were a mere bagatelle, and to be had at will? — and moreover offered the actual money on any day they desired it. Had he discovered the philosopher's stone? — and could he convert all before him into gold? If so what assurance had they that he would not reduce themselves to "filthy lucre," and thus deprive them of their privilege of becoming more common and less valuable dust? Trust me for it, they trembled at the thought, and on the heads of such as wore no wigs the hair was strangely bristled! From this surprise the mayor first recovered, and began to question the stranger concerning himself, and what assurances he could give that his contract would be fulfilled. To this the man replied, that he would leave it to their wisdom to determine who he might be; that the money should not be a loan but an actual gift, for all time; that it should be paid immediately and thus no doubt be left of their receiving it. But for all this he made two conditions: One, that the Cathedral should be finished. Another, that on the day of its dedication, the first entering by the open door should belong to him, "skin and hair, body and soul!" As he said this the senators fled to the farthest part of the hall, for they well knew with whom they talked. The mayor indignantly commanded him to go away, and not flatter himself that they, men of dignity, were so foolish as to fall into the same trap that with another plausible device caught Mother Eve, and had since her day, by means of changing the bait, seduced so many of her descendants. But in spite of this, he only moved the nearer to them, and courteously demanded the cause of their strange conduct. He reasoned with them if it were not better that one should be given for all; and reminded them how little kings and governments hesitated to sacrifice thousands in war, to obtain some good for those remaining. Thus at last the senators recovered from their surprise and began to consider him with some favor. Their great need of money also influenced them, and finally the bargain was made. Then the Devil, after recommending himself to their kind consideration, vanished by way of the chimney with peals of satanic laughter. It was not long before many well-filled sacks descended this same chimney and thus secretly reached the council chamber. At first the senators were suspicious of the money, but examination proved it to be of genuine metal and exact weight. Then they agreed that the whole matter should remain a secret among themselves, and went on to finish the cathedral. But some of them whispered it to their wives, and some told other men, and so it happened that soon their secret was everybody's secret, and the whole city in deep anxiety concerning the result. When all was ready and the day for the dedication had arrived the door was opened, but none would enter; and though the bell tolled to call them, and all heartily desired to see the splendid temple, yet not one advanced to go in. The mayor and senators knew not how to proceed, when suddenly a little priest appeared who had a plan by which he hoped to cheat Satan out of his soul and his gold, and for once make him an instrument of good. The contract had indeed been that the first entering should be his, but it had not been stated what it should be, whether man or beast. By this oversight he hoped that the Devil might be outwitted. It happened that the day previous a wolf had been taken, and now the trap was so placed that if let out the wolf must run into the church. Then it was opened, and Satan, who watched for his prey, chased the devoted wolf with lightning speed; but when he found how he had been cheated his anger was terrific. He broke the wolf's neck, he spat fire and howled terribly, he banged the cathedral door with such force as to split it, and vanished in smoke, leaving the cathedral filled with the odor of brimstone. On the door an image of a wolf in brass is yet shown, and a fir-cone which represents a lost soul. The crevice also remains, a lasting memorial of the little priest who was so wise as to outwit the Devil.

The Hunchbacked Musicians. Long ago there lived at Aix-la-Chapelle two musicians both of whom were hunchbacked. But a great difference existed in their faces and characters. Friedel was well looking and amiable, and a fine musician, for his soul was full of goodness and it found expression through the tones of his violin. But Heinz had ugly red hair and a more ugly temper, and his playing was so unmusical that none ever listened to him for pleasure. Thus it happened that Friedel and his violin were always in demand for all occasions of merry-making and frolic, while Heinz was left unemployed. Now Friedel loved Agatha, the daughter of a rich wine-merchant, and she, perceiving his soul and forgetting his deformity, returned his love. All went well with the lovers themselves, but knowing the pride and love of money of the maiden's father they determined not to speak to him until they should be compelled so to do. At last a very rich suitor desired Agatha for his bride, and obtained her father's consent. Then it was that Friedel was obliged to speak, though with sinking heart. The wine mer chant cruelly ridiculed him, and drove him away with harsh words. Poor Friedel, quite distracted, wandered, he knew not whither. It was late when the chilling dews recalled him to his senses and he sought the town. As he approached it strange sounds were in the air and sights more marvelous met his gaze. Daws and all sorts of night-birds were screaming, and above the tops of the houses the broom-riding witches were trooping. And all making their way to the fish-market, or Perwisch, as it was called, in Aix-la-Chapelle. Friedel also went there, and great was his amazement at what he saw. The square was illuminated by little flames in the air, and crowds of female figures were moving about. Then Friedel remembered that this was quarter-day, and the witches were said to hold a picnic on that day at midnight in this very square. As he thought of this a woman, who looked very much like the mayoress of the town and seemed to be the leader of the others, advanced to meet him and led him to a table loaded with all kinds of delicacies and delicious beverages. She invited him to eat, and after he had refreshed himself, placed in his hand a violin and asked him to play music for dancing. As soon as the violin sounded they moved away the tables and seats and prepared to dance. It gave Friedel a very novel sensation to perceive that while all appeared to be busily talking and laughing together, no sound reached his ears. Soon the lady-president gave the signal to begin; then the violin of Friedel seemed as if bewitched, for in spite of him it would go quicker and more quickly, and the dancers whirled faster and more swiftly till all was as witchlike as could well be. At length Friedel fell on a seat exhausted, and the lady-president thanked him for his sweet music, and commanded him to kneel to receive his reward. Then she whispered words of strange sound above him, and laid her hand upon his poor deformed shoulders, and quickly removed the hump from them and placed it in a dish which she instantly closed. As she did this the clocks sounded the hour of one and in a twinkling all vanished and Friedel was alone. Weary and confused he hastened home, and to bed, where for the remainder of the night strange dreams came to him. But in the morning he found the most wonderful part of all, to be true. He was straight and comely in form as in face; moreover, a goodly sum of money was in the pocket of his jacket; enough to make him equal to any of the suitors of Agatha. As soon as possible he repaired to the house of the wine merchant, and told him his story under promise of secrecy. Now his reception was quite different from the former one, but it was more the sight of the money that decided the merchant to make Friedel his son-in-law, than the loss of the hump. Then were the lovers made happy. Although this adventure of Friedel's was to be a secret, it escaped in some way, and among others Heinz heard the story. His envy and hatred of Friedel, which had been bitter enough before, were increased, and he reported wicked stories of Friedel and accused him of the most immoral intercourse with the witches. But he secretly determined to attend their picnic on the next quarter-day and try his fortune among them. Now as he came to the fish-market the same scene met his gaze as that which Friedel had beheld, and Heinz advanced boldly, bearing his own violin, and making signs that he was willing to play. The dance was formed as before, but Heinz was so occupied in gazing avariciously upon the plate on the tables that he forgot his music, and played even more discordantly than was his custom. Soon the dance became a race, and Heinz believed he was doing so well as to give the witches great pleasure, when they all ran to him in a fury and shook their fists at him. He had also been so unwise as to call by name some wives of the town whom he thought he recognized. When the lady-president commanded him to kneel he thought it the time to claim a reward, so he seized a large gold drinking-cup. The lady gave him so smart a box on the ear that he gladly dropped the cup; she then took from a tightly covered dish the very hump she had taken off the shoulders of Friedel, and fastened it on the breast of Heinz. At that instant the clock struck one and he was left alone. Who can describe the rage and despair of Heinz? He added also to his misfortune by foolishly telling the story, and thus became the laughing-stock of the whole city. Only Friedel felt sorry for him, and he, out of his goodness of heart, maintained Heinz comfortably all the rest of his days.

All Saints, or **Allerheiligen.** See Baden-Baden.

Alsace and Breisgau, "*The Holy Odilie.*" Attich, Duke of Alsace, had a lovely and amiable wife, with whom he lived in great happiness, desiring but one thing more than he possessed; this was, the blessing of children. But his prayers remained unanswered until he vowed that if the Lord would grant him a child he would dedicate it entirely to his service. At length a daughter was born to him, but his joy was alloyed by the fact that she was blind. She was christened Odilie. When she was grown she was a beautiful maiden, and as good as lovely. Very early she showed singular piety and devoutness of character, and was the delight of all who knew and loved her. Often she lamented that she could not see, and the more delightful the descriptions that were given her of God's creation, the more sad her blindness seemed to her. She was accustomed each day, and many times a day, to ask God to bestow on her the gift of sight; and this she did with the same confidence and faith with which she would have asked her father for a new robe. At length, to the great astonishment and joy of all, this prayer was answered. Beautiful before, the new expression of her eyes enhanced her loveliness, and while previously she had no lack of suitors, now she was wooed by many and most noble youths. This so dazzling prospect, affected the mind of her father and led him to repent the vow he had made to give his sweet child to God. He had almost determined to announce that he had changed his intentions, when Count Adelhart, a brave man, and one who had done much service for Attich claimed the hand of Odilie as his reward. Then the duke resolved that she should be his bride. Odilie heard this with terror. She told her father how wrong she believed it to be, and how she much feared the vengeance of Heaven if they thus disregarded his vow. But when she saw that they would marry her by compulsion, she fled, she knew not whither. Then Attich called out his servants and huntsmen to pursue her; she ran through the forest like an affrighted hare, and at last came to a wall that she could not pass. Her pursuers were close upon her, and despair filled her soul, when lo, a rock opened before her! She glided in and it inclosed her from the sight of her father and his men. All were amazed. Soon Odilie called out from the bosom of the rock and declared that unless her father would fulfill his vow he should never see her again, but that if he would consent that she should be the bride of Heaven, she would come to him. Attich, who now plainly saw the will of God concerning Odilie, promised all she asked, and the rock opened that she might come forth. In remembrance of this miracle, Attich built there where the rock had opened, a cloister. Odilie was the first nun who took the veil in it, and was afterwards abbess of the convent. After her death she was made a Beato by the pope. This is the popular legend. The religious one will be found by reference to St. Ottilia, in the preceding portion of this book.

Alten-Aar. "*The last Knight of Alten-Aar.*" On one of the precipitous, cone-shaped hills that overlook the river Aar, may be seen the ruins of a once magnificent castle. This was formerly the home of a powerful and noble family of knights; but the end of Kurt, the last of his race, was so horrible, in its sadness, that no one would again inhabit the castle, and though for many years it remained stately and grand in its desertion, it at last crumbled and fell, no longer able to survive the adverse fate of the race it had shielded. Kurt of Alten-Aar, the last knight of his name, was a noble champion of liberty. He opposed the oppressions of Church and State, and thus offended princes and bishops. He had two lovely daughters who so cheered his stern, warrior life, that he often trembled lest the time should come when they would leave him. At length he received on the same day two letters demanding them in marriage. Pale and tearful he read these letters and with sad heart gave them to his children. When they had read them he asked their decisions. The eldest threw down the letter with scorn, and declared, "The daughter of the Count of Alten-Aar is too proud to give her hand to a robber!" "And you, my darling?" asked the father of the other. She threw her arms about his neck, and kissing him said, "Father, my sister has spoken for both." Then was the old knight proud of his children. "It is true," exclaimed he, "these knights are robbers. They will attack and besiege us, but it is better that we should die than to make these unholy alliances." Then he tore the letters and delivered the pieces to the messengers who had brought them and bade them return to their masters. Soon the castle was besieged. The brave Kurt called all his followers together, and gave permission for those who desired to leave the castle. But none would go, all preferred to die with him rather than desert him. The strength of the castle was such that the besiegers knew they could not attack it with any profit, and they determined to subdue it by famine. Thus weeks passed on, no relief came, and at length the provisions were spent and death was lurking in every nook of the vast castle, sure of victims. Again the knight assembled his retainers, and the second time offered them the opportunity to go forth from the castle. But not one was ready to leave him whom they loved as well as served. Then they determined upon a sally, but this failed and death alone was left to them. One by one they dropped away. Fevers broke out among them and the hunger-weakened ones could not long endure. Soon all save the old knight were gone. He stood by the dead bodies of his children, and determined that he would not wait for death which was so slow in claiming him. He put on a full suit of armor, and descended to the stables; his favorite horse remained. He mounted it and rode to the highest tower of the castle. It was early morning, and the rising sun irradiated all the scene, and showed plainly to the besiegers this wonderful sight. The commanding figure of the noble Kurt, his long silver hair, his stern face shaded by the plume of his helmet, the glistening steel of his armor, his beloved milk-white charger, and all standing out against the sky, as does the angel on the Castle of St. Angelo. Those who beheld were breathless with horror, but could not turn away their gaze. At length he waved his hand, as if to speak. "Here you behold the last man and the last steed that live in my castle! Hunger and disease have taken all. Wife, children, comrades, all, all are gone! Gladly would I have died an honorable death, to give them an honorable life. But sooner would I see them die, than that they should live beneath your oppression. Thank God, they have died free, even as I will die!" So saying he spurred his steed to the edge of the rampart. The animal started back and reared; but soon perceiving the will of the master he had loved and obeyed, he gave the fatal leap into the air. Down, down the deep abyss, from rock to rock, and into the dark river rolled the noble beast and his more noble rider, and the waters hid from view the old knight Kurt, the last of Alten-Aar! Hastily, and overcome with horror the besiegers retired, nor could any find courage to enter the vast castle-tomb, which seemed to frown, as if ready to fall upon them, should they dare to pollute by their presence its ghastly, death-strewn halls.

Auerbach. As a poor peasant was one day passing the old castle of Auerbach, he thought of the stories he had heard of the rich treasures supposed to be concealed in such old castles; and as he regarded the vineyards all about, he thought that there might well be wines also, for why should not they be preserved as well as gold and jewels? As he thus reflected there came towards him an old man, with smiling face and shining eyes, and wearing a cooper's leather apron. He thus addressed the peasant. "Would you not like to taste the wine of the noble lords of Auerbach? Aye, I thought so. Well, follow me." And he led the way through the vineyards towards the castle. The peasant was only too ready to follow, and he smacked his lips, and fancied he could smell the luscious wine. They stopped at an old, rickety cellar-door, and when this was opened, descended some steps, slippery with moss and partly decayed. At the bottom the old cooper took a huge bowl, a lever, and a candle from a niche, and proceeded over the moist, uncertain ground with careful step. As they advanced, and their eyes became more accustomed to the gloom, the flickering candle disclosed a row of gigantic, jolly, comfortable looking wine-tuns. The old cooper began to talk fluently of them all, as if they were his friends, and in fact had names for them, such as Bulgegood and Cheer-me-quick, Warm-me and Lay-me-down. He said that this was his kingdom, and the tuns his loving subjects. The astonished peasant was filled with admiration, which he expressed by varied exclamations and continually clapping his hands. "And then," said he, "the tuns shine like real burnished gold!" The old cooper declared that it was true, and explained that this was because the tuns were formed from the wine; that those made by man had long since dropped away. "But," he added, "looking is not enough; you must taste." So saying, he filled his bowl, and first drank himself to the health of the peasant. Then came the peasant's turn, and so good was the wine, that he stopped not short of emptying the bowl. He smacked and lapped his mouth, declaring the wine to be fit for the pope himself. Then the old cooper, though pleased, declared, that the wine which they had tasted was quite plebeian, and his aristocracy were farther on. Thus they proceeded, and soon the peasant was hugging and kissing the casks, and cutting all manner of ridiculous capers. But the old cooper only laughed, and at each bowl declared that he had still better, farther and farther on. At length the tears gushed from the eyes of the happy peasant as he tipped the last bowl, and sank down in a deep sleep. Next morning when he awoke, he found himself in a ditch behind the old ruin, and when he arose and searched for the entrance to the wine cellar, it could not be found, and since that time though many have sought, none have discovered it; but sometimes they perceive an odor of wine which causes them to exclaim, "Behold the cooper is tasting his wine!"

Bacharach. *Palatine Count Hermann of Stahleck.* On a mountain above Bacharach lies the ruin of Stahleck. Here, in the middle of the twelfth century, lived Hermann, Count of Stahleck, nephew of the Emperor, Conrad III. He was remarkable for his wisdom and learning, but was exceedingly avaricious, and possessed of an unquiet spirit. His wife succeeded in persuading him not to join the Crusades; but he could not rest, and was carried away by his desire to possess a large tract of country which was under the rule of the Bishops of Mayence and Trier. Many other knights joined him, and at length he stormed the stronghold of Treis, a castle on the Moselle, belonging to Adelbert, of Monstreil, Archbishop of Metz and Trier. Now this bishop, fearing for the strength of his arms, had recourse to a spiritual ruse which assisted him immensely. He presented himself to his troops with a crucifix in his hand, which he declared to them was brought to him by the Archangel Michael; and he added that this heavenly messenger had assured him of success, if only his troops would fight bravely and well. This served to inspire his soldiers with confidence, and when those of Hermann saw the bishop advancing with the crucifix in his hand, they did not stand firm, and their cause was lost. But Hermann, not yet discouraged, continued the war, and attacked the Archbishop of Mainz, Arnold of Selnhofen. And here he would have succeeded, but for the employment against him of treachery, and a great abuse of spiritual power. The archbishop, by means of dazzling promises of preferment, seduced the chaplain of Stahleck Castle. He refused absolution to the countess, because her husband was battling against the Church, and it was her duty to try by all the means at her command to put an end to this unholy conduct. He urged her to write to Hermann, persuading him, which she did; but as this failed, he hired two assassins who enlisted among Hermann's soldiers under false pretenses; and the bishop promised them full absolution for all their past and future sins, if they would rid him of his enemy. These wicked ones fulfilled their mission but too well. They waited until they were on watch together, and then entering Hermann's tent, they struck off his head, and fled with it to his own castle in order to prove to the confessor that they had fully executed his will. Here a true follower of the countess saw the dreadful sight, and hastened to inform his mistress of the truth. She, with dagger in hand, rushed to the apartment of the chaplain and took a meagre revenge by stabbing him on the spot. She then lavished tears and caresses on the head of her murdered husband. But suddenly all reason fled. She ran wildly about the castle, threatening all who attempted to approach her with the same fate as that of the confessor. At last she rushed to the highest part of the castle, and threw herself down to instant death. But the principal cause of all this wrong was still left, — the archbishop, Arnold of Mayence. It was not long before the punishment of his sins overtook him. He had excited the hatred of the people by his hardness and oppressions, and soon they razed his palace about his head, and he was forced to escape for his life. His friends warned him, and even the Abbess Hildegarde wrote to him, urging him to repent, but all in vain. He retired to the Abbey of Jakobsberg. The abbot was his enemy, and betrayed him to the people, who came by night and murdered the archbishop, even as he had caused to be murdered the Palatine Count Hermann of Stahleck.

Baden-Baden. *All Saints, or Allerheiligen.* The abbey of this name was celebrated in bygone days for the learning of its monks; and the school connected with the monastery was frequented by the sons of the most illustrious families, as well as by those of lesser consideration. At one time there came hither a well-born youth of Strasbourg. He excelled in the pursuits of literature, and had a soul keenly sensitive to the beautiful, and in harmony with nature. The scenery in the vicinity of Baden-Baden was his delight; and the forest depths, and the falling waters of the Grindbachs held him spell-bound for many hours. One day as he sat watching the snowy waterfall, lost in thought and admiration, a lovely maiden issued from a cave near by, and seemed to seek peace and rest as he had done. She was a gypsy, and a perfect child of Nature. She knew it all by intuition; by having learned it in her earliest years; by having breathed and lived its truth and simplicity with every moment of her life. Thus was she suited to all about her, and seemed to the young student to be the one element which had been wanting to make the perfection of the scene. From this time his wanderings had a purpose, and soon the gypsy Elmy and the student had plighted their faith and love forever and forever! Her childish heart was more than full of happiness, and she spent many hours of his absence in gazing on the plain gold ring, which he had given her in pledge that she should be his bride. One day she laid it down before her that she might see it glisten in the sun. A raven sat upon a tree above her, and suddenly he seized the ring, and bore it to his nest. Then was Elmy sorrowful, for her grandmother, a learned gypsy, had often told her that all her happiness depended on the safe-keeping of this ring. When her lover came, she begged that he would devise some means for its recovery. He dispelled her sadness, and assured her that his love depended not on any gift or bauble, on nothing save her own good and truthful heart. But next day as she walked near the grotto a frightful scene presented itself to her. The student, anxious to comply with the request of Elmy, had obtained the assistance of some of his friends, and had come to try if it were possible to recover the lost ring. They had lowered him over the cliff in a basket, and just as Elmy came in sight, he had almost reached the nest. She was rigid with fear. She would have screamed, but her voice was gone; it would not warn him of her love and nearness. And now he approaches the nest; he reaches out; the ring is his. But whence that fearful shriek, that agonizing cry that comes but when the very soul is rent asunder, and is the wild death-knell of hope? It was Elmy; for even then, just then, when it seemed that all was well, and the joyous thought had flashed through her, that he had done all this for her, and soon she should thank him for it, the rope gave way — a single crash, a dash from rock to rock, and Elmy bent over the lifeless body of her faithful lover!

Baldreit. This was the name of one of the most celebrated old hotels in the vicinity of Baden-Baden. It was acquired in the following manner: One of the princes of the Palatinate was a great sufferer from gout, and was sent by his physician to try the effect of the hot springs of Baden. His cure was very slow, and his patience almost exhausted, when one morning he awoke and found himself free from all pain, and able to move with perfect ease. His delight was so great that he determined to test his recovery even at this early hour. He dressed and ordered his horse, and descended to the court-yard to mount. As soon as he was in the saddle the court-yard door was opened, and he spurred his horse; but the animal went prancing about for some minutes in the paved court; this noise, so unusual at this hour, woke all in the house, and the landlord and several servants appeared at the windows. Waving his hand to them the prince said, "See, how soon I can ride." But the noise was such that "soon ride," were the only words that they could hear, and this has remained the sign of the house to this day.

Burkhardt Keller of Yburg. Many years ago a margravine of Baden-Baden determined to pass the days of her widowhood at the Castle of Hohen-Baden. In her suite was young Burkhardt Keller, a most noble knight. The steward of the margravine had a lovely daughter, Clara von Tiefenau, with whom Burkhardt was soon passionately in love. She lived at Kuppenheim, and the young man was accustomed to go to and from the castle and town sometimes very late at night. It happened that as he passed one night near twelve o'clock, he saw a lovely lady sitting beneath the trees, whose face was only covered with the thinnest of veils. He was spell-bound by her beauty, and at length stretched out his hand as if to touch her, when she vanished like the dew from a flower. The knight returned to Hohen-Baden and related this strange vision to the old warder of the castle. Now this particular old warder fully realized the accepted idea of old warders in general, and was not a whit lacking in garrulity, and knowledge of all that was wonderful for leagues about his castle, or in the love of telling it. So he told Burkhardt whom he had seen. That on or near the spot where the airy lady sat there had formerly been a heathen temple; that nymphs and such-like dangerous and bewitching ones often came there by night; and that no sane people ever ventured there, and added that now it even seemed unsafe for love-sick and dazed ones, like our young knight. But Burkhardt could not rest: the vision he had seen came constantly before his sight and deprived him of all peace. So he determined to try if he could solve this mystery. He took with him men and implements for digging. Soon after they commenced the excavations they found an altar which had been dedicated to the Nymph of the Forest, and a little farther down an exquisitely chiseled statue in marble. It represented a lovely and richly dressed lady, full of grace and attractiveness. It acted as a spell on Burkhardt. He remained motionless before it. He caused it to be placed upon the altar, and at last went away. But still the strange spell was on him; he returned next day to see the statue, when to his surprise he again beheld the same lovely being he had first seen at midnight. And now she did not vanish; she greeted him kindly and with sweet smiles, and as she listened to his burning words of love and wild devotion she clasped him in her arms. Alas, that death should lurk in anything so sweet as were her kisses and embraces to the infatuated knight! His horse returned to the castle without his rider, and next morning his dead body was found at the foot of the altar; but the beautiful marble statue was gone. The brother of the knight destroyed the altar, and erected on the spot a cross on which may be seen the name of Burkhardt Keller, and not far from the cross is a stone statue called Keller's Bild.

The Convent of Lichtenthal. Kloster Lichtenthal. Long ago, in one of the German wars, the enemy approached so near this convent that the good Abbess of Lichtenthal was rightfully alarmed. She had heard much of the wrongs inflicted upon helpless women and children, and she feared for the chastity and the lives of her nuns if they remained in the cloister. So she called them all together and told them of her decision to seek safety in flight. They then went in procession to the chapel to pray for grace and protection in this hour of need. When the service was ended the abbess stood before an image of the Blessed Virgin, which was carved in wood. In a loud voice she besought her kind care, and hung the keys of the convent on her arm, begging her to protect their loved home from the rage and fury of the approaching foe. Just then a peasant rushed in. He was bleeding from wounds, and his clothing torn and soiled. He announced that the soldiers were so near that only minutes, not hours could elapse before they would reach the gate. Then the nuns hastened to go out by a side door which led in an opposite direction from that of the coming troops, and they were soon out of sight of the convent. The soldiers came, they found none to oppose, and made their way through the silent corri dors to the chapel, hoping to find there rich plate and other booty such as they desired. But as they would have entered, the image of the Virgin, surrounded by a dazzling light, came towards the door of the church. At first they were fixed to the spot, but as she moved on and came nearer they were filled with awe, and when she seized the convent keys and offered them with a threatening air, none dared to take them, and they fled from the convent with far more readiness than they had entered it. Thus was the Kloster preserved, and when the nuns returned they found everything undisturbed, and but for the testimony of those who had seen they could not have believed that the army had been there. The wonderful miracle-working Madonna is still in the choir of the church. It is evidently a production of a master of the Byzantine school of art.

Eberstein, Old. After the Emperor Otho I. had conquered Strasbourg, he besieged the Castle of Eberstein which the counts of that name held against him. But they were brave warriors, and after a siege of nine months Otho was apparently no nearer his hopes than at the beginning. Then one of his knights advised him to proclaim a tournament at Spiers and promise the counts of Eberstein safe-conduct if they should choose to attend, and meantime, while they were absent, the castle could be surprised. Otho profited by this advice, and the tournament was held. The counts of Eberstein appeared and did themselves great credit. After the tournament there was a ball, and the counts danced with many of the chief ladies of the company. During one of these dances the Count of Eberstein was told by his partner of the ruse of the emperor; she advised him to confer with his two brothers, and that they all should leave as early as possible. He acted on the advice of the fair lady, but after telling his brothers, they returned again to the dance, and after a little Count Eberstein proposed that the knights and ladies should reassemble next day to repeat the tournament, and proposed to leave a hundred guldens in honor of the noble ladies. The emperor consented, and all separated with great good-will, but the three counts of Eberstein hastened to their castle. Next day all were assembled and waited for the tournament to begin. At length it came out that the counts of Eberstein had returned home and the emperor was outwitted. Then he sent men to try if they could not reach the castle before them; but they were already there, and repelled the assault in such a manner as to convince all that it was worse than useless to contend against them. Then Otho sent three ambassadors to negotiate terms with them. The castellan conducted them through the castle, and showed them casks of wine, heaps of fruit, and an abundance of flour. Now the casks had false bottoms, and the flour covered a mass of chaff; but the ambassadors told Otho that the castle contained provisions for another nine months, and that it was vain to think of subduing it. They advised him the rather to propitiate them by giving one of his sisters in marriage to Eberhard, the youngest Count of Eberstein. This was done, and their union was celebrated by joyous festivals throughout all Saxony.

Eberstein, New. The Knight's Leap. The counts of Eberstein were ever a bold and fearless race, who preferred liberty before life, and death sooner than imprisonment. They were also adventurous, and frequently engaged in wars and battles. A deadly feud existed between Count Wolf of Eberstein and the counts of Würtemburg. He was obliged to flee for his life, and found an asylum with his uncle William at the Castle of New Eberstein. But his retreat was discovered, and it was again necessary that he should flee. He arose one morning and mounted his horse to do so, when he found that the castle was already surrounded by his enemies, except on the side which overhung the Murg. There was no other way of escape, and this was apparently the way of death. He considered but a moment. He would not fall into the hands of his enemies. He thought of the mettle and spirit of his faithful horse, and he turned his head in the direction of the rocks; when he reached the edge, he spurred the noble creature to take the leap. One moment and it was done. He had gone into the deepest part of the river, but he was rewarded by success. His enemies had seen his leap with wonder and shouted with excitement. They now saw him gain the opposite bank and ride away, with oaths and cries of rage. He made his way to the Castle of Pfalzgraf Ruprecht, who joyfully received him, and helped him to regain his possessions.

The Fremersberg. This eminence commands a very extensive view of the Valley of the Rhine even as far as the Vosges. Here in 1411 a hermit, called Brother Henry, built a cell and chapel. He was soon joined by others, and they felt the need of more extensive buildings. At length it chanced that the Margrave James, who was an untiring huntsman, was one day separated from his friends and servants, and could not find them again. He wandered for hours, but found no way of escape. His path was ever closed by some craggy height or dangerous precipice. He sounded his horn again and again with no effect, and at length a moonless night seemed to end all hope. But the barking of his dog and the sound of the horn reached the ears of the hermits of Fremersberg. They went out with torches and found the good Margrave, whom they conducted to their cells. They gave him all the comforts their poverty would allow, and though vastly different from his accustomed fare, the supper was eaten with keen relish, and he slept better than ever before. He was charmed with the spirit of the hermits and grateful to them for their kindness. But words were not the only testimonial of this, for with such liberality as becomes the rich and royal, he built here in 1451 a fine monastery, and it was filled with monks governed by the Franciscan rule. In 1689 it escaped destruction, and was a monastery until 1826, when the number was so small that it was sold. A portion of the estate is now in vineyards. On another part there was an inn, now a chateau, the delightful situation of which could not well be surpassed. In 1838 a cross was erected where the high altar had formerly been.

Hohen-Baden. At the end of the fifteenth century a fearful plague broke out through all Germany. The Margrave, Charles I., died at Pforzheim. The Margravine, Catherine of Austria, fled with her two children, Frederic and Margaret, to the Castle of Hohen-Baden. Here she passed her time in the care of her children, and in prayer to the Blessed Virgin that she would preserve the lives of the little ones. Each day the plague came nearer and nearer, and the reports of its ravages grew more frightful. At length Catherine took her children into a room in the highest tower. Here she carried a large supply of provisions, and allowed no one to come near her, save an old man who came each morning to the foot of the staircase with fresh bread and water. The children played several hours each day upon the turret, and seemed to thrive in the pure air they breathed. One evening they fell asleep in each other's arms upon a carpet in the corner of the turret, and as the mother watched them she was moved to praise and thanksgiving for the goodness that had spared them thus far, and at the same time she earnestly prayed for further protection. Suddenly as she was kneeling upon the stone pavement, with her clasped hands raised towards heaven, a beautiful vision was before her. The Blessed Mother of Mercy was near her on the clouds, which on each side of her were formed into radiant pictures. That on the right represented the convent and Lichtenthal, that on the left the hot springs of Baden-Baden. She bent her head lovingly towards the margravine, and pointed with her right hand to the sleeping children, and then to the convent and church. With the left she pointed to the springs of Baden. Then she disappeared instantly as she had come. The pious Catherine pondered long on the meaning of this and what it demanded of her. She decided that she had been instructed to devote her children to the Church if they survived the plague, and that the hot springs would be the means of their preservation. Praying that her mind might be enlightened with heavenly wisdom she slept till morning. She then commanded that the water from the springs should be allowed to flow through all the streets. As soon as this was done a thick vapor was spread through the town and its surroundings. From this time the plague was stayed. The water was then freely used, and soon no traces of the dreadful disease remained save the sorrow in the hearts of those whose dear ones were gone. The Princess Margaret afterwards took the veil at

Lichtenthal, and Frederic entered the Church. He became Bishop of Utrecht, and his monument is in the great church at Baden-Baden.

The Mummelsee. At some distance from Baden-Baden, between Sassbachwalden and Oberkappel, in the northern portion of the Black Forest, there is a long range of hills, — they are about 3,800 feet high. They are called Hornisgrinde, and the southern point is Greuzberg. Here is the Mummelsee, a large lake whose waters are generally calm, but at times stirred as from the very depths and tossed in billowy waves. This occurs too when all is peaceful on the land and scarcely a leaf stirred in the forest; when the silence is unbroken, save by the raven's cry, and it would seem that some fearful tumult must exist within the lake and thus manifest itself upon the surface. It is in short a gloomy and soul depressing spot. It takes its name from the water-nymphs who are said to dwell there, — beautiful Undines, whose homes are in ever-verdant and luxuriant gardens, where the orange blooms among the blood-red coral, and a thousand flowers and glistening crystals combine to make a scene of untold beauty. The nymphs, themselves so ethereal and lovely, are as if formed of snowy lilies with the exquisite blush of a delicate rose. Every month, when the moon is at the full, they rise to the top of the lake to revel in the moonlight which cannot penetrate to their subterranean home. They frolic and jest, swim and dive hither and thither with the utmost *abandon* of joyousness. But when the cock crows and the first streak of dawn appears, they must descend to their sea-home and wait until Madame Luna again puts on her broadest smile of invitation. Sometimes they are forgetful of the hour, and the cock's crow and the morning light are equally unheeded by these frolicking nymphs. Then there appears an ugly old water dwarf who orders them home with such a voice and manner as cannot be disobeyed; and the waters are left as dull and gloomy as if there were no joy and beauty in all the earth.

The Pulpits of the Angel and the Devil. One of the finest views near Baden-Baden can be had from what is called the Devil's Pulpit. It is a high rock on the road to Gernsbach, just where it turns off to Ebersteinburg. It is surrounded with beautiful trees and not difficult of ascent. It gained its name from the following circumstances: About the time that the Christian Gospel was first preached in Germany and many were converted, the Devil was so much disturbed, that he decided to make some great exertions to stop the progress of these new doctrines, so fatal to his dominion in Rhineland. So he was accustomed to leave the lower regions near the source of the hot springs (which place on this account was called Hell), and proceed to the rock before described to teach and preach his dangerous and seductive doctrines. He is, as all admit, a fine orator, and employs every art that can increase the power of what he says. He described the good gifts he lavishes on his devotees: the pleasures of the world, the gratifications of ambition, the glories of pomp and power, the comforts of wealth, the revels of the gay and licentious, — and all this in language so fascinating, with touches of poetic inspiration, always in exactly the right place to catch the ear of the sentimental hearer, with arguments of apparent reason, for the satisfaction of the cooler headed ones, with a metaphysical mystery for those who would appreciate that style of thing, and in short, with some nice, little, well-turned sentence, exactly suited to tickle the ears of each one who listened. Many were affected by all this, and just prepared to take him for their leader, when a strange sound was heard through the air, and lo, a bright and glistening light was seen on a rock opposite to that on which the Devil stood, and as it separated a little, there appeared in its midst a glorious angel, holding in his hand the branch of peace. Then he addressed the assembly in a manner so unlike the other as to chain the attention from the very first word he spoke. He showed the value of what had been offered in comparison to happiness and lasting peace. He told them how one life brought death, the other life, — and both eternal. Wonderful was the effect of all he said. He strengthened the weakened, gave courage to the hopeless, and faith to the doubting, and even touched the hearts of those who disbelieved. Then Satan raved in his madness, and attempted again to address the listeners, for he saw that his cause was fast being lost. Just then the thunder roared, the lightnings flashed, and the winds blew from every point. The confusion of earth and sky was fearful. The angel held the branch threateningly toward the Evil One. A fearful shriek rent the air; the devil fell over the dread precipice, and was lost in the earth which yawned to receive him. Then all fell on their knees, and the air now calm was filled with praise and prayer, in the midst of which the Heavenly Messenger vanished from the sight of those whom he had saved from sin and death.

The Rocks. Many long years ago there stood a lonely castle not far from Baden-Scheuern. It was the home of Immo, the wild huntsman. No one dwelt with him save an old man and woman who attended to his wants and comforts. His only companion was his faithful dog. So fond was Immo of hunting that it never lost its charm, and filled in his life the place of society and friends, of business and literature, of love, wife, and children; in a word, it was his all. And his skill was such that he seldom failed to hit the mark at which he aimed. What then was his surprise one day, when he fired with perfect confidence at a white doe, to see his arrow fall far short of his intended game? He was astonished and annoyed, and at the same time he felt a singular admiration for the beautiful creature he would have slain. He determined to follow it. When the doe reached a place where the rocks rose abruptly toward the clouds it sprang into an opening in the crags. Immo now felt sure of his prey, but suddenly as he advanced a lovely woman stood before him. With one hand she softly petted the frightened doe, and with the other pointed toward the hunter as if to threaten him She spoke in a low, sweet voice: "Immo, why followest thou my doe?" The wild hunter was overcome with admiration and surprise. He knelt before her, but he shaded his eyes from the dazzling light which beamed around her. When he again looked up both doe and maiden had vanished, and ugly goblins looked mockingly down on him from all the rocks. But in these few moments the life of Immo was changed. He went home with pensive heart, and from that day he never hunted more.

The Wildsee. Not many miles from the Mummelsee toward the south there lies another gloomy lake called the Wildsee. From it flows the Schönmünzach, which empties into the Murg. Upon its shores are vast fir forests which cast a gloomy shade far over the lake. Here dwell water-sprites who come more frequently to the surface than do those of the Mummelsee. They leave the water and sit on the banks weaving garlands, playing their lutes and singing, or amusing themselves by telling stories, talking of each other and the fashions, very much as ladies do. For while these nymphs know little of flounces or puffs, and have no conception of drapery and its effects; yet the manner of weaving their garlands, the width of their bracelets and anklets plaited of finest grass, and the most becoming shade of coral, are topics as inexhaustible and full of interest as are those Paris styles of which we hear so much. Now it happened once on a time, that Bernfried of Schönengrund tended his flock quite near this lake; and as he lay stretched upon a moss bank thinking and dozing away the autumn day, he heard a strain of music more sweet than ever before had met his ear. The clear tones of the voice thrilled to his very soul, and he sprang up with flashing eyes and beating heart to listen with delight. Long time he waited, until it seemed that some spell was on him, and then sprang forward toward the lake from which the sound proceeded. A woodman who saw him, and who well knew the nature of the singer and the sad effects of gazing on her, tried to detain him, but in vain. Bernfried dashed on until he saw a lovely maiden upon the rocky shore. Beside her was a white doe, decked with garlands, while she played a sweet-toned harp. He knew not which most to admire, her beauty or her grace. Luxuriant blonde hair fell in waves about her neck and bosom, and as she sang her coral lips and pearly teeth were more bewitching than his wildest imagination could have conceived. But what was more wonderful than all, as soon as she heard the step of Bernfried, she gave but a glance toward him, and sprang into the middle of the lake. The dark waters hissed and bubbled over her, and she was hidden from the gaze of the young shepherd. But alas, that single glance had deprived him of his reason! From that moment he was wild and under the effect of a strange madness. He wandered from place to place, and at length so far away that he never more was seen by those who knew and loved Bernfried the Shepherd.

Windeck. The castle of this name stands high above the town of Bühl, about eight miles from Baden-Baden. It is said to be haunted by the spirit of a beautiful girl who appears here from time to time. A young sportsman once saw her, and she offered him a glass of delicious wine. He was so charmed by her that he returned day after day in hopes again to meet her, but each day he was disappointed. At length he took up his abode in the lonely place and was called the "Lord of the Castle." One morning he was found dead, but on his face was a smile so radiant that all who saw believed he must have died while gazing on the face of his much loved spirit maiden. On his finger was a ring never seen there before. This confirmed the opinion that he had seen her, and some believed that her kiss had been fatal to him. He was solemnly buried in the vault of the castle by the side of his unearthly bride.

The Marriage of the Ghost at Castle Lauf. This is another name for Castle Windeck, and the present legend refers in all probability to the same girlish spirit. Long time ago a young page who had wandered out of the right way sought the shelter of the castle. He saw a light in one of the rooms and made his way to it. It was a reception-room, and in it was a beautiful girl. She seemed buried in thought and did not notice the entrance of the page. Her beauty was only equaled by her sadness, which gave a sorrowful air to face and form, and seemed to have stolen all color from her cheeks. When the youth spoke she raised her eyes and nodded gently to him. He asked for lodging and a supper, and begged pardon for his intrusion, for which his only excuse must be that he had lost his way in the darkness. She answered nothing, but left the room. Soon she returned and brought venison, fowls, and other delicious viands, as well as wines, of which she motioned him to partake. After refreshing himself and becoming more cheerful from the effects of the wine, he ventured to address her: "You are the daughter of the house, if I mistake not." She nodded assent. "And your parents?" asked he. She pointed to the portraits which hung upon the wall, and sadly said, "I am the last of my race." The youth continued to regard her with ever-increasing admiration, and the more wine he drank, the more he found in the pale maiden to approve and the more lovely she appeared. At length he reflected that this was an opportunity of making his fortune such as seldom occurred, and not to be slighted. He then asked her if she had a lover or was promised in marriage, and when she answered in the negative, he immediately begged that she would be his bride, and declared the passion with which from the first moment of his entrance she had inspired him. At this her pale, sad face was illumined with light and joy. She arose instantly and took from a drawer two rings and a rosemary wreath. She then made a sign for him to follow whither she should lead. At this moment two old and venerable men, dressed in rich gala attire entered the apartment. They accompanied the young couple to the chapel of the castle. In it there were many monuments and splendid memorials of the family who had formerly dwelt here. Among them was a statue of a bishop. This the maiden touched as she passed on, and it instantly rose and proceeded to the altar. The candles which were apparently arranged for some impressive service, had meanwhile lighted themselves, and all was ready for the marriage. The face of the bishop lighted up, and his eyes shone as if he was full of joy. Then in a deep, impressive voice he said, "Kurt of Klein, are you resolved to take Bertha of Windeck, to be your wedded wife?" The heart of the youth died within him and he could not answer. Just then a cock crew, and a gust of wind swept through the place as if it would destroy the chapel and all that it contained. Instantly the whole company disappeared, the candles were out and the bishop had again become a brazen statue. Kurt fell senseless to the floor, but when he recovered himself he was lying in the court-yard of the castle, and his horse was quietly feeding by his side.

The "Henneyraben." Near this same Windeck Castle the traces of a deep ditch are to be seen. The neighboring farm was named from it, and the legend connected with it is as follows: Many long years ago when a certain Dean of Strasbourg was the prisoner of the knight of Windeck, there lived at Wolfshag an old woman, who was called through all the country round, "The Woman of the Woods." One evening as she sat at the door of her cot, two delicate looking and pleasing youths passed by. "Whither go you?" questioned the old woman. "We go to the Castle Windeck," replied the elder with a blush; "our uncle, the Dean of Strasbourg, is prisoner there and we desire to give ourselves as hostages for him until he can pay his ransom." "What!" exclaimed she, "do you expect the knight will receive such hostages as you? and how could you bear imprisonment?"—saying which she looked with cunning eyes at the elder of the two, who only blushed and looked away, then quickly said, "God will assist us, for our dear uncle is the only one to care for us, and all our support." Then the younger of the two cried out, "But I will challenge the Knight of Windeck! Indeed, I will! for I too am a knight, and I will deliver our uncle." "Gently, Cuno, we must entreat, we cannot defy," said the elder brother. "Pshaw! Imma; you may sue and pray, but I will not!" Then the maiden blushed painfully at the careless words of her brother, which thus revealed her sex. But the old woman said, "Do not be troubled, maiden. I saw through your disguise at my first glance; but you are honest, and I like you and will assist you. Go to the castle and tell the Knight of Windeck that I sent you to warn him that the people of Strasbourg have agreed to attack him and he must hasten to make a ditch on the only side where ascent is possible. And as his time is short, I will give you something which will help him." She then gave a peculiar whistle, whereupon a gray hen came to her, and perched itself upon her shoulder. "Here, my child, take this. Bring it to the castle, and when it is dark and the moon risen, carry it where the ditch should be and leave the rest to us." The brothers were amazed, but the old woman was so kind they could not refuse obedience. She then said something to the hen in a strange tongue, and gave it to them with other charges to take care of it, and do as she had commanded them. So they went on until they reached the castle and were presented to the knight. He was young and handsome, and received them with kindness. The maiden hesitated and blushed, and could scarcely find words to make her request. The knight seemed to enjoy this confusion, and did not in the least assist her, but gazed on her in such a way as not at all to reassure her. At length she explained why they were come, and begged him to accept them as hostages. She also gave him the hen and the message of the old woman. A strange emotion stirred the soul of the knight as he listened to her proposition, and with great kindness promised to take them to their uncle. Meanwhile the younger boy had touched the belt and arms of the knight and expressed his childish admiration for them. The knight spoke kindly to him and took him in his arms, bidding the elder to follow. The Dean was a prisoner in but a single respect, — he could not leave his prison. He was confined to a certain suite of apartments, but they contained all he could desire for comfort or amusement. In spite of this he was gloomy and dejected. The thought that he was in the power of his enemy oppressed him, and the many duties he was detained from performing weighed heavily upon his mind. Often he thought of Imma and Cuno, and prayed the Holy Mother to guard them from every danger. At times he succeeded in losing himself in books, and mental activity dulled the pain of his grief. It was at such a moment that the knight entered with the maiden and her brother. The heart of the former beat with such force beneath her doublet as she stood before him that she feared lest it should burst. But the boy sprang forward and cried out, "O, uncle, darling uncle! See, Imma and I are come to set you free!" The knight was much astonished when the maiden's secret was thus revealed, but he did not allow his surprise to betray itself. He only reached his hand to the Dean, saying, "Do you hear? If you will yield these children to me as hostages you are free, but I will not promise to return them to you soon." Then to the maiden he said, "Now my fine page, which will you choose to be, a soldier or to take a place in my household? You seem more fitted for the latter." Imma looked at him with a glance of such tender reproof that he could no longer resist his desire to embrace her, and tenderly pressing her to his heart he said softly, "Tell me, will you have my home for yours, and me for your husband and protector, or will you leave me with your uncle?" She spoke not, but as he gazed on her he read his answer in her face, and in the tears she shed upon his bosom, for he cheerfully summoned the Dean to change his prisoner's dress for the surplice, and to become his uncle in place of his enemy. The Dean hesitated to consent, but Imma added her persuasions to those of the knight, and at length he joined their hands with solemn blessings. The hen was placed according to the directions of the old woman, and when the men of Strasbourg came they found a ditch filled with the soldiers of Castle Windeck, and in place of the battle they had come to fight, they joined in the wedding-dance and drank to the good health of the Knight of Windeck and his young Strasbourg Bride.

Baldreit. See the legends of Baden-Baden.

Basel or Bâle. "*One hour in Advance.*" A great many years ago when Basel was surrounded with enemies, there were also traitors in the town, and they had agreed together that at a certain time they would combine in their movements and thus gain possession of the city; the signal agreed on was the striking of twelve by the clock in the tower, on a certain night. Fortunately the watchman in the tower was informed of this plan before it was too late to prevent it, but not soon enough to consult with any others as to what should be done. Some cunning device alone could interfere with the success of the undertaking. So after a little thought he advanced the clock one hour, and in place of midnight, it sounded one o'clock. This confounded all, and made both those outside and those within the city doubtful what to do. Meanwhile the watchman hastened to inform the magistrate, and the commandant, and their united efforts prevented any result from the treacherous device, and at length the enemy being weary of the siege retired, and left Bâle without having obtained any advantage. The magistrate ordered the clock to remain as the good watchman had set it, and for many years, until 1798, it struck one o'clock in Bâle when in other places it sounded twelve. From this the saying arose, that "Though the inhabitants of Basel are a century behind, yet they are one hour in advance of all the world." At Basel was also the carved head called the Lallenkönig. It was placed on the clock of the Basel Bridge steeple, and with each motion of the pendulum the head turned its eyes and thrust out its tongue. This singular thing was made and placed upon the clock after a dispute among the inhabitants, and was intended to ridicule those of Little Bâle. This tower was taken down and the Lallenkönig destroyed in 1839.

Bingen. *The Mouse Tower.* Bishop Hatto of Fulda was a man of high ambitions, and much desired to obtain the vacant archbishopric of Mayence. The Emperor Ludwig and the Duke Otto ruled the country as regents, and Hatto was so much a favorite of the emperor that he was called the "heart of the king." He was at the head of the German clergy, and was governor of twelve rich and powerful abbeys. He made heavy taxes in order to erect magnificent buildings, and he it was who first established the temporal power of the bishopric of Mayence. Among other devices for raising the revenues he built a tower near Bingen, in the midst of the river, and all passing ships were obliged to pay a toll. This was considered extremely oppressive. Soon a dreadful famine visited the bishopric; drought, hailstorm, and vermin destroyed all the crops, and this was rendered more distressing to the people because the bishop had bought up all the grain and sold it only for the highest prices. For this the tradition makes him suffer a terrible death, inflicted miraculously as a direct judgment from Heaven. This legend is related in the following lines by Southey: —

"The summer and autumn had been so wet,
That in winter the corn was growing yet;
'Twas a piteous sight, to see, all around
The grain lie rotting on the ground.

"Every day the starving poor
Crowded around Bishop Hatto's door,
For he had a plentiful last-year's store,
And all the neighborhood could tell
His granaries were furnished well.

"At last Bishop Hatto appointed a day
To quiet the poor without delay:
He bade them to his great barn repair,
And they should have food for the winter there.

"Rejoiced such tidings good to hear,
The poor folk flocked from far and near,
The great barn was full as it could hold
Of women and children, and young and old.

"Then when he saw it could hold no more,
Bishop Hatto he made fast the door;
And while for mercy on Christ they call,
He set fire to the barn and burnt them all.

"'I' faith, 'tis an excellent bonfire!' quoth he,
'And the country is greatly obliged to me,
For ridding it in these times forlorn
Of rats that only consume the corn.'

"So then to his palace returned he,
And he sat down to his supper merrily,
And he slept that night like an innocent man; —
But Bishop Hatto never slept again.

"In the morning as he entered the hall
Where his picture hung against the wall,
A sweat like death all over him came,
For the rats had eaten it out of the frame.

"As he looked there came a man from his farm:
He had a countenance white with alarm;
'My lord, I opened your granaries this morn,
And the rats had eaten all your corn.'

"Another came running presently,
And he was pale as pale could be, —
'Fly! my Lord Bishop, fly,' quoth he,
'Ten thousand rats are coming this way, —
The Lord forgive you for yesterday!'

"'I'll go to my tower on the Rhine,' replied he,
''Tis the safest place in Germany:
The walls are high, and the shores are steep,
And the stream is strong, and the water deep.'

"Bishop Hatto fearfully hastened away,
And he crossed the Rhine without delay,
And reached his tower, and barred with care
All the windows, doors, and loop-holes there.

"He laid him down and closed his eyes; —
But soon a scream made him arise:
He started, and saw two eyes of flame
On his pillow, from whence the screaming came.

"He listened and looked: it was only the cat:
But the Bishop he grew more fearful for that;
For she sat screaming, mad with fear
At the army of rats that were drawing near.

"For they have swam over the river so deep,
And they have climbed the shores so steep,
And up the tower their way is bent, —
To do the work for which they were sent.

"They are not to be told by the dozen or score:
By thousands they come, and by myriads and more.
Such numbers had never been heard of before;
Such a judgment had never been witnessed of yore

"Down on his knees the Bishop fell,
And faster and faster his beads did he tell,
As louder and louder drawing near
The gnawing of their teeth he could hear.

"And in at the windows, and in at the door,
And through the walls, helter-skelter they pour,

And down from the ceiling, and up through the floor,
From the right and the left, from behind and before,
From within and without, from above and below,
And all at once to the Bishop they go.

"They have whetted their teeth against the stones;
And now they pick the Bishop's bones;
They gnawed the flesh from every limb,
For they were sent to do judgment on him."

Another legend of the Mouse-tower (Mäusethurm) relates, that when during the Thirty Years' War, the Swedes took possession of all the castles on the Rhine, the Mouse-tower was held by the knights of the Teutonic Order. It was a very important point, commanding as it did the passage of the river. The knights well knew this, and defended it with great courage. At length all but a single one were killed. His enemies were filled with admiration of his valor, and could not have the heart to murder him. They called on him to surrender, but his reply rang out, "Mercy neither for you nor for me. Knights can die, but cannot surrender." Then he seized the tricolor, and cutting a way through the foe he plunged into the river. The Swedes made earnest endeavors to recover his body, and sought especially for the flag, but neither could be found. The Rhine remained the faithful guardian of what was thus consigned to its care.

The Holy Rupert. During the reign of the pious Ludwig, Saxony was governed by the Duke Robolaus. He was wild and full of courage, and possessed of great skill in arms and all manly exercises; but he was not favorable to the Christians. In spite of this he was deeply in love with Bertha, the daughter of one of the most powerful dukes upon the Rhine; and his passion was ardently returned, although she was a quiet, amiable, and devout maiden. She flattered herself with the hope that under the influence of her love, Robolaus himself would become a Christian. But her endeavors to effect this change enraged him, and he became so sulky and unkind that Bertha was obliged to leave him, and went to a distant castle where she gave birth to a son, whom she called Rupert. Him she determined to so educate, that he should as greatly excel in virtue as did his father in courage and arms. Robolaus fell in battle while the child was still young. Then Bertha forgot all his faults, and magnifying his virtues mourned him sincerely. She determined to remove to the ducal palace of her father at Bingen. Here she refused many offers of marriage, and devoted herself entirely to the little Rupert. He fully repaid her cares, and was early distinguished by many graces of character, but by none so much as that of charity, and love of doing good to the poor and suffering; he divided all he had with them, and when Bertha would have built a church he opposed it, saying, "First feed the hungry and clothe the naked." When he was older, although universally beloved, he was urged to acquire such knightly accomplishments as befitted his rank, and was frequently rallied on account of his lack of them. But neither advice or raillery moved him. He still devoted himself to works of charity. One day as he slept on the bank of the Rhine he had a wonderful vision: A venerable old man stood in the river surrounded by a troop of boys; he dipped them, one after the other in the stream, and they emerged more lovely than before. Then a beautiful island, well realizing in its fruits and flowers, its birds and their sweet songs, his idea of Paradise, rose in the midst of the stream. Thither the old man led the boys, and clothed them in shining garments. Then Rupert hastened to request that he too might be allowed to go to the lovely island, but the old man solemnly replied, "This is not a place for you, Rupert; your life of charity and holiness renders you worthy of the life in heaven, and to see the face of the Transfigured." At these words there arose from the island, a beautifully brilliant rainbow, and Rupert saw a band of angels with golden wings, and in their midst the Infant Christ appeared in indescribable glory. At his side knelt St. John, and two angels soared above him, holding a garment which Rupert had recently given to a poor child. With this they clothed the divine child, who said, "You have fed the hungry, and clothed the naked; for such works are given the higher rewards of eternal glory." Rupert in an ecstasy, stretched out his hands to the lovely vision. It vanished, and he awoke. From this time he determined to resign all worldly honors. He told his mother of his intention to visit Rome and the Holy Sepulchre, after which he would return to Rome, there to pass his days in religious labors. Now although his mother had educated him religiously, she had intended that he should be a knight, and support the state and dignity which was his right. But no persuasions could obtain from him more than a promise to return to her for a short time, and he renounced all honors of rank and riches, preferring thereto the staff of the pilgrim. After a year of wandering he returned. His privations had destroyed his health, and he came to his mother to die in her arms. He was not yet twenty years old. The pious Bertha did not long survive him. Rupert has since been canonized, and the Convent of Eubingen is said still to contain the garment which he gave to the poor child, and which was represented in the vision.

The Prophetess Hildegarde. After the death of Bertha and her son, their estates were divided among several relatives, and the Castle of Sponheim was built. Here the Knight of Bökelheim lived with his wife Matilda, and their only child, Hildegarde. This child was sent to the Convent of Dissibodenberg to be educated. It was soon evident that she was one set apart for the service of Heaven. She was a prophetess, and had many visions. She wrote much, and was especially severe in her exposures of the corruptions of the priesthood. When St. Bernard preached his Crusade he visited her, and gained her approbation and assistance in his great undertaking. He presented her with a ring, inscribed, "I suffer willingly." This is still to be seen at Wiesbaden. She was made abbess of her convent. Many of her writings were in Latin, and she was a learned woman. She has been canonized, and her festival is on the seventeenth of September.

Bonn. *The Treasure-seeker.* After the siege of Bonn, in the last part of the seventeenth century, there was much building and repairing to be done, in order to make good that which had been destroyed during the war. All classes of workmen were prosperous, and among them none more so than young Conrad, the locksmith. His father had been a sheriff at Endenich, but had lost his property by the war. His house was burned, and his eldest son had perished in his attempts to save some portion of their valuables from the flames, and now the old man had come to pass his remaining days with Conrad. All went well until the young man fell in love with Gretchen, the pretty daughter of another sheriff, named Heribert. This wooing did not promise well, for the father had declared that none save a man of wealth should be his son-in-law. He himself had grown very rich since the war. No one knew how, and all were full of surmises concerning it. Some believed he had gained wealth by supplying the enemy; some that he had discovered hidden treasures, and some that he had dealings with evil spirits; and this last opinion found the larger number of disciples. But the lovers did not disturb themselves about the father or his consent. They were happy without it, until on an occasion, he surprised them at their love-making, when his fury was great and he struck Conrad on the head so violently that he fell to the ground, and marched Gretchen off in great displeasure. From that moment Heribert hated Conrad, and vowed to ruin both him and his father; and he had the power to do them great injury. Soon their creditors were clamorous, unwilling to await their payments; their property was to be sold and ruin staring them in the face, and all the result of the hatred of the rich Heribert. But do all he would he could not change the heart of Gretchen nor prevent her seeing her lover. One evening Conrad had climbed to her chamber window, and at midnight when all others slept they softly discussed the sorrows of their lives, and different plans for accomplishing their desires. Suddenly another window opened, and the voice of the father called, out, "Rogue, thief, off instantly or I shall shoot you dead!" Conrad alarmed sprang to the ground, and then cried out fearlessly: "Although you have found me at night at your window, you know that I am honest, and that love for your daughter alone brings me here. You hate me because I am not rich, but who can tell how you obtained your wealth? I too could have as much from the devilish Lapp, if I would consent to hold intercourse with him. Would you not be willing to give me Gretchen if I wooed her, laden with wealth?" A shot was the only reply to this speech. The bullet missed its aim, but despair went to the heart of Conrad, and he felt that money alone could help him to wed with his beloved Gretchen. As he was thus returning home the clock struck twelve. Temptations came to him and he reflected, "How would it be if I were to call on Lapp, who lives under the graves in the church-yard, and answers those who call at this hour? Be it so!" and he hastened to the spot. Thrice he called the fearful name, and a dreadful figure with flaming eyes rose from the ground and stood before him. "What is your wish?" it asked in fear-inspiring tones. "I seek gold, help me to it!" exclaimed Conrad. Then the figure beckoned him to follow and led the way to the forest; when there it pointed to a certain spot and put its finger on its lips in token of silence, then it disappeared. Conrad returned home, and this great excitement threw him into a fever. When he recovered from this, he went to the place which had been pointed out, and dug for gold. After some time he came to a chest filled with coins. Next day he bought in Bonn a nice house; he furnished it to his fancy and increased his business. He went each night to his treasure-house to bring away the gold, and soon excelled Heribert in his style of living. He also paid his father's debts and released his mortgaged property. When all this was done he repeated his wooing, and this time with very different results. The father was now but too ready to receive him, and the marriage was celebrated. But all was not now as smooth and happy as he had anticipated. Gretchen had all the curiosity of her sex, and greatly desired to know how Conrad had obtained his sudden wealth, and used all the bewitching arts which are so effective when employed by a lovely wife during the honeymoon, to find out the secret. Conrad was about to confide all to her when suddenly one evening he was arrested and thrown into prison. He was called on to account for the change in his circumstances, and as he refused all explanation, the torture was used to extort a confession from him. He then declared that he had found a treasure. With this the court let him rest from farther torture, and was apparently satisfied. His wife was allowed to visit him, and listeners were set to obtain, if possible, the whole truth. Then Conrad told Gretchen all, and the listeners reported to the judges how he had obtained his money. This produced no immediate effects, for although the treasury could claim money so obtained, the elector decided that if Conrad could prove what he had said to be true, he would allow him to retain his riches. Just then when he was considering how to prove this, a great cry was raised by the Jews of Bonn. One of their number, Old Abraham, who was very rich, had disappeared, was probably murdered. Of course Conrad was suspected, again arrested, and tortured. He confessed, and said he had an accomplice, whom he declared to have been Heribert, his father-in-law, who had killed Abraham by shooting. In this way he hoped to be revenged on him whom he regarded as the cause of all his troubles. The frightened sheriff also confessed under the torture, and they were condemned to be hung. The day of the execution came, and they were dragged forth, when a most unexpected person appeared, none other than the Jew Abraham. The prisoners were conducted to their homes in joy. But although he had escaped death, all these experiences had sadly affected Conrad. He could neither work nor be happy at leisure. Gretchen too was sorrowful. They returned to Endenich where they lived in the closest retirement. They had no children, and Conrad left his property to churches and charities, in order to atone as much as possible for having obtained the aid of the spirit Lapp, in his greediness for gold.

Boppard. *The Convent of Marienburg.* In the days of Frederick I. there lived in Boppard a young knight, Conrad, a descendant of "Bayer of Boppard." He was in love with a maiden also of noble race, and determined to marry her as soon as her brother who had accompanied Frederick to Palestine should return. During the absence of the emperor, robbers infested all the country and attacked Conrad several times. He repulsed them successfully, and also assisted other knights to do the same. This caused him to lead a wild and irregular life, and he came to feel that marriage would perhaps prove a certain kind of slavery, and his love for Maria gradually grew less. At length he wrote her that he would release her from her promise. But as soon as this was done, his conscience reproached him and he was most unhappy. He tried to drown sorrow in wine, and went frequently to the chase. As he was hunting one day, he was more joyous than usual, all nature seemed beautiful, his spirits rose and he was like his former merry self. The hounds soon found a track, the chase became exciting and mad, the stag disappeared in an underwood and the dogs followed, but Conrad took a more open path. He soon found that he had been misled and was separated from the chase. He was disappointed, and dismounted to rest. Just then a knight in full armor came up and challenged him to combat. He demanded who thus addressed him, and asked that he should raise his visor. Then the knight replied, "I am the brother of Maria, and challenge you to atone for the insult you have offered her." This, added to his ill-temper at losing his way and the reproofs of his conscience, rendered him furious. He turned his horse directly and charged at the knight His adversary sunk down and covered his bosom with his hands, for the blood was flowing copiously. Then Conrad's heart misgave him, and he hastened to take off the knight's helmet, when he was filled with horror at the sight of Maria's own sweet face. Faintly she spoke, "By your hand I wished to fall, since life without you is a burden." In vain he essayed to stop the life-blood; one moment and she was gone. Then he cursed himself, and fell senseless upon the body of his beloved Maria. So he was found, and it was with much difficulty that he could be taken away from her. She received a splendid burial, and above her remains Conrad erected a convent which he called Marienburg. To this he gave all his property, and hastened away to Palestine to seek death, which could alone reunite him to Maria. He fought without armor and exposed himself in every way. He won much renown, but death came not. At length at the storming of the fortress of Ptolemais, he was the first to ascend the ladder, and was killed by a deadly thrust from a spear.

Bornhoven. *The Brothers' Hatred.* Near the Convent of Bornhofen, on the Rhine, are the ruins of a castle with nothing of the romantic beauty that characterizes so many such localities on this charming river. Here dwelt a very rich knight, who, when dying, left two sons and a daughter. Their mother had long been dead, and they had received no loving care; for the old knight was a wicked man, and had gained his wealth by oppression and injustice, at the expense of all love and respect from equals or inferiors. At his death, besides his estates he left a large amount of gold. The brothers inherited all the avarice and selfishness of the father, while the sister was gentle and loving, and was, moreover, very religious in life and thought. The brothers were unjust to her in the division of the property, but she would not expose them to the world, and having employed that which they chose to give her in founding religious houses, she entered a convent where she lived in retirement. The brothers, who had been agreed in robbing the sister, now quarreled regarding the division of the booty between themselves, and their hearts were filled with hatred which was ever ready to blaze forth on the slightest occasion. At length the spark necessary to kindle the flame was added in the fact that both loved the same maiden, and she being a coquette, was happy in the attempt to fascinate them both. Jealousy added the last particle of hatred that they could endure, and they drew their swords in a duel, which ended in the death of both; for in their blind rage they ran upon each others' swords, and both were murderers, while both were murdered. Since this event gloom and melancholy have seemed to preside over this spot, like avenging spirits of the unnatural crimes of the inimical brothers.

Burkhard Keller of Yburg. See Baden-Baden.

Carlsruhe (Charles' Rest). The Margrave Charles of Baden was a victorious warrior, and returned to his home determined to devote himself to the arts of peace and the improvement of his possessions. He desired to commence with the embellishment of Durlach, but court intrigues so opposed him that he gave up the idea. One day as he was hunting in the Haardt forest, he laid down beneath an oak and fell asleep. In a dream he saw high above his head, a crown set with precious stones, and inscribed, "This is the reward of the noble." All around the crown was a splendid city with towers. A noble castle, well fitted for a royal residence, was there, and churches with spires, springing lightly toward heaven. When he awoke his courtiers surrounded him, for they had sought and found him while asleep. He related his dream, and declared his intention of founding there just such a city as he had seen. He would also dwell in it, and his place of burial should be beneath the tree where he had rested when the vision came to him. Thus was Carlsruhe founded, for Charles accomplished all that he proposed to do.

Caub, Castle Gutenfels. This splendid castle was the scene of a very romantic love-story about the middle of the thirteenth century. Count Philip of Falkenstein and his lovely sister Guta then resided here. They attended a great tournament which was held at Cologne. Guta had been courted by many brave knights, and had refused all offers of marriage. On account of her beauty she had been selected to bestow the prize on the victor of the day. Among those who contended for the honors was a knight known only to the Bishop of Cologne, whose guest he was, and he assured those assembled that the stranger was worthy to contend with any in the land. This knight was splendidly armed and mounted, and so skillful that it was soon seen that he would carry off all prizes. He soon fixed his eyes on Guta with admiration, and when he rode around the lists as victor, he lowered his lance to her. This unexpected attention so confused her that she dropped her glove, which the knight quickly caught, and begged that he might retain it. This she could not refuse, and he fixed it upon his helmet. Falkenstein, much pleased with these attentions to his sister, invited him to call on them at their castle. This he did a few days later, and then declared his love to Guta, begging her to trust him and wait a few months until he should be able to tell her of his name and circumstances. This she promised to do, and after exchanging vows of love and faithfulness, they parted. Soon a war broke out, and Richard of Cornwallis was declared emperor and crowned at Frankfort Falkenstein, who had been absent with the army, found on his return that his sister was sad, and apparently drooping in health, which greatly troubled him, but she concealed the cause of her grief and shut herself in her own apartments much of the time, where she mourned the falseness of her lover, for as the time he had named for his return had long since passed, all hope of seeing him again had left her. One lovely morning there appeared before the castle a troop of cavaliers magnificently dressed and mounted on spirited horses. Falkenstein hastened to meet them, and as the leader dismounted he exclaimed, "Be welcome, my king!" and they entered the castle, but scarcely were they within the walls when Richard asked for Guta. "She is ill," replied the brother, "and sees no one." "Tell her that King Richard demands her hand,— that will cure her." "No, no," said Falkenstein, "I believe it not, for she will not marry, though many and brave men have sought her hand." But the brother, well pleased, conveyed the message, and even urged his darling Guta to accept this honor, although it would separate them. But she was immovable, and he returned to Richard with a refusal. "God be praised!" said the emperor. "Now know, my dear Falkenstein, that Guta plighted her troth to me after the tournament at Cologne. She knew not my name, but she loved me. I have tested her faith. She has refused a king. Bring her now this glove and tell her a knight of the king's train sent it to her. Let her come to me that I may fulfill my promise." Falkenstein did so, and as soon as Guta saw the glove she hastened to welcome her lover. "You are still faithful, as I myself am," said Richard, tenderly embracing her. A sweet smile was her only answer. "Should I deserve to be emperor if I kept not my promise?" Then looking at her brother she exclaimed, "You? Emperor?" "Our emperor and your husband, my sweet sister," answered Falkenstein, while tears flowed from his eyes. Then were they married, and Richard changed the name of the castle, which had been Caub until now, and called it Gutenfels in honor of his true and loving wife.

Cleve. *The Swan Knight.* The young Countess of Cleve was in great distress because a strong and daring vassal had announced his rebellion, had made her a prisoner in her own castle, and would restore her to freedom only on condition that she would marry him. She saw no way of escape, for no other knight would venture to challenge this traitor, so strong and powerful was he. And she prayed to Heaven to send her release. Now on her chaplet was a silver bell which had a surprising power. Its sound increased by distance in one especial direction; and this sound came to the ears of a distant king, who regarded it as the cry of some one up the Rhine who was in deep distress and greatly needing assistance. He also believed it to be an occasion for his only son to make his name known and respected, for these knights of olden time regarded exploits in aid of the defenseless, especially if women, as worthy of great praise, and by them they established a reputation for bravery and prowess. Then a swan appeared on the river drawing a boat by a golden chain. It placed itself on the bank before the king's son, as if demanding to be used. This appeared to the young man like a signal from a higher power; he entered the boat, and immediately the swan proceeded up the Rhine drawing the boat after it. Now the day had arrived on which the rebellious vassal of the young countess had determined to marry her in spite of all repugnance on her part. She knew she could not escape this hateful union unless she could find a knight who would challenge him to mortal combat, and of this she had no hope. While she was sadly reflecting on her sorrows, and preparing to array herself for this marriage, she saw a boat drawn by a swan in which was a sleeping knight. It approached her domains on the river. Instantly she called to mind that an old nun had once told her that a sleeping youth should save her from some imminent danger. Just then the knight sprang to the shore, and the swan and the boat instantly disappeared. He came directly to the castle and kneeling before the countess begged that he might be allowed to combat for her hand. She consented joyfully, and preparations were instantly made for the trial. All who witnessed it were filled with fear for the young knight, who seemed wholly unable to contend with his proud and powerful opponent; but justice triumphed and the rebellious vassal fell, pierced through by the sword of the young knight. Then the countess thanked him most earnestly, and so great was her gratitude that a few days after she willingly conferred her hand upon him. He proved a fond and faithful husband, and there was but one thing which could have added to the happiness of the countess. She much desired to know who her husband might be, and of his former life; most of all what fate or fortune had brought him to her relief. But before he had promised to marry her, he required of her that she should never question him of these things, and assured her, that should she disregard his wishes he should leave her forever. Time passed on, and their happiness was increased by the birth of three sons who bade fair to be an ornament to chivalry and the pride of their family. But now the countess could no longer repress the cravings of her mother's heart. She felt that her husband was of noble origin, and she begged him to give his name to his children. She urged that the lowest of parents gave that at least, to their sons, and she feared lest her noble boys should be regarded and mocked as bastards. Then was the knight sorrowful, and exclaimed, "Woe, woe, unhappy mother! What have you done? By these words you have destroyed our happiness. I must now leave you, never to return!" Then he had his silver horn blown on the waters, and at daybreak the swan appeared drawing the boat as before. The knight entered, and was borne forever away from the terrified and despairing countess. She soon died of grief, but her sons lived and were founders of noble families, who are still distinguished by the swan upon their arms.

Cologne. *The Building of the Cathedral.* About the middle of the thirteenth century, the Archbishop of Cologne, Conrad of Hochsteden, determined to build a magnificent cathedral. He had large sums of money which he was willing to spend for the purposes of religion, and he was sure of liberal contributions. So as there would be no lack of means, he desired that it should be more imposing in its splendor than any cathedral in the world. The first difficulty was to find an architect who could conceive and execute a plan worthy of the acceptance of the archbishop. Now there was in Cologne an architect of great reputation; for him the archbishop sent and requested him to make such a plan as he desired, and to have it ready for his approval in one year. The architect was greatly flattered and determined to devote himself most heartily to this work, which if successful would make his name known throughout all time. He thought of nothing else, and renounced all other employment. How it should be arranged, how vaulted, what columns, and where to be placed, and a thousand other things, were revolved in his mind again and again, and plan after plan put upon parchment. But nothing pleased him. He had in his mind a more noble conception than any he could commit to paper, and although a vision of splendor and sublimity in style and ornament floated always before his eyes, it never could be made to appear where he could show it to others. Thus ten months had passed and nothing was done. The poor man began to be almost insane. He knew at the appointed time not only the archbishop but all his fellow-citizens would look for his promised plan, and he feared greatly the ridicule which failure would bring upon him. At length he had but three days remaining. He wandered far away among the Siebengebirge. There night overtook him, and a fearful tempest. The darkness was such as could almost be felt, and the lightning when it came, gave an unearthly appearance to all around him. The trees seemed like giants with their arms stretched out to seize him, and contending with each other concerning him. But he was too engrossed in his thoughts for fear to find any room in his overtasked nature. He remembered but one thing, and that the nearness of the day when he should be disgraced in his profession. He cursed himself and his destiny, and raved like one mad. Just then a flash of lightning set on fire a large oak, and the thunder which followed seemed to rock the very earth. Then from the flame of the tree stepped forth a figure which advanced toward the architect. At another time he would have been startled by this frightful scene, but now his mental agony had blunted all feeling, and he received his new companion as he would have done any acquaintance. He wore a fire-red mantle, and a broad-brimmed hat with a long plume. His face was like what one would expect on a poacher or highwayman. "A fearful storm, Dom-architect," said he. "How could you wander out in such a night? If you will follow me I will show you a short way to a place of safety." The architect felt the bitter mocking of this speech. There was that in the tone with which he said "Dom-architect," which cut him to the heart, and he turned and walked away without a word. But nothing daunted, the stranger seated himself as for a conversation, and drawing a bottle from his pocket, said, "Drink, master, to our better acquaintance, and if you have a sorrow or should be reflecting on anything, this beverage will do you good." "My grief," answered the builder," is not removed by any beverage, neither can it give me insight into that which I vainly endeavor to discover." "You are an unsocial fellow," answered the stranger, "but that does not frighten me, nor prevent my offering to assist you, as I have done others. Still again, drink, and forget your sorrow." Then he held the bottle close to the face of the architect, who to be rid of his importunity, tasted the preparation. No sooner had he done so than it seemed to flow through all his veins. He felt a new confidence and an unknown strength, and he exclaimed as he sat down by the stranger, "A genuine nectar! An incomparable cordial!" "Ah! my beverage is good, let that convince you that I have other good qualities. I know that you reflect on a plan for a splendid cathedral; you cannot succeed unless I assist you." The architect gazed at him with astonishment. "I see you have no confidence in me, but I am the only one who can and will help you. Take another draught, and you will see that it is the best you can do. My conditions, too, are easy, and I keep my word as faithfully as men do their oaths." The master had tasted the contents of the bottle again, and asked how all this could be done in three days. Upon this the stranger laughed and pulled from his pocket a parchment, which he unrolled before the eyes of the builder. It was the very thing he had so long attempted in vain to draw. "Yes, that is it!" exclaimed he, "that is the beautiful thought that always escaped me just when I believed to have it fixed." "Well," said the other, "here it is, — the plan is perfect in every part, you can have it on one condition: sign this contract and all is done. Sign it with a little of your blood. I have many such, and it is my hobby to increase the number." The builder was overcome with horror. He had read to whom he should give himself; but the desire for renown overcame all, and he signed. Instantly the fiend disappeared and he was left with the dearly bought plan. He returned home. His plan was viewed by the archbishop with delight, and he was courted and admired by all. As the building of the cathedral went on, fêtes were made in his honor, and great attentions lavished on him; but he was the victim of an uncontrollable sadness in the midst of all. The bishop ordered a plate engraved with his name to be inserted in the wall of the dome, but nothing aroused him to cheerfulness. He only reflected on hell and eternal torments, and saw the quick completion of the church with anxious terror. At length he could endure his agony no longer, and told all to his confessor. This good man promised to do everything in his power by prayers and atoning services, but advised the master to seek a hermit who dwelt in the Eifel mountains and had power to exorcise evil spirits. This he did, and the hermit assured him that by prayers and penances his sin could be removed. He remained with the hermit for weeks, and performed a great number of penances. At length he returned to his home and continued his penitential life. He was not allowed to finish his work, for disputes arose among the electors and all went wrong, and at length full of grief and shame the master died. On the same night the tablet which bore his name disappeared, and soon the disputes became so important that the work on the cathedral ceased altogether. The Devil sowed seeds of discord, determined that as he had been cheated of his booty the work should not be done; and it is only in later years that it has been possible to undertake its completion. This is one version of the legend. Another relates that the architect agreed to give the Devil not only his own soul, but that the first who entered the cathedral after its completion, should also be his; and that this compact becoming known he was the horror of all the city, and deserted and wretched, awaited the time when his bargain must be fulfilled. When at length it came there was in Cologne a woman of bad reputation, who had been sentenced to punishment, which she awaited in the archbishop's prison. When she heard of the perplexity of the citizens, and that no one dared be the first to enter the cathedral, she offered to be the one, if by so doing she could gain her freedom. This was assented to, and on the day appointed, large crowds were assembled to witness the strange spectacle. Six men came from the palace with a large box, which they placed before the door of the cathedral, which being opened, a woman apparently crawled out on her hands and knees, and passed through the door. She was seized by Satan, and her neck broken with a horrible yell; — he then fled. No sooner had he gone, than a woman stepped out of the box, and entering the church, kneeled down to pray. The archbishop saw that the evil one had been exorcised, and entered with the people in the midst of alleluias and rejoicings. The servants removed from the cathedral the carcass of a pig, with which the woman had cheated Satan. But the poor architect was found sitting in his library, horribly disfigured, his neck broken, and the fatal plan spread out before him, while his prayer-book was thrown in a corner. He was buried privately. The wicked woman was so overcome by the sight of the Devil, that she became converted and entered a convent.

The Burgomaster Gryn, the Lion-slayer. When Engelbert II. was Archbishop of Cologne, there were very serious disputes between himself and the people of the town. He was determined to subject them to his will, and they equally so to rule themselves. He built the Bayenthurm to assist him in his designs, but the citizens stormed and took it very shortly after it was finished. Among his persistent opposers the bishop found the family of Overstolz and Herman Gryn, and his hatred of the latter was such that he determined on his destruction. Two of his canons were set to entrap Gryn by a pretended friendship. This they succeeded in doing; and at last invited him to a banquet to be held in the domecloister. When he arrived, the other guests whom they feigned to expect had not appeared, and they proposed that he should visit the curiosities of the place. Accompanied by the canons, he had examined several apartments, when as he entered another the door was suddenly closed behind him and he found himself a prisoner. He had scarcely time to realize this when he perceived a lion in a corner of the room. He had but a moment, in which he drew his sword, and wrapped his cloak about his left arm. The lion had not been fed for several days, and immediately sprang toward him with flaming eyes. With wonderful presence of mind, Gryn ran his left arm down the throat of the monster while with the right hand he plunged his sword into his breast, and he fell dead. Meanwhile the canons, who could not doubt the success of their plans, called loudly for help, saying that the lion of the archbishop had attacked Gryn. What was their surprise, when after a crowd had collected they entered the room and found the lion dead and Gryn still alive? Their treachery being exposed, they attempted to flee, but were seized by the people and hung near a door of the cathedral, which since that day has been called the "priests' door." The heroic action of Gryn is commemorated in a bas-relief, still to be seen on the portal of the town hall.

The Legend of Herman Joseph, who was a native of Cologne, will be found in the preceding portion of this book.

The Wife, Richmodis von Adocht. When the plague visited Cologne in 1357, Richmodis von Lyskirchen, wife of the Knight Mengis von Adocht was attacked by it. She fell into a deathlike swoon, and was thus buried in the Apostles' Church. A beautiful ring had been left on her finger and had not escaped the notice of the grave-digger, who came at night to possess himself of it. She was awakened by this, and arose and went home. When she arrived there all in the house were asleep, but a servant, aroused by her knocking, asked from a window who thus disturbed his repose. The lady replied, and the servant much frightened told his master who had come. Adocht replied that it was impossible, and added that he would as soon believe that his gray horses would leave their stable and come up-stairs to him. No sooner were these words spoken than the horses started and were about to mount to the garret. Then Adocht hastened to welcome his returning wife. By careful nursing she was restored, and lived to present her husband with three sons. She was evermore thoughtful and serious in her manner. A modern house now stands on the spot where that of Adocht stood, but the heads of two horses made in wood are still seen affixed to an upper window in commemoration of this remarkable event.

Legend of St. Ursula. See preceding portion of this book.

The three Kings of Cologne. See the Madonna, "Adoration of the Magi," preceding portion of this book.

Darmstadt. *Walter of Birbach.* This young knight distinguished himself above all others of his time by his great piety. He was especially devoted to the service of the Blessed Virgin. On one occasion he rode to Darmstadt to strive for the honors of a tournament. His lady-love was to be present, and he was extremely anxious to win, but he knew that many knights more skillful than he would endeavor to excel him. As he rode on thus thinking of his wishes and chances of success, he came to an altar upon which was a statue of the Virgin. He immediately dismounted and performed his devotions, and entreated the aid of Our Lady in the accomplishment of his desires. In the fervency of his prayers, he lost his senses, — a convulsion seized him, and he became insensible at the foot of the altar. Then the Virgin descended, clothed herself in his armor, and rode to the lists, where she conquered all the knights who contended. She then returned to Walter, replaced his armor, and resumed her place on the altar. Soon the pious knight awoke, and bowing once again to the Virgin, proceeded to the tourney. As he approached the town, all whom he met congratulated him as the victor of the day, and lavished praises upon him. At first he was amazed, but soon as by an inspiration, he understood who had fought for him. In consequence of this success he married his lady-love, and in gratitude to Mary he erected on the spot where the altar stood, a commodious and elegant chapel, and remained devoted to her service to the end of his life.

Drachenfels. "The castled crag of Drachenfels," commands one of the finest views on the Rhine. The Siebengebirge, the basaltic rocks near Honnef, the villages of Unkel, Erpel, Rhöndorf, Rheinbreitbach, Remagen, and the Church on the Apollinarisberg, the ruins of Olbrück and Tomberg, and the volcanic Eifel, the islands of Nonneworth and Grafenwerth, the ruin of Rolandseck and the farm-house of Roderberg, and still further away Kreuzberg, Bonn, and a shadowy view of Cologne, — make up a picture such as is seldom seen. Drachenfels, or Dragon's Rock, is also famous for having been the home of a huge dragon, who in his day did much mischief in all the surrounding country. In the midst of his ravages a war broke out between the heathen and Christian tribes. The heathen were victorious, and brought to their homes much booty and many prisoners, among whom was a lovely maiden. All wished to possess her, but especially Ottfried. In order that this difficulty might be settled they determined to consult the priestess of night. She declared that as the maiden was so beautiful as to create enmities and hatred, none should have her, but she should be thrown to the dragon. All were filled with horror; but the command must be obeyed. Ottfried was in despair when the maid was led forth to the dragon's cave; but she advanced with firm and resolute step, as if fearing nothing. The dragon came out and rushed toward her, but suddenly fell to the ground, and Ottfried who had kept near her plunged his sword into the monster and killed him. All shouted for joy, and congratulated Ottfried that he had destroyed the monster and rescued the maid. Afterward Ottfried desired to know why she had been so fearless, and how she, a delicate maiden, had dared more than strong men could do. Then she showed him a cross which she wore in her bosom, and told him that it always gave her strength and courage; and that any one who believed in Jesus who had died on the cross, had no fear of death or the grave. When she had explained all to Ottfried he was converted and baptized, and at length was married to the maiden, and built for her the Castle of Drachenfels. It is also said that he bathed in the dragon's blood and thus became invulnerable. He was a good ruler, and made not only his wife but his people happy. The stone for the Cathedral of Cologne was taken from Drachenfels, and the quarry is called Dombruck. The wine of the vineyard is Drachenblut, — Dragon's blood.

Dünwald near Mühlheim. "*The Oak Seed.*" The monks of Dünwald were very rich and not less avaricious. They desired much wealth in order that they might be able to gratify their desire for luxurious living. They were determined to annex to their possessions one hundred acres which belonged to the young nobleman of Schlebusch. They made many claims out of their old parchments, and thought to prove that they had a right to it. But the young man knew it had been the estate of his family for many long years and he would not resign it. Then it was referred to the judges, but they fearful of the Church dared not give a decision, and so the young man saw no hopes of a settlement. He then proposed to the monks that if they would agree that he might sow one more crop and harvest it when ripe, he would then relinquish the land. To this they joyfully agreed, and a contract legally written and worded with great exactness was signed by the monks and the nobleman. Then he sowed his seed. The monks watched with great interest to see what kind of grain he preferred for his last crop upon the land; but when it appeared it was neither wheat, rye, or any grain — the ground was covered with tender green leaves. What was their consternation when they found that they were those of young oaks! There was nothing to be done; they were fairly outwitted, and before the trees reached the top of the cloister the monks were all dead, and before the oaks decayed the cloister itself had crumbled into dust.

Eberstein. See Baden-Baden.

Eginhard and Emma. See Ingelheim.

Ehrenfels. In this castle, at the window of her chamber, sat the maiden Uta. She wept bitterly, for her father had called the knight of Castle Reichenstein, whom she tenderly loved, a robber, and declared that he had been outlawed by the emperor. As she gazed toward the home of her lover, and watched the waves of the Rhine dancing in the moonlight, suddenly the flames leaped from the castle, and in the fire-light, dark figures could be seen fighting desperately. "Holy Mother, protect him!" she ejaculated. "O, my God! it is not possible. He a robber, and his castle burning!" But it was all too true. The emperor had sentenced him, and Reichenstein was destroyed. Just then she saw a small boat cross the river, and she heard the knight say, "Uta, Uta, O come to me once more, ere I leave you forever." She hastened to throw herself in his arms. "I am an outlaw and fugitive, my Uta. I was only able to save a few jewels to keep me from starving in the distant lands to which I go. My life too, was in great danger, but though all others curse me, you will still love me. Farewell, I must leave you forever!" She sobbed and tenderly clung to him, saying, "O, my beloved, it would have been better that we had died while happy, than to suffer this fearful separation." "Ah, Uta! I cannot leave you, I cannot live without you. Fly with me, my darling maiden." "I cannot desert my father. I will take the veil, and in the cloister give all my thoughts and prayers to you." "Never!" exclaimed Reichenstein. He took her in his arms, and stepped some paces back, then with a leap plunged into the river. No sound was heard as the waves closed over them, and the waters flowed calmly on, as if it were nothing that in their midst two breaking hearts had ceased to beat. Next day the lovers were found locked in a close embrace.

Eppstein or **Eppenstein.** This town lies in the Taunus, at the extremity of the Lorsbacher valley. The knights of Eppstein were of great renown, and five archbishops and electors of Mayence were from their family between 1059 and 1284. The castle rises from a rock above the town, and the legend of its foundation is as follows: The Knight Eppo was one day lost in the forest while chasing a boar. He sounded his bugle and cried for help in vain. At length worried and discouraged he alighted from his horse, and reclined beneath the trees. Suddenly he heard a sweet song, sung with much taste and expression. He went in the direction from which it proceeded, and saw a maiden, who, with eyes raised imploringly to heaven, was singing a sacred melody. Eppo stopped to listen, but when she saw him she begged for his assistance with many tears. She told him that a giant had stolen her, and brought her here; that he was now in a deep sleep, but she was chained to a rock. The knight asked her how he could assist her. "Return to my castle: bring me a consecrated net which I have there; in it I will entrap the giant in the name of the Holy Trinity, and when I utter that sacred name, he will not have power to move." Eppo did this, and awaited at the grotto a favorable time to use the net. When the giant awoke he went out of the grotto to cut a pipe. Then the maiden ran out and spread a bed of mosses and sweet herbs, and told the giant to lie down to see if it was comfortable. As soon as he did so, she threw the net over him in the name of the Holy Trinity. His horrible howls and yells of rage drove her away with fright, but he was powerless to free himself. The maiden desired the knight to fly with her instantly, but he demanded that she should wait a little while. He ran to the giant and rolled him off the precipice, where he was dashed in pieces. Then the knight married the maiden whom he had saved, and built the Castle of Eppstein for her; and there the giant's bones are still to be seen, and this of course makes the tale quite true, if any proof were needed.

Falkenburg. This ruin, called also Reichenstein, stands on an eminence above the village of Trechtingshausen. The castellan of this fortress had a lovely daughter named Liba. When he died he left her not only with a fine education, but also considerable fortune. She lived in retirement with her mother, but nevertheless had many suitors and offers of marriage. But Liba was betrothed to a young knight, Guntram, who only waited to be invested with his fief in order to marry her. One lovely May morning, Liba told her mother how much she wished that Guntram might come to her that day. Scarcely was the wish uttered when he rode into the courtyard, and Liba rushed down to welcome him with smiles and kisses. They spent a happy day, not the less joyous because Guntram was even then on his way to the Pfalzgraf to obtain his estate; for this seemed to bring nearer the time when they should be united; and he left her with a smiling command that she should hasten the preparation of the bridal dress. Saying this he kissed away her tears, which always came when parting from him, and rode hopefully away. He was a noble fellow, and handsome as good, and Liba gazed after him with a full heart, and a happy mingling of love and pride. He immediately obtained the favor of the count, and as he desired an ambassador for Burgundy, he selected Guntram for the honor. He could not refuse this, and sent a messenger to Liba to announce his appointment and excuse his prolonged absence. She received this news with heavy heart; she could not explain her sadness, but since her last parting with Guntram she had been depressed and gloomy. Meanwhile he, with all a lover's eagerness, hastened to dispatch his commission, and soon finished the affairs of his embassy. He was on his return, and so great was his impatience that he hastened before his companions, and missed his path. He was on a side road, and constantly thought he should meet some person who would direct him aright, but he came first to an old, half-decayed castle. He entered the court-yard, and threw his reins to a boy who gazed at him with strange surprise. Guntram inquired for his master, and the youth pointed to an old tower, moss-grown and falling to decay. The knight dismounting experienced a strange sensation, and felt as if he were in fairy-land. He was met by an old man who declared himself to be the steward of the castle, and led him to a gloomy apartment where he desired him to await the entrance of his master. The knight was surprised at his strange and solemn reception, and was attracted by the sight of a veiled picture on the opposite wall. He drew aside the drapery, and was startled by the face of a beautiful girl who seemed to smile on him, and at the same moment a harp sounded through the room. He had scarcely reseated himself when the old steward returned, and announced the lord of the castle. The old man advanced, and in a proud, grave tone said, "We seldom entertain a stranger, but though we live in retirement, we forget not the customs of hospitality. Be assured that you are welcome." Guntram was chilled and thrilled by a strange fear, but this was soon dispelled by the politeness of the old man; and a few glasses of excellent wine enabled him to converse in his usual agreeable manner, concerning warfare, chivalry, and various topics of political interest. At length he referred to a harp which was there, thinking by this means to learn something of the picture he had seen. But the old man became instantly sad, and covered his face with his hands. Immediately he excused himself, wishing Guntram a good-night, and refreshing sleep. The old servant retired with him, but soon returned to the young man. "Sir Knight," said he, "my lord begs you to pardon his sudden leave-taking, but you touched a chord which makes him gloomy and sad." "Some strange mystery reigns here," said Guntram, "can you explain it to me?" "Why not, Sir Knight. Come to your apartment, and on the way I will tell you what you desire to know." They arose and proceeded to the room where hung the veiled portrait. "Stop here," said the knight, "and tell me first of all, why this lovely portrait is veiled." "Then you have seen her," said the old man; "how beautiful she is. She was the daughter of the house, and when with us most lovely and bewitching. But alas, she was a coquette. She had many suitors, and she treated them all in such a way, and demanded such impossibilities of them as to drive them all from her. All save one, — he was the last of a noble race, and the only support and hope of an infirm, old mother to whom he was devoted. But his love for the maiden was so true as to endure where others failed. At length as a last task she demanded of him to descend to the family vault, and bring to her a crown of gold which would be found upon one of her ancestors. He did so, and the profanation was punished by death, for a stone from the roof fell on him, and he was found dead with the crown in his hand. His mother survived him but a few days, and died cursing the foolish maiden. From that time she drooped, and died a year from the day on which her lover had descended to the tomb. But when we would have buried her, the body had disappeared, and her coffin was empty." As the story was ended they reached the bedroom of the knight. The old man wished him "Good-night," and turned to go away, but at the threshold he said, "Sir Guntram, if during the night any strange thing should occur, say but a paternoster, and go again to sleep." When Guntram was alone he found himself strangely excited by all this, and filled with wonder at what the warning might mean. Nevertheless in his weariness, he could but sleep. Suddenly he seemed to hear a rustle as of a lady's dress from the adjoining room, and then a harp, accompanied by a sweet, sad song. He arose, and through a crevice beheld the original of the picture, who, as she ended her song, dropped the harp on the ground with a cry of sharp distress. He could wait no longer; he opened the door and stood before her, — she regarded him with tender kindness, and when he knelt and would have kissed her hand she embraced him passionately, and abandoned herself to his caresses with a sweet rapture. "You love me," said she softly. "More than my life," replied the knight. She drew from her hand a ring, and put it on his own; he pressed her to his heart, and instantly he heard the death-cry of an owl, and in his arms he held a corpse. He staggered to his couch where he fell in a swoon. In the morning when he awoke all seemed a dream, but for the ring. This he would have thrown away, but he could not remove it from his hand. He was almost distracted, and resolved to fly from this hated place. The old lord entered to inquire for his health. "Where are we? What room is this?" demanded Guntram. "It was my daughter's, and the only inhabitable one in the castle." "Yes, yes," said the knight, "and I have seen her; she herself gave me this ring." "Then God help you sir," exclaimed the old servant, "in three times nine days you will be a corpse." With a loud cry Guntram fell to the floor insensible. When he revived, though fever was in his heart and brain, he proceeded on his way, and the joy of Liba could not be told when she saw him once more. But she soon perceived his sadness, although she questioned him not. He pressed her to hasten their wedding-day, which she did but too gladly. When the hour arrived he had persuaded himself that all would yet be well; his love for Liba remained unchanged, and he approached the altar with a firm step; but as the priest joined their hands he screamed, tottered, and fell. When he recovered he told

Liba all, and that the dead girl had put her hand in his as he stood at the altar; but he still begged her to become his wife before he died. She called a priest, and at his bedside pronounced the holy vows. A few moments after he pressed her to his bosom as his wife he breathed his last. Liba soon retired to a convent, where she did not long survive him.

Falkenstein. This ruined castle is on a mountain, remarkable even on the Rhine for its difficulty of ascent. The following is the legend concerning the zigzag path which leads to it: A rough old knight dwelt here, who, as is the custom with rough old knights, had a lovely daughter. He drove away her suitors by his harsh manners, for in spite of the steepness of the ascent many cheerfully climbed to the castle in the hope of obtaining a reward in the hand of the daughter. But one Kuno von Sayn was never weary of coming, for he was rewarded by the maiden's love and smiles. One day he ascended with difficulty, almost overpowered by the heat, but determined to brave the stern knight and demand the hand of the daughter in marriage. He did so, and the old knight replied, that if he would make a road up to the castle by which a carriage could come before the next morning, he should possess the daughter. The knight went away in despair, not even seeing his love again. He told his miners of the strange condition, and offered immense rewards if it could be done, but they declared it impossible. Then he wandered away into the forest, almost frantic with love and disappointment. Suddenly an old man stood before him and offered to assist him. Kuno returned home to await the result, and next morning rode his horse up the present crooked way. The old knight was quite overcome, and his roughness all dispelled. He related how all night a dreadful storm had raged about the castle, and continually the sound of hatchets and hammers could be heard coming nearer and nearer. Much alarmed they had passed the night in prayer, and only slept about day-break. The horse of Kuno awoke them, and he joyfully demanded and received his bride. Even now one cannot doubt that the wood sprites made the path, so difficult would it be for any others to construct it. See also Taunus.

Flörsheim. Many years ago a knight of Flörsheim, called Bodo, was left a widower with an only child, named Adeline. She was sought in marriage by many men of rank and worth, but she loved her father too well and was too happy in her home to leave it except for one she dearly loved, and such a person she had never seen. One day a young man of cultivated manners and great beauty came to the castle in the garb of a shepherd, and wished Knight Bodo to employ him as superintendent of his flocks. He showed so much good sense, and knowledge of agriculture and cattle-raising, that Bodo did not hesitate to engage him. Soon he began to see the wisdom of his decision, for never before had he been so prospered in all connected with his herds and flocks. But one thing disturbed him. Otto, as he was called, refused to give his name or tell anything concerning himself, saying that he had good reasons for not wishing to speak of these things. He was sad and kept alone, thinking apparently of some grief. Adeline had heard much of Otto from her father, but had never seen him, until they met one day in the forest. He was so affected with her appearance, that he stood for a time speechless. Then recollecting himself he begged her pardon and to be allowed to attend her, as she was alone in the forest. He was respectfully attentive to her words, and when they neared the castle, ventured to express a hope that they might meet again. After leaving her, Otto retired to his humble apartment and reflected on what had occurred. The resemblance of Adeline to a sister he had lost, affected him deeply, and he thought that if he could determine again to enter the world from which he had so early retired, if there existed happiness for him, Adeline could lead him to it. The maiden too, reflected upon the interview; and one who had closely watched her could have detected that love was awakened in the heart so long unmoved. From this time scarcely a day passed that they met not, exchanging thought for thought, aye, and heart for heart. At length Otto told her of his past life. He was the son of a most noble knight of Thuringia, who died while he and his only sister were very young. His mother married again, and dying herself left her children to one of the most cruel of step-fathers. Otto escaped to an uncle, and was educated as a knight. After several years he returned to find his sister dead, murdered by ill-treatment, and as some believed, by poison. Otto demanded the restoration of his property, and challenged the wicked wretch to answer for the death of his sister. He received an insulting reply, and in a rage stabbed him whom the world regarded as his father. He then fled, and now even his uncle turned against him, and shared his property with another relative. One can understand how this story moved the very soul of Adeline, how truly she loved him when she knew all his sorrow, and how she planned different methods by which he should again be made happy. And she had decided that her father should be made their confidant, should assist Otto to recover his property, and make them happy by consenting to their union. But very soon the pinions of this delightful fancy were most effectually clipped, for a high-born and rich knight, Siegbert, now demanded her hand, and it was an alliance well pleasing to Bodo. He commanded Adeline to prepare to receive him as her husband, and said much of the renown and fame which he had gained in Palestine, and of the honor which had come to her, in that she could be the bride of such a knight. Adeline was as one turned to stone and refused to see Siegbert. Then

Bodo grew angry and harsh, and even confined her to her apartments. When Siegbert came he was greatly disappointed at the coolness with which Adeline received his courtly attentions and declarations of burning love, for he found her even more attractive than report had made her. Then Bodo confined her in a dark room, and threatened to send her to a convent if she did not give her promise to Siegbert that very day. He went on to prepare for a magnificent wedding. Otto meantime was in agony; he could not see Adeline; he had heard of the visit of the stranger, and feared all the dreadful truth. He wandered in the woods, but at last went irresistibly toward the castle, when he heard of the approaching marriage. Believing Adeline false, he went to a deep stream and threw himself into it. Meanwhile Adeline had told her love to her father, and had been more strictly guarded on account of it. But when all was ready and she was in her bridal dress, she found an opportunity of escape. As she rushed through the forest in search of Otto, she saw the shepherds taking some one from the water. Instantly the truth flashed on her mind, and glancing at her lover's face, before any one could detain her, she plunged into the same stream and was swallowed by the friendly waves. A few days later she was washed ashore, and her beauty as she slept the death-sleep in her bridal robes was such as none had seen before. The wretched father buried her in the arms of her loved Otto, and did not long survive his repentance and sorrow.

Frankfort. *The foundation of the city.* When the Emperor Charlemagne contended with the Saxons the fortune of war was often against him. On one occasion he was forced to retire before them along the banks of the Main. There was a heavy fog and it was not possible to discover a vessel, neither did he find any place where his army could make a passage. At length a doe sprang from the thicket in great alarm. She bore a young one, and plunging into the stream swam over as if to escape an enemy. Charlemagne followed the example thus offered him, and delayed not to cross at the same place. The fog concealed the army, and they escaped. When the emperor reached the shore he struck his spear into the earth and exclaimed, "Here shall a city arise, to be called Frankenford;" and as in consequence of this crossing the river, he overthrew the Saxons, he here built the town, afterwards the scene of the imperial coronations, and which is now the beautiful, commercial city of Frankfort-on-the-Main.

The Knave of Bergen. All was gayety at the Römer. There was a great masked ball which made a part of the coronation festival. The rich toilets of the ladies and the glistening costumes of the princes and knights, united with the joyous music, made up a scene of brilliant, exciting merriment. There was but one in all the throng who gave an idea of gloom or sadness. His armor, all black, and the manner in which he moved, excited general attention and curiosity. None could guess his personality, for his visor was completely closed. Tall and graceful, with much of pride and modesty, he advanced and bent his knee before the empress, requesting the favor of a waltz with the queen of the festival; it was granted, and he danced easily and gracefully through the hall with the sovereign, who thought she had never seen so elegant and excellent a dancer. But this was not his only attraction, for he well knew how to please in conversation, and the queen was most impatient to know with whom she waltzed, and graciously accorded him even the fourth dance. All regarded him with envy, and the other knights suffered in the eyes of the ladies in comparison with his easy elegance. Even the emperor was excited with curiosity to see him unmasked. At ast the moment came, and all were breathless, but while others removed their masks, his visor remained closed. At length the queen commanded that his face should be seen. He opened the visor; not one of all the lords or ladies knew the handsome man on whom they gazed, but from the crowd advanced the officials who declared that he was the executioner of Bergen! Then was the anger of all great, and the emperor declared that he who had thus insulted the empress should die. The culprit threw himself at the feet of the emperor and said: "Indeed I have greatly sinned against all this noble company, but most of all against you and my queen. But no punishment can take away this insult. Therefore, O my sovereign, allow me to suggest a way in which the disgrace may be removed, and as if never received. Raise your sword and knight me. Then will I throw down my gauntlet to all who dare to speak with disrespect of my king or his most gracious lady." The king hesitated, overcome by surprise and amazement at this bold proposition. But soon he said, "You are a knave, but your advice is good, and (raising his sword) I make you knight even while you kneel to me for pardon. Like a knave you have acted, and Knave of Bergen shall you henceforth be called." The black knight rose gladly; three cheers were given for the emperor, and the queen danced still once again with the Knave of Bergen.

The 9 in the Vane. At the end of Eschenheimer Street rises a tower with five points, and having a vane on its gable, in which nine holes form the figure 9. The origin of this singular thing was as follows: Hans Winkelsee was a troublesome poacher, and so skillful a shot that it was believed the Devil gave him charmed bullets. At length he was taken prisoner, and suffered much in his confinement, for freedom and the range of the forest were necessary to his happiness. When the time came that he was to be hanged he expostulated, and said it was a sin to kill a man for having shot the animals which were made for his use. Then one of the judges accused him of being leagued with the Devil and using charmed bullets; whereto he replied, that he would shoot nine shots through the vane, and with them form a figure, and this he would do with bullets that had been blessed. He was assured that if he could do this, one principal cause of his condemnation would be removed. He insisted on the trial, and all became so interested, and especially the foresters, that they declared that if he could do this he should go free, and the judges assented. On the day of the trial large crowds, assembled both outside and inside the gates; the foresters were ranged upon the rampart, and their master cast the bullets on which the life of Hans depended. Now a monk again warned Hans not to trifle with them, and if the Devil had been his assistant he promised him that he would now fail him. But Hans declared that God and St. Hubert would help him and all would be well. Then the master-forester loaded the gun and gave it to him. The first shot went through the vane, and the next, and so on, and after each one the people cheered, and when all was done, and the figure "9" was seen on the vane, their enthusiasm knew no bounds. Then it was that Hans fell on his knees in hearty thankfulness to God, in which the people joined him. The mayor offered him the honor of being captain of the shooting corporation, but Hans declared that when once out he would never enter Frankfort again. So he went forth loaded with presents, and lived an honest life ever after, but it was always outside the walls of the city.

Frederick and Gela. See Gelnhausen.

Fremersberg. See Baden-Baden.

Gelnhausen. *Frederick and Gela.* The ruined fortress of Gelnhausen was in the twelfth century a majestic and imposing structure, and here dwelt Frederick, a descendant of the Emperor Barbarossa, and later in life himself an emperor. The old castellan had two charming daughters, and one of them, Gela, was beloved by the young prince. One day he could restrain his speech no longer, and abruptly declaring his love to her, he as abruptly left her. For several days they did not meet, and Frederick was agonizing between hope and fear. At length they met in the fields, where Gela had gone to gather flowers. At first she turned away as if to avoid him, but seeing his look of sorrow, she frankly gave him her hand saying, "Frederick, I love you, and will wait for you this evening in the church." Frederick was there before her; and when she came they softly whispered their love with all its hopes and fears, for Gela well knew the wide distance which separated her station from that of her lover. Here they met every evening for months; together they paid their devotions to the Blessed Virgin, and each sought her blessing for the other. But soon the noise of war and the preaching of the Crusade broke in upon their dream, and when Frederick wished to assume the cross and go to the Holy Land, Gela was brave enough to encourage him to do so. He returned covered with honors and anxious to lay them at the feet of Gela, for he felt that to her influence and prayers he owed much of the success which had attended him. But instead of seeing Gela, he received a letter which the noble girl had written, saying, that now he was a duke he must marry a princess, suitable to his rank and place in life; and adding that she had retired to a convent, where her love for him should ever remain pure and unviolated. When Frederick became emperor he did not forget his noble Gela. Her letter he wore always on his heart, during all his life; and in remembrance of her he built the town of Gelahausen or Gelnhausen.

Gernsbach. *The Klingelkapelle.* In the early days of Christianity in Germany, a hermit established himself in a deserted cell near Gernsbach, on the road to Castle Eberstein. He performed the duties of a missionary preacher in that part of the country. One stormy night he heard a supplicating voice outside his cell. When he opened the door he saw a beautiful young female, scantily clothed and apparently suffering from her exposure to cold and storm. She begged that she might enter and warm herself. The hermit willingly permitted this, and gave her wine and honey. When he had made her as comfortable as his poverty would allow, he asked the cause of her wandering alone on such a night. She then told him that she was devoted to the service of Hertha, that she once lived in the cell where they then were, and had been driven from it by the persecutions of the Christians. While she was speaking the monk had drawn closer to the maiden and was more and more charmed with her beauty, but when she announced herself as a heathen, he started in horror. "You are shocked," she cried, "to find me other than a Christian. But am I not a human being like yourself? Reflect! this cell was once mine, although I am now obliged to beg a shelter in it. Is it any less comfortable for you that I have lived here? Do you sleep less soundly, or does the sky look less bright because I have been happy here? The world was made for all. Why do you persecute me?" Then he told her of Jesus and how much he would rejoice over her conversion, which he determined to accomplish if possible. He uttered a short prayer, and again attempted to talk to her, but his heart was not in what he said, for the beauty of the maid had dazzled all his senses. She affected to listen but constantly drew nearer to him, until her breath was warm upon his cheek, and his blood flowed like fire in his veins. The maiden saw her power, and continued to caress him until at last with apparent innocence she asked him to break the cross before which he was accustomed to perform his devotions. He was about to do so, and had stretched out his hand to take it when a little bell rang outside his cell; this sound restored him to his senses, and instantly he fell on his knees to thank God for his goodness. When he raised his eyes the "Saga" had vanished. Some unseen hand had placed the bell in the bushes near by. He carried it to his cell, and from that time it was called, "The Klingelkapelle."

Gerresheim, near Düsseldorf. *Gunhilde.* This beautiful nun in the Convent of Gerresheim had become the object of the passionate love of her confessor. She did not imagine the existence of this sentiment, and when at length he declared it to her she was overwhelmed with surprise. But even then she did not suspect him of any impure desires, and when he begged her to fly with him and promised to marry her, she consented. He now thought her completely in his power, but Gunhilde resisted all his importunities to sin, and demanded the fulfillment of his promise. This he did not hasten to keep, but fell into all sorts of evil ways, and at length joined a band of robbers. During an excursion he was seized, and at length hanged for his crimes. The news of his dreadful death was a fearful blow to Gunhilde. She had remained virtuous and had preserved her chastity, but who would believe this? After some time spent in the closest retirement she went to her cloister and threw herself before the abbess begging to be again received; acknowledging her great wickedness, and promising amendment in life and to atone for her sins by constant penance. The abbess chided her for thus distressing herself, and said that she had been more holy and pleasing to God than she herself could be. Gunhilde was led bewildered to her cell, and as she entered it she saw an angel rise from her bed and disappear. She then knew that he had been sent as her substitute, and had performed all her duties while she was away, and thus her sin was known only to God and herself.

Gertruidenberg. *The Holy Gertrude.* Years ago there lived in the Netherlands a holy maiden named Gertrude. A knight of rich and illustrious family was deeply in love with her from merely seeing her, and entirely without her knowledge. At length he declared himself to her, and wooed her with the most zealous attentions and unwavering devotion. But Gertrude had already determined to be the bride of Christ, and was about to make her profession as a nun. Her only grief was her poverty; because on account of it she was not able to gratify her desire to do what she wished for the various charities in which her heart was interested. This she expressed to her lover, and he resolved that since his heart must be buried with her in her seclusion he would supply her wants as far as possible. Often he had seen her in tears and sorrow on account of her inability to give aught but consolation and hope to the poor whom she visited. She was but eighteen when, in spite of her lover's entreaties, she took the veil, and daily he sent her a sum to be expended in charity. And this devotion continued for years until his property was exhausted — his estates had been sacrificed, and he saw with sorrow that the time was not far distant when he could neither give his accustomed aid or receive her smile and grateful thanks, which was the only reward his faithful heart desired. When he carried her the last sum that he possessed he bade her farewell, saying that he was going on a journey, but in fact determined to make money in some way in order to supply the demands upon the charity of Gertrude. But so unaccustomed to labor was he, and so unfitted for it, that he knew not how to commence his new life. He wandered for days in the forest frantic with grief. One night about twelve o'clock a man suddenly stood before him. He was repulsive in his appearance, and in a harsh voice demanded of the knight what he desired, at the same time assuring him that if it was gold he could supply his need, as he had done that of many others. He promised that for seven years there should be an inexhaustible store in his chest if he would sign his contract with a drop of his blood. This provided that at the end of seven years they should again meet at the same place where they then stood. The knight well knew to whom he spoke, but so great was his need that he hastily signed, and delayed not to return home to see if in truth the gold would be supplied. His joy was great to find a good amount in his chest, and from day to day he lavished large sums upon the convent. Thus the seven years passed, and the time had arrived when he must go to meet the author of so much wealth, and alas, of how much agony! Who could tell what was in store for him? Again he bade Gertrude farewell, under pretense of a journey. She begged him to drink a cordial under the protection of her patroness, St. Johanna, and assured him that it would defend him from all danger. He drank, and as he emptied the flagon a life and strength coursed through his veins such as he had never known before. He bade adieu to Gertrude, and hastened to the spot where he was to meet the devil. He was awaiting him, but as soon as he came near the knight he sprang away with a fearful howl, and tore the contract in pieces, scattering it to the winds. "Woe is me!" cried Satan. "I have no power over you, for riding behind you is St. Gertrude, whose happiness you last drank." Then the devil vanished, leaving behind him an odor of brimstone and a thick vapor. The knight returned to his home, where he found an immense treasure awaiting him. This he devoted to a new charity which Gertrude desired to undertake, and then entered a cloister, where he passed the remainder of his days.

The Hague. *Three hundred and sixty-five Children.* A beggar-woman came once to Countess Henneberg, with twins in her arms. The noble lady was angry at the interruption, and upbraided the woman for want of virtue, declaring that twins could not be the children of one father. The beggar cursed her, and expressed the wish that she might bear as many children as there are days in the year. Then she retired, bitterly weeping. Nine months later the countess did, indeed, give birth to three hundred and sixty-five children successively. As they were born they died, and she herself went mad and did not long survive them. The graves of all are shown at a village church near the Hague, as well as the font in which they were baptized!!

Hammerstein. *Count Otto and Irmengard.* The Castle of Hammerstein is said to have been founded by Charles Martel. Early in the eleventh century it was occupied by Count Otto, who had a quarrel with Archbishop Erkenbold of Mayence. The brave count always maintained himself in battle, and the bishop determined to ruin him in some other way than that of open warfare. He had married Irmengard, his cousin, without a dispensation from the Pope. On account of this, Erkenbold published his excommunication from the Church and declared his marriage invalid. Otto did not allow this to disturb his happiness. Next the bishop applied to the emperor, Henry II., to interfere. Henry was ever ready to listen to the clergy. He therefore laid siege to the Castle of Hammerstein. It was not possible to reduce it except by famine. This proved to be a long and tedious undertaking, and after a time the emperor gladly embraced an opportunity to settle all difficulties by a compromise. Otto made a sally with Irmengard by his side. They were both carried back to the castle wounded. Then Henry declared to the bishop, that as both had shed their blood in defense of their union, he thought it right that they should be pardoned, and even married by himself. To this the bishop at length consented, and this second marriage was celebrated with great pomp, and was the occasion of a hearty and enduring reconciliation between the Bishop of Mayence and Count Otto of Hammerstein.

The Wish of the old Castellan. After the death of Otto the emperor gave his castle to the archbishops of Cologne. One evening as the old castellan was sitting with his two daughters, listening to their merry jokes and sweet songs, he became suddenly thoughtful, and when they rallied him and asked if their songs did not please him, he answered sighing, "Ah yes, my darlings, your songs are sweet; but I often wish you wore jackets rather than petticoats, and could manage a sword as well as you do a spinning-wheel. If I but had a son I should indeed be a happy father!" Then they answered him with merry repartee, and the younger one told how she would play soldier, and danced about her father with such roguish airs as banished all his seriousness. In the midst of this a servant announced two pilgrims who begged rest and lodging. "Bring them in," said the castellan, "none shall want at this castle while I have bread and wine." So they came in, an old and a young man. The castellan approached them, and as he did so the elder pilgrim threw back his hood. The castellan fell on his knees and exclaimed, "My lord, and my emperor!" "Even so," said Henry IV., "and I come as a fugitive to claim your hospitality." "A fugitive! Who has dared to commit this crime against his emperor ?" demanded the castellan, as his hand sought his sword. "My son! even my son!" answered Henry, and he covered his face to conceal his tears. "Thank heaven, my friend, that you have no sons, but these loving daughters to cheer your old age. How gladly would I exchange my lot for yours, my brave friend!" The emperor resided here for some time in order to escape from Henry V., and here he kept the royal insignia, until it was removed by the same usurping son. When he left, the old castellan accompanied him to Cologne, and he often reflected on the words of the good emperor, and never again desired a greater joy than to live and be happy with his charming daughters.

Heidelberg. *The Jettebühl or Wolfsbrunnen.* A road from the east of the Castle of Heidelberg leads to a spot where the water of a spring flows off into five different ponds. Here many years ago, according to tradition, the priestess Jetta died. She lived in an adjacent grove, where she was accustomed to make sacrifices to Hertha and reveal the will and wisdom of that divinity. One day as Jetta sat by the altar, a young man advanced from the wood and desired her to tell his fate. The maiden raised her eyes to his, and instantly he felt that all he had heard of her wondrous beauty was more than true, and a strange charm was over him. The priestess too was confused and unable to answer as was her custom. "You have come," said she, "at a time when the spirit of prophecy has left me. Return at this hour to-morrow. Meantime I will offer a sacrifice, and demand of Hertha that which you would know." The youth assured her that he should return, and added that in leaving her he left more than the future could possibly give him. When a short distance away he stopped to admire the beauty of the maiden as she sat unconscious of his gaze. When he came next day Jetta was in the same place and attitude as before, and he knelt at her feet and kissed the border of her robe. "You have come to hear your fortune," said Jetta. "Yes, from the lips of her I love, but not from a prophetess," replied he tenderly. She was not angry, even when he drew her to himself and passionately kissed her, but he soon perceived that she was weeping piteously, and his efforts at consoling her were quite unavailing. She told him that his love was fully requited, but that it was forbidden a priestess of Hertha to love or be the wife of any man, and she feared the punishment which the outraged divinity would inflict on her. Then she promised to meet him often in secret at the spring near by, and when he left her it was with the hope of seeing her there the next evening. He carried with him a light heart and did not fail to keep the tryst, but what was his horror, as he approached the fountain, to see Jetta lying dead, and a wolf drinking the blood from the wounds he had made in her bosom! He rushed upon the ferocious monster and thrust it through. Raising Jetta, he lavished caresses upon her, and called her to answer him in vain. Hertha had indeed punished her faithless priestess!

Heisterbach. *The Sleeping Skeptic.* The old Convent of Heisterbach is situated in a ravine in the midst of the Siebengebirge. Here many years ago dwelt a monk, Aloysius, quite celebrated for his learning and untiring study of the Scriptures. But there was one passage which he could never understand and which so staggered his faith as to make him very unhappy, and at times the abbot and his brother monks feared for his reason. The difficult passage was this: "One day is with the Lord as a thousand years, and a thousand years as one day." This constantly occupied his thoughts. At length as he wandered in a wood near the cloister he fell asleep, and when he awoke he heard the vesper bell. He returned to the convent; the monk who admitted him was a stranger, but he did not stop to think of this, and entered the chapel. He found his seat occupied, and by one whom he knew not, and who regarded him with the same astonishment that he felt. Meanwhile the singing ceased, and as he gazed about him he found that all the monks were unknown to him. They also wondered at him, and gathered about him to inquire his name. When he answered them and declared that he belonged to the convent, they regarded him with great surprise and believed him insane. Then one remembered to have read that a monk Aloysius, of great learning, had disappeared in the wood, and when Aloysius mentioned the name of his abbot they found it was three hundred years since he had gone to sleep in the forest. God had done this miracle to convince him of his power, and his doubts were banished from that hour.

Heppenheim. See Lorsch.

Hohenbaden. See Baden-Baden.

Ingelheim. Below Mayence, near where the villages of Nieder-ingelheim and Oberingelheim now stand, the Emperor Charlemagne had his favorite palace, some of the ruins of which still remain. There lived then in the Rheingau, a hermit who cured all manner of diseases and gave every patient who visited him some small present. The emperor was very curious to see him, and sent a messenger to request his presence. The hermit replied that his visits were more needed at the cottages of the poor than at the palaces of the rich, and added that as the emperor had much better conveniences for travelling than himself, it would be better that he should come to him. This much surprised his majesty, and he laughingly determined to pay him a visit. One night he was restless and uneasy, and after vainly endeavoring to sleep he determined to go then to the hermit. He arose and dressed in an ordinary suit of armor, went to the stables and saddled a horse, and rode away without being seen by any one. He had not gone far into the forest when he met a knight in black armor. He addressed Charlemagne, desiring to know whence he came and whither he went. The emperor replied that he came from Ingelheim in search of an adventure. The knight questioned him still farther concerning the lateness of the hour and the fact of his being alone, and at last demanded his name. The emperor answered that he was called Charles, and asked the name of the stranger. "Elbegast," was the reply. "What," said Charles, "are you the robber whom the emperor has sentenced?" "Softly, more softly, my friend, the emperor is not to blame, for he is misinformed by those about him. But if I could meet him here as I do you, I would soon tell him by what a set of thieves and liars he is surrounded." "You speak like an orator," said the emperor. "I am frank and sincere, at least, but if you will ride with me to-night we must away. I am on a track, which if it misleads me not, will break the necks of some of those rascals, whether Charles thanks me for it or no." "Perhaps you feel the emperor should reward you for your skill in breaking necks!" "If I do it to-night, it will be for his benefit and he ought to do so." Then the emperor decided to accompany him, and they proceeded like friends. Soon they reached a fortress where Elbegast alighted, and signed for Charles to do so. They proceeded to a small door, which the robber opened with an implement which he carried for the purpose. They entered a dark corridor and proceeded through a gloomy apartment, separated only by a folding-door from one brilliantly lighted, in which men were talking. As they listened one was speaking of the emperor and his power, and declaring that a stop must be put to it. "To the devil, with you!" murmured Charles, as he tried to see the speaker. What was his surprise as he recognized Count Eggerich of Eggermonde, for whom he had done so much. What would Charlemagne say to that?" asked Elbegast. But Charles motioned him to be silent. They listened thus until they heard a plan made for the murder of the emperor. All swore to it upon a crucifix in the hands of a high prelate. As they retired Charles asked Elbegast to come next day to the palace to tell the emperor what they had heard, saying that he would be there as a witness. But the robber replied that he would do no such thing, as it would be sure to cost him his life. "Is the emperor so unjust?" asked Charlemagne. "Not he, but his vassals; they would cut my throat before I reached the emperor." "Then I will tell him. But tell me where I can meet you." "No, no! Elbegast is not so foolish as to be thus caught!" and the robber laughed merrily. "Elbegast, I summon you in the emperor's name to appear before him to-morrow morning." "Who are you to speak thus?" "Your former enemy and present friend. Elbegast, I am the Emperor Charlemagne!" Then Elbegast leaped from his horse and came joyfully to Charles, exclaiming, "My emperor, and my lord!" "Come then to me in the morning, I will prepare all for you." Saying which Charles rode quickly away to Ingelheim. In the end the traitors were hanged, but Elbegast was made rich and loaded with honors. Some time after the emperor again set out to visit the hermit, and this time Elbegast accompanied him. As they rode on they met the daughter of a charcoal-burner who was very pretty. The emperor, who was ever fond of beauty, patted her upon the cheek and stooping from his horse clasped her with an arm, and would have kissed her. She drew back and ran to a tall man who then appeared, and who was in fact no other than the hermit. He looked at the emperor. "Have you daughters?" asked he. "And if I have?" replied Charlemagne. "Then do not forget what you have now done to this girl, and censure not others if the same thing should happen to your own." "Elbegast," said the monarch, "I believe I cannot put on this attire, but I receive some salutary lesson like this." "And I know, my master, how well you profit by them."

Eginhard and Emma. The favorite of Charlemagne was young Eginhard, his private secretary, and he dearly loved Emma, the daughter whom the emperor idolized, and this affection was fully returned. They were frequently together during the day, but in so cold and constrained a manner as not at all to satisfy their lover's hearts; so the young man was accustomed to go at night to the maiden's apartments. One night while he was there, a snow fell and when he would have crossed the court he did not dare to do so, as his foot-prints would betray his visit and expose Emma to unworthy suspicions. After much discussion Emma persuaded him to allow her to carry him to the other side of the court, upon her shoulders. Of course he at first refused, but as no other plan could be thought of by which to avoid exposure, he at length consented. Now the emperor had arranged his own apartments so that none could pass the court unseen by him. This night he could not sleep, and as he walked his chamber he saw the strange sight which Eginhard and Emma presented, and also recognized them. At first he was furiously angry, and would have killed Eginhard, then he remembered the admonition of the hermit. "If such a thing should happen to your daughter censure no one," and he could but laugh at his child's cunning and determination. Next morning he sent for Eginhard and asked him what punishment was due one who abused the confidence of his patron and seduced his child. Eginhard could not endure to hear his love called seduction, for he respected Emma as much as he loved her. "Death, if the father cannot pardon the love," was his reply. "Then you love my daughter. But I well know why; it is because she is the child of Charlemagne." Eginhard declared that he would love Emma, were she any other. The emperor then led him to her apartments and threatened her with the death of her lover. She begged that any punishment might be inflicted upon herself if only he could go unharmed. When Charlemagne saw that she truly loved him, he told them that if they married they must go far away; that Emma would no longer be considered as his child, neither could he give her any dowry. They begged his blessing, and he answered that while he would give them nothing else, that he could not refuse. Then they went away. They crossed the Rhine, and prepared to lead an humble life, far from the palace of Charlemagne. Years after, as the emperor hunted in the Odenwald, he was separated from his huntsmen and friends. While he was alone, he came to a neat cottage, where he saw a lovely young mother playing with her child. He watched them some time, quite undiscovered, and he thought he had never seen so beautiful a domestic picture as this young woman and all her surroundings presented. Suddenly she turned towards him and he saw that it was Emma. Then she ran lovingly to him, and begged his blessing for her child. She told him that Eginhard tilled the land for their support, and that he would soon return to his cottage home. The emperor pressed her thankfully to his heart, and when Eginhard came, he freely forgave them all. When the emperor's train arrived, they found him at supper with his children, and more happy than for years previously. He took them home with him and made Eginhard secretary of state, but though from this time all was prosperity, the young couple did not forget the cottage where they had been so happy, and often visited it for the sake of its sweet associations.

Queen Hildegarde. Once upon a time when Charlemagne marched against the Saxons, he left the knight Thaland in charge of the Castle at Ingelheim, and to him especially commended Queen Hildegarde, desiring him to protect her from every danger, and to report to him on his return, all that had occurred in his absence. Now Thaland had been educated at the Grecian Court, and had so mean an idea of female virtue that he believed that every woman could be unfaithful to her lord and husband. But at the court of Charlemagne he had devoted himself to no lady, for since the day when he first saw Hildegarde, no other had any charms for him. She so far outshone all, as to render him indifferent to others, and thus his conduct had been such as to win the respect and confidence of the emperor. But now, having the opportunity, he resolved to gain the favor of the queen. He began to show his regard by many little attentions and glances which Hildegarde could not fail to understand. She allowed this to pass without remark, and at length when an opportunity offered, he declared his love in the most passionate language, and swore that life was valueless if this affection were not returned. Hildegarde repulsed him with all the anger and contempt which he merited; but he believed this to be a ruse, and could not understand that she was in truth a loving wife and virtuous woman. Next day he repeated his offense, and the queen determined not to be subject to this insult during all the absence of her husband, but to rid herself of it by a harmless deceit. She feigned to listen to him with some favor, and made an appointment to meet him the following evening in a part of the palace quite unfrequented, where they could converse without fear of interruption. The knight was delighted with what he considered his success. He proceeded to the appointed place and the queen was not long in coming. She desired him to enter an apartment to which she led the way. No sooner was he within than she closed the door and he found himself her prisoner. She declared that there he should remain until the return of the emperor. Thaland was devoured with rage, but he was also powerless to free himself. Each day a discreet servant of the queen brought him a frugal allowance of food; this was passed through a small grated door, and then he was left in solitude. He constantly sent the most earnest entreaties to Hildegarde to set him at liberty, as well as assurances of his hearty repentance. When Hildegarde heard that the emperor was at hand, she determined to free the knight, and did so the very day that Charlemagne entered the castle. She made a pretense that he had been on a secret mission, to those who had noticed his absence. The knight was determined to be revenged on the queen, and proceeded to excite the jealousy of Charlemagne. He declared that Hildegarde had been so shameless in her conduct with a strange knight, that he had retired to a distant place rather than witness the infidelity of the woman who was left in his charge, by a man whom he esteemed as he did the emperor. Charles loved his wife so fondly that he was easily enraged by jealousy, and he commanded that the queen should be taken to a neighboring forest and there decapitated. Thaland gladly undertook the execution of this sentence, and gave the queen to two villains who were sure to do his will. These men dragged Hildegarde away, but just as they would have completed their dreadful task, a tall white figure approached them, and in a hollow voice, commanded them to release their victim. The assassins fled affrighted, but they declared to Thaland that his command had been executed. It was the faithful waiting-maid of the queen who had thus saved her; she had felt herself powerless at the court and under the eye of Thaland, but had followed the queen, determined to save her life. Convinced that there was no safety in returning, they proceeded to the cell of a hermit, where they remained some time, and the queen learned from him the art of curing diseases by the use of herbs. At length the two women proceeded to Rome, where Hildegarde supported them by her skill in medicine. She soon became very noted, and even the pope consulted her. She assumed the name of Arabella, and her fame extended even to Germany. Charlemagne had known no peace since his separation from the queen, and was constantly brooding on her death, tormented by the reflection that possibly she was not guilty. At length he determined to visit Rome, and Thaland, who was also ill in body and mind, begged to be allowed to accompany him. When they reached Rome, Thaland decided to consult the wonderful woman of whom he had heard. Hildegarde had seen the wretch by the side of her husband when they made their public entry into the city. She now assured him that if he had committed any crime it must be confessed, or her remedies could have no power, and he must surely die. Thaland was greatly distressed. He deferred his confession from day to day, but at last becoming seriously alarmed for his life, he sent for the emperor to attend his bedside and at the same time summoned Arabella. He then confessed how he had sinned against Charlemagne, and the innocency of the queen. Charles was convulsed with agony, and when Hildegarde entered she could not restrain herself from exclaiming, "O, my lord and husband!" and she fell at his feet. Charlemagne raised her joyfully, and held her in a loving embrace. Gladly they returned thanks to God who had thus brought them out of all their sorrows. The wretched Thaland had sunk upon a chair, and when Charles turned to him life had already flown. Then was there a feast made in Rome such as none had seen before, and at this festival Charlemagne and his queen were blessed by the pope and returned to Ingelheim in great happiness. The faithful waiting-woman was by no means forgotten, and with joy returned to her home on the Rhine, where the queen ever honored her as a dear friend. The Abbey of Kempton was founded by Hildegarde as a token of her gratitude to heaven for returning her to her husband and home.

Kevelaer. *Foundation of the Town.* According to the religious traditions, this town was founded in the seventeenth century. As Heinrich Buschmann journeyed over Kevelaer plain at a certain Christmas-time he came to a cross by the road-side. He stopped and prayed earnestly, and as he did so, heard a voice cry out, "Here you are to build me a shrine." A few days later the same thing occurred in the same place. Then Buschmann resolved that he would save a portion of his earnings for the purpose of fulfilling this command, but as he was not a rich man, he could not hope to erect any other than a simple shrine. The winter passed, and when spring came the good man had put aside the necessary sum, when one day his wife related to him a vision which came to her nightly. It was that of a shrine on which was a figure of the Holy Virgin. They then told their story to some monks who inhabited a cloister near them, and they assisted them in the performance of their heaven-directed labor. The shrine was completed, and the statue of the Virgin and Child unveiled, June 1, 1642. So many pilgrims visited it, and so wonderful were the miracles there performed, that houses were erected near by, and from this beginning, the town of Kevelaer gradually arose. In 1842 the two hundredth anniversary of the consecration of the shrine was celebrated, at which time two hundred thousand persons visited it as pilgrims.

The Klingelkapelle. See Gernsbach.

The Knight's Leap. See Baden-Baden.

Königsdorf. *The Election of Bishop Hildebold.* During the reign of Charlemagne, there arose a great dispute at Cologne concerning the election of a bishop. The emperor heard so much of it that he determined to go himself to decide the difficulty and appoint such a bishop as should seem best to him. So he went without a retinue, and as he reached Königsdorf, the bell called the people to hear mass. The pious monarch dismounted, and entered the church. When the service was ended, he approached the priest to give him a piece of gold as an offering. This the priest refused, saying that he had no need of such money, and that it was not the custom of his church to receive it. "But," he added, "you have the appearance of a hunter, and if you will give me a hide from a stag or roe, you will do a good work; for my mass-book is in sad need of a binding." This simplicity and earnestness impressed the emperor and he resolved to remember the priest. When he was come to Cologne he summoned the clergy, and told them he would himself appoint the new bishop. Then each party attempted to influence him in their favor, and large sums of money were paid him to secure his interest. The gold he ordered to be used to pay the debts of the bishopric, and at length he told them that they had endeavored to bribe him in vain, and that he found none so worthy as the priest of the forest chapel at Königsdorf, for he despised his gold, and seemed only intent upon his mass-book. He had therefore determined to make him bishop. The astonishment of the priest was great when he learned the high dignity to which he was called; but he possessed the grace of God, and by it was instructed how to conduct himself in his new office, and the name of Bishop Hildebold is still remembered in Cologne, where he founded the dome of St. Peter's, on the same spot as that on which the present cathedral stands.

Königswinter. See Drachenfels.

Kreuznach. *The Ebernburg.* There are two legends connected with the name of this castle. One relates that during the fifteenth century it was besieged, and when the provisions were almost exhausted and they had come to the last boar, the master of the castle had it taken out every day and bound as if for slaughter, and then put again in its pen. Thus each morning the besiegers heard the sound as of a boar being killed, and reasoned that it would be long ere the provisions could be exhausted, and as they were already weary they raised the siege. From that time the castle was called Ebernburg. Another tradition recounts that when the robber knight Rupert possessed the castle, he desired to marry the Countess of Montfort. She had refused him and preferred the

Rhine Count Heinrich. Rupert desired to be revenged, and until he could devise some measure to accomplish his end, he retired to his estates and passed much of his time in hunting. One day he was coming from the chase when he met a large fierce boar near the Rheingrafenstein. So thick was his skin that the weapons thrown at him only rebounded, and Count Rupert having lost all he carried stood unarmed before the savage beast, expecting to be killed instantly. Suddenly the monster fell dead at his feet, killed by a well-directed blow, and when he looked around to thank his deliverer, he saw only the Count Heinrich. This was the cause of a perfect reconciliation between the two counts, and soon the Count Heinrich was married to the beautiful Montfort. In commemoration of this event, the head of a boar was carved in stone and placed above the door of the castle which was called Ebernburg. This castle has many interesting historical associations. Here Ulrich von Hutten wrote his letters to Charles V. and the German nation. It was the stronghold of Franz von Sickingen and in it his noble wife, Hedwig, received and cared for many outlaws and fugitives, and it was sometimes called the "Asylum of Justice."

Laach. Near Laach is the Frauenkirche founded by Geneviève of Brabant, in thankfulness for her restoration to her husband after having been separated from him by the treachery of his steward Golo, with whom her husband, Count Siegfried, had left the care of his wife while he was absent in war. See legend in preceding portion of this book.

Lahneck. The Order of Knight Templars founded by Godfrey de Bouillon, for the protection of the Holy Sepulchre in 1118, in a short time became rich and powerful, and spread all over Europe. The clergy were jealous of it, and Pope Clement V. determined to exterminate them with the help of Phillippe le Bel. Molay was lured to France with sixty knights, and there they were all executed and their property confiscated. Then the pope commanded the Archbishop of Mayence, Peter of Aichspalt, to exterminate the knights in his diocese. The Templars held the Castle of Lahneck, and they there defied the bishop. They were besieged, and as their number was small they were surrounded. At length all save one were killed, and he was summoned to surrender; but he declared that he would never do so, and pointed to his fallen comrades with pride. At this juncture a messenger arrived, who proclaimed a truce from the emperor. The besiegers laid down their arms, and the messenger respectfully approached the remaining knight, saying: "Surrender to me your arms, noble sir. I regret not having come in time to save your brethren, but to you I can promise safety of life and property." "Think of Molay and his murdered followers! Think of my comrades slain here?" replied he. "As they had no mercy, I desire none!" Then he rushed upon the enemy and fell pierced with many wounds.

Lichtenthal, Convent of. See Baden-Baden.

Liebenstein and **Sterrenberg.** These two castles, called "The Brothers," are situated not far from the village of Camp, upon a sharp ledge of rocks at the foot of which is the Convent of Bornhofen. In Liebenstein lived the noble Bayer of Boppard with his sons, Conrad and Heinrich, and their beautiful foster-sister, Hildegarde. The father was anxious that one of the brothers should wed with Hildegarde, but he was pained to see that both were enamored of her. Heinrich with true generosity determined to leave the prize to Conrad, and joining the Crusades fought with such bravery as to cause his name to resound through all Europe, as well as in the East. The wooing of Conrad was successful, and soon he was betrothed to Hildegarde. Then the old knight, in order that the young couple should be near him, commenced the erection of Castle Sterrenberg. But he died before its completion, and the marriage was deferred for a year. During this time Conrad was much with gay companions who represented marriage to him as slavery; he also greatly envied the fame of his brother, and finally he too, determined to join the Crusades. Hildegarde passed her days in close retirement, mourning the absence of her lover, and praying for his safe return. Meantime Sterrenberg was finished, and made ready to receive the young people. Suddenly Hildegarde was startled by the news that Conrad had returned with a lovely Grecian bride, and would be received at Sterrenberg with great festivities. This proved but too true, and the heart-broken girl shut herself in the most lonely chamber of Liebenstein, and refused to see any one save her attendant. Heinrich hearing of his brother's treachery returned to Liebenstein, determined to avenge the wrongs of Hildegarde, and one morning suddenly appeared before her. He challenged Conrad to mortal combat, which was about to begin, when Hildegarde stepped between them and begged them to desist and be reconciled to each other, leaving vengeance to God alone. She soon entered the Convent of Bornhofen. It was not long ere the Grecian proved as faithless as Conrad had been, and eloped with a friend of her husband's. Then the brothers became fully reconciled, and lived together at Liebenstein, while Sterrenberg was forever deserted. This tradition and that of the Lurlei, are the most popular of all the legends of the Rhine.

Lorch. *The Devil's Ladder.* Near Lorch is a steep cliff called the Kedrich, or "Devil's Ladder." This was the home of mountain spirits who did much mischief in the surrounding country, and could never be assailed or punished, as their retreat was inaccessible. The knight Sibo, of Lorch, had become gloomy and morose after his wife's death, and lived in retirement with his only child, a beautiful maiden of fourteen. One evening some strangers requested his hospitalities, and he drove them away with abusive language.

The next day his daughter went to the fields and did not return. A search was made, and the father was wild with grief, for this child was his idol. At length a shepherd lad said he had seen two little gray men who led a maiden toward the Kedrich. Hither the father hastened, and there high above him he saw the little spirits who led away his child, and they cried out to him, "This is the reward of your hospitality; when you know how to show it better we will restore her to you." Years passed on, and every morning and evening the maiden could be seen walking on the top of the inaccessible cliff. Now a young man who had loved her from childhood returned from his wanderings, and went at once to the Castle of Sibo. When he heard what had happened he was inconsolable, and spent much time in examining the Kedrich to see if he could not discover a way to climb its heights. One day while thus occupied, a little woman came to him and asked if he still loved the maid. The young man desired to know who she was, and if she could help him. "I have taken care of her since she came here, and with a mother's tenderness. She loves you, and if you are inclined to marry her I will help you," said the funny little woman. The young man swore that his love was unchangeable. Then she told him to return the next day and she would assist him, for it was time they should marry, and the father was sufficiently punished. When the next day came Sibo went with the young knight, and they found a ladder reaching from the bottom to the top of Kedrich. This the young man mounted, while the father anxiously watched him. Arrived at the top he found an enchanted region. Gardens and beautiful groves with fountains and rare flowers met his gaze. Wandering on he entered a grotto where he saw the maiden asleep on a mossy bank. She awoke with glad surprise, and ran to embrace him lovingly. Now a gnome stood before them who regarded them maliciously, but the woman who had made the ladder appeared, and speaking to the dwarf in an unknown tongue, they both laughed, and told the lovers that they should soon be made happy. The young man was in haste to depart, and the dwarf told him to descend the ladder, but the maiden should go down more easily. He obeyed, and found her before him, and in her father's arms. The spirits gave the maiden a box which they said contained her dowry, and assured her they should come to her wedding, and so they did, and brought rich and rare gifts to their foster-daughter. From this time the melancholy of the old Sibo disappeared, and happiness reigned in the castle, where grand-children soon played about the old man. The ladder fell to pieces in time, and as the people called it the "Devil's Ladder," the cliff has always retained that name.

Fürsteneck. Knight Oswald and his revenge. Between this knight and Wilhelm von Saneck there existed a deadly feud, and the latter had greatly desired to get Oswald into his power. This he succeeded at last in doing and carried him to his castle, where he not only imprisoned him, but with fearful cruelty deprived him of his sight. At his own castle it was thought that Oswald had fallen into the hands of robbers, but as there were no proofs of this, young Edwin, his only son, did not believe it, and greatly feared he had been taken by the Knight of Saneck. He determined at all events to ascertain, and disguised as a minstrel approached the castle. Arrived there he found that a great banquet was being given, and in his character of a musician he penetrated even to the room where the knight sat at table with his guests. He listened attentively to all that was said, hoping to hear something of his father. At last when all were merry with wine and their tongues well loosened, one said to Saneck, "Do you know that you are suspected of holding Oswald of Fürsteneck prisoner?" "Hum," said Saneck, "all tales are not lies." "And some believe," added the first, "that you have blinded him." "Well, well, what then? Does it make any difference whether a candle goes out or is blown out?" "But it is a great pity in one way," said a third, "for Oswald was a most skillful archer." "I will wager," said another, "that he could still hit his mark if one made it known to him." "And I will wager that he cannot," said Saneck, now quite drunk; and he ordered the prisoner to be brought in. Young Edwin was almost overcome by what he heard, and when his father was brought could scarcely resist the impulse to declare himself. But he heard Saneck tell him the wager and command a bow and arrows to be brought for him. Then Oswald said, "Knight Saneck, give me the sign of what I am to hit." "Here on the table I place a cup," said Wilhelm von Saneck, and it was his last word, for Oswald sent his arrow when he heard his voice, and it entered the heart of the knight. A wild cry arose throughout the hall, but Edwin sprang quickly to his father and cried out, "I am the son of this poor man! Whoever loves honor, will approve his act, and to any who do not, I will answer with my sword." Then the knights declared their horror of the cruelty of Saneck and the justice of his punishment. Edwin conducted his father to his home, where although he could not restore his sight he nursed him with the tenderest care.

Lorsch. *The Emperor and the Monk.* Once upon a time the Emperor Charlemagne being on a journey, stopped at the Abbey of Lorsch to pass the night. He was kindly received, and entertained with a banquet by the good monks. But after retiring to his bed he could not sleep, so harassed was he, and full of care. At last he arose and went to the church to pray. While there he saw a venerable monk who was blind come into the church, being led by a boy. He tottered along to a place near the emperor and sank on his knees. There was something in his manner that fixed the attention of the emperor, and he watched him as he prayed. He was very devout in his manner, and his prayers were often interrupted with sighs and groans, and it seemed to Charlemagne that a halo of light surrounded his head. In the morning the emperor related what he had seen to the abbot, and inquired concerning the monk. The abbot said he knew not who he was or whence he came. That he called himself Bernardus, but had always refused to tell anything concerning himself, although he had been some years with them, and was growing old. This excited the curiosity of Charlemagne, and he went to the cell of the monk, where after a little he recognized in him Thassalio, duke of Bavaria, whom he had banished years before on account of political difficulties. As the emperor remembered all this he called him by name, announced that he was Charlemagne, and assured him of his forgiveness for his past wrong-doing. Thassalio was deeply moved, and told the emperor how sincerely he had repented. He declared that he believed God had pardoned him, and that his last earthly wish had been that he might receive his forgiveness also. Next morning Charlemagne wished again to speak with him before his departure, but the abbot told him that the excitement of their interview had deeply moved his already exhausted nature, and in the night he had quietly died.

Lurlei. The rocks known by this name are just above St. Goar, and rise four hundred and twenty feet above the Rhine. The legends tell that in days of yore a charming maiden lived on the top, and each evening sat there and combed her golden locks, or played the lute and sang melodiously. All who saw or heard her were passionately in love with her, and many boats were drawn into the Gewirre, or whirlpool, while attempting to near her home. She did much good to the fishermen, showing them the best places to fish, and did not seem to be wholly wicked. The fame of her beauty and goodness attracted the son of the Pfalzgraf to see her. He ordered his boatmen to row toward the Lurlei; they remonstrated, but in vain; they went and could see nothing on the rock; but returning, they heard a song coming from the depths of the river. Then the waves rose as if with a storm, and raised the boat towards the rock where now the virgin appeared dressed in white and veiled. Then the youth would climb to her. The boatmen sadly tried to near the rock, but he leaped out and was swallowed by the foaming waters. His father was determined to revenge the death of his son, and sent soldiers to take the undine prisoner, that she might be burned as a witch. She stood on the rock smiling while they climbed up, and when they commanded her to come down, she said, "The Rhine will receive me and that will be better." When they had almost reached her, she bent toward the river singing, —

"Hasten hither, lovely waves,
Take me quickly to your caves."

The waters rose, and two waves took her away while she sweetly sung. But the men were thrown down on the rocks, and were glad to escape with their lives to the Pfalzgraf, who was convinced he had no power over her. The undine was never seen again. Another legend relates that at Bacharach dwelt an orphan maiden whose exquisite beauty gained for her such numbers of admirers that it became a great trial to her, for she loved one who had gone to Palestine to acquire renown before he should marry her. She lived in strict retirement, and yet many duels were fought concerning her; and so great was the love and jealousy which she occasioned that she was accused of exercising a magical art. At length the case was referred to the Archbishop of Cologne, who went to see her; and told her he would take her to a place where she could peaceably await the return of her lover, or in case of his death take the veil. He ordered three knights to conduct her, and give her every attention on the way. When they were come to the Lurlei she ascended it to take a parting look at the Rhine, and while there perceived a boat coming toward her, bearing the flag of her lover, and in fact he was in it. She was overcome with joy and fell on her knees, extending her arms toward the boat. As it came near a splendidly dressed knight stood on the deck waving his hat, and when he saw and recognized his love he was full of joy. In his anxiety to reach her no one thought of the whirlpool, and suddenly the boat was swallowed up in it. All were filled with horror, and a pale figure with fair hair appeared on the surface of the water. Then the maiden with a frightful shriek leaped from the rock and sank where the body of her lover had disappeared. They were afterwards found locked in an embrace, and this confirmed the belief in the existence of the Nymph of the Lurlei.

The Maiden Leap. Many years ago there lived in the Haardt Mountains a giant of great power who had built a castle on one of the highest peaks, and from his towers could overlook the whole country. A few miles distant from him lived a maiden who had large estates and many servants. She was very beautiful in person, and fond of the chase and all such things as are called manly exercises, and in these she excelled. She also managed her household with great skill and judgment, and could do herself credit at the spinning-wheel. Now the giant loved and was determined to possess this maiden. So he sent his servant with rich jewels to ask her hand in marriage. The servant, who was a cunning fellow, deemed it a pity that these riches should be given the maid, and she refuse his master as he was sure she would do, and felt that it was better for him to retain them for himself. He turned aside into the forest to find a place to conceal them, where he saw a knight who was weeping. When the servant inquired the cause of his grief and offered his assistance, he told him of his love for the same maiden to whom the giant had sent his proposals, and that he dared not approach her on account of his poverty. Then the faithless servant told his errand, and offered to divide the jewels with him if he would assist to conceal them. This the knight assented to and they commenced to dig a hole. When this was done the servant attempted to kill the knight, fearing he might disclose his treachery. The knight had left his sword on a rock while at work, and as the servant had seen him in tears, he took him for a coward, but he realized his mistake most perfectly, for he threw down the servant and was about to kill him, but he decided to take his part of the booty and leave him alive. He then sped toward the castle of the maiden. Meanwhile the giant had become impatient at the long absence of his servant, and set out himself for the maiden's home. When he arrived he declared that he would kill her if she would not marry him. She and her maids fell on their knees beseeching him to leave them in peace, but nothing could move him or change his decision, so the maiden determined to make a desperate trial for life, and told him that if he would wed her he must prove himself worthy by running after and overtaking her. To this he consented, and she leaped on her horse. She rode many miles and still the giant pursued, and now the horse was giving out and the giant gaining on her. Just then she reached a fearful chasm and determined to risk all on a leap over it. She did so, and landed safely on the other side. The giant was furious. He saw her kneeling on the bank. He ran up and down seeking a place to cross, and soon his triumphal shouts announced that he had found one. The heart of the maiden grew cold, but at that moment the young knight came up and attacked the giant, who weary with his chase was easily overcome. While on his way to the castle he had seen the pursuit of the maid and had followed as quickly as possible. In consideration of the great service he had thus rendered her and the wealth he had acquired he no longer feared to tell his love. He was accepted, and in a few days the wedding was celebrated with much gladness.

Mayence. *The Heads of Stone.* On the wall of Mayence, just by the gate called "Gauthor," two heads are engraved. They commemorate the following events: In 1462 Dethier of Isenburg was Archbishop of Mayence. The pope and the emperor were opposed to him and desired to give his office to Adolf of Nassau. As Mayence remained faithful to Dethier, Adolf besieged the city, and misery and suffering soon reigned there. One evening Walderer, the fisherman, sat gloomily in his cottage; his wife was dying, he and his child starving. At length he declared he would fight for Adolphus rather than die for Dethier. His wife began to repeat the "Lord's Prayer," and at the end, the sweet voice of his daughter Gertrude said, "Amen." She tried to console her father, but the spirit of hopelessness was in his heart. While he uttered traitorous sentiments and the others argued with him for right and duty, three men entered the house. One of them, a young fisherman, hastened to Gertrude and her mother, while the others conversed with the father. Soon he came to the daughter with money and commanded her to go and buy food. Then the truth flashed through the mind of the dying wife, and she knew that her husband was about to betray the city to the enemy. The girl went out with the young man, who was her lover, and her mother attempted, with all the impressive solemnity of one about to die, to dissuade Walderer from the crime. But all in vain, and even while she talked, she died. Next day when the monk who had been her confessor came to bury the poor wife, he too was persuaded to assist in betraying the city by allowing the soldiers of Adolf to pass the gate. He was a wicked hypocrite, and had withal the most infamous designs upon the unprotected Gertrude. One of the strangers who had come to the cottage the evening previous, had remained, and the monk brought him a habit like his own, and thus disguised they together walked through the town. That evening their plans were matured. Walderer was to be the watchman at the Gauthor, and the lover, John, was to conduct the soldiers there, by ways known to few. At length the stranger departed, much to the joy of Gertrude, for she feared lest he should be discov ered in their cottage. When she was alone the monk came to attempt the accomplishment of his designs against her, and when she scorned him, he threatened to expose the treachery of her father. The poor girl was in distress, when John came to her rescue. He declared the only way was to make the monk a prisoner, and being the stronger, and moreover armed, he soon placed the priest in a room from whence he could not escape. Gertrude was then commanded to remain in her chamber. At night John led Adolf and several of his soldiers to the house of Walderer, in the disguise of monks. They swore to a solemn compact. Gertrude heard the unusual noise and then the departing steps as her father led them to the Gauthor. Instantly she knew the truth, and determined to save the city if possible. She went to the monk and besought him to lead her to Dethier, but he only caught her in his arms and declared she should pass the night with him. With the strength of despair she broke away and rushed into the street, crying, "To Arms! To Arms! The enemy! The enemy!" Thus arousing those near her she told them all her suspicions, and begged them to hasten to the Gauthor. But the brave girl was too late to prevent the entrance of the enemy, and soon a desperate struggle was going on all over the city. The women fought as fiercely as the men, and Gertrude fell pierced by an enemy's lance at the feet of her father. Adolphus was victorious, and his punishment of those he had conquered was fearfully cruel. But that of Walderer and John was sent by a higher power. The father went mad, and the lover threw himself into the river with the corpse of the noble Gertrude. The heads were carved on the wall to commemorate the bravery of the maiden, and the treachery and punishment of her lover.

Arnold of Walpode. In the middle of the thirteenth century there was a tournament at Mainz, and nothing was left undone to make it as magnificent as possible. The beautiful Anne of Walpode was selected to confer the prize, and when the victor, a noble and handsome youth, knelt before her, an unspeakable happiness lighted both their faces, and he tenderly kissed the reward she blushingly conferred upon him. Then her father, the brave Arnold, led the young man to the archbishop, who received him with kindness, and declared him his chamberlain, saying, "Now salute your betrothed, for you have gained a right to her hand. Is it not so?" asked he of Arnold. The old knight smiled, and commanded the young Sir John to meet him at his castle, and dine with him that day. Now it happened that Dethier of Katzenelnbogen, had been present at the tourney and had seen and admired the lovely Anne. He coveted her fortune also, for his own had been lessened by the building of Castle Rheinfels. He so presumed on his rank and power that he doubted not his acceptance. But Arnold declared that his child should not wed a Gaugraf, who levied taxes on citizens and merchants; for Dethier had rebuilt Rheinfels in order to exact customs from all who passed on the river. The count was full of anger, and left Arnold declaring, "You appreciate my castle rightly; it shall be a stumbling-block to bring your proud citizens to ruin! Most noble knight!" said Walpode, "do not forget that Schwarz has discovered powder, and the strongholds of robbers can be destroyed by it!" For a long time Arnold had striven to persuade the towns to make a confederation to oppose those counts and barons who from their castles, demanded customs and oppressed all who came in their way. Now he gave his entire energies to this purpose, but although many approved his theory, they were slow to action. Meanwhile the lovers were happy; the wedding-day was fixed, and guests were invited from great distances, for Arnold hoped to make it an occasion to persuade his friends to arouse themselves to the forming of the confederation. The news of the preparations reached Count Dethier, and he cursed himself that he had not been able to be revenged upon the noble knight of Mainz. While thinking of this a horn sounded, and he was told that a troop of armed men approached. He hastened to put himself at the head of his retainers and proceed to ascertain who they might be. It proved a train of the noblest and wealthiest families of Cologne, Bacharach, and St. Goar, on their journey to the wedding at Mainz. When Dethier learned this he determined to make them prisoners, and though they would have fought, being much embarrassed by the presence of ladies, they were soon led into the castle. They were expected at Mainz with impatience and surprise, which were not lessened when the truth was known. Then Arnold of Walpode felt that the time had indeed come for the maturity of his scheme. He addressed the citizens with such power, and so depicted the abuses from which travellers and merchants suffered, adding a vivid picture of the way in which these prisoners, their friends, the first and best in the land, were even then suffering, that all were at last aroused; a league was made and money raised; and all swore that an end should come to the power of such robber knights as Dethier of Rheinfels. The third day his castle was attacked, and the prisoners rescued. Then was the marriage celebrated with great joy, and after-events proved that the noble Arnold had not overrated the value and importance of the confederation.

Count Henry of Meissen was a Minnesänger of the fourteenth century. Many of his songs were in honor of the Blessed Virgin, and all of them so filled with the praise of woman, that he acquired the title of "Frauenlob" (woman's praise), by which he is still known in German literature. He died in 1317, and received such a burial as no other ever had, before or since his time. The ladies of Mayence assembled in mourning, the cathedral bells and those of all the churches tolled from the break of day; eight ladies of the highest rank bore the coffin, covered with myrtle and flowers, and followed by a long train of women whose songs mingled with the music of the bells. The cathedral was splendidly decorated, and the archbishop pronounced the benediction. The coffin was lowered to the tomb in the midst of sobs and tears, while the young maidens strewed it with roses and poured into the tomb the most delicious wines, from golden cups. Then a song which Frauenlob had written was sung and followed by a high mass, after which the maidens intoned a hymn, expressing the hope of immortality. A monument was erected to him in the cathedral, and again in 1842 a beautiful one by Schwanthaler was placed there by the ladies of Mayence, to perpetuate the memory of the poet. It represents a female figure decorating a coffin with a wreath, and is on the south wall of the cathedral.

Rabbi Amram was a Jew of Mayence, who founded a school in Cologne, where he died. He expressed a wish to be buried near his parents in Mayence, and being told that the bigotry of that city would render it impossible, he commanded that after death his body should be placed in a small boat on the Rhine, and allowed to go where it would. This was done, and the boat went directly to Mayence. The whole population came out to see the strange sight, but when the truth was known, the Christians would not allow the wishes of Rabbi Amram to be fulfilled. The bishop commanded that the coffin should remain where it was, and a crypt be built over it. Many believe that from this arose St. Emeran's Church. But the Jewish students stole the body at night, leaving the coffin, and gave the Rabbi the burial he so much desired. There was a fresco, representing the drifting of the strange ship, upon a house in Mayence, which remained until 1850.

Marriage of Ghosts at Castle Lauf. See Baden-Baden.

Mousetower. (Mäusethurm.) See Bingen.

Mummelsee. See Baden-Baden.

Niedeck Castle. *The living Toy.* Many years ago, Rhineland was the home of numerous giants who were good-natured, and never employed their vast strength for the injury of men. Such an one lived at Castle Niedeck. One day his little daughter went for a walk, and as she strolled along, she saw a husbandman with a horse and plough. She had never seen one before, and she clapped her hands with joy, so that the mountains echoed. "What a fine toy!" said she, "and living too! So much better than my dolls, which are but leather, and cannot move." And she hastened to snatch up horse, plough, and husbandman, and returned to her father with them all in her apron. She put them down on the table before him with great exultation and danced about in glee. Then her father explained to her that she had interrupted most important labor. That the husbandmen who tilled the fields and supplied food for men should ever be respected, and commanded her to return the toy she so admired to the field from which she had taken it.

Oberwesel. *The Seven Virgins.* Above Oberwesel rise the picturesque ruins of Castle Schönburg. This was the birth-place of the famous Marshal Schomberg who fought under the Prince of Orange and compelled the Spaniards to acknowledge the House of Braganza. After being high in office in Prussia he went to England and perished in the battle of the Boyne. He is buried in Westminster Abbey. In this same castle once resided a knight who was so devoted to his wife that when she died nothing could interest him or arouse him from his grief. She had left seven daughters; they grew up with little or no training, and when their father died they lived a life of coquetry and folly. They were all beautiful, and as they possessed vast estates many suitors flocked to their castle. Here they were hospitably entertained, and gayety reigned triumphant in their halls, but no sooner did a suitor speak with earnestness than he was dismissed with laughing raillery. At last at a banquet two knights fell into a dispute concerning the sisters which ended in a challenge for a duel, and all the young men present declared that it was time to end this folly, and demand of the sisters an explanation of their flirting and fickleness. So a request was sent to them to meet the knights next day and make a choice for marriage. They consented to the gathering, and a vast number went to the state-saloon where they thought to find the sisters; but a servant announced that they desired them to repair to an arbor on the Rhine. When the young men reached the spot the seven virgins were in a boat and at some distance from the shore. One of them stood in the stern and told the knights that they had never intended to marry; that they loved liberty too well to be the slaves of any, and that as this decision had been forced on them they had decided to leave their castle for a long time and go to an aunt in the Netherlands, where they would play the same comedy with the knights of that country that they had so enjoyed here. This speech was hailed with laughter by the sisters, and the boat moved off. But suddenly a storm arose, and even in sight of the suitors the boat was upset and all were drowned. On the spot where this occurred seven rocks appeared above the water. They are a terror to navigators, and are called the "Seven Virgins," to this day.

Oggersheim. *Hans Warsch, the valiant Shepherd.* During the Thirty Years' War, the Spanish troops approached Oggersheim. All the citizens fled save a poor shepherd, Hans Warsch. He would not leave his wife who was very ill, having just given birth to a child. When Hans found himself alone, he closed the gates of the town, according to the usages of war, and placed himself on the watch-tower with a trumpet, ready to answer the summons of the enemy. When the Spanish trumpeter demanded the surrender of the town, Hans replied that this should be done on condition that the commander would insure the citizens the protection of their property. If this was not granted they were determined to defend themselves *to the last man!* The Spanish commandant gave his word of honor that the condition should be observed, and Hans hastened to open the gates. When the warriors entered the town they were surprised to see no one in the streets, and more so when they became aware that the poor shepherd with his sick wife and wee baby were the only persons left in all the town. The commandant admired the brave shepherd, kept his promise, and stood godfather to his child, whose christening was kept with joy.

Oppenheim. The ruined Castle of Landskron is all that here remains of the imperial fortress, once so famous. In the church-yard of the town are the remains of many Spaniards and Swedes who fell during the Thirty Years' War. One evening, not long before the commencement of the Seven Years' War, in 1756, a young artist entered Oppenheim, and proceeded to an inn, at the door of which stood the daughter of the landlord, a beautiful girl. The young man was not long in becoming very friendly with the maiden. When she learned that he was an artist, and making pictures of Rhineland, she begged him to paint one of her "dear Oppenheim," and told him how beautiful it was when seen from the castle by moonlight. He promised to go that very night to select the spot from which his picture should be made. He kept his word, and as he walked past the church-yard was occupied with thoughts of the decay of pomp and power, and exclaimed, "All vanishes save Glory! and happy he alone who succeeds in gaining that." Just then his foot knocked against a skull and sent it whirling along before him. Socn the clock sounded the hour of midnight, and instantly he heard 'a strange noise through all the church-yard. The bones began to unite and form skeletons, and these to form in line of battle — Spaniards with Spaniards, and Swedes with Swedes, while commands were given in an unearthly voice. They fought furiously and more furiously, until the scene was most frightful. At length one was thrown down at the feet of the artist, and when he looked at the hollow cavities where once eyes had been, a strange light seemed to shine in them, and a voice said, "Mortal, you have seen our dreadful contest! Tell to all how we still suffer and are forced thus to contend, because in life we were enemies instead of loving each other." As this was said the clock struck one, and the bones were again scattered about the church-yard as at first. Then the artist hastened to the inn, full of fear and excitement, and told his strange adventure. The people of Oppenheim afterwards regarded it as a forerunner of the war which soon broke out. The artist, though he gained not the glory he so earnestly apostrophized, married the innkeeper's daughter, and to the end of his days was called on to tell his story to every stranger who visited Oppenheim.

Pfalzgrafenstein. In 1194 the Emperor Henry VI. wished to marry the daughter of the Count Palatine Conrad to some member of his own family. The count had great wealth and no sons, and Henry desired to secure these riches to some near relative. But the princess was deeply in love with Henry of Brunswick. Her father, dreading the anger of the emperor, would not hear of the alliance, and sent her to be kept a close prisoner in the Pfalzgrafenstein, which rises from the Rhine "like an immense stone ship, forever at anchor." It is situated a little below Bacharach and not far from Caub. Now the wife of Count Conrad sympathized with her daughter, and did not admit the right of the emperor to select a husband for her. So she sent for Brunswick, who came in disguise, and the marriage being solemnized in secret, the young couple enjoyed a quiet and blissful honeymoon. The mother at length told her husband what she had done, and so tenderly pleaded for her daughter, who was about to become a mother, that she overcame his anger at being thus outwitted. He in his turn told the emperor, who then commanded the marriage to be celebrated with great festivities. Count Conrad passed sentence upon the young couple that they should remain at the Pfalzgrafenstein until the princess bore a son; and tradition relates that hence came a law that all future Countesses Palatine should go to this castle to await their accouchements, and from this it derives its name of Pfalzgräfin-stein.

Philippsburg. *The Brave Recruit.* When this place was besieged by the French, a storm attack was ordered on a lonely and apparently undefended portion of the works, and twelve grenadiers selected to make it. Now it happened that a recruit had been made sentinel on this spot where no attack was anticipated. He was watchful, however, and stood with his halberd ready for defense. Suddenly the face of a mustachioed grenadier appeared above the parapet, and the owner of it was about to set his foot upon the wall, "Ho, ho! I will show you the way!" called out the recruit, and gave him a push which sent him from the storming ladder. But scarce a minute had elapsed, when the same face (as the recruit thought) appeared again, and again was pushed away. This was repeated to the twelfth time, and the raw soldier thought he had never seen such persevering determination as that of the inimical grenadier. When the guard was changed, the sergeant asked the recruit if anything had occurred there, and he answered, nothing save that a grenadier had been determined to come upon the wall, and he had pushed him back, but he always returned until he had thrown him down twelve times. The sergeant went to see what this could mean, and found the bodies of the twelve grenadiers in the trench where the recruit had thrown them, and the storming ladder still hanging on the wall. When the commandent knew this, the recruit was handsomely rewarded.

Pulpits of the Devil and the Angel. See Baden-Baden.

Rheinfels. See Mayence. Arnold of Walpode.

Rheinstein. *The Ride to the Wedding.* In the early part of the thirteenth century this castle was inhabited by a very wealthy knight named Siegfried, who was noted for his robberies and wickedness. Returning from one of his expeditions he brought much booty and a beautiful woman named Jutta, whom he had taken in Frankenland. The knight soon yielded himself to her charms and married her. From this time the life at Rheinstein was changed in all its aspects: merchants who passed on land or sea were undisturbed; Siegfried went on no more expeditions, and his wild and rough comrades ceased to visit him. But, alas, this quiet happiness was of short duration, for Jutta died in giving birth to a daughter. Then the knight thought only of this child and gave his life to her care and education. She was called Gerda, and inherited the character and beauty of her lovely mother. Though Siegfried entertained no guests, the pilgrims and travellers who received the hospitalities of the castle carried abroad the report of her beauty, and this as well as the riches of the knight, attracted many suitors. At length in order to free himself from their importunities the old knight promised to meet them all at a tournament at Mayence, and declared that the victor should be the husband of Gerda. Never had a larger number striven in any tourney. Now among those who contended were Kurt of Ehrenfels, which castle is not far above Rheinstein, and Kuno of Reichenstein, which last fortress is near to Rheinstein, the Church of St. Clement being between them. The last-named knight was beloved by Gerda, and when he had conquered all in the list save Kurt of Ehrenfels her hopes rose high. But Kurt, who on account of his riches was her father's favorite, was more skillful than they all, and was declared the winner of the prize. The wedding day was then appointed, and though Gerda attempted to move her father by prayers and tears, he would not listen to her. The fatal day having come, she was decked in her bridal attire, than which nothing could have been more magnificent. But when all was ready, Gerda knelt before the Virgin in the castle chapel and begged earnestly of Our Lady to provide some way of escape for her. Kurt was so impatient of waiting that he even interrupted her devotions to ask that she should hasten to join the marriage procession. She arose from her prayers with a feeling of confidence and requested the knight that her white palfrey, which was a gift from Kuno of Reichenstein, might be saddled for her to ride to the church. It was done, and the long and brilliant cortége at length began to move. Kuno sat in a tower of his fortress, watching all this with breaking heart. The procession had nearly reached the Clemenskirche, when, look, the horse of Gerda becomes unmanageable; it breaks away from those who hold it and dashes with lightning speed toward Reichenstein! Scarcely had Kuno time to lower the draw, when she had reached it, and was soon in the court and in his arms. He then barred all entrance and refused to open to her pursuers. But Heaven freed them from their troubles, for Kurt, maddened at seeing Gerda fleeing to Kuno, was so rash in his pursuit that he fell and broke his neck. Siegfried now gladly consented to the union which was so plainly according to the will of God and the Blessed Virgin. Kuno, too, was the heir of Kurt, and his great wealth was after all united to that of Gerda.

Clemenskirche. There is an interesting legend connected with the foundation of this church. The beautiful Ina was an orphan of great wealth who lived in the Sauerthal. The knight who then inhabited Rheinstein was a brave, resolute fellow, and little given to love-making. He was resolved to have Ina for his bride, and as she had refused his offer, he marched to her home with his men, determined to seize her forcibly. They succeeded in taking the castle, and carried the maiden to a boat which waited for them on the Rhine. A furious thunder-storm now came on, and in spite of all their efforts they were driven on the rocks. At this time Ina recovered her senses, and kneeling down to pray, she vowed to build a church to St. Clement, if he would save her from death and the robbers. Just at this moment there was a crash, and she closed her eyes, to avoid the sight of the drowning men and the fearful waves. Soon she felt herself borne through the air, and when she opened her eyes they rested on such a blaze of light as she had never seen.

When she became accustomed to it, she found herself in the arms of the saint, who bore her safely to the shore, and gently laid her on the bank. The knight and his men had all perished. She hastened to fulfill her vow and built the church, and when it was done she stood before its altar, the happy bride of the knight she loved.

Rhense. Toward the end of the fourteenth century the Bohemian emperor Wenzel ascended the imperial throne of Germany. His temperament did not fit him for the cares of royalty; he much preferred to pass his time with agreeable friends at the Königstuhl, drinking Rhine wine and listening to jest and song. The Count Palatine, Rupert III., had long coveted the imperial crown, and lost no opportunity of showing Wenzel all the troubles and cares of the empire, and exaggerated them, hoping that he would cede his crown to him. One evening as they sat together with other jovial companions drinking their delicious Assmannshausen wine, Wenzel thus addressed Rupert: "You have long aspired to my crown; give us now a wine which we shall find more delicious than this, and it shall be yours." Rupert gave his orders, and a barrel was soon rolled in from which their cups were filled. He begged them to give their opinion freely, saying that it was Bacharach wine. The company declared it superior to Assmannshausen, and they sat later than usual at the Königstuhl, and drank deeply of this delicious wine. Wenzel kept his word, and the crown was ceded to Rupert, who sent his accommodating predecessor four wagon-loads of Bacharach wine. Thus runs the popular legend, but history declares that the Rhenish Electors, on the 20th of August 1400, deprived Wenzel of the crown at a little chapel which is seen at the south gate of Oberlahnstein, and crossed next day to the Königstuhl and elected Rupert in his stead, and that the town of Nürnberg obtained its freedom by a yearly tribute to Wenzel of four tùns of Bacharach wine.

Rocks, The. See Baden-Baden.

Rolandseck. The beautiful legend connected with this castle is believed to have suggested the "Ritter Toggenburg" to Schiller. The young knight Roland, the supposed nephew of Charlemagne and peer of France, had won great renown by his valorous deeds. Riding one day on the banks of the Rhine, he came to the Castle of Drachenfels, where Count Heribert, the lord of the Siebengebirge, resided. When he announced his name Roland was received with great honor, and the count introduced him to his daughter Hildegunde, who according to the custom of welcome, offered him bread, wine, and fish. The heart of Roland, until now unmoved by beauty or wit, was immediately surrendered to Hildegunde, and soon they were betrothed: but their happiness was interrupted by a summons from Charlemagne, desiring Roland to join the Crusade. Time passed, and news came of the fierce battle of Roncesvalles, and also that Roland had fallen by the hand of the Infidels. Hildegunde was inconsolable, and begged her father to allow her to enter the cloister at Nonnenwerth, which was an island within view of his castle. He consented, and each morning the count and his wife looked down to the convent, from which Hildegunde waved her hand to them as she passed on to the chapel. Now the rumor of the death of Roland was untrue; he had indeed been severely wounded, but recovered, and one day presented himself at Drachenburg to claim his lovely Hildegunde. His sorrow when the truth was told was uncontrollable. In despair he built the Castle of Rolandseck that he might be near her and sometimes see her loved form as she passed to the chapel. One morning he missed her from among the nuns, and the tolling of the Kloster bell told him only too plainly that for her suffering was ended. From that day Roland never spoke again. He sat much of the time with his eyes fixed on the convent, and thus was he found dead. Only a single arch of the castle is to be seen, but the mountain on which it was built is still called Rolandseck.

Rüdesheim. *The Maiden Gisela.* When Bernard of Clairvaux preached the crusade on the Rhine, the knight Brömser of Rüdesheim determined to go to fight for the recovery of the Holy Sepulchre. He was a widower with an only child, the maiden Gisela. She bade her father farewell with much sorrow. Knight Brömser won great renown by his bravery. He killed a terrible dragon who lived near the source of the spring which supplied the army with water, and poisoned it, so that the soldiers suffered much. But so dreadful was the monster that none save the valiant Brömser dared attack him. As he returned to the camp he was seized by the Saracens and made prisoner. He was given to an emir and kept a captive for many years. He earnestly longed for freedom, and made a vow that if he could but return to his home, he would build a convent, and Gisela should be the first to enter it. At last deliverance came, and Gisela welcomed her father with rapture; but when he told her of his vow, her distress was most pitiable. She told him that during his absence she had been betrothed, and begged him not to insist upon the fulfillment of his vow at the expense of hers. But he was inexorable, and the grief of Gisela soon deprived her of reason. One dark and stormy night, she threw herself into the Rhine, and was lost to father, lover, and convent. According to tradition she still hovers about the ruined tower of her home. Knight Brömser built the convent, and tried by every means in his power to divert his mind, but his whole life was wretched. One day his husbandmen, when ploughing, turned up in the furrow an image of the Virgin, which cried out for help. The knight regarded this as a sign from heaven, and built a chapel where it was found, and placed the Virgin in it. It was soon said to work miracles, and pilgrims flocked to the chapel. The knight called the church "Noth Gottes" (God's need), and he died soon after its completion.

Schönberg. See Oberwesel.

Schwanau. In the fourteenth century, the affairs of Germany were at a strange pass. The robber knights who inhabited feudal castles were able to pounce upon merchants and travellers and do them great injury. And so powerful were they that the towns were obliged to make confederations, in order to defend themselves against single knights. In these days Walter of Schwanau had a feud with the citizens of Strasbourg. He intended to attack the town, and felt sure of a safe retreat in his castle should not all go well. But on this occasion the citizens determined to make the attack themselves, which was contrary to their usual custom; and without ever dreaming of such a thing, Knight Walter found himself besieged. At last when his provisions failed he sent messengers to the enemy, but as he had at first received their propositions with scorn and contempt, so now they thought fit to refuse to listen to his proposals. Then was he in despair. At this juncture, his lovely wife insisted that he should tell her all the causes of the grief which she saw so plainly written on his face. At first he refused to do so, but at length yielded to her entreaties. Then she declared that she would go to the camp of the besiegers. The commandant could not refuse to see a woman. Her husband strongly opposed this, but she assured him that she would preserve his honor unimpeached; and at length he consented. She then took her little son, and having prayed to the Blessed Virgin, she went to the camp. She was taken to the commander, and he could not long remain insensible to the eloquent words which she spoke. At length they agreed that the castle should be given up, and she should pass out with all her treasures, free to go where she willed. "Then," replied the noble wife, "take the castle. My husband is saved, for he and my child are my first and greatest treasures. All else I willingly leave to you. I know that my husband has incurred the displeasure of the citizens of Strasbourg, and they desire to possess him in order to punish him; but since he is to go free by your promise, you will not revenge yourselves on his soldiers who have but obeyed his will." The commander turned away to hide his tears. But he kept his word. The wife went forth with her husband and child as well as their other treasures, and most of the soldiers joined the forces of the confederate towns, but the castle was destroyed.

Seckenheim. *Frederick the Victorious.* When the Elector Louis IV. died, his son, not one year old, was left the heir to the Palatinate. A powerful regent was necessary, for the affairs of the government were much disturbed by the lawlessness of the robber knights who attacked all who passed their castles, taking their money and making them prisoners. The choice fell upon Frederick, the uncle of the little prince. This choice was not pleasing to the emperor, and Frederick had other enemies, who from jealousy and other motives made an alliance against him. At length a decisive battle took place near Seckenheim, where the regent was victorious and took many prisoners, among whom were the Bishop of Metz and the Earl of Würtemburg, with many other nobles. Frederick made a triumphant entrance into Heidelberg with his prisoners and his victorious army, but he treated the former with kindness and consideration, and that same evening invited them to a grand banquet. The entertainment was magnificent, but there was no bread. The Earl of Würtemburg asked a servant for it, but the Elector Frederick took him by the hand and led him to a window, saying, "The warriors who devastate the fields, stamp down the seeds, and burn the mills, should not ask for bread. It does not belong to them." Frederick then resumed the lively conversation which had been interrupted; but his lesson had touched the heart of his prisoners. After a time a considerable ransom was paid, a bond was signed in which the prisoners agreed never again to invade the Electoral-Palatinate, and they went free.

Seebach. *The Spinning Undine.* One evening when the lasses of Seebach were all gathered in the spinning-room to twist the linen thread, and the lads were there to repeat jokes and tell stories, and all were as merry as one could wish, a beautiful young lady entered, bearing an ivory spinning-wheel. She asked to be allowed to join their society. They received her very kindly, gave her the best seat, and enlarged the circle to take her in. At first they were a little embarrassed by her presence, but soon they resumed all their former merriment. From the moment of her entrance the son of the house was fascinated, and his eyes were riveted upon her. When she had departed and all the others were filled with speculations concerning her, he said not a word. From this night she came every evening for a long time. She always went away at a certain hour, and nothing could induce her to remain a moment later. The son of the house was sad when she left, and joyous when she appeared, and one could tell that he loved her. She had a perceptible influence too, on all. The maidens were neater and more tasteful in their dress, and their work was better, while the lads were softened and more gentlemanly in their deportment, and all had come to love her gentle face and manner. One night the lover determined to change the hands of the clock, that he might have the joy of gazing on her for another hour. When she rose to go he followed her. She went hastily to the Mummelsee, and threw herself into the waters. Then a complaining, mournful sound was heard, and the waters foamed and boiled angrily. At this the lover also rushed into the lake and disappeared. Next day his corpse was found, and the spinning undine came no more.

Solingen. The art of blade-making had not reached its perfection in Solingen in the tenth century. Among its blade-makers was one, Ruthard, who had all his life greatly desired to discover a process by which he could equal the blades of Damascus. He had spent much time and in fact much money in fruitless experiments. One Christmas eve he returned to his home more discouraged than ever before, for a trial on which he had greatly depended had failed like all the rest. His daughter Martha upbraided him for thus working and wearying himself, and, quite unsuspicious of the waste of his money, declared that he should give up labor altogether and that it was wicked to work on this holy eve. But she could not rally him, neither did he eat the supper she had served to please his taste, and went out gloomy and sad. She sighed, and reflected that in this humor he would not smile on the wooing of young William, his chief workman, who was about to ask him for her hand. Soon after the lover came to her, pale and sad. He told how her father had made it a condition of their marriage that he should go to Damascus and learn the secret he so wished to know. He had shown him a blade with which he had easily and smoothly cut off a nail from the wall, and declared that no one should be his son-in-law who could not make a blade like that. This caused Martha deep grief; but William was determined to try all in the hope of gaining the reward. So the next morning he departed. The tenth day of his journey he was in a solitary mountain as night approached, and just as he despaired of finding a lodging he saw a hut, in which was a frightful old crone. He begged a lodging and she promised him one, adding that she expected another visitor. She was extremely ugly, her eyes squinted and were red, while her voice was almost a shriek. As she was preparing his supper William told her the object of his journey. After he was in bed he could not sleep, and about midnight he heard such strange sounds that he arose and peeped out to see the cause of them. A man was sitting with the old woman by the hearth and over the fire was a pot in which something was boiling and seething, while from it rose at times a blue flame. The man was no more agreeable in his personnel than the woman, and his feet were concealed in the ashes. Suddenly the old woman started towards William, and he had scarcely time to get to his bed, when she screamed to him to get up and see a man from the far Orient who could tell him all he wished to know. The strange appearance of the man and woman, the flame-colored mantle which he wore, and the manner in which he peered at William, filled him with fear and he trembled as he stood before him. "I know what you seek," said the man — "and can help you. But I do nothing without pay. If you receive the knowledge which you desire from me I will give you seven years and seven days. Then you will belong to me. If you agree, well and good. If not, you shall never return to your Martha." William was too frightened to think and too anxious to see Martha to refuse, so he signed a contract with a pen dipped in the contents of the kettle, and having received a letter from the man he went again to bed. In the morning the old woman had disappeared as well as the man. William returned home and told his master all his experience. After thinking much upon the matter, he advised William that he should not open the letter, but lay it carefully away. He consented that he should marry Martha, and if a son should be born to them he could open the letter, for over him the Devil could have no power. Then were William and Martha happy, and as he was honest and industrious he mended the fortunes of the family, and all went well. Many years after, when Ruthard and William were both in their graves, the letter was opened by their descendant, and the blades made by its direction were equal to the Damascus blades, and from that time those of Solingen have been excellent and world-renowned.

Speyer. The Cathedral was founded in 1030 by Conrad II., as a burial-place for himself and his successors, and here many royal personages have been buried. The following legend relating to the death and burial of Henry IV. is not without interest. The poor monarch had died while under the sentence of excommunication from the pope. His unnatural son, Henry V., had treated him most wickedly, and even obliged him to live in exile, and he died at last in poverty and wretchedness. Five years elapsed before this son requested the pope to remove the ban, so that his father might receive Christian burial. All this time the faithful servant of the old emperor had stayed by the body of his master, and devoted much of his time to praying for his soul. It would be impossible to tell his joy when at length his beloved lord was interred with all the honors and ceremonies which attend the burial of crowned heads. Kurt did not long survive these solemnities, and when he died all the bells of Speyer were tolled by unseen hands, as if an imperial burial were taking place. Henry V. lived to sadly repent his cruelty to his father, and died a horrible death in Speyer, at which time, one bell, and that the sharp, clear bell of the poor sinner, was miraculously rung. Those in the street who heard it asked each other what criminal was to be executed that day, and when the truth was known horror filled every breast, and many prayers were offered for the repose of this wicked son.

Staufenberg in Ortenau. In the fine old times, when fairies lived in dells and streams, dressed Cinderellas for balls, and helped Aladdins to live in style, the Rhine was not without some most bewitching specimens of this order of beings. But charming as they were when pleased, their revenge was dreadful when reason was given for its exercise, and this was strikingly illustrated in the case of the young Count of Staufenberg. He was a very Apollo. So much so that the fame of his beauty preceded him wherever he went. He was devoted to the pleasures of the chase, and rode often to the banks of the Rhine in pursuit of game. One day while there he fell asleep, and when he awoke a lovely maiden sat near and saluted him in the most friendly manner. When he asked her of her home, she said she was a nymph and lived in the rocky bed of the river. The count was thoroughly bewitched by her, and did not say farewell until he had a promise from her to meet him next day at the same time and place. And now he renounced the chase and all his former pleasures, and spent his spare hours with the enchantress. The fairy demanded and received an oath of true and eternal love, which he willingly gave; and she often told him, that were it broken nothing would remain to her but endless sorrow, for nymphs could love but once. She also said that were he false he could never rid himself of her plaintive cry, for it would be heard through all his castle or wherever he might be, and that although she should be invisible he would some time see her foot, and that would be a sign that he could live but three days longer. The count paid little heed to all this, for he was at that stage of love when lovers are sure they shall be ever true, and are ready *so to swear* by all on earth or in heaven, fairy-land not excepted. And this love was an advantage to him, for whatever he undertook was successful through the magic art of his fairy sweetheart. Did he leave her for the chase, his arrow never missed the mark, did he ride in the lists, he was ever the victor, and in serious battle his lance or sword was always sure, while his life seemed to be a charmed one. His fame was widely sounded, and numberless damsels had set their hearts on him, and him alone. But this moved him not; he was always anxious to return to his loved nymph, ever so sweet, so pure, so fresh, with all the refinement, and none of the airs of the high-born maidens who so loved him. But at length the only daughter of the emperor desired to marry him, and her father, well pleased, made the count acquainted with her wish. The young man appreciated the honor thus offered him, and assured the emperor of his earnest desire to accept it, but at the same time told him of his vows to the maid of the Rhine. The emperor assured him that a promise to such a being was not binding, and added that the bishop could release him from any vows he had made. Thus persuaded, the count consented to the union, and the marriage was soon celebrated with great festivity. As they sat at the wedding-feast, the count most happy in gazing at his loving young bride, and the guests proposing the health of the newly wedded, suddenly, from the wall opposite the festive board, an extremely beautiful female foot protruded, visible nearly to the knee, and at the same time a heart-rending wail sounded in all the air. Then the count cried, "Woe is me!" and declared that in three days he must die. He became mad, and rushed into the forest, where he could not be found until after three days, when his lifeless body was borne to his virgin bride. She retired to a cloister, where she passed her life in inconsolable grief.

Stavoren. Six centuries ago, according to tradition, Stavoren was the first commercial city of Holland. High life and magnificence prevailed there, and among those who attempted to excel in splendor none exceeded the Virgin Richberta. Her wealth was enormous. Her ships ploughed all seas, and brought home, not only merchandise, but the rarest articles for her house, as well as rich clothing, jewels, and ornaments for her person. She was vain of her wealth, and especially so of the rich feasts she gave. On one of these occasions a strange guest was announced to Richberta. He sent her a message that he had been in all countries, had seen the splendor of many courts, and had come to admire that of Richberta, of which he had heard much. The lady was flattered, and commanded that he should be seated beside her. He was an old man in oriental costume, who advanced toward Richberta with ease and elegance. He expected her to offer him the welcome of bread and salt, but while hundreds of expensive dishes loaded the table, there was no bread. He conversed agreeably, and told many interesting stories of what he had seen and heard in all the world. Richberta listened for a word of praise of her and her feast, but she heard none. At last her impatience overcame her wisdom, and she asked what impression it had made on him. He declared that only in the halls of kings had he seen such splendor, but added that he had been surprised to find the best thing in the world wanting. Then all desired that he should explain himself, but he would not. This rendered Richberta miserable, and she could not imagine what the precious thing could be which she had not. She sent ships to every clime, but could hear of nothing that satisfied her. Now it happened that the vessel in which the commander of her fleet had sailed, made a leak, and the flour was spoiled. There was enough of meat and wine, but no bread, and the want of it was so dreadful that he decided that bread was the best and most indispensable of all things on earth. So he steered to a Baltic town and took a cargo of the finest wheat, with which he returned to Stavoren. He told Richberta of his decision, and that the missing bread must have been that to which the stranger had referred. But Richberta was in a rage, and demanded on which side of the vessel the cargo had been received, and commanded that it should all be thrown overboard from the opposite side. In vain the commander expostulated with her; she only repeated her orders, and although crowds of the needy flocked to her she would not allow them to receive an ounce of the grain; and it was thrown into the sea amidst their curses. But soon the grain germinated, and a forest of stalks shot up and formed a sort of net-work to which the sand and dirt could cling, and soon an impenetrable bar was formed before the harbor of Stavoren, and all vessels that made the attempt to enter were lost. Richberta was reduced to poverty. Moreover, a passage through which the sea had been accustomed to flow was closed up, and at last in a tempest it broke through the dykes and flooded the city, and all was lost. Where Stavoren stood the Zuydersee now tosses its many waves, and when the water is clear those who sail behold with horror the towers and palaces of the once flourishing city.

Sterrenberg. See Liebenstein.

St. Goar and **St. Goarhausen.** These towns, though on opposite sides of the Rhine, are both named for the holy St. Goar, who came here about the middle of the sixth century. He built a hut below the Lurlei, where the river, forced into a narrow channel, rushes on with noisy speed. Just above is the ledge of rocks called the "Bank." In those early days many fishermen were attracted to this spot by the great numbers of salmon abounding there. St. Goar devoted himself to the work of a missionary among this people, and especially cared for those who were shipwrecked in the "Gewirre" or whirlpool. The fishermen thus came to regard him as a messenger from God, and loved him accordingly. The attention of King Siegbert was drawn to St. Goar by his enemies, but when he watched his life he so much admired his piety and good living that he appointed him Bishop of Trier. But this, and all other preferments, St. Goar refused, and died where he had lived. The king commanded a chapel to be built over his cell and tomb, which became a place of pilgrimage, and was in the end enlarged into a convent, the monks of which devoted themselves to hospitality and charitable labors, as St. Goar had done. Robbers plundered and burned this, but the Count of Arnheim rebuilt it and inclosed it with walls, and gradually the town of St. Goar was built around it. So many offerings were made at this tomb that it became very splendid, and it was believed that misfortune would follow those who passed it without a visit. On one occasion Charlemagne did this and was enveloped in a thick fog which did not clear until he had retraced his steps and prayed in the chapel. His sons when at variance met there accidentally and became reconciled, and his wife Fastrada was there healed of a severe illness. In consideration of all these benefits, Charlemagne built a court and a new church for the monks of St. Goar.

Stolzenfels. This castle was much improved if not founded by Arnold von Isenburg, Archbishop of Treves, in the middle of the thirteenth century. Its highest point is four hundred and ten feet above the river. Many years ago the treasurer of Archbishop Werner of Falkenstein resided here with his daughter Elsbeth, a maiden both beautiful and good. Her father was infatuated with the pursuits of alchemy, astrology, and kindred subjects. One night a pilgrim begged the hospitalities of the castle, and was admitted. Before long he declared himself learned in alchemy, and immediately the treasurer was fascinated with the idea that possibly this man could teach him something of the black art, which he did not know. He fitted a room in one of the unoccupied towers, with everything needful for their use, and in this the two often passed their nights as well as days. Elsbeth watched her father grow troubled and nervous until at last he no longer noticed her or her endearments. One day a messenger announced the approach of the archbishop. Then was the treasurer most wretched; he was as one mad, and walked the castle weeping. Elsbeth had watched him sorrowfully, and was about to approach him to endeavor to comfort him, when he rushed to the apartment of the alchemist. She followed to the door and listened to see if she could ascertain the true cause of his grief. He upbraided the pilgrim with having deceived him, and caused him to spend not only his own gold, but that of the archbishop. The other replied in measured tones that if he would comply with his request and bring him a virgin who had never loved any man he could have gold to his heart's content. The treasurer declared in one breath that he would not add murder to his sins, and with the next, that he must have gold if he suffered eternal torments for it. Then he rushed away. Elsbeth now approached the pilgrim, and said that having heard all she was ready to sacrifice herself for her father. He at first regarded her with all his wickedness depicted on his face, then remembering himself he changed to a tender manner, and would have taken her hand. She repulsed him, shuddering, and declared that she could plunge a dagger to her heart, but she would not suffer the profanation of his touch. Then he told her to return at midnight and all should be prepared, and added that at sunrise her father should possess all he desired. The maiden demanded if he could swear this. Instantly he took a cross from his bosom and solemnly swore that if she obeyed him, her father should be rich and honored. "I shall come," said Elsbeth, and withdrew. Then the monk gloated over his wickedness; he laughed at the cross, saying it had done him much good, and touched a spring which sent a dagger out of it. He proceeded to make fast the doors, and to raise a stone from the floor where he had concealed the gold the treasurer believed to have been lost in the crucible. He fastened the bag containing it beneath his gown and waited for the night. Meanwhile the bishop and his train had arrived, and all was confusion about the castle. Elsbeth, pale and sad, directed the servants, till the bishop desired to see her. He told her how pretty she had grown, and presented her to his knights, warning them jestingly that all must not fall in love with her, while she, blushing, could not raise her eyes. Among the knights was one of the family of Westerburg, whose heart was given to Elsbeth even while the bishop spoke, and he could think of nothing save the maiden, and wonder whether fortune would favor their better acquaintance. So wakeful was he with these thoughts that he made no attempt to sleep. Looking from his window at midnight, he saw Elsbeth cross the court to the most remote part of the castle. Impelled as by an irresistible power, he followed her, and arriving at the place where she disappeared he looked into the apartment of the alchemist. He saw the maiden on her knees and the monk bent over a crucible. He turned to her saying, "Are you resolved to do all as I shall bid you?" The knight could not hear her low reply, but the pilgrim said, "Then will your father be happy and able to restore the gold he has taken from the archbishop. The sacred book of science declares, blood for blood; honor for honor. By the sacrifice of the latter you can make your father honorable among knights, and with the former you can obtain gold to rescue him from infamy! Prepare then for the sacrifice!" Thus speaking, he approached as if to embrace her. Elsbeth drew herself proudly back, and said, "Away, wretch! I came to shed my blood for my father, but I will not suffer insult even for him!" She seized a dagger and would have plunged it to her heart, but the knight burst in and snatched the fatal weapon. The maiden fainted, and the monk was for a moment stupefied; then while the knight restored Elsbeth he hastened to escape. The maiden woke as from a frightful dream in sobs and tears. The knight endeavored to console her, and at length she confided all to him. Then he assured that he would supply the gold for her father, and all should yet be well. "Rejoice," added he, "as I do, that this has occurred, for by it have I not found a treasure more precious than that which the alchemist seeks?" Their eyes met, and through them heart spoke to heart as they sealed their betrothal with a kiss. Next day the knight sought the treasurer, to confess his love for Elsbeth and to offer the gold he so much needed. But the necessity was supplied in another way, for the body of the pilgrim was found in the Rhine, and on it all the gold that the treasurer had lost. The marriage of Elsbeth and the knight was soon celebrated. Her father gave her a large dowry, and never forgot the love and courage she had shown by resolving to sacrifice her life for him.

Strasbourg. There lived in Strasbourg, many years ago, a mechanic who had gained great celebrity by the finish and delicacy of his works. He was a widower with an only child. She managed the affairs of the house and all was happiness. But the mind of the father was ever occupied with the desire and endeavor to produce some work more perfect than any he had yet done. He secluded himself and gave little attention to business. His friends expostulated in vain, and finally left him to what they called his folly. But two persons out of all his acquaintances continued to visit him. One of these was an old man, rich and disagreeable, who after years of maneuvering had obtained the appointment to a magistracy. The other, a young and worthy mechanic, who came often to converse with the learned master upon topics connected with his art. He also loved to watch the daughter as she performed her various duties, and often tarried by her side, much longer than by that of the abstracted father. At length the rich old man, in all the satisfaction and pride of his new office, came to demand the hand of the daughter in marriage. The father was overcome with surprise, and the daughter by distress, for she well understood the revengeful disposition of her suitor, and feared he would not easily forgive her refusal. This proved to be so, for he left them with threats of vengeance. In the midst of all this excitement the young mechanic came, and inquired the cause of her distress, and when he heard her declare how hateful the thought of such a marriage was to her, his heart was full of joy, and he was bold enough to ask her, if since she scorned the wealth of the magistrate, she could accept his poverty and devotion. Her answer was all he could desire; but she begged him to wait a time before speaking to her father on this subject, as he had not recovered from the surprise and unpleasantness of the late event. But the young man, now sure of the maiden's love, dared asked the father to make him a partner in his business, which he readily consented to do. Thus the lovers were more together and all their affairs were more prosperous than formerly, for the young man looked out for the interest of the old one, while he dreamed over his schemes. Together the young people made the father very happy. One day they were startled by shouts of joy from the apartment of the father, and when they reached him found him standing before a clock which although altogether new and surprising in its construction, moved lightly and easily and with wonderful exactness. The excitement of the master was intense. He pressed his daughter to his bosom, while the young man held his hand in silent admiration and respect. When the work was shown to the public, there was no more ridicule of the master and all ideas of his madness were dispelled. The rejected lover now saw an opportunity to revenge himself, and was able for a long time to prevent the mayor of the city from approving the work. But the fame of the clock went abroad, and commissioners were sent from Basel to examine it. Then the mayor was forced to approve the clock, and when those from Basel desired to buy it, the corporation of Strasbourg bought it and agreed to place it in a chapel in the cathedral. The city of Basel then ordered another to be made for them, but this greatly excited those of Strasbourg, for they were unwilling that any any other city should have such a clock. The discarded lover was loud in his declarations that it would be treason in the master to make another. The latter was called before the authorities and a promise that he would not make a second clock required of him. He replied that God had given him his talents for use, that when he studied and labored for years they turned from him sneeringly, and derided his work when done, that only when those of Basel came to admire, did they approve; that he had been loyal in that he had given the first to his native city, but he would promise nothing which could hamper his future labors. He retired from the tribunal, and they then determined (being led on by the offended magistrate) to destroy the sight of the master in order to gain their end. Cruel as was this decision he received it without a word, and when asked if he desired anything before the execution of the sentence, he answered that he wished to suffer before his work, and asked that he might be allowed to give it some final touches. These requests were granted, and he gazed long at his darling clock; even in this sad moment his persecutor reminded him that others waited, and the old man, after busying himself a moment with the works, declared that all was finished. The dreadful deed was done, but while he writhed in agony there came a strange buzz from the clock, and lo, the weights fell to the ground and it was destroyed. He had removed the principal spring, and his revenge was complete. Then the lovers led him away and being married devoted their lives to the master, while the wicked magistrate was given up to scorn and contempt and expelled from society. Thus the clock remained until 1842, when parts of it were used in the new one constructed by Schwilgué; and the old master shares the honors with the new and more fortunate one of later days.

Taunus. When Rudolph of Hapsburg was emperor he published a decree that any robber knight taken with arms in his hands should be executed, and his accomplices also. At this time there lived in the Taunus, at the Castle of Falkenstein, a knight named Kurt, who had seven sons, and their depredations were so numerous and bold that great complaints were made to the emperor at Worms. He took with him a large force and proceeded to invest Falkenstein. The knight and his sons fought bravely, but were taken by a storm attack. Then the emperor's edict must be obeyed. A circle of soldiers was formed on the platform of the castle, and Kurt and his seven sons were led out for execution. So sad a spectacle moved even the heart of the emperor, but he could not violate the law. Much sympathy was felt for the sons from the fact that they had obeyed their father and been led on by him. The emperor then said (in order to give them a chance, however slight), that liberty should be given to the son toward whom the father should advance after execution. A light beamed on the face of Kurt as he bowed his head to the sword, and, mirabile dictu! as soon as the head rolled on the ground the form advanced to the eldest, the next, the third, and sc on until it fell at the feet of the youngest. A strange sensatior o mingled horror and amazement filled the hearts of all who beheld this wonderful sight. The emperor gave the seven young men places in his army, in order that they might prove their loyalty and efface the disgrace which had heretofore attended them.

Thann in Alsace. *The Lyingfield.* This is a barren waste on which no vegetation flourishes, avoided by all, and literally a field of death, upon which lie the bones of those who there fell. One night a wanderer who had lost his way, entered on this plain. When the hour of midnight sounded, he heard a strange subterranean noise and a rattle of swords, with other sounds like those of a battle. An armed knight came to him, and sternly demanded what he sought in this accursed place. When the wanderer declared himself a stranger, the knight told him that many years before Louis the Pious had there arranged his soldiers to fight an enemy. His sons who were with him persuaded his troops to abandon him and leave him to his antagonists. When the old monarch realized his betrayal he raised his hands to heaven and called down curses on his sons, his soldiers, and the field which had witnessed their treachery. From that time the plain had been deserted and the perjured men who fell there could obtain no repose, but were ever forced to fight each other again and again. When the story was ended the earth opened and the knight disappeared. Then the wanderer hastened in great terror to leave the place and when he at last reached Thann recounted his experience on the Lyingfield.

The Mortar that was mixed with Wine. There is a tower in Thann which is said to have been built in a season when there was a scarcity of water, but such a supply of wine that casks and vessels enough to hold it could not be found. So the mortar was mixed with wine, which gave it a delicious fragrance. It is said that it was of an extraordinary solidity, and that to this day, when the vines are in blossom the walls sometimes exude a pleasant substance; and some go so far as to say that at such times the sound of the bells is more musical than usual. This legend affords a more pleasing association with Thann than that of the Lyingfield.

Treuenfels. Upon this height, which rises above one of the valleys of the Siebengebirge, is an altar upon which the name of Liba may still be read, it having formed a part of the inscription, for the altar was built to commemorate the devotion of the maiden Liba to her father, Knight Balther, who inhabited a castle not far distant from Treuenfels. He lived in the days of Engelbert I. when that bishop attempted to stop the depredations of the robber knights. Liba was his only child, and betrothed to the young Schott of Grünstein. Now Balther was not a robber, but he felt that the laws of the archbishop were oppressive and an insult to the independence of knights. One evening when entertaining a large party, these subjects were discussed, and Balther declared that were he young he would not submit to these insults, and taunted those about him with want of courage and independence. They all sat for a time in silence, when one arose and said that Balther was right, and challenged those who would prove their claim to knighthood to fill their goblets and drink to an alliance against the tyrant. They were inflamed with wine and passion, and all drank to the success of their undertaking. Not long after, these knights waylaid and murdered the bishop. This roused the indignation of all the land, and the emperor ordered the arrest of the assassins. All evidence tended to make Balther their leader, and the command was given to burn his castle and make him prisoner. The castle was on fire before any alarm of the approach of the troops had been given. Liba had barely time to arouse her father and lead him through a subterranean passage to a place of safety. They entered a thick forest and there lived. Balther grew rapidly blind, and their only subsistence was the berries and herbs which Liba gathered. One day in their wanderings they came to a cave, where she made moss couches, and henceforth remained. Often Balther told how earnestly he repented his crime, and begged Liba to forgive the deed which had resulted so unhappily. One day they were sitting upon the rock and the old man took her head in his hands as was his custom, kissing her and smoothing her hair, when Liba saw a tall young hunter behind some bushes near by. She would have suddenly called out "Schott!" — but she feared the effect on her father, and she knew not if he would still care for the child of a criminal and outlaw. The tears gathered in her eyes, and raising her hands to heaven she prayed: "O God, forgive our sins we pray Thee, and let our punishment be ended." "Amen," responded the old man, and as they spoke a sharp flash of lightning came and the heavy thunder reverberated through the mountains. The good Father had heard their prayer, for when Schott went toward them both were dead. He buried them where he had found them and erected a chapel, the altar of which still remains, and the height was from that time named Treuenfels.

Trifels, Castle of. *Richard the Lion-hearted.* In the Haardt mountains in the Bavarian-Rhenish Palatinate rises the mountain on which stands Castle Trifels. The views from this and the neighboring heights are the finest in all the Palatinate. It takes in the borders of the Rhine from Strasbourg to the Odenwald with the Black Forest also in the distance, while the towers of Worms, Mannheim, Speyer, Carlsruhe, and Strasbourg are all to be seen with the eye alone, and near at hand are the grotesque and many colored peaks of the Vosges. But this is not the place even if we had the power to picture these beauties. This castle was formerly a prison, a fortress and royal residence, and a treasury of the royal jewels and insignia. About Easter time in 1193, Richard Cœur de Lion was sent to Trifels by Henry VI., who had received him a prisoner from Leopold of Austria. He was here more than a year, during which time his faithful Blondel with some English knights had travelled far and near to discover the prison of the king. At length they came to Trifels, and when Blondel in the rôle of a minstrel sang a song which Richard had composed, the king answered him by singing another strain. Blondel introduced himself into the castle under some pretext, and won the affections of the daughter of the jailer.

At length they together contrived a plan by which, with the coöperation of the other knights who remained at hand outside the castle, they liberated the king, and all reached England in safety. There Blondel married the beautiful Mathilda, and was largely rewarded, with the other knights, for the services they had rendered the brave Richard Cœur de Lion.

Wildsee. See Baden-Baden.

Windeck, Castle of. See Baden-Baden.

Worms. *Siegfried.* After the adventures of Siegfried in the Nibelungenlande he determined to go to Worms to see Chrimhilde the sister of King Gunther. He took with him twelve well-chosen and brave knights. When he was come to Worms, the king, who had heard of his prowess, received him surrounded by his court. Siegfried was amazed at the immense size of those he saw here and especially that of the brothers of the king, and Ute, his mother. Siegfried here passed a year in tournaments and feasts, but never saw Chrimhilde as he so much wished. At length messengers arrived from the Saxons and Danes to declare war against Gunther. Siegfried immediately undertook to assist the Burgundians and promised to go forth with his twelve knights. He persuaded Gunther to remain at home. Siegfried fought with the two northern kings, and conquered the first while the second surrendered to him. They with much booty were sent to Worms, and Siegfried was received there with the highest honors. He then saw Chrimhilde, and from that day they were much together. About this time the report reached Gunther of the beauty and prowess of Brunhilde, queen of Iceland, who would marry any one who could conquer her in wrestling, and many had fallen in the attempt. Gunther was resolved to go to see her, and Siegfried promised to go with him and that he should succeed if he would give Chrimhilde to him on their return. To this Gunther assented, and with two other knights they set out for Isenstein the capital of queen Brunhilde. She received them with great ceremony and respect, and soon all was arranged for Gunther's trial. His courage would have failed him after seeing the great strength of the queen, but Siegfried encouraged him with hopes and promises of success. When the day came, Siegfried put on his Tarnkappe, which he had taken in the Nibelungenlande, and which made its wearer invisible, and stood beside Gunther. He whispered to him that he was there to aid him, and thus inspired him with confidence, and in every trial of skill or strength Gunther was by the help of Siegfried victorious. When all was over, Gunther claimed the hand of Brunhilde, but she answered him evasively, saying, "This cannot happen without the consent of my generals and princes." Her answer did not please Gunther or Siegfried, and they feared the queen intended some treachery, so Siegfried took their ship and hastened away to Nibelungenlande, and requested assistance from the dwarf Alberich, and he gave him a thousand of the best fighting giants of the land, and ships to take them to Iceland. When Brunhilde saw them come she asked Gunther who they were, and he answered that they were his suite whom he had left on the way. Then she felt it was of no use to contend with such a force, and prepared to go to the Rhine. When the fleet reached the mouth of the river, Siegfried and some other knights hastened on to make preparations for the reception of Gunther and Brunhilde. All went well and they were affectionately welcomed by Dame Ute and Chrimhilde. Then the marriage was celebrated and at the wedding feast Siegfried claimed of Gunther the fulfillment of his promise that Chrimhilde should be his wife. The king turned to his sister for her consent and she gave it most heartily, and the two were united and lived happily. But with Gunther it was not so, for the truth was, that Brunhilde was in love with Siegfried rather than the king, and when they were come to the bridal chamber she refused him the reward of love, and when he would have insisted she bound him and hung him on the wall where she left him until morning. Then Gunther told this to Siegfried and he promised to assist him, so he again donned the Tarnkappe and went with Gunther to his chamber. There he threw Brunhilde down and tore off her magic girdle and a ring which gave her such great strength, and she believing herself to be overcome by her husband could make no farther resistance. Now shortly after all this Siegfried and his wife went to the Netherlands to the court of his father, where he was gladly received with feasts and festivals, and the hearts of his parents were glad. Here he remained two years, during which time Chrimhilde bore a son, his mother died, and his father transferred the kingdom to Siegfried. Then a messenger came from Brunhilde urging them to come to Worms. Now Brunhilde did this with evil intentions, because she had always been jealous of Siegfried and his power over the Nibelung nation. But the invitation was accepted, and Siegfried set out with his wife, his father, and a hundred knights. Arriving at Worms they were received with great splendor, and feast succeeded feast; but one day when in the open space now in front of the Cathedral at Worms the two queens had a fierce quarrel concerning the strength and bravery of their husbands. Each declared that their own excelled the other, and finally they waxed so warm that Chrimhilde declared that even in the bridal night Siegfried had assisted Gunther. Now her brother was grieved to find that Siegfried had not kept this a secret, but he was so thankful to him for all he had done that he could not think of resenting this. But Brunhilde determined to be revenged, and she enlisted the Knight Hagen and several others in her cause who were bent upon killing Siegfried. They knew that he had been rendered invulnerable with dragon's fat, but that like Achilles he had one spot remaining which was sensitive to injury: this was his shoulder. So they arranged a great hunt, and when all were thirsty they went to a spring, and as Siegfried stooped down to drink, Hagen pierced the shoulder with a spear and a great stream of blood gushed from the wound. Siegfried seized Hagen and threw him to the ground, but fell immediately himself, and only lived to recommend Chrimhilde to the care of Gunther, who with all the right-minded of his court greatly lamented this act of treachery. For other adventures of Siegfried see Xanten.

The Combat of Maximilian I. When this emperor called together all the knights of his dominion to consult concerning the measures to be employed to maintain peace and good order, a great tournament was announced, and knights of all nations were invited to contend for the prize. Immediately there came a Frenchman of great renown, Claude de Barre, and he hung his arms over the door of his lodgings, and sent out a herald to invite all to a combat for life or death. Time passed on and none dared accept the challenge, and Maximilian saw with sorrow that no one would vindicate the German against the French arms. When the time arrived and the challenger had become extremely vainglorious and disagreeable, the emperor himself hung the arms of Ostriech and Burgundy beside those of the Frenchman. The day arrived, and many thousands gathered to witness the combat. While mounted, both lances were broken, but neither combatant unhorsed. They then dismounted to contend hand to hand. At first de Barre seemed the best man, but suddenly Maximilian called up his strength and fire, and soon overcame the giant boaster. The emperor offered his hand to his humbled opponent, and invited him to a banquet that night, but de Barre thought it well to leave Worms that very evening.

The Captive Jews at Worms. The lord of Dalberg, whose castle was at Hernsheim, near Worms, and who belonged to one of the oldest and most noble families of the German empire, served with the Romans at the destruction of Jerusalem. He was a centurion, and received as his portion of the booty a number of Jewish prisoners, whom he took home with him to form a Jewish colony. Among them was an old man, almost blind, who was led by his daughter, whose beauty was beyond description. The old man was both learned and holy, and he, together with his daughter, cheered the other prisoners and encouraged them to trust in the power of Jehovah. As soon as Dalberg arrived there were many feasts and banquets to welcome him, and to give his friends an opportunity to hear of all he had seen. Among his friends was a distinguished Roman officer who belonged to a cohort stationed at Mayence. He no sooner saw the lovely Jewess than he determined to possess her. To this he knew he could not obtain the consent of Dalberg, so he resolved to run away with her. He prepared a refuge in the forest, and watched his opportunity. One day he seized her as she was drawing water, and leaping on his horse with her, carried her away. But when he reached his hiding-place he could not accomplish his base designs, and at last as he grew wild with passion and rage the maid fell on her knees praying God to protect her, and preserve her virtue. "To hell with your God!" shouted the Roman. "Mine you shall be though the heavens fall!" and he approached her with wicked determination. Then came a lightning flash, and a stone which killed the blaspheming wretch. The maiden was saved; but when she regarded the stone, she saw the features of Jehovah, and so dazzling was the sight that she became blind. Her father and Dalberg at length found her, and on the stone was the name of Jehovah in Hebrew, but the brightness was gone. When she told her story all regarded her with reverence. But neither she or her father long survived this sad event. When these poor Jews left their homes they brought with them sacks of earth, that they might be interred in their native soil, and these were the first who were thus buried. The stone which marked their graves, was later built into the synagogue at Worms, and in a part of the Jewish burial-ground is still shown a spot, said to be formed of the earth brought from Judæa.

The Coquettish Maiden of Wampolder Hof. This house, which is at present divided, belonged to the distinguished lord of Wampold, and was in charge of a castellan who was also a nobleman, but not rich. He had a coquettish daughter, who although fondly in love and solemnly betrothed to a young man whom her father approved, could never be done with teasing him. One Walpurgis night when a company of young people were assembled at Wampolder Hof, they told many stories of witches, and the maiden imposed on her betrothed the task of watching the witches' procession, and telling her of it afterwards. The youth laughed, and promised to do so, for he was a good Christian and feared nothing. When the company separated he went to a crossway in the fields for this purpose, and was never seen again. His mother was a widow, and overcome with grief, she cursed the maiden, who went mad, and it is said still haunts the town, and runs about each night calling her lover. Some believed that he was torn to pieces by the witches, but others, that he was thrown into the Rhine by his rivals, and as a body was found which appeared to be his, there is nothing in this legend which incontrovertibly establishes the fact of the existence of witches.

Liebfrauenmilch. Milk of Our Good Lady. There was an old Burgundian noble who was a great wine-drinker; he was also a good Christian and gave much in alms and charity. This troubled the Devil, who wished to possess him entirely, so he disguised himself as a strolling knight, and visited the nobleman. When the old man gave him a bowl of his best wine, Satan described a most delicious beverage which he said he had drank in the south. The noble then said that if he would bring him such wine as he described, he would do anything in his power for him. Satan promised to plant him a vineyard which would yield it, but only on condition that he should give him his soul. The vines were started, and grew as by magic, and when the noble first tasted the wine, he christened it Liebfrauenmilch, meaning that there could be nothing better. The Devil was furious at hearing this name, but still hoped to gain the soul of the old man. Then the "good lady," who pitied him, sent an angel to drive the Devil away. The noble, who now began to realize that wine may cost men their souls, built a chapel in his vineyard and dedicated it to the Virgin, and for many years under her protection enjoyed the Devil's delicious wine, which must have deteriorated since the first vintage, although all who drink it agree that the knight was pleased with good reason, when his Satanic majesty made him a vineyard which produced so good a wine as the Liebfrauenmilch.

Xanten. This town is about two and a half miles from the Rhine, and is very ancient. It was called by the Romans, Castra Vetera and Colonia Ulpia. Here stood the Castle of Nibelungen, and in Xanten, Siegfried the dragon-slayer was born. He was the son of Siegmund, King of the Netherlands. When but eleven years of age he became weary of the quiet life at his father's castle, and set out in search of adventures. He wandered to the Siebengebirges where he met the famous armorer Mimer, and decided to go with him as an apprentice. He quarreled with the workmen; and was of no use as an armorer, for he cut through all the iron he tried to work, and drove his anvil into the ground by his powerful blows. In order to get rid of him, Mimer sent him into the wood to burn charcoal. Near the place was a fearful dragon who had formerly been the giant Fafner, but on account of his cruelty, had been transformed, and now watched some jewels and treasures which were in a hollow cave. Just as Siegfried had his kiln well burning the dragon came to attack him, and it afforded him great pleasure to see the monster, for it gave hope of just such an adventure as he desired. He came on with jaws wide open, intending to swallow Siegfried, who, however, was of quite a different mind, for he thrust a burning oak down his throat, which threw him into great agony. The dragon then endeavored to kill him by a blow from his tail, but Siegfried, full of courage and strength, managed to cut off his head, and threw the carcass into the fire. Soon a stream of fat ran out, and a little bird, sitting on a tree above him, sang to him that if he should bathe in the dragon's blood, it would render him invulnerable and no sword could harm him. He did not fail to profit by this advice, and threw himself naked into the stream and anointed himself completely, with the exception of a spot on his shoulder, where a leaf had fallen from a tree and adhered without his knowledge. He took the head of the dragon and returned to the forge, where he killed the malicious Mimer, and selecting a fine sword and complete suit of armor, he mounted the racer Grani, and rode in search of still other adventures. He travelled down the Rhine until he came to the sea, where he embarked on a vessel ready to sail. A storm drove it upon a rocky, rough coast. His good horse climbed well and brought him to a castle surrounded with flames. He knew not what to do, but the little bird again sang and directed him to leap into the flames, and he would find a spell-bound maiden whom he should release from the power of the magician who held her. Siegfried obeyed, and as soon as he made the leap the flames were extinguished and he entered the castle. Everything here was as rich and splendid as could be imagined, but the stillness of death was on all, the servants were in the position in which they had been at the moment of enchantment. The cook before the fire; the butler pouring a glass of wine; the grooms before the horses, and even the animals immovable before their mangers. At length he entered a hall where a beautiful maiden slept on a divan, and was bound with brass bands. Siegfried cut the bands; he then kissed the rosy lips, and instantly everything began to move, for his kiss broke the spell which had endured for a century. Then Siegfried hoped for the rewards of love, and that Brunhilde would consent to be his; but she wished not to be too easily won, and she enchanted him for a long time without consenting to his wishes, until finally his restless spirit demanded more change, and the little bird constantly sung to him of the delights of Nibelungenlande; of great deeds to be performed; of other beautiful women to be loved, and of daring adventures to be enjoyed. So he left the enchanted castle, stealing away by night, with the bird for his guide, who hopped from limb to limb, and sang when he rested, of the beautiful country to which he went, and of the great treasures hidden there; of a sword and cap which he could obtain. The first should kill all his enemies, and the latter make him invisible whenever he chose to put it on. Siegfried became impatient to reach this land. When at last he did so he stretched himself on the ground fatigued from his long journey. As he laid there a troop of dwarfs surrounded him to make him a prisoner. But he bound Alberich, their leader, and compelled him to tell where the cap and sword were kept. But to gain possession of them was not easy even then, for he had to overcome the giant Wolfgrambär, who was the keeper of a subterranean treasury. But he was forced to deliver the sword Balmung to Siegfried, and when he had also obtained the cap he released Alberich. Here he slew another dragon which guarded immense treasures. After a time he longed for home and returned to Xanten, where his parents received him with joy. For other adventures of Siegfried, see Worms. To those interested in German legendary lore, the "Nibelungenlied" offers much entertainment.

Yburg. Many ghost stories are connected with this castle, and it seems a fitting home for such people. Besides it is said that the monks put all the ghosts and goblins of Baden in a bag and transported them to Yburg, which was certainly a clever proceeding, and the locality for their future home well chosen. Here too the descendant of Gustav Wasa had his laboratory and in connection with Pestalozzi pursued his alchemical studies. The last representative of the family who built Yburg was a wild and reckless fellow and largely in debt while still a young man. After a violent scene with his creditors, he dreamed that he had discovered great treasures in the sepulchral vaults of his ancestors. He descended there, and finding nothing, though he broke open many coffins, he began to curse his ancestors that they did not furnish him with all he needed. In the midst of his fury a dreadful figure rose from the earth, and towered to the roof. The young man fell on his knees imploring God and all the saints, while the goblin laughed. Then he made a vow that he would become a hermit and lead a holy life from that day, and from one of the coffins came a voice like that of a child, reminding him to seek only his salvation, as his days were numbered. The demon vanished in a flash of lightning which split one of the towers from top to bottom. The knight kept his word, and though the vault supplied him no earthly treasures, his visit there so changed his life as to gain for him those of heaven.

Yburg. *Burkhardt Keller of.* See Baden-Baden.

Zähringen. *Origin of the Castle.* Many years ago a young charcoal-burner lived in the valley at the foot of the Rosskopf. He was worthy and industrious but never liked his employment, and would many times have resigned it but for the sake of his aged parents. After their death he was one day at a town where a tournament was held, and was so in love with what he saw that he determined to try if he could not enlist in the service of some brave knight. As he thought upon this after reaching home, an old man came to him and said that he well knew what he meditated, but that the time had not yet come for him to go away, but that he must change his location to a place that he would show him. He followed the old man, who led him to a neighboring forest and vanished. The young man made a kiln where he had been directed, and when it was burned he found several pieces of gold which the fire had drawn from the rocks, and this result he obtained time after time. He became so rich that he began to be anxious as to how he should remove his gold and in what he should invest it. One evening a man knocked at the door of his hut, desiring lodging and refreshment. At first the young man hesitated, but the stranger told him that misfortune alone had driven him there, and at length he admitted him. He remained several days, and by observing the young coal-burner he saw that he was honest and trustworthy. He then told him that he was his emperor, and having lost a battle his treasure had fallen into the hands of his enemy, and he desired the young man to guide him to a place of safety where his friends awaited him. Then was the young man glad, and falling on his knees he told the emperor of his gold, and begged him to accept it, and allow him to become his servant. The emperor was overcome with emotion at this unexpected fortune. They proceeded with the treasure to where his friends awaited him, and by means of it he was able to levy a new army and retrieve his lost fortunes. The charcoal-burner won many honors during the war and was knighted on the field of battle. The emperor gave him the name of Zähringen and commanded him to build a castle on the loftiest peak near his former charcoal-burner's hut, which should be for him and his successors.

Zuydersee. See Stavoren..

ANCIENT MYTHS

WHICH HAVE BEEN ILLUSTRATED IN ART.

Achelo'us. The largest river in Greece, the god of which is the eldest of the three thousand sons of Oceanus and Tethys. He fought for Deïanira with Hercules, and being conquered took the form of a bull and fought again, when Hercules took away one of his horns. Ovid says that the Naiads changed this horn into the cornucopia or horn of plenty. Achelous was a great god in ancient Greece and represented all fresh water. Sirens are called Achĕlōïădes, daughters of Achelous.

Achil'les (Pelides, Peleiades or Pelion, Æacides). Son of Peleus king of a part of Thessaly, and Thetis. Educated in eloquence and war by Phœnix, in medicine by Chīron. His mother foretold that he would die early with great glory, or live long without it. He chose the first. He led his troops to the Trojan war in fifty ships. He was favored by Minerva (Athena) and Juno (Hera). When Agamemnon was forced to give Chryseïs to her father he wished to take Briseïs from Achilles. Minerva persuaded him to surrender her, but he shut himself in his tent and refused to fight. Jupiter (Zeus) promised Thetis that victory should attend the Trojans until the Achæans should honor Achilles. So the Greeks were unsuccessful. At last they offered him rich presents and the restoration of Briseïs in vain. But Patroclus persuaded him to allow him to use his men, horses, and armor. Patroclus was slain, and Achilles filled with grief. Thetis promised him new arms made by Vulcan (Hephæstus), and Iris implored him to recover the body of Patroclus. When he had his new armor he put the Trojans to flight by the sound of his voice and chased Hector three times about the walls, killed him, bound him to his chariot and dragged him to the Greek ships; but afterwards gave the body to Priam.

Achilles fell in battle before Troy was taken. He was ambitious, the bravest and handsomest of Greeks; hero of the Iliad; affectionate to friends; revengeful to enemies, and obedient to the gods. Various traditions relate that his mother concealed him in the fire to burn out the mortal he had inherited from his father and render him immortal. His father discovered him, and Thetis fled. Peleus gave him to Chiron to instruct. He taught him hunting, riding, and music, and fed him on the marrow of bears and hearts of lions. Another way in which it is said Thetis tried to make him immortal was by dipping him in the river Styx; his ankles, by which she held him, were not wet, and thus remained vulnerable. When but nine years old Calchas declared Troy could not be conquered without him, and Thetis disguised him as a maiden and he remained with the daughters of Lycomedes at Scyros, where he was called Pyrrha from his golden hair. Ulysses came here with female dresses to sell and arms concealed among them. Achilles betrayed himself by seizing the arms with great eagerness, and then accompanied Ulysses to the war. While at Scyros Deïdamīa became by him the mother of Neoptolemus or Pyrrhus. While in the war Achilles slew an Amazon, Penthesilēa, and fought with Memnon and Troilus. There are various accounts of his death, but all agree that he died not by mortal hands but by the assistance of Apollo. Some say this god killed him, others that Apollo assumed the appearance of Paris to kill him, and again that he directed the weapon of Paris; while again it is related, that he loved Polyxena, daughter of Priam, and went to the temple of Apollo at Thymbra without arms and was there assassinated. Ajax and Ulysses rescued his body, and his armor was promised by his mother to the bravest Greek (see Ajax). After his death he became a judge of the lower world and dwelt in the islands of the blest, where he was married to Medēa or Iphigenīa.

Achilles seizing arms at Scyros
(Painting found at Pompeii).

A'cis. Son of Faunus and Symæthis, loved by the nymph Galatea. Polyphemus the Cyclop, being jealous of Acis, crushed him beneath a huge rock. The nymph changed his blood into the river Acis or Acinius at the foot of Mount Ætna.

Actæ'on. Son of Aristæus and Autonoë. Celebrated as a huntsman. One day coming suddenly upon Diana (Artemis), when she was bathing with her nymphs, she changed him to a stag, and he was torn to pieces by his fifty dogs on Mount Cithæron.

Actaeon. (British Museum.)

Admetus. King of Pheræ in Thessaly. He asked Pelias for his daughter Alcestis, who made a condition that he should come in a chariot drawn by lions and boars. Apollo assisted him to do this. Apollo persuaded the Fates or Moiræ to grant freedom from death to Admetus. They consented if his father, mother, or wife would die for him. Alcestis did so, and was brought back from the lower world by Hercules.

Ado'nis. Son of Cinyras by his daughter Smyrna or Myrrha. He was very beautiful, and beloved by Venus (Aphroditē). He was wounded in the chase by a boar so that he died. The anemone sprung from his blood. Venus so mourned his death that the gods of the lower world allowed him to pass six months of each year with her on earth. His death and return were celebrated by games called Adonia in Egypt and Greece, and referred to the death of nature in autumn and its revival in spring, as he passed six months in the lower and six in the upper world.

Death of Adonis. (Painting from Pompeii).

Adras'tus. Son of Talaus, king of Argos. Expelled from Argos by Amphiarāus, he fled to Polybus of Sicyon, to whose throne he succeeded. He established the Nemean games; was reconciled to Amphiaraus and returned to Argos; married his daughter Deipyle to Tydeus of Calydon, and Argīa to Polynīces of Thebes. Both husbands fugitives from their native countries. He attempted to restore Thebes to Polynices, who had been expelled by Eteocles, his brother. Amphiaraus foretold that all who fought should perish, save Adrastus, who had six companions, Polynices, Tydeus, Amphiaraus, Capaneus, Hippomedon, and Parthenopæus. Adrastus only escaped, and that by the fleetness of his horse Arīon, which Hercules gave him. Ten years later Adrastus led the six sons of those who fell to Thebes, and it was then taken and destroyed. This war is called that of the "Epigoni," or descendants, while the first is styled that of the "Seven against Thebes." Ægialeus was the only Argive hero who fell, and his father, Adrastus, so grieved at this that he died at Megara before he reached Argos, and was there buried.

Æ'geus. Son of Pandion. He was King of Athens, and was driven away by the fifty sons of Pallas. He was father of Theseus by Æthra at Trœzen. Theseus came to Athens and restored his father to the throne. When Theseus went to Crete to deliver Athens from the tribute to Minos he promised that if successful he would hoist a white sail on his return. He forgot to do so, and Ægeus threw himself into the sea from grief, supposing Theseus to be dead. From this, according to tradition, comes the name Ægean Sea.

Ægis'thus. Son of Thyestes by his daughter Pelopia. Atreus, his uncle, had dethroned his father, and Ægisthus restored Thyestes to the throne by killing Atreus. He did not go to the Trojan War, and while Agamemnon was gone he seduced his wife Clytæmnestra, and murdered her husband on his return. He reigned seven years in Mycenæ, and then Orestes the son of Agamemnon slew him to avenge his father's disgrace and death.

Æne'as. Son of Anchises and Aphrodīte (Venus), born on Mount Ida. Beloved of gods and men. Did not go to the war till Achilles drove away his flocks from Mount Ida. From that time he appears with Hector as hero of the Trojans. When wounded by Diomedes, Venus carried him off, and when about to perish by the hand of Achilles, Neptune (Poseidon) saved him. Homer evidently represents Æneas as reigning at Troy after the fall of the house of Priam, but other accounts say that he went to Mount Ida with friends and the images of the household gods, especially Pallas (Palladium), and thence crossed to Latium in Italy, and thus became the ancestral hero of the Romans. Virgil makes him first visit Epirus and Sicily, and then Dido on the coast of Africa (See Dido). Then arriving at Latium he married Lavinia, daughter of Latinus, king of the Aborigines. He founded the town of Lavinium. Turnus had been betrothed to Lavinia, and made war on Æneas, who slew him.

Latinus was also killed in the battle, so that Æneas was king of the Trojans and Aborigines. Soon after he was killed in a battle with the Rutulians. His body could not be found, and it was believed that he was carried to heaven, or perished in the river Numicius.

Æs'chines. Son of Atrometus and Glaucothea. Born B. C. 389. Athenian orator. Sent on embassies to Philip of Macedonia with Demosthenes. Deserted to the Macedonian party. Established school at Rhodes. Died at Samos.

Æscula'pius (Asclēpīus). God of Medicine. Homer does not make him a god, but a "blameless physician." His father Apollo was told by a raven before his birth that his mother Coronis was false, and loved Ischys an Arcadian. Apollo killed them both, and when the body of Coronis was to be burnt Æsculapius was saved from the flames. Chīron cared for him, and taught him hunting and medicine. He not only healed the sick, but raised the dead, and Zeus (Jupiter) killed him with a thunderbolt, fearing lest men should learn to escape death; but he placed him among the stars at the request of his father. He was married to Epione, and Homer speaks of his sons Machaon and Podalīrius as physicians in the Greek army. He was worshipped as a god, for medicine was held to be a sacred and secret knowledge. His chief temple was at Epidaurus. His worship was introduced at Rome B. C. 293, to avert a pestilence. Cocks were sacrificed to him, and serpents were sacred to him, for they were believed to discover healing herbs, and were a symbol of renovation. His descendants were called Asclepiadæ.

Agamem'non. Son of Plīsthenes and Aëropē or Eriphȳlē. Grandson of Atreus, king of Mycenæ. Homer makes him son of Atreus and grandson of Pelops. He was reared in the house of Atreus, together with his brother Menelaus and Ægisthus, the son of Thyestes. After Ægisthus murdered Atreus (see Ægisthus), Agamemnon and his brother went to Sparta. Agamemnon married Clytæmnestra, daughter of Tyndareus. His children were Iphianassa (Iphigenīa), Chrysothemis, Laodice (Electra), and Orestes. The way in which he acquired the kingdom of Mycenæ is variously related. Homer says he ruled all Argos, but this means Peloponnesus, for Diomedes ruled the city of Argos. When Helen was carried off by Paris, and the Greeks went to recover her, Agamemnon was their leader. They spent two years in preparation, and then the fleet assembled at Aulis in Bœotia. Here Agamemnon killed a stag sacred to Artemis (Diana), and she to punish him, becalmed the fleet and brought a pestilence upon the army. To appease her he consented to sacrifice his daughter, Iphigenīa, but at the moment of the sacrifice, Artemis put another victim in her place, and carried her to Tauris. Then the fleet sailed for Troy. Quarrel with Achilles (see Achilles). Though not the hero of the Iliad, Agamemnon was commander of the Greeks, and though inferior to Achilles, he was great in dignity and majesty. His eyes and head like Zeus (Jupiter), girdle like Ares (Mars), breast like Neptune (Poseidon). Cassandra, the daughter of Priam, was given to him after the fall of Troy.

Agla'ia. "The bright one." [See Charites].

A'jax (Aias). (1.) Grandson of Æacus. Son of Telamon, king of Salamis. Sailed to Troy with twelve ships. Achilles only excelled him. He fought with Ulysses for the armor of Achilles; and Homer says this occasioned his death, but later writers say it made him insane, and he rushed upon the flocks of the Greeks, fancying them to be men, and at last killed himself. From his blood a flower bearing his initials (Ai) sprung up. He had Tecmessa for his mistress, who bore a son, Eurysaces. (2.) Ajax, son of Oïleus, king of Locris. Sailed to Troy with forty ships. Though small, was swiftest of the Greeks next to Achilles, and skilled in throwing the spear. Returning from Troy was shipwrecked, but was put on a rock by Neptune (Poseidon). He boasted that he would escape in spite of the gods. Neptune then split the rock, and Ajax was drowned. This is the account of Homer. Virgil says he violated Cassandra in the temple of Minerva (Athēna), on the night of the fall of Troy, and thus incurred the anger of that goddess.

Ajax (Ægina Marbles).

Alces'tis (Alceste). Wife of Admetus. See Admetus.

Alcme'ne (Alcmena), daughter of Electryon, king of Mycenæ. Her brothers were slain by Pterelaus, and she promised to marry Amphitryon if he would avenge their death. While he was gone to do this Zeus (Jupiter) visited Alcmena, and pretending to be her husband, told how he had punished Pterelaus. She became the mother of Hercules by Jupiter. Next day Amphitryon returned. To him she bore Iphicles.

Althæ'a, daughter of Thestius, and called Thestias. Wife of Œneus and mother of Meleager, called also Thestiades. She killed herself when Meleager died.

Amaz'ones (Amazonides). A mythical race of warlike women.

Said to come from the Caucasus and to found Themiscyra in Asia Minor. Often occur in Greek mythology. Ruled by a queen. Had their right breasts cut off to enable them to use the bow with ease.

Amazons. (Sarcophagus at Rome.)

Achilles killed the Queen Penthesilēa at Troy. They invaded Attica in the reign of Theseus. One of the labors of Hercules was to deprive their Queen Hippolyte of her girdle. See Hercules.

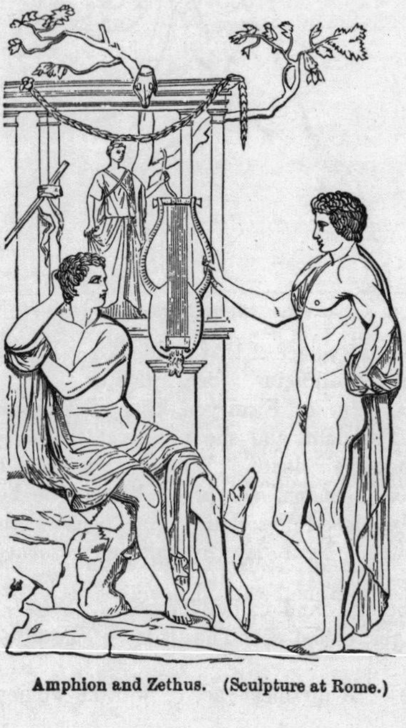
Amphion and Zethus. (Sculpture at Rome.)

Amphi′on. Twin brother of Zethus. Son of Jupiter (Zeus) and Antiŏpē. Born on Mount Cithæron, and reared with the shepherds. Lycus, the husband of Antiope, had treated her with great cruelty and married Dirce in her stead. He then reigned at Thebes; and the twin brothers, marching against him, killed both him and Dirce to avenge their mother. They tied Dirce to a bull, who dragged her to death. They then threw her body into a fountain, which was afterward called by her name. Hermes (Mercury) gave Amphīōn a lute, and he played it so skillfully as to charm the stones, and they moved and built a wall about Thebes. He married Niobe, and when Apollo killed the sons she had borne him, Amphion destroyed himself. See Niobe.

Amphitri'te. Wife of Neptune (Poseidon). An Oceanid or Nereid. Mother of Triton. Goddess of the sea, especially of the Mediterranean.

Dirce. (Naples).

Anchi'ses. Son of Capys and Themis, daughter of Ilus, King of Dardanus. His great beauty won the love of Venus (Aphrodītē). She bore him Ænēas, who is also called Anchīsĭădēs. The goddess struck him blind with lightning for boasting of his intercourse with her. When Troy was burned by the Greeks, Æneas bore Anchīsēs away on his shoulders. He died at Sicily and was buried on Mount Eryx.

Androm'ache (Andromacha). Daughter of Eëtion, king of the Cilician Thebes. Wife of Hector and mother of his son Scamandrius (Astyanax), who was hurled from the walls of Troy when it was captured. Andrŏmăchē fell to the share of Neoptolemus (Pyrrhus), son of Achilles. He took her to Epirus and she afterward married Helenus, brother of Hector, and ruler of Chaonia.

Androm'eda (Andromĕde) Daughter of Cepheus, king of Æthiopia, and Cassiopēa. Her mother declared her to be more beautiful than the Nereids, and in revenge Neptune (Poseidon) sent a sea-monster to ravage the country. The oracle of Ammon said that Andrŏmĕda must be given to the monster to save the country. Cepheus chained her to a rock by the sea, it is said where Jaffa now stands. Perseus slew the monster, and took her for his wife; but as she had been promised to Phineus, he came with his associates to the wedding to fight with Perseus, who slew him and all his friends. After death she was placed among the stars.

Antin'ous. Son of Eupīthes of Ithaca. A suitor of Penelope. Slain by Ulysses.

Anti'ope. (1.) Daughter of Nycteus. Mother of Amphion and Zethus. (See Amphion.) (2.) An Amazon and sister of Queen Hippolytē. Wife of Theseus and mother of Hippolytus.

Antis'thenes. An Athenian and founder of the Cynic philosophy. Disciple of Gorgias and Socrates, at whose death he was present. His mother was a Thracian, and he taught in the Cynosarges, a gymnasium for those born of foreign mothers, on account of which his followers probably received the title of Cynics. He opposed Plato, as he did not allow speculation, and taught that virtue is the sole necessity of man. The Stoics sprung from his school. Died at Athens, aged seventy.

Aphrodi'te (Venus). Homer makes her the daughter of Jupiter (Zeus) and Diōnē. But later writers relate that she sprung from the foam of the sea. Wife of Vulcan (Hephæstus), to whom she was faithless, and loved the gods Mars (Ares), Bacchus (Dionysus), Mercury (Hermes), and Neptune (Poseidon), also the mortals Anchises and Adonis. She received the prize of beauty (see, Paris.) She had the power to grant beauty, and whoever wore her magic girdle became an object of love and desire. The sparrow, swan, iynx, swallow, and dove, served her as messengers, and to draw her chariot. The rose, poppy, myrtle, and apple were sacred to her. She is seldom represented without her son Eros (Cupid). Her worship came from the East, and the islands of Cyprus and Cythera were the places in Greece where she was most considered, and from these her worship spread to all the country. She is thought to be identical with Astarte or the Ashtoreth of the Hebrews.

Apol'lo. Celebrated Grecian divinity. Son of Jupiter (Zeus) and Leto (Latona). Twin brother of Diana (Artemis). Born in the island of Delos, where the jealousy of Juno (Hera) had driven Leto. (See Leto.) He has many offices, and is — (1.) The god of punishment; represented with a bow and arrows. Sudden deaths were attributed to his arrows, and with them he sent plagues into the Greek camp before Troy. (2.) He wards off evil and grants aid. In this character he is father of Æsculapius and was identified with Pæëon, god of the healing art in the Iliad. (3.) God of prophecy. He had numerous oracles, the chief one being that of Delphi; hence he is called the Pythian Apollo, as Pytho was the ancient name of Delphi. He gave the power of prophecy to gods and men. (4.) God of music. In the "Iliad" he plays the phorminx, and gave the power of song to the Homeric bards. In this office he is in close relation with the Muses, and is styled Musagetes. He is said to have invented the flute, and to have received the lyre from Mercury (Hermes). (See Midas, Marsyas.) (5.) Protector of flocks and herds. Homer says little of this attribute of Apollo, but later he is represented as tending the flocks of Admetus. (6.) The especial deity of those who found towns and make civil constitutions. The Greeks never founded a town or colony without consulting his oracle. (7.) God of the sun. Homer makes him entirely distinct from Helios, but later writers and the influence of other nations maintain this attribute. He was the chief Grecian god, but not worshipped by the early Romans, which latter nation were in later times instructed concerning him by the Greeks. The ludi Apollinares were instituted in 212, during the second Punic war.

A'res (Mars). Son of Jupiter (Zeus) and Juno (Hēra). Greek god of war. One of the Olympian divinities. So savage in his nature, and so delighting in war and destruction, that he was hated by other gods, and even by his parents. He was wounded by Diomedes, assisted by Minerva (Athena), and he roared like ten thousand warriors. The Aloīdæ conquered him and kept him confined thirteen months, till Hermes (Mercury) released him. He fought concerning his son Cycnus with Hercules, who conquered him, and compelled him to retire to Olympus. Aphroditē (Venus) loved him. Later traditions relate that when Halirrhothius, the son of Neptune (Poseidon), offered violence to Alcippē the daughter of Ares, he was killed by her father. He was for this accused by Poseidon before the Olympian gods who were assembled in the Areopagus. He was acquitted, and it is believed that this event gave rise to the name Areopagus. See Mars, for Roman god of war.

Argonau'tæ. These were the heroes who sailed to Colchis (Aea) for the capture of the golden fleece. Pelias, king of Iolcus in Thessaly, wished to get rid of Jason (see Jason), and persuaded him to go for the golden fleece, which was hung on a tree in the grove of Mars (Arēs) in Colchis and guarded by a dragon. Jason bade Argus, son of Phrixus, to build a vessel with fifty oars. It was called Argo in honor of the builder. Minerva (Athena) superintended the building of the Argo. Hercules, Castor, Pollux, and many other heroes, went with Jason, and after many adventures they reached the mouth of the river Phasis. The king of Colchis, Æëtes, promised the fleece to Jason if he would yoke to a plough a pair of oxen with brazen feet who breathed out fire, and sow the dragon's teeth which Cadmus had not used at Thebes. Medēa the daughter of this king, loved Jason, and gave him power to resist fire and steel, and put the dragon to sleep. Jason then took the fleece and sailed away at night with his Argonauts, taking Medea with them. They were driven in a storm to Italy, but at length reached Iolcus. See Medea, Jason.

Ariadne. (Painting from Pompeii.)

Ariad'ne (Arĭadna). Daughter of Minos and Pasiphaë. When Theseus was sent to Crete to free Athens from tribute to the Minotaur she fell in love with him and gave him the thread to guide him out of the labyrinth. Theseus took her away under promise of marriage, but at Naxos she was slain by Artemis (Diana), according to Homer, but more commonly it is said, that Theseus deserted her and Dionysus (Bacchus) found her, married her, and placed the marriage crown he gave her among the stars.

Ari′on. (1.) Born at Methymna in Lesbos. Inventor of dithyrambic poetry and a wonderful musician. Lived about B. C. 625, spent many years at the court of Periander at Corinth. Went to Sicily to contend in a musical combat, and being the victor embarked for Corinth laden with presents. The sailors intended to kill him to obtain his treasures. He begged permission to play the cithara once more, which he did, invoking the gods for aid. The music attracted many dolphins about the ship, and he threw himself into the sea and got upon the back of one of these, which took him to Tænărus, from which he reached Corinth, and told all to Periander. When the vessel arrived, and Periander inquired for Arion, the sailors said he had remained at Tarentum. Then Periander called him, and the lying sailors were confounded at the sight and punished by Periander. (2.) A fabulous horse said to have been begotten by Neptune (Poseidon).

Ar′temis (Diana). According to the ancient traditions twin sister of Apollo, daughter of Zeus (Jupiter) and Leto (Latona), born at

Artemis (Diana). Gorii, Mus. Flor. vol. ii. tav. 88.

Delos. She appears in several characters. (1.) *As sister of Apollo*, she is a female likeness of him. She has a bow, quiver, and arrows, and like him sends sickness, plagues, and sudden deaths. Also averts evils and alleviates suffering. In the Trojan war she was, like Apollo, the friend of Troy. She watched especially over the young, and because she guarded the young of flocks came to be considered a huntress. She was never conquered by love. She turned Actæon into a stag, because he had seen her bathing, and slew Orion because he had made an attempt upon her chastity. With Apollo she slew the children of Niobe. When Apollo is represented as Helios or the Sun, Diana is made Selene, or the Moon; hence she is represented in love with Endymion and kisses him in his sleep; but this is not in character with Diana, and is probably Selēnē. (2.) *The Arcadian Artemis* was not connected with Apollo. She was goddess of the nymphs of the Arcadian mountains, and her chariot was drawn by four stags with golden antlers. (3.) *The Taurian Artemis.* The Greeks identified this goddess with their own Artemis. She dwelt in Tauris, and all strangers thrown on the coast were sacrificed to her. Iphigenīa and Orestes brought her image from Tauris and landed at Brauron, from which she was called the Brauronian Artemis, and worshipped at Athens and Sparta, at which latter place boys were scourged before her altar until it was sprinkled with blood. (4.) *The Ephesian Artemis* is quite distinct from the Greek goddess. The Greeks found her worship established when they settled in Ionia, and they gave her the name of Artĕmis. She is often represented with many breasts (multimammæ.) The attributes of Diana vary according to her different characters. As a huntress she wears the chlamys, and her breast is covered; legs bare to the knees. Has the bow, quiver, arrows, spear, stags, and dogs. As goddess of the moon she wears a long robe, a veil, and above her forehead a crescent. She often bears a torch.

Asca'nius, son of Æneas and Creusa. Other traditions say this was the name of the son of Lavinia. He went with his father to Italy, founded the city of Alba Longa, and was succeeded by his son Silvius. He was also called Iulus or Julus, and the gens Julia at Rome traced its origin to him.

Aspa'sia. (1.) Daughter of Axiochus of Miletus. She was the most celebrated of the Greek Hetæræ. Having gained the affections of Pericles, as much by her mental as her personal charms, he parted from his wife, and lived with Aspasia until his death. Her house was frequented by Socrates and all the most learned men of Athens. She was accused by the enemies of Pericles of impiety, but his influence procured her acquittal. After the death of Pericles it is said that she attached herself to a cattle-dealer named Lysicles, and so instructed him that he became a fine orator. (2.) The favorite mistress of Cyrus the younger, and later of his brother Artaxerxes. Her name was Milto, but Cyrus changed it to that of the mistress of Pericles. At length Darius, son of Artaxerxes, loved her and his father made her a priestess in a temple at Ecbatana, where strict celibacy was enforced.

Atalan'ta (Atalante). The Arcadian Atalanta was daughter of Iasus, Iasion or Iasius, and Clymene. Her father exposed her in infancy, but she was suckled by a she-bear, a symbol of Artemis (Diana). When older she joined in the Calydonian hunt. She slew the Centaurs, who pursued her, and preserved her chastity. Her father acknowledged her and desired her to marry, but she made a condition that he who would be her husband must excel her in a foot-race. She was the fleetest of mortals. She outran many, but was overcome by Milanion, who was assisted by Aphroditē (Venus). They married, but were changed to lions because they profaned the grove of Zeus (Jupiter) by their embraces. *The Bœotian Atalanta* has precisely the same history, with change of names and localities. Daughter of Schœnus, married to Hippomenes. The race was in Onchestus in Bœotia, and the temple of Cybele the place profaned; which goddess not only made them lions, but compelled them to draw her chariot.

Athe'na (Athene, Minerva, Pallas, and Pallas Athena). Daughter of Zeus (Jupiter), and Metis, whom Zeus swallowed before the birth of the child. Athena sprang from the head of Zeus in complete armor, and with a war-shout. As her father was most powerful, so her mother was wisest of all gods, and she herself a combination of power and wisdom. She was protectress of the state, and all useful arts, such as agriculture, weaving, and others. Invented the plough and rake. As goddess of wisdom she maintained law and order, especially in courts, and is said to have founded that of the Areopagus. As a warlike divinity she protected the state from enemies. Was a friend of the Greeks in the Trojan war. When the giants fought Zeus she slew Pallas, and buried Enceladus beneath the island of Sicily. She never loved. Hephæstus (Vulcan) was compelled to flee for making an attempt upon her chastity, and Tiresias was made blind for seeing her in the bath. She was the special protectress of Athens and Attica. She contended with Poseidon (Neptune) for the possession of Athens. The gods declared that the one who produced the best gift for man should have it. Poseidon produced the horse, and Athena the olive. The city was given to her. As goddess of war she is in armor, and bears the ægis and a golden staff. The head of the Gorgon Medusa is in the centre of her breastplate. The olive, cock, serpent, and owl were sacred to her. The magnificent *Panathenæa* was celebrated in her honor, and it is the procession of this festival which is represented on the frieze of the Parthenon.

At'las. Son of Iapetus and Clymĕnē; brother of Prometheus and Epimetheus. He was sentenced to bear heaven on his head and hands, for having joined the Titans in making war on Zeus (Jupiter). Another tradition relates that Perseus, by means of the head of Medusa, changed him into Mount Atlas which supports heaven and all the stars, because he refused him a shelter. Male descendants of Atlas are called Atlantĭădes, especially Mercury and Hermaphroditus; and females Atlantias and Atlantis, particularly one of the Pleiades and Hyades. He was father of the Pleiades by Pleiōnē or by Hesperis; of the Hyades and Hesperides by Æthra; of Œnomaus and Maia by Sterŏpē. Calypso, Diōnē, Hesperus, and Hyas, are all called his children.

Atlas. (Farnese collection. Naples.)

Auro'ra (Eōs). Daughter of Hyperīon and Thia, or Euryphassa; Ovid says of Pallas. Wife of Tithonus, whom she carried off and to whom she bore Memnon. She also carried away Orion and Cephalus. She is goddess of the dawn, and each morning leaves the couch of Tithonus to ascend to heaven from the river Oceanus, in a chariot drawn by swift horses to announce the coming of the sun.

Aus'ter. See Notus.

Bac'chæ, called Mænades and Thyiades. The female attendants on Bacchus (Dionysus), in his wanderings in the East. They carry the *thyrsus*, are crowned with vine leaves, and dressed in fawn skins. Also the priestesses who by wine and other exciting causes threw themselves into a frenzy at the festivals of Bacchus. See next.

Bac'chus (Dīonysus). Son of Zeus (Jupiter) and Semele, daughter of Cadmus, king of Thebes. Hera (Juno) appeared to Semele in disguise before the birth of the child, and urged Semele to persuade Zeus to come to her in the same manner as that in which he approached his own wife Juno. The god complied most unwillingly, and came in thunder and lightning. Semele gave premature birth to the child, but Zeus sewed him up in his thigh till he had come to maturity. After birth he was reared by nymphs of Mount Nysa, who were made Hyades among the stars by Zeus to reward them for this service. When he was grown, Hera took away his reason, and he wandered mad in all parts of the earth. He went to Egypt, Syria, India, and all Asia. He taught the people the cultivation of the vine and some elements of civilization. At Thrace, Lycurgus, king of the Edones, received him ill (Lycurgus). At Thebes he punished Pentheus, who attempted to prevent his worship, and compelled the women to go to Mount Cithæron, and celebrate Bacchic festivals. The mother and aunts of Pentheus, when in the Bacchic frenzy, believed him to be a wild beast and tore him in pieces. At Argos the people refused to receive him as a god, until he drove all the women mad to convince them of his power. At Icaria he hired a vessel which belonged to Tyrrhenian pirates to go to Naxos. They attempted to take him to Asia to sell him for a slave. Then he changed the oars and masts into serpents and himself into a lion; flutes were heard, and ivy grew over the vessel. The sailors went mad and plunged into the sea, where they became dolphins. After thus showing himself a god in various places, he took his mother out of Hades, and carried her to Olympus. Many fabulous beings are said to be the offspring of this god, but of all whom he loved, Ariadne is most noted (Ariadne). In the earliest times Bacchus was not worshipped, and Homer makes him merely the teacher of men in the cultivation of the vine, but as this cultivation increased, his worship spread, and his festivals assumed a wilder and more frenzied character. He represents the productive and intoxicating power of nature, and wine is called the fruit of Dionysus, and is a symbol of this power. He also has a more pleasing phase, for as cultivation of soil leads to civilization, he was regarded as a lover of law and peace. The drama arose from the dithyrambic choruses of his festivals; thus he was considered the patron of theatres. He was accompanied by Bacchantes, or women who are represented as frenzied, heads thrown back, disordered hair, with serpents, swords, cymbals, and thyrsus staffs. Satyrs, Pans, Sileni, and Centaurs were his companions. The ram was the sacrifice usually offered him. The dolphin, ass, lynx, serpent, and panther were sacred to him, and in nature, the vine, asphodel, ivy, and laurel. He is represented as youthful, languishing, and as one slightly intoxicated.

Dionysus (Bacchus) (Painting at Pompeii).

Beller'ophon (Bellĕrŏphontēs). Son of Glaucus, king of Corinth, and Eurymede. His name was Hipponous, and changed because he slew the Corinthian Belerus. He fled to Proetus, king of Argos, to purify himself from the murder of Belerus. Antea, wife of Proetus, loved him, but he rejected her advances. She then accused him to Proetus of having attempted her virtue. Proteus did not wish to kill him, but sent him to Iobates, king of Lycia, father of Antēa, and desired him to kill him. Iobates sent him to kill the Chimæra. Bellerophon obtained Pegasus and slew the monster.

Bellerophon slaying the Chimæra (Hamilton Vases).

(See Chimæra, Pegasus). Then Iobates sent him to fight the Solymi, the Amazons, and the bravest Lycians. But he conquered all. Iobates then gave him his daughter, and made him his successor. At length the gods came to hate him, and he wandered, inconsolable, in the Aleïan field and avoided men. Homer relates nothing of his death, but later writers say he attempted to fly to heaven on Pegasus, when Zeus sent a gad-fly to sting the horse. Bellerophon was thrown to the earth and became lame and blind from the fall.

Bo'reas. Son of Astræus and Eos (Aurora). Brother of Hesperus, Zephyrus, and Notus. Himself the north or north-northeast wind. He carried Orithyia, daughter of Erechtheus, king of Attica, to his cave, which was in Mount Hæmus in Thrace. By her he begot Zetes, Calais, Chione, and Cleopatra, wife of Phineus. They are called Boreades. In the Persian war Boreas assisted the Athenians and destroyed the fleet of the barbarians. At Athens the festival of the Boreasmi was in his honor.

Boreas.
(Bas-relief. Athens. Temple of the Winds.)

Brise'is. Her real name was Hippodamia; was called Brīsēis from her father, Briseus of Lyrnessus. She fell into the hands of Achilles, from whom Agamemnon took her. This made the quarrel between the two heroes. See Achilles.

Busi'ris. A king of Egypt who sacrificed to Zeus (Jupiter) all strangers who fell into his hands. Hercules slew him.

Ca'cus. Son of Vulcan. A huge giant. Lived in a cave on Mount Aventine and preyed upon all the surrounding country. When Hercules brought the cattle he stole from Geryon in Spain, to Italy, Cacus stole a part of them and dragged them to his cave by their tails while Hercules slept. When those remaining were driven near the cave, the others began to bellow, and Hercules killed Cacus for the theft. In honor of this event Hercules dedicated the *ara maxima* at Rome.

Calli'ope. The muse of epic poetry. Her attributes in art are a tablet and stylus, and a roll of paper or a book. See Musæ.

Callir'rhoe. (1.) Daughter of Achelous, and wife of Alcmæon. She induced him to bring from Psophis the peplus and necklace of Harmonia. For this act he was slain. (2.) Daughter of Scamander, wife of Tros and mother of Ilus and Ganymedes. (3.) The most celebrated well of ancient Athens, was in the southeast part of the city and is still called Callirrhoe.

Callis'to. An Arcadian nymph, called *Nonacrina virgo* from Mount Nonacris in Arcadia. A companion of Artemis (Diana). Zeus (Jupiter) loved her, and in order to conceal this from Hera (Juno), he changed her into a she-bear. But the truth did not escape Hera, and she caused Artemis to slay Callisto while hunting. Arcas was her son by Zeus. He placed her among the stars under the name of Arctos or the Bear.

Cal'ydon. A town of Ætolia, said to have been founded by Ætolus, or his son Calydon. In the neighboring mountains, the hunt of the Calydonian boar took place, and in the poets we read of *Calydōnis*, a woman of Ætolia, who was Deïanīra, daughter of Œneus, king of Calydon; *Calydonius heros*, Meleager; *Calydonius amnis*, the Achelous, which separated Ætolia from Acarnania; and *Calydonia regna*, Apulia, for Diomedes grandson of Œneus, king of Calydon obtained Apulia.

Calyp'so. A nymph of the island Ogygia. She loved Ulysses, who was shipwrecked here. She promised him immortality if he would remain, but he refused, and after detaining him seven years the gods compelled her to release him.

Can'ace. Daughter of Æolus. Loved her brother Macareus unnaturally, and was compelled to kill herself by her father.

Caryat'ides are female figures that support burdens in architecture, and are so called from the women of Caryæ, a town of Laconia, who were reduced to abject slavery and degradation by the Greeks, because they joined the Persians who invaded Greece.

Cassandra and Apollo (Pitture d'Ercolano).

Cassan'dra. Daughter of Priam and Hecuba. Twin sister of Helenus. Her beauty won the love of Apollo, who promised her the gift of prophecy if she would comply with his desires. She consented, but having received the gift, still refused to yield herself to him. He then ordained that no one should believe her predictions. When Troy fell she fled to the temple of Athena (Minerva), but Ajax tore her away from the statue of the goddess. She fell to the lot of Agamemnon in the division of the booty, and he took her to Mycenæ, where she was slain by Clytæmnestra.

Cas'tor. Son of Zeus (Jupiter); brother of Pollux. See Dioscuri.

Ce'crops. Said to have been the first king of Attica. Husband of Agraulos, daughter of Actæus. Father of Erysichthon, Agraulos, Herse, and Pandrosos. It was during his reign that Athena (Minerva) and Poseidon (Neptune) contended for Attica, and Cecrops decided for the former. (Athena). The citadel of Athens was called Cecropia for him, said to have been its founder. The division of Attica into twelve communities, the introduction of civilization, the institution of marriage, the abolition of bloody sacrifices, and the worship of the gods, are all attributed to Cecrops. Another and later tradition makes him a native of Sais in Egypt, who led Egyptians to Attica and thus introduced arts and civilization there; but this is rejected by those best able to decide.

Centau'ri, which name signifies Bull-killers, inhabited Mount Pelion in Thessaly. Homer calls them savage beasts, but later they are represented as half men and half beasts, and are said to have

Centaur. (Bas-relief, Parthenon, Athens.)

proceeded from Ixion and a cloud. They are celebrated for their contest with the Lapithæ. This arose at the marriage of Pirithous, and is sometimes connected with a combat between the Centaurs and Hercules (Hercules.) They were expelled from their home and fled to Mount Pindus. Chīrōn is most celebrated of their number (see Chiron). They are represented as men from the head to the loins, and the remainder of the body like a horse with four feet and a tail.

Ceph'alus. Son of Deion and Diomede. Husband of Procris or Procne. Eos (Aurora) loved him, but could make no impression on him because of his love of Procris. Eos then advised him to test Procris, and gave him the appearance of a stranger. He thus visited his wife with rich presents which so tempted her that she yielded to him. Cephalus then discovered himself, and she fled to Crete in shame. Artemis (Diana) then gave her a spear and a dog, which were never to miss their mark. She disguised herself as a youth, and then returned to her husband. In order to obtain the dog and spear Cephalus promised to love the youth. Procris then made herself known, and they were reconciled; but she was ever jealous of Eos, and watched her husband when he went out hunting, and at length he killed her accidentally with the unerring spear.

Cer'berus. Son of Typhaon and Echidna. He is the dog that guards the entrance to Hades, and his den is placed on the farther side of the Styx where Charon landed the shades of the dead. He has been represented by poets as having fifty and one hundred heads, but later writers give him three heads with serpents twined about his neck and the tail of a serpent.

Cerberus. (Bronze Statue.)

Ce'res. Goddess of the Earth. See Demeter.

Char'ites (Gratiæ, Graces), were three in number. Daughters of Zeus (Jupiter). Euphrŏsynē, Aglaia, and Thălīa. They are the personification of grace, beauty, and refinement. They were in the service of other divinities and lent enjoyment to life by gentleness and all that elevates and refines. They were companions of the Muses and dwelt with them in Olympus. They especially favored poetry. In most ancient representations they were draped, but in later art they are nude. They usually embrace each other, and are maidens in the bloom of life and beauty.

Cha'ron. Son of Erebus. He is represented as an old man, dirty and meanly clad. He carried the shades of the dead across the rivers of the lower world in his boat. To recompense him for this service an obolus or danace was placed in the mouth of every corpse.

Charyb'dis. See Scylla.

Chimæ'ra. A fire-breathing monster of Lycia. The idea probably originated in a volcano of this name near Phaselis in Lycia. It is represented with the fore part of a lion, the middle part of a goat, and the hind part of a dragon. She made great havoc in all the country about her home. Bellerophon having obtained **Pegasus**, rose into the air and killed the monster with arrows. In some works of art found in Lycia the Chĭmæra is represented like one species of the lion of that country. See Bellerophon.

Chi'one. (1.) Daughter of Boreas and Orithyia; mother of Eumolpus, who is called Chionides. (2.) Daughter of Dædalion. Killed by Artemis (Diana) because she compared herself to the goddess in beauty. Mother of Autolycus, by Hermes (Mercury), and of Philammon by Apollo.

Chi'ron. Son of Saturn (Cronus) and Philyra. The best of the Centaurs. Lived on Mount Pelion. Was instructed by Artemis (Diana) and Apollo, and so excelled in medicine, hunting, music, gymnastics, and prophecy that the most distinguished Grecian youths were given to him for instruction, such as Peleus, Achilles, and Diomedes. The other Centaurs would have killed Peleus, but Chīrōn saved him. He was a friend of Hercules, but while the latter fought with the other Centaurs one of his poisoned arrows hit Chiron. He was immortal, but he gave his immortality to Prometheus and would live no longer. Zeus placed him among the stars as Sagittarius.

Chryse'is. Daughter of Chryses, priest of Apollo at Chryse. Taken prisoner by Achilles in the capture of Lyrnessus. She fell to the share of Agamemnon in the division of the booty. Her father sought to ransom her, but Agamemnon harshly repulsed him. Apollo then sent a plague among the Greeks, and she was released to appease the god. Her right name was Astynome.

Cir'ce. Daughter of Helios (the sun) and Perse. Dwelt in the island of Ææa. Her mother was celebrated for her magic arts. Ulysses was cast upon her island, and when his comrades drank of the cup she offered them they were changed to swine with the exception of Eurylochus, who remained to tell the truth to Ulysses. The latter had received from Hermes (Mercury) the magic root *moly* which preserved from enchantment. He drank the cup of Circe without effect, and he then compelled her to restore his companions. He stayed with her a year, and she bore him a son Telegonus, said to have founded Tusculum.

Cli'o. Muse of History. Represented standing. Her attributes, an open roll or a chest of books. See Musæ.

Clytæmnes'tra. Sister of Castor, Pollux, and Helena. Wife of Agamemnon. Mother of Orestes, Iphigenīa, and Electra. During the absence of Agamemnon at Troy she lived adulterously with Ægisthus and assisted him to murder her husband after his return. Orestes slew both her and Ægisthus to revenge his father's disgrace and death.

Coryban'tes. These were priests of Cybele or Rhea in Phrygia. They danced to the sound of drums and cymbals to celebrate her worship. They are sometimes said to have been the nurses of Zeus (Jupiter) in Crete, because they are identified with the Curetes and the Idæan Dactyli.

Cro'nus (Saturnus). Son of Uranus and Ge (Heaven and Earth). Husband of Rhea. Father of Hestia (Vesta), Demeter (Ceres), Hera (Juno), Hades (Pluto), Poseidon (Neptune), and Zeus (Jupiter). He dethroned his father and was in turn dethroned by Zeus. See Rhea, Zeus.

Cu'pid (Eros, Amor.) Son of Aphroditē (Venus) by either Ares (Mars), Zeus (Jupiter), or Hermes (Mercury). See Eros.

Cy'ane. A Sicilian nymph. A playmate of Proserpine, at whose death she was changed into a fountain through grief.

Cyb'ele. See Rhea.

Dæd'alus. He personifies the earliest manifestations of sculpture and architecture in Athens and Crete, and both these places are credited with having been his home. He excelled in sculpture, and taught Calos, Talus, or Perdix, the son of his sister; but when he excelled his master, Dædalus killed him. Dædalus was tried for this murder by the Areopagus and sentenced to death. He fled to Crete, and by his skill made a friend of Minos. He made the wooden cow for Pasiphaë, and when she gave birth to the Minotaur he constructed the labyrinth at Cnossus in which to keep the monster. For this Minos imprisoned him, but Pasiphaë released him, and as Minos guarded all the vessels on the coast, Dædalus made wings for himself and Icarus, his son (see Icarus). Dædalus flew over the Ægean Sea and alighted at Cumæ. He then went to Sicily to King Cocalus, who received him kindly, and when Minos pursued him he was killed by Cocalus or his daughters. Many works of art in Italy, Greece, and Libya were attributed to him as well as in the islands of the Mediterranean; and the earliest images of the gods, which were made of wood, gilded and dressed in draperies of cloth, were called Dædala by the Greeks.

Dan'ae. Daughter of Acrisius, king of Argos, who confined her in a brazen tower, because it had been prophesied that her son should kill his grandfather. But Zeus (Jupiter) came to her in the form of a shower of gold, and she became the mother of Perseus. Then Acrisius placed her and the child in a chest and cast it into the sea. The chest was sent ashore at Seriphus and they were saved by Dictys. (See Perseus.) Italian traditions relate that Dănăē went to Italy, married Pilumnus, built Ardea, and gave birth to Danaüs the ancestor of Turnus.

Dana'ides. These were the fifty daughters of Danaüs son of Belus. His twin-brother Ægyptus had fifty sons, and Danaüs fled to Argos with his daughters because he feared the sons of his brother, but they pursued him to Argos and demanded his daughters as wives. He consented, but he gave to each daughter a dagger, with which to kill her husband in the bridal chamber. All did this save one, Hypermnestra, who spared her husband Lynceus. He afterwards killed Danaüs. The Danaids are obliged to constantly carry water in the lower world, and to pour it into a sieve as a punishment for their crime.

Danaids. (Mus. Pio Clem. Visconti.)

Daph'ne. Daughter of Peneus, the river god of Thessaly. Apollo loved her and pursued her, but when about to reach her, she prayed for aid and became a laurel tree. On this account the laurel was the favorite tree of the god.

Daph'nis. Son of Hermes (Mercury) by a nymph. He was a Sicilian shepherd, and learned to play the flute of Pan. The inventor of bucolic poetry. He was faithless to a Naiad, and she made him blind. His father then translated him to heaven.

Deme'ter (Ceres). Goddess of the earth. Daughter of Cronus (Saturnus) and Rhea, mother of Persephŏnē (Proserpine) by Zeus (Jupiter). Without the knowledge of her mother Jupiter promised Proserpine to Aïdoneus (Pluto), and one day as she gathered flowers on the Nysian plain, the earth opened and she was carried off by Aïdoneus. Demeter searched for her, until Helios told her the truth. Then she left Olympus in anger, and came to dwell on earth, where she blessed all who received her kindly, and punished those who did not. Then the earth produced no fruit, and Zeus sent Hermes (Mercury), to bring back Proserpine. Pluto consented, but gave Proserpine part of a pomegranate, which she ate. Then Demeter returned to Olympus with her child, but the latter having eaten in the lower world, was obliged to pass one third of the year there with Aïdoneus. Now again the earth brought forth fruit. This is the account of Homer. Latin writers place the rape of Proserpine at Enna in Sicily, and say that Demeter changed Ascalaphus into an owl because he was the only witness of the eating of Proserpine in Hades. The signification of the legend is, that Proserpine carried off is the seed placed in the earth; when she returns, she is the grain rising from the ground to feed men. Again others make it refer to the burial of man and immortality. Other incidents in the life of Demeter are these: Poseidon (Neptune) pursued her and she changed herself to a mare, but he accomplished his desire, and she bore the horse Arion. She was in love with Iasion, and conceived in a thrice-ploughed field in Crete; Plutus (Wealth) was the offspring. Erysichthon cut down her grove, and she so punished him with hunger that he devoured his own flesh. The Athenians claimed that agriculture originated in their country, and that Triptolemus of Eleusis was a favorite of Demeter, and first sowed corn and invented the plough. The festival of the Eleusinia at Athens, and of the Thesmophoria in all Greece, were in her honor. The Romans kept the festival of Cerealia in honor of Demeter, and gave the property of traitors to her temple, where the decrees of the senate were deposited for inspection by the tribunes. In art she is fully draped, a garland of corn-ears or a ribbon upon her head, and a sceptre with corn-ears, or a poppy in her hand. Sometimes she had a torch and basket.

Dia'na (Artemis). At Rome her temple was on the Aventine. There she was goddess of light, and represented the moon. See Artemis.

Di'do (Elissa). Daughter of Belus, King of Tyre. She was married to her uncle, Acerbas. Her brother Pygmalion killed him, and Dido with many noble Tyrians, left their home secretly, and took away all the great wealth of Acerbas. They went to Africa. She bought as much land as could be surrounded by the hide of a bull. She cut this into narrow strips, with which she measured the spot where she built the citadel of Byrsa. This was the commencement of Carthage, which rose rapidly. A neighboring king, Hiarbas, being jealous of her power, asked her in marriage, but she was determined to be true to the memory of Acerbas. When she saw that all around her expected her to marry the king, she made a pretense of sacrificing to the manes of Acerbas, and when the pile was lighted, she mounted it and stabbed herself in the presence of the people. Virgil gives another version, and makes Æneas land at Carthage and gain the affections of Dido, so that when he sailed away she killed herself as above. But the anachronism is most glaring, as Troy was taken B. C. 1184, and Carthage not founded until B. C. 853.

Diog'enes was born in Sinope in Pontus, B. C. 412. A celebrated Cynic philosopher. As a youth he was a disciple of Antisthenes (Antisthenes), and became eminent for his moroseness and self-denial. In summer he rolled in hot sand, and in winter he embraced statues covered with snow. He lived a most austere life in every particular: slept in porticoes, or in the streets, and finally lived in a tub belonging to the Metroum, or temple of the Mother of the Gods. On his way to Ægina he was taken by pirates and sold as a slave, and when asked what he could do, his answer was, "I can command men." Xeniades of Corinth bought him, gave him his freedom, and made him instructor of his children. At Corinth he saw Alexander, who said to him, "I am Alexander the Great." The philosopher answered, "And I am Diogenes the Cynic." Alexander so admired him that he said, "Were I not Alexander, I should wish to be Diogenes;" and when he asked him if he could do anything for him, he said, "Yes, you can stand out of the sunshine." Diogenes died at Corinth, B. C. 323.

Diome'des. Son of Tydeus and Deïpyle. He is called Tydides. Succeeded Adrastus on the throne of Argos. His father died in the war of the Seven against Thebes, and Diomedes fought in that of the "Epigoni." He went to Troy with eighty ships, and was second only to Achilles among the Greeks. Athena (Minerva) was his special protectress. He fought with Hector, Æneas, and even the Trojan gods; and thus wounded Ares (Mars), and Aphroditē (Venus). Later traditions teach that he, together with Ulysses, carried off the Palladium from Troy, because it was said Troy could not be taken while it remained within the walls. When he returned to Argos after the fall of Troy, he found his wife Ægialea living adulterously with Hippolytus, or according to others with Cometes or Cyllabarus. Aphroditē (Venus) had sent him this misfortune. He therefore left Argos and went to Ætolia. Later he attempted to return, but a storm sent him on the coast of Daunia, Italy. Here he settled, and married Evippe, daughter of Daunus. He lived to be very old and was buried on one of the islands off Cape Garganum, since called Diomedean Isles. His companions so mourned his death, that they were made birds, *Aves Diomedēæ*, and would fly toward the Greek ships, avoiding those of the Romans. A plain of Apulia was called *Diomedei Campi*, and several towns in the eastern portion of Italy were said to owe their origin to him. (2.) King of the Bistones in Thrace. He had mares which he fed on human flesh, and for this Hercules killed him.

Diony'sus. See Bacchus.

Dioscu'ri. Sons of Zeus (Jupiter), named Castor and Pollux. Called Polydeuces and Castores by the Romans. Homer makes them the children of Leda and Tyndareus, and the brothers of Helen. They were called Tyndărīdæ. But others make them the sons of Leda and Zeus, and born out of the egg at the same time with Helen. (See Leda.) Again Castor was called the son of Tyndareus, mortal and subject to age and death; while Pollux and Helen, children of Zeus, were like him, immortal. They had disappeared before the Greeks went to Troy; and were buried; but Homer says, came to life every other day and enjoyed the honors of gods. Their lives were made remarkable by three events: (1.)

An expedition to recover their sister Helen, who had been carried off by Theseus, and placed in Aphidnæ. (2.) They joined the expedition of the Argonauts, during which Pollux killed Amycus, king of the Bebryces, in a boxing-match, and they founded the town of Dioscurias in Colchis. (3.) Battle with Idas and Lynceus, sons of Aphareus: Castor being mortal, was killed by Idas, whom Zeus (Jupiter) then killed by a flash of lightning. Pollux slew Lynceus. He then asked Jupiter to allow him to join his brother, and his request was granted, so that he lived one day among the shades of the lower world, and the next among the gods. Another tradition relates that Zeus rewarded their brotherly love by placing them among the stars as *Gemini.* They were first worshipped in Sparta, then in all Greece and Italy. Neptune (Poseidon) so admired their affection for each other, that he gave them power over the waves, and they were especially honored by sailors. They were also regarded as patrons of poets, presidents of public games, and inventors of the war-dance. They always rode on magnificent white horses, and are thus represented in art, with egg-shaped helmets surmounted by stars. They carry spears. They were worshipped from the earliest times at Rome. A temple was erected in their honor opposite that of Vesta in the Forum. On the 15th of July the Equites visited this temple in a magnificent procession.

Dir'ce. See Amphion.

Dis. Pluto and the lower world are sometimes called by this name, which is a contraction of Dives.

E'cho. A nymph who amused Juno (Hera) by constantly talking to her while Jupiter (Zeus) sported with other nymphs. When Juno discovered the trick she changed Echo into an echo; in which state she fell in love with Narcissus, and this love not being returned she pined away so that nothing remained but her voice.

Ege'ria (Ægeria). The goddess by whom Numa was instructed concerning the worship to be introduced into Rome. She was one of the Camenae or prophetic nymphs of the religion of ancient Italy. The grove in which she met the king was dedicated by him to the Camenæ; in it was a well which gushed forth from a dark recess. Tradition points out two localities as sacred to Egeria: one near Aricia, and the other near Rome, at the Porta Capena.

Elec'tra (Laodice). Daughter of Agamemnon and Clytæmnestra. Sister of Iphigenīa and Orestes. When her father was murdered by her mother and Ægisthus, she sent her brother Orestes to King Strophius to be reared. When older she excited him to kill their mother to avenge the death of Agamemnon, and herself assisted to do the deed. Afterward Orestes gave her in marriage to Pylades. Electra signifies "the brilliant one."

Endym'ion. A beautiful youth who was always asleep. As he slept on Mount Latmus his beauty touched even the cold heart of

Selene (the Moon), and she came down to him, kissed him, and laid at his side. Various causes were assigned for this eternal slumber, but it was usually believed that Selene kept him thus that she might caress him without his knowledge.

E'os. See Aurōra.

Epicu'rus. Greek philosopher, born at Samos B. C. 342. Removed to Athens 306, purchased a garden and established the school known as Epicurean. He taught that happiness is the *summum bonum*, and that, the happiness which results from virtuous living; and that virtue should be followed, not for its own sake but for the happiness it brings. His doctrines were degraded and misrepresented by men of sensual natures who attributed to him the doctrine that pleasure and indulgence were the highest good.

Epimen'ides. A prophet and poet who lived in Crete and whose history has been interwoven with many fables. It is thus given: As a boy he was sent in search of a lost sheep, and becoming weary, he fell asleep in a cave and slept fifty-seven years. When he awoke and returned home, he was greatly surprised to find how long he had slept, and also at the changes which had taken place. But his visit to Athens was a reality. A plague had been sent upon the city on account of the crime of Cylon, who had seized the Acropolis intending to become tyrant of the city. Epimenides being sent for purified the city by certain mysterious ceremonies and sacrifices. Many writings were attributed to him, and Paul referred to him (Titus i. 12): "One of themselves, even a prophet of their own, said, 'The Cretans are always liars, evil beasts, slow bellies.'"

Er'ato. The muse of Erotic Poetry. See Musæ.

Erichtho'nius. King of Troy. Son of Dardanus. Father of Tros.

2. Erichtho'nius or **Erech'theus I.** Son of Vulcan (Hephæstus) and Atthis. Minerva (Athena) reared the child secretly and concealed him in a chest which she gave to Agraulos, Pandrosos, and Herse with the command that they should not open it. But they disobeyed, and when they looked in saw the child entwined by serpents or in the form of one. They went mad and threw themselves down from the Acropolis. This child was afterwards king of Athens and his son Pandion succeeded to his throne. It is said that he introduced the worship of Athena (Minerva), built her temple on the Acropolis and established the festival of the Panathenæa. He also decided in favor of the goddess when she contended with Poseidon (Neptune), for the possession of Attica. He was the first who used a chariot with four horses, and for this reason was placed among the stars as *auriga*. After his death the temple called the Erechtheum was erected on the Acropolis and he was worshipped as a god.

E'ros (Cupid, Amor). His mother was Aphroditē (Venus). His father is not known; was either Ares (Mars), Zeus (Jupiter), or Hermes (Mercury). God of Love. He was a boy full of tricks, and troubled gods and men alike. He carried arrows in a golden quiver, and torches that none could touch with impunity. His arrows were of various sorts. If golden, they kindle love, if lead they produce the opposite effect. He had wings of gold and fluttered as a bird. He often had his eyes covered, and was as one blind. He is usually with his mother. Anteros was the opposite of Eros, and punishes those who do not return the love they inspire. See Psyche.

Eros (Cupid).

Euphros'yne. See Charites.

Eurip'ides. Born at Salamis, B. C. 480, on the day that the Greeks defeated the Persians off that isle. He was in reality an Athenian, as his parents fled from Athens when Xerxes invaded Greece. He became distinguished as a tragic poet. He pictured men and women as they are, not as they should be. Socrates greatly praised him, on this account. His especial excellence was in the tenderness and pathos of some of his writings. There are eighteen of his tragedies yet known, omitting the "Rhesus," which is not positively known to be his. In youth he excelled as a gymnast. He was a friend of Socrates. He took prizes for his plays in Athens. He died at the court of Archelaüs of Macedonia, aged seventy-five. It is said that he was killed by the dogs of the king.

Europa. (Stosch Coll., Schlichtergoll.)

Euro'pa. Her parentage is disputed, and she is called daughter of Agenor, king of Phœnicia, and of Phœnix. Zeus (Jupiter) fell in love with her beauty, and assuming the shape of a bull, mingled with a herd near where she played with her maidens. The tameness of the animal attracted her, and she got upon his back. Then he went into the sea and swam to Crete, where he begot by her Minos, Rhadamanthus, and Sarpēdon.

Euryd'ice. Wife of Orpheus. See Orpheus.

Euter'pe. Muse of Lyric Poetry. See Musæ.

Fau'nus. Son of Picus, grandson of Saturnus, and father of Latinus. He gave oracles, and protected agriculture and shepherds. He was identified with Pan, after the introduction of the latter into Italy, and represented with horns and goats' feet. Later writers use the plural Fauni. This idea of plurality arose from the fact that he manifested himself in various ways; and in the end the Fauni came to be considered the same as the Greek Satyrs. Faula, his wife, was the same to the female sex that Faunus was to the male.

Faus'tulus. A shepherd who saved the lives of Romulus and Remus. See Romulus.

Flo'ra. The Roman goddess of spring and flowers. Her festival was kept from the 28th of April to the 1st of May, and attended with excessive dissipation and lasciviousness.

Fortu'na (Tyche). Worshipped both in Greece and Italy. She has different attributes, according to the characteristic represented. With the horn of Amalthea, or with Plutus, she personifies the plentiful gifts of good fortune; with a rudder, she is guiding the affairs of the world; with a ball, she represents the uncertainty of fortune. She was more considered by the Romans than the Greeks, and at Antium and Præneste her oracles were celebrated.

Fortuna. (British Museum.)

Galate'a. Daughter of Nereus and Doris. See Acis.

Ganyme'des. Son of Tros and Callirrhoë. Brother of Ilus and Assaracus. The most beautiful of mortals, and on this account carried off to live with the gods and be the cupbearer of Zeus (Jupiter). This is the account of Homer, but others are very different. He is made the son of Laomedon, of Ilus, of Erichthonius, or of Assaracus. And it is said Jupiter, in the form of an eagle or with the aid of one, bore him away, and remunerated his father for his loss with a pair of divine horses. The place from which he was taken is also variously given, but the greater number agree upon Mount Ida. He is placed among the stars under the name of Aquarius. In Latin he is sometimes called Catamitus.

Genius. A protecting spirit, corresponding to a guardian angel. Both Greeks and Romans believed in them, and the former called them Dæmons. They were believed to be the agents of Zeus (Jupiter), dwelling on earth to fulfill his will and enforce justice. The Greek philosophers taught, and the Romans believed, that such a being was appointed for each mortal at birth, and the Romans worshipped them as gods most holy, especially on their birthdays, when they offered them libations of wine, garlands, and incense. The bridal bed was called *lectus genialis*, and was consecrated to the genius on account of his connection with generation. Every place, too, had its genius, and on many merry festivals sacrifices were offered to them. A genius of place is represented as a serpent eating fruit.

Wine Genius. (Mosaic. Pompeii)

German'icus, Cæsar. Son of Nero Claudius Drusus and Antonia, daughter of the triumvir Antony. He was early raised to the honors of the state by his uncle, Tiberius, who adopted him. After being in various battles he had command of the forces in Germany, and had nearly subdued the whole country, when Tiberius became jealous of his power, and recalled him to Rome. He then gave him command of all the Eastern provinces, but placed Cn.

Piso to watch and thwart him. He died in Syria, and he and others believed that Piso had poisoned him. So great was the indignation at Rome, that Tiberius was forced to sacrifice Piso to it. Germanicus was a writer, and some of his works were poems. He had nine children, the most famous of whom were the Emperor Caligula, and Agrippina, mother of Nero.

Ge'ryon (Geryones). Son of Chrysaor and Callirrhoë. King of Spain. He had three heads, or according to some, three bodies united. Hercules stole his oxen and carried them away. See Hercules.

Gor'gones. These were Stheno, Euryale, and Medusa, three frightful maidens, sometimes called Phorcydes, from their father Phorcys. Their mother was Ceto. They had claws of brass, wings, and enormous teeth, and hissing serpents about their heads in place of hair. Medusa was the only one who was mortal, and some legends relate that she was at first beautiful, and was the mother of Chrysaor and Pegasus by Zeus (Jupiter), in one of the temples of Athena (Minerva), for which the goddess changed her hair to serpents, and all who looked at her were turned to stone. Athena then placed her head in the centre of her breastplate. See Perseus.

Medusa. (Marble, Munich.)

Gra'tiæ. See Charites.

Ha'des (Aides, Pluto, Dis, Orcus, Tartarus). Son of Cronus (Saturn) and Rhea. Brother of Zeus (Jupiter) and Poseidon (Neptune). Husband of Persephone or Proserpina [Demeter]. When the world was divided between the three brothers, Hades obtained the abode of the shades. He was hated by mortals, and fierce in character. Black sheep were the sacrifice offered him, and the person offering turned away the face. He bore a staff with which to drive shades to his dominion, and to show his power. He had a helmet, which he sometimes lent to gods and men, which rendered the wearer invisible. Being king of the lower world, metals and all the productions of the earth are his gifts. He was in love with the nymph Mintho, whom Proserpina changed to the plant called

Hades. (Vatican, Rome.)

mint; and with the nymph Leuce, whom he made a poplar after death. He is represented as seated on his throne with Proserpina. He resembles Zeus and Poseidon, except that his hair falls over his forehead. He is dark and gloomy, and has the keys of Hades. Cerberus is usually near him.

Harpy'iæ (Harpies). These are the robbers or spoilers who carried off persons. They are said to have stolen the daughters of Pandareos. They tormented Phineus when he was blind, by darting down and stealing his food from before him, or rendering it unfit to eat. After being driven away from Phineus they went to the Strophades, islands in the Ionian Sea. They are represented as maidens with fair hair and wings; also, as most disgusting birds, with heads like maidens and long claws, apparently pale with hunger.

He'be (Juventas). Daughter of Zeus (Jupiter) and Hera (Juno). Wife of Hercules after he was received among the gods, to whom she bore two sons. Goddess of Youth. She filled the cups of the gods before Ganymedes became cupbearer. She was said to have the power to make the aged young again.

Hec'ate (Perseis). The only Titan who retained power under Zeus (Jupiter). Called the daughter of Persæus or Perses, and Asteria. All the gods honored her, and she is identified with three divinities. Selene (Luna), in heaven; Artemis (Diana), on earth, and Proserpina (Persephone), in Hades. Hence she is called *Triformis*, *Tergemina*, and *Triceps*. She became a goddess of the lower world by searching for Proserpina [Demeter], and remaining with her as an attendant, when she was found. She taught sorcery and dwelt near tombs, and where people were murdered; also where two roads crossed. She wandered about with shades of the dead, and the whining of dogs was said to give warning of her approach. She sent demons from the lower world at night. Black female lambs, honey, and dogs, were offered to her at Athens; dishes of food were set out to her where roads crossed, at the end of each month. She is represented with three bodies and three heads.

Hec'uba (Hecube). Daughter of Dymas of Phrygia, or of Cisseus, king of Thrace. Wife of Priam, king of Troy. Mother of Hector, Paris, etc. After the fall of Troy she was made a slave by the Greeks. She was metamorphosed into a dog, and threw herself into the sea at a place called Cynossema, or the "tomb of the dog."

Hec'tor. Son of Priam, king of Troy, and Hecuba. Husband of Andromache. Father of Scamandrius. The Trojan hero in the war with the Greeks. He slew Patroclus. This aroused Achilles, who chased him three times around the walls of Troy, slew him, fastened him to his chariot, and dragged him to the Grecian camp. Other accounts say he dragged him three times round the city. Zeus (Jupiter) commanded Achilles to give the body to

Priam, and it was buried with great honors. Hector is one of the noblest of all who are mentioned in connection with the siege of Troy. He made even Achilles look to his laurels, and withal, was a good son, husband, and father.

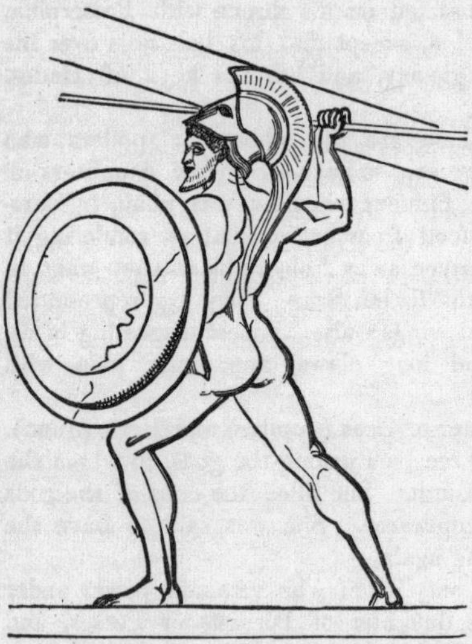

Hector. (Ægina Marbles.)

Hel'ena (Helenē). Daughter of Zeus (Jupiter) and Leda. Sister of Castor and Pollux. Exceedingly beautiful. While young was carried away to Attica by Theseus and Pirithous. While Theseus was in Hades, Castor and Pollux went to liberate Helen, took Athens, and carried to Sparta not only Helen, but Æthra, the mother of Theseus, whom they made a slave to Helen. When she was sought in marriage by all the noblest Greeks, she chose Menelaus, and by him became the mother of Hermione. She was then seduced, and carried away by Paris. The Greeks who had been her suitors resolved to avenge this, and sailed against Troy. This war lasted ten years, and Helen is represented to have had great sympathy for the Greeks. On the death of Paris she married Deiphobus, his brother, whom she betrayed to the Greeks on the fall of Troy. She then became reconciled to Menelaus, and returned with him to Sparta, where they lived happily for some time. There are various accounts of her death. Some relate that she and Menelaus were buried at Therapne in Laconia; again, that after the death of Menelaus, his sons drove her out of Peloponnesus, and she fled to Rhodes; here she was tied to a tree and strangled by Polyxo. The Rhodians built a temple, and dedicated it to her in the name of Helena Dendritis, in order to atone for this crime. Again it is related that she married Achilles in the island of Leuce, and by him became the mother of Euphorion. But Proteus in the "Odyssey" declared that Menelaus and Helen would not die but would be conducted by the gods to Elysium.

Hel'icon. A range of mountains in Bœotia crowned with snow almost constantly. Sacred to Apollo and the Muses, the latter being called *Heliconiades* and *Heliconides*. Here were the sacred fountains Aganippe and Hippocrene.

He'lios (Sol, Hyperionides, Hyperion). He is represented as having two splendid palaces, one in the East and one in the West. He starts in the morning in a chariot drawn by four horses, which feed at night upon herbs growing in the islands of the blessed. He sees and knows all that is done on earth. He it was who disclosed to Vulcan (Hephæstus), the faithlessness of Aphrodite (Venus), and to Demeter (Ceres), the truth concerning Proserpina. He is sometimes identified with Apollo. His daughters Phætusa and Lampetia tended his flocks, on the island Thrinacia, which was sacred to him. In many parts of Greece he was worshipped, and the Colossus at Rhodes was a statue representing Helios. The cock was sacred to him, and bears, bulls, white rams, and horses. Goats and honey were sacrificed to him.

Hel'le. Daughter of Athamas and Nephele. Sister of Phrixus. His stepmother Ino had intrigued to sacrifice him to Zeus (Jupiter), but his mother saved him, and Helle, by riding away upon the ram with the golden fleece which Hermes (Mercury) had given her. But Helle fell into the sea, which has since been called Hellespont (Helles-Pontus), or Sea of Helle.

Hephæs'tus (Vulcanus). Son of Zeus (Jupiter) and Hera (Juno). Another tradition relates that he had no father, and that Hera gave birth to him independently, on account of her jealousy of Zeus in giving birth to Athena (Minerva) without her aid. She so disliked him on account of his being lame and weak, that she threw him down from Mount Olympus. Thetis and Eurynome received him, and kept him nine years in a grotto beneath Oceanus. He then returned to Olympus, where he became a great artist among the gods. His palace in Olympus was imperishable, and glistened like stars. In it was his workshop, with an anvil and twenty bellows which worked at his bidding. He made all the palaces of Olympus, the arms of Achilles, the necklace of Harmonia, and the bulls of Æëtes. Later traditions place the workshop on some volcanic island, and represent the Cyclops as his workmen. At first he was merely the god of fire, but as that was necessary to the working of metals, he became an artist in metals. Although so cruelly treated by his mother, he took her part in a quarrel with Zeus, when that god seized him and hurled him from Olympus. He was a day in falling, and landed on the island of Lemnos. He again returned to Olympus, and acted as mediator between his mother and Zeus. On this occasion he offered nectar to his mother and the other gods, who were much amused, and laughed loudly at his hobbling from one to another. In the "Iliad," Charis is his wife; in "Hesiod," Aglaia, but in the "Odyssey" and in later accounts, Aphrodite (Venus) is his wife, and when she was in love with Ares (Mars), Helios disclosed it to Hephæstus, who caught the guilty pair in an invisible net, and exposed them to the ridicule of the gods. He preferred Lemnos for an earthly home, but many volcanic islands have been called his workshops, such as Sicily, Lipara, Imbros, etc. He was represented as a vigorous man, with a beard, bearing a hammer or some implement of his art, and wearing an oval cap and a chiton, which leaves the right arm and shoulder bare.

He'ra (Here). Juno. Signifies, Mistress. Daughter of Cronus (Saturn) and Rhea. Sister and wife of Zeus (Jupiter). She was reared by Oceanus and Tethys, and became the wife of Zeus without the knowledge of her parents, according to Homer. Others say that Cronus swallowed her, as he did his other children, and afterwards restored her. She was treated with great respect by the gods, and Zeus consulted her, and told her his secrets, but she was obliged to obey him, and the idea of her as queen of heaven is much later than the "Iliad." She was unlovely in character, jealous, quarrelsome, obstinate, and revengeful. She quarreled with Zeus at times, and once made a plan with Poseidon (Neptune) and Athena (Minerva) to put him in chains. He often beat her, and once hung her in the clouds with her hands chained and anvils tied to her feet. She was mother of Ares (Mars), Hebe, and Hephæstus (Vulcan). Hera was the only goddess who was really married, and is therefore the divinity of marriage and of births. She is mother of the Ilithyiæ, the goddesses who aided mothers in childbirth. She was hostile to the Trojans on account of the judgment of Paris. She persecuted the children of Zeus by mortal mothers. She was especially worshipped at Argos, and to a less extent all over Greece. She was represented as very beautiful and majestic. She wore a diadem and veil to signify that she was the bride of Zeus. The sceptre and peacock are her attributes. See Juno.

Her'cules (Heracles). Son of Zeus (Jupiter) by Alcmene, wife of Amphitryon of Thebes, whom Zeus deceived, pretending to be her husband. On the day he was to be born, Zeus boasted that he was about to become the father of one, destined to rule over the race of Perseus. Hera (Juno) persuaded him to swear that the first descendant of Perseus, born that day, should be the ruler; then she hasted to Argos and caused Eurystheus, a grandson of Perseus, to be born; so Hercules was robbed of his kingdom. Zeus was angry, but he had sworn. Alcmene gave birth to Hercules, and Iphicles, begotten by Amphitryon one night later than Hercules by Zeus. Hera sent two serpents to destroy Hercules, but the child killed them. Castor instructed him in fighting in armor; Linus in music; Eurytus in archery, and Amphitryon in driving the chariot. He killed Linus because he censured him, and Amphitryon sent him to tend his cattle. When eighteen years old, he killed a huge lion, which made great havoc among the herds of Amphitryon and Thespius. The latter had fifty daughters. He made Hercules his guest, and delivered his daughters to him, so long as the chase for the lion lasted. After he had killed him he wore his skin as a garment, the head and mouth being a helmet. Others say his lion-skin was that of the Nemean lion. His next achievement was that of killing Erginus, king of Orchomenos, to whom the Thebans paid tribute. In this battle Amphitryon was killed. Creon rewarded Hercules with his daughter Megara, who bore him several children. He always carried a club he had cut near Nemea, and his arms were presents from the gods. Hera now drove him mad, in which state he killed the children of Megara and two of the children of Iphicles. He went to Thespius, who purified him, and he sentenced himself to exile, and consulted the Delphic oracle to find where he should settle. Before this his name had been Alcides or Alcæus; the oracle now named him Hercules, and commanded him to live at Tiryns, and be the servant of Eurystheus twelve years, when he should become immortal. Later writers tell of twelve labors which he performed for this master, but Homer mentions only the conquest of Cerberus; a fight with a sea-monster; his expedition for the horses of Laomedon, and the war with the Pylians, when he killed the entire family of king Neleus, except Nestor. These twelve labors are, (1.) *The fight with the Nemean lion..* This was the offspring of Typhon and Echidna. Hercules used his club and arrows in vain, and finally strangled him with his hands, and carried him to Tiryns on his shoulder. He had ravaged the vale of Nemea between Phlius and Cleonæ. (2.) *Fight with the Lernean hydra.* This monster sprang from the same source as the lion, and was reared by Hera (Juno). It ravaged all the country of Lerna, near Argos, and lived in a swamp by the well of Amymone. It had nine heads, and the centre one was immortal. Hercules struck off the heads, but in place of every one he took away, two new ones appeared. At length with the help of Iolaus, his servant, he burned its heads, and buried the immortal one beneath a huge rock. He dipped his arrows in its bile, which was an incurable poison. (3). *Capture of the Arcadian stag.* Eurystheus ordered him to bring this alive. It had golden antlers and brazen feet. After pursuing it a year, he wounded it with an arrow and bore it away on his shoulders. (4.) *Capture of the Erymanthian boar.* He was also commanded to bring this fierce animal alive. He chased it through the snow until it was exhausted. and then took it in a net. With these immense labors smaller ones are connected, called *Parerga.* For instance, while pursuing the boar, he encountered the centaur Pholus, to whom Dionysus (Bacchus) had given a cask of wine. Hercules opened it contrary to the wishes of Pholus. Its fragrance attracted all the other centaurs. Hercules drove them away, and in his eagerness wounded his friend Chiron. (See Chiron). He also killed Pholus by accident. (5.) *Cleansing the Augean Stables.* He was ordered to perform this labor in one day. They belonged to Augeas, king of Elis, who had three thousand cattle, and the stalls had not been cleansed for thirty years. Hercules then went to Augeas, and did not mention the name of his master, but offered to cleanse the stalls in a day if he would give him a tenth part of the cattle. Augeas gave consent, to which his son Phyleus was witness. Then Hercules turned the rivers Alpheus and Peneus, so that they ran through the stalls. Augeas, however, refused him the cattle, and exiled his son because he witnessed against him. Hercules afterwards killed both him and his sons. After this it is believed that Hercules founded the Olympic games. (6.) *Destruction of Stymphalian birds.* These birds had brazen claws, beaks, and wings. They used their feathers as arrows, and ate human flesh. They had been reared by Ares (Mars). Hercules was commanded to expel them from lake Stymphalus in Arcadia. Athena (Minerva) gave him a brazen rattle with which he frightened the birds, and when they flew into the air, he killed them with arrows. Some say that he merely drove them away, and that the Argonautæ found them at the island of Aretias. (7.) *Capture of the Cretan bull.* This bull had been sent to Minos for a sacrifice by Poseidon (Neptune). Minos so admired it that he kept it and sacrificed another. Neptune then drove the bull mad, and he made great havoc. Hercules caught the creature and carried it home on his shoulders. He let it go again, and it appeared later at Marathon. (8.) *Capture of the mares of Diomedes.* These mares were fed on human flesh, and Hercules was commanded to bring them to Eurystheus. With a few assistants he seized them and took them to the sea-coast. Here he was overtaken by the Bistones, the subjects of Diomedes. While fighting he gave the horses to Abderus, whom they killed. Hercules conquered the Bistones and slew Diomedes. He threw his body to the horses. Eating the flesh of their master tamed them. Hercules founded the city of Abdera in honor of his friend, and then took the mares to Eurystheus, who set them free, and they were destroyed by wild beasts on Mount Olympus. (9.) *Seizure of the girdle of Hippolyte.* This queen of the Amazons had a girdle which Mars (Ares) had given her. Admete, the daughter of Eurystheus, desired it, and he sent Hercules for it. He had many adventures in reaching her country, where the queen received him kindly

Hercules and horses of Diomedes. (Museo Borbonico.)

But Hera excited all the Amazones against him. A quarrel ensued, in which Hercules killed Hippolyte, and seized her girdle. On his return he stopped at Troas and rescued Hesione from the monster sent by Neptune (Poseidon). Her father, Laomedon, promised him the horses Zeus had given him when he took away Ganymedes. He did not keep his word, and Hercules afterwards made war on account of this. (10.) *Capture of the oxen of Geryones in Erythia.* The fabulous island of Erythia (the reddish), was so called because it was in the west beneath the setting sun. Here lived Geryones, the monster with three bodies. He had magnificent oxen, which were guarded by Eurytion, the giant, and the two-headed dog Orthus. These oxen Hercules was commanded to bring to Eurystheus. After traversing many lands he reached the borders of Europe and Libya, and erected two pillars, Calpe and Abyla, one on each side of the straits of Gibraltar, since called the pillars of Hercules. He so suffered from the heat of the sun, that he shot at Helios, who admired his boldness, and gave him a golden boat in which he sailed to Erythia. He slew Geryones, Eurytion and his dog, and sailed with the oxen for Tartessus. Here he returned the golden boat to Helios. On his journey through Gaul, Italy, Illyricum, and Thrace, he met with many hindrances, but at last brought his booty safely to his master, who sacrificed the oxen to Hera (Juno). (11.) *Bringing the golden apples of the Hesperides.* Ge (the earth) had given these apples to Hera as a marriage gift. Hera gave them to the Hesperides, and the giant Ladon on Mount Atlas, for safe keeping. (Hesperides). Hercules did not know where they were kept, which made the task a difficult one. When Hercules arrived at Mount Atlas he bore the weight of heaven, and commanded Atlas to bring the apples. This he did, but refused to take the weight again. Hercules, however, took the apples, and hastened to Eurystheus and gave him the apples. He dedicated them to Athena (Minerva), who restored them to their former place. Some accounts say that Hercules killed the giant Ladon. (12.) *Bringing Cerberus from Hades.* This was the most difficult task. He entered the lower world near Tænarum in Laconia. Hermes (Mercury) and Athena (Minerva) accompanied him. He liberated Theseus and Æsculapius from torments, and obtained permission of Pluto to carry Cerberus to Eurystheus if he could do it without force of arms. This he did, and

Hercules and Cerberus.

after showing the monster to his master he returned it to Hades. These twelve labors being ended, Hercules returned to Thebes. There he gave Megara to Iolaus in marriage, and wished himself to obtain Iole, daughter of Eurytus, king of Œchalia. Her father promised her to any one who should excel himself and his sons in shooting with the bow. Hercules excelled them, but they refused, (with the exception of Iphitus), to give Iole to him because he had killed his own children. He soon killed Iphitus, his friend, in a fit of madness, and although purified from this murder he was attacked by a severe illness. The Delphic oracle declared that he could be restored to health if he would serve three years for wages, which he must give to Eurytus to atone for the murder of Iphitus. He became the servant of Omphale, queen of Lydia. Tradition says that here he lived effeminately, spun wool and dressed like a woman, while the queen wore his lion-skin. Others relate that during this time he undertook an expedition to Colchis; met the Argonauts; took part in the Calydonian hunt; and met Theseus on the Corinthian isthmus when he returned from Trœzene. At the end of three years he sailed to Troy, killed king Laomedon, and took the city. About this time the gods sent for him to assist them to fight the giants, who had made war against them. After his return to Argos he marched against Augeas; against Pylos, and killed the entire family of Neleus, with the exception of Nestor. He went to Calydon and fought with Achelous for Deïanīra, daughter of Œneus. After being married to her three years he accidentally killed the boy Eunomus at the house of Œneus. Hercules then went into exile, taking Deïanīra.

Hercules and Omphale. (Farnese Group, Naples.)

When they came to the river Evenus, where Nessus ferried travellers across, Hercules crossed and left Deïanīra to follow him. Nessus then attempted to violate her, but Hercules hearing her cries shot an arrow which pierced Nessus through the heart. Before he died he told Deïanīra to take his blood with her as a sure means of preserving the love of her husband. Hercules then dwelt at Trachis, and attacked Eurytus of Œchalia. He took his kingdom, killed him and his sons, and carried his daughter Iole away a prisoner.

On his return he landed at Cenæum, a promontory of Eubœa, and erected an altar to Zeus. He sent Lichas to Trachis to bring him a white garment to use during the sacrifice. Deïanira, fearing lest Iole should rob her of his love, sent a garment steeped in the blood of Nessus. The arrow of Hercules had poisoned the blood, and when Hercules put on the garment and it became warm, he was seized with the most excruciating agony. When he pulled it off pieces of flesh came with it. He seized Lichas and threw him into the sea. He was conveyed to Trachis, and when Deïanira saw what she had done, she hung herself. Hercules commanded his eldest son by Deïanira, Hyllus, to marry Iole as soon as he should reach manhood. He then raised a pile of wood on Mount Œta, placed himself on it and commanded it to be set on fire. While it was burning, a cloud descended and carried him to Olympus, where he was made immortal; was reconciled to Hera, and married Hebe. He was worshipped at Greece and Rome. The sacrifices offered him were rams, lambs, bulls, and boars. The poplar tree was sacred to him. He is variously represented in art as a child, youth, hero, and god. In every case he personifies energy, courage, and strength.

Hermaphrodi'tus. Son of Hermes (Mercury) and Aphroditē (Venus). Grandson of Atlas, and therefore called Atlantiades, or Atlantius. He inherited great beauty from both parents. The nymph of the fountain Salmacis near Halicarnassus loved him, and tried in vain to win his affections. One day as he bathed in the fountain she embraced him, at the same time praying the gods to unite them forever. Her prayer was answered, and their bodies united, retaining the characteristics of both sexes.

Her'mes (Mercurius). Son of Zeus (Jupiter) and Maia, daughter of Atlas. Born in a cave on Mount Cyllene in Arcadia, and called Atlantiades or Cyllenius. When but a few hours old he went to Pieria, carried off the oxen of Apollo and drove them to Pylos. When he returned to his cave he found a tortoise at the mouth of it, which he made into a lyre, by placing strings across its shell. Apollo knew who had stolen the oxen and came to demand them, but Maia showed him the infant asleep in his cradle. The god took him to Zeus, who compelled him to give up the oxen, but when he played the lyre Apollo was so charmed that he returned them to him and became his friend. Hermes was made the herald of the gods, es-

Hermes. (Museo Borbonico.)

pecially of Zeus; and as the heralds speak publicly, he was the god of eloquence, — the god who protected travellers, and the god of commerce. His statue was erected on roads, at gates, and doors. He was the god of luck, and presided over games with dice. He invented sacrifices, and protected animals used for them. For this reason he was connected with nymphs and with Pan, and was honored by shepherds. He was the god of cunning, and even of deceit and treachery, and his shrewdness caused him to invent many things, such as measures, weights, the alphabet, numbers, astronomy, the art of fighting, and gymnastics, music, the cultivation of the olive, as well as the lyre and syrinx. Some of his important duties as a herald were to lead Priam to Achilles to recover the body of Hector; to rescue Dionysus (Bacchus) from the flames after his birth; to sell Hercules to Omphale; to carry off Io, who was changed into a cow and guarded by Argus; to tie Ixion to the wheel; and to conduct Hera (Juno), Aphroditē (Venus), and Athena (Minerva) to Paris. Arcadia, his native land, was the first place where he was worshipped, but at length he was honored throughout all Greece. All gymnasia were under his care, and he was always represented as perfectly developed in limb and person, as if by gymnastic exercises. His festivals were called Hermæa. The palm, the tortoise, various fishes, and the number "4" were sacred to him. Young goats, lambs, pigs, honey, cakes, and incense were sacrificed to him. His attributes are a hat with a wide brim, and sometimes with wings; sandals which carried him swiftly on sea or land, having wings at the ankles, from which he is called *alipes;* and the herald's staff given him by Apollo, which in early art was adorned with white ribbons, but later twined with two serpents. See Mercurius.

Hermi′one. Daughter of Menelaus and Helen. Very beautiful. Was promised to Orestes before the siege of Troy, but after the end of the war Menelaus married her to Neoptolemus (Pyrrhus). At his death she married Orestes and bore a son, Tisamenus.

He′ro. See Leander.

Hersil′ia. Wife of Romulus. After death worshipped as Hora or Horta.

Hesper′ides. Their parentage is disputed, but some call them daughters of Atlas and Hesperis, hence called Atlantides or Hesperides. Some mention their number as three, and their names as Ægle, Arethusa, and Hesperia; others give them as four: Ægle, Crytheia, Hestia, and Arethusa, and again they are said to have been seven. Very early writers say that they lived on the river Oceanus in the West, but later they are placed near Mount Atlas and in Libya, where they guarded the golden apples which Ge (the earth) had given Hera (Juno) at her wedding. The giant Ladon assisted them. See Hercules.

Hes′tia (Vesta). Daughter of Cronus (Saturn) and Rhea. She was the first born of Rhea, and thus the first swallowed by Cronus. She was one of the twelve great divinities. Goddess of the fire on the hearth. When Apollo and Poseidon (Neptune) sought her in marriage she swore by the head of Zeus to remain a virgin. She was believed to dwell in the inner domestic life, as the hearth was the centre of that life. As goddess of fire she had a part in all sacrifices. She was goddess of the public hearth, as of the private; when colonists went forth they carried fire, which was to burn in the new home they went to found. The public hearth was usually in the prytaneum of a town, where Hestia had a special sanctuary. See Vesta.

Hieron′. Tyrant of Syracuse. Brother and successor of Gelon. A friend and patron of literature. Æschylus, Simonides, and Pindar dwelt at his court. (2.) King of Syracuse and descended from Gelon. A friend and ally of the Romans. Succeeded by Hieronymus, his grandson.

Hippol′ytus. Son of Theseus and Hippolyte, Queen of the Amazones, or of her sister Antiope. Theseus afterward married Phædra, who fell in love with Hippolytus, and when she found that he would not return it, she accused him to Theseus of having attempted to dishonor her. Theseus cursed him and gave him over to destruction. As Hippolytus rode near the sea, Poseidon (Neptune) sent out a bull which frightened the horses, who upset the chariot and dragged Hippolytus to death. When Theseus later learned the deceit of Phædra she killed herself. Artemis (Diana) and Æsculapius attempted to restore Hippolytus to life. The accounts concerning their success differ. Some relate that they could not restore him; others that they succeeded, and under the name of Virbius he dwelt in the grove of Aricia in Latium under the protection of Egeria, and was worshipped as a divinity.

Ho′ræ. Daughters of Zeus (Jupiter) and Themis. Goddesses of the seasons and of the order of Nature. They kept the door of Olympus and controlled the weather. Thallo (Hora of spring) and Carpo (Hora of autumn) were worshipped at Athens from very early times. They are usually represented as four in number. Hesiod calls them Eunomia (good order), Dice (justice), and Irene (peace). In art they are represented as blooming youths or maidens bearing the products of the seasons.

Hyacin′thus. Son of Amyclas, King of Sparta. A beautiful youth, beloved by Apollo and Zephyrus. He loved Apollo, but as he played quoits with him Zephyrus through jealousy caused the quoit of Apollo to hit Hyacinthus and kill him instantly. The hyacinth sprang from his blood, and on its leaves was the woful exclamation AI, or Υ, which is the initial letter of Ὑάκινθος. He was worshipped at Amyclæ as a hero, and his festival was called Hyacinthia.

Hydas'pes. The most northern of the five rivers which form the Indus, and water the great plain of northern India.

Hy'dra. See Hercules.

Hygie'a (Hygea; Hygia). Daughter or wife of Æsculapius. Goddess of health. In art she wears a long robe, and feeds a serpent from a cup.

Hy'las. A beautiful youth whom Hercules loved and took with him in the expedition of the Argonauts. He went to draw water on the coast of Mysia, and was carried off by the Naiads. Hercules sought him in vain.

Hy'men (Hymenæus). Son of Apollo and a Muse. God of marriage, who was invoked in a bridal song. In art he is young, but more serious in expression than Eros (Cupid), and bears a torch.

Hypsip'yle. Daughter of Thoas, king of Lemnos. When the Lemnian women killed all the men, she saved her father, and when this was discovered she was compelled to quit the island. She was taken by pirates when escaping, and sold to Lycurgus the Nemean king. He gave her to his son Archemorus or Opheltes.

Ic'arus. Son of Dædalus. When they wished to escape from Crete, the father made them wings and fastened them with wax, and he flew safely to Italy; but Icarus flew too near the sun so that the wax was melted, and the wings coming off he fell into the Ægean Sea.

Dædalus making wings for Icarus. (Bas-relief).

I'ole. See Hercules.

Iphigeni'a. Daughter of Agamemnon and Clytæmnestra, or as others say, of Theseus and Helena. Agamemnon killed a hart sacred to Diana (Artemis), and she becalmed the Greek fleet in Aulis when they would sail to Troy. Calchas, the seer, advised Agamemnon to sacrifice Iphigenīa, but Artemis put a hart in her place and bore her to Tauris, where she made her a priestess. When her brother Orestes was to be sacrificed to Artemis she rescued him and carried him to Grecce with the statue of the goddess. Iphigenīa was probably the same as Artemis originally. She was worshipped in Athens and Sparta.

I'ris. Daughter of Thaumas and Electra. Sister of the Harpies, — called also Thaumantias. In the "Iliad" she was the messenger of the gods. She is a virgin in the earlier traditions, but later the wife of Zephyrus and mother of Eros (Cupid). She was the personification of the rainbow, which was considered a swift messenger of the gods. In art she wears a long and full tunic, over this a light garment; wings on the shoulders; — bears the herald's staff in her left hand and sometimes a pitcher.

Iris. (Ancient Vase.)

I'sis. Chief female divinity of Egypt. Wife of Osiris. Mother of Horus. Originally goddess of the earth, later of the moon. Her worship was introduced into Rome and became popular. Her temple was in the Campus Martius, and she was called Isis Campensis. She is also called *linigera*, because her priests wore linen garments.

Ixi'on. King of the Lapithæ. Father of Pirithous. He murdered his father-in-law, and when no one would purify him, he went to Zeus (Jupiter) who took him to heaven and purified him. But Ixion was ungrateful to Zeus, and tried to win the love of Hera. Zeus then made a phantom like Hera, and by this Ixion became the father of a centaur. Ixion was punished for his impious ingratitude by Hermes (Mercury), who chained him to a wheel which revolves perpetually in the air.

Ja'son. Son of Æson, king of Iolcus in Thessaly. Pelias, uncle of Jason, took the kingdom from his father, and attempted to kill Jason. His friends saved him, and he was cared for by Chiron the centaur. When older he demanded his kingdom of Pelias, who made the condition that he should bring him the golden fleece. (See Argonautæ.) While Jason was absent,

Medea and her children. (Museo Borbonico.)

Pelias slew his father. Medea, the wife of Jason, in order to revenge this murder, persuaded the daughters of Pelias to cut him up and boil him, to make him young again. He died thus, and his son Acastus drove Jason and Medea out of Iolcus. They went to Corinth, where they were happy until Jason deserted Medea for Glauce or Creusa, daughter of the king of Corinth. Medea sent her a garment which burned her up when she put it on; and her father, Creon, also perished in the flames from it. Medea then killed her children by Jason, and fled to Athens in a chariot drawn by winged dragons. Several traditions are given concerning the death of Jason. One says he killed himself from grief; another, that he was crushed beneath the poop of the ship Argo.

Ju′no (Hera). Although the Roman Juno and Greek Hera are considered the same goddess, there was a difference regarding her in the opinions of the two nations. Juno was queen of heaven, as Jupiter (Zeus) was king, and had the surname *Regina*. Her other surnames were, *Virginalis*, *Matrona*, *Sospita*, *Opigena*, *Juga* or *Jugalis*, *Pronuba*, *Cinxia*, *Lucina*, *Moneta*, and others. She was believed to watch over every woman from birth till death. On birth-days she was invoked as *Natalis*. The *Matronalia* on the first of March was her great festival. It is said that June was originally called *Junonius*, and was considered the most favorable month for marriage. Women in childbirth, and newly born infants were her special care. She also guarded the finances, and had a temple on the Capitoline Hill dedicated to Juno Moneta.

Ju′piter (Zeus). The Roman lord of Heaven. His surnames are *Pluvius*, *Fulgurator*, *Tonitrualis*, *Tonans*, *Fulminator*, *Victor*, *Imperator*, *Invictus*, *Stator*, *Opitulus*, *Triumphator*, and many more. Being the highest god, he was called Optimus Maximus. He was called *Capitolinus* and *Tarpeius*, from the fact that his temple was on the Capitoline Hill. He was regarded as the special protector of Rome, and recognized on all important occasions, such as victories, the assumption of office by new consuls, etc., etc. There were almost numberless temples and statues sacred to him in Rome, under his various surnames. As *Capitolinus* he presided over the great games; as *Latialis* or *Latiaris* over the Feriæ Latinæ. He was *Prodigalis*, because he caused all wonderful events besides determining the usual course of all human affairs. Nothing was undertaken without seeking his blessing, and he was regarded as the protector of justice, and the

Head of Olympian Jupiter.

enforcer of faith and oaths. Fides and Victoria were his companions on the capitol; hence were traitors thrown from the Tarpeian rock. As prince of light, and lord of heaven, white was sacred to him. White animals were sacrificed to him; his chariot was believed to be drawn by four white horses; his priests wore white caps, and the consuls wore white when they sacrificed to him upon assuming their office. The *Flamen Dialis*, who had the care of the worship of Jupiter, was the highest of all the flamens. See Zeus.

La'don. The dragon who assisted the Hesperides to guard the golden apples of Juno. See Hercules.

Laoc'oon. A Trojan priest of the Thymbræan Apollo. He endeavored to prevent the Trojans taking the wooden horse into the city. As he was about to sacrifice a bull to Neptune (Poseidon), two serpents came from the sea, and destroyed him and his two sons.

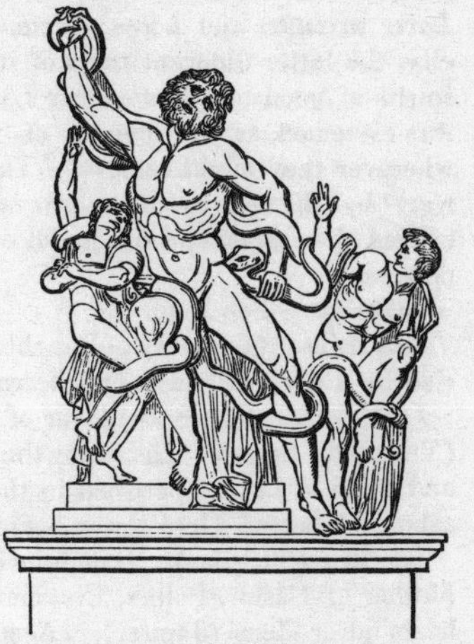

Laocoön. (Vatican.)

Laodami'a. Daughter of Acastus. Wife of Protesilaus. Her husband was slain before Troy, and she obtained permission of the gods to converse with him three hours. Hermes (Mercury) led Protesilaus back to the upper world, and when he died again Laodamia died also.

Laom'edon. Son of Ilus. Father of Priam, Hesione, and others. King of Troy. Poseidon (Neptune) and Apollo had displeased Zeus (Jupiter), and he sentenced them to serve Laomedon. Apollo tended his flocks on Mount Ida, and Poseidon built the walls of Troy. When they had done, the king refused the wages he had agreed to give, and in revenge Poseidon sent a sea-monster who preyed on the country, and the Trojans were forced to sacrifice a maiden to him from time to time. It fell to the lot of Hesione, the king's daughter, to be thus slain, and Hercules killed the monster to save her. Laomedon promised to give him, as a reward, the divine horses which he had received from Zeus as payment for Ganymedes. Again the king was faithless, and Hercules sailed against Troy, took it, killed the king, and gave Hesione to Telamon.

Lap'ithæ. The mythical subjects of Pirithous, son of Ixion and half-brother of the centaurs. This race were said to dwell in the mountains of Thessaly. The centaurs demanded a share of the kingdom, and being refused there was war between them and the Lapithæ. They at length made a peace, but when Pirithous married Hippodamia, the centaurs became intoxicated at the wedding-feast, and urged on by Ares (Mars), they attempted to carry off the bride and other women. A bloody contest ensued. The Lapithæ were victorious. It is said that bridles for horses were invented and first used by this people. They were probably a Pelasgian race, who drove the less civilized centaurs away from Mount Pelion.

La'res. These inferior gods of Rome were of two classes: *Lares publici*, and *Lares domestici*. The *publici* were also divided into *Lares præstites* and *Lares compitales*. The former protected all the city, the latter different parts of it. The *Lares domestici* were the spirits of good men honored as Lares. They were led by Lar, who was esteemed as the founder of the family, and went with them, wherever they might remove. The images of Lares in large houses were by themselves in a *lararia*. A portion of the meals was offered the Lares, and on joyful occasions they were adorned with flowers.

Lato'na. See Leto.

Lavin'ia (Lavinia). Daughter of Latinus and Amata. Married to Æneas, although first betrothed to Turnus.

Lean'der. The brave lover of Hero, the priestess of Aphrodite (Venus) in Sestus. He swam the Hellespont each night to see her, and when at last he perished in the waves, and his body was washed ashore at Sestus, Hero threw herself into the sea and thus perished.

Le'da (Thestias). Daughter of Thestius. Wife of Tyndareus. Mother of Castor, Pollux, Clytæmnestra, and Helena, either by her husband or Zeus (Jupiter). According to the tradition, the latter visited her in the form of a swan, and she brought forth two eggs. From one Castor and Pollux issued, and Helena from the other.

Le'to (Latona). Daughter of the Titan Coeus and Phœbe. Mother of Apollo and Artemis (Diana) by Zeus (Jupiter). Juno (Hera) hated and persecuted her, and at last she went to Delos, a floating island. Zeus fastened it to the bottom of the sea with chains of adamant, and here she gave birth to her children. She was worshipped in connection with her children, and principally at Delos. From her Apollo is called *Letoïus* or *Latoïus*, and Diana *Letoïa*, *Letoïs*, *Latoïs* or *Latoë*.

Leucip'pus. 1. Son of Œnomaus and lover of Daphne. 2. Son of Perieres. Prince of the Messenians. Father of Phœbe and Hilaria, who are called Leucippides. They were betrothed to Idas and Lynceus, sons of Aphareus, but they were stolen by Castor and Pollux.

Lips. The Southwest wind. Corresponds to the Latin Africus.

Lucre'tia. Wife of L. Tarquinius Collatinus. Her rape by Sextus Tarquinius led to the dethronement of Tarquinius Superbus and the founding of the Republic.

Lips. (Athens. Temple of the Winds.)

Lycome'des. King of the Dolopians. Achilles was sent to his court as a maiden. (See Achilles.) Lycomedes killed Theseus by thrusting him down a rock.

Lycur'gus. Son of Dryas and king of the Edones in Thrace. He is celebrated for his persecution of Dionysus (Bacchus). The gods made him mad on account of his impiety. He was killed, but the manner of his death is variously related.

Mars (Ares). Next to Jupiter the highest god at Rome. He was considered the father of Romulus. Often called Father Mars. He was one of the three tutelary deities, and to him Numa appointed a flamen. He was god of war, and war itself was often called Mars. The Campus Martius being dedicated to warlike exercises, was named for him. His priests, the Salii, danced in full armor. He was also the protector of agriculture and watched over the Roman citizens as Quirites, he being identified with Quirinus. In each character he has an appropriate name. As war god he is *Gradivus*, as rustic god, *Silvanus*, and as civil god *Quirinus*. His wife was called *Neria* or *Nerĭēnē*, the feminine of Nero, signifying strong. Many temples in Rome were dedicated to Mars. The most important was that on the Appian Way, beyond Porta Capena, and Mars Ultor, built in the forum by Augustus. The wolf and woodpecker were sacred to him.

Mar'syas (Marsya). A satyr of Phrygia. He found the flute which Athena (Minerva) had thrown away, because it distorted her face. Marsyas finding that it emitted sweet music, challenged Apollo to a musical contest on condition that the victor should do what he chose with the loser. Apollo played the cithara, and the Muses decided in his favor. Apollo bound Marsyas to a tree and flayed him alive. His blood formed the River Marsyas, and Apollo hung his skin in the cave from which that stream flows. The statues of Marsyas were erected as a warning against presumption. That in the Roman forum was often spoken of by the poets.

Mede'a. (See Argonautæ, Jason.)

Medu'sa. (See Gorgones.)

Melea'ger (Meleagrus). Son of Œneus, king of Calydon, and

Althæa. He was in the expedition of the Argonauts, and was afterwards leader of his companions. He slew the Calydonian boar. He gave the hide to Atalanta whom he loved, but the sons of Thestius, brothers of Althæa, took it away from her. Meleager slew them in revenge. Althæa had been told by the fates when Meleager was seven days old, that he would die when the firebrand then on the hearth was consumed. Althæa took, it, extinguished the flames and carefully preserved it. She was so angry at the murder of her brothers, that she again lighted it, and as soon as it was burned Meleager expired. His mother then repented, and killed herself. The sisters of Meleager wept for him so continually that Artemis (Diana) metamorphosed them into guinea-hens and placed them on the island of Leros.

Meleager. (Pompeii, Painting.)

Melpom'ene. Muse of Tragedy. See Musæ.

Menela'us. Son of Plisthenes or Atreus. Brother of Agamemnon and king of Lacedæmon. Husband of Helen. Father of Hermione. (The rape of Helen and expedition to Troy, see Agamemnon.) In the siege of Troy Menelaus killed many Trojans, and would have slain Paris, had not Aphrodite (Venus) carried him away in a cloud. Helen married Deiphobus, brother of Paris, after the death of the latter. As soon as Troy was captured, Menelaus and Ulysses hastened to the house of Deiphobus, whom they killed. It is said that Helen introduced them secretly to his chamber, and thus was reconciled to Menelaus. He sailed from Troy with Helen and Nestor, but was eight years in reaching Sparta, where he afterwards lived with Helen in happiness, and surrounded by wealth and luxury. One tradition relates that they never died, but were translated to Elysium. Another that they went to Tauris, and were sacrificed to Artemis by Iphigenia. Menelaus is represented in art with a noble and athletic form. The poets describe him as silent, brave, gentle, intelligent, and hospitable.

Mercu'rius (Hermes). Roman god of commerce and gain. He is identified with Hermes, but the Fetiales did not recognize the identity, and gave him the branch of peace in place of the *caduceus*. His name, connected with *merx* and *mercari*, sufficiently indicate his office. His festival was kept on the 25th of May, and observed principally by merchants who went to his well near the Porta Capena, said to have magic powers. A temple was built in his honor, near the Circus Maximus B. C. 495.

Metrodo'rus. The most distinguished disciple of Epicurus.

Mi'das (Mida). Son of Gordias. King of Phrygia and famous for his riches. He was so kind to Silenus that Bacchus (Dionysus) allowed him to ask a favor of him. He asked that all he touched should be turned to gold, but he soon begged that the permission should be taken away. Bacchus ordered him to bathe in the river Pactolus. Midas was saved, and ever after the river had much gold in its sands. Pan and Apollo had a musical contest, and Midas was the judge. He decided for Pan, and Apollo changed his ears to those of an ass. He concealed them by a Phrygian cap, but his barber saw them. The man dared not tell this, and he could not keep such a secret; so he dug a hole in the ground and whispered the fact to the earth. He filled up the hole, but a reed grew from it, and in its whispers it told the truth.

Minerva (Athena.)

Miner'va (Athena). At Rome she was a great divinity and regarded as the thinking power, her name containing the same root as *meus.* A chapel was dedicated to her in the capitol. She protected trade and the arts; guided men to conquer in war by prudence and courage, and invented musical instruments, which were much employed in her worship. Her festival, called *Quinquatrus*, lasted five days from March 19. Besides the chapel at the capitol she had one at the foot of the Cœlian Hill, where she was called *Capta*, and another on the Aventine. The booty taken in war was often dedicated to her. She is represented in a coat of mail with helmet and shield.

Minotau'rus. A monster which was half man and half bull. Offspring of Pasiphaë and a bull. Minos compelled Athens to send seven youths and seven maidens to be given to this monster, each year, until Theseus killed him, aided by Ariadne.

Mi'thras. Persian god of the sun, worshipped also at Rome. He is represented as young and handsome, wearing the Phrygian cap and costume. Usually kneeling on a bull and cutting its throat.

Mnemos'yne. Goddess of Memory. Daughter of Uranus (Heaven). Mother of the Muses by Zeus (Jupiter).

Moi'ræ (Parcæ; Fates). They were three in number. Clotho, the spinning Fate. Lachesis, the goddess who assigns his fate to man. Atropos, the inevitable fate. These different offices are not always strictly observed in their representations, for sometimes the three are described as spinning the thread of life. At death they cut it. They are sometimes said to be ugly and aged, but in art they are grave women. Clotho with a spindle or roll (the book of fate). Lachesis points to a globe with her staff. Atropos bears a pair of scales, a sun-dial, or some cutting instrument.

Mor'pheus. Whose name signifies the fashioner or moulder, was son of sleep, and god of dreams. Thus he shapes the dreams of the sleeper.

Mu'sæ (Muses). Daughters of Zeus (Jupiter) and Mnemosyne. Born at Pieria at the foot of Mount Olympus. They were nine in number.

(1.) *Cli'o.* Muse of history. Represented standing or sitting with a chest of books or an open roll of paper.

(2.) *Euter'pe.* Muse of lyric poetry. Attribute, a flute.

(3.) *Thali'a.* Muse of comedy and idyllic poems. Attributes, a comic mask and wreath of ivy or a shepherd's staff.

(4.) *Melpom'ene.* Muse of tragedy. Attributes, a tragic mask, a sword or club of Hercules. She wears the cothurnus and is crowned with vine leaves.

(5.) *Terpsich'ore.* Muse of dance and song. Attributes, the lyre and plectrum.

(6.) *Er'ato.* Muse of erotic poetry and mimic imitation. Attribute, the lyre.

(7.) *Polym'nia*, or *Polyhym'nia.* Muse of the sublime hymn. Is represented in a thoughtful, pensive attitude, without attributes.

(8.) *Ura'nia.* Muse of astronomy. Usually represented pointing to a globe with a staff.

(9.) *Calli'ope*, or *Calliope'a.* Muse of epic poetry. Attributes, tablet and stylus, or a roll of paper or a book.

The favorite localities of the Muses were Mount Parnassus, with the Castalian spring, and Mount Helicon, with the fountains Aganippe and Hippocrene. They were invoked by poets; but all who endeavored to compete with them were punished. The Sirens who had done so were robbed of the feathers of their wings, which the Muses wore as ornaments, and the nine daughters of Pierus, who aspired to be their rivals were changed to birds. They were connected with Apollo, who is said to have been the leader of their choir. He was sometimes called *Musagetes.* The offerings made them were libations of water, milk, or honey.

Myr'rha (Smyrna). Mother of Adonis.

Narcis'sus. Son of Cephissus and Liriope. He was very beautiful, but incapable of love. The nymph Echo, who was enamored of him, died of sorrow. Nemesis, in order to punish him, showed him his own image in a fountain, with which he was so charmed that he too pined away, and was at last changed into the flower which bears his name.

Neces'sitas (Ananke; Necessity). A powerful goddess. Neither gods nor men can resist her. She has brazen nails in her hands with which she fixes the decrees of fate.

Nem'esis. A goddess who in the earlier times was believed to measure out the lot of mortals, to control their happiness or misery, and to send suffering to those who have too many good gifts. Later she has been regarded as more like the Furies or Erinnyes, who punished crimes. Her surnames are Adrastia and Rhamnusia or Rhamnusis; the last from an Attic town Rhamnus, where she had her most celebrated temple.

Neoptol'emus (Pyrrhus). Son of Achilles and Deidamīa, daughter of King Lycomedes. He was called Neoptolemus, on account of going to Troy late in the war, and Pyrrhus on account of his golden hair. He was reared in the palace of his grandfather at Scyros, and was taken to Troy by Ulysses, on account of a prophecy which said that Neoptolemus and Philoctetes were necessary to the taking of Troy. He was one of the heroes concealed in the wooden horse, and was a brave warrior. He killed Priam and sacrificed Polyxena to the spirit of Achilles. In the distribution of the booty, Andromachē, the widow of Hector, fell to his share. He abandoned his native Thessaly after this war and lived in Epirus, where he became the ancestor of the Molossian kings. He married Hermione, daughter of Menelaus, but was killed in a combat with Orestes to whom she had previously been betrothed. From his father he is sometimes called *Achillīdes*, and *Pelīdes* and *Æacīdes* from his grandfather and great grandfather.

Neptu'nus (Poseidon). The chief maritime god of the Romans; identified with the Greek Poseidon. The early Romans were not a maritime nation, and little is known of the worship of this god. At his festivals the people made tents, *umbræ*, of the branches of trees, and enjoyed feasting and drinking. See Poseidon.

Nere'ides (Nereids). The fifty daughters of Nereus and Doris. Nymphs of the Mediterranean, and distinct from *Naiades* who were nymphs of fresh water, and from *Oceanides*, nymphs of the great oceans. They were very beautiful, and dwelt at the bottom of the sea. They were kind to sailors. Thetis, the mother of Achilles, was a Nereid. They are usually represented as beautiful maidens but sometimes as half maidens and half fishes, especially on ancient gems.

Ne'reus. Son of Pontus and Gæa. Husband of Doris and father of fifty daughters. He dwelt at the bottom of his empire the Mediterranean Sea, or especially the Ægean Sea, and he is hence sometimes called the Ægean. He acted an important part in the story of Hercules. He had the gift of prophecy, and was wise and unerring. He is sometimes represented with sea-weed in place of eyebrows, beard, and hair.

Nes'sus. The centaur who carried travellers across the river Evenus. See Hercules.

Niobe and her children. (Florence.)

Ni'obe (Nioba). Daughter of Tantalus. Wife of Amphion, king of Thebes. She was so proud of the number of her children that she boasted herself as superior to Leto (Latona) who had but two children. The number of those of Niobe is usually given as seven sons and seven daughters. Apollo and Artemis (Diana) so heartily espoused the cause of Leto that they killed the children of Niobe with their arrows. Zeus (Jupiter) metamorphosed Niobe into a stone, and placed it on Mount Sipylus in Lydia. During the summer this stone always shed tears. The story of Niobe was a favorite subject of ancient art.

Notus. (Athens.)

No'tus (Auster). The South or Southwest wind. It brought rains and fog.

Oce'anus. Son of Uranus (Heaven) and Gæa (Earth). Husband of Tethys and father of all the river gods and water nymphs in the whole earth. He was especially the deity of the Atlantic, or the water without the Pillars of Hercules, in distinction from the Mediterranean, or the sea within them. Hence the Atlantic was often called Oceanus.

Œd'ipus. Son of Laius, king of Thebes, and of Jocasta, sister of Creon. His father exposed him on Mount Cithæron, because an oracle had said that he should die by the hand of his son. His feet were pierced and tied together, and when he was found by a shepherd of Polybus, king of Corinth, they were so swollen that he was on that account named Œdipus. Polybus reared him as his own child, but when he was grown the Delphic oracle declared to him that he was fated to kill his father and commit incest with his mother. Believing that Polybus was his father, he determined not to return to Corinth, and on his way to Daulis he met Laius whom he killed without knowing that it was his father. About this time the celebrated Sphinx appeared near Thebes. The monster was seated on a rock, and put a riddle to every Theban that passed. If not able to answer he was killed. The Thebans proclaimed that he who would answer the riddle should have the kingdom and Jocasta for his wife. The riddle was as follows: "A being with four feet, has two feet and three feet, and only one voice; and when it has most it is weakest." Œdipus declared that it was man: that in childhood he went upon all fours, in manhood upon two feet, and in old age supported himself with a staff. The Sphinx threw herself down from the rock. Then Œdipus married his mother and was made king. She bore to him Eteocles, Polynīces, Antigŏnē, and Ismēnē. A plague was sent upon Thebes in consequence of this incest. The oracle was consulted and declared that the murderer of Laius must be expelled. Tiresias, a seer, told Œdipus that he was the guilty one. Then he put out his own eyes, and wandered away from Thebes, accompanied by his daughter Antigone. Jocasta hung herself when she knew the truth. Œdipus went to Attica, whence he was taken away by the Furies or Eumenides. His fate was the subject of many tragic poems.

Œno'ne. Daughter of the river-god Cebren. Wife of Paris before he carried Helen away.

Om'phale. Daughter of Iardanus. Wife of Tmolus, and queen of Lydia, after his death. (See Hercules).

Or'cus. See Hades.

Ores'tes. Son of Agamemnon and Clytæmnestra. Husband of Hermīonē. When Ægisthus and his mother murdered Agamemnon, his life was saved by his sister Electra, who sent him to Strophius, king of Phocis, who had married the sister of Agamemnon. He became the dear friend of Pylades, the king's son, and when a man went to Argos with him and avenged the death of his father. He slew both Clytæmnestra and Ægisthus. After killing his mother he was mad, and went from land to land pursued by Furies. Apollo at length advised him to go to Athens and have his case judged by the court of the Areopagus. This he did, and took refuge in the temple of Athena (Minerva). He was acquitted by the court. Another tradition relates that Apollo told him that he could only recover his reason by bringing the statue of Artemis (Diana) from the Tauric Chersonesus. He went there with Pylades. The natives seized and were about to sacrifice them, when Iphigenīa who was the priestess, and also the sister of Orestes, recognized him. She saved their lives, and the three escaped, bearing with them the image. After their return Orestes obtained his father's kingdom of Mycenæ, and after killing Neoptolemus married Hermione.

Ori'on. Son of Hyrieus of Hyria in Bœotia. He was a giant hunter and very handsome. He went to Chios, where he loved Merope, daughter of Œnopion. He so treated the maiden that her father with the help of Dionysus (Bacchus) put out his eyes. An oracle told him that he could recover his sight by exposing his eyes to the rising sun. He went to Lemnos, and Hephæstus (Vulcan) sent Cedalion as his guide to the east. After his sight was restored he lived with Artemis (Diana) as a hunter. His death is attributed to various causes. One tradition relates that Aurora (Eos) carried him away, and as this displeased the gods, Artemis shot him with an arrow in Ortygia. Another, that he was loved by Artemis, which displeased Apollo, and he challenged her to hit a mark that he pointed out to her on the water. She aimed but too well, for the mark was the head of Orion who was swimming. Horace relates that Orion offered an insult to Artemis, who then killed him. Again it is said that he was stung by a scorpion, and Æsculapius was killed by lightning sent by Zeus (Jupiter) when he attempted to cure him of the poison. After his death he was set among the stars, where he is represented as a giant with a lion's skin, a club, a sword, and a girdle. His constellation set at the beginning of November, the season of rains and storms. Hence his names are *nimbosus* or *aquosus* and *imbrifer*.

Orithy ia. Daughter of Erechtheus, king of Athens, and Praxithea. Boreas carried her off to Thrace, where she became the mother of Cleopatra, Chione, Zetes, and Calais.

Or'pheus. A mythical poet, called the son of Œagrus and Calliope. He accompanied the Argonautic expedition. Apollo gave him a lyre, and the Muses taught him how to play. He enchanted everything that had life, and even trees and rocks, so that they would follow him. After his return from Crete he married the nymph Eurydice and dwelt in Thrace. She died from the bite of a serpent. Orpheus followed her to Hades, where the charm of his music caused the torments to cease. Pluto consented that Eurydice should accompany him to the upper world, on condition that he should not look back while upon his way. This he refrained from doing until he reached the threshold, when he turned his head and Eurydice fell back to Hades. His grief for his wife was so great that he scorned the Thracian women, and they in revenge tore him to pieces in their Bacchic feasts. The Muses collected the fragments of his body and buried them at the foot of Mount Olympus. His head was thrown into the Hebrus and rolled to the sea, and was carried to Lesbos. His lyre was also said to be carried there, but these two stories are only illustrations of the truth, that Lesbos was the first place where the music of the lyre became noted. Another tradition relates that his lyre was placed by Zeus (Jupiter) among the stars.

Orpheus. (Mosaic.)

Pal'las. One of the names of Athena or Minerva.

Pan. Son of Hermes (Mercury). God of flocks and herds. Arcadia was the source and principal place of his worship. From here it was carried to all Greece. He is identified with Faunus, and like him represented as sensual, with goats' feet, pug nose, and horns. He is merry, and often dances and plays the syrinx, which he invented. He was mischievous and dreaded by travellers, whom he often surprised with some sudden fear with no apparent cause, hence called a Panic.

Pan. (Bronze Relief. Pompeii.)

Pando'ra. The first woman on earth. When Prometheus stole the fire from heaven, Zeus (Jupiter) in order to avenge himself, caused Hephæstus (Vulcan) to make a woman out of earth, whose charms should bring misery on men. Aphroditē (Venus) gave her beauty, and Hermes (Mercury) gave her cunning boldness. She was called the all-gifted, or Pandora. She had a box containing every human ill. Hermes brought her to Epimetheus, who was so charmed with her that he forgot that Prometheus had told him not to accept any gift from the gods, and took her for his wife. She opened the box and the ills spread over all the earth. Hope was the only blessing which was there. Later writers say that the box contained choice blessings destined for humanity by the gods, but that when she opened the box these blessings being light and having wings escaped.

Par'cæ. (See Moirae).

Par'is (Alexander). Son of Priam and Hecuba. Before his birth his mother dreamed that she had brought forth a firebrand which set all the city on fire. Hence he was exposed on Mount Ida, but was taken and brought up by a shepherd who named him. When grown he so defended the shepherds and flocks that he was called Alexander, the defender of men. He at length discovered his parentage and was received by Priam as his son. He married Œnone, the daughter of the river-god Cebren, whom he soon deserted for Helen. The reason of his going to Greece, was that he offended Hera (Juno) and Athena (Minerva). He went away under the protection of Aphrodītē (Venus). The cause of this anger arose from the wedding of Peleus and Thetis, to which all the gods were invited save Discordia. She being angry threw a golden apple among the company, inscribed "To the fairest." Then Hera, Athena, and Aphrodite claimed it, and Zeus sent Hermes (Mercury) to conduct them to Paris that he might decide between them. He gave the apple to Aphrodite, which was the cause of all the ensuing troubles, for the two rejected beauties persecuted Paris until he was driven to Greece, where being received at the house of Menelaus he loved Helen and carried her to Troy. She was the most beautiful woman in the world, and had been wooed by many suitors, who now joined her husband to assist him to redress this wrong. Hence the ten years' siege of Troy. Paris would have been killed by Menelaus with whom he fought, but Aphrodite carried him away in a cloud. He is said to have killed Achilles. (See Achilles). At the capture of Troy he was wounded by Philoctetes with one of the poisoned arrows of Hercules. He then returned to Œnone and desired her to cure the wound, which she refused to do, and he died. Then Œnone repented and killed herself. Paris is represented in art as young, without a beard, and in a Phrygian cap.

Parnas'sus. A mountain range in Doris and Phocis. Its two highest summits near Delphi were called Tithorea and Lycorea; these are the parts usually referred to, and from them is Parnassus called "double-headed." It contained many caves, ravines, glens, and romantic spots. The sides were wooded, the top covered with snow, while olives, myrtles, and laurel grew at its foot. It was the favorite home of Apollo and the Muses. Here song and music were inspired. The Muses are called Corycian nymphs, from the cave of that name on Mount Lycorea. The famed Castalian spring issued from between two cliffs near Delphi. These cliffs, named Nauplia and Hyamplia, were called summits of Parnassus. They are in reality but small peaks and near the base of the mountain. The Thyades held their Bacchic revels on a summit of Mount Parnassus, for it was sacred to Dionysus (Bacchus) as well as to Apollo. The sacred road to Daulis and Stiris from Delphi ran between Mount Cirphis and Parnassus proper. Where this road branched was the scene of the murder of Laius by Œdipus.

Pasiph'ae. Daughter of Helios (the sun) and Perseis. Wife of Minos. Mother of Androgeos, Ariadne, and Phædra. Mother also of the monster Minotaur, half man and half bull.

Patro'clus (Patrocles). Son of Menœtius of Opus and Sthenele. Grandson of Actor and Ægina, hence called *Actorides*. He accidentally committed murder while a boy, and his father took him

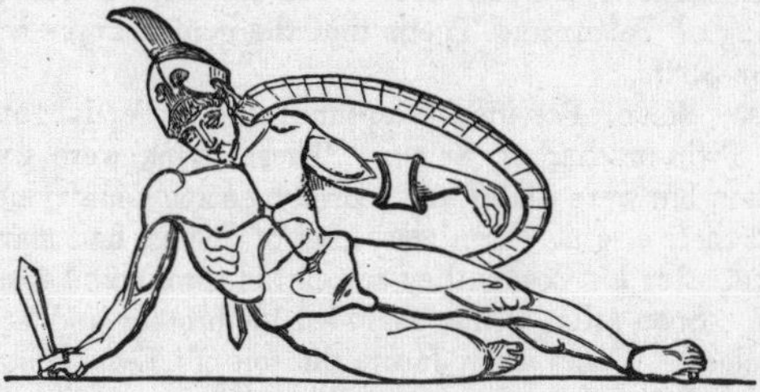

Patroclus (Ægina Marbles).

to Peleus at Phthia. Here he became the friend of Achilles. He accompanied the latter to Troy, and when Achilles retired from the fight Patroclus did the same. At length Achilles lent him his arms, and he led the Myrmidons to battle. He was slain by Hector, and a desire to avenge his death led Achilles again to take the field.

Peg'asus. The winged horse which sprang from the blood of Medusa, when Perseus struck off her head. While he drank at the fountain of Pirēnē on the Acrocorinthus, Bellerophon caught him with a golden bridle which he had received from Athena (Minerva). It was on account of having Pegasus, that Bellerophon was able to kill the Chimæra, but when he attempted to fly to heaven he fell and was killed. (Bellerophon). Pegasus kept on to heaven and dwelt among the stars. The fountain of Hippocrene in Mount Helicon in Bœotia, sacred to the Muses, sprang from the spot where Pegasus struck the ground with his hoof. He is regarded as the horse of the Muses and in later times he is most considered in this connection.

Pe'leus. Son of Æacus and Endeis. King of the Myrmidons at Phthia in Thessaly. Husband of Antigone and Thetis. Father of Achilles. Together with his brother Telamon, he murdered his half brother Phocus. For this he was expelled from Ægina, and fled to Thessaly. Here he was purified by Eurytion, son of Actor, who gave his daughter Antigone and a third part of his kingdom to Peleus. He then went to a boar-hunt where he accidentally killed his father-in-law. Again he became a wanderer and took refuge at Iolcus; was again purified by Acastus, the king of that country, and inspired Astydamia, wife of Acastus, with a wicked love. When she found no return to her passion she accused him falsely, and he was driven to Mount Pelion, where he almost perished. There he met Thetis, a Nereid, whose fate was to marry a mortal. She had the power to assume any form she chose, and she attempted to escape Peleus by becoming an animal, but he had been instructed by Chiron, and he held her fast while he persuaded her to marry him. By her he became the father of Achilles. He was too aged to go to the siege of Troy, and survived his heroic son. It was at the wedding of Peleus and Thetis that the golden apple was thrown by Eris, or Strife.

Pe'lias. Son of Poseidon (Neptune) and Tyro, daughter of Salmoneus. Twin-brother of Neleus. These twins were exposed by their mother, but were found and reared by some countrymen. They discovered their origin. Cretheus, king of Iolcus, had married their mother, and after his death, they seized his throne and excluded his son Æson. Soon after, Pelias excluded his brother and became sole ruler of Iolcus. Years after, Jason, the son of Æson, came to claim the throne. Pelias, in order to get rid of him, sent him to Colchis to obtain the golden fleece. He fitted out the Argonautic expedition for this purpose, and returned with Medea, who persuaded the daughters of Pelias to cut their father to pieces and boil him, in hopes to restore him to youth. His son Acastus held funeral games in his honor at Iolcus. He expelled Jason and Medea from the country.

Pe'lops. Son of Tantalus, king of Phrygia. Grandson of Zeus (Jupiter). Husband of Hippodamia, daughter of Œnomaus. He brought with him so much wealth, and acquired so much influence, that Elis was called the "Island of Pelops." The principal events of his life are: (1.) *He was cut to pieces and boiled.* Tantalus, his father, was a favorite of the gods, and once made a repast to which he invited them. On that occasion he killed Pelops and cooked him that the gods might devour him; but they, knowing all things, immediately perceived of what the dish was composed, and would not eat it, except Demeter (Ceres) who was so absorbed in grief at the loss of Proserpina, that she heeded not and ate a shoulder. The gods commanded Hermes (Mercury) to put him in another cauldron and restore him to life. This was done, and when Clotho took him out of the cauldron the shoulder was wanting. Demeter

(Ceres) made one of ivory, and the *Pelopidæ*, his descendants, were believed to have an ivory shoulder. (2.) *Contest with Œnomaus and Hippodamia.* An oracle had declared that Œnomaus should be killed by his son-in-law, therefore he vowed that no one should marry his daughter unless he could conquer him in a chariot race, moreover all who attempted to do so and failed, were to suffer death. He thought himself safe in this, as his horses were the fleetest in all the earth. Many suitors had been sacrificed when Pelops came to Pisa. He promised Myrtilus, the charioteer of Œnomaus, one half the kingdom if he would help him to conquer. Myrtilus took out the linch-pins of the chariot so that it broke down, and Pelops was victorious. Thus Hippodamia became his wife, and he threw Myrtilus into the sea to avoid fulfilling his promise of dividing his kingdom. As the charioteer sank, he cursed Pelops and all his race. Pelops then went with Hippodamia to Pisa in Elis, where he restored the Olympian games with great splendor. His son Chrysippus was his favorite, and this so roused the jealousy of Atreus and Thyestes that they killed him with the assistance of their mother, and threw him into a well. Pelops suspected the truth, and drove them from the kingdom. After death, Pelops was honored at Olympus more than all other mortal heroes. His name was so celebrated that it was used as often as possible in connection with his descendants. Hence his son was called *Pelopeïus Atreus*, and his grandson *Pelopeïus Agamemnon.* Iphigenia and Hermione were called *Pelopeïa virgo*, while Virgil calls the cities in Peloponnesus which Pelops and his descendants ruled, *Pelopea mœnia.* Mycenæ is called *Pelopeïades Mycenæ* by Ovid.

Penel'ope. Daughter of Icarius and Peribœa of Sparta. Wife of Ulysses king of Ithaca. Her father had promised to give her to the conqueror in a foot-race; but when Ulysses won it, Icarius tried to persuade his daughter to remain with him; she blushingly covered her face with her veil, thus intimating that she would follow Ulysses. She had one child, Telemachus, an infant, when Ulysses sailed for

Penelope. (British Museum.)

Troy. During his absence she was besieged by suitors, but she deceived them by declaring that she must finish a robe for her father-in-law, Laërtes, before she could listen to them. She worked upon this robe by day and unraveled it at night, and thus put off her lovers, until the stratagem was exposed by her servants. Then was she more pressed than before. Ulysses returned at the end of twenty years, and was most joyfully received by Penelope. Homer represents Penelope as thus faithful to Ulysses, and it is the character usually attributed to her, but later writers charge her with being the mother of Pan by Hermes (Mercury), or by all her suitors; and these add that Ulysses repudiated her on his return, and that she then went to Sparta and thence to Mantinea. Another tradition relates that Telegonus killed Ulysses and then married Penelope.

Penthesile'a. Daughter of Ares (Mars) and Otrera. Queen of the Amazons. She assisted the Trojans after Hector was killed, and was herself slain by Achilles. He mourned sincerely over his victim on account of her youth, beauty, and bravery. When Thersites ridiculed this grief, Achilles killed him also. Then Diomedes, who was a relative of Thersites, threw her body into the Scamander. Others say that Achilles buried her on the banks of the Xanthus.

Perseph'one (Proserpina). Daughter of Zeus (Jupiter) and Demeter (Ceres). In Attica she was called Κόρη, *i. e.* the daughter, and when with Demeter, they were often called "The Mother and Daughter." She was the wife of Hades (Pluto), queen of the lower world and the shades of the dead. Hence she is called *Juno Inferna*, *Averna*, and *Stygia*. Mother of the Eumenides, Erinnyes or Furies. For story of the rape of Persephone, see Demeter. She is represented in works of art grave and severe, as would become the queen of the lower world.

Per'seus. Son of Jupiter (Zeus) and Danaë. Grandson of Acrisius. Husband of Andromeda. Acrisius had been warned by an oracle that he should perish by the hand of the son of Danaë, so he shut her in a brazen tower. Zeus visited her here in the form of a shower of gold and became the father of Perseus. Hence he is called *Aurigena.* When Acrisius discovered the birth of the boy, he put both him and his mother into a chest, and cast it into the sea, but Zeus carried it ashore at Seriphos, one of the Cyclades, where they were found by a fisherman, Dictys, who carried them to king Polydectes. He received them kindly, and fell in love with Danaë. He desired to be rid of Perseus, and sent him to kill Medusa and bring to him her head. With the assistance of Athena (Minerva) and guided by Hermes (Mercury) he went to the Grææ, sisters of the Gorgons, and took away their one tooth and one eye, and would not restore them till they showed him where the nymphs lived who had the helmet of Hades (Pluto), the winged sandals, and the magic wallet. He obtained all these. Hermes gave him a sickle, and Athena a mirror.

He then flew to Tartessus, the abode of the Gorgons. He arrived when they were asleep, and cut off the head of Medusa by looking in the mirror, for if he had looked at her he would have become stone. He placed the head in the magic wallet which was on his back. The other Gorgons pursued him, but by his helmet he became invisible and thus escaped. He then went to Æthiopia, where he saved Andromeda, and married her. (See Andromeda.) It is said that he changed Atlas to a mountain by the sight of the head of Medusa. On his return to Seriphus he found that Polydectes had so persecuted Danaë that she had sought refuge in the temple. He then turned the king and all his guests to stone. He at length gave the head of Medusa to Athena, who put it in the centre of her breast-plate. He took Danaë and Andromeda to Argos. His grandfather, fearing lest the prophecy of the oracle should be fulfilled, escaped to Larissa. Perseus followed him in disguise to endeavor to persuade him to return, but while taking part in the games there he threw the discus in such a way that Acrisius was killed by it without his intention. Then Perseus took the government of Tiryns and left Argos to Megapenthes, son of Prœtus.

Phæ'dra. Daughter of Minos. Wife of Theseus. She falsely accused her step-son Hippolytus. After his death her treachery became known and she destroyed herself.

Pha'ethon (*i. e.* "the shining"). Son of Helios and Clymĕnē. He teased his father to allow him to drive the chariot of the sun across the heavens for one day. Clymene added her request, and Helios yielded to them, but the boy was too weak, the horses went out of their course and came so near the earth as almost to set it on fire. Then Zeus (Jupiter) killed Phæthon with a flash of lightning and hurled him into the river Eridanus. The *Heliadæ* or *Phaethontiades*, who were his sisters and had yoked the horses, were turned into poplars and their tears into amber.

Philocte'tes. Son of Pœas and called *Pœantiades.* He was the most skillful archer in the Trojan war. The friend and armorbearer of Hercules, he had lighted the pile on Mount Œta on which Hercules died, and for this service received the bow and the poisoned arrows of the hero. On his way to Troy, when on the island of Chryse, he was wounded by one of these arrows or bitten by a serpent on his foot, and the stench from this wound was so unendurable, that Ulysses advised his companions to leave him at Lemnos. He remained there until the last year of the Trojan war, when an oracle declared that Troy could not be taken without the arrows of Hercules. Then Philoctetes was brought and his wound healed by Æsculapius. He slew many Trojans, Paris among the number. He went from Troy to Italy.

Phin'eus. (1.) Son of Belus and Anchinoe. Slain by Perseus. See Perseus. (2.) Son of Agenor. King of Salmydessus.

A soothsayer. He put out the eyes of his sons who had been falsely accused by their step-mother, Idæa. The gods then made him blind and sent Harpies to torment him. (See Harpyiæ.) Zetes and Calais, sons of Boreas, freed him from these tormentors. In return he explained the course which the Argonautic expedition should take. Some say he was slain by Hercules.

Phœ'be. (1.) The feminine of Phœbus, and one of the appellations of Diana when Luna or the goddess of the Moon. (2.) Daughter of Tyndareus and Leda. Sister of Clytæmnestra.

Phœ'bus. One of the appellations of Apollo, meaning bright or pure.

Ploti'na (Pompeia). Wife of the emperor Trajan. She persuaded him to adopt Hadrian.

Plu'to (Pluton). The giver of wealth. A surname of Hades, afterward used as the name of a god. See Hades.

Plu'tus. Son of Iasion and Demeter (Ceres). God of wealth. Zeus (Jupiter) took away his sight, that he might distribute his gifts blindly and without regard to merit.

Pol'lux (Polydeuces). See Dioscuri.

Pol'ybus. King of Corinth, who reared Œdipus. See Œdipus.

Polym'nia. See Musæ.

Polyx'ena. Daughter of Priam and Hecuba. Loved by Achilles. When the Greeks lingered on the coast of Thrace on their homeward voyage, the shade of Achilles appeared and demanded that she should be sacrificed to him. Neoptolemus slew her on the tomb of his father.

Pomo'na. Roman goddess of fruit. Called also *Pomorum Patrona.* Silvanus, Picus, Vertumnus, and several other rustic divinities, loved her.

Posei'don (Neptunus). Son of Cronus (Saturn) and Rhea. Called also *Cronius* and *Saturnius.* Brother of Zeus (Jupiter) and Hades (Pluto). When the universe was divided between the brothers, the sea was given to Poseidon. He was equal to Zeus in dignity, but not in power. He once conspired with Hera (Juno), and Athena (Minerva), to put Zeus in chains, but usually he was submissive to the more powerful god. His palace was in the depths of the Ægean Sea, and there he kept his horses. These had brazen hoofs and golden manes. He rides over the waves in a chariot drawn by these horses, and the sea becomes smooth at his appearance, while the monsters of the deep gambol and play around him. Troy was called *Neptuna Pergama,* because Poseidon assisted Apollo to surround it with walls for king Laomedon, who refused to give them their promised reward, and Poseidon sent a sea-monster to ravage the country, which was killed by Hercules. He always hated the Trojans, and assisted the Greeks against them. He prevented the return of Ulysses, in revenge for his having blinded Polyphemus, the son of Poseidon. When he contested with Athena for the naming of Athens, he created the horse for man. He was the originator and patron of horse-races, and taught men to manage horses with bridles. When he pursued Demeter (Ceres), he changed himself into a horse. His wife was Amphitrītē, and by her he was father of Triton, Rhode, and Benthesicyme. He was also father of many others by mortal women, and by other divinities. The horse and chariot races on the Corinthian Isthmus, were held in his honor. The animals sacrificed to him were usually black and white bulls; but wild boars and rams were sometimes used. The trident or the spear with three points was his weapon and the symbol of his power. With it he shattered rocks, shook the earth, and brought on storms. In art he is often represented in groups with Amphitrite, Tritons, Nereids, etc., etc., and is easily recognized by his attributes, which are the trident, horses, and dolphins.

Pri'amus (Priam). Son of Laomedon. His real name was Podarces, the "swift footed," but he fell into the hands of Hercules, and was ransomed by Hesione, his sister, hence he was called Pria mus, "the ransomed." Husband of Arisba and Hecuba. Father of fifty sons, nineteen the children of Hecuba. He was too old to be active in the Trojan war. He superintended the contest between Paris and Menelaus. He went to the tent of Achilles to ransom the body of Hector. At the fall of Troy he was slain by Pyrrhus, son of Achilles.

Pria'pus. Son of Dionysus (Bacchus) and Aphrodite (Venus). Born on the shores of the Hellespont, and hence called Hellespontiacus. God of fruitfulness. Especially the protector of flocks, of bees, of the vine, and fruits of the garden. Usually represented in the form of hermæ, a sickle or horn of plenty in his hand, and carrying fruit in his garments.

Prome'theus. Son of the Titan Iapetus and Clymene. Brother of Atlas, Menœtius, and Epimetheus. The name of the latter signifies "after-thought," and that of Prometheus "fore-thought." In spite of Zeus (Jupiter) he was a great benefactor to men. He stole fire from heaven in a hollow tube, and taught mortals many useful arts. Zeus gave Pandora to Epimetheus (see Pandora), and chained Prometheus to a rock on Mount Caucasus. Here an eagle consumed his liver by day, which was restored each night. Zeus consented that Hercules should kill the eagle, and thus liberate the sufferer. Zeus did this in order that his son might gain never ending fame. There is a legend that Prometheus created man by fashioning him from earth, and giving him a portion of every quality possessed by other animals.

Proser'pina. See Persephone.

Protesila'us. Son of Iphiclus and Astyoche. Born at Phylace in Thessaly. Called *Phylacius* and *Phylacides*, either from his birthplace, or his grandfather Phylacus. He was the first Greek who leaped upon the shores of Troy, and the first one killed. He was slain by Hector.

Pro'teus. The old man prophet of the sea who tended the seals which made the flocks of Poseidon (Neptune). At mid-day he rose from the water, and slept on the rocks with sea-monsters all about him. He did not like to prophesy, and in order to compel him to do so it was necessary to catch hold of him while thus asleep. He could change his shape, and would assume all manner of hideous forms to escape, but if one persevered and kept a hold on him, he at length prophesied, told the truth, and then returned to the sea. Homer says he lived on the island of Pharos, but a day's journey from the river Ægyptus (Nile) ; but Virgil places him on Carpathos between Crete and Rhodes.

Psy'che, "The Soul," was one of the three daughters of a king. She was so lovely that Venus was jealous of her and commanded Cupid to inspire her with love for the most contemptible of men. Cupid hastened to obey, but when he saw Psyche, he was so enamored of her that he carried her to a charming retreat where he spent each night with her, but fled at the approach of day. Her sisters being jealous of her declared that she was receiving the embraces of a hideous creature. So she approached him with a lamp as he slept, and was enraptured at beholding the beautiful god. She dropped from her lamp a bit of hot oil, which fell on his shoulder. Awaking, he reproached her for her distrust, and left her to return no more. She was wretched, and wandered from place to place searching for him. At length she came to the palace of Venus, who made her a slave and treated her with great cruelty. Cupid, who still loved her, helped her secretly to bear her burdens, and at last she overcame the hatred of Venus and won her love. Then she was received among the gods, and united to Cupid forever. This allegory plainly represents the soul that is purified by trial, and at length made happy in heaven. Psyche is represented in art as a maiden with butterfly wings, and often together with Cupid in the various circumstances of the story above.

Pudici'tia. Personification of Modesty. Worshipped in Greece and Rome. At Rome two sanctuaries were dedicated to her: one in the name of *Pudicitia patricia;* the other *Pudicitia plebeia.* At Athens an altar was dedicated to her.

Pyl'ades. Son of Strophius and Anaxibia, sister of Agamemnon. His father was king of Phocis. After the murder of Agamemnon, Orestes was carried to the court of Strophius, and there originated his friendship for Pylades, which became proverbial. He assisted Orestes to murder Clytæmnestra, and married his sister Electra.

Pyr'rhus. See Neoptolemus.

Re'mus. See Romulus.

Rhe'a (Cybele). Daughter of Uranus and Ge (Heaven and Earth). Wife of Cronus (Saturn). Mother of Hestia (Vesta), Demeter (Ceres), Hera (Juno), Hades (Pluto), Poseidon (Neptune), and Zeus (Jupiter). Cronus swallowed all his children, but when Rhea was about to give birth to Zeus, she went to Lyctus in Crete. She gave Cronus a stone wrapped up like a child. He swallowed this supposing it to be the infant. Many places claim to have been the birth-place of Zeus; but undoubtedly, Crete was the earliest place where Rhea was worshipped. She was in truth the great goddess of the eastern world. In Asia Minor she was identified with "The Great Mother" or the "Mother of the Gods." Also called Cybēlē, Agdistis, Dindȳmēnē, etc., etc. Her worship became wild and exciting from the introduction of eastern rites, and in the and it was closely connected with that of Dionysus (Bacchus). As Cybele she was worshipped in Phrygia; as Agdistis at Pessinus in Galatia, and under various names she was honored even as far as Bactriana. The Romans from the earliest times worshipped Ops, the mother of Jupiter and wife of Saturn, who was identical with Rhea. In European countries she was supposed to be accompanied by Curētes, who were connected with the birth and rearing of Zeus in Crete. In Phrygia she was associated with the Corybantes, Atys, and Agdistis. The Corybantes were her priests. They danced on the mountains and in the forests in full armor, having drums, cymbals, and horns. In Rome her priests were called Galli. The lion was sacred to her, and in works of art her chariot is sometimes drawn by lions, or they crouch on each side of her throne, where she is often represented as seated with a mural crown and a veil.

Rhea or Cybele.

Rhe'a Silvia. See Romulus.

Rom'ulus. Son of Mars (Ares) and Rhea Silvia. She was a daughter of Numitor, and a Vestal Virgin. Her father was a descendant of Iulus and Æneas, and was excluded from the throne of Alba Longa by his brother Amulius. Rhea Silvia and her twin sons, Romulus and Remus, were condemned to death, for it was not lawful for a Vestal Virgin to bear children. The babes were thrown into the Tiber, but the cradle containing them was stranded, and the children were suckled by a she-wolf who carried them to her cave. Here they were found by Faustulus, the king's shepherd, who carried them to Acca Larentia, his wife. When they were grown up, they decided to found a city on the banks of the Tiber, but a strife arose as to which brother should give his name to the city, and Remus was slain. Romulus soon found that he had too small a number of people, so he made a sanctuary for runaway slaves and homicides, on the Capitoline Hill. Soon he had men enough, but women were wanting. Then he instituted games, and invited the Sabines and Latins, and when all were assembled, the Roman youths rushed upon them and seized the virgins. Hence arose a war; but when the Romans and Sabines were formed for battle, the Sabine women who had been stolen rushed in and begged their fathers and brothers to lay down their arms, declaring themselves happy with their Roman husbands. Then they made peace, and agreed to unite to form one nation, with both a Roman and a Sabine king; but soon after, the Sabine king, Titus Tatius, was slain, and Romulus reigned over all. He reigned thirty-seven years, when his father, Mars, took him to heaven in a fiery chariot. Not long after, he appeared to Julius Proculus in immortal beauty, and bade him instruct the Roman people to worship him under the name of Quirinus. This is the genuine legend. Another tradition relates, that the senators, displeased at his tyranny, murdered him during a tempest, cut him in pieces, and carried away his remains beneath their robes.

Sabi'na (Poppæa). Daughter of T. Ollius, who took the name of her grandfather, Poppæus Sabinus. Wife of Rufius Crispinus, and then of Otho, who was the intimate friend of Nero. She was of wonderful beauty, but wanting in virtue. Nero soon became enamored of her and sent Otho to Lusitania as governor. Poppæa then became the mistress of Nero, and governed him absolutely. She was resolved to be the wife of the emperor, and persuaded him to murder his mother, Agrippina, who would not hear of the marriage, and soon after to divorce and at length to kill his wife Octavia. Then she accomplished her designs and married Nero who, three years later, killed her by a kick when she was pregnant.

Sabi'nus, Fla'vius. Brother of the emperor Vespasian. Was *præfectus urbis* during the last eleven years of the reign of Nero. He was removed under Galba, and restored under Otho and Vitellius. During the struggle between Vespasian and Vitellius, Sabinus took refuge in the capitol. The capitol was burned, and Sabinus put to death, in the presence of Vitellius, who tried in vain to save him. He was a man of unspotted character and distinguished reputation.

Sap'pho. A native of Mytilene or of Eresos in Lesbos. A contemporary of Alcæus, Stesichorus, and Pittacus. Together with Alcæus she led the Æolian school of lyric poetry. Her own poetry and that of Alcæus proves them to have been friends. Ovid alludes to her flight from Mytilene to escape some danger, between 604 and 592 B. C. It is also said that she threw herself from the Leuca dian rock because her love for Phaon was not returned. But this is not probable. She was the centre of a female literary society in Mytilene, the members of which were her disciples in gallantry, poetry, and fashion. Her lyric poems made nine books, of which we have but scanty fragments; but the most important part, a splendid ode to Venus, we probably have entire. The ancient authors were unbounded in their praise of her writings.

Sardanapa'lus. The last king of Nineveh. The account of Ctesias concerning him has been followed by most writers. It contradicts Herodotus and the Old Testament writers, but is preserved by Diodorus Siculus, and is the one commonly referred to in connection with its subject. It represents him as effeminate, luxurious, and licentious. He passed his time in his palace with concubines, himself in female attire, and unseen by his people. At last Arbaces, satrap of Medea, and Belesys, a noble Chaldæan priest, renounced their allegiance to him and marched against Nineveh. Then Sardanapalus was roused from his luxurious idleness and showed himself a brave warrior. He twice defeated the rebels, but was then obliged to shut himself up in Nineveh. He held out against the besiegers two years, and when this was no longer possible he collected his treasures, his wives, and concubines in an immense pile which he set on fire, and throwing himself therein he thus destroyed all together. B. C. 876.

Satur'nus. See Cronus, Rhea, and Zeus.

Sat'yri. A class of beings who personify the luxuriant vitality of nature. Inseparably associated with the worship of Dionysus (Bacchus). Said to be the sons of Hermes (Mercury) and Iphthima or of the Naiades. The older ones are called Sileni, the younger Satyrisci. They were greatly dreaded by mortals. Originally they were quite distinct from the Fauni, but have been confounded with them in later writings. They had two small horns growing out of the top of the forehead, bristling hair, and pointed eyes, round and turned up noses, and a tail like a horse or a goat. They were fond of wine and all sensual pleasures. They wore the skins of animals and wreaths of ivy, fir, or vine leaves. In art they are of all ages, and are sleeping, dancing voluptuously with nymphs, and playing on pipes and flutes.

Scyl'la and **Charyb'dis.** Two rocks between Italy and Sicily. Scylla was a daughter of Cratæis and dwelt in a cave on one of these rocks. She was a fearful monstrosity. She had twelve feet, six necks and heads, with three rows of sharp teeth in each, and she barked like a dog. A great fig-tree grew on the other rock, and beneath it dwelt Charybdis. Three times each day she swallowed all the waters of the sea and threw them up again. This is Homer's account, but later writers differ. Hercules is said to have killed Scylla because she stole some of the oxen of Geryon, and Phorcys restored her to life. Virgil speaks of the plural, Scyllæ, and places them in the lower world. Charybdis is made the child of Poseidon (Neptune) and Gæa (Tellus), and described as a voracious woman who stole the oxen from Hercules, and was thrown into the sea by a thunderbolt from Zeus (Jupiter).

Semir'amis. Daughter of Dercĕto, fish-goddess of Ascalon, and a Syrian youth. Derceto, wishing to conceal her frailty, killed the father and exposed the child, who was fed by doves until found by some shepherds. The shepherd of the royal flocks, called Simmas, brought her up, and from his name hers was derived. The wonderful beauty of Semiramis attracted Onnes, a general, who married her. She displayed such bravery and military skill at the siege of Bactra that Ninus was attracted to her, and also charmed by her beauty so that he determined to make her his wife. Onnes killed himself in despair. She had a son by Ninus called Ninyas. Upon the death of Ninus she succeeded to the throne, and reigned forty-two years when she resigned the kingdom to Ninyas, and leaving the earth flew to heaven in the shape of a dove. Her fame far exceeded that of Ninus, who built the city of Ninus or Nineveh. Semiramis erected a tomb for him in that city, nine stadia high and ten wide. She built other cities and magnificent buildings; she conquered Egypt, some part of Æthiopia, and many nations of Asia. She built Babylon and made the hanging gardens of Media, but she failed to conquer India, which she attacked. The foundation of this story, so evidently fabulous, is probably this: Semiramis was a Syrian goddess, perhaps identical with the heavenly Aphrodite or Astarte who was worshipped at Ascalon. The dove was sacred to this goddess, hence the story of the heavenly flight. There were accounts of her voluptuousness which would also prove this identity.

Silenus. (Bronze of Pompeii.)

Sera'pis (Sarapis). An Egyptian goddess whose worship was introduced into Greece during the reign of the Ptolemies, and into Rome with that of Isis.

Sile'ni. See Satyri.

Sile'nus. Son of Hermes (Mercury, or of Pan and a nymph, or Gæa (Tellus). He always accompanied Dionysus (Bacchus), whom he is said to have instructed when a youth. Nysa was said to be his birthplace. He slew the giant Enceladus. He was a fat, jolly old man, and usually intoxicated; generally supported by other satyrs, or riding on an ass. He was withal an inspired prophet, and when drunk or asleep was in the power of mortals, who could compel him to prophesy and sing by surrounding him with chains of flowers. He is mentioned as the inventor of the flute, as are also Marsyas and Apollo. Silenus is often represented playing upon it; there is also a certain dance called by his name.

Sire'nes (Sirens). Called the daughters of Phorcus; of Acheloüs and Sterope; of Terpsichore; of Melpomene; of Calliope or of Gæa. Some say they were two in number: Aglaopheme and Thelxiepia; others that there were three: Pisinoë, Aglaope, and Thelxiepia, or Parthenope, Ligia, and Leucosia. They were sea-nymphs, and charmed all who heard their songs. When Ulysses came near their home he stuffed the ears of his companions with wax, and tied himself to the mast until they were beyond the sound of the voices of these singers. They were connected with the rape of Proserpina. When the Argonauts sailed past their home, their attempts to charm them were unavailing, for Orpheus excelled them in the sweetness of his music; and as they were fated to die, when one who heard their song passed by unmoved, they then threw themselves into the sea, and were changed into rocks.

Sisyphus, Ixion, and Tantalus.

Sis'yphus. Son of Æolus and Enarĕte, and called *Æolides*. Husband of Merope, the daughter of Atlas or a Pleiad. Father of Glaucus, Ornytion (Porphyrion), Thersander, and Halmus. Later traditions make him the son of Autolycus, and father of Ulysses by Anticlea. Hence Ulysses is sometimes called *Sisyphides*. Sisyphus was said to have built the town of Ephyra, or Corinth. As king of Corinth he did much for commerce, but was deceitful and avaricious. In the lower world, his punishment is to roll a huge stone up hill, which always rolls down again as soon as it reaches the top.

Sy'rinx. An Arcadian nymph. Pan pursued her, and she fled to the river Ladon. At her own request, she was metamorphosed into a reed, from which Pan made his pipe or flute.

Ta'ges. Son of a Genius, Jovialis, and grandson of Jupiter (Zeus). He was like a boy with the wisdom of an old man. He rose suddenly out of the ground, and instructed the Etruscans and Tarchon in the use of the haruspices. All that he said was written down, and was said to fill twelve books, called the books of Tages.

Tan'talus. Son of Jupiter (Zeus) and the nymph Pluto. Husband of Euryanassa, or of Taygete or Dione, or of Clytia, or of Eupryto. Father of Pelops, Broteas, and Niobe. All traditions agree that he was a wealthy king; some say of Argos, others of Lydia, and again of Corinth. One tradition relates that he divulged the secrets of Jupiter, and is punished in Hades with burning thirst, while he is in the midst of a lake whose waters always recede if he attempts to drink; bunches of fruit hang over his head in such a way that he cannot catch them, and a great rock is suspended as if just about to fall and crush him. Again it is said, that in order to test the power of the gods he cut up his son Pelops, boiled him and gave him to them as a repast; again, that he stole nectar and ambrosia from the gods, for which he was punished. Still another account says, that when Pandareus stole a golden dog, which Rhea had appointed to watch Zeus (Jupiter) and his nurse, Tantalus received and kept it. From his name and punishment comes the English verb "to tantalize."

Ta'tius, T. King of the Sabines. (See Romulus.)

Tel'ephus. Son of Hercules and Auge daughter of Aleus, king of Tegea. Husband of Laodice, or Astyoche, daughter of Priam. He consulted the Delphic oracle in order to learn his origin, and was told to go to Teuthras, king of Mysia. There he found his mother, and succeeded to the throne of Mysia. He endeavored to prevent the Greeks from landing there, but Dionysus (Bacchus) caused him to stumble over a vine, and he was wounded by Achilles. He was told by an oracle, that the wound could only be cured by the person who had inflicted it; and the Grecians were also told that they could not take Troy without the aid of Telephus. Hence when he came to the camp, Achilles cured him with the rust from the spear with which he had been wounded, and he in turn pointed out their course to them.

Terpsich'ore. See Musæ.

Thali'a. See Musæ.

The'seus. Son of Ægeus, king of Athens, and Æthra, daughter of Pittheus, king of Trœzene. He was reared in Trœzene, and when old enough took the sword and sandals which had been left by Ægeus and went to Athens. He made the journey by land, and did many brave deeds on the way, such as killing monsters and robbers which infested the country. Ægeus recognized Theseus by the sword; and made him his successor, excluding the sons of Pallas. Then Theseus captured the Marathonian bull which had laid waste the country. Next he went to Crete as one of the seven youths which were sent every year, together with seven maidens, as a tribute to the Minotaur. He was determined to free Athens from this necessity. Ariadne, the daughter of king Minos, loved him, and gave him a sword with which he killed the monster, and a thread by means of which he made his way out of the labyrinth. He then left Crete with his companions whom he had preserved, and Ariadne also. Accounts vary, but the usual one relates that he deserted her at Naxos. (Ariadne). He is said to have had two sons by her, Œnopion and Staphylus. Before leaving Athens he had promised that if successful he would on his return hoist a white signal. This he forgot to do, and Ægeus, believing that his son had been slain, threw himself into the sea. Thus Theseus became king of Athens. One of his exploits was an attack upon the Amazons, which he is said to have made before they had recovered from that of Hercules. Theseus carried off their queen Antiope. The Amazons in turn attacked Attica, and went even to Athens itself, where Theseus finally defeated them. By Antiope he was father of Hippolytus or Demophoon. After her death he married Phædra. He was in the Argonautic expedition; he joined the Calydonian hunt; he assisted Adrastus to recover the bodies of those slain before Thebes; he aided his friend Pirithous and the Lapithæ against the Centaurs; together with Pirithous he carried Helen to Aphidnæ when a young girl, and placed her in care of Æthra; he attempted to assist Pirithous to recover Proserpina from the lower world, but Pirithous perished, and Theseus was held a prisoner, until freed by Hercules. During this time Castor and Pollux carried off Helen and Æthra. At the same time Menestheus endeavored to influence the people against Theseus, and when he returned he was not able to resume his government. He then went to Scyros, where he was treacherously slain by Lycomedes. He is believed to have appeared at the battle of Marathon. He is without doubt a purely legendary character, but later Athenians regarded him as an historical personage, and the founder of many of their institutions.

The'tis. Daughter of Nereus and Doris. Wife of Peleus. Mother of Achilles. She dwelt with her father in the bottom of the sea. She received Dionysus (Bacchus) there when he fled from Lycurgus, and in gratitude he presented her with a golden urn. She also protected Hephæstus (Vulcan) when thrown down from heaven. Hera (Juno) had brought her up, and when she was old enough, Zeus (Jupiter) and Hera gave her to Peleus against her will. Poseidon (Neptune) and Zeus himself desired to marry her, but Themis declared that the son of Thetis should excel his father, and the gods withdrew their suit. Another tradition relates that Thetis rejected Zeus because she had been reared by Hera, and in revenge Zeus declared she should marry a mortal. Thetis had power like Proteus to assume any form she chose, but Chiron instructed Peleus, and he held her fast until she promised to marry him. It was at their marriage-feast that Eris, who was not invited, made the famous quarrel by means of the golden apple. (Paris). Thetis bestowed much love and care upon Achilles.

Tire'sias. A renowned soothsayer. A Theban, and blind from his seventh year. He lived to be very old. The cause of his blindness, and the origin of his prophetic power, are variously related. He was connected with many important events in the history of Greece, and it was believed that after death, while other mortals were mere shades, he retained his powers of perception. During the war of the Seven against Thebes he declared that if Menœceus would sacrifice himself, Thebes would be victorious. In the war of the Epigoni, after the Thebans were defeated, he advised them to make a ruse of commencing negotiations for peace, and then to take the opportunity to escape. He fled with them, or was carried captive to Delphi, but on his way drank of the well of Tilphossa and died.

Triton.

Tri'ton. Son of Poseidon (Neptune) and Amphitrītē (or Celæno). He dwelt with his father in a golden palace at the bottom of the sea, or at Ægæ. He is described as riding over the waves on sea-horses and monsters. The plural, Tritons, is mentioned and their appearance described. They were men in the upper portion of their bodies, and fish in the lower. Their attribute in poetry and art is a shell, *concha*, which they blow at Neptune's command to calm the waves of the sea.

Ulys'ses (Ulyxes, Ulixes, Odysseus). Son of Laërtes and Anticlea, or of Sisyphus and Anticlea. Husband of Penelope and father of Telemachus. He was distinguished for his valor and eloquence. He is said to have invented the wooden horse, and was one of the heroes concealed in it. He assisted in carrying off the Palladium. He fought with Ajax for the arms of Achilles and gained the prize. Homer's "Odyssey" is an account of the adventures of Ulysses after the fall of Troy. He visited the Cicones and Lotophagi, and then sailed to the west coast of Sicily, where with twelve companions he entered the cave of Polyphemus, the Cyclops. The giant ate six of the companions of Ulysses, and reserved him and the remaining six as prisoners. Ulysses succeeded in making Polyphemus drunk, and with a burning pole put out his single eye. He then concealed himself and his companions under the bodies of the sheep which the monster let out of his cave, and in this way they escaped. He next went to the island of Æolus and the god gave him a bag of winds to take him home, but his companions opened the bag and the winds all escaped, and they were driven back to Æolus, but he refused to assist them again. He then visited Telepylos, and next the island where dwelt the sorceress Circe. Ulysses sent a part of his number to explore the island and she turned them

Ulysses and Tiresias.

into swine. Eurylochus however escaped, and told the sad truth to Ulysses, who while hastening to his friends was taught by Hermes (Mercury) how to resist the power of the sorceress. He succeeded in freeing his companions from her spell, and was treated kindly by her. She advised him to cross the river Oceanus. He landed in the country of the Cimmerians and went to Hades, where he consulted Tiresias concerning the way in which he could reach home. He then returned to Circe, and she gave him a wind that sent him to the island of the Sirens, but he filled the ears of his companions with wax and tied himself to the mast until beyond the sound of their song. In passing between Scylla and Charybdis, the former carried away six of his companions. Next he landed on Thrinacia, and here his companions, in spite of the warning of Tiresias, killed some of the oxen of Helios. In punishment of this, when next they put to sea, Zeus (Jupiter) destroyed their vessels, and all save Ulysses perished. He clung to a mast, and after ten days reached the island of Ogygia, where the nymph Calypso lived. She loved him, and promised him immortality if he would remain with her, but after eight years he longed for his home, and Athena (Minerva) requested Hermes to carry to Calypso a command from Zeus to let Ulysses go. Calypso showed him how to make a raft, and in eighteen days he came to Scheria, the home of the Phæacians. Then Neptune (Poseidon) raised a storm which threw him from his raft, but Leucothia and Athena assisted him to swim ashore. Here he fell asleep from exhaustion. He was awakened by the voices of

Ulysses and the Sirens.

Nausicaa and her maidens. She was the daughter of Alcinous and Arete. She took him to her father's palace, where the minstrel Demodocus sang the fall of Troy. The hero wept, and when questioned of the reason of his grief, related his whole history. Then king Alcinous prepared a ship to take him to Ithaca, from which he had been absent about twenty years. During this time Laërtes had withdrawn into the country. Anticlea had died. Penelope had rejected many suitors, and Telemachus had grown up. Athena metamorphosed Ulysses into a beggar, and he was kindly received by Eumæus, a faithful servant. Soon Telemachus returned from Pylos and Sparta, where he had been to inquire concerning his father. Ulysses made himself known to him, and together they arranged a plan for the death of the suitors of Penelope. She was induced with much difficulty to promise herself to him who should excel in shooting with the bow of Ulysses. None of the suitors could use it on account of its size and weight. Ulysses then took it and shot all the suitors. He then made himself known to Penelope, who received him with great joy. He also visited his aged father. The relatives of the suitors now rose against him, but Athena assumed the appearance of Mentor and succeeded in effecting a reconciliation between the king and his subjects.

Ura'nia. (1.) A muse. Daughter of Mnemosyne by Zeus (Jupiter). The bard Linus is said to be the son of Apollo and Urania. Hymenæus was also considered her son. She was the muse of astronomy, and her attributes are a celestial globe and a small staff. (2.) Daughter of Oceanus and Tethys, and a nymph in the train of Proserpina (Persephone). (3.) A surname of Aphrodite (Venus), meaning "the heavenly," and intended to distinguish her from Aphrodite Pandemos. Wine was never offered in her libations. Plato represents her as the child of Uranus, begotten without a mother.

Venti. (Vatican Virgil.)

Venti (the Winds). They are personified, and yet are the phenomena of nature. The master and ruler of winds is Æolus, who lives in the island of Æolia. Other gods have power over them, especially Zeus (Jupiter). Boreas is the north wind; Eurus the east wind; Notus the south wind; and Zephyrus the west wind. The beneficial winds, Notus, Boreas, Argestes, and Zephyrus, were sons of Astræus and Eos. The destructive winds, such as the Typhon, were sons of Typhœus. Between Boreas and Eurus are placed the Meses, Caicias, and Apeliotes. Between Eurus and Notus, the Phœnicias. Between Notus and Zephyrus, Lips; and between Zephyrus and Boreas, the Argestes (Olympias or Sciron), and the Thrascias. This is the arrangement of Aristotle, who also says that Eurus is not east but southeast. There is a different arrangement upon a monument in the Museum Pio-Clementinum. The Venti are represented in art with wings at the head and shoulders. Black lambs were sacrificed to the bad, and white ones to the good winds.

Ve'nus (Aphrodite). Goddess of Love. At Rome she was not important until she was identified with the great Aphroditē. But

Venus (Aphrodite) and Eros (Cupid).

she was at length worshipped in various characters. The surname of *Murtea* or *Murcia*, referred to her fondness for the myrtle. That of *Calva*, to the fact that on her wedding-day the bride cut off a lock of hair to sacrifice to Venus. She was worshipped as Venus Erycina, Venus Verticordia, Venus Obsequens and Postvorta, Venus Genitrix, and Venus Victrix. Cæsar favored her worship because he traced his descent to Æneas, said to be the son of Mars (Ares) and Venus. The month of April was especially sacred to the goddess of love.

Vertum'nus (Vortumnus). The Romans connected this god with everything to which the verb *verto*, to change, could be applied; such as change of seasons, purchase and sale, etc., etc. But the transformation of the blossom to the fruit was in reality his proper care. When he was in love with Pomona, he changed to all manner of forms to please her, and at last succeeded as a blooming youth. Gardeners offer him the first fruits, and especially budding garlands. The *Vortumnalia* was celebrated on the 23d of August. The worship of Vertumnus at Rome was so important that it was attended by a special flamen.

Vesta (Hestia). Goddess of the hearth, and connected with the Penates. It was believed that Æneas brought her eternal fire from Troy with these gods. The prætors, consuls, and dictators sacrificed to her before assuming their offices, as well as to the Penates. As every house had a hearth, so each one was a temple of this goddess, but her special temple was in the Forum, not far from that of the Penates. There was no statue to represent her, but the eternal fire on the hearth personified her, and was kept alive by Vestal Virgins, chaste and pure. The 1st of March was the day when the sacred fire was renewed, and also the laurel tree which shaded the hearth. The 15th of June the temple was purified. The dirt removed was placed in an angiportus, and this locked by a gate so that none could enter. The first half of this day was thought so inauspicious, that even the priestess of Juno did not comb her hair or cut her nails, but the last half was thought very favorable for marriage or the commencement of any important thing. On the 9th of June the *Vestalia* was kept, when only women went to the temple, and they barefooted.

Virgin'ia. Daughter of L. Virginius, a Roman centurion. She was betrothed to L. Icilius, but the decemvir Appius Claudius, enamored of her beauty, was determined to possess her. One of his clients claimed her as his slave, when her father was away with the army; but her lover summoned her father, and he arrived the very morning that judgment was to be rendered, and Virginia delivered to the decemvir. When Virginius found that he had no power to control the decision, and that Virginia would be delivered to Appius Claudius, he asked to be allowed to speak to her and her nurse. This was granted, and drawing them aside, he seized a butcher's knife from a stall near by, and plunged it into the breast of his daughter, exclaiming, "There is no way but this to keep thee free!" Then holding the bloody knife on high, he rushed to the Roman camp. Then the people arose, the decemvirs were deprived of their office, and the tribunes restored. Virginius was the first elected. He sent Appius Claudius to prison, and there he killed himself.

Vulca'nus (Hephæstus, Vulcan). His worship was important at Rome, and his temple was regarded as a kind of centre of the state. The temple of Concord was built upon the site of the temple of Vulcan. His most ancient festival was called Fornacalia or Furnalia, he being the god of furnaces. His great festival was Vulcanalia, on the 23d of August.

Zeph'yrus. The West Wind. Dwelt with Boreas in a palace in Thrace. By the harpy Podarge, he became the father of the horses Xanthus and Balius; these belonged to Achilles. The wife of Zephyrus was Chloris, whom he carried away by force, and who was the mother of Carpus.

Zephyrus. (Athens.)

Zethus. Twin brother of Amphion.

Zeus (Jupiter). The greatest Olympian god. Son of Cronus (Saturn) and Rhea. Brother of Poseidon (Neptune), Hades (Pluto), Hestia (Vesta), Demeter (Ceres), and Hera (Juno), to which last he was married. When the world was divided between the three brothers, Hades received the lower world, Poseidon the sea, and Zeus the heavens and upper regions of air, while the earth was equally free to all. Mount Olympus in Thessaly was believed to pierce heaven itself with its lofty summit, and this was the home of Zeus. Everything, both good and bad, came from Zeus. He possessed all power over gods and men, and founded all law and order. Dice (Astræa), goddess of justice, Themis, goddess of order, and Nemesis, who measured the misery and happiness of mortals, were his assistants. Even fate was subject to him. He was armed with thunder and lightning, and called "the thunderer," "the gatherer of clouds," etc., etc. The shaking of his ægis produced storms and tempest. By his wife Hera, he was father of Ares (Mars), Hephæstus (Vulcan) and Hebe. Mount Dicte or Ida, Thebes in Bœotia, Ithome in Messenia, Ægion in Achaia, and Olenos in Ætolia, have all been called the birthplace of Zeus, but the common account, and the one generally followed is, that because Cronus swallowed his children as soon as born, Rhea applied to Uranus and Ge (Heaven and Earth) for assistance before the birth of Zeus, in order that the child might be saved. They sent her to Lyctos in Crete. At his birth she hid him in a cave of Mount Ægæon, and gave Cronus a stone wrapped up as a child, which he swallowed, believing it to be the infant. At last Cronus was made

Zeus. (Medal in British Museum.)

to bring up the children he had swallowed: first came the stone, which was afterwards set up at Delphi by Zeus. The Cyclopes whom Cronus had fettered were liberated by Zeus, and in gratitude they gave him thunder and lightning. He also freed Briareos, the one hundred armed Gigantes, Cottus, and Gyes, all of whom assisted him to conquer the Titans. When these last were overpowered they were shut up in Tartarus and guarded by the Hecatoncheires. Then Typhœus was born of Tartarus and Ge. He struggled desperately with Zeus, but was conquered. The god now being ruler over all took Metis for his wife. When she was pregnant, by the advice of Uranus and Ge, he took the child from her body and placed it in his head, that thereby he might preserve his power; for if Metis had given birth to a son, that son would have displaced Zeus. Thus Athena (Minerva) sprang forth from the head of Zeus. He was also father of the Horæ and Moeræ by Themis; of the Charites (Graces) by Eurynome; of Persephone (Proserpina) by Demeter; of the Muses by Mnemosyne, and of Apollo and Artemis (Diana) by Leto (Latona). It is said that Hera gave birth to Hephæstus (Vulcan) independently, in revenge for the birth of Athena without her aid. The Cronidæ, or the twelve Olympian gods, were Zeus (Jupiter) the greatest of all; Poseidon (Neptune) god of the sea; Apollo, god of prophecy, of song and music, protector of flocks, god of punishment, god who gives help and turns away evil, and who establishes civil governments and founds cities and towns; Ares (Mars) god of war; Hermes (Mercury), the messenger of the gods; Hephæstus (Vulcan) god of fire; Hestia (Vesta) goddess of the hearth; Demeter (Ceres) goddess of the earth; Hera (Juno) goddess of love, marriage, and births; Athena (Minerva) goddess of war and of wisdom, and patroness of arts and trades; Aphrodite (Venus) goddess of love; and Artemis (Diana) goddess of light, of flocks and the chase, and in short representing the same idea as a female that Apollo does as a male, the especial protectress of the young. Both Greeks and Romans recognized these gods, and the poets of both nations gave Zeus or Jupiter many surnames derived from the powers which he exercised, and from the places where he was worshipped. The oak, the heights of mountains, and the eagle, were sacred to him. In Arcadia and Dodona, the oak and prolific doves were sacred to him, and the Dodonæan Zeus has a wreath of oak-leaves, while the Olympian Zeus sometimes has a wreath of olive. In art he is represented as the father of gods and men, and his attributes are the eagle, thunderbolt, sceptre, cornucopia, and a figure of victory in the hand.

[*March* 15, 1871. — The following carol, from an old song-book, was sent to the author of this book too late for insertion in the first edition, and is now given here as an appendix to article St. Clement. See page 79.]

CAROL FOR ST. CLEMENT'S DAY.

It was about November-tide,
A long, long time ago,
When good St. Clement testified
The faith that now we know.
Right boldly then he said his say
Before a furious king:
And therefore on St. Clement's day
We go a-Clementing.

Work in the mines they gave him then,
To try the brave old Saint;
And there two thousand Christian men
With thirst were like to faint.
He prayed a prayer, and out of clay
He made the waters spring;
And therefore on St. Clement's day
We go a-Clementing.

An anchor round his neck they tied,
And cast him in the sea;
And bravely as he lived, he died,
And gallantly went free.
He rests a many miles away,
Yet here his name we sing,
As all upon St. Clement's day
We go a-Clementing.

Our fathers kept it long ago,
And their request we make,
Good Christians, one small mite bestow,
For sweet St. Clement's sake;
And make his feast as glad and gay
As if it came in spring,
When all upon St. Clement's day
We go a-Clementing.

GENERAL INDEX.